Retreat from Empire

By the Same Author

Johnston's Administration: A History of the British Central Africa Administration, 1891–1897

Education and Research in Public Administration in Africa (with A. Adedeji)

The Evolution of Local Government in Malawi

Ife Essays in Public Administration (with M. J. Balogun)

Seeds of Trouble: Government Policy and Land Rights in Nyasaland, 1946–1964

Development Governor: A Biography of Sir Geoffrey Colby

State of Emergency: Crisis in Central Africa, Nyasaland, 1959–1960

Retreat from Empire:
Sir Robert Armitage in Africa and Cyprus

COLIN BAKER

BLOOMSBURY ACADEMIC
LONDON • NEW YORK • OXFORD • NEW DELHI • SYDNEY

BLOOMSBURY ACADEMIC
Bloomsbury Publishing Plc
50 Bedford Square, London, WC1B 3DP, UK
1385 Broadway, New York, NY 10018, USA
29 Earlsfort Terrace, Dublin 2, Ireland

BLOOMSBURY, BLOOMSBURY ACADEMIC and the Diana logo
are trademarks of Bloomsbury Publishing Plc

First published in Great Britain by Tauris Academic Studies 1998
An imprint of I.B. Tauris
Paperback edition published by Bloomsbury Academic 2021

Copyright © Colin Baker, 1998

Colin Baker has asserted his right under the Copyright,
Designs and Patents Act, 1988, to be identified as Author of this work.

All rights reserved. No part of this publication may be reproduced or
transmitted in any form or by any means, electronic or mechanical,
including photocopying, recording, or any information storage or retrieval
system, without prior permission in writing from the publishers.

Bloomsbury Publishing Plc does not have any control over, or responsibility for,
any third-party websites referred to or in this book. All internet addresses given
in this book were correct at the time of going to press. The author and publisher
regret any inconvenience caused if addresses have changed or sites have
ceased to exist, but can accept no responsibility for any such changes.

A catalogue record for this book is available from the British Library.

A catalog record for this book is available from the Library of Congress.

ISBN: HB: 978-1-8606-4223-4
PB: 978-1-3501-8297-4

Copy-edited and typeset by Oxford Publishing Services, Oxford

To find out more about our authors and books visit
www.bloomsbury.com and sign up for our newsletters.

Contents

	Maps and Plates	vi
	Abbreviations	vii
	Glossary	x
	Preface	xi
1.	Early Years	1
2.	Kenya	18
3.	The Gold Coast	73
4.	Cyprus	98
5.	Nyasaland I	170
6.	Nyasaland II	216
7.	Nyasaland III	281
8.	Retirement	312
9.	Missions Impossible	340
	Biographical Notes	355
	Notes	363
	Sources	396
	Index	401

Maps and Plates

Maps

1. Africa and the Mediterranean –
   Kenya, the Gold Coast, Nyasaland and Cyprus
2. Kenya
3. The Gold Coast
4. Cyprus
5. Nyasaland

Plates

1. Muriel and Frank Armitage with Robert, Madras, 1911
2. Sir Charles Arden-Clarke, Kwame Nkrumah and Robert Armitage, 1952
3. Government House, Nicosia, Cyprus
4. Government House, Zomba, Nyasaland
5. Lady Armitage, Cyprus, 1955
6. Sir Robert Armitage, Nyasaland, 1957
7. Sir Robert Armitage, Nyasaland, 1960
8. Sir Robert Armitage, in retirement, 1984

Abbreviations

ADC	aide-de-camp
AFC	Air Force Cross
BBC	British Broadcasting Corporation
BSAP	British South Africa Police
CB	Cavendish-Bentinck
CBE	Commander (of the Order) of the British Empire
CDP	Christian Democratic Party
CDSC	civil defence and supply committee
CDWF	Colonial Development and Welfare Fund
CH	Companion of Honour
CIE	Companion of the Order of the Indian Empire
CLP	Congress Liberation Party
CMG	Companion of the Order of St Michael and St George
CPP	Convention People's Party
CVO	Commander of the Royal Victorian Order
DC	district commissioner
DP	Devlin Papers
DSO	(Companion of the) Distinguished Service Order
EEC	European Economic Community
Eoka	Ethniki Organosis Kypriakou Agonos (National Organization of Cypriot Struggle)
Ex. Co.	executive council
FCO	Foreign and Commonwealth Office, Research and Analysis Department
FRS	Fellow of the Royal Society
GBE	Knight *or* Dame Grand Cross of the Order of the British Empire
GCMG	Knight *or* Dame Grand Cross of the Order of St Michael and St George
GCVO	Knight *or* Dame Grand Cross of the Royal Victorian Order
GOC	General Officer Commanding
HE	His Excellency

HMG	His/Her Majesty's Government
HMS	His/Her Majesty's Ship
HRH	His Royal Highness
KAR	King's African Rifles
KBE	Knight Commander of the Order of the British Empire
KCB	Knight Commander of the Order of the Bath
KCMG	Knight Commander of the Order of St Michael and St George
KCVO	Knight Commander of the Royal Victorian Order
KG	Knight of the Order of the Garter
KPM	King's Police Medal
Kt.	Knight (Bachelor)
Leg. Co.	legislative council
LMY	League of Malawi Youth
MBE	Member of the Order of the British Empire
MC	Military Cross
MCP	Malawi Congress Party
MI5	Military Intelligence, section five (British counterintelligence agency)
MI6	Military Intelligence, section six (British intelligence and espionage agency)
MLC	member of legislative council
MP	Member of Parliament
MV	merchant vessel
NATO	North Atlantic Treaty Organization
NCO	noncommissioned officer
NRR	Northern Rhodesia Rifles
OBE	Order of the British Empire
ODRP	Oxford Development Research Project
OM	(Member of the) Order of Merit
PC	provincial commissioner/Privy Counsellor
PM	prime minister
PMF	police mobile force
RAF	Royal Air Force
RAR	Rhodesia African Rifles
RHL	Rhodes House Library, Oxford
RNVR	Royal Navy Volunteer Reserve
RRAF	Royal Rhodesian Air Force
RRR	Royal Rhodesia Regiment
RSA	Republic of South Africa
SFC	standing finance committee
UFP	United Federal Party

ABBREVIATIONS

UGCC	United Gold Coast Convention
UN	United Nations
UNO	United Nations Organization
USSR	Union of Soviet Socialist Republics
VIP	very important person

Glossary

askari	policeman, soldier or guard
baraza	public meeting
boma	district headquarters
duka	Indian shop
enosis	union of Greece and Cyprus
ethnarchy	national leadership: in Cyprus, the Orthodox Church
kipande	labour registration certificates
kitoi	short wrapover skirt
laibon	witchdoctor
muktar	Turkish village headman
ngoma	drum ceremony with dancing
posho	maize meal flour
shauri	complaint
Sokole	shouted salute

Preface

Few colonial administrators who reached the top of their profession were as well prepared for gubernatorial office as was Robert Armitage. By background, experience and training his preparation was extremely thorough. He came from a family that served the crown overseas. He went to a preparatory boarding school, a major public school and a major university – all in England. He served in four colonies, was a district and secretariat officer in Kenya, a minister in Nkrumah's Gold Coast cabinet, Governor of Cyprus and finally Governor of Nyasaland. He acquired a deep understanding of rural African problems in his early days in Kenya and of economics and finance during his later days there. In the Gold Coast, this economic and financial understanding and the skills that went with it were developed further. As Britain began its imperial retreat from Africa, he became intimately familiar with rapid progress towards independence and the highly charged politics accompanying it. Yet, having reached the top of his profession, after only 19 months in Cyprus he was peremptorily replaced by a military governor and he only narrowly escaped being replaced prematurely in Nyasaland. Why was this? Why, after a quarter of a century of such thorough preparation and clear suitability for high office, were his years at the top – it may appear – unsatisfactory?

As Governor of Cyprus and of Nyasaland there was no way, short of indefinite repressive autocratic rule, that he could accomplish the tasks with which he was charged by the British government. Given the changes in British colonial thinking – eventually exemplified rather extremely by Macleod's appointment as secretary of state for the colonies – such rule was out of the question. Consequently, there was no way he could introduce a constitution in Cyprus that excluded the possibility of self-determination – which is what he was asked to do – or lead Nyasalanders to accept staying in the federation – which, again, is what he was asked to do. In Cyprus, he knew this to be so, though he hoped that by indicating the possibility of eventually conceding the principle of self-determination he could – given time – persuade the Cypriots that union with Greece was not in their best interests. In

Nyasaland, he hoped that if he could persuade the federal and British governments to grant regional autonomy, given time, he would be able to persuade the Africans that they were better off remaining part of the federation.

But the avalanche of nationalism, triggered by violent political activism, had begun to roll and was gaining momentum. The British government plucked Armitage from its path in Cyprus as they themselves moved to one side by involving Greece and Turkey in what Britain had previously adamantly argued was a domestic matter and, shortly, by conceding the principle of self-determination, contrary to their persistent stance up to that time. In Nyasaland, British ministers decided that for a few years they would try to ride on the accelerating avalanche's surface, with little expectation of influencing its path and with still less inclination to slow it down. But Armitage was not the sort of man to ride on the surface in this way and his term of office was not, as might have been expected, extended. The British government were escaping from the avalanche and, lest he impede their escape, they ensured that he did not stand in their way.

His service in the colonies spanned a remarkable period of change. It covered half the interwar years, including the depression and the rise of fascism. It covered the deprivations and worries of the Second World War. It encompassed the early postwar period with colonial emphasis on economic development, and the early stirrings of nationalist political advance. It spanned, also, the 1950s and early 1960s as those stirrings became turbulent and as Britain's retreat from empire became clearer and its pace quickened.

Armitage's contribution to Africa was exceptional. His work in Kenya, particularly at Isiolo and in the secretariat, was outstanding. Even more clear was his contribution in the Gold Coast in the crucial years of early African government preceding independence, where his political role as a member of the cabinet and his economic role as minister of finance were vitally important. His service outside Africa, for a brief period as Governor of Cyprus, also covered crucial years – the outbreak of violence and the internationalization of the issue of the island's future. That he did not succeed in what he set out to do – to introduce a constitution that excluded self-determination – was because the mission itself was impossible. In Nyasaland, it would be a serious error to conclude that he was unsuccessful. It is true that he was unable to fulfil his initial instructions – to win the Africans over to accept federation – but this was again because the mission was impossible. None the less, he diligently and skilfully built good relationships with, if not always between, the various communities. By declaring a state of emergency he brought to a swift end the escalating grave disorders, pre-empted plans for further and more extreme violence and set the conditions in which – although he disagreed over timing – constitutional progress was to be made. Even with this firm action he retained the respect of the Africans and his good relationships with them, most valuably with Dr Banda. Finally, and supremely importantly, he skilfully, firmly and successfully devoted his final few months in Nyasaland to laying the foundations of amicable and trusting relationships and preparing and smoothing the path along which the protectorate's peaceful progress to secession and independence was shortly to be taken.

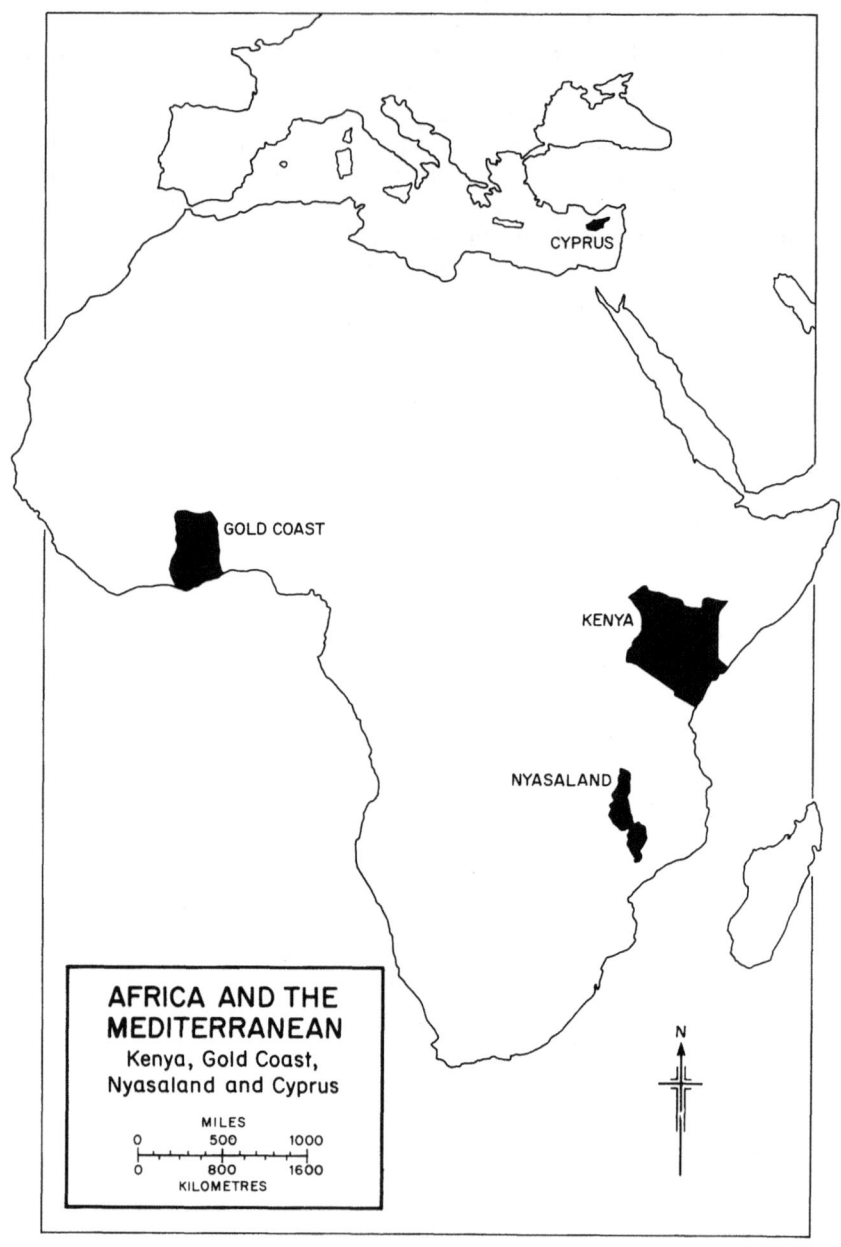

Map 1 Africa and the Mediterranean – Kenya, the Gold Coast, Nyasaland and Cyprus

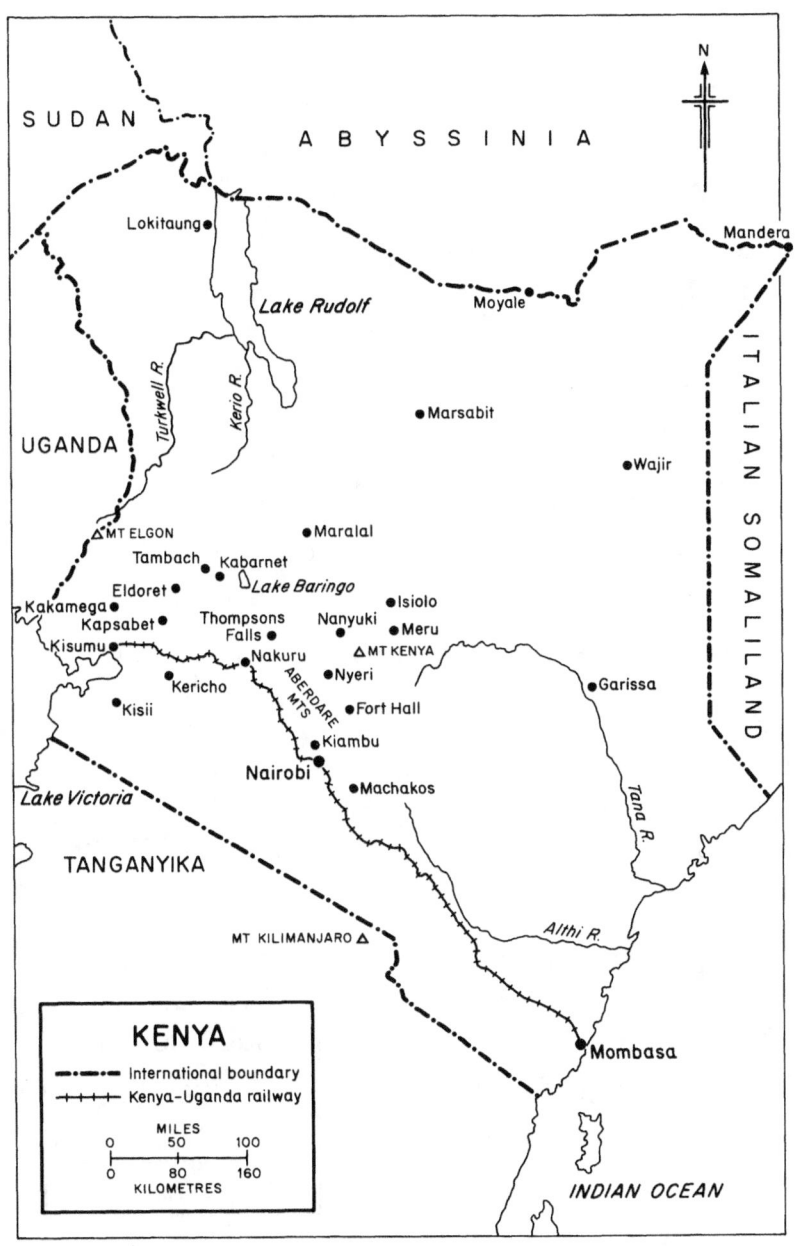

Map 2 Kenya

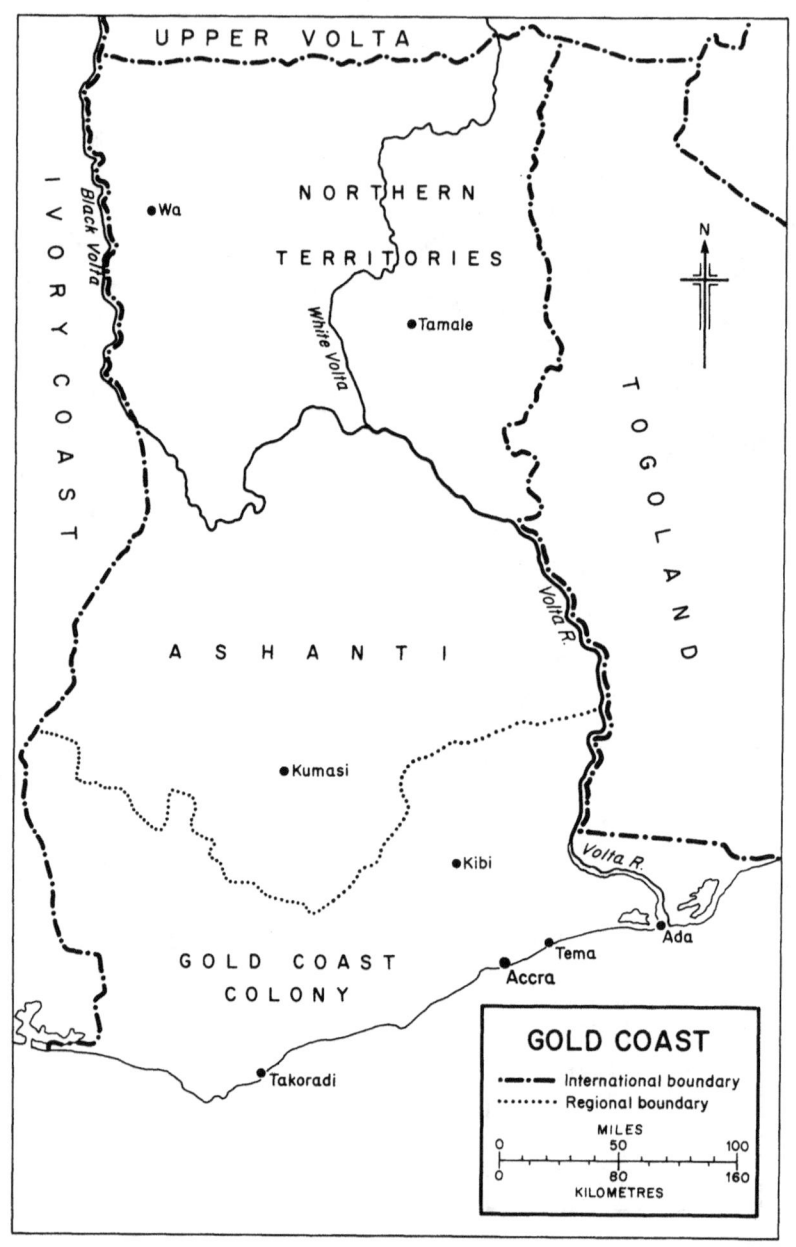

Map 3 The Gold Coast

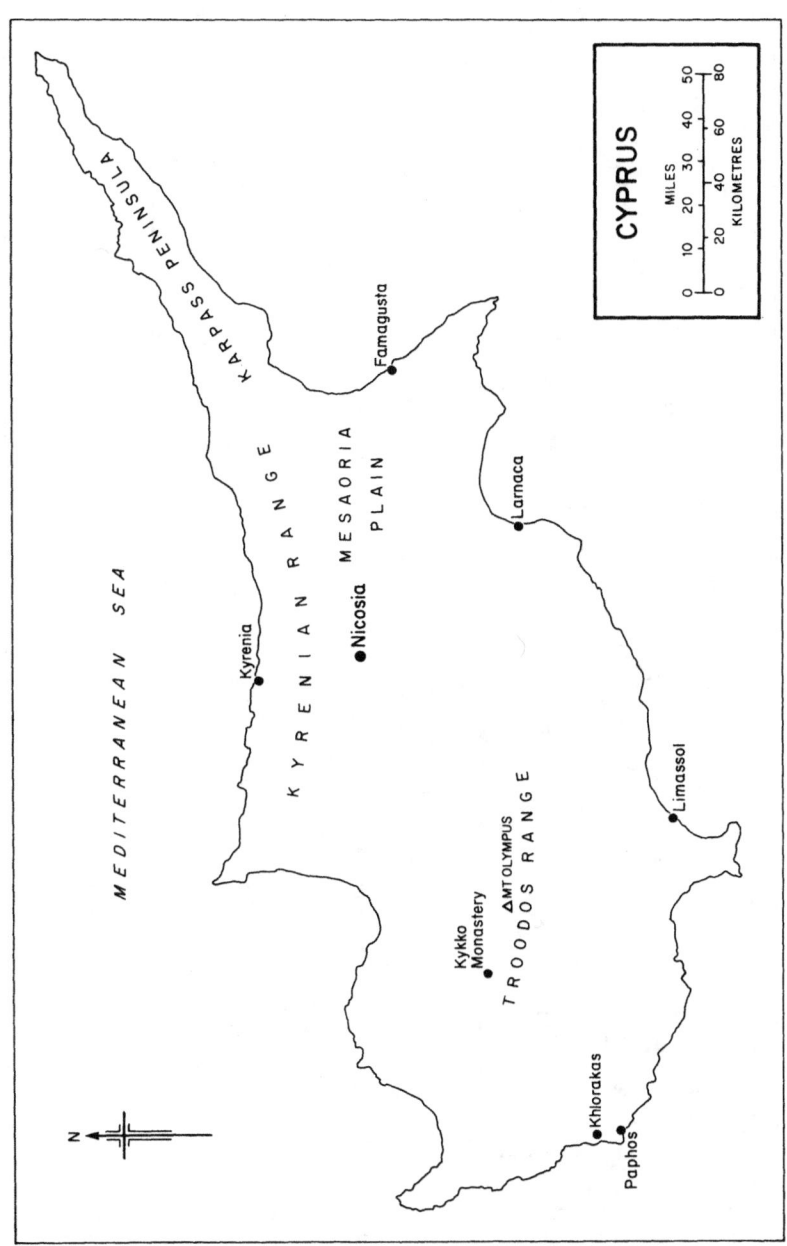

Map 4 Cyprus

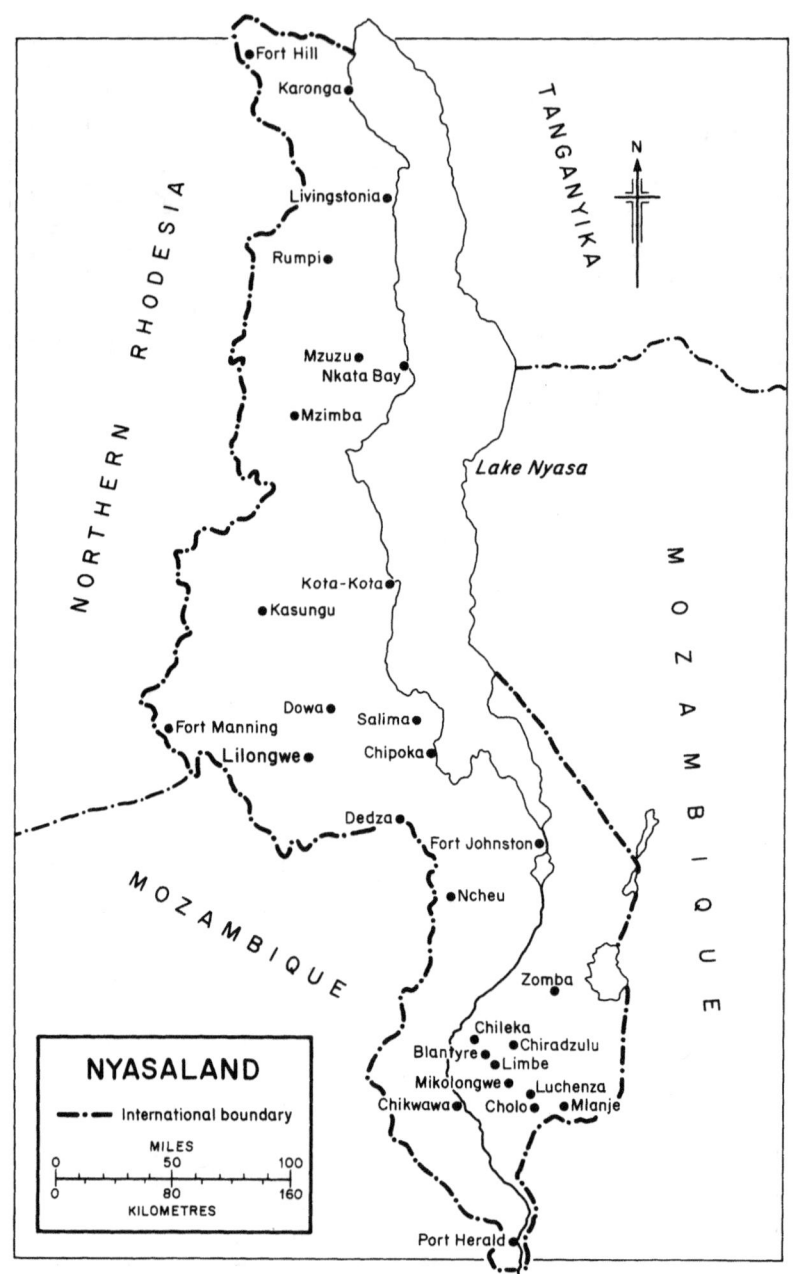

Map 5 Nyasaland

1

Early Years

I believe the colonial service is the thing for me.

Saint Thomas the apostle is traditionally believed to have been martyred on Mount San Thome in India and to have been buried in what is now part of Madras city. Madras itself was founded by Francis Day of the English East India Company in 1639 and grew in size as the commercial and government population expanded. By the beginning of the twentieth century it was a flourishing city, the main port of India's southeast coast, and there was a large community made up of traders and those in the 'civil, military, naval and ecclesiastical service of the crown'. The expatriate population created a remarkable western-type existence for themselves. There were cricket and polo matches, they hunted to hounds, held balls and receptions, worshipped at one of the many Christian churches – there were three cathedrals – and held grand evening concerts.

The extent to which they recreated their 'home' society, an essentially English society, is seen at its clearest in their preparations each year for Christmas. In December, with temperatures ranging between a minimum of 75°F and a maximum of 85°F in the shade, and with a humidity of 86 per cent, the Madras European society perused the local *Madras Mail* to see what was available in the shops ready for the festive season. The leading stores had a plenteous assortment of provisions: Christmas cakes, plum puddings, nuts, turkeys, ham, Oxford sausages, mince pies, dessert fruit, cards, decorations, crackers, toys, games and Santa Claus stockings.[1]

It was into this society, four days before Christmas 1906, that Robert Perceval Armitage was born at Nungumbankum, Madras. His father must have been very quick off the mark because Robert's arrival was reported in the *Madras Mail* on the very day he was born. It was the only birth reported that day and usually reports appeared several days after the event.

Robert was the first child of Frank and Muriel Armitage.[2] A second son, Harry, was born in 1911. Two strands of the family, on the paternal side, had been joined in 1851 when Arthur Armitage, a justice of the peace and doctor of letters, married Isabel Jane Perceval. Arthur's ancestry could be traced back to at least the early seventeenth century and Isabel's almost as far – at least to the marriage of John, Earl of Egmont, to Catherine, Baroness Arden, in 1756. Robert's great-great-grandfather, Spencer Perceval – John and Catherine's son – was prime minister of Great Britain, and was assassinated in the House of Commons in 1812. Arthur, like his father – Spencer Perceval's son – was land agent for the Guy's Hospital estate at Bridstow near Ross in Herefordshire, and he lived in the large estate house, Moriston, until he married and bought Dadnor on the edge of the estate.

Dadnor became the family home and Arthur and Isabel's four spinster daughters lived there, three of them for the whole of their lives. They also had four sons, one of whom was Frank, Robert's father, born on 19 January 1872. Frank was educated at Marlborough College and at the age of 18 joined the police department in Madras, India. He was promoted to be superintendent in 1901 and commissioner of police, Madras city, in 1910. He became inspector general of police of Madras presidency from 1921 until he retired in 1927 when he was awarded the CIE. In November 1905, at Bombay cathedral, he married Muriel Byrde, daughter of the Reverend Frederic Louis Byrde and the adopted daughter of Henry Bidewell Grigg of the Indian Civil Service. Her parents lived in India, she spent a good deal of time with the Griggs and at a later stage added their name to her own: Byrde-Grigg. Frank's family also had close connections with India: his cousin, Selina, married Sir Horatio Walpole, assistant under-secretary of state for India, two of his aunts were married to officers of the Bombay Artillery and a number of relatives were in the Indian Civil Service. There were other overseas connections: his eldest brother, Robert, worked in Barbados, South Africa and Egypt, and his younger brother, Arthur, worked in Ceylon.

Robert's parents took leave in Britain every three years and when he was ten years old they sent him to Highfield School at Liphook in Hampshire, where he began in the Lent term of 1917. The school had been founded in 1903 in the Highfield district of Southampton, but when the buildings were burned down it moved to Liphook in 1907.[3] The school prospered and by the time Robert started there, the buildings were three times as extensive as the original and the premises had expanded from 32 acres to 160. The original 32 boys, mainly from Southampton, had grown in number to 70, 'from every part of the country'. Highfield was a typical preparatory school of the period, but generally considered to be in the top class. In those days it was normal among the professional and middle classes, from whom the Highfield boys were drawn, to send their sons to boarding school at the age of eight or nine, and there was one case of a boy of only six years when Robert was at Highfield. The headmaster was the Reverend W. D. Mills, a wealthy and generous man who took a great interest in the education of his pupils and in their lives after they left his care. He believed that 'the real test lies in the life of each boy when he leaves here'.

Preparatory schools, including Highfield, were primarily places for laying the early foundation of a classical education: Latin and Greek were taught in the top form, and boys were prepared not only for common entrance but also for scholarships to public schools where most were expected to go. Highfield's standard of scholarship in classics was high because the headmaster, although not professing to be a scholar, shrewdly appointed good scholars to his staff to take the top form. During Robert's time at the school there were old boys studying at 18 major British public schools.

Robert won a number of book prizes for academic work and he 'treasured' these throughout his life. An annual general knowledge competition was held for the whole school and the results were prominently published. In his first year he came 45th out of 70 with a grading of 38 per cent. In his final year he came 2nd out of 80 with 76 per cent.

Outside the academic field – classics and the 'three Rs' – Highfield boys lived a robustly physical existence. Their day began with compulsory cold showers supervised personally by the headmaster, who directed them under the shower for the prescribed period. Games were compulsory: football in the autumn, rugby in the spring and cricket in the summer. Swimming and diving in the unheated swimming bath were important in the summer. Physical training was a curriculum activity, which varied with the staff available, but during the First World War there was less than previously. There was a physical drill competition each year and Robert represented his form – which won – in 1918. Games were taken very seriously and it was compulsory for boys who were not themselves playing to watch first team matches. When the cricket second eleven were all out for 15 against a neighbouring rival school, they were treated in disgrace for a whole week.

In his final year Robert captained the school cricket team – he had been a member of the first eleven during the two previous seasons – and, in anticipation of this, the editor of the school magazine wrote: '[Armitage] has another year in the team and if he tries hard he should be both a good captain and cricketer next season. He has not opened out much this year, but his batting shows promise.... Should stick to his bowling as it may be useful. Is quite a good catch and field.' In a match against the ladies of South Hampshire he was bowled by Miss Day – possibly a descendant of the founder of Madras – for a duck! Early in his cricket career he batted low down on the list, but when he became captain he opened the batting! By his final season, the editor of the school magazine said that he was a conscientious captain, would improve with experience and his batting was much improved. He also played football for the school and did 'a lot of good work, [being] indefatigable though somewhat slow and erratic in his kicking'.

Parents and, in the case of boys from overseas, guardians were not encouraged to visit their sons and wards more than once or twice a term; and there were no exeats. The masters – who lived in houses around the school – were all bachelors – even Mills married only early in the war and his wife died in 1918 – so they were more involved in after-school activities; and almost every moment of the boys' time was directed and supervised by masters. The sole female on the staff besides the matron taught the lowest form only.

> The complete isolation from women except the rather dragon-type Matron; and the complete lack of expression of affection, throughout the whole organization, naturally led to masters sometimes having special friends; but ... I don't remember any sort of accusation of being 'teachers' pets'. There was a little ... mild bullying – rather from the point of view that you ought to be able to take the various tortures which boys inflicted on each other.

Boys entered a life totally different from home – socially, emotionally and intellectually. Much depended on the sort of 'inner person' they were whether they would be happy or not and on whether they were unlucky enough to be punished. Beating with a cane by the headmaster was the normal punishment for serious offences and smacking with a slipper on the bare buttocks for mild offences. Below that level, the punishment was writing lines – the same sentence written over and over again. One of Robert's contemporaries recalled: 'Some people thought that Mills was too fond of beating; and with reflection I think that was true. But I don't think he was a monster or a sadist: he thought, and we all thought, that to take a beating was a test of one's courage and manhood.' At least one local rival school practised beating more than did Mills. Highfield boys despised its headmaster not because he beat his boys excessively but because, when umpiring at cricket matches, he advised and coached his own side during the game from the umpire's position: 'That was really unforgivable.'

There were seventy to eighty boys at Highfield and virtually all went on to public schools or the Royal Navy via Osborne College where they went at the age of 13. Highfield had a much stronger connection with the Royal Navy than with the army. Robert's time at the school coincided with the later stages of the First World War. 'All old boys serving in the forces, and at that time they would all have been in the officer class, were prayed for regularly in chapel, and Mills spoke and wrote about them with genuine emotion when they were killed.' The school magazine carried frequent obituaries of old boys who had died on active service.

Highfield had no particular religious 'accent'. Although Anglican, it was neither high Church nor low Church – but rather less than 'evangelical'. There was a beautiful school chapel and choir singing, school music and concerts – all in the curriculum – were among the most popular activities. Mills gave places to the sons of clergy for lower fees and there was a substantial church connection. The headmaster tried to inculcate Christian faith, behaviour and virtue while at the same time mixing in with it considerable worldly shrewdness and earthly wisdom.

Robert was remembered by his head boy as 'a rather quiet, shy sort of boy who was in no way outstanding, but then many prep school boys are not outstanding at the age of eleven, just nice ordinary types'. Because he was quite a large boy with a prominent gap between his front teeth, he was known at Highfield as 'Gorilla'. In his final year, he himself became head boy.

In 1919, at the age of 13, Robert sat the Winchester College scholarship examination in which candidates were expected to translate passages from Greek and Latin authors, to pass papers in arithmetic, algebra and geometry, English, French and divinity and a combined paper in history and geography, 'with a distinct imperial flavour'.[4] The examination, taken at the college over three days, was devoted to intensive written tests and followed by viva voce interviews. It imposed 'considerable strain on everyone involved, boys, parents and teachers'. He narrowly missed securing a scholarship, but was given a headmaster's 'nomination'[5] and, in September 1920, now nearly 14 years old, he went to Winchester where he spent the next five years.

Throughout Robert's first four years the headmaster of Winchester was Montague John Rendall, 'an extraordinary person to look at, with his large ungainly figure, his bristly piratical moustaches, and his peculiarities of manner and dress'. 'Monty' Rendall was a markedly eccentric man and during the last years of his headmastership – when Robert was at Winchester – 'his idiosyncrasies were taking gigantic steps'. His eccentricity and unpredictability extended to disciplining schoolboy malefactors. He might flog one in which case 'it hurt him very much more than it hurt the headmaster' or dismiss the errors of another with the enjoiner that he leave 'once and for all, the murk of sin and the confusion of error' and come back to look at the headmaster's Botticellis. Perhaps his oddest, if most endearing, habit was to get people's names wrong. Addressing three boys, he said, 'Of course I know your names. I know you, A, and you, B, but which of you is C?' It is likely that his real knowledge of the boys was profound and that he secretly enjoyed his 'humorous infirmity'.

Rendall's successor was Alwyn Williams who had previously been second master. He was, therefore, an important master during the whole of Robert's time at Winchester. Williams was held in high esteem. A fellow of All Souls and headmaster of Winchester at the age of 36, he was subsequently Dean of Christ Church, Bishop of Durham, and finally Bishop of Winchester. 'Though a man of great stature both physically and intellectually, he was never overbearing or condescending, but always sympathetic, courteous and kindly... his humanity and sure judgement left their mark on the school.' Known as 'History Bill', his teaching of history was 'brilliant'. Under him the subject rose in popularity and status.

Other masters – 'dons' – with whom Robert was in close, and in some cases daily, touch included Malcolm Robertson. Known as 'the Bobber', he was housemaster of Turner's House – known as Hoppers, Turner's nickname – opened about 1870. It was in this house that Robert was placed. Robertson had a 'first-class mind', was a good and popular housemaster and his tenure of office was long. During his time at Winchester

> The House became ... a castle to be defended against the assaults of the despot (in the person of the headmaster, however benevolent), while its inmates were vigorously trained for skirmishes with the rival barons. Competition was fierce, unqualified loyalty was demanded, and the rights claimed by the housemaster over his boys were little less than proprietary.... [The] autocratic style of housemastering was for the most part successful in winning the affection of the boys themselves.

Even so, despite the autocracy of the housemaster, prefects also took part in the government and discipline of the school. Rendall relied heavily on the prefect of hall and the senior commoner prefect, Winchester's two head boys. Robertson went to Winchester with the rank of major and was put in charge of the officers training corps. A year or so before Robert went to the college, Robertson, with three other masters, returned from the war, with an OBE and an MC.[6] He was also a form master, teaching English.

He was an enthusiast who delighted in teaching the language and in the fruits of its literature. He... felt deeply that his charges were to be citizens of the future and, while respecting the past, should not be laced too tightly into the strait-jacket of tradition. He was... fundamentally more interested in the whole boy than in any talented part... he required the best performance in any field in which one happened to operate... he was sincerely concerned to try and develop whatever was best in a boy's character rather than just a general drive onward and upward.

The new boys' examination troubles were not over when they passed the entrance examination and arrived at Winchester, because shortly after arrival they were expected to pass the 'notions' examinations: 'notions of language' – the school vernacular – and 'notions of behaviour'. It was an initiation process of considerable antiquity. Each new boy was allocated a junior mentor to show him 'the ropes' and teach him the 'notions'. Wykehamists have many words, often obscure to outsiders which they themselves use frequently, almost automatically and with complete understanding – at least of their meaning if not always their etymology. Notions of behaviour had also to be learned: 'the conventions based on petty privilege, which determine what a boy should or should not do' such as having all buttons on his coat done up during his first half – half means term – and being allowed to unbutton one button for every half he was at the school. After two weeks new boys were expected to pass an examination in these notions conducted by the prefects of the house. The notions were taken very seriously and frequent letters to the editor of *The Wykehamist* during Robert's time guarded against any decline in adhering to them.[7]

At the time Robert (or Armite, as he was now sometimes called) was at Winchester, there were 470 boys. Of these, 70 were scholars who lived in the Old School buildings, wore black gowns and were 'generally brainy'. There were ten boarding houses, each with 40 commoner boys, dispersed at various distances from the school itself. Robertson's spinster sister kept house for him and fed the boys well. Domestic life was centred in the house rather than the school and it was in the house that boys ate, relaxed and slept. Hoppers was generally reckoned to be a very good house and had the reputation of being exceptionally 'British', a slightly derogatory way of saying it was over-conscientious.[8]

In Hoppers, discipline was strict and, although individuality was encouraged to some extent, non-conformity was not. It was easy for a boy to run up against 'the network of traditional shibboleths that abounded on all sides' and many boys spent their first few years with apprehensions that they might transgress without knowing it. There were four or five prefects in each house and the fags were at the beck and call of any of them. 'For the first two or three years one was a fag with certain duties on behalf of a particular prefect and general dogsbody to the others. The prefects had powers to beat the juniors for one or other of the many errors in behaviour into which it was only too easy to fall.' The prefects had a communal study and each prefect had his own small study, which it was the job of his particular fag to keep clean and tidy. The fag also cleaned his shoes. 'A cry of "boy" would summon any available fag to the main study at any time. The first to arrive got the job, whatever it was, connected with the wellbeing of the caller. Any rush to obey was likely to be noisy rather than rapid.'

In a typical day, the boys rose quite early and, for the compulsory showers, there was a plentiful supply of cold water – 'pretty parky in winter'. In the summer only, there was a short period of class work before breakfast at 9.00 a.m. After chapel, there was a seven-minute walk to the school – known as 'going up to books' – where the classrooms were located. At 1.00 p.m., lunch – 'a square meal' – was taken in house and the boys returned to two periods of classwork in the afternoon. It was an inflexible rule that every boy took some exercise every afternoon and what each did was carefully recorded. The minimum requirement was a run round a nearby block of streets, which took about a quarter of an hour; otherwise, one could play fives, squash or racquets. In the summer, cricket was 'the constant order', with a multitude of games progressing in various parts of the grounds. During one of the two winter terms soccer was played and, in the other, Winchester football: 'a hybrid sport played with a round ball, with scrums but no handling. It needed a special pitch with enclosed sides.' Tea was at 6.00 p.m. – 'unlimited bread and butter and jam and tea but nothing more unless you ordered something more solid, e.g. eggs and chips from the school shop. This was delivered and paid for by yourself.' After tea, a period of leisure was followed by study from 8.00 p.m. until 10.00 p.m. At 10.15 p.m. prayers were taken by the housemaster or one of the prefects. This was followed by cocoa and biscuits and lights out were at 11.00 p.m.[9]

Beating, an accepted part of Winchester life, was administered by boys except in the case of the headmaster, 'who had the power to beat anyone who stepped too far beyond the limit of what was deemed decent behaviour'. When the headmaster did perform this task, which was rare, with a birch he would open with the warning, 'Ahem, hold your vitals.' The more normal beating was by house prefects with a three-quarters of an inch thick ash stick and the recipients were juniors of less than two or three years in the school. Pressures on academic achievement were considerable and weekly orders of merit in class were issued. If a boy went down the order for three weeks running without a valid excuse he could be beaten for it. 'As one progressed up the school tensions certainly relaxed and after three years life became less grim.'

Robert's first report – for March 1921 – was a good one and he came third in a class of 26.[10] In 'Division subjects', in which he came fourth, Dickenson – a master reputed not to hand out bouquets easily – said that he was a 'sensible worker with a clear brain' who would have no difficulty in 'getting up the school': it was a 'good performance'. In Greek, in which he came tenth, his work was 'good', but he had lost a little through absence; none the less he was said to 'hold his own well'. He came eleventh in mathematics and did 'very well'. He did 'well throughout' in French, coming third. He took no science. The headmaster commented, 'A capital place: he is coming on well.'

Towards the end of the summer term of 1921, Robert travelled from Winchester to watch the annual cricket match against Eton. The railway company was unable to let them have their usual train, so the boys travelled by motor bus – a new experience for many of them. He stayed with Sir Edward Grigg, 'Uncle Ned', in London. Grigg – who also had been born in Madras and had gone to Winchester before going to New College, Oxford – was private secretary to David Lloyd-George and was too busy to go to Eton on the first day of the match. Instead, he took Robert to 10 Downing Street while he had meetings with the prime minister. 'I went to 10 Downing Street and saw the PM while I was waiting for Uncle Ned. I had lunch and tea with the Astors and dinner with Uncle Ned at the Oxford and Cambridge Club.' The next day the prime minister 'kept Uncle Ned till 1.00 p.m.', and by the time they motored down to Eton they arrived at the end of Winchester's second innings. When Grigg went on to Chequers, Robert returned to Winchester by bus. Motor buses in the early 1920s were a novelty and journeys in them an exciting experience:

> Nearly the whole school came back by them. I got on top luckily. We were due to start at 7.00 p.m. We started at 7.45 p.m. First of all we took the wrong turning then we stopped every now and then for water, our bus broke down, was mended and so after a very enjoyable ride of six hours we arrived [at Winchester] at 1.40 a.m.

He spent much of the summer holiday – as he did throughout most of his years at school – with his aunts at Dadnor where he developed a lifelong enjoyment of gardening. He did a good deal of shooting: rabbits, partridges, pigeons and ducks and spent the end of the holiday in London with Grigg.[11] At Easter 1922, he spent a fortnight with Harry at Saint Germain in France while Uncle Ned went on to Genoa. In the few days in London before he left for France, he sorted his stamp collection into an album with the aid of a catalogue he had bought at school. This was another interest that was to last the rest of his life. They went to the Coliseum in London and 'saw people riding bicycles on one wheel and ventriloquists and Russian dancers'. In Saint Germain they went for long walks, played card games and danced a little. He wrote to his parents, 'I am reading a French book and I can read it perfectly except for the hard words I have never heard of.' In Paris they did a good deal of sightseeing, had tea at the Lyceum Club and 'watched the Parisian crowd in the Bois de Boulogne and the "bourgeois" go to the races at Longchamps'.[12]

During the summer half, he had a 'frightfully good leave-out day at Highfields', visiting his old school:

> [We] went by train and were met by Mr Mills' new 6 cylinder Buick, a very smart affair. I saw [two old friends], they both looked flourishing. In the morning I went round the old place. The grounds are so different now.... After lunch we changed and played cricket ... Bonham and I opened our innings and the bowling was so bad we could have hit off the runs in a quarter of an hour but we were told to get out. I got myself out [leg before wicket] and Bonham allowed himself to be bowled.[13]

Robert was a member of the officers training corps at school and passed the musketry and general efficiency tests, attended two annual camps and was made a corporal. In June 1922 he attended a field day when they marched on to the downs, had a parade and were then given '15 rounds of blank'. When they were in position they were attacked by Marlborough College.

> Our platoon was right in front and we had the first scrap. We completely wiped out Marlborough before they reached us yet nevertheless they came on and we had to retreat which we did in a masterful manner. We then occupied a position in the rear and had another small scrap at the end. It was huge fun and going and coming we sang songs etc.[14]

This was an annual event, the venue being near Winchester, Marlborough, Wellington and Bradford in turn and the boys being taken in specially hired trains. On this particular occasion the boys were lucky that the weather was too cold for them to be obliged to do 'the projected bathing in Gunner's Hole'.[15] A week later he played cricket for his house in 'the match of the season'. Having lost the toss, his team did well, opened their 'attack with uncanny command of length and spin and by dint of brilliant fielding' soon got the other side out. Later they needed only six runs to win 'and two absolute rabbits in, who took four overs to add one run before one of them hit a four: We were equal!' The next ball hit the batsman on the leg and they ran two byes: 'We had won!' In enthusiastically recounting this match to his parents he did not tell them that in the second innings he scored 47 not out, the highest score. In internal matches at school at this time, he was scoring 15 to 20 and taking up to seven wickets in an innings. A year later he opened the batting for Hoppers. He also played Winchester and association football for his house.[16]

He and Harry spent much of the 1922 summer holiday at Craigmaddie in Scotland. Although it was very wet they managed to play some tennis, went for long walks, boated on the pond, went shooting, went for motor drives and enjoyed seeing the old churches and the lovely views. They visited Glasgow, went to the art galleries and saw 'pictures and models of ships and engines and beasts and birds of all descriptions'. Later in the vacation he stayed near Bishop's Stortford and with Uncle Ned he played cricket for Furneaux Pelham against Brent Pelham, the pair of them opening the batting. The standard of this village cricket was not high, but they both enjoyed the match and the company. Grigg scored two and Robert three in the first innings out of a total of 49. In the second innings, Sir Edward scored a duck and Robert again three, out of 17. They none the less beat Brent Pelham! He also played for a local farmers' team. During this part of his holidays he had lunch with the prime minister and Grigg. Lloyd-George 'was very jolly and drank Bass'. He spent the last part of the vacation at Dadnor where he played patience, billiards and tennis – he claimed his service was 'quite demon like' – went cycling, watched football, ferreted with a local boy and went shooting hares and rabbits – he was 'mad on shooting'.[17]

At the end of September 1922 he travelled back to Winchester and wrote to his parents: 'Being a two year man I need not get up till after first peal, five minutes later than last term and I can come in before 3.00 p.m. on Sundays. Also, I can "brew" and heaps of other things – I have changed my [study] and now have a chair.'[18] He played a good deal of football, sometimes four times a week, and squash, getting into the handicap competition semi-finals. On a leave-out day he went to London 'to 10 Downing Street and saw Uncle Ned. I felt frightfully important as I rang the bell. I have been there so often you see.' He went again to Downing Street a few days later and talked with the prime minister for about five minutes.[19]

In his school report for November 1922, the headmaster, who taught Latin, was surprised to find him 'so low' in this subject – third from bottom of the class.[20] The staff thought he had 'got a bit discouraged lately', especially in Latin, although they quite expected him to 'come on a good deal before the end'. His Greek also was poor, history was better and he was 'a little languid' in modern languages, but 'coming on fairly'. In mathematics he had worked very well, and in chemistry, in which he was interested, he was making good progress.

Lord and Lady Astor, close friends of Grigg, invited Robert and Harry to spend Christmas 1922 with them at Cliveden. Sir Edward was supposed to be with them too, but instead he 'went to his bride-to-be's home'. The boys went to the cinema, played tennis, football and ping pong, and went shopping to buy Christmas presents. Robert had only partly been looking forward to Christmas at Cliveden, but in the event he found it enjoyable and interesting: 'Christmas passed as a dream. Among the guests were Earl Winterton, two MPs and Mrs Wintringham, the other lady MP. We had great fun and terrific political discussions.'[21] The Astors owned race horses and it was they who were instrumental in interesting Robert in horses and racing – and betting on them – which were to become a lifelong passion.[22]

In April 1923, his school report was something of a mixture: 'Not brilliant in any way, but uniformly thorough. He is always alive, very often helps with a good suggestion. On paper he is improving; but his expression (v spelling) still needs care.'[23] In modern languages he was 'always well prepared' but was still 'a very poor hand at pronunciation'. In mathematics he was 'interested and intelligent' and worked well. Chemistry was weak: 'He obviously finds the work rather beyond him, but he always shows interest and willingness to learn.' The headmaster's overall comment was that he had good all-round ability, 'which may carry him some way in life' and he tackled all his work 'with good will'. In a letter to Mrs Armitage, the house master said that this was 'a very satisfactory report'. He was confident he would manage 'Certificate' the following half and might have a chance of an exhibition in 1925. 'He is a steady, reliable fellow and I look to him to be a leader in the house before he leaves.' In his school certificate, awarded in July 1923, he passed with credits in scripture knowledge (Greek text), history, Latin, French and elementary mathematics. Although he had also studied geography, Greek and science these were not mentioned in his certificate. In the July 1923 school examinations he came sixth out of 25 in Latin, ninth out of 16 in Greek, and fourth out of 25 in divinity.[24]

Early in the autumn term of 1923 the Prince of Wales visited Winchester College and Robert wrote enthusiastically to his parents.[25] The visit passed off 'magnificently' and the school was given an extra week's holiday. The prefect of hall gave an address in Latin to which the prince replied, in English, and later that day the prince watched a game of football.

> There were three benches reserved for the Prince and his train, etc. Uncle Ned took me along to these and I sat on a sort of bench the Prince used as a footstool.... After the game Uncle Ned took me along and ... introduced me. Then HRH said 'What did you say your name was?' [I replied] 'Armitage' [and he said]: 'Armitage – ah', as if trying to remember where he had heard it before.

Grigg, who had accompanied the prince on a number of commonwealth tours, explained that Frank Armitage had been in Madras when the prince was there. The prince replied 'Ah, yes. I remember' and asked Robert if he had been born there and if he wanted to go back, to both of which questions he replied 'Yes.' 'Then we shook hands again and he went to have some tea and I went to the school shop.'

He was made a school prefect in 1924 and his summer examination results were good: he came seventh out of 21 in Latin, fourth out of 17 in history and fifth out of 16 in divinity.[26]

In Robert's final year at Winchester, 1924/5, he was senior commoner prefect: '[He] stood between august authority with all the gravitas of tradition and the subject citizens of whose behaviour he was theoretically in charge. Being representative of the masses and at the same time responsible to the management he was a sort of proconsul in microcosm.'[27] A fortnight before Christmas 1924 he spent a week at Oxford, 'making a vain attempt', as he saw it, to pass the university entrance examinations.

> The essay quite finished me, we had to write on 'Pedantry'. We did not even have a choice. I do not know what it means really and I had to write for three hours on the subject. It was the pink penultimate with a vengeance. But I had a great time up there. I took the opportunity to have a good bath every morning. ... My exam took place in University Hall and lasted from 9.30–12.30 and 2.00–5.00. I had essay, general European and English history papers and a French, Greek and Latin unseen, making seven papers in all. One piece of French was full of the most abstruse words ever invented, but I managed to make a little sense of it.[28]

After 5.00 p.m. each day, he 'staggered away for a cup of tea' and then, since 'there was nothing else to be done', went to a cinema. On Thursday he had his viva, 'an awful ordeal'. He was not frightened until he got to the door and then he 'got acute wind up, but it soon passed once [he] was inside'.

There were about eight men all sitting at a table, and I felt as if I had come there to be condemned. After a few moments my examiner ... asked me what I thought was the greatest boon the middle ages had left us. My mind became a complete blank on the spot but I tried to look composed and answered Cathedrals.... He then asked me what was the best specimen of Norman I had seen. That was a poser! Suddenly I remembered an expedition I had made to Romsey Abbey [in the course of an annual visit by the archaeological society at Winchester[29]] and mentioned it. He said, 'I thought you would say that, it is the finest bit I have seen.' He then made me discourse on the different forms of Norman and tried to draw me off onto Romanesque, but that was too much for me. I stalked out of the room thanking my lucky stars for that expedition to Romsey. On Friday morning I did a Greek unseen quite quickly and picking up two more men who were up for exams, we went off and played billiards. It was the best fun I have ever had.

He had lunch, went again to a cinema and then returned to Winchester. At Reading he was 'ravenous and bought vast bags of buns and pork pies etc.' He did not know when the results of the examinations would be out, but was convinced – incorrectly – that he had 'not got a chance'.

In July 1925 he left Winchester and his last few days there were full. He had to make a speech at House Supper and did so rather better than he had expected, although he said nothing would ever induce him to get on his hind legs again! 'Thus ended another phase of my life. Finis.'[30]

He then went to stay with the Griggs in London and, in a letter to his parents, he gave the first indication of what he wished to do for a career: 'I believe the colonial service is the thing for me. Uncle Ned advises it and it seems quite hopeful as there is no exam and if I can get a good degree, I ought to be all right. I should like to go to Kenya.'[31] Grigg had been knighted in 1920, became secretary of the Rhodes Trust and in 1925 was appointed governor of Kenya.[32] During Robert's second year at Winchester, Grigg had lectured to the school on the 'problems and destinies' of the British Empire, in the interests of which he had 'spent long years of his life in persistent and disinterested work'. Lord Chelmsford, formerly Viceroy of India, also gave a lecture and in the course of his speech said: 'Winchester always stands *ad portas* to her sons; they pass out and are scattered over the world.' Another visitor spoke about central Africa and Kenya. *The Wykehamist* carried several reports of Old Wykehamist reunions in various parts of the empire: Simla, Calcutta, Cairo, Khartoum and Nairobi. These and other imperialist influences may well have helped to shape Robert's ideas on a career in the colonies.

What other part might Winchester have played in his development during his five years there? The beatings, cold showers, male environment and staff eccentricity seem to shave left no lasting adverse mark on him. On the positive side, from Williams he may have learned a 'sympathetic, courteous and kindly' approach to life's problems and have developed sufficient of a liking for history to study it at university. From Robertson, he may have learned more about loyalty and have responded to his housemaster's attempts to encourage an open and enquiring mind and to develop whatever was best in his character. The tone of the college, however, and thereby the influence it might have on the boys, was set by the headmaster. For four years, this was Rendall.

> Rendall constantly put before his boys the ideal of free and responsible obedience to law. Preaching [a few years before Armitage's time] he said ... It seems to me the special work of the Public Schools of England to carry on that tradition of duty and discipline which is day by day vanishing from sight, to manifold fields of service at home and abroad.[33]

He believed that 'the real thing is mastering ... the power to use the world and its resources, and to hand it on improved to those who come after you.'[34] From the many letters sent to him on his retirement, one in particular indicates the effect his headmastership may have had on his pupils: 'No boy who has been under you can think of you and at the same time harbour any thought of self-indulgence, insincerity or purposelessness ... your own qualities have formed the high tone which the outside world recognizes in Winchester boys.'[35]

From Robert's letters to his parents one detects a gradual and confident growing up, yet one that retained a marked schoolboyishness with its excitement and enthusiasm. This showed through in his accounts of the Winchester scholarship examination, his visit to Highfield, the army field operation and his cricket. Academically, he was middle-of-the-road except in history, but his personal qualities were more outstanding and he became senior commoner prefect. Socially, he also developed a good deal, mildly hobnobbing with the prime minister, the Prince of Wales, the Astors and the Griggs, yet playing village cricket and going ferreting with a local lad at Dadnor.

Of the 68 boys entering Winchester at the same time as Robert, 48 went on to university, all to either Oxford or Cambridge. Of the 34 who went to Oxford, 16 went to New College. A further nine went to either the Royal Military Academy or the Royal Military College. Only 11 did not go to university. Later, when they went into careers, 13 went into school or university teaching, eight into banking, insurance or the stock exchange, four each into the colonial service and medicine, three into the law – one becoming a Lord of Appeal in Ordinary – two into the civil service and two into politics, both becoming ministers.[36] In 1924, for example, there were 154 Old Wykhamists among the 4750 students at Oxford, 52 of them at New College.[37]

In October 1925 Robert went up to Oxford, to New College, where he read history. He played soccer during his first year but not thereafter, preferring hockey and becoming a member of the college first eleven. He was a member of the New College and Magdalen beagles.[38]

During the summer vacation of 1927, which he spent at Ross, he met a young lady, Lyona Meyler, who was visiting her three boy cousins – friends of Armitage – when on holiday from her work in London. She had left school at the age of 17 and had studied art at Reading University for two years. At the age of 19 she went to work in London, did a variety of jobs including modelling for Miss Gray in Brook Street. Robert and Lyona corresponded frequently during the autumn and she was invited to stay at Ross for a few days after Christmas. During this holiday they became engaged to be married. Robert's parents – who probably did not realize that they had known each other for four months – had recently retired to Herefordshire and his mother was 'horrified' that they became betrothed so soon after meeting and at so young an age, and she refused to allow Lyona to wear an engagement ring.[39] Until he met Lyona, Robert's contact with young women had been limited and, while he recognized the attractions of some of the few he had met, he seems previously also to have noticed their defects, as he saw them:

'The daughter is 17 and very nice only she has one dark brown eye and one light eye.'[40]

'The daughter ... is 15, grim and very independent and dances at L'Opéra, she is rather pretty and was brought up in England and speaks English very well. She has varicose veins or something of that nature in her left leg so she has to be *très* careful and not do too much.'[41]

'There is a friend staying here, a Turkish girl of 16 years, she is very nice and full of spirits but talks French too fast for me.'[42]

Early in 1928 – now in his final year and engaged to be married – he applied for a post in the colonial administrative service. He used as his referees, Robertson from Winchester, Fisher, warden of New College, and Woodward, his final year history tutor and a fellow of All Souls.[43] Robertson reported that Robert 'had an honourable record', was a house and school prefect, played all games for his house and 'took his full share of its general activities'. Fisher recommended him as 'extremely fit to hold a position of public trust' and said that he had an excellent character, was conscientious in his work and was 'of more than average ability'. Woodward said he was 'a man of vigorous personality, quick and good intelligence and excellent character. He would be well able to undertake responsibility and could be trusted to maintain the best traditions of the colonial service. He is a very pleasant man and would be a good tempered and reliable colleague, and a valued member of any community to which he belonged'.

In the summer of 1928 he graduated with a second class honours degree in history, and on 16 August he received a letter from the Colonial Office saying he had been selected as a cadet administrative officer in Kenya at a salary of £400 a year.[44] Fisher, in giving permission to return to New College for the tropical services course, said, 'A fine career opens out before you and I have every confidence that you will make your mark.'[45]

He spent the 1928/9 academic year at Oxford on the course preparing cadets about to take up careers in Africa. He recalled almost 40 years later how his instructor in agriculture said that he knew all about farming in South America and the Pacific islands but nothing at all about farming in Africa. He was not impressed with the quality of his fellows: 'The entrance to this colonial service has got to be made harder. Some of these men...are a disgrace.'[46] Others found the course 'great fun' and the most useful parts those that dealt with surveying and law, although it gave little 'idea of what the service was really like'.[47] Others over the years also found the course enjoyable and particularly valued the more practical aspects. He was a member of the 'Gridiron Club' and was remembered by a colleague on the course as 'a rather reserved type of whom we did not see a lot', probably because he 'preferred the company of members of his college and old school friends'.[48] It was the case, too, that he spent a good deal of time with Lyona who drove up from London in her 'snub-nosed Morris' car to visit him.[49] At the end of the course he travelled out to Kenya.

2

Kenya

I should be very unfeeling if I did not do my best to get on.

Kenya in East Africa is 225,000 square miles in area and broadly comprises six geographic regions.[1] The coastal plane, 270 miles long and 20 miles wide, bears marsh and mangrove forests with patches of high grass and scattered groups of trees. The highlands, inland, are broken by the Rift Valley, 50 to 60 miles wide and containing a number of freshwater and saline lakes. To the east of the rift the highlands are dominated in the south by the Aberdare mountains and the volcanic Mount Kenya, both of which include large areas of moorland with thick forest between, while in the north, the northeast plateau of Kenya lies between 800 and 3500 feet above sea level. To the west of the rift the Cherangani range and Mau hills rise to 11,000 feet with plateau lands to the west including the Kericho highlands and Nandi hills. The Lake Victoria basin lies to the west of the highlands and contains the northeast corner of that lake.

Rainfall averages less than 20 inches annually in the northern desert areas and 40 to 80 inches along the coastal strip. Elsewhere, averages are between 20 and 40 inches. On the coast there is usually a single rainy season from April to November, but elsewhere there is a long rainy season from April to June and a short season from October to December. The coastal areas are tropical but the highlands are cool and invigorating.

In 1929, when Armitage arrived, Kenya's African population was 3 million, its Asian 42,000 and its European – found mainly along the line of rail from Mombasa to Lake Victoria – 13,000. The country was administered by the governor, then Sir Edward Grigg, and an executive council of 11 others, including three non-officials. The legislative council comprised 11 ex-officio, 10 nominated – one representing African interests – and 17 elected members – 11 European, five Asian and one Arab. There were no African members of either council. The secretariat, the central government office under the chief secretary, had

24 officers and attached to the secretariat were the treasury, customs, audit and attorney-general's departments. In the district administration there were 107 officers – provincial, district and assistant district commissioners. Kenya was well blessed with the size of its administrative staff. In British Africa as a whole in the 1930s there was one administrative officer for every 35,000 population; in Kenya there was one for every 20,000. Specialist departments included police, prisons, medical, education, agriculture, veterinary, forestry, game and public works.

Administratively, the country was divided into six provinces and 36 districts. District officers were moved roughly every 18 months to experience a variety of environments: agricultural, pastoral and European settlement areas. District commissioners were transferred about every five years so as not to become too settled in any one area. The district commissioner was responsible for all government staff in his district including personnel of the main specialist departments.[2]

Armitage travelled to Kenya on the *Matiana* from Southampton on 6 July 1929.[3] He sailed via the Bay of Biscay where the ship 'rolled a bit'. He felt ill at lunchtime so lay on his bunk for the rest of the day, passing Gibraltar and on to Marseilles. Travelling via Crete, he spent the night at Port Said, where he danced aboard a French destroyer. He found the Red Sea nights very hot and slept on deck. Shipboard entertainment included bridge, which he played frequently, and a sweep, which he won and had to organize thereafter. On 4 August, a month after leaving Britain, he 'Arrived [at] Mombasa in the good ship *Matiana* [at] 4.00 p.m. . . . Mombasa looking too wonderful and green.' His first impressions of Kenya were 'distinctly good'.

The following day he spent 'an awful morning' getting through customs and the next travelled by rail to Nairobi, noting of his travelling companion, also a new cadet, 'He is very quiet [and] I doubt if he will have enough push to succeed': from the outset Armitage had his eye on the personal attributes needed to succeed in the colonial service. He travelled by rail via Nakuru to Kisumu on Lake Victoria, where he stayed the night, and was privately critical of a number of people on the station. He thought the district commissioner 'an inconsequential blighter' who knew nothing useful and shouted at his servants. Of a couple with whom he played cards he said she talked all the time and he was the worst player he had ever played with. He confided to his diary: 'I don't like Kisumu: government officials too many and third rate.'

He was pleased to move on the next day to Kakamega. He started the trip by lorry, which had to stop to cool only once in the first four miles, after which a public works officer picked him up and took him by Chevrolet, 'driving like the wind' at 35–40 miles an hour. He immediately liked Kakamega, his first posting: 'a wonderful place on top of a ridge'. After a few months he found the district, though attractive, 'too thickly populated to be very interesting except as regards the natives'. He was also initially pleased with his first district commissioner, C. B. Thompson, who was 'quiet with flashes of humour. The perfect boss, [he] is friendly off duty and correct when office hours are on.'

Kakamega district, in the Nyanza province, was a low steamy station not far from Lake Victoria. Its large population of Luo tribesmen were agriculturalists and 'reasonably law abiding'. The total African population of the district was 385,000, divided into 17 sub-tribes. The *boma* – the district headquarters – stood in a blue gum grove and the immediate area was 'green and pleasant, the gardens full of colour and drought almost unknown, for it rained almost every afternoon'. The principal administrative problems related to clan disputes over land boundaries. There was a European gold-mining population employed as lowly paid compound managers – bankrupt farmers financially ruined after three years of locust attacks – although the real gold rush did not start until shortly after Armitage's time there.[4]

He was quickly into Kakamega's social swim. On his first full day he dined with the district commissioner and went to a dance, followed by sausage and eggs at the doctor's house. The doctor was very drunk. The district commissioner's wife was 'very Scotch' and, although she was extremely kind to Armitage, he understood that she tried 'to run the *boma*'. The assistant district commissioner, W. R. McGeagh, and his wife 'could not have been kinder'. Others on the station knew of his relationship to the governor and felt that this somewhat 'set him apart' from the other bachelors. One colleague at Kakamega saw him as 'a Wykhamist smoothie ... good looking and dressed tidily but ... a bit stand-offish'. He was called at 6.30 each morning and, although this sounded 'frightfully early', it did not worry him, but after a full day's work and a social evening he felt quite tired and was in bed by 9.30: 'I have never wanted my bed so much as I do here.'[5]

He was soon into the office routine and, in his role of magistrate, convicted his first African tax defaulter – one of the most frequent tasks of a young colonial administrator.[6] He sentenced him to a month's penal labour to be performed on the golf course where he joined five others on the first fairway planting it with grass. His first civil case was a simple one – 'some miserable man had sold a bicycle for a couple of heifers' – but others were vastly complicated and he had to reprimand a chief for sending him cases 'which no European could deal with'. He was unhappy with his court procedures:

> I have been trying some cases ... and I should hate the high court to see

the mess I make of them. I am always forgetting to write things down in the right order and then have to put them in afterwards quite illegitimately.

Got hopelessly tied up in a theft case. All the witnesses were called for the wrong people and new people kept on cropping up. An awful mess.

He found the office badly off for accommodation and had to share with a fellow assistant district commissioner, Colonel E. L. B. Anderson – 'a one-legged war veteran'[7] – whom he thought 'took life rather seriously'. This sharing had its advantages because he could ask Anderson questions he himself could not answer. In the office each day he signed a number of labour contracts and settled a number of *shauri*s or complaints. There were times when he had little to do in the office: 'Nothing ever seems to happen in the office. I merely signed some *kipande*s [labour registration certificates], receipts and contracts. So I read Swahili and the Indian Penal Code. How I wish I could get out on safari.'

He quickly changed his first impression of Thompson: 'The District Commissioner is far too easy going to make me do any work. Really a bad first boss to have.' 'He does not work hard enough here. Leaves letters too long unanswered and dislikes [court] cases and is very casual. Best thing is to do things on one's own and he will only grunt and let it go. I should say a man who can only concentrate on the matter in hand.' When McGeagh asked the district commissioner about Armitage going on safari, he said it was an excellent idea but seemed to have 'no ideas as to where I should go. Vague again'.

The district commissioner, conscious that Armitage had not enough to do in the office, gave him the tasks of filing the district annual reports – since 1902 – copying McGeagh's map of the district and collecting the dates of accession of all the chiefs in the district! Shortly, he found himself so busy that he 'had not even time to yawn': 'My days here are so full and I have hardly any time for reading. The office and tennis take up the daylight hours and then I have to do some Swahili and law and really this place makes me long for bed at 9.30. I am told it's the altitude.'

Indeed, he now periodically had so little time for reading that he asked his parents to stop sending him copies of *The Times* and send only cuttings of 'interesting articles on history or biography'. Not all days were busy, however, and he found time to study accounts of local customs, especially matrimonial customs. He found he had more to do when his fellow assistant district commissioners were on safari. McGeagh was a great help to him and he would 'miss him like anything' when he left. He also liked Mrs McGeagh – provided he did not have to play bridge with her. She helped him measure the curtains he had made by a local Indian tailor with material Lyona had bought before he left. He saw McGeagh as a man who knew his mind, had a deep understanding of the local Africans and was popular. He hoped he himself would be able to apply the wisdom he had obtained from him.

Outside the office his work entailed supervising brick-making for the new prison, marking out maize mill plots, looking after road works and supervising the breaking-in of oxen. After 'the old bullock died... another very stubborn ox began to be broken in. He had to be dragged everywhere. He would not walk of his own account.' He was soon to learn about one of the more important practical aspects of public finance procedures when, towards the end of the financial year, the public works department suddenly offered the Kakamega administration significant sums of money with which they thoroughly resurfaced and ditched the station roads, before the funds could revert to the treasury at the closing of the annual accounts.

He undertook his first safari early in September and this was largely taken up in tax collection, travelling by lorry and collecting well over 20,000 shillings on each of several successive days. On his return he paid the money into the bank and reconciled the accounts – sometimes he was a few shillings up, sometimes a few down. Safari carried its problems, often difficulties with transport: 'Of course the bloody lorry never turned up [to take me back from safari] and I sought out another knock-kneed old thing. But by stint of filling up with water every mile we managed to reach Kakamega.' On a later occasion he kept a vehicle going by filling up the radiator with ginger ale.

For relaxation he played tennis most afternoons and at weekends, unless it rained, in which case, once it eased off, he normally did some gardening. Usually, 'the whole community' turned out for tennis: four men and three women. The rain was often very heavy and they had a number of hail and thunder storms: 'The lightning played all round and literally made the landscape as bright as day.' But he did not find the house damp 'except where the roof leaks'. The rain added clarity to the views, which he appreciated: 'The most lovely morning. Elgon was clear as a photo. You could see the white cliffs in places. All the hills around were breathtaking in their blueness and greens. A nearness and the whole earth moist with dew and smelling fresh.'

Almost every day he had drinks in the early evening at either his own or a colleague's house. His garden gave him a great deal of pleasure. He soon had the borders weeded, his roses tied up and cornflowers, lettuces, beans, mulberry cuttings, pineapples and lemon trees planted. He was worried by the lack of fruit, and tried to remedy it with these plantings. His mother sent packets of seeds – by registered mail –

but he thought it better if she just sprinkled a few in each envelope when she wrote to him, thereby avoiding customs duty.

In the seclusion of his private diary he was quite critical of his colleagues and their wives and of non-officials who lived nearby. Eventually, however, he concluded that he would have to be polite to them. If they had to live together there was no point in having rows 'and it is not as if they are intolerable'. He found that after a drink they got quite friendly. He also acknowledged that he and they were 'bad at criticizing [their] superior officers ... quite against all the advice given me by mother'.

He missed Lyona a great deal and was anxious when mail was late or did not bring letters from her: 'Mail, no English letters, damn it'; 'No English mail. Curse it bitterly'.[8] He wrote to her frequently and on one occasion 'wrote to Lyona all night'. He was also much troubled by difficulties, as he saw them, over his marriage. It appeared that the old rule under which an officer could not get married and have his wife with him in the colony within his first six months of service had been replaced by one with a much longer period, and although the governor was his uncle the rule looked as if it could not be bent: 'Uncle Ned wrote and said impossible Lyona and me to be married. He is a swine. I'm not going to sit down under it. I joined under the six month rule. ... I've a good mind to chuck the job if we cannot be married before next July. The suspense is killing.' The suspense also did little for his tennis because he lost his temper and broke six strings in his racquet.

Both the Colonial Office[9] and the government of Kenya had formally and clearly published their views:

> Cadets are strongly advised not to marry during their first two tours. Should they do so, and should they be posted to remote stations such as those of the Northern Frontier Districts their wives will be unable to accompany them since these districts are not at present suitable for European women. A further consideration is that a married couple unless possessing private means of their own will probably find it difficult to live on the pay of a cadet.[10]

He was not really comforted when the district commissioner thought his application to get married would be successful: 'I know [it will] not. Luck has turned. I can feel it.'[11] Shortly, however, things brightened considerably when Grigg wrote to say he would not stop the marriage:

> He said I had misunderstood his letter and he would not stop anyone marrying after six months though he advised them not to ... I cannot see anything for it but for Lyona and me to get married in February and hope

that we get left here in peace for some time. . . . Lyona will sail at the end of January. I do not really think it will be fair to let her endure the home life that she now has to put up with.

He cabled Lyona as soon as he received the governor's letter but was still anxious because leave for the wedding had not yet been granted and he feared she would be 'quite distracted' wondering whether to book her passage or not. She did not receive his cable and Armitage exploded: 'That bloody little [man] could not have sent that cable. God, I will get him.' His plans to marry so soon disturbed his parents and he sought to justify his wishes. He discovered that cadets stayed about a year in their first station and only during their second tour were they usually sent to a bad station. With an inexperienced understanding of the pace of economic development in Africa he hoped that by his second tour 'with the development going on there will be no bad stations or very few'.

If we are sent to a bad station, Lyona has a cousin and brother out here she could stay with. . . . I would be letting Lyona down more by not marrying her soon and even being parted for a bit later than by waiting for some time. . . . I know I am being a worry to you but it has been terribly difficult.

He was concerned, too, about finances: 'Really my financial position is awful. I just cannot save money. Oh God this life!' When he did his accounts he found himself 'sinking deeper and deeper into the mire!' He had borrowed money from his parents, which he was gradually paying back, although more slowly than he had hoped. He was relieved to find his travelling allowances a help: 'I certainly do make on the travelling allowance. I get 8 [shillings] a day. . . . My expenses on my last safari were only such things as I could not get given me by the chiefs – oil, flour, potatoes, coffee, etc. Meat, milk and vegetables were always brought me.'

He was 'cheered up no end' when he received the 'joyful news' that his request for leave had been granted,[12] and he immediately discussed the wedding plans with the district commissioner who advised Nyeri as a honeymoon spot. He had previously thought of the Mountains of the Moon in Uganda, but uncertainty over acquiring a car ruled this out. He asked the ladies on the station about what Lyona should wear on safari. He still felt sore about Uncle Ned, and when he received an invitation to spend Christmas at Government House he refused.

His parents were unhappy about his marriage and his attitude towards the governor and he hastened to reassure them that he would not repeat his comments to anyone in Kenya.[13] His dissatisfaction with Grigg's opposition, however, showed through: '[Uncle Ned] objects to anyone marrying in their first tour *at all* and he would hardly tolerate them marrying in their second.' He knew their objections were that he would not get to know the country as well as he ought, but he did not think an extra six months would appreciably alter that and, as for waiting three or five years as the governor wished, 'that was impossible'. Recognizing that his parents felt his stance was unlikely to enhance his career prospects, and wishing to be both appropriately humble and determinedly optimistic, he continued:

> I know you want me to make the best of my life and after the wonderful start that you have made so many sacrifices to give me I should be very unfeeling if I did not do my best to get on and I do not think that being married would have such a bad effect on me.... I am finding myself getting very interested in the job and I see no reason why I should not go on getting more and more so.

At the end of December 1929 he was able to look back, in the privacy of his diary, on his five months in Kenya:[14]

> First, it is nothing like as hot as I had expected and of course we get more rain. Then the work would tend to monotony if it were not that I have become interested in the mind of the native though so far I have not even scratched the surface and I want to find out how he thinks.... [Station] life is boring and only to be borne because of safari. I consider that the station has been badly laid out and as regard the native bazaar and African staff houses, really it is quite disgraceful.... But even since I have come here the improvements have been great. Bush has been cleared. Roads have been improved but the roads of the district will never be satisfactory until they have all been murrummed and the place cleaned up.

He counted himself lucky as regards the people in the station except for 'two large drawbacks'. The first was the district commissioner's lack of interest in his subordinates, leaving them to find their own way in 'the tangled maze of office routine and work that is entirely new'. He was critical of the district commissioner's lack of sympathy with the difficulties of newcomers and his lack of foresight in providing the right sort of work for them and arranging their programme. The other drawback was social: 'the amount of alcohol that is drunk'. He had 'a very bad head' and much preferred soft drinks to alcohol. It took him some time to persuade his hosts of this but eventually he succeeded.

As regards individuals ... the Thompsons are very friendly. McGeagh was most helpful whatever his failings and I shall always be grateful for the advice he gave me. ... The DC has been a perfect gentleman to me away from the office. Kind, considerate and very helpful and interested in the great difficulties I have had with my marriage – difficulties that have undoubtedly prevented me from enjoying this life as I should otherwise have done. The [doctor and his wife] are now very friendly but nonentities. [Another couple] bored me at first; when she went he bored me more but he has undoubtedly good stuff in him though he talks too much and is very bigoted and unreasonable. [The nurse] is a queer, independent creature, rather proud which causes her violent outbreaks when she is thwarted. Finally the Andersons. No one could have been more kind than they have been to me. In the office I cannot help condemning him for every breach of etiquette in not recognizing the DC's position ... but I thank God that I came here and pray that it will see Lyona and me successfully launched in the life of married love.

The first six weeks of the new year, 1930, saw his attention overwhelmingly concerned with his forthcoming marriage, especially the practicalities of arranging it: 'Well, thank God we have got into this new year. Every day will count now. I never thought we should get here.'¹⁵ 'The crab now is what day to get married on. We can hardly rush off from the train to the cathedral and I do not suppose they will marry us on a Sunday so it looks rather as if we shall have to wait till the Monday. A nuisance as Saturday would have been the ideal day.'

He explained to his parents that 'the drawback now is Uncle Ned' who would not say whether he would attend the ceremony. If he was not attending they would get married in Mombasa which 'certainly would be far simpler'. He anguished over the few letters he was getting from Lyona – busily arranging to leave England – but was relieved when Roddy, her brother, wrote to say that he could get leave in order to give Lyona away. He learned from his family that Lady Grigg had said Lyona would be married quietly from Government House, but he was disturbed that his refusal to spend Christmas there 'had evidently bitched the issue completely'. 'Oh God, what a life. This marrying business nearly puts one in one's grave before one is married. What will it be like after? What won't I give to be married and at peace?'

He tried to calm his parents' continued fears about his refusal to spend Christmas at Government House:

I did not know that Uncle Ned was keen for me to go after the way I had been worrying him about the wedding. My only idea having got the leave was to drop out of the limelight and sit quietly and hope that the episode would be quickly forgotten. Instead of that I seem to have completely finished things.

In none of his previous letters had Grigg mentioned Christmas, and since he had not heard from him for two months 'undoubtedly things have gone beyond the breaking point'.

He was cheered when his marriage licence arrived by mail on 13 January and when he received a telegram a week later from Grigg saying the wedding would indeed be from Government House. His relief was abundant: 'Thank God is all I can say, and pray hard and sing psalms of joy and gladness and thanksgiving.' The telegram 'just saved the situation when [he] was getting desperate'. He was pleased, too, when Lyona wrote to say the presents were 'rolling in well', even though there were not enough cheques for his liking! It is unlikely he ever learned that some of his colleagues believed his early marriage was the result of 'favourable treatment' from the governor. Certainly Armitage himself thought Grigg had been very difficult over the matter. He was embarrassed when the governor asked him whom he wanted invited to the wedding. 'I only know five people in the colony and half won't come. Very awkward.' He was sceptical when the doctor raised his hopes by saying that he would get a free rail ticket to meet Lyona – 'Not a bloody earthly' – but was elated the next day to discover 'God, the doctor was bloody right about the ticket. Free all round.'[16]

Although he was being given more work to do in the office – maybe in an attempt to divert his attention from his marriage – he found it very difficult to focus his mind and get on with his work. Instead he read Tennyson's love poems and remarked to himself, 'I have the disease badly.' A little earlier he had read Galsworthy's *Forsyte Saga* and had become emotionally involved in it: 'I would not have given up Fleur, I swear it. Love with me is too strong.' By 7 February he was finding the suspense 'awful', every day was an effort to get through and it was extremely difficult to concentrate. The new suit he had ordered had not yet arrived, although it had been dispatched 'ages ago'. The following day was his 'last day at work, thank God' and the next, a Sunday, was 'taking ages to go'. On the Monday he got his free railway pass and on Tuesday left Kakamega by local native council lorry – which contrasted with the gubernatorial Rolls-Royce in which Grigg's private secretary met him at Nairobi the following day.[17]

Things continued to go wrong. The governor was delayed at the coast, so the wedding was postponed from Saturday to the following Monday. Also, he was unable to get a car for his honeymoon. He met the people who were trying, with difficulty, to arrange the decoration of the church. He now discovered that executive council was to meet on Monday, so the wedding was postponed to Tuesday: 'What a honeymoon we shall get!' 'Good Lord, what a mess this all is.' 'Would that a registry in Mombasa had been our goal.' His first choice as best man, a fellow cadet, had been refused leave because he was late back from a previous leave, and his second choice, a doctor from Kakamega who should have been in Nairobi at the relevant time, could not make it. He hoped Lyona would not be too disappointed by it all. He travelled down to Mombasa by train and was anguished by it being four hours late getting there. Lyona's ship, the *Madura*, was also four hours late so he arrived just in time to meet her – on Saint Valentine's Day. He was ecstatic with their reunion: 'What a day of rapture!' Lyona stayed at the provincial commissioner's and he at Government House where he met Neville Chamberlain who was visiting Kenya and had a few talks with him: 'a simple, enquiring, rather rustic looking soul with a brain crammed with knowledge'. They dined at Government House on 16 February and felt they had 'at last been taken to their bosoms' by the Griggs: 'Everything looks more cheerful as their excellencies are assuming control.'[18]

They were married at the Highlands cathedral of All Saints, Nairobi, on 18 February 1930.[19] The ceremony was conducted by the dean. The best man was John Coryndon, son of a former governor of Kenya. Lyona was given away by her brother Roddy. The pageboy was John Grigg, the governor's small son. Governor and Lady Grigg were in the congregation. The reception was held at Government House and was 'quiet and informal in character as befitted a family occasion'. The bridegroom's account, committed to his diary, was:

> I can remember eating a hearty breakfast and something about a cocktail, a band and a church where I waited in crushing suspense. Lyona looked too wonderfully divine and calm and we got through the ordeal not too badly.... What a day. Agonizing in the waiting but actually not as terrifying as we had both imagined. We have now entered heaven.

They spent their honeymoon at the Outspan Hotel, Nyeri, described as actually being in a tree with six camp beds and little else. The charges were £5 a day per couple and the money was returned if the visitors did not see elephant, buffalo or rhinoceros at the salt-lick below. On their return to Nairobi they bought a second-hand Chevrolet 4 box-body car and drove back to Kakamega in it.

Armitage now returned to his normal district work, frequently taking Lyona with him on safari. She was soon busy sewing curtains, cushion covers and a new cover for the sofa, as well as putting up pictures in the various rooms. He spent a good deal of time studying for his government law examinations, which he passed with distinction in October. A few days earlier he had been told that he would shortly be posted to Kericho as assistant district commissioner: 'Could be worse but we shall not enjoy the cold and wet very much.'[20]

After four days packing their property, which was taken ahead of them by lorry, they left for Kericho on 25 October to join district commissioner P. J. de Bromhead and D. O. Brumage, his assistant. The Brumages were very kind to them when they first arrived: she frequently sent them flowers and fruit and he – although 'a South African of the "no nonsense" school of administration [was] very jolly ... always pulling one's leg'.[21]

Kericho was in the 'White Highlands' on the western flank of the Mau hills, a 'lush and fertile region' about a hundred miles northwest of Nairobi, where European agriculture dominated. It was a buffer zone between two hostile tribes: the Luo in the lowlands near Lake Victoria to the west, and the Kipsigis in the highlands to the east. There were two 'really enormous' tea companies close to the township, with over a score of quite sizeable units within 20 miles of it. It was a well-developed area with good roads and buildings and 'prodigious sums were invested in buildings and machinery'. Thousands of Luo labourers were employed by the big companies and their terms of service were a 'model'. Although flax and coffee both failed, tea and mixed farming were great successes.[22]

A year later, in 1931, there was a new district commissioner, C. Tomkinson. Armitage was senior assistant district commissioner and Richard Turnbull junior assistant district commissioner.[23] As Turnbull later described it, 'I was the dog's-body and he was the dog's-body bar one.' Armitage and Tomkinson were both Wykehamists, 'each of them with the beautiful manners that you would expect from that establishment'. Turnbull confessed to feeling 'somewhat inadequate', largely because his two colleagues were 'so extremely kind' to him. This was Turnbull's first posting in Kenya. Having been somewhat neglected by Thompson at Kakamega when he arrived at his first station, Armitage was keenly aware of the desirability of someone with experience teaching newcomers their job. He quickly took the new cadet under his wing, and Turnbull recalled:

> I thought at the time how outstandingly lucky I was to have as my immediate senior a man so admirably suited to instruct me. He had been two years in Kenya and I did not see how anybody could be more ready to get down to the task of telling me what to do and how to do it. . . . But as well as answering the questions that were put to him, he inspired one

with his patience, sharpened one's wits and opened one's eyes in all kinds of ways.

It was as well Armitage was there to help Turnbull because on his first day the district commissioner introduced him to the work by saying, 'Well, this is the office. You had better get on with it.' It was as well, too, because, as Armitage saw it, 'Turnbull seems to put his feet into everything badly, holding forth on subjects when he is new to the country.'[24] Turnbull, who later became governor of Tanganyika and of Aden, long remembered his apprenticeship under Armitage, and half a century later he wrote: 'I look back on my introduction at your hands to the arts of administration in Kericho in 1931 with much gratitude and appreciation. I am uncomfortably aware, too, of what a particularly odious young man I was and how much I am indebted to you for your kindness in those days.'

The work of the district administration concentrated on preserving peace and good government, administering the law through routine court work, collecting African tax and improving sanitation. Armitage and Turnbull considered themselves extremely fortunate to be 'brought up by an immensely skilful tax man', Tomkinson, who had a squad of Kipsigis tax collectors, 'all of them proud to be serving under him in this way'. They were seldom in the station together because it was usual for one to be out on a tax-collecting or peace-keeping safari, while the other was at the *boma* where he was responsible for court work, station upkeep and maintaining the station roads.

Armitage was soon immersed in the administrative work and the life of Kericho. Within days he had to deal with an incident in which 200 Maasai warriors 'nearly massacred' a Luo, who had murdered another Maasai; with an old man who was beaten by 400 women who then wrecked his house and property because he had raped his own small daughter; and with a local missionary who had been badly beaten by his labourers – 'a bad show'. 'So the district is not exactly quiet.' He heard numerous labour disputes and spent quite a lot of time trying criminal and civil cases. He supervised the digging of pit latrines for the local prison and was particularly proud of one that was 30 feet deep, was dug by two men in nine days, and 'should take some filling up'.[25]

Although, 'with a dozen officials at the *boma*, tea planters nearby and farmers at Sotik, Kericho did not lack social life', the Armitages seem rarely to have gone to the club. This was largely because of the drinking, scandal-mongering and good deal of pettiness that went on there. One of the stalwarts resigned from a golf competition 'for bad tasting remarks made' after he had beaten his opponent. A special meeting was called at which 'each hurled abuse at the other'.

The club days here are Wednesday and Saturday and that means when it is fine the whole world comes in and plays golf, tennis or polo.... After the games people forgather in the club house which consists of a verandah cold and drafty, a fairly large room with a fireplace but no fire, and a bar.... The men sit in the bar or on the verandah and the women in the room and both freeze. As a result we do not often patronise the place and then never for long.

The Armitages 'took the usual pleasure that socially minded people find in small dinner parties and small luncheon parties, and from time to time would take the plunge of a larger party'.[26] 'Larger parties with various games were particularly up his street, and those that had with them an element of gambling were his favourites. He was, in addition, a skilful and enthusiastic dancer and one that set a splendid example to those who were not as enthusiastic as they might have been.'

Armitage was an avid race-goer at the local track. He was a 'keen and very competent lawn-tennis player, proved himself a most useful performer in all kinds of station tournaments' and was a 'thoroughly competent' player on the squash court. His attitude to golf is revealing. It was the only ball game of which he was not a strong player: 'My drive is like my serve at tennis, most erratic.' He confided to Turnbull that he was not going to allow himself to occupy such a depressing standard of play and was determined to make his mark in the game. Kericho was well endowed climatically and this led to the development of a good golf course, on the greens and fairways of which Armitage devoted hours and hours a week. It was largely due to his enthusiasm and organization that the Kericho golf course became one of the best in Kenya. His determination was successful and by the time he left Kericho he had become one of its champion players – runner-up in the vice-captain's cup – and this in a club with several top class golfers.

Safaris at Kericho were not easy and 'in this backward station [they] were done by ox cart', which was slow and meant they had to pack their kit for it to depart early on Saturday so as to precede them and be ready when they went out on Monday.[27] Nor did things always go smoothly once they were out on safari:

> Was up at 6.00 a.m. and confusion reigned supreme while... donkeys kicked and cattle wandered and men shouted and some slacked and some were too eager and it was not till after 8.00 a.m. that we got off.... Then we found a good camping spot.... More confusion putting up the tent, then lunch and rain.... African day ended in billows of mist.

Out in the district he tried numerous stock theft cases and he spent many full days dealing with the plagues of locusts affecting Kenya and with the European farmers affected who 'stormed' about the government's 'feebleness' in failing to deal adequately with them. He spent a great deal of often frustrating time putting down poisoned bran bait and hoped it would kill the hoppers and nothing else but felt rather mean 'sneaking off' without seeing the result. 'A fruitless day spent in waiting for bait that only came after tea in heavy rain. However, we were able to have it boiled before dark. The camp was infested with locusts. We dug a ditch but not deep enough and were defeated. Saw that they do eat each other [and] they ate my red blanket.' The locusts destroyed the Africans' grain crops, leaving only planted potatoes, and they 'cleaned out' a good many European farms. He also had to handle the difficulties of widespread witchcraft: 'The natives are completely under the thumb of the *laibon* whose power is due to witchcraft alone, without the use of poisons. A man denounced by a *laibon* can get no one to do anything for him.'

There were grave concerns in the Kenya civil service over the effects on government finances of the world economic depression in the early 1930s. Safari allowances were reduced by a quarter, mileage allowances by almost a half and free dental treatment was abolished. Armitage and his colleagues were alarmed by the rumour that the cut in pay was to be increased from 5 to 15 per cent and were worried by news of individual officers who were retrenched, often for dubious or unclear reasons, fearing 'someone had blundered or allowed private interests to prevail'. The Armitages themselves had to economize because they did not know how secure his salary was.[28]

The financial stringencies had a particular effect on district travelling. Tomkinson and Armitage had box-body cars but there was no government lorry any of them could use for carrying kit on tax-collecting or peace-keeping tours. Instead, they took station ox wagons and up to 20 head of oxen, which were 'very clumsy and cumbrous', although the Kipsigis ox drivers were 'prodigiously skilful'. At best, these ox wagons covered only two and a half miles an hour, and if he wanted to get to any particular place within a certain time, Armitage had to make an agreement with an Indian trader who owned a lorry. The trader hired out a space in his lorry and used the remainder to carry his own goods, but these arrangements often led to disagreement because the owner tried to charge more than Armitage's Goanese clerks thought proper. On occasion, too, especially when travelling in forest areas, head porterage was the only means of carrying kit. This involved bringing a dozen or more head porters from the station and, since they needed to be clothed, sheltered and fed, the operation became 'tiresomely elaborate'.[29]

Early in 1932, the Armitages began packing their goods ready to go on leave, and they boarded the *Madura* at Mombasa on 16 January. They had a quiet trip largely because Lyona, now pregnant, was unwell and spent several days in bed. They decided not to risk the Bay of Biscay and instead travelled by rail from Marseilles via Paris, Boulogne and Folkestone to Victoria where they arrived on 2 February.[30]

On leave they stayed at Bournemouth with Lyona's mother and at Whitchurch, Herefordshire, with his parents who had retired there in 1927. He frequently played golf and hockey – which made him 'stiff and short of breath'. He went to several horse races, including a number of point-to-point meetings, the Derby and Grand National. Later in the summer he played tennis, croquet and went swimming. On 13 June Lyona went into a nursing home and, after an unpleasant three days, their first son, Robert Jeremy, was born. His family 'fussed' Lyona, who was not feeling too well, and Armitage remonstrated, making himself unpopular with them although, as he thought, 'in a good cause'. They were soon able to take short rides in the car with Jeremy on the back seat in a basket and looked after by a young nanny.[31]

After 'a very successful leave though not a very exciting one for Lyona', he returned alone to Africa. He stayed with the Griggs in London, travelled overland to Marseilles and boarded the *Llandovery* on 21 July. In Genoa he commented on how clean the city was and the smartness of the police who were automatically obeyed by the traffic: 'All the handiwork of Mussolini'. He was disappointed when he arrived at Mombasa that only a colleague's wife was there to meet him 'and no one else', which brought a lump to his throat. Colonial officers quickly became accustomed to their friends taking relatively little interest in them when on leave, but were less accustomed to their return being ignored. He caught the train to Nairobi and Kisumu, his new station.[32]

The general atmosphere in Kenya was now even more heavily dominated by the world depression and government economies.[33] On the ship, Armitage met three cadets going to Tanganyika and commented on their very high quality and how the Colonial Office could afford to select only the best. A high level of tension between officials and settlers was created by the *East Africa Standard* starting an economy campaign aimed at government and its servants. There were proposals to reduce the number of provinces to three, abolish the post of chief native commissioner and decentralize the administration; further to reduce pay and allowances and remove the right of families to free housing and medical attendance: 'All very annoying and makes life harder.' The general fear of retrenchment was still considerable. There were fears, too, that tours would be extended from three to four years. Armitage took to cycling on safari, which was more economical than a car. The effect on tax collection was marked. Collection became much more difficult and payments were often late. The number of low denomination coins offered in payment also increased, reflecting the low prices secured for African produce. There was a general shortage of money and a rundown in trade. Armitage spent many a 'breathless afternoon' on Sundays trying to sell cattle that had been seized or surrendered in lieu of cash payment of the tax, often at low prices. At one stage, he had over 400 cattle waiting to be sold and this led him into conflict with the 'conservation people' because there was inadequate grazing and accommodation for so many.

> Some more tax [collected] with enormous difficulty. The elders are subjects of my wrath but it makes no difference. Miserable cattle only brought. The general [harangues] I have here seem to make no difference at all. . . . Spent the whole day collecting a few shillings and dealing with cases and collecting a number of prisoners. They are not ransomed so there is no [doubt] of the shortage of cash.

The increased number of cattle theft cases caused greater tension between African groups and more court work.

Kisumu is on the shore of Lake Victoria and this meant that Armitage encountered a number of features he did not meet elsewhere.[34] These included the Imperial Airways flying boats setting down on the lake *en route* from Britain to South Africa, and the beginning of a few officers travelling on leave by air rather than by sea. Most, of course, preferred their longer, more restful, sea passage to which they clung for many years. The flying boat also brought mail more quickly from England and this pleased him, especially in Lyona's absence. The airways employees formed a cricket team against whom Armitage played for Kisumu. He enjoyed watching the flying boat set down and take off – 'very simple but impressive' – and he enjoyed a short flight in one of them on a radio test. Other unfamiliar features included travelling to some parts of the district by launch, a large number of African fishing boats and a trade in making canoes.

Since there was a considerable European population at Kisumu – employees in government, commerce, the port and railway – there was a very active and varied social life. Much of it centred on the club, though people continued to have drinks and to dine at each other's houses. In the club he played billiards, snooker, bridge, crown and anchor and enjoyed the cinema. Outside he played golf, tennis, cricket and hockey, the last two frequently against Indian teams. He also played soccer for the first time since his first year at Oxford.

On safari he collected tax and heard cases; for relaxation he used his newly acquired rifle to shoot guinea fowl – not always successfully. After a few weeks following their return in October, Lyona and Jeremy accompanied him on safari.

Health dangers were a worry. There were outbreaks of rabies and of sleeping sickness. The rabies was tackled by poisoning wild animals and quarantining domestic animals, and he 'heard that a dog had bitten two children so had it shot and took the corpse' to be examined. Locusts continued to destroy food crops and diets suffered as a result. Armitage himself endured miseries with frequent boils on the back of his neck, which had to be lanced – not always successfully – and Lyona and the doctor, among others, were similarly tormented.

There were times when he had very little to do in the office: 'So little to do at the office, we went to the hotel and played snooker'. There were, however, other days that were heavy with work, especially when he had many court cases to hear or numerous complaints to be looked into. He noted the optimistic progress of gold mining in the Kakamega district, where miners were flooding in, where small fortunes were being made and where Roddy began to prospect and mine. As the Kisumu district was opened up to gold prospecting, they had to reorganize the district office to accommodate four new mining officers.

In March 1934 he was transferred from Kisumu back to Kericho: a 'splendid idea for the family if it ever stops raining'. Here he found that Percy Wyn-Harris, the other assistant district commissioner, took all the court cases – many of which were concerned with the very large number of cattle thefts – and Brumage, now district commissioner, did most of the rest of the work. This left little for Armitage to do except go on safari; but even then Wyn-Harris wanted to go out, so Armitage had to stay in rather more than he wished. He was, however, able to learn Luo and to pass the government examination 'nearly with distinction'. He was not satisfied with this near miss and thought he might 'have another shot at it' by improving his oral work. Five months later he passed the examination with distinction and was awarded a £25 bonus.[35]

Just as Armitage had taken care to help Turnbull learn about district administration at Kericho in 1931, so now he took equal care with another new officer, Lambert, who wrote to thank him 'for the excellent way in which you initiated me into the mysteries and difficulties of Kericho district. I'd like you to know how very much your consistent hard and sound work was appreciated. We could do with a few more like you.'[36]

During July the provincial commissioner told Brumage that Wyn-Harris was not to go to the secretariat as had been planned, but that

Armitage was to be transferred in his stead. Since both Wyn-Harris and Armitage wanted to go to the secretariat, Brumage wired the provincial commissioner to say so and to indicate that the provincial commissioner should make the decision. Curiously, the provincial commissioner said they should toss a coin for it. This seemed far too casual to Armitage who refused to join in the toss and, as a consequence, stayed in Kericho while Wyn-Harris went off to the secretariat in Nairobi.[37]

The Armitages' social life at Kericho became more varied than at Kakamega and even at Kisumu. They went to the cinema and they joined the dramatic club; he was made secretary – 'damn it' – and they were soon busy with the stage, opening chorus and dress rehearsals. They attended horticultural show committee meetings and the gymkhana races, played a good deal of golf and tennis, and thoroughly enjoyed 'a great celebration' for the twenty-fifth anniversary of the King's accession.[38]

Lyona and Jeremy went on leave three months ahead of Armitage, mainly so Jeremy could go into hospital in England for an adenoid and tonsils operation. Armitage sold his car to a merchant who hoped to trade in fish: 'poor boob. However he got it cheap.' He himself left Kericho on 2 April 1936. On board the *Matola* he found 'no organized sports, thank god, but we have good gin and other parties and bridge'. He formed a sweep syndicate but failed to make money. In the canal he commented on an Italian aircraft carrier and vessels carrying tanks, military lorries and cars. He travelled by rail from Marseilles and, having forgotten his passport on the ship, relied on his driving licence to get through to Victoria. He was in Britain from 23 April to 23 October and spent some of his time studying for part one of the Bar examinations in Roman law, contract and tort and part two in criminal law and procedure, which he sat and passed in September, earning himself a champagne dinner from Lyona's mother. He had been admitted as a student in 1928 and by 1936 had kept eight terms. He watched tennis at Wimbledon – with tickets bought in Nairobi – and saw the finals there. He also played a good deal of golf and tennis and went to several race meetings. He stayed for a while with the Griggs and watched the Winchester–Eton cricket match. Then, it was time to say goodbye to Lyona and return to Africa: 'She was not feeling well and these partings of ours are so bitter and we have to keep on doing them.'[39]

He landed at Mombasa on 13 November 1936, travelled by rail to Nairobi and then on by road – commenting on the 'marvellous views of Mount Kenya as [he] went round the foothills' – via Isiolo to Wajir in the Northern Frontier Province, his new posting and for the first time as district commissioner. As he went through Isiolo he met Crozier, 'now employed looking after the Eritrean internees who came across and surrendered last March – 490 of them in a camp'. These were the early refugees from the areas north of Kenya, fleeing from the Italian army, which, late in 1935, invaded Abyssinia and moved forward with tanks, poison gas, artillery and bombers. Shortly, the number of refugees was to increase alarmingly.[40]

It took him two days to drive from Isiolo to Wajir. The overnight stop on this stretch was at Archer's Post – simply the name of the camping site since there were no inhabitants there – where lions and snakes could be a danger. The first 60 miles were through rough lava rock and then over clay. It was a nearly straight road completely through bush. There were no hills on this route until 100 miles beyond Wajir, which he reached at midday on 22 November and took over from M. W. Low two days later.[41] He recorded in his diary: 'Began taking over. Checked stores ... Medical Officer is here and two KAR houses with food, stores etc. but they are all out at Moyale now. ... District in very good order. Very prosperous from selling stock to the Italians, lira being exchanged every day. Tax well over the estimate.'[42]

Wajir district was towards the remote northeast corner of Kenya, a hot and arid area. Elspeth Huxley caught its essence:

> Wajir, lying on those great dry scorching plains that stretch towards the Juba River ... had an aura of romance about it created partly by the white crenellated walls of its fort, guarded night and day by smart *askaris* of the King's African Rifles; by its tall arched doorways; by bugle calls at dawn and sunset; and by tall Somalis in chequered *kitois* (short wrapover skirts), finely woven shawls, and turbans in bright tomato-red and gentian-blue – lean men with clever bony faces stamped by pride and authority. Lines of camels roped nose to tail converged on the wells astride the fort's perimeter, uttering half-roaring, half-moaning cries as they awaited their turn. The constant clattering of their wooden bells was the signature tune of the North.[43]

It was a lonely district because there were no senior departmental officers stationed there except a doctor. In Armitage's first year there, four doctors succeeded each other, only one being stationed at Wajir at any one time. The police unit consisted of a sergeant, two corporals and 27 constables. There was only an officer and small maintenance party of the KAR, the company usually stationed there having recently been removed to the northern border. There were no mission stations in the district and, apart from a few small bush schools where the elements of the Koran were taught, there were no schools. So far as transport was concerned, stores were carried by KAR convoys and commercial lorries, and mail was taken and brought by whatever vehicles happened to be going in the appropriate direction. Delays of over two weeks in Nairobi awaiting transport to Wajir were not uncommon. The RAF landed there from time to time to bring stores or on a special mission. He had three government camels for carrying water and firewood, and two station mules. Colleagues believed that he would have found Wajir the most lonely and physically exacting time of his life. A decade earlier the district was seen as a punishment station for those who had incurred official displeasure and 'a posting to Wajir [was] roughly the world's end so far as a career in the Kenya administrative service was concerned'. Fortunately for Armitage, this was no longer the case in the mid-1930s.[44]

The government's view of the life of an administrative officer in the Northern Frontier Province was:

> In this province a man must be inured to loneliness and have the makings of a 'bush-whacker' in his soul to appreciate the work and life. He must be prepared . . . for hard marching, hard work and the task of inuring himself against the tedious monotony of the endless bush-covered country. He needs a strong sense of humour, patience, common sense and a love of the wild and its denizens. If he is known as one who must have company or is not strong and cannot take an interest in nature in all or in some of its forms he is unlikely to be suitable for the Northern Frontier Province.[45]

The people were pastoral nomads, Somalis and Galla, owning sheep, goats, camels and some cattle, constantly on the move in search of fresh pastures and new grazing areas. The main problems of administration were keeping law and order among the rival clans by preventing the Somalis encroaching on the Galla grazing; preventing the Wajir tribes moving towards the Tana River; and preventing the incursions of alien Somalis from Jubaland. The district provided excellent grazing for camels and fair grazing for sheep and goats but was not really suitable for cattle. During and immediately after the rains, pools were plentiful but were soon exhausted, and the stock were then dependent on the well areas and the Uaso River. If the river showed signs of drying up it had to be reserved for cattle only and camels were made to use the well areas. There were 20 well groups in the Wajir area with 250 wells and it was usually necessary to restrict stock access to them. This inevitably led to frequent acrimonious disputes and Armitage had to keep a firm hold on them. It was important for him to spend a good deal of time on safari by camel or lorry visiting the various watering places in order to talk to the tribesmen to find out what was going on and where people were going. The provincial commissioner was very keen that Armitage should 'get the hang of the way the people live' and urged him to make 'a long camel safari' one of his earliest tasks. It was a reasonably safe place because Wajir had the Mandera district as a buffer between itself and the Abyssinian border, a much more dangerous district where the district commissioner was speared to death by Shifta marauders from across the border in 1937.[46]

On one occasion Armitage visited Mandera, where Turnbull was district officer, to inspect the Kenya–Italian Somaliland border.[47] The border was marked with a 12-foot 'cut' and the various district commissioners along it – Garissa, Wajir and Mandera – were responsible for clearing and stumping the cut and keeping it in good condition. It was important they should coordinate the work at the points where their districts joined, especially where, as in the case of Wajir and Mandera, the straight line border took an angle turn. Turnbull finished his section more quickly than Armitage and the district officer of Mandera felt good-humouredly that the district commissioner of Wajir was keen to see the 'polished article' so that he himself did not achieve a lower standard. Turnbull recalled that meeting:

> I introduced Bob Armitage to our Police Inspector and our Superintendent of Police. He made an excellent impression upon them. Our policeman said 'Debonair is how our old Commissioner would have described him, debonair in manner and debonair in appearance.' Bob certainly made a splendid impression upon all of us in Mandera. The policeman said 'If you or the District Commissioner ever felt like changing your style you could do far worse than copy our debonair colleague.

The distances between district headquarters in the northern frontier were enormous, but even so Armitage occasionally received visits from his neighbour at Mandera. On one occasion Turnbull walked 200 miles – which he later described as 'a longish foot safari' – to confer with him at Wajir and, conforming to northern frontier etiquette, he camped overnight a few miles outside Wajir so as to arrive at a civilized hour the next morning. At dawn, however, he changed his mind and walked the 200 miles back to his own *boma*.

Wajir was normally a very dry district in which wells were important for the Somalis and their camels.[48] Indeed, the importance of Wajir was due to its wells, the underground water travelling from Moyale and reaching the surface in limestone outcrops – which provided cement, rubble and limewash for the flat-roofed houses – with no water in between. During his time there, however, he experienced some very heavy rain:

My house leaked from the roof in two places and the windows are so formed as to lead the water in not keep it out. The gaol and hospital swamped but on whole not too bad.... Another three quarters of an inch rain yesterday morning making 3 inches in the 24 hours 2.00 p.m. to 2.00 p.m. Wajir has not had such rain for 3 or 4 years. Nothing can reach us for a week.

Although he did not specifically comment on it, Armitage's private diary for his time at Wajir shows clearly that the place, the work and the type of life he led were very different from those of his earlier stations in the Nyanza province. He saw more wild animals here than on any of his other stations: giraffe, elephant, leopard, ostrich, zebra, oryx, lion and rhino. There were also cheetah, antbear and snakes. Armitage and his two colleagues were very dependent on each other's company in this remote and lonely station. They took it in turns – not apparently by conscious design – to have drinks in the house of one and dinner in the house of another. They played a little squash – in a court with no roof so the ball was liable to fly out – even though one of his partners had never played before. They played even less golf. They whiled away the time playing 'battleships' and they enjoyed shooting sandgrouse and attempting to shoot the lesser bustard. They shared books and discussed various aspects of them. Some of their discussions were of a relatively trivial philosophical nature, for example a classical education as a basis for a career and 'the single track minds of soldiers as they have to be taught not to think, to get machine-like efficiency then cannot stimulate their minds later'. Armitage found time to study, take and pass the government language examination in Swahili. He reorganized the office filing system – largely for something constructive to do. The triviality of his life in Wajir is illustrated by a number of entries in his private diary:

Less than ever to do today. Played squash with Hunt. He is not much good ... Watched a couple of mongooses playing around in house most of the afternoon ... Harris and Hunt to drinks. Harris suggests a sign post on Mandera road to commemorate coronation. Good idea ... Played some golf then listened to wireless ... Office work is getting less and less. I managed to account for a lesser bustard. Kingston came and played battleships ... Harris has a cucumber ready to eat ... Very little to do these days except the desire to drink!

Even Christmas Day was quiet – inevitably so. He spent the morning writing to Lyona. He then went to Hunt's house, where the three of them drank two bottles of champagne before going on to lunch at

Harris's. He took a walk after tea across the well area and discovered that it was bigger than he thought. Hunt and Harris joined him for dinner and they then 'went to *Ngoma* [dance] just outside [the] wire. Somalis [were] doing a forbidden one or two men dance – a reel – in a circle clapping.'

There were, however, a number of highlights to his life at Wajir. First there was a New Year's Day party at Moyale on 1 January 1937: 'Drinks ... Good turkey and champagne. Then on to roof after and sang songs. Then to fort and fired off 67 Very lights after Italians had been warned and three bugles going all they could. Ended up with dancing and talk and got to bed at 4.30 a.m.' Then his second son was born on 30 May 1937. He was delighted with the baby but disappointed it was not a daughter – as they had both hoped – and was irritated by his father's insistent views on the child's name:

> Found large mail and letters about my new son, Simon. Father calls the name 'Only a joke' so I wonder whether I too would not prefer Michael. I hate the Armitage names but Lyona and I both feel we should like Father's name carried on so second name to be Frank. ... Father strongly dislikes Simon as a name, so Jewish and reminds him of bad characters so cabled him to give Lyona his reasons and to Uncle Arthur to be godfather.

Later the child was named Richard Hugh Lyon. Finally there were the coronation day celebrations:

> Parade of KAR at which endless salutes, *baraza* of chiefs, bazaar sports, some sack races and tug-of-war. I gave away prizes, distributed food to chiefs and all government employees and boy scouts. Lunch Harris, dine with me. Tea party at Koja mosque of Wajir merchants' association. Band sang God Save the King. Football match KAR v. Bazaar. Kingston refereed. Bonfire and *Ngoma*s all evening. How civilized Wajir!

The economy had now begun to pick up and the levy on public salaries – formerly 2.5 per cent – was removed: 'Nice, this.' African tax also began to come in a little better. He commented that 70 people came in to pay on one day and the headmen were beginning to collect the tax from their people to hand over to the district commissioner. There were collecting difficulties, however, when the rains fell, grazing became easier and the tribes were scattered over a wider area away from the wells.[49]

His predecessor had intended to dam the Lag Bogal to retain water after heavy rains, but realized that it would require a large spillway to take off the surplus water. Armitage decided on a different approach.

Like most district commissioners, he kept a 'goat-bag'. This was an unofficial – indeed officially unknown – collection of money from irregular and unaccountable sources, from which district commissioners paid for officially unauthorized works and services of their personal choosing. From his goat-bag Armitage began to dig a water hole in the dry river bed at a site where there was a depression and dry, trampled mud. Some two months later just before the rains broke, there was deep water over the whole area of his tank and he was pleased, but three months later still he noted with sadness that the sides, which had been dug vertically, had caved in.[50]

On 20 August, Armitage received a telegram from the provincial commissioner, V. G. Glenday, and learned of his next, and early, posting: 'Wire ... saying stand by to take over Isiolo District and refugee camp. I must ask this: what have I or Rimmington done[?] ... I was sitting pretty here till end of October. Anyway it is a more expensive place to live in.'[51] Glenday assured him that the transfer would not affect his planned move out of the Northern Frontier Districts and his ability to meet Lyona and his sons in November. He also told him that the transfer was 'a personal tribute' to him and his organizational abilities. The challenge ahead of him, especially the refugees, was enormous. The influx had become a considerable concern to the government, and the *East Africa Standard* graphically brought the problem to the public's attention.

> There are now nearly 8000 uninvited guests in Kenya and they include people representative of almost every class in the one-time Ethiopian empire. Some of them come from good families who have fled from the regime which they feel holds out little hope for them; some are peasants whose reason for flight is less obvious; others are slaves belonging either to members of the parties or collected on the remarkable trek of over 300 miles to security. There are others – deserters from the Italian native forces – whose homes are in far away Eritrea ... included too are men who at one time served in the Abyssinia army. Together they represent perhaps as difficult a problem as was ever placed before the government of this country.... The bare hot plains of Isiolo may not be very attractive compared with their homes in far off Harar but they mean peace and kindness and skilled attention. There is something in this story of which Kenya may be modestly proud.... Thousands of people, physically exhausted, emaciated by starvation, exposure and thirst, many of them dying where they stood, practically crawled over the frontier with their equally wretched mules, horses and cattle but they brought with them smallpox, typhoid and fever resulting from their incredibly unclean condition. They were a menace to the country. No words of praise are

fulsome enough for the handful of European officers and their African assistants who tackled that problem risking their own wellbeing, bringing order out of disorder and restoring some measure of discipline and self respect into one of the most extraordinary rabbles that ever wandered the face of the earth in these modern times.[52]

Gerald Rimmington took over Wajir district at the end of August. He arrived with an ostrich – being trained to pull a cart – dog, parrot, monkey, zebra and young giraffe – which was saddled and trained to be ridden. On 2 September Armitage left early in the morning in the rain and had a good trip as far as Garba, where he stayed overnight. He was not sorry to leave and to see what he hoped would be the 'last signs of those parts'. Early next morning he arrived at Isiolo.[53]

A month or two before Armitage arrived there, Elspeth Huxley visited Isiolo from the south and described it:

> You approached it through a row of scruffy Indian *duka*s along a road deep in dust; past the barrier [a pole balanced on two posts] came the police and other quarters built of local sunburnt bricks with tin roofs; then a few mud-and-wattle offices and finally bungalows for the handful of white officials, who I think consisted of the DC, a policeman, a doctor and a vet. A rather half-hearted attempt had been made to plant pepper trees and eucalyptus for shade. That was about all there was of Isiolo.[54]

Armitage's two months' stay at Isiolo was in very marked contrast to his time at Wajir, since he was now faced with the enormous challenge of quickly and effectively organizing the camp in which refugees from Abyssinia were beginning to be housed and this involved him in a great deal of hard work. Unlike Wajir, he now had scarcely a moment's relaxation – no games, no reading, no grouse-shooting and little social entertainment.

His predecessor, Rimmington, had been unable to cope. He was 'muddle-headed' and had refused to accept responsibility. Everywhere Armitage found signs of his inefficiency.[55] Armitage thought he 'should have concentrated on animal training!' Rimmington, however, was not well. He had been attacked in the eye by a spitting cobra, ate aspirin and quinine and drank salts instead of meals to feel better. His condition was made worse by the heavy mineral content of the local water, which gave rise to excessive micturition known as 'Wajir clap'. There were already over 2000 refugees in the camp at Isiolo – a sharp increase on the 490 Armitage had seen less than a year earlier on his way to Wajir – and the numbers were growing daily. From the outset, he was told that another 6000 were on their way to Isiolo from

Marsabit. The flow – or flood – of refugees was unlikely to abate, because the Italians were increasing their harshness, as Glenday reported from Moyale:

> The [Italian] has already closed all the wells on the west side of here to our tribesmen if they refuse to move on to his side. He's doing it east of here as well. You can imagine what chaos is likely to occur. I have tried to intimidate the commissario but the order comes from the high command. There is no question but it is a reprisal for our harbouring refugees and they are, I believe, greatly incensed.[56]

Armitage responded immediately and extremely well to the challenge confronting him. It was as if his mind and body suddenly clicked automatically into a higher gear. Within hours of arriving he had taken over the district and camp from the assistant district commissioner, Lockhart, and was walking around to 'get the hang of some of the features and problems [and] get some idea of the refugee camp into [his] head'. The inactivity of Wajir had not dulled his energy or ability. Not only had he to put right things that were going wrong, but he had also to move forward and cater for the future running of the camp – both enormous tasks waiting to defeat the person tackling them, but not Armitage. All the basic needs of a large and fast growing number of people had to be met: housing, health, food.

Possibly fearing that a relative newcomer to the northern frontier would aim at ultimately achieving near perfection rather that concentrating on the immediate practical essentials, Glenday told him:

> I appreciate only too well that the camp cannot be a garden city. There is far too much wind and dust for that. The important thing is that they have some sort of shelter before the rains break. All the local oracles, soothsayers and wise men predict early rains and the only other thing to do is to make the camp as sanitary as possible to avoid disease. With one trained in such a respectable and advanced part of the world at Nyanza you will know far more about it than I do.[57]

Armitage was fortunate in having Cormack to help him, a doctor who had 'dealt with these conditions for many years in various places and is very helpful'. He relieved the district commissioner of a great deal of work in the camp, which enabled Armitage to do his ordinary district administrative work in addition to being responsible for the refugees. Lockhart was also a great help to him. The same could not be said, however, of Mackintosh, whom he found 'full of piss and wind [when] what is wanted is painstaking attention to detail'. Nor was he favourably impressed with Harrison when he arrived because he knew 'the joys of drink' and at dinner the first night 'got quite whistled and then peacefully and snoringly went to sleep'. And he found Wylie 'hopeless' and dangerous: 'Wylie shot at two natives the other day who he says squatted down in front of his wife. She should have looked the other way.' Turnbull later claimed that Wylie was not his name nor she his wife, and that the police 'knew him well and kicked him out'.[58]

He had to deal with the camp's multifarious problems virtually all at the same time; the difficulties were so numerous and pressing that he could not afford to deal with them in order piecemeal. The housing was a first priority, a race against time before the rains. Some had been started haphazardly. He organized gangs to cut grass 'in great quantities' and lorries to transport it to the camp where the huts were erected in orderly lines – which he measured out himself. He saw that it was important to get everyone into the camp as quickly as possible rather than have them scattered in an unorganized fashion all over the place. Within days he had an office built and the area laid out in wards, and he began to feel that 'order will come out of chaos.'

Health was also a major problem. From Marsabit, where refugees gathered before being sent down to Isiolo, Harris – who had been with him at Wajir – told him: 'The outbreak of smallpox has been followed by the epidemic of dysentery which has killed and is killing many of them. It is an awful shambles here at the moment. Rather like the last scenes in Hamlet.'[59] At Isiolo there was smallpox, dysentery, relapsing fever and typhoid and he was concerned that the early arrivals had not all been shaved and had their clothes boiled. Water supplies had to be arranged and pit latrines dug. He had the river cleaned out, by hundreds of labourers, because 'the shit in some places [was] inches deep'.

The refugees had also to be fed and he organized regular issues of *posho* – maize meal flour – and meat. When, soon after his arrival, he 'found complete chaos in the issuing of *posho*', he immediately tried to make the operation smoother. After this, though he was far from happy that the issues were as well organized as they should be, he was sure 'we will get it.' To speed things up, he made the issues himself. The distribution of meat seemed to go rather better, although even this did not always run smoothly: 'The meat issue was delayed because the cattle ran away. Then White said he had no cattle for next week's issue so the game goes on. . . . Saw the meat issue. Beyond being unsanitary it goes quite well and quickly.' He was concerned too about the lack of cultivable land nearby on which the refugees could grow their own vegetables, but this was a longer term problem. No one knew how long they would be there and his immediate problems were too numerous for him to devote much time to considering the long-term future.

He also took the early steps needed to organize the refugee community. He used their own tribal organization of elders and gave thought to how disputes – especially over cattle and marriage – would be dealt with. 'Thinking about camp organization and wondering whether we shall not have to have some sort of tribunal except there is no stock to quarrel over and [there are] only the women in the camp to marry or in most cases simply live with.'

Bringing order to the chaotic conditions he met on arrival and catering for the housing, health, food, community and other pressing needs of the fast growing number of refugees required a great deal of labour. Acquiring labourers was not easy but over the course of a few weeks he succeeded in doing so. He was pleased in his early days that he got as many as 300 labourers out to work, and a little later commented: 'Had 520 labour out today. So the position is getting better and I should be able to get labour for the police lines if it keeps up like this. I am beginning to feel hopeful that our labour troubles are ended.' By the end of October he had 900 labourers turning out daily.

He did not have, nor did he have time for, many visitors, but he was quite pleased to see Turnbull, who 'arrived before breakfast and stayed the night', largely because Turnbull wanted to take over Isiolo from him, and Armitage was anxious to be relieved by November when Lyona returned. He had less patience with a lady visitor – 'Plump, highly scented female came in and wanted to go and see the camp ... she did not get past my defences' – and no one had much time to devote to a missionary visitor – 'The Reverend Morgan came down with me in the afternoon to see his flock who were far too busy to see him and so he had to go away.' The governor, Air Chief Marshal Sir Robert Brooke-Popham, also paid a visit and Armitage told the provincial commissioner:

> Cormack and I both stressed the water scheme but it did not appeal to him very much though he made a note of it. ... HE was very taken with the native tribunal and asked what punishments they imposed. Quick quote 'Did they order everyone to be beaten? Did I just put down anyone who was a nuisance and just thrash him?' I told him I did not allow anyone to be punished except by myself, but there had been some cases of people having to be beaten. This did not often happen. ... HE asked me if I had any ideas how the refugees could grow their own food. He was very keen on this and I told him there was a certain amount of cultivable land here but that if it was to be used working teams would have to be established outside the main camp. He did not seem at all keen on paying these working parties anything [and] seemed surprised that I had permission to do so. ... However, he told me it was not at all a bad place this. A dust

devil of course went through the place just after he had left and he certainly had no idea of the difficulties under which the camp started.⁶⁰

The wind and the dust were a menace: 'an unrelenting, vicious wind that whirled dust around in choking eddies, shrivelled the skin and howled like a thousand dogs.' The wind also increased the fire hazard: if one house caught fire, others nearby would rapidly catch fire too. When, at the end of his visit, the governor asked the community leaders if they had any complaints, one replied that they would like to be moved to a more sheltered area because, as he explained, 'the wind aggravates my syphilis.'⁶¹

For two months Armitage worked ceaselessly and with speedy improvisation to get the refugee camp organized, to get order out of chaos. By the end of October he was reasonably satisfied with the progress, even if he judged it cynically: 'The camp is assuming normal proportions now as there is a fair amount of ordinary crime which has to be dealt with.'

At one time he had 8000 refugees in his camp. When they arrived they were in a desperate state of health, suffering from malnutrition, dysentery and smallpox: 'They had no food, no means of shelter, no medicines, nothing but pathetic bundles of possessions carried on backs or heads.' When Turnbull took over from Armitage, there were 6000 in the camp, 2000 having died. When it was finished, it was the third largest township in Kenya with two churches, a hospital, several clinics, a handicraft centre, courthouse and school at which every child received a daily ration of milk, meat, bread and vegetables.⁶²

Just as the *East Africa Standard* had described the refugee position at the time Armitage took over Isiolo, so also did the *Mombasa Times* describe the position at the time of his departure. The difference was very marked:

> The last of the refugees have now been brought in from the outlying districts of the Northern Frontier Province and have arrived at the special camp near Isiolo. The camp is pleasantly situated on the banks of the Siolo River and ... within the great rectangle marked out for the camp there is probably a bigger population relative to space than in any centre in Kenya.... This new Kenya town is a very temporary affair and the dwellings laid out in long lines on the most modern planning and sanitation principles are only made of grass with wooden supports....
> The smallpox has now been eliminated but the staff of the camp ... are constantly engaged in preventing any further epidemic of any kind of infectious disease. The largest building or group of buildings in the camp is the hospital. It has accommodation for 300 beds which with the

necessary blankets, sheets, pots and pans, cutlery and all the essential equipment of so large a hospital were despatched from Nairobi. Surgical cases are moved to Meru thirty miles away. At present there are about 170 hospital cases in the camp many of whom are recovering from deficiency diseases, malaria, dysentery etc.[63]

At the end of October Turnbull arrived to take over from him, and during the next two days Armitage packed his goods and handed over the station. He felt ashamed that the stores were in something of a mess, but he had not had time to attend to them better. He left Isiolo early in the afternoon of 3 November and, after a relatively short trip by car, had dinner at the hotel in Nanyuki, the railhead, and then boarded the train, hoping this would be the last he saw of the northern frontier.

After the hectic time he had spent at Isiolo he was now able to relax a little and reflect on how his career was progressing:

> I think I have done well out of it though that cannot really make up for the weary months without Lyona. I hope that no crises arise out of my administration of the two districts [Wajir and Isiolo]. I have certainly got more confidence in myself and I shall have to be careful not to annoy people by being abrupt and telling them to 'get to hell or bloody well do it'.[64]

This untypically abrupt ordering of people was the result of the magnitude and urgency of his work at Isiolo where the pressures were so great that extremely firm and positive leadership was required. His private diary while at Isiolo contained rather more profanities – all of them mild – than at other times, and for the same reason.

At Nairobi the provincial commissioner told him that being posted to Tambach, the headquarters of the Elgeyo district, was 'definitely a good mark'. Armitage hoped that he could keep up his good work. The chief native commissioner had been at Tambach for about eight years and Armitage felt a personal responsibility in trying to do his best there. His only doubt was whether with Lyona and the family he could be as efficient as he should be. A little later, a neighbouring district commissioner told him that 'experience in a settler area [was] capital laid out to secure future promotion'. He looked forward to Tambach and, although he did not relish the prospect of the rain, fog and cold, he quite liked the idea of having fires in the house to keep warm. It had been intended – once again – that on leaving the northern frontier he would be posted to the secretariat, but he was not too disappointed by the change of plans. Perhaps he felt that further experience as a district commissioner would be to his ultimate advantage.[65]

In Nairobi he bought a second-hand car and then went by train to

Mombasa, excited by the prospect of meeting his wife and sons, but his excitement was soon dampened:[66]

> Nearly died when told by [British India] agent that the *Malda* [was] not due until 15th at dawn. This must be the latest the boat has ever been and is a damned scandal I think. What the hell can I do for five days here? No car. No money. Me very dispirited you see, not even heard from Lyona since Marseilles.

Over the next few days his depression deepened and he had 'no desire to spend any money' and so did not hire a car or entertain anyone – indeed, he knew no one at Mombasa to entertain – and he was embarrassed by being seen walking in a town where Europeans habitually travelled even short distances by car. In his diary he remarked, 'God this is a weary life' and he passed his time reading Winston Churchill's *World Crisis* and a book on *Hitler the Pawn*: a far cry from the Tennyson and Galsworthy of a few years earlier, which reflected changes both in his own life and in international affairs. At last his waiting came to an end and his family arrived on 15 November. He had not seen Lyona and Jeremy for over a year and he saw Richard for the first time: 'quite a model child'. It was 'good to have our family back again'. The following day they travelled by train to Nairobi and by car to Eldoret where they left Lyona's mother – who had travelled out with them – with Roddy, and then drove on to Tambach.

His new district was a fairly remote one on the western rim of the Rift Valley.[67] It was a peaceful spot but cold, misty and rainy, with many steep hills: an area that was 'ghastly precipitous' and heavily forested. He had two assistant district commissioners: Hennings and W. H. Hale. There were a number of settlers – 14 of them were resident in the district – the African population was 36,763 and there were four Indians.[68] From some locations the views were extraordinarily impressive and beautiful: 'Got a marvellous view from a hill near camp. Mount Kenya, Elgon, Aberdares, Cherangani, [the] whole line of the plateau, Lake Baringo and the Mau forest.' It was a district in which he walked a great deal – up to four hours at a time, sometimes not eating for 12 hours, which he did not find uncomfortable. Others travelled by donkey, and his sons learned to ride – and fall off – a mule.

Much of his routine fieldwork was the same as in other districts: collecting tax, holding *barazas* – which were well attended by up to 800 people and especially by old men hoping the new district commissioner would grant them tax exemption; chairing meetings of the local native council; and supervising building works. He tried a large number of civil and criminal cases including the usual stock theft cases

– in one of the 19 cases which he personally tried in 1938 he convicted his first woman cattle thief. He had to deal with numerous boundary disputes and conscientiously insisted on walking along the boundaries himself in every case: 'The trouble with these boundaries is that previous officers have never walked along them.'

The building works he supervised included a new detention camp where he had difficulty with the pit latrines, one of which filled with water as it was being dug and another of which had to be abandoned because huge boulders were encountered a short distance below the surface. The detention camp work was slow because there were insufficient detainees to build it. He selected a site and built a house in a fairly remote area where the chief native commissioner was keen that someone from Tambach should be stationed. Armitage thought he might have to take up residence there himself, was none too enthusiastic about the idea and was relieved when the country's financial position made it extremely unlikely that a permanent station would ever be established there.

The office work varied a great deal from one day to another, as it had in Kisumu, alternating from days of almost complete inactivity to days of extreme pressure:

> Very little to do in this office some days. . . . Find that so much routine to do no time for other and important things . . . Luckily there is not too much to do at the office these days. . . . Writing! I seem to spend all my time at the office doing it. . . . Spent a lazy morning doing nothing. Also afternoon reading bridge book. . . . Seems to be more work here than one realizes. The mail is so much more than I imagined.

His judicial workload was heavy. He investigated a case in which a large number of people were involved in illegally killing elephants and he applied pressure on them to confess or inform on the culprits: 'The hunters, who will not confess, are adamant so I have told them I want goats or the culprits.' Some 69 people were later arrested and punished for this offence. On the other hand, he authorized the killing of a number of elephants at another location because of the damage they were causing to crops in irrigated fields.

He had to deal with a number of murder cases – he personally heard seven preliminary inquiries for murder in 1938 – work that he had not directly encountered before. Some of these were complicated by witchcraft. An early case was of a chief who had quarrelled with his father and shot an arrow at him. It missed him, but killed another man. In two other cases, 'the wrong man was killed each time.' One case arose out of the custom of taking debt by force: 'Tempers rose and A tried to spear B but missed and hit another who died.' He also had to travel nearly 100 miles to arrest a murderer who was in hospital with wounds in his legs, which he had self-inflicted with poisoned arrows: 'Unfortunately the poison had no effect!' A particularly unpleasant task was exhuming and holding a postmortem on a corpse buried over a week previously. And there were several other cases:

> Began the investigation into the Metkei murders with 53 people concerned. They all persist that they did not hang the two men but they hanged themselves and I am sure they did but with physical pressure put on them, they could not resist. The old man would hang himself quite quickly but the young man was obviously beaten severely before he did.

There were also some narrow escapes — for both the assailant and the victim: 'An *askari* ... got drunk and wanted to shoot another *askari* whom he suspected of lying with his woman. They had a fight and luckily none got shot. He forgot to push the safety catch forward.' In a number of instances, the delay in having cases reported to him meant that he could take no action: 'I completed the Metkei enquiries and heard of another hanging from there but the man who brought the complaint said he had waited four weeks to tell us as he was too busy. ... Find alleged stock thieves also murderers at Metkei of course but the offence took place months ago awaiting me.' In his annual report for 1938 he dealt at length with witchcraft and its deep-rooted prevalence:

> Shortly after the beginning of the year numerous charges of practising witchcraft were brought against individuals. ... After investigation, sentences of imprisonment were passed on a number of people but it must often have happened that many of those who were accused of these practices suffered at the hands of their accusers without their cases being brought to the notice of the tribal authorities. ... The hold that witchcraft has over the tribe is unshakable. No death of humans or stock or sudden misfortune is ever attributed to natural causes unless a medicine man, who is invariably consulted, decides that it was so.[69]

A major theft case involved him much more directly and personally than did the murders with which he had to deal, and in this case he was able to use witchcraft to his own advantage.[70] He was awakened about 3.30 one morning and told his office had been burgled, the window forced, the bolt and glass pane broken, and the padlock on the counterfoil receipt book box broken. The cashier had put 2000 shillings in another box instead of in his safe; and this box, with its contents, was missing. Armitage and his staff searched the office and surrounds and he reported the theft to the police who arrested a new Luo driver and suspected that one of the Luo *askari*s was implicated. Shortly afterwards they found the broken and empty box behind the driver's hut. A meeting of local elders interviewed all the station staff but got nowhere. The police continued their interrogations, but found no further clues.

It was at this point that Armitage turned for help to his neighbouring district commissioner at Kabarnet and to a well-known witchdoctor there. Tambach and Kabarnet were situated on opposite rims of the Rift Valley, 20 miles apart by direct distance but very much further by track down into the rift, across it and up the other escarpment. Armitage and his colleagues across the valley, E. M. Hyde-Clarke the district commissioner and J. L. H. Webster his assistant, had evolved a system whereby at sunset each evening they drove their cars to the escarpment edge, pointed the bonnets across the valley and signalled to each other in Morse code with their headlights. Usually this worked well, but on occasions 'we could not understand a word they said'. Much of what they communicated was of no great importance – the results of local football matches for instance – but they enjoyed the contact and the experiment.[71] On the occasion of the theft from Armitage's office, however, this means of communication was invaluable because it was in this way that Armitage was able quickly to seek the help of the witchdoctor. As Webster recalled many years later:

> Kabarnet was able to be of considerable help to Bob. He flashed a message to the effect that [a large sum of money] had been stolen from his office safe.... As he would have to repay, in instalments, every penny of it to the Government, he asked if we would send over a noted witchdoctor called Kimwengoi, who was held in Kabarnet under house arrest. His powerful curses had killed quite a number of people. Hyde-Clarke authorized me to arrange for Kimwengoi to go over to Tambach on the following day, under guard. Armitage arranged a *baraza* of all the inhabitants of Tambach. Kimwengoi duly put a curse on the culprit who had stolen the money.[72]

The story was taken up by Armitage who explained in his diary what Kimwengoi did:

> The [witchdoctor] cursed all the thieves and the office staff, tribal police and police [who] passed under an arch of spears with sansevieria on top and flowers and a hole below with poison arrows.... [The] old man chanted and poked with spear and after, naked, flung spear forward and

himself after it. Said he would come again if I rewarded him well and that thief and money would appear within a week.

The very next day Armitage was awakened at 2.00 a.m. to be told the money had been found abandoned. He went out and saw a bag on the ground, but there was 'no trace of the depositor'. As he remarked, 'What price a guilty conscience!' By midday a policeman confessed to taking the money by himself and hiding it. He was utterly petrified of the curse and pleaded for the witchdoctor to take it off him. 'The elders did not want to take the curse off the thief but eventually agreed and said that the [witchdoctor] must return and then with [the] elders helping [him they could] absolve the whole crowd.' This was done. Kimwengoi had another day out, the crowd was relieved of the communal curse and the policeman was tried, pleaded guilty and gaoled. For decades Armitage and Lyona were relieved that they had not had to repay the cash stolen – equivalent to half a year's salary. Armitage was deeply conscious that failure to recover the money might have severe repercussions on his career. So far this career had progressed well and he certainly did not want a black mark on his record. His provincial commissioner went out of his way to give a warning and advice:

> I am very pleased to hear that the [money] has been recovered. I imagine it has been an awful worry to you but for goodness sake do see that financial orders re custody of cash are carried out and do not assume that the cashier is doing what he should. See for yourself that cash is locked up in the safe.... It happens at times that so much tax comes in that it is impossible to put it in the safe and it cannot be taken to the bank. In that case chain all the boxes together and padlock them, if possible to the safe door handle. Mount a full guard of police or if you have the men a double guard... under a reliable NCO.... If this money hadn't been recovered there was every likelihood of you being made to pay.[73]

Their social life at Tambach was in some respects rather more restricted than elsewhere, other than that which Armitage had experienced without Lyona at Wajir and Isiolo: 'These days we lead a very domestic life, office and garden only.'[74] They visited Eldoret, a fairly easy ride, for shopping and the races, and while he recognized that 'one must be prepared to put on several pounds at these meetings', he often lost money. Although he later became a master of racing form with an encyclopaedic knowledge of it in Britain, he seemed to have been at least a little superstitious and to attribute ill fortune at races to bad luck: 'Went again to the races after Lyona had broken her pocket mirror and had no luck. Found we had been overpaid in the sweep by 100 [shillings]. Backed no winners and day time cold.'

They played a good deal of tennis together – almost every evening – and even kept their golf going albeit on a much restricted scale. 'We have got a patch of bush down the front of Williams's house cut and can drive golf balls onto the rough below. So far have hit no one although narrow escapes! ... Bad for losing balls.' They did not possess a radio but visited a neighbour to listen to the Grand National and boat race.

They were thrown much more into depending on their own family relations than in the past and derived great pleasure and support from them: 'Our wedding day. Eight years married and I am confident we are more happy than we have ever been.' When he met Lyona and his sons, who had been away on a short local holiday, he remarked, 'The house lives again!' Lyona began to teach Jeremy at home and she dealt with a great variety of subjects, to create interest rather than to teach factual matters. And a little mild excitement was caused by Lyona's mother's remarriage: '[They] announced their engagement ... and wanted me to marry them but unfortunately I cannot.' On the whole, despite the general damp and cold – 'as cold as charity at this place in the morning and night and sun does not come too early' – they enjoyed good health, ailments being confined to sore throats and earache.[75]

Although Tambach was relatively isolated and although the Armitages had no radio and their social life was somewhat restricted, they kept in reasonable touch with affairs developing in Europe in the year leading up to the Second World War.[76] He commented in his diary on Sir Anthony Eden's resignation, on Hitler's activities and on the way in which the prime minister was 'bent on talking with Italy and bent on showing the world we are weak minded if not weak armed'. He was sceptical of Kenya's military expenditure, which he felt was 'enormous': 'The military expenditure is crippling the economy and HE came out to fortify Kenya. Though against whom?' He did not think of the governor, Brooke-Popham, in exclusively praiseworthy terms. Indeed, on occasions, at least in his diary, he was highly critical of him. When the governor visited his district, he gained the impression that 'HE had little personality and was very hard to talk to and appeared rather heavy', but he attributed this to him feeling ill, 'having inhaled alcoholic fumes from a broken compass'. He was particularly irritated when the governor, as Armitage saw it, tried to interfere with the running of his district:

> Had three minutes from HE who went to Kapsona at Christmas with no official warning. First wanted to know why the forest [was] being

cleared. This is [not my] baby. Next, what about soil erosion at Sunbeaet which I am told has been like it for years. And finally what about the Union Jack and picture of King and Queen for Kapsona? Well, what about it? I don't see why [it is] any concern of mine.... As [Glenday] says, HE was the finest inspecting officer in RAF. He is nothing else. ... He listens to all sorts of talk and pokes his nose into things which are no concern of his.

Early in 1939 he received a letter telling him he was to be transferred to the secretariat in Nairobi and that he should arrive within two weeks. This came as a surprise because, although he had anticipated being transferred to the secretariat at some stage, he 'did not expect it so early'. He had been in the colonial administrative service nearly ten years and had spent all his time in district work, work he enjoyed with its variety, independence and challenges. He was never to serve again in the districts of any of the four colonies in which he worked.[77]

Young administrative officers arrived in their first colony with very little property, but their possessions increased considerably over the years, especially after their marriage when they built a home and began to bring up a family. It now took the Armitages several days to pack, but eventually they got all their luggage into three lorry loads, 'which was an effort'. He handed over the district to Hale, his assistant district commissioner, who long remembered how impressed he had been with Armitage's ability as a district commissioner, how much he learned from him and how much this stood him in good stead in his career. The Armitages set off for Nairobi on 9 February 1939. They had a little difficulty in settling into the house allocated to them. The previous incumbents did not leave for another ten days and the house was smaller than they had expected: they felt their seniority entitled them to something larger. They began their rounds of calls by signing the book at Government House, leaving visiting cards at the houses of the most senior civil servants and timing their calls – not always successfully – when the people on whom they called were not in. They were disappointed that for five weeks no one called on them.[78]

An interesting and marked change now occurred in Armitage's private diary. Whereas in the districts he had noted a great variety of information about his work and the area in which he was working, for most of the time he spent in the secretariat his diaries contained relatively little about his work and instead concentrated largely on social and domestic matters. There were also several days when there were no entries at all in the diary.[79] This was not because the subject matter he dealt with was generally less interesting or less important, though much was both. Rather, it was because the matters he dealt with were less immediately fascinating and because the processes behind them were spread over many days, weeks or indeed months before decisions were reached. In any event, the decisions were made by others – more senior officers and non-official members of executive council. Nor was the lack of diary entries on his professional work the result of there not being much work involved, as had been the case in Wajir, where the often tedious inactivity had also resulted in sparse entries. In fact, he was heavily pressed with work for most of the time in Nairobi. The factors that had led to fuller comment on his work in the districts were largely absent in the secretariat. Fewer and less varied visitors passed through his office; there were few departmental specialist officers with whom he was directly in contact; the physical environment in which he worked – an urban office with no safaris – was less fascinating, varied and unusual; and more of the work was of a confidential or secret nature than was the case in the districts.

On the family side of their life, Jeremy went to school first in Nairobi and then at Gilgil where there was a large boys' preparatory school attended by the sons of administrative and other government officers. Armitage took a keen interest in his progress in football: 'the only boy who can kick the ball at all'. They all enjoyed their 'new' car, a 1937 Opel Olympic, a German car, which Armitage regretted, but since 'no one would look at [their old] car it could not be helped'. They both enjoyed their garden, although more of the work now fell to Lyona, and they enjoyed the occasional picnic with the children. They led a full social life and played bridge and a good deal of tennis together and with others. He played squash and after a while played tennis almost every Tuesday, hockey almost every Thursday and cricket almost every Saturday. They frequently had guests in and went to friends' houses for drinks or dinner. They enjoyed their fairly frequent visits to the cinema and to the races, now sometimes accompanied by Jeremy, although in the case of racing not always financially to their advantage: 'Went to the races and never backed a placed horse and no luck on sweep either. A good day however.'[80]

The secretariat was headed by the chief secretary who had under him a deputy chief secretary and two assistant chief secretaries, the chief native commissioner, the financial secretary and his deputy, and five assistant secretaries. Armitage was assistant secretary 'B' and his portfolio dealt with transport, game and supplies. All files were submitted by clerks direct to the assistant secretaries, each of whom was told on arrival to make as many decisions as possible without referring the matter upwards, so long as he felt confident in his judgement.[81] The game policy committee – which was in the early days of discussing the idea of a national park – and the Supply Board – which dealt with price and export controls – involved him in a great deal of work: 'Meeting of Game Policy Committee all morning. ... I am undoubtedly going to have a hell of a lot of work. ... Got the Supply Board scheme just about fixed but it has meant a terrific amount of correspondence.'

When he learned that an Italian agent intended to export all the rice he could get hold of by dhow to Italian Somaliland, he had the export of rice stopped, together shortly with most other foodstuffs. The sellers were raising commodity prices. To start with, the government only controlled the prices of foodstuffs, although before long this was considerably extended. In their price fixing they attempted to avoid export parity, so as to keep local prices down, but Armitage wondered 'who will make the profit if that is adhered to? Surely the merchants and not the producer, which is wrong. So, [perhaps we should have a] selling agency?' Soon he was working every evening when they were not going out or entertaining at home, and he worked on Sunday mornings.[82]

In their early months in Nairobi, preparations and precautions were being taken in case war should be declared against Germany and Italy. As early as April 1939, the secretariat received the first of several lectures in a short course on air raid precautions, but many elements were still unclear. The role of these precautions would depend upon the Kenya Defence Force and on whether there was to be general mobilization, but no one could discover whether this would be the case. Lyona attended a series of first aid and bandaging lectures. There were also plans to create a pioneer corps and to get money for strategic roads. He had talks with a senior army officer who said that Southern Rhodesia had 5000 European men under the age of 35 who would be mobilized as soon as war broke out and who could be in Kenya within ten days. A defence scheme booklet was produced and Armitage attended frequent meetings of the chief secretary, attorney-general, solicitor-general and other senior officers to decide when the orders in the scheme should be brought in.[83]

As August 1939 drew to a close, anxiety and uncertainty about war increased. There was a lack of news and a number of people thought war might be avoided, although Armitage's view was 'that is no use unless disarmament comes along and we get a lasting European peace'. On 3 September, he was at the secretariat when news arrived that Britain had declared war on Germany: 'So the die was cast and the only relief was that Italy so far was out of it.'[84]

Early excitement and concern in Nairobi at the very beginning of the war had nothing to do with Germany or Italy and everything to do with the deputy financial secretary making himself a cup of tea in the secretariat, an old one-storey wood and iron set of buildings.[85] Armitage was awakened by the attorney-general at 6.30 one morning to learn that the secretariat had been burnt down. He found only the chief native commissioner's block standing, while the financial secretary's block and half of the main block were in flames.

> All records and registry went up, not a thing saved except files we had at hand. I had 11 out of 27 Supply Board files saved. Several files in my safe were not burned, only scorched. . . . Thus the consummation that all have wished [has] come to pass but too drastically actually, and will the spirit change? No it can not.

They immediately sought new accommodation, turned out the agriculture and education departments and took over the top floor of the law courts. This provided quite a good room for the Supply Board, which was soon 'working in discomfort but at pressure'. A colleague explained how the conflagration had come about and its effects:

> [The deputy financial secretary] was working late in his office when he decided to make a cup of tea. He put a kettle on and forgot it. By morning the secretariat had been destroyed by fire, and the Government files were in ashes. . . . [An officer] was given the task for several weeks of opening a file for each letter as it came in. The fire had both good and bad results for the assistant secretaries. On the bad side was the fact that there was no precedent available to help them to make a decision or to support a suitable one. They were not allowed to submit a file without recommending a course of action. On the good side they did not have to spend time searching for precedents. Their seniors did not expect to get any.

Early in October 1939 Armitage's portfolio was altered so that he no longer dealt with the Supply Board – which relieved him of a good deal of work – and he took over censorship, broadcasting and information.[86] To start with, he found he got through his work quite quickly and had time to look through copies of dispatches from the secretary of state and to read files on his new responsibilities. The strain of an increasing workload and the disruption the fire had caused began to show on some officers. Armitage, however, thought there was a genuine feeling that things ought to move more quickly than they did, 'and the old secretariat habit of years ago that three months [to deal with matters] was OK' was not shared by himself and many of his younger colleagues.

He envied the unmarried officers who were able to spend more time on their work without worrying about their wives and families, and he found 'lately, it ha[d] been more and more of a strain working at home'. He admired and very much enjoyed working with the chief secretary, whom he saw as having 'a brain and the right methods of presenting argument in despatches etc., and with the least verbiage'. He contrasted this with another senior officer, who 'just spurts words without any consecutiveness' and nearly all of whose draft dispatches were rejected by the chief secretary. He was pleased, too, there was a new governor, Sir Henry Monck-Mason Moore, who had been governor of Sierra Leone before spending the last three years as assistant under-secretary in the Colonial Office.

Armitage's own work included drafting the final report of the game policy committee, a memorandum on requisitioning motor transport, another on African broadcasting, a long minute on reducing overtime in the secretariat, discussions on the fares to be charged to passengers in the forces, and the selection of a bombing and firing range. 'It is a devil of a weary life these days.' He now had an office to himself and a typist of his own, and found 'it strange to concentrate on a reasoned minute after having to make most decisions and hold long conversations on the telephone'. He preferred dictating to drafting by hand: 'Spent the whole [morning] dictating and still have a crowd of files to deal with. Having only one typist on hand here is a bore as I find I can dictate memoranda these days but cannot write and my brain seems to work better the other way.'

Until May 1940, few direct physical effects of the war were felt, though rumours abounded. For example, there were rumours that the Italians had entered Kenya, that there was to be a native rising in Kenya and that the Dutch were rebelling in South Africa. In May, however, anxieties increased and Nairobi introduced a compulsory blackout scheme. He and his colleagues volunteered to keep watch over government buildings during daylight hours. They formed a 'quite adequate force', even though they did not have 'much idea of what to do'. He attended many refresher course parades as an instructor in infantry training, but his office work prevented him from doing much instructing and 'there [was] no refresher about it. It is all new, even standing to attention and at ease and the terms.' There were also courses on using stirrup pumps, filling sandbags, warden duties, bandaging and artificial respiration. He found these sessions 'very tedious at times'. Italy entered the war on 11 June. A week later there were a number of air raid warnings in Nairobi: 'We were cursed with two air raids.... In neither did any raiders appear near my post but we heard bursts of machine-gun fire which we imagined was practice only.' The news that France had capitulated made him wonder whether Britain should 'get her colonies and fleet and continue the struggle with [the] US.'[87]

In mid-June 1940, he changed jobs in the secretariat and became clerk of legislative and executive councils and responsible for preparing the budget. His predecessor had done the job for four and a half years and could not 'face another estimates session'. Executive council met every two weeks, usually from 10.00 a.m. to 1.00 p.m. Items for the agenda, averaging 20, were approved by the chief secretary. The clerk circulated the agenda to the governor and members, took the minutes and circulated them. Legislative council was more time consuming, involving several days away from the office during each session and many other days on standing finance committee (SFC) work.[88]

Armitage's first impression that in this new job he was not overworked but soon would be, proved correct and he was wise to conserve his strength during the first few days. Office hours were now formally extended from 4.00 p.m. to 4.30 p.m. daily and one day a week officers were required to work till 6.30 p.m. This did not greatly worry them because many had a good deal of work to do and were able to get on with it in the extended hours. Armitage found that his late afternoon duty from time to time prevented him playing cricket — 'a damned curse!' He resented only slightly more the removal of public holidays: 'I know we all have to work as hard as we can these days, war time efforts and all that, but I think that a rest is advisable sometimes.'[89]

His clerkship of the standing finance committee took up a great deal of his time.

> SFC finished at 5 o'clock and I worked till 1.30 a.m., my latest night so far.... Got proof of SFC report from printer.... Finished correcting the proof and left a copy with the [chief secretary].... Leg. Co. started again. SFC report put on table and railway estimates debated.... Leg. Co. went on and quite a breeze over the report of the SFC.[90]

And, in addition to this work directly related to the finance committee, there was the ongoing work of getting the annual budget through the legislative council at the same time: 'Leg. Co. to finish the railway estimates.... I have started on the budget despatch.... Spent the [morning] correcting the draft estimates.... Got the proof of the estimates to the printer at last. [We also have] the draft despatch so we progress.'[91]

The pressure of work continued through 1941 and he was called back from his local leave at Roddy's farm early in the new year. He was made secretary of a commission enquiring into the workings of the custodianship of enemy property, which took up even more of his time. And at the next round of finance committee and budget deliberations he worked late into the night: 11.00 p.m. correcting the draft committee report and 3.00 a.m. to complete it another night. Lyona thought he was looking very tired although he would not admit it.[92] Meetings of executive council – including finding the answers to the numerous questions asked by the non-official members – and of legislative council were a constant drain on his time:

> Last weekend was my worst weekend of the year. It always is as I have to get my standing finance committee report. We sat on December 1st to 4th all day till 5.00 p.m. or 7.00 p.m. and then there was a squabble as to the final paragraph and we had to sit again on the 9th. The mornings of the 5th and 12th were taken up with Executive Council and the mornings of the 9th to 11th were spent in Legislative Council. Thank goodness we have only three more days of Legislative Council this next week and then ... I can get down to finishing off the offshoots of the budget.[93]

He was embarrassed but pleased when the chief secretary spoke in legislative council of how very careful and correct he was in his work and how much one 'felt for him in his long hours of overtime'.[94]

Executive council turned its attention to developments after the war, and Armitage found these discussions of great interest.[95]

> Ex. Co. very occupied with postwar vocational training and so on. Committees are being appointed and they will be able to collect statistics at any rate, but the difficulties are how to deal with the demobilized soldiers who may be better suited for the jobs which are held by people in Kenya and whose employers may want to get rid of them! Then there is the added complication of women having done so many men's jobs.

Other matters discussed in council included military exemptions, voluntary cuts in civil service salaries, control of agriculture and who should exercise the extensive powers proposed, reserve occupations, government's purchase of a bacon factory, guaranteed prices for produce, postwar reconstruction, land tenure, defence regulations, pensions for European soldiers, part-time training for the Kenya Defence Force and the conscription of women. He was also

> involved in working out the scheme recently announced by Government for the granting of bonuses for the breaking of new land, advances for cultivation and a guarantee against loss of production costs in order to help farmers produce more wheat, maize, rye and flax which are all wanted in the Middle East and elsewhere to help the war effort. The scheme is so large that ... the detailed work is considerable.[96]

The large influx of Commonwealth servicemen into Nairobi and surrounding stations had a marked effect on the social life of the more permanent residents. They provided a larger and more varied pool from which to draw dinner guests. Many were keen sportsmen and they supplied additional high quality teams against whom to play cricket, hockey and tennis. On the other hand, they packed the cinema and made attending films there less attractive to a number of residents, and the Armitages found it more difficult to place bets at the very crowded local horse race meetings.[97]

War conditions required that the bulk of government decision making be done executively; consequently the role of the legislative council declined.[98] For example, the only business at the April 1942 meeting was the presentation of insignia to those receiving awards in the New Year's honours list. At the same time, the role of the executive council increased as the use of defence and other executive regulations expanded. Kenya had long made use of committees and boards – largely to involve European non-officials in the business of government – and in the first two years of the war over thirty new and often powerful committees and boards were set up. In this way, the whole economic life of the country came under executive control in which non-officials played a major role, often acting as controllers of various primary products. Armitage was concerned about the relationship of the most important and powerful of these new bodies, the civil defence and supply committee (CDSC), with the finance committee, of which he was secretary, and with the executive council, of which he was clerk.

> Executive Council set up [the CDSC] to advise HE on defence. [A leading non-official] expects to be executive and to get things done and if any man does not do things he is to be removed but SFC and Ex. Co. will often have to be [consulted]. I am not sure that with a little larger personnel it should not take [the] place of the two latter bodies.

> I had SFC all [morning]. They are worried about lack of financial examination of projects put up to CDSC, remarking that Leg. Co. is the ultimate authority for voting the money. HE in his broadcast said that he would leave the routine side of government to the civil service and leave himself free for CDSC matters.

> Had Executive Council. It still seems to get a lot of work although the [CDSC] has stolen the thunder.

To start with, the only direct effect on Armitage was that he had to take over some of the work of a colleague who was sent to work with the CDSC. However, he was pleased even then to acquire a new filing cabinet to go with the files he took over. Although legislative council work declined and that of the executive council increased, it was the work of the finance committee that imposed the most onerous burden on him. Although the CDSC made most of the important decisions – rather than executive council *per se* – these decisions invariably involved finance, which had to be provided, or approved, by the finance committee. The changes were already indicating possible constitutional developments later. By May 1942 Armitage himself was wondering whether they could develop a ministerial system so as to avoid a centralized secretariat and give each head of department a secretariat-trained secretary.[99] Although new structures were emerging the organization of the secretariat was not changing in step with them: 'Finding life in office as hectic as ever. There is too much not seeing the wood for the trees which is why our secretariat is not in favour at Government House. Also some sections are undoubtedly too over worked.'[100]

Allied to his finance committee work was the preparation of the annual estimates of revenue and expenditure and the presentation of the budget. From July to November each year from 1940 to 1943, this involved Armitage in an increasingly heavy and anxious burden.[101] 'I am trying not to have to bring work home to do. I find that I must get rest and conserve myself for the budget which I am afraid is going to be a tiresome one.... Having to start and tackle estimates problems [a little early is] a nuisance but it will save congestion later.'

The chief secretary recognized the virtual impossibility of one man now doing both the increased volume of executive council work and at the same time handling the 'terrific pressure of work with [the] estimates' and he arranged for Armitage to be relieved of the former during the busiest period of the latter: 'The decision was taken that [K. W.] Simmonds should do my Executive Council work whilst I concentrate on the estimates.... The Executive Council sitting all day last week prevented me doing any estimates that day and time is pressing. I don't like ... giving up my own work or putting more on another person but things are difficult this year.'

This relief, with Lyona's help, enabled him to cope with the 1942 round of estimates work: 'I worked from 9.00 a.m. to 9.45 p.m. [on Saturday] and Lyona helped with the adding machine in the [afternoon] and we really made progress with these ruddy estimates but it left me quite exhausted.' On the King's birthday, a bank holiday, they 'spent the morning by working on the estimates and Lyona played the adding machine'. He was so busy with the estimates during the second half of October that for a whole week he made no entries in his diary. Even so, he narrowly missed catastrophe because having just completed the estimates he broke his wrist playing hockey and was away from the office for over a week. On his return he took back his executive council work, attended the budget session meetings of the legislative council and then immediately started his standing finance committee work again:

> Had Executive Council in [morning] and we started SFC in [afternoon] ... SFC 9.30–4.30 and then I go back to finish my office work ... SFC the whole day again. Talk ranged from meat control to traffic control. The secretary gets somewhat tired but the members seem able to keep going and the deficit grows ... SFC all day ... Executive Council but got my report off to the printer and so had peace of mind.

Any relief was but a temporary remission and by the very beginning of the new year the pressure was on again, exacerbated by his wish to clear his desk before going on leave, which, if he took it, he was now obliged to take on the coast: 'Huge amount of work and don't know how to get through it.... Going flat out to get all my work done in the hopes of getting my leave on 8th February. It is amazing how much one has left over from the budget session always, and this year in particular.'

Even at the coast, however – where he spent the days 'very easily, sleeping, eating, reading and playing on the beach and gradually acquiring a tan' – he was not safe from the demands of officialdom. He received 'an unpleasant telegram' peremptorily recalling him to duty. Having his much needed, restful and happy holiday so rudely interrupted seems to have affected his total preparedness to work himself, regardless of the personal cost: 'We had an early evening. I am averse to overworking since my return from leave!' But old habits die hard, as did his sense of duty and his career aspirations. He was soon back to working enthusiastically and at full tilt.

The task of being secretary of the finance committee and preparing the estimates was given for a while to another officer to gain 'experience so that he can qualify for Deputy Financial Secretary in due course'.[102] He may have been mildly disappointed that it was another officer being prepared by these means for promotion rather than himself, but he was relieved not to have to do the estimates work and felt sure he would benefit: 'I have done them for 3 years so shall not be sorry but I am sure to get something in return.' He enjoyed his new work of dealing with development proposals, especially those to be financed from the Colonial Development and Welfare Fund (CDWF):

> [The chief secretary] put me on to getting out schedules of schemes for which we want money from loan or CDWF. Got to £6.1m. already. We are going hard on this subject now.... Spent morning getting files about

CDWF ready for SFC next week. Dreadfully overworked. . . . Still spending the time reading files dealing with the proposals for the CDWF and finding we have a lot to explain away. . . . Spent the whole day on CDWF draft despatch which has to be a general development plan. As we have no plan and no intention of making one yet the secretary of state is certain to demand one. . . . One idea is to get the schemes off now so that we shall have time to take what's coming to us. Luckily my ordinary work [is] not too heavy.

Traces of mild disillusion remained for a while and he no longer felt compelled to work on public holidays. He found 'the pall of work which [hung] over [him] most depressing'; he had 'a complete revulsion from doing any of the work [he] had meant to do and so went and gardened before lunch' and remarked: 'Such a good weekend that I drank myself out of beer!'

He continued as clerk to the executive council. Not all its meetings went smoothly – some were 'snappy' – and colleagues' tempers began to fray:

A most unfortunate day as Executive Council papers were delayed and some went astray and others were not sent me in time and so on. Then [the typist] spelt HE's name without a 'C' in Monck and that was [seen as] a crack and the [chief secretary] went off the handle because I opened his door to put some papers in and he returned and I left the door open. People's nerves are getting rattled and they fly off the handle.[103]

In mid-June 1943 there was a rearrangement of duties in the secretariat and Armitage again took over responsibility for the finance committee and estimates: 'So am where I was 2 years ago, but better as then the arrears were dreadful.'[104] Even so, his work with the committee and the estimates kept him under immense pressure:

This is the third night having stayed up until after midnight. Estimates are going better. . . . Had a SFC meeting all the [morning]. I was very sleepy and the meeting talked a lot about things which the [chief secretary] wanted more complete picture of . . . Just work all the afternoon, evening and night to 10.15 when I could go on no longer. . . . Just kept on all day with the estimates and other things; never stopped. . . . Spent the day rushing about getting the last half of the draft estimates and the whole of the memo to the printer.

Having found one last mistake in the approved estimates, he got them also off to the printer. With relief, he remarked: 'So all my worries are over ... if anyone finds mistakes at this stage well it is just too bad.' He found the relaxation after working at full pressure curious – 'rather like shock after an accident', even though relaxation meant 'being able to read up arrears of papers and so on'. He was awarded the MBE in the 1944 New Year's honours list, primarily for his work on the estimates.[105]

Further secretariat reorganizations were in the air and Armitage felt that he might get the new post of personal assistant to the chief native commissioner.[106] As things turned out he did not take this post and instead, at the beginning of 1944, began work at the agricultural produce and supply board, working closely with a leading non-official member of both the legislative and executive councils, F. W. Cavendish-Bentinck, often referred to as 'CB'. He immediately and enthusiastically entered into working with him and getting the office – which was 'quite good [but had] more files than [he] liked the look of' – in order: 'Long session going through files with CB. I'm keen to know of his views as I must represent them. ... There is a lot of important work to be done getting mass production with the existing labour supply, getting more use of labour, more work out of the labour, bigger yields and so on.'

Some six weeks after taking up this job, however, he learned that officers who wanted to go on leave to Britain should apply to their head of department and it would be for the head to say whether they could be spared. 'We are going to apply. Lyona is very tired and we want to get Jeremy home before Winchester. We realize the dangers [and acute discomfort] and that we shall not be able to buy things and go places but the mental rest is what we want and Lyona particularly. CB of course might not let us go.'[107] Arranging leave was not a smooth and guaranteed affair. However, to start with it seemed that things were promising and that he was likely to be given priority – largely because he had been due for leave at the beginning of the war, had not had home leave for eight years and his local leaves had been cut short in the interim. He gathered he was to 'have the honour of being the first administrative officer to go on leave and to go in May'.[108] 'HE is supposed to support policy of getting some of us away and back refreshed and so keeping the fort when everyone is bats and tired and longing to get home. The [provincial commissioners] are ... against it as it means denuding the districts.'

He was working very hard indeed and feeling exhausted: 'The work is still as flat out as ever. I have never known anything like it. However, we shall win through.' 'I feel so tired these days, I can't initiate a conversation.' By mid-May the situation was very uncertain. The establishments officer said there was no space for the Armitages on the next boat leaving Mombasa because it would be full of military and merchant navy personnel. Also, he could see no accommodation for civilians being available on subsequent sailings. For a while they explored the possibility of travelling down the Nile or by air to Cairo and catching a boat from Egypt. However, they were advised against this, mainly because there had been earlier troubles over similar proposals involving a wife and children. None the less, they did go on leave:

> We sailed from Mombasa in a cargo ship in May 1944. There were 12 staterooms – not converted. We zigzagged up the Indian Ocean and were in the Red Sea on D-Day. We spent 3 weeks in a camp in Suez waiting for a Mediterranean convoy. Best event every day was swimming on a beach. Later in June we sailed from Port Said on the liner *Orion*. It had been converted into a troop ship and the four of us were in one cabin. We were all civilians on board. Two sittings for meals and great competition to find a place to put a rug down on the deck for the day. We were in a large convoy with a naval escort and zigzagged all the way to Liverpool where we arrived on about 10 July 1944. No enemy was encountered. The *Orion* did leave the convoy for a few hours to pick up hundreds of Italian prisoners of war in Algiers who came to work in the British harvest.[109]

While Armitage was away on leave a new governor, Sir Philip Mitchell, arrived at the end of 1944. Mitchell was 'possibly the ablest of the governors who had come and gone in East Africa up to that date' but he was no longer at his peak: 'Sir Philip had returned from the wars an exhausted man, having had no leave for seven years. He was on the verge of a nervous breakdown.... Shortly afterwards he went on three months' leave and returned apparently rested, but ... he was [n]ever quite the same again. The cutting edge of his intellect had been blunted.'[110] Even so, Mitchell immediately turned his mind to constitutional change. He was particularly interested in bringing an end to the anomaly in which non-officials were privy to government secrets and shared responsibility in the executive council, yet outside and in the legislative council were free to attack the government and frequently did so strongly.[111] He intended that in future all non-official members of the executive council should support the government or resign. To achieve this, he proposed to abolish the system of all government business being channelled through the chief secretary and to introduce a system in which members of the executive council, whether officials or not, would be placed in charge of groupings of departments, be responsible for their work and have a senior official as secretary to the grouping. This was a development Armitage had foreseen over two years earlier.

During the first few months after Armitage's leave, when he had returned to his old job with Cavendish-Bentinck, these plans of the new governor were being actively discussed and Armitage took a keen interest in them. There was some hope he might be made deputy financial secretary or assistant chief secretary, but both these posts were filled from outside Kenya, and the governor decided he should become secretary of a new department headed by Cavendish-Bentinck.

> Saw [the chief secretary who] said conclusion reached by HE [was] that I was better required in new [job] which he felt would be better prospects. I saw HE who repeated same. Eyes of world on this experiment [of members heading departments]. Gave me undertaking to look into the position in two years' time if I wanted him to. CB has accepted so if all is well I should get the job from 1 August. That will suit me.

On 1 August 1945 the new system was introduced:

> CB becomes Member for agriculture, animal husbandry and natural resources today and I secretary.... Spent most of [morning] talking... about the new reorganization. I get all appropriate files minuted to me and will have to consult [senior finance officials] according to importance of financial implications.... I'm afraid it means much more work and at night for me.

Armitage's work with Cavendish-Bentinck was in substance very similar to that with him before the reorganization. Now, however, he was the official head of an embryo ministry, the member's chief adviser, and his work did not have to be channelled any longer through the remainder of the secretariat and ultimately via the chief secretary. Cavendish-Bentinck took matters directly to executive council for approval. The pressure of work, as so very often – in fact normally – over the past several years, continued to be relentless:

> Unremitting toil is my lot and I am browned off with it.... Got back to my awful feeling of strain again dealing with 12 things at once.... By working flat out I managed to get all done by 4.30.... I am so tired and overwrought that I can't bring myself to do anything that means a real effort.[112]

He was pleased with his promotion and with the work he was doing, but concerned about the salary. He had been told that, as secretary to the member for agriculture, his salary would be the same as that of the deputy financial secretary, £1100, but when the estimates appeared before the budget session of the legislature early in November, he found that the deputy financial secretary got £1200 and he only £1000. Eventually, a salary of £1100 was agreed by the secretary of state.[113]

He developed a close, professional and protective relationship with Cavendish-Bentinck, rather like that of a permanent secretary with his minister:

> Discussed ... getting CB away for two months. He is so tired he goes to sleep in evening at his desk.
>
> CB spent two and a half hours with HE. I think he is gradually taking these high ups into his way of thinking. He wants to change the mind of the administration.
>
> Managed to get CB to attend to his files. He has habit of brooding on too many. I agree that one should a bit. He's getting to office earlier now and I think should get through quite a lot of work in next three months and then [he] goes home I hope on leave.[114]

Armitage's career in Kenya had developed well and on fairly traditional lines. He had served as an assistant district commissioner and then as a district commissioner in a variety of types of district – African agricultural, African pastoral and European settled areas: only the coast was missing. From the very beginning at Kakamega, he had used his initiative by doing 'things [his] own way' when the district commissioner – who he thought did not work hard enough – gave him no guidance, and learning as much as he could from his fellow assistant district commissioners. He had worked well in the three districts of which he had been district commissioner. Wajir had been a fallow period – inevitably so – and he had done an exceptionally good job in the difficult tasks that faced him at Isiolo. Turnbull described it as a 'magnificent job' and both the governor and the provincial commissioner thanked him for it.

He was conscientious and careful to pass his government law and language examinations as quickly and as well as he could: he was critical of a fellow officer who had 'failed in his language examination ... which is bad for an ADC.' He recognized that an extra period as district commissioner when he left the Northern Frontier, rather than going straight into the secretariat, would provide beneficial experience. The only potential blot on his copybook had been the theft of cash at Tambach, but this had inflicted no lasting damage, if any damage at all. He had been taken into the secretariat after ten years in the districts. In Nairobi, he had a wide range of experience as an assistant secretary, the clerk to the executive and legislative councils, the secretary of the standing finance committee and as the person responsible for compiling the annual estimates and preparing the budget. Especially in the secretariat he had shown himself to be a competent and hard worker, one who could withstand the drudgery and enormous pressures of work, albeit on occasions only just.

Although he frequently pushed himself almost to the limit and felt that his family commitments might prevent him from doing even more work, he was careful not to overdo it and risk his health and thereby his ability to work efficiently: 'I shall bust myself if I go too hard at it.' He was acutely aware of the need for change, doubting whether the 'spirit' in the secretariat would alter as a result of the fire. He felt that things could move much more quickly. He did not share the 'old secretariat habit' of taking months to deal with matters. He recognized there was too much not seeing the wood for the trees. His experience in the secretariat sharpened his awareness of organizational and constitutional development possibilities: he wondered if a selling agency might be set up to control prices and if the CDSC could replace the executive council and standing finance committee. He was quick to see that a ministerial system – an early stage in the loosening of imperial control – might emerge.[115]

He had always been an officer with career aspirations. This was partly taken for granted because he came from a family that had done well in its careers and partly because he felt he owed it to his parents after the sacrifices they had made to educate him. This showed through when he responded to their fears about the possible effect on his career of an early marriage and of friction with the governor. We have seen too how, after scarcely a day in the country, he had doubted a young colleague's possession of 'enough push to succeed'. Also, much later he commented privately on another colleague whom he doubted had his sights on more than becoming a provincial commissioner.

He was never in the slightest degree sycophantic, taking on the governor over being allowed to marry after only six months in the service. In 1934 he stood against Wyn-Harris in wishing to be posted to the secretariat, withdrawing only on the principle that decisions by numismatic chance are too casual, even though Wyn-Harris was three years his senior. It is likely, too, that he recognized that if one went into the secretariat at too early a stage one was likely to be moved out of it again and consequently that path to advancement would be interrupted and possibly broken completely. He was quick to sum up the abilities of those with whom he worked, including his seniors. Although he occasionally had 'malicious scandal-talks' with Turnbull, he normally kept his criticism strictly to the privacy of his personal diary.

From about 1942 the comments in that diary concerning his career progression – and the related question of the progression of colleagues – became more numerous and clear. For example, when he learned that the post of chief secretary in the Falkland Islands was vacant, he asked to be considered for it: 'It could be a chance to get out of the rut here' and a stepping stone: 'One should get a good appointment from it so I should be very glad [although surprised] to get it.' When an officer from Northern Rhodesia got the job Armitage was content that the Kenya government had recommended him for it: 'That is good.' He took heart when more senior officers were moved on or sidelined, for example when the financial secretary gave up his finance work to concentrate on food supplies and did not then return to the treasury, 'which pleased everyone'. He was disappointed when the honours lists contained no names of secretariat officers. When the chief native commissioner asked him if he would leave his post with Cavendish-Bentinck and join his staff – which would have meant a move from being concerned with policy matters at the centre to being concerned with administration in the field – Armitage told him he 'would have to make it worth [his] while'.[116]

Not only was the work he did in the secretariat good experience, but after the first few years it was work that brought him into contact with the governor and thereby brought him and his attributes to the attention of the person most likely to influence his future. This applied especially, but not exclusively, to his work as clerk to the legislative and executive councils, of both of which the governor was president. For four months in 1946 he was a nominated official member of the legislative council.[117] Working directly to the most senior non-official, especially when Cavendish-Bentinck became member for agriculture, was also a help in bringing Armitage and his work before the governor's eye. He acted as supernumerary aide-de-camp and found the governor 'kindly' and 'affable'. It may be, however, that Cavendish-Bentinck valued his work so highly that he was reluctant to let him go too soon, even on promotion.

> CB and I took [the white paper] up to HE who approved all our alterations. He was very chatty. CB raised the question of chairmanship of the African settlement board and he mentioned [Wyn-Harris] and although HE did not agree he did not refuse and also said what about me and how CB must prepare me to get promotion and go away. So that is good.

> CB heard from Sir P. Mitchell ... asking who is to succeed CB and [saying] that I shall have to get a move up which is pleasant but CB will try and keep me for a year I know.

None the less, in March 1947 Armitage was further promoted to become administrative secretary of Kenya. He did not, however, take up this post until his return from leave at the end of the year. The administrative secretary was the permanent secretary in the chief secretary's 'ministry'. A colleague who worked with him in this capacity described him as 'a quiet, unassuming person with a good sense of humour and complete composure. He was well liked and respected.'[118]

Lyona flew on leave to Britain in March to be with their sons who had not returned to Kenya after the war. She travelled 'in a converted York bomber, twelve passengers, no heating or air conditioning. They had a very bumpy flight from the Mediterranean to Heathrow'. Armitage followed a little later in July. In the meantime, he wrote:

> Since she left I have been trying to concentrate on getting my work done and write a comprehensive white paper on our agrarian plan – a hopeless task. I have given up games almost entirely. . . . I am now a nomad laying my head wherever a friend will take me in. The club unfortunately has such limited accommodation that one can't stay there for long.[119]

While he was on leave in August 1947, he attended the Colonial Office conference in London of all the African governors. He was a member of the governor of Kenya's team and chairman of one of the discussion groups, for which he was warmly thanked by Sir Andrew Cohen.[120]

Soon after he returned from leave he was offered, and accepted, the post of financial secretary in the Gold Coast.

3

The Gold Coast

The most dramatic years that any African colony can have seen.

The Gold Coast, now Ghana, in West Africa is 92,000 square miles in area. It has three main geographical zones.[1] First, a narrow coastal plain of between five and 50 miles wide intersected by rivers, only three with permanently open mouths, guarded by shallow bars. Second, a tropical rainforest belt extending northwards from the coast for almost 200 miles near the western frontier and petering out towards the east. It is broken by heavily wooded ranges rising to 2000 feet, intersected by many streams negotiable only by canoes. It is from here that most of the country's timber, cocoa and minerals are derived. Third, north of the forest belt, an undulating area 300 to 1300 feet above sea level. This is mostly covered with orchard bush, but contains stretches of treeless plains and a range of hills along the eastern boundary, which rise to 2900 feet.

In the south, there are two annual rainy seasons with a short dry spell in July and August and a longer dry spell from December to February. In the north, the rainy seasons merge to exclude the short dry season; and the major dry season is longer. The harmattan, bringing hazy and dusty conditions, reaches the country from the north in January and February.

In 1948 the African population was 4,111,000 and the non-African 6770. Most of the population was engaged in peasant agriculture. More than a third of the world's supply of cocoa came from the Gold Coast. Cocoa formed over 90 per cent of the country's agricultural exports and almost 70 per cent of all its exports. The main food crops were millet, maize, guinea corn, plantain, yams and cassava. Other important agricultural products included palm oil, palm kernels, cola nuts, coconut and copra. Sea fisheries were a major source of food.

The Gold Coast had long contact with western Europe. Gold attracted the Portuguese in the 1470s, the English came in 1553, the Dutch in 1595, and the Swedes and Danes in about 1640.[2] Western education, for both sexes, was much more advanced than in any other African country.[3]

Administratively, the country was divided from south to north into the Colony, Ashanti and the Northern Territories. Each was headed by a chief commissioner under whom were a number of district commissioners in charge of administrative districts.

On 17 June 1948 Armitage left Kenya and flew to the Gold Coast, arriving there the following day. He arrived at a crucial point in the country's political history.

At the end of the Second World War, Governor Alan Burns introduced a new constitution with a legislature of nine officials and 22 Africans: 13 nominated by the chiefs, four nominated by the governor and five directly elected by coastal town ratepayers. One of those nominated by the chiefs was Dr J. B. Danquah. The 65,000 African soldiers and others returning to their homes after the war, full of hope and expectations, were soon disillusioned. With no army pay, without jobs and with greatly increased prices in the shops they became deeply discontented. Demobilization was too rapid to absorb them and unemployment increased. To harness this discontentment to his political advantage, Danquah set up a new political party, the United Gold Coast Convention (UGCC) and invited a dynamic, young, politically active African to return from his studies in London, after 22 years' absence, to organize the party as its paid secretary: this was Kwame Nkrumah who arrived in December 1947.[4]

A month later, and five months after Burns's departure, Sir Gerald Creasey arrived in Accra as the new governor. After a quarter of a century's service entirely in the Colonial Office, he 'knew virtually nothing about the Gold Coast'.[5] He was then aged 51 years. One of his tasks was to implement the new constitution. A month after his arrival he was faced with a dangerous situation.

A procession of ex-servicemen, objecting about not receiving their war bonuses, decided to complain directly to the governor. Instead, the police persuaded them to hand in a petition at the secretariat. The route and timing were agreed, but when the procession started the leaders lost control and the marchers turned towards Christianborg Castle, the governor's residence. The police tried to stop them, but were attacked and eventually opened fire, killing two and wounding five. Some of the fleeing marchers went to the trading quarter where youths, taking advantage of the sensitive situation caused by a recent boycott of European firms' goods – the result of high prices and inflation – burned down and looted a number of stores. The rioting spread over the next few days and in all 29 people were killed and 237 injured. The mob took over Accra for 48 hours and the trading area was in ruins. The

UGCC sent a telegram to the secretary of state claiming that since civil government had broken down they should be allowed to take over control.[6]

Creasey declared a state of emergency and banished Danquah, Nkrumah and four other UGCC leaders to the Northern Territories. Two sloops sailed from Cape Town and took up station off Accra. In Gibraltar three troop-transporting planes and a battalion of the Cameronians were placed on stand-by. A detachment of Nigerian troops was brought in. The governor gave a broadcast message designed to quieten things down, but it 'was really a bit of a disaster [and] created all kinds of problems', including the rumour that the governor had fled the country or was in hiding somewhere – for example at 'the bottom of a gold mine a couple of thousand feet down'. The rioting came as a shock to colonial officers: 'The vast majority of us were taken completely by surprise and were puzzled that there should be so much dissatisfaction in the African mind over the established order of things.'[7]

In London there was 'enormous excitement' – panic as one official, J. K. Thomson, saw it.[8] Many telegrams were exchanged and Colonial Office officials worked over the weekend discussing the riots with the Gold Coast chief secretary, who had flown in to report to the secretary of state. There was a feeling in the Colonial Office that Creasey had not reacted calmly and, although they knew him well from his service in the Office, they 'were sorry for him but felt that there were plenty of people on the spot who could have handled things more calmly'. The Labour government decided a commission of inquiry should report on the disturbances and make recommendations.

They appointed as chairman, Aiken Watson, a junior judge and former Labour parliamentary candidate. A research officer in the Colonial Office at the time recalled of Watson: 'In one sense we were scraping the bottom of the barrel ... and an extraordinary search was made by Cohen all over the place. Everyone who had African experience was busy so in the end they had to settle for a [person] with no African experience whatsoever.' Another Colonial Office official was also struck by Watson's lack of knowledge of Africa: 'Briefing him was a trifle laborious.' In a narrative of events, which the government issued as evidence to the commission, it was claimed that the UGCC had links with overseas communist organizations and had revolutionary plans that included assassination and terrorism. Watson rejected these elements of the government's appraisal.

Armitage read of these events while he was on leave in Britain and he recalled a recent conversation with George Sinclair, who was a member of the governor of the Gold Coast's team at the Colonial

Office conference. Sinclair said: 'what a marvellous colony the Gold Coast was, the relationships between black and white and between the government and the population were absolutely superb, there was harmony and goodwill and good nature prevailing and nothing could ever go wrong.' Recalling this glowing description of the Gold Coast, he was 'very surprised' and he 'went with some trepidation'. By the time of his arrival, however, 'everything was quite quiet and peaceful [and] people had ceased being stunned by what had happened'.[9]

Watson's report was published soon after Armitage arrived in the Gold Coast. It resulted in a widespread condemnation of the Burns constitution as 'outmoded at birth' and acceptance by the British government that 'the constitution and government must be so reshaped as to give every African of ability an opportunity to help govern the country'. Although Watson did not propose to draft a constitution, he none the less set out clearly the requirements in detail for local authorities, the legislature, the executive council and the role of the governor. The proposals were for fast progress towards African government. Armitage was concerned that in the absence of an effective public relations department the people would continue not to understand and not to trust the government.[10]

Another result was Creasey's quiet removal to Malta after little more than a year in office. The governorship again remained vacant for five months, until Sir Charles Arden-Clarke arrived in August 1949. The secretary of state warned that the Gold Coast was on the edge of revolution: 'We are in danger of losing it.' The new governor was told to do something about it. In the interim before his arrival, five of the six detainees, now released – but not Nkrumah who refused to serve – had been appointed to a committee, comprised entirely of Africans, to recommend constitutional changes, under the chairmanship of judge Sir Henley Coussey.[11]

Arden-Clarke's three most senior civil servants and his official advisers in executive council were Reginald Saloway (chief secretary), Armitage (financial secretary) and Patrick Branigan (attorney-general). Saloway, 'with high level experience of the handover of power in India', replaced Sir Robert Scott as chief secretary within three months of the new governor's arrival. Branigan, with a first-class honours degree in law and political science, had served in several colonies and had considerable experience of arbitration and conciliation. And Armitage came from Kenya, where a ministerial form of government – the 'member' system – had been introduced. With the departure of the three regional commissioners, the six members of the governor's top team of advisers changed between November 1948 and the spring of 1952.[12] Armitage recalled: 'We were none of us old Gold Coast stiffs as

I used in private to refer to the civil servants who were Gold Coast based. Remember, once in the Gold Coast you never left the Gold Coast and the Gold Coast resented any outsiders coming in.'[13]

Two related aspects of Armitage's life over the five years he was in the Gold Coast need to be examined: his role in the political development of the country and his financial work. First, there was the political development that took place during Armitage's service in the Gold Coast and with which he was closely involved as a member of the executive. As Arden-Clarke said, it is 'in the political sphere that Ghana's chief importance lie[s], as the spearhead of politically emergent Black Africa'.[14] The political scene Armitage encountered on his arrival was outlined a few years later by Saloway:

> Before I went to the Gold Coast in 1947 I was assured that it was regarded as a model colony where everything was going according to plan. I arrived there to find political and racial feeling as tense as I had ever known it in India, and in February 1948 there were violent riots ... the government had virtually no effective support among the people and the forces of law and order were utterly inadequate to control the situation. [The chiefs] were powerless against nationalist agitators who stirred up the militant young men amongst whom respect for traditional authority was already waning. The 1946 Constitution ... accorded overwhelming preponderance to the representatives of the traditional authorities. There were direct elections in the five municipalities only. What was intended to be, and indeed was, an important step towards self-government did in practice put a clapper on a head of steam emanating from the postwar nationalist fervour among the semi-educated youth and particularly among the ex-servicemen. [Nkrumah's] aim was immediate self-government based on adult suffrage. The Gold Coast was thus all set for a social and political revolution.[15]

Two months before Arden-Clarke arrived, Nkrumah set up his own political party, the Convention People's Party (CPP), with its slogan 'full self-government now'. Anything less would be regarded as 'bogus and fraudulent' and be met by 'positive action'. All the other major leaders were fully occupied with the Coussey committee and had little time left for practical politics. It was into this vacuum that Nkrumah strode. Coussey's report, published in October 1949, although recommending a very far-reaching set of constitutional proposals, fell short of the CPP's demands and consequently positive action was adopted. In January 1950, the Trades Union Congress, set up by the CPP, declared a general strike and Nkrumah announced the beginning of his campaign to demand 'self-government now'. The governor feared that further trouble would follow and, in response, spoke with Armitage and Branigan.

They agreed that a state of emergency should be declared and: 'All the ringleaders were immediately arrested. Almost overnight about a hundred people were taken into custody ... and the whole affair fizzled out in a matter of a few days,' although Nkrumah's followers threatened and jostled people in the streets, which 'were full of very insolent and violent young men ... and the Europeans were molested and had bad language used to them'. Lyona Armitage 'had to have an orderly [accompany] her whenever she went out shopping' because of her husband's 'position in the government, which could have put her in danger'.

The CPP *Accra Evening News* was shut down. Nkrumah was arrested and charged with sedition: he served eight months in gaol. In the meantime, CPP branches were organized throughout the Colony and Ashanti. In the Northern Territories the chiefs did not want independence since this, they thought, would mean domination by educationally more advanced southerners.[16] As the governor recalled:

> A general strike was called but did not receive the support of the workers to the extent expected by the CPP. There was some rioting. Prompt and firm action was taken to restore the situation and to maintain law and order. Within three weeks, the country was almost back to normal and those chiefly responsible for the trouble were in prison.[17]

With the CPP in eclipse, Arden-Clarke and his executive council worked out the details of the new constitution based on Coussey's recommendations. In February 1951, a general election – at which the Armitages, who much admired Danquah, and Europeans generally voted for the UGCC – resulted in a sweeping victory for the CPP.[18] Nkrumah, however, was still in gaol and it was clear his party would refuse to cooperate in working the new constitution in his absence. Arden-Clarke decided to release him. Armitage was 'very disturbed' about what would happen under the new constitution with a United Kingdom-type cabinet and a majority of African ministers. His concern was whether the CPP would participate constructively, for it did not grant 'self-government now' as they had demanded. The governor recalled the first few meetings of the new executive council, now comprised of eight Africans elected to the legislature, including Nkrumah, and three officials – Saloway, Branigan and Armitage – presided over by the governor:

> The officials were suspicious of the politicians and the African Ministers mistrusted the 'European agents of Imperialism', as they were said to

regard them. But the members of the Council were all reasonable men, and this soon passed as we got to know each other better. There were wide differences of opinion as to the best pace and the best means of achieving full self-government, but no differences that full self-government within the Commonwealth was our objective and that it should be achieved, if at all possible, with goodwill on both sides.

Their meetings gradually became 'more like family affairs', with members arguing and quarrelling happily (and occasionally violently) with each other privately, but maintaining a united front publicly. Within three months council was working harmoniously as a team. Armitage approached the first meeting of executive council with 'a certain amount of trepidation':

> I expect the African ministers were as apprehensive as we were because we hadn't met socially or in any other way. But as one did, one began to talk and [after the first meeting] there was an agenda and we had to go through the agenda and gradually [we progressed as] we met week by week. The Governor and Nkrumah had established a position of complete mutual trust and this spun off onto the rest of us. We all worked together. The white ministers, who had more experience of this naturally, helping black ministers when asked to do so and the black ministers giving us advice and certainly telling us what they wanted done. So basically the affairs of executive council went on smoothly.

Branigan recalled that he approached the first meeting of executive council with 'expectancy'. This was largely because, although the expatriate ministers had met the leaders of the UGCC, they had not met the CPP leaders, whose policy it had been to shun 'fraternizing with the imperialists'. There was no seating plan and no agenda and no important business was discussed at the first meeting. Although there were some sensible examples of close colleagues sitting next to each other – Saloway on the governor's left and Nkrumah on his right with K. A. Gbedemah next to him – Armitage and Branigan sat on opposite sides of the table between African ministers.

During the next three years or so they 'lived in an atmosphere of perpetual crisis', when 'everything [was] happening at once' and Saloway 'felt like a man laying down a track in front of an oncoming express train'.[19] Dennis Austin has given a characteristic description of this atmosphere, in an illustration involving Armitage:

> The University College [Accra] arranged a conference on 'Parliamentary Government' for the newly-elected assemblymen. [Austin] was chairman

for a senior government officer [Armitage] who tried to explain what lay behind the preparation of government estimates and the drawing up of a budget. It slowly dawned on the largely CPP audience that the budget they would be asked to approve had been prepared before they were elected – while many of them indeed were still in prison. They would have none of it therefore: they wanted their own, and not an 'Imperialist' budget. Order was restored only when [Armitage] suggested that the new government could, if they wished, introduce an 'anti-Imperialist' supplementary budget in the 'autumn', and thereafter goodwill prevailed once more.[20]

Austin concluded that, for the day-to-day conduct of government business, the new constitution worked 'surprisingly well'. He claimed that this was largely because the need to cooperate led to a working alliance between 'the CPP ministers who knew nothing and the officials who knew very little' about the operation of a parliamentary system of government. Armitage himself recalled:

We found that as we went along we [the expatriate ministers] never directly opposed any particular minister in any of the things he wanted. We found that by talking through and round a subject we got general agreement. I have no recollection of the Governor having at any time to put any question in executive council to a vote so I think that shows we were able to establish an extremely good relationship with the African ministers.[21]

The three European ministers 'accepted Arden-Clarke's lead and helped to make the Executive Council into an effective working committee'. 'Once Nkrumah had been released from prison and the CPP had won the 1951 elections the main responsibility of the Colonial power was to maintain sound government and at the same time introduce democratic procedures against a background of strident demands for immediate self-government from the new political parties.'[22] The governor had to balance stable government and constitutional advance at a pace sufficient to satisfy the CPP.[23] 'Most [expatriate officials] thought Arden-Clarke was going too fast and caving in to the demands of the CPP too readily.' He was, however, able to establish and retain good relationships with Nkrumah and his colleagues and, at the same time, move the country peacefully towards independence. This was despite the 'quite serious problems' in Ashanti, where the traditional authorities were strongly opposed to the CPP and stoned the governor when he visited the area. The expatriate officials were very conscious of the speed with which the country was moving, and Arden-Clarke's secretary wondered if the pace was at least partially due to his age: 'He wasn't a young man any longer. He was a magnificent Governor, very strong physically and mentally but he was beginning to get tired ... and wanted to see the thing finished soon.'

The African ministers continued to make wild and inflammatory gestures in the country, but their contact in cabinet with men of Armitage's, Branigan's and Saloway's experience was an important part of their political (governmental) development, which they seemed to appreciate. In most cases, the African ministers 'hadn't done any kind of government job before and they hadn't really understood that they had to work regular office hours. ... They didn't understand about reading their briefs and one had almost to stand over them while they read them.' Armitage's relationship with Gbedemah, who succeeded him as minister of finance, was particularly good. Gbedemah's experience was that: 'It's not an easy transformation from an agitator to a responsible government position.' It was also not easy to realize that they were 'no more on the soapbox' but had to ensure that the country's affairs were properly conducted. In quickly effecting this transformation himself, he found Armitage 'very good ... very, very cooperative, very helpful'; he especially appreciated Armitage's occasional warnings that money for certain projects could not be found unless they increased taxes.[24]

As an expatriate secretariat officer saw it: 'The great problem facing British officers at the top of ministries in Nkrumah's cabinet was simply how to restrain the wholly inexperienced, but boisterously self-confident African Ministers from acts of folly of various descriptions. There was a remarkable amount of goodwill towards the 'British colonial servants, and a willingness at first, at any rate, to listen.'[25] Another recalled that 'many of the aspects and stages of decolonization were evolved by the Gold Coast administration, sometimes in the teeth of opposition from the Colonial Office.' Arden-Clarke sent a minute to officers in the secretariat: 'Correspondence with the Colonial Office should be kept to the minimum. Invariably it should be conducted in the past tense!'[26] This point is also made by another officer: 'The Colonial Office in London often hadn't a clue about how to deal with the various situations which arose, and had at times to be firmly led by the hand of [the] Governor'.[27] And another officer has said:

> This was the fundamental problem facing the colonial government in the early 1950s – how to implement an orderly transition from colonial status to independence. There were few guidelines and the Gold Coast was the first British territory to tread this path. ... The question was to strike a balance: if progress were too slow, the hotheads might take matters into

their own hands, and doubt might be cast on the good faith of [the British government]; if progress were too rapid, chaos might ensue.[28]

Executive council met once a week and decisions were reached by consensus. In general the minister of finance and the attorney-general spoke less than other members partly because the timetable for achieving independence was the most important subject in the minds of the African ministers. Once they accepted that the governor and the Colonial Office genuinely intended that independence should be granted reasonably soon they were content to toe the governor's line, feeling that what they did not like they could put right later. 'Though not usually a leader in executive council discussions, Armitage was not aloof from them. He was always well prepared; he was patient and he was respected as one who knew his business and stuck to it.'[29]

Armitage had a dual role. Many of the political changes in which he was involved as a member of executive council – creating ministries, Africanizing the civil service and setting up district councils, for example – had financial implications with which he had to deal as financial secretary and later minister of finance.[30] In this second role he was a head of department, responsible for the country's finances and economy – initially the finance branch of the secretariat and later the Ministry of Finance.

The finance branch was one of several secretariat branches.[31] All were staffed by colonial service officers, mostly expatriate, though there was an increasing number of African officers in the administration. Like all branches, it was very small, with a deputy secretary and three assistant secretaries, one of whom was a former banker in charge of exchange control. The other two divided between them the work of the branch, which included the treasury, income tax, customs and excise and the custodianship of enemy property. There were also links with the audit, commerce and industry, and statistics departments. The staff was enhanced annually by one other officer, also an assistant secretary, who was responsible for drawing up the estimates of revenue and expenditure – as Armitage had been for several years in Kenya.

The routine work of the finance branch was dominated by the annual budgetary cycle. The financial year ran from 1 April. New major expenditure proposals were formulated by departments by midyear and their main elements were put to the finance committee of the legislature for approval. Finance committee normally met monthly. With the exception of Armitage, who chaired it, and the secretary, its members were African. On it sat the most prominent elected legislative assembly members, including those from the opposition. There was thus no prospect of the civil service being able to steamroller a proposal through the committee. Armitage had considerable experience as secretary of standing finance committee in Kenya, his relaxed and friendly style in the Gold Coast disarmed his critics and he usually got his way.

By about October the departments submitted their estimates of expenditure — and revenue, if any — based on the current level of service and those new proposals already approved by finance committee. These were examined and checked, invariably involving meetings with the department concerned. After that the final figures were approved by the financial secretary and sent to the printer.

Income estimates were prepared by the revenue departments — income tax, customs and excise — and it was after their preliminary figures were received that the financial secretary was intimately involved. It was known how the economy was progressing during the year and if things were not going well this was reflected in the attitude of finance branch to new proposals. Even so, there was always a tendency for expenditure to run ahead of revenue based on current rates of tax. So, by January, the financial secretary was usually faced with a gap between anticipated revenue and expenditure and had to decide how the shortfall would be made up. The room for manoeuvre was not great. To his official colleagues, Armitage never appeared to be anxious about issues: they saw him as relaxed, imperturbable, approachable, supportive and reassuring. As a result, he was a much respected, quiet and encouraging leader of the finance team. He never made people feel small.

He kept in close touch with his heads of finance departments by monthly meetings with them.

> The main [general] thrust [of his contacts with his heads of department] was to imbue them with the need to get their department organized for independence and to ensure that they understood the need for political change, the transfer of power and localization [of the civil service]. . . . Armitage welded his departments into a forward-looking team, largely by his skills of leadership and quiet persuasion.

Within the finance branch he generally left meetings to his deputy, but frequently walked into his colleagues' offices to ask questions or to see how the budget, for instance, was getting on, or to suggest some change in presentation or emphasis he thought desirable. The pace of developments was such that quite junior officers, once they had secured the trust of their seniors, were encouraged to use their initiative and make their own decisions except on the most difficult or politically dangerous matters: a practice Armitage was used to in Kenya. He was a good delegator and got the best out of his officers as a result. He did not spend a great deal of time committing his views to paper and within the finance branch he discouraged it. He expected proposals to reach him in a form in which he could agree on the basis of the arguments supporting them; if he did not agree he indicated what was needed and sent them back for further work.

His colleagues found him quick to grasp a point or to say what changes were needed. His general approach was to be helpful. This did not mean he accepted what others wanted to do, but he was widely regarded as open-minded, fair and ready to deal with each matter on its merits. 'He was full of common sense and free of all pomposity.' He had a good sense of humour and his colleagues did not recall him being anything other than courteous and certainly he never lost his calm demeanour. 'Though a great man in the land, he was a kindly soul . . . a quiet and reserved man.'[32] An officer posted to work with him in the finance branch recalled:

> I had virtually no experience of finance or of a large office set-up. People were very patient with me, no one more so than Bob Armitage. I enjoyed working for him and was lucky to do so even if during the preparation of the estimates one often did not get home till 9,00 p.m. Somehow the result was worth it. He taught me a lot.[33]

When the Coussey report was published there was widespread pleasure that in the legislative assembly nearly all the members would be elected and that the executive council would be comprised largely of African ministers. The *Accra Evening News*, published by Nkrumah, viewed with 'grave concern' the fact that Armitage's ministry – 'this most important portfolio' – should still be entrusted to a person whom they claimed was not responsible to the elected assembly.

> How long shall we continue to entrust our money to people over whom we have no control? If really this New Constitution is to give us the chance to participate in the Government of this country, and if honestly this Constitution is to place this country on the right road to fast nationalism, then we see no reason why such a big post which is the pivot of any government should not be given to us now without delay.[34]

Of the three ex-officio posts retained in executive council, it was Armitage's that came most under fire, but he was not alone, for all three came in for attack: a little later Oliver Lyttelton, the new secretary of state, went to the Gold Coast and recalled that he saw there, by the roadside, 'two boys whose combined ages could not have been twenty and who were completely naked, holding up a large blackboard. On it in impeccable copperplate was written in chalk "Away with the three ex-officios".[35]

Cabinet government was introduced in 1951.[36] It was now the cabinet who decided the financial allocation within which each ministry would frame its estimates and if one minister wanted more he had to argue for it with his colleagues; if more was needed for one service then this required reducing expenditure elsewhere, or increasing revenue, or higher taxation, or raising loans. Ministers accepted this and Armitage – whose standing with ministers was high – soon convinced them that an expatriate minister of finance was an ally. His integrity and quiet unassuming approach were appreciated and the allocations he proposed were usually accepted although not always straightaway:

> My only trouble every now and then was that I wanted to get something through on the financial side so I had to lobby African ministers and if I couldn't always get them immediately, then when it came up in executive council, we three white ministers used to throw the ball about, if I may use the expression, and by the end of the discussion we probably got what we wanted.

It was important that his advice was usually accepted because there was always in the background a suspicion that the British were not taking the demand for early independence seriously. But at an early stage Armitage was able to gain Nkrumah's confidence that he was working to give early independence to the country, but to do so with sound finances.

He persuaded Nkrumah that not every scheme to which ministers attached political importance could go ahead at the same time or at the same speed. Planning, coordination and establishing priorities were essential. 'Armitage kept a tight rein on the budget and stood up to the more dotty ideas of some of the new ministers; some other ministers were quite sound.'[37] Armitage handed over the chair of the finance committee to Nkrumah at a very early stage and thereafter piloted its business through him. 'At that time Nkrumah was a very good chairman; he had much charm, handled business quickly and effectively, was well briefed and kept members to the point.'[38]

Nkrumah at this stage was remembered as 'still reasonable, balanced and prepared to take advice'.[39] Armitage found him 'a most charming man to work with, he was always busy but he was one of those people who never appeared too busy to see anyone who wanted to talk to him. ... He was charming, he was efficient and he never stopped working.'

Armitage did not always get what he wanted because Nkrumah 'was apt, at times, to say yes to the last person he saw on any particular subject and if I wasn't the last person on one of my subjects, I didn't always get what I wanted'.

The finance committee felt the policy of localization was much too slow. There was a major row when the ministries were set up and the top posts in each were allocated to expatriates. The committee refused to cooperate and a crisis persisted for several weeks. It was resolved only with great patience, tact and much persuasion by Armitage. He played a major role in creating a localization office with its own African head. This proved to be the key to settling what threatened to be a major constitutional crisis. Localizing the civil service with sufficient time for a large number of them to gain experience by working with expatriate officers before independence, was extremely important. It was they who helped to add stability and in some ways to restrain 'the more rampant antics' of some of the politicians.[40]

> [Arden-Clarke] did not act without consulting the most senior officials of whom Armitage was one of those close at hand and ... they supported his actions.... From the introduction of the Ministerial system in February 1951 this ... included the inculcation of British colonial financial orthodoxy into the new ministers most of whom were bright but all of whom were entirely without experience of exercising governmental power. Of course the actual control of expenditure was vested ... in the permanent secretaries. But putting over the basic idea of keeping Government funds separate from Party funds, and not exercising power to augment the latter was something that ... concerned Armitage greatly. There were also lots of honest but hare-brained suggestions for the use of official funds that needed to be resisted.[41]

The main financial and economic issues during his time as financial secretary and minister were the level of cocoa production; the establishment of local industries – because almost everything was imported; and the expansion of the infrastructure, especially port, rail and road capacity to accelerate the movement of imports and exports.[42] There was also an argument about continuing the monopoly of the Cocoa Marketing Board. This had been established by the Ministry of Food during the war and it fixed the cocoa price annually in advance. It had built up large reserves, held in sterling, which Britain was anxious to retain but which producers wished to reduce severely so as to give them a higher price. The board accumulated huge profits during the Korean war and Armitage convinced his African ministerial colleagues to divert these to finance a major development plan: the construction of

Tema harbour and new town, railways, roads, the university, an institute of technology, a teaching hospital, higher education, scholarships to accelerate localization, and the Volta River project feasibility study.

Important as these projects were, they were only complementary to the important objective of bringing the Gold Coast peacefully to independence. Under Arden-Clarke, Armitage was a major contributor by providing the funds to finance the ambitious programmes of development to which ministers attached enormous importance and in securing their confidence and support in such unpopular programmes as cutting out diseased cocoa trees. Under his stewardship, too, the funds were available to promote Africanization of the civil service without losing the services of expatriate officers. When he arrived, there were 1068 expatriate senior officers and 171 African. When he left, there were 1490 expatriate senior officers and 916 African.[43]

The fact that the Gold Coast became independent with substantial financial reserves, a well-developed infrastructure, no political rancour, and a competent and almost entirely Ghanian-staffed civil service was due to Arden-Clarke as the prime leader, Nkrumah who trusted him, and his most senior advisers – Saloway, Armitage and Branigan. About a year after Armitage left the Gold Coast, Saloway spoke of the difficulty of overemphasizing the extent of the 'social and political revolution' that had taken place there: 'That it has not produced chaos but has achieved some reasonable results is due to the mutual goodwill and confidence which has been built up between the Gold Coast leaders and their British advisers.'[44]

It was generally accepted at the time that a colony could become independent only if its economy and finances were in sound condition and sufficiently firmly based to support an independent political existence. In the early 1950s there was no, or very little, international aid and the Colonial Development and Welfare Fund had been established but a few years earlier. Until then, colonies had only the services for which they could pay. A vital element for constitutional development was for a colony to demonstrate that it had the fiscal and economic resources to sustain a separate existence, including adequate financial reserves. It was the yield from cocoa export duty, in particular, that gave the Gold Coast the financial strength to proceed to independence, and Armitage managed the finances to ensure that this was so.[45]

He was also responsible for compiling the country's development plan. This was initially worked on between 1949 and 1950 following the riots of February 1948.[46] The early draft was not very bold in concept and even-handedly gave something to each department. Its aims were based on modest growth, but financial and economic growth, together with political demands, changed rapidly in the early 1950s and the plan quickly became outdated.[47] Thereafter, decisions on the plan were taken by ministers and against political needs in which politicians had to be seen to deliver. It also had to meet nationalist aspirations and 'Armitage was very much involved in the excellent progress towards satisfying Nkrumah's hunger for economic development.'[48] For instance, a bank of the Gold Coast was established to create more credit and to provide competition with the overseas banks: an institution not envisaged in the earlier plan.[49] Armitage quickly saw the value of using academic economists as consultants to examine specific aspects of the economy and its development, and he regularly used local university staff to complement the resources of the administration. As academics, they were able to think rather more widely and imaginatively and to suggest more innovative solutions than the more traditional approach of some civil servants, and Armitage encouraged this.[50]

In pioneering the road to independence in Africa, the Gold Coast produced a blueprint of the action needed in a wide variety of fields, such as the civil service (with compensation for loss of career for expatriates), the establishment of overseas missions and the machinery for diplomatic representation. All this required a good deal of outside help. Some of this came from the Colonial Office, but it also came from elsewhere, including a banker from India and advice on a public service commission from Ceylon.[51] Nearly all of it involved major considerations of finance, in which Armitage played a leading – often the leading – part. The officer Armitage specifically recruited to handle exchange control had over 20 years' previous experience in banking. He recalled Armitage's ability to delegate and his willingness to give advice based on his earlier field experience in Kenya and his dealings there with tribal leaders:

> He made it clear by delegation of banking matters and . . . the operation of exchange control that he trusted me to lighten his load of responsibility. . . . For example, he accepted that drafting new exchange control legislation was a priority and he left the necessary drafting entirely to me. [Armitage], with his knowledge and experience, advised me that the Paramount Chiefs, especially the Asantahene of Ashanti, would appreciate the courtesy of being told verbally at personal gatherings of the need for these new currency restrictions.[52]

Armitage had scarcely been in the Gold Coast three months before he was working hard on the preparation of the first annual estimates of expenditure under his financial secretaryship. The procedures and techniques, save for minor local variations, were familiar to him: he had spent several years in Nairobi doing the donkey-work of preparing the estimates and developing them into the annual budget. He knew the pitfalls and difficulties and he knew the pressures under which his junior colleagues had to work in the months leading up to the budget session of the legislature. As clerk to legislative council he had watched at close quarters how the financial secretary had presented the budget and answered his critics. He also had experience, in his later years in Kenya, of devising and submitting schemes for financing from the Colonial Development and Welfare Fund.

During the late months of 1948 in Accra, he oversaw the preparation of departmental budgets and then, early in 1949, he and his colleagues in the finance branch discussed them.[53] 'The unending problems of the day-to-day financing of government services... always came to a head at the time of financing the annual budget. The conflicting and irreconcilable claims... could only give rise to one agonizing decision after another.'[54] He was then responsible for having the departmental estimates collated and the draft estimates of expenditure prepared for presentation to the legislature.[55]

He prepared his own budget speeches. He frequently made requests for facts, figures and supporting material, much of which was later published. He then presented the budget and the legislature considered it in committee over a period of two to three weeks. In his early days this was a select committee, which summoned heads of departments to appear before it and which he chaired. Later a committee of the whole house decided which estimates were to be examined and on which they would concentrate.[56]

He presented his first budget on 15 March 1949 at the beginning of the longest budget session in the Gold Coast's history.[57] He opened on a happy note. The expected supplementary budget during the year had been unnecessary. Also, he did not anticipate there would be the expected deficit on the current year's budget because 'heads of department are notorious as to overestimating' how much they would spend by the end of the financial year. He had three main considerations in mind in preparing the budget. First, the business of government – the work of the departments – had to be efficiently organized and designed to give a wide range of services to all the people of the country. Second, new forms of wealth had to be created, new revenue-earning works constructed and large-scale capital expenditure wisely planned to meet the ever-increasing demand for services. Third, the incidence of taxation had to be so devised to yield the revenue required for running the government machine, providing services and meeting sinking fund and interest charges. In the revenue he proposed to raise, he included £0.5m. for a campaign to intensify the cutting out of diseased cocoa trees and a further £0.5m. to devote to the development plan during the coming 12 months.

The time had come to stop the practice of financing development out of the surplus on recurrent account. Instead, he set up a separate development fund with the development estimates drawing on that fund, made up of deliberate contributions from the recurrent budget, a portion of the surplus, and grants and loans for example from the Colonial Development and Welfare Fund. He was making development an integral and ongoing part of government's work rather than contingent on surpluses on recurrent account. In any case, financing major development works does not fit well into a system of annual appropriation. He had already asked the Cocoa Marketing Board to lend money to the government and so avoid an early approach to the London money market. International demands on the London market in the years following the war were heavy and interest rates high. He also made provision to pay advances for development ahead of raising loans: 'Whilst we have surplus cash it is unnecessary to raise a loan and we can thus avoid the payment of interest.' At the time he had £3 million surplus but a 'simple sum' would show that at current rates of expenditure there would be no surplus at all in two years' time.

He then turned to how he proposed to raise the required revenue. A week earlier, 'in the absence of any other forms of taxation which [could] bring in substantial sums', he had increased import duties on a wide range of non-essential items, by an order of the governor in Council that required the legislature's confirmation within 21 days. There was no direct tax collected from all the people in the Gold Coast. Income tax was largely derived from companies, 'the salaried classes and professional men'. He recognized the need to widen the income tax net to include wealthy farmers and individual traders, but until that could be done there was 'only one way to make it reach the man of moderate means' and that was to raise import duties. It was 'from import duties on cotton piece goods that the incidence of taxation [could] best be spread'. Concerning export duty, he aimed mainly at cocoa and changed it from a specific to an *ad valorem* duty so that its yield would vary with the value of sales rather than with their weight. 'There can be no doubt that the cocoa industry can well afford to bear this additional taxation. It has just experienced the most profitable year of its existence. Sums dispersed to the growers have been larger than ever before and more than they could possibly have expected to receive in the past.'

Armitage's draft estimates revealed a deficit of £1.1m. With the £0.5m. for cutting out cocoa trees and £0.5m. for development he needed to raise an extra £2.1m. He designed his budget to cover this by bringing in an extra £1m. from the changed duty on cocoa exports and £1.1m. from customs duty increases. He was, in fact, using the buoyant cocoa market to government's advantage both directly by taxing cocoa exports on their value and indirectly by taxing cotton piece goods purchased by individuals with income derived directly or indirectly from cocoa sales. Only twice did he raise a laugh during his speech. The first time was when he thought some members would consider cigarettes and cigars essentials to life, and the second when he announced an increase in the import duty on them: 'Individual smokers will congratulate themselves that they will contribute more to the national income.'

Armitage's second budget speech was delivered on 1 March 1950.[58] In reviewing the previous 12 months he was pleased that, despite the trading losses resulting from the 1948 riots and the consequent dislocation of business, trade had not suffered too badly and income tax returns were higher by £0.5m. than he had expected. Also, the recovery in the world price of cocoa had led to a high yield from the *ad valorem* tax he had imposed. He was pleased, too, that there was little increase in government expenditure, though worried that this was largely due to a lack of sufficient experienced and skilled supervisory staff in the departments and to lack of materials:

> At present in some departments the position can be described as on the verge of calamity. The shortage of agricultural officers, doctors and engineers of various categories is such that in some cases ordinary departmental activities cannot be carried out. Hospitals are in fact closed, districts are deprived of the services and advice of an agricultural officer and the main roads cannot be maintained to the standards required by modern conditions.

In these unfortunate circumstances, however, he derived comfort from the fact that money that would otherwise have been spent would be retained in the surplus and be available for future spending, especially on development schemes. He was, in fact, able to add £3m. to the accumulated surplus to make a total of £8m., from which he proposed to devote £1.75m. to development. He was able to reserve so large a surplus because of the lack of staff and materials, but the time would come when it would be the lack of money that held them back. Then the surplus would come into its own to pay for development, including the servicing of loans. He had not yet approached the loan market and – giving a warning about the need for political stability – he felt that the credit of the Gold Coast did not stand high in financial circles: it was not easy to raise money for a country that had suffered from 'a series of political crises, strikes, looting and rioting'.

Regarding the expectations that might arise from the proposed new constitution, he gave another political warning and stressed that:

> Contrary to the view held in some quarters, Government under the new constitution will not provide a situation where everyone will be paid more for less work, taxation will be decreased, if it does not disappear altogether, and Government departments will run themselves without any control or supervision. ... Political agitators who lead people to imagine that they can get something for nothing merely lead to ruinous economics.

Shortly after the 1950/1 budget session, Saloway went on leave and Armitage acted in his stead as chief secretary. In writing to Saloway in May 1950, he commented on the poor health of a number of senior officers. Saloway himself had to extend his leave because of blood pressure. Branigan was 'somewhat under the weather'. The governor had an operation to remove gall stones. Of three others, one was in hospital with jaundice following malaria, another had been in hospital 'with undefined pains in the stomach' and a third had to go to England for an operation and would not be returning. 'Fortunately the Governor was [now] keeping very fit' and Armitage himself was well.[59] Armitage was awarded the CMG in the New Year's honours list, 1951.[60]

He laid his budget for 1951/2 – his third – before the legislative assembly on the last day of March 1951 only seven weeks after the first general election on an adult franchise ever held in black Africa.[61] The CPP won 34 out of 38 seats filled by popular ballot. It was the first meeting under the new constitution: Nkrumah was leader of government business and there were five elected and three ex-officio ministers. Armitage, now minister of finance, got off to a good start by announcing there would be no increases in taxation: the annual revenue had risen from the wartime level of £4m. to £10m. in 1947/8, £18m. in 1949/50 and he expected it to rise to just over £20m. in the coming year. Although some of the increase was due to depreciation in the value of money, this did not account for all the increase:

> During the last four years the Gold Coast has been going through more favourable times than previously. This prosperity has encouraged the Government to plan a programme for the expansion of economic development and of the social services with some degree of confidence. That is a major blessing that has been conferred on the Gold Coast by this prosperity which has enabled the Government revenue to increase.

Four-fifths of government revenue came from import and export duties and income tax, and their yield was dependent on the country continuing to sell its cocoa, timber, coffee, palm products and minerals at good prices. 'Fortunately there is no sign at present that the world does not want these products.'

He emphasized the major and crucial dual role of cocoa, the price of which had risen from £50 a ton in 1946 to £204 in 1950. First, it produced very large amounts of export duty, devoted to running the government machine and financing development projects. Second, money from selling cocoa was earned by farmers, brokers, farm labourers and transport owners and was devoted to purchasing internal products and imported goods many of which were taxed. Their incomes in many cases were also taxed. Income tax, which had yielded less than £2m. at the end of the war, was nearly £3m. in 1948/9 and was expected to be £5.25m. in the coming year – mostly from mining and trading. 'Only a few thousand persons have so far entered the clutches of the income tax department. Every effort I can assure you is being made to find out how those who are liable can be traced and assessed.'

On the expenditure side Armitage pointed out that during the war the limit was about £4m. a year. This increased to £9m. in 1947/8, £12m. in 1949/50 and was estimated to rise to £20m. in the coming year. The rate of increase in expenditure was rather less than that in revenue earning. Two visiting British parliamentarians who attended the budget session said to Armitage afterwards, 'Well, we've never [before] attended a parliament where the minister of finance did not propose a single tax or a single increase in tax!'

Very soon after he delivered his 1951/2 budget speech, he received a letter of congratulation from a London director of a mining company in the Gold Coast who considered the speech 'a masterful economic survey that surpasses anything I have ever read. It is extraordinarily clear, concise and comprehensive – full of interest and information.'[62] He asked for a spare copy so that he could send it on to Hugh Gaitskell, leader of the opposition in the Commons, whom he knew. Gaitskell had been a year ahead of Armitage at Winchester. Armitage, 'somewhat overwhelmed' by this praise, explained: 'I did try to cover a wide range of economical matters in particular as we now have a Legislative Assembly of 84 members of whom only about half a dozen were members of the old Legislative Council. I felt that I must try and get some background against which they would judge the Annual Draft Estimates.'

Armitage's fourth budget speech, for 1952/3, was made on 5 February 1952.[63] Whereas in the past he had presented the estimates in two volumes – the government ordinary estimates and the estimates for the government-owned railway and harbours – he now presented three, the additional one, for the first time, being the estimates of expenditure on development. He was again careful to explain the recent history of government finances and, in simple terms, the economics behind them and their trends. He re-emphasized cocoa's pivotal role. World supplies were not increasing but other countries were looking to begin or expand production. It was vital to maintain the total quantity of cocoa picked in the Gold Coast: 'Any downward trend in the yield of cocoa over several years will deal the finances of this country a blow the effects of which it would be difficult to envisage at present.'

Of the total export value of £91m., cocoa contributed £60m. and minerals £22m. In 1952/3, cocoa would contribute just over £6m. to government's ordinary revenue, £1.8m. to the special development fund and £2.4m. to the reserve development fund. He pointed out that the increasing revenue from income tax indicated the general level of prosperity in the country and, because he believed that prosperity would continue to expand, he proposed to increase the rates fairly heftily for the higher earners – up to 75 per cent on incomes over £10,000. To his astonishment and irritation, however, the legislature did not accept this proposal. He had put his proposals to the cabinet, as was customary, and they were accepted, but when Armitage sat down at the end of his budget speech, the CPP chief whip, Krobo Edusei, who was a member of the cabinet, got up and said that he was not going to vote for the proposal – having already put a three-line whip on it to ensure its safe passage through the assembly. 'His opposition was naturally followed by a number of people very cheerfully and so the proposal for that year did not get approved.' It was clearly taking rather longer than some have suggested for the principle of collective responsibility to be accepted.

Armitage's fifth and final budget in the Gold Coast was for the 1953/4 fiscal year, introduced into the legislative assembly on 12 February 1953.[64] This was the longest, most detailed and most sophisticated of his budget speeches. Again, he was at pains to explain what was happening and why he was making the proposals he was introducing. He was, in effect, continuing to teach the members of the assembly and the public about the Gold Coast economy and its public finances. He saw this as an important part of his role as minister of finance. He gave annual broadcasts on the local radio outlining and explaining his budget soon after introducing it in the assembly, and he addressed extramural seminars at the University College.

At one such seminar he gave an address on the economic and financial position of the Gold Coast in which he said that it was not generally known just how much the country's prosperity depended on cocoa. There were 300,000 farmers employing 250,000 labourers and providing employment for many others, for example in transport. In the record year of 1948/9, 268,000 tons of cocoa were sold and £35m. distributed to the growers. He spoke of the way in which the distribution of this 'stupendous amount' of money affected a wide range of people and the way in which imported commodities, in short supply, such as cotton piece goods changed hands quickly at ever increasing prices: too much money chasing too few goods. He spoke also of the way that only 'with the greatest of good fortune and with a certain degree of organization' was he able to ensure that enough money was available: 'The currency board had, in fact, to charter planes and fly out from England currency notes hot from the printing press in order to keep the banks supplied and through them the firms purchasing cocoa. There were moments when stocks of notes in the banks were down to a bare minimum.'

A month after Armitage steered the 1953/4 budget through the legislature, the assembly spent three days debating the Volta River scheme,[65] a proposal which even in the very earliest days of consideration 'had the most widespread implications' for the Ministry of Finance.[66] Ministers were trying to allay fears about the scheme which was in an early stage of debate. Primarily they sought, and received, consent to set up a preparatory commission after which the government and assembly would make up their minds as to whether to proceed. Many of the large number of questions asked were answered by either Nkrumah or the minister of commerce and industry, but a number of important financial questions were handled by Armitage. He was at pains to assure the assembly that although it was proposed that the British government would contribute, by loans, £46m. and the Gold Coast £8m., the Gold Coast government would itself control the power project. He carefully explained the difference between equity capital and loan capital, the former being contributed by the Gold Coast government and involving control of the project, the latter being loans involving no control over the project. He also handled questions on the taxation of the aluminium companies and the labour – 30,000 – required for the scheme. When he was asked what the particular need was for developing the Volta, Armitage replied:

> If it is decided to go ahead with it, it will take some ten years before the aluminium ingots are rolling off the smelter delivery line. Well, the Gold Coast in ten years' time will be looking for an industry which will put into the country the money to enable the standard of living of this country to be kept going higher and higher. This is an agricultural country and depends on the mono-crop of cocoa. We are seeing a downward trend in cocoa; we must do something to supplement it.[67]

In his five years as financial secretary and minister of finance in the Gold Coast – a period which coincided with a boom period in cocoa prices and production – Armitage presided over a great expansion in the public finances. Government revenue rose from £18m. in 1949/50 to £50m. in 1953/4, while government expenditure rose from £14m. to £44m. Imports rose in value from £45m. in 1949 to £74m. in 1953, while exports rose from £49m. to £88m., with a peak of over £93m. in 1951.[68]

Although Armitage's work was onerous and important – both politically and economically – he was not as heavily pressed as he had been in Nairobi, and he was able to enjoy the full social life of Accra, which was 'well developed'.[69] There was no colour bar in the Gold Coast, but social mixing depended on one's occupation and cultural level. There were a number of well-educated African businessmen and at drinks and dinner parties it was usual for the Armitages to have both black and white guests.

He was a governor of the University College, and their particular African friends – 'exceedingly attractive and pleasant companions' – were often academics, many of whom had good degrees from Britain or the USA. They tended to marry educated women, and wives usually accompanied their husbands. 'And so we really had a very easy social life [but] this did not extend to occasions where African ministers were involved because they did not give parties and did not come to many of our parties. We met them at dinner parties and other functions given by the Speaker [and] by the Governor.'

There were quite a lot of dances, invariably mixed, and the Africans were especially keen on a dance called the 'High Life', which Armitage found 'particularly attractive but very vigorous'. There was a mixed race dining club to which Armitage and his colleagues went. He and his wife entertained a good deal and went out of their way to include even the most junior officers from the finance branch. At their dinner parties there was a ritual that each guest entered his name on the day of his birthday in a five-year diary.

Towards the end of his time in the Gold Coast, Armitage spent some weeks on his own – Lyona having preceded him on leave – and one of his assistant secretaries and his wife invited him, rather diffidently, to dinner. They asked who else he would like to come and he replied, 'It would be rather fun it there were just the three of us.' This was seen by his host and hostess as a typical gesture from a man who knew the cost of entertaining and the pressure on the salaries of junior officers and who enjoyed informal, family, occasions.[70]

Arden-Clarke liked playing tennis and invited senior officers to play on the Government House courts with him, including Armitage, who was considered to be 'a most useful partner and a good-tempered player'.[71] In the office in the afternoons on which he played tennis he came in his tennis kit, unless he had important meetings, and this illustrated his informality. To his finance branch colleagues, 'he was the most unstuffy of senior officers and his staff would do anything for him.' The junior African officers noted the gap between his two middle top teeth and regarded this a sign of good luck.[72]

In mid-1953 Armitage was offered the governorship of Cyprus and readily accepted.[73] In September 1953 he left the Gold Coast and sailed back to Britain on board the Elder Dempster Line's flagship the MV *Aureol*.

In looking back over his five years in the Gold Coast – years in which the early positive steps in Britain's retreat from empire in Africa became very clear – Armitage said: 'I had lived through the most dramatic years I think that any African colony can have seen. They had been years when the situation had changed from a completely officially dominated Government to an African-controlled government and ... this had taken place without any real trouble.'[74]

4

Cyprus

The problem of enosis is like the velvety blackness of a nightmare, it clutches one everywhere and one strains to see a glimmer of light to guide one to safety but nowhere is there light.

Cyprus,[1] an island of 3572 square miles in the northeastern corner of the Mediterranean, is 140 miles east to west, and 60 miles north to south. Parallel to its northern coast is the long and narrow Kyrenia range, rising to 3000 feet and terminating eastward in the Karpass peninsula. In the centre and west of the island is the Troodos massif, reaching 6400 feet in Mount Olympus. Between these two mountainous areas lies the 15-mile-wide central plain, the Mesaoria. To the north of Cyprus lies Turkey, 43 miles away; to the east, Syria, 64 miles away; to the south, Egypt, 200 miles away. The Greek mainland is 500 miles away to the northwest.

The climate is varied. Summers are hot and dry in the plains, with a mean maximum temperature of 78°F and a mean minimum of 55°F although temperatures of over 110°F are often experienced. Winters vary from mild on the coast to well below freezing in the mountains. There is a rainy, cool season from October to March.

In 1954 the population of Cyprus numbered 515,000, of whom 80 per cent were Greek orthodox and 18 per cent Turkish Muslim. Most of the 626[2] villages were either Turkish or Greek, although about 15 per cent were mixed. Turks were most numerous in the north and west. There were six urban areas: Nicosia (40,200), Limasol (27,000), Famagusta (20,500), Larnaca (16,300), Paphos (6500) and Kyrenia (3400). Some 400,000 people lived in rural areas. The Orthodox Church was autocephalous and had been since at least AD 488, and thus was 1000 years older than either the Turkish or the Greek states. The church elected its own archbishop and governed itself independently.

Overwhelmingly, the main occupation was agriculture, which occupied 153,000 people. The service industries employed 51,000; manufacturing 44,000; mining and quarrying 6300; and government service 6000. The main crops were wheat, barley, potatoes, cotton, deciduous and citrus fruit and olives. The main exploited minerals were cupreous and iron pyrites and asbestos. Half the imports came from, and a third of the exports went to, the United Kingdom. Tourism was a major invisible export.

Although Ancient Greece extensively colonized Cyprus, the island was never part of Hellenic Greece and the Greek claims to it were based on the Greek language, membership of the Eastern Orthodox Church and strong emotional ties.[3] In 1571, the Turks conquered the island. They settled and retained it until 1878 when, retaining nominal sovereignty, they gave Cyprus to Britain as a base to deter further Russian encroachment on the Ottoman Empire and to protect British routes to India. Remembering that Britain had recently restored the Ionian Islands to Greece, the Greek Cypriots welcomed Britain's arrival, confident that their plea for union with Greece – enosis – would be granted. In 1882, a legislative council was introduced with six officials and nine Greek and three Turkish elected members. The Greek members' constant disruptive demand for enosis led to an alliance of Turks and officials regularly outvoting them.

In 1914, when Turkey entered the war, Britain annexed the island, offered it to Greece – who declined rather than join the Allies – and, under the treaty of Lausanne, Turkey renounced sovereignty in favour of Britain by recognizing the annexation. In 1925 the island formally became a British colony and the high commissioner became the governor, now assisted by a nominated executive council and a legislature comprised of the governor, nine officials and fifteen elected members, three chosen by the Muslim community and twelve by the non-Muslim community.

In 1929 a Greek Cypriot delegation asked Britain to cede Cyprus to Greece and was met with a sharp refusal: the matter was not to be discussed. It returned disgruntled to the island. In October 1931 pro-enosis disturbances followed stringent measures to secure a balanced budget, imposed over the heads of the legislature, and attempts to curb the use of schools for nationalist propaganda by transferring control of schoolteachers from Greeks and Turks to British officials. There were widespread riots by Greek Cypriots, refusal to pay taxes, boycott of British goods, burning a police car and the governor's residence, killing six civilians, wounding 30 civilians and 38 policemen, and 400 arrests. Governor Storrs reacted severely and called in the army and navy from Egypt.

The Greek members of the legislature resigned and, consequently, the constitution was revoked and direct powers of legislation were given to the governor. The elected municipal councils were abolished and meetings of more than five people required official permission. The flying of Greek flags and the ringing of church bells other than for religious services were banned and press censorship was imposed. All the bishops, save one, and the archbishop of the Greek Orthodox Church, who had led the demonstrations, were exiled. The governor ruled, advised by an executive council of four officials, one Greek and one Turkish non-official. The white paper on the disturbances recorded, prophetically: 'Until the shadow of union [with Greece] is finally removed from the political horizon the leading inhabitants [of Cyprus] are not likely to come forward in large numbers to support the Government, to cooperate openly in the progress of their country under British rule.'[4]

During the Second World War, 30,000 Cypriots joined the British army, being assured that they were fighting 'for Greece and freedom'.[5] Many thought this included the freedom for Cyprus to join Greece, although the colonial secretary in Cyprus remarked that little was heard of enosis outside Cyprus and 'we hope to keep it that way'. The governor added: 'The Colonial Office has many more important things to think about than a remote island half the size of Wales.' With Greece an ally of Britain, there was a spontaneous outbreak of Greek nationalism on the island, which it was not in Britain's interest to restrain. 'The laws were relaxed and ... displays of Greek nationalism became [a] normal manifestation of political life. This led to some complacency on the part of Government.' Municipal elections were restored in 1943, in accordance with British policy that successful experience in local government should precede constitutional advance at the centre. To those returning after the war, Cyprus

> was still a quiet little island, one might say a sleepy island, but this was on the surface ... there were strong undercurrents of dissatisfaction with the continuation of the British administration ... because people had expected that after the Second World War, and having made [out] so much that this war was for freedom etc. the Greek Cypriots would be given the opportunity to exercise the rights of self-determination which in their mind meant the equivalent to decide to unite with Greece.

In 1947, Lord Winster became governor and established a consultative assembly to draw up a constitution. When the constitutional proposals were published in May 1948, both right- and left-wing Greek, but not Turkish, Cypriots rejected them. They included a legislature of four officials and 22 non-officials, 18 elected on a general roll and four on a Turkish roll, and an executive council, including three Greek and one Turkish elected members. There were also to be

Cypriot under-secretaries in some government departments. The proposals would have given the Greeks a majority in the legislature the governor could not easily have overruled. They could have been the basis for further development. They made no provision, however, for enosis. Indeed, they barred discussion of the status of Cyprus and threatened to remove political leadership from the Church. The governor was to have reserve powers only over defence, external affairs, finance and laws affecting minorities and the constitution itself. The rejection of the proposals was followed by disturbances: strikes, marches, demonstrations, dynamite attacks, arson and assaults. Winster resigned – 'solely on the grounds that, efforts to secure acceptance of the Constitution ... having proved unavailing, the primary purpose for which he undertook the appointment ... no longer existed'. He was replaced by Sir Andrew Wright, instructed by the British government to 'keep things quiet' and to 'keep Cyprus out of the news'.

In April 1951, in response to a somewhat inept Commons statement by the Foreign Office minister of state that no formal demand for enosis had been made by Greece, the Greek government formally asked Britain to negotiate to cede the island to Greece in exchange for bases in Cyprus and Greece, or for Britain to announce a willingness to determine in a reasonable time the wishes of the Cypriot people. At this time the Turkish position became clear. There was a growing anti-Greece-enosis press and radio propaganda campaign and the emergence of Turkey-enosis claims. Turkish Cypriots sent a delegation to Turkey, and the normally good relations between Greek and Turkish Cypriots showed early signs of breaking down with demonstrations on both sides. The Turkish government reassured the delegation that the island would not be surrendered to Greece and that sovereignty would remain with Britain, and they told Britain they would expect to be consulted on any future moves. Britain, however, did not try to enlist Turkey's support because, in the official view of both countries, there was no Cyprus question.[6]

On 1 May 1951 a secret meeting in Athens between George Stratos, a former war minister, Savvas Loizides (who had been exiled to Britain after the 1931 riots), Socrates Loizides and George Grivas proposed that Grivas 'should undertake the leadership of an armed struggle to throw the British out of Cyprus'.[7] Two months later, following a plan he had drawn up in detail a year earlier for a terrorist campaign, Grivas visited Cyprus and made a preliminary study of the terrain. It was 'a military reconnaissance ... to spy out the land'. He met the ethnarch, Archbishop Makarios, who agreed with the proposal, although Grivas felt he was not really convinced.

Indeed, he did have reservations about the timing and methods of the struggle, preferring to limit it to small-scale sabotage. 'In July 1952 Makarios [secretly] became chairman of a revolutionary committee that met in Athens and recruited as its military organizer Colonel George Grivas [who] had a reputation for harshness and cruelty and a fanatical commitment to the extreme right in politics.' Makarios was sceptical, telling Grivas 'not fifty men will be found to follow you.' Archbishop Spirindon of Athens, primate of all Greece but junior to Makarios, promised the committee his full support and, countermanding Makarios's instructions, authorized Grivas's return to Cyprus.

In October 1952, now at Makarios's invitation and following his July 1951 reconnaissance visit, Grivas began a five-month clandestine visit to Cyprus to plan arms smuggling, recruit guerrillas and lay the groundwork for terrorism. On his return to Athens, he drew up a detailed plan to which Makarios gave grudging support and accepted the need for violence, estimating that it would soon be brought to an end by a political settlement. The plan's objective was to mobilize international opinion on the Cypriot side and ultimately achieve their claims through diplomatic pressure on the UN.

Makarios wanted to restrict operations to sabotage and to exclude guerrilla activities, but Grivas insisted on his full plan. The archbishop agreed to smuggling in mines and grenades but not guns or personnel. For some time – influenced by Mahatma Gandhi's peaceful policies – he continued to hope that the struggle could be confined to sabotage and he believed that he could stop it at any time he wished, although the abbot of Kykko warned him that these things were easy to start but difficult to stop. Under pressure from other members of the committee, Makarios finally accepted the full plan and an initial consignment of arms was landed at Khlorakas, Cyprus, on 2 March.

By the end of 1953, Greece's opposition to Britain's continued sovereignty over Cyprus was increasing. The retiring Greek permanent delegate to the UN said that 1954 would 'be for Greece the year of Cyprus'.[8] 'Priests, prelates and politicians, no doubt encouraged by the more direct approach to the Cyprus question which Greece seem[ed] lately to have adopted, hailed the New Year as the decisive one in their struggle for Enosis.'[9]

When Governor Wright left on 9 February 1954 the Greek press, 'adhering to its practice and policy of criticizing each successive Governor', wrote: 'Now that the Governor is preparing to leave the island there is nothing to be counted to his credit' and 'Sir Andrew is leaving behind him a people who did not want him. His administration was marked by decisions and activities which constituted an obvious disregard for Cyprus realities.'[10] It was onto this scene, with this historical background that the new governor arrived early in 1954.

The Armitages spent the last few days of their leave in London, in the snow, staying – as they usually did – at the Royal Empire Society. Life was 'rather a rush', Armitage attending meetings with Colonial Office officials, the chairman of Cyprus Airways and MPs. At the Colonial Office he was told 'to introduce a new Constitution in Cyprus', which if not accepted would be imposed. He dined with his old friend, Oliver Woods, colonial correspondent of *The Times*, and lunched at the Ottoman Bank, the government's bank in Cyprus, and at the Carlton Club. He squeezed in a number of West End plays and went to the Sandown races. Finally, he bought a new uniform. He was looking forward to getting 'back into a job again'. His instructions were clear: introduce a new constitution, and he seemed to be in a strong position because if he could not secure acceptance for the constitution, Britain would none the less impose it.[11]

They left London by air on 18 February 1954 – their wedding anniversary – and took six hours to reach Athens where they spent the night and were entertained by the British ambassador, Sir Charles Peake. Peake spoke to him 'about the Greek Government's attitude to enosis':

> It looks as if this time they will take it to the UNO if they feel that the UK will not settle the matter in bilateral talks. Papagos wants to go to the UK but we will not let him unless he agrees not to raise enosis. The King is also being asked and he could be conditioned but he has no influence with Papagos. The only hope is to involve Turkish influence to stop Greece.

Early the next morning they made a quick visit to the Acropolis then boarded a Dakota for Cyprus. Just before their arrival, Armitage changed into his uniform behind a curtain screen, having a good deal of trouble with his cocked hat and its white plumes. He stepped down the gangway and was welcomed by a 17-gun salute while a number of jet fighters 'whistled past' overhead. After the national anthem, he inspected army and Royal Air Force guards of honour and was driven off in a 'huge Daimler with military jeep and wireless car in front [and] a mass of Cypriots lining the roads'. He was pleased, and relieved, that people waved to him on his way in from the airport. At Government House – with which they were 'charmed' despite finding it cold – he was sworn in as governor.[12]

The following day they had a large lunch-time reception at Government House for the heads of department and their deputies, with the police band playing in the garden. On Sunday they went to church and were met by the Anglican bishop from Jerusalem and Archdeacon D. N. Goldie. The next day the commissioner of Nicosia,

W. F. M. Clemens, held a reception for them to meet people they had not met on Saturday.[13]

The local press made much of his previous experience having been in Africa, which they felt would be of little help in dealing with Middle Eastern politics, and some saw his appointment as 'a slur on such an enlightened public as the Greek Cypriot community believed itself to be'.[14] His position in the Gold Coast as minister of finance was 'an important post without a doubt, but scarcely one to make him a suitable candidate for the much more important position of Governor of Cyprus'.[15]

The opinion of a leading Cypriot newspaper was that there must be some 'cogent reason for [his] rapid and surprising promotion which is at present known only in Whitehall'. They interpreted his appointment as indicating that 'a sound and strong man will for the next five years be in charge of affairs in Cyprus'. They did not believe that Britain's traditional policy would be changed, but rather that Armitage's instructions were: '[The] enosis question is dead, but be kind and tolerant towards those who clamour for union with Greece, do everything possible for the welfare of Cypriots and try to make them appreciate the benefits of British rule, and, above all, do nothing to upset them or to cause the Colonial Office difficulties or trouble.' It seemed to Armitage that there was 'the most general apathy in the population about a new Governor', but he thought this might also be the case elsewhere.[16]

Armitage was soon – indeed 'within a few days of arrival' – 'ready to sally forth' and he started the first of a series of visits to see and be seen by people in different parts of the island. For a while, he was 'very rushed'. He visited an orange-packing station, a factory producing edible gum, a wine and brandy factory, a brewery, a sanatorium, copper mines, an asbestos company, an agricultural farm and research station, a teacher training college, a pottery works, a printing works, a reservoir, a Turkish farm school and numerous other schools. He had expected to be greeted by demonstrations in favour of enosis since he understood that it was 'a habit of the country to take the opportunity of a new face to express displeasure', but he was relieved during this first tour to be faced by none:[17]

> Only one Greek flag flew, that was over a coffee shop owned by a right-wing nationalist, otherwise it was all myrtle branches on the road, union jacks, triumphal arches, portraits of the Queen and lines of schoolchildren singing what they were taught as God Save the Queen ... speeches of welcome were made on each side and on we went.[18]

He was received 'everywhere ... with courtesy and friendliness, though care had been taken not to invite people to meet him who might have declined to do so on political grounds', and, a little later, to ensure that he avoided villages in which Greek flags might be waved. He met leaders of the Greek and Turkish communities, held his first meeting of executive council and was shown round the secretariat – 'which is the old Turkish police stables still almost in original form'. He had early individual meetings with each of his heads of departments.[19]

He very quickly turned his mind to considering a constitution.[20] His early meetings with heads of departments produced a variety of opinions from those who thought that development should be via local government institutions with no constitution being produced, and certainly not imposed, to those who felt the only way forward was to decide on a constitution involving elections and if necessary impose it. Only a month after his arrival he recorded privately:

> I try to get ideas [but] one can hardly expect anyone really to give me advice. It appears that we shall have to muzzle the press if we are to give the middle of the road man a chance. No one can stand up against the present vitriol. Also that UNO will have had to make some pronouncement, we hope not in favour of enosis, before anyone can be expected to commit themselves in favour of any constitution or government scheme.

By the end of March he had worked out in his own mind a number of basic considerations concerning constitutional advance. Some of these views were formed after discussions with Paul Pavlides, a member of his executive council, and, separately, others. He felt that both the ethnarchy and the communists feared a constitution because whoever lost might suffer seriously: the church feared it would lose its lands – which were 'generally absentee owned and badly farmed' – and its hold over the Cypriot people, and the communists feared they might be proscribed 'and even shot, which of course they would be in Greece'. The press was 'so violent that no man who [held] views against enosis [could] stand against it'. There was a body of opinion, too, which felt that the enosis campaign had gone on long enough but until the matter had reached the UNO they would not come into the open.

Armitage was convinced that the British government must declare that it was not going to leave Cyprus, as a means of getting loyal Cypriots to take part in a constitution without jeopardizing their careers and prospects, and in order, too, to assure Turks there would be no enosis. The Communist Party, he felt, were few in numbers, but were well organized and would win any election based on popular votes. Members of the nationalist party were 'quite fluid', some were fanatic

– like the Bishop of Kyrenia – while others were merely anti-communist. In these circumstances it was difficult for him to gauge the nationalist strength. The 'clerical intimidation' the Church could wield was 'a tremendous influence', but if it could be split they might be able 'to intrude and hope to prevent general excommunication by winning over the Archbishop'.

He was unsure whether the nationalist leader, Dr T. Dervis, the Greek Cypriot mayor of Nicosia, and his colleagues were careerists or die-hards, but suspected the former. Because he could not deny the cultural relationship with Greece, he thought it unwise to attempt to do so, but rather he should possibly try to build it up. 'The Cypriot, like the Greek, loves the election, it gives him something to talk about, he is a great sitter, and he thinks they are fun. So [we should] give him some elections somewhere.' He felt it was important to recapture the goodwill of the loyal Cypriots and 'show by a large cheque, i.e. for ten million pounds, that HMG is determined to continue to develop Cyprus'.

A little later he added to these considerations a number of others. It seemed to him that a large number of the right-wing nationalist objects were originally formed by the communists: the plebiscite, the clamour for an appeal to the UN, an approach to the USSR to sponsor enosis. As a consequence, the communists acted as a goad to the right wing. Extracts from the Greek press – which was fanning the flames – formed the main mass of material in the Cyprus press, and he felt it vital that the Greek government should be won over to control the enosis campaign and to stop demonstrations in Greece: 'That is the fount of all the agitation now.'

Armitage's early general views were also indicated in an interview a few months after he arrived. In answer to a question about why the Cypriots were so pleasant to the British, despite their enosis demands, he replied:

> The Enosis disagreement has never disrupted relations between the British and the Greeks in Cyprus. Indeed official Ethnarchy policy has always emphasized the peaceful and orderly nature of the struggle. Greek Cypriots who feel a psychological need for Enosis are not blind to the material consequences. Many dread union with Greece for this alone. . . .
> The Cypriot leaders have repeatedly emphasized, as indeed the metropolitan Greeks have too, that there is nothing anti-British about the Enosis movement.

He recognized that ties of language and religion and the methods of teaching in the schools predisposed the Cypriots towards enosis: 'A psychological problem of Enosis would always exist [but] its political aspect would not have assumed serious proportions without the active campaigning of the Press and the Church.' Without this, enosis would be 'a shadow rather than a reality'.

He was, however, already concerned about international interference and accepted 'the general opinion' that if the Greek government, urged on by Makarios, raised the Cyprus question at the UN, the Latin American and Arab countries would help to pass a resolution that Britain should consult with Greece as to constitutional advancement. 'This is the sort of occasion when the small nations like to take the opportunity to annoy the larger.'[21]

He was under few illusions that his job would be easy, and when his parents asked about ancient monuments he replied, somewhat sharply: 'I have had no time yet to study the past, the present is giving me sufficient headaches.' He had an early taste of public demonstrations particularly by students towards the end of March, when the anniversary of the Greek day of independence from Turkey in 1821 was celebrated with 'crowds of students, schoolchildren, cars, flags and sermons'. The demonstrations were peaceful and neither Armitage nor his advisers were particularly concerned with security, believing that no precautions were necessary, so none were taken: 'Whatever they may write in their papers or say in their pulpits, the individuals are friendly and pleasant.'[22]

He was much concerned about the constitution and its practical effect on government.[23] The legislature had not met since 1931 and he believed executive council was a thoroughly bad system, for it was autocratic and did not allow issues to be subjected to popular criticism: 'This was a pretty inefficient body to decide how the island should be run.' One of his senior officials, however, felt that 'the British administration wasn't as remote as people sometimes made out': 'The Governor's executive council had Greek Cypriot members ... they were all men of distinction whose advice was ... taken very seriously and given great weight, so I think that in policy making ... the British administration did take account of Cypriot opinion to a very high degree.' Although he did not have discussions with the two main political parties, the communists and the nationalists, because neither had been willing to operate the 1948 constitutional proposals, Armitage took every other opportunity to meet people with all shades of opinion.

Within three months of their arrival, the Armitages had invited to dinner all heads of government departments and those 'highest level Cypriots' who were prepared to dine with them and they had several cocktail parties, each with well over 100 guests. His father thought him neither frugal nor hard worked. Over 1000 people had signed their visitors' book – the traditional form for calling at Government House without actually meeting the governor – despite 'active enosists' and 'many who sit on the fence' declining to sign. Of Turkish attitudes he was soon convinced of a fundamental obstacle to progress: 'The Turks don't want a constitution here, as they will be in a permanent minority to the Greeks. They like a benevolent British autocratic rule. What a country this is!'

He held a series of meetings in an attempt to persuade Greek Cypriots that it would not be in their economic interests to unite with Greece and become 'a dumping ground for mainland Greeks'. Although a fair number were prepared to discuss the issues with him at first, later they became far fewer as pressure was put on them by the Greek government, press and radio, the local press, Makarios, the bishops and the Church.[24] He was personally highly respected by his civil servants: 'He was admired for his efficiency, gentleness, frankness and easy approach.' The only Turkish Cypriot district commissioner long remembered the governor's kindness when his father died in 1954: 'He kindly visited me at my house and at my office, and made sure that the Government was well represented at the funeral.'[25]

By the end of April the position was that 'Cyprus continue[d] to sit back, watching and commenting on the steady advancement of the Enosis cause, but making little or no contribution to its progress.' Three distinct attitudes towards the colony's future had become apparent. First, enosis was a foregone conclusion and Britain was 'merely attempting by every possible expedient to prevent the inevitable'. This was the attitude of the Greek government and press and the Cypriot nationalists and their press. Second, enosis was a foregone conclusion, but Greece was 'ill-advisedly attempting to force the inevitable at an inconvenient moment'. This was the attitude of the British press and the local *Cyprus Mail*. Third, enosis might appear to the Greeks to be a foregone conclusion but they would find 'some surprising opposition from the Turks if they continue[d] to press the matter'. This was the attitude held in Turkey and by the Cypriot Turkish politicians and press. The political situation appraisal that reported these attitudes continued: 'Nowhere from any local quarter, official or otherwise is it suggested that Cyprus is British territory, that the Cypriots are British subjects and that the only development in the colony will be along accepted constitutional lines.'[26]

There were clear signs of the Greek government being disappointed at Britain's recently repeated refusal to discuss the status and future of Cyprus.[27] They announced on 20 April that they would appeal to the UN if bilateral talks were not agreed by 22 August. Clear too was 'the rising demand for enosis and the rising repugnance to it from the

Turks', and the Turkish government made it clear that a change in Cyprus's status was not desirable but when the time arrived for it to be discussed by Britain, Turkey would expect to have its views expressed. 'The Cypriot Turkish politicians' ... hopes repose[d] more and more in Turkey.' Ankara British embassy staff visited Cyprus in June to 'get the hang of Turkish opinion', but like Armitage they found 'very few respected Turks whom one can entertain and [with whom one can] discuss Turkish affairs'.

The Turks strongly objected to union with Greece and, indeed, did not want a democratic constitution, fearing Greek majority oppression: 'A benevolent autocracy is really what everyone wants.' In truth, however, Armitage did not yet know what best should be done and he found the problems deeply intractable. 'It early became clear to me that no constitution would be accepted unless self-determination in future was conceded.' He made his frustration, amounting almost to anguished despair, known to his parents:

> The problem of enosis is like the velvety blackness of a nightmare, it clutches one everywhere and one strains to see a glimmer of light to guide one to safety and nowhere is there light. The more one studies it and the ramifications which as every month goes by it provides, the more difficult it seems to find a solution which will not make everything temporarily much worse.[28]

As he explained, 'this fearful problem called Enosis' made effective cooperation between people and the government quite impossible. He could see no solution to a problem that had existed for 78 years, 'but it [was] now more acute than ever' and he thought the situation would have to get worse before it got better.[29] The feeling of the inevitability of enosis became more widespread, Armitage's commissioners reporting in June:[30]

> Nearly everyone – Turks, villagers, officials, possibly even the politicians themselves – have come to believe that enosis is on the way.
>
> The conviction that British rule on the island is nearing its end is steadily taking its hold and ... there are now few people, even amongst the most loyal of government supporters, who think otherwise.

On 27 June, Armitage flew to Britain. He had been summoned at very short notice to report to the cabinet on the current situation in the island. The departure was a closely guarded secret and 'not a single flag was out'. They discussed introducing a new constitution, to be announced a month later, which, on Armitage's advice, would include nominated Greek Cypriot ministers. He had concluded from his numerous soundings that many Greek Cypriots were indifferent to enosis and could fairly easily be won over to a constitution that included Greek Cypriot ministers. They had contemplated having a legislature elected by constituencies, or by functional organizations such as cooperative societies, trade unions and farmers' associations, but concluded that the electors and constituent bodies could not be well enough defined. They came back, therefore, to the 1925–31 arrangement of having 12 Greeks and three Turks. He felt Britain needed to make a clear statement of policy as soon as possible and he argued that two things were needed: first, 'Cypriots must be convinced that British rule is not about to be exchanged for Greek rule [and second] the law especially in relation to sedition should be enforced; the Cypriot is not a natural resister when confronted by firmness.' He forecast that some arrests would be necessary to introduce his constitutional recommendations.[31]

While in London he had an audience with the Queen – in place of an investiture – at which she dubbed him on being made a KCMG in the birthday honours list a few weeks earlier: a 'most unexpected honour' he attributed to his Gold Coast work because Branigan was also knighted.[32]

He returned to Cyprus to face a busy time on constitutional issues, about which there was much speculation. He had a hard task ahead of him and was anxious that the current civil service salary revisions should go well. He wanted the service firmly on his side 'when we have the much more complicated problems which will shortly face us on the constitutional aspect' and he feared there might be strikes and other disruptions. Locally, the newspapers were firmly saying that a constitution could not be accepted.[33]

There now 'followed an event which stands high in the mythology of Cyprus and of the British Empire'.[34] On 28 July, Eden told the Commons that Britain was to withdraw her troops from Suez and that Cyprus was to be the new Middle East military headquarters. Armitage had been aware of this for several weeks. A large number of Conservative members threatened to vote against the government, seeing the withdrawal as capitulating to Egyptian violence, and this could have brought down the government. Henry Hopkinson, the Colonial Office minister of state, speaking on behalf of Lyttelton who was resigning as secretary of state that very day, was anxious to make it clear to Conservative backbenchers and Britain's allies in the Middle East that there would be no further withdrawal from Cyprus. This was in accordance with the agreement Lyttelton made in cabinet that morning, under great pressure from the chiefs of staff, that there would be 'no fudging the issue'. In doing this, however, and taking 'his instructions perhaps a little too literally', Hopkinson – who had not been at the cabinet meeting – used the word 'never' in referring to the island's advance to full independence.[35]

This 'never' outraged the Labour Party and deeply antagonized the Greek government, which had already been insulted by Eden. In November 1951, in response to a Greek suggestion that in exchange for the union of Cyprus with Greece, Britain should have bases in both Cyprus and Greece, Eden said 'the British Empire is not for sale. The Cyprus question does not exist.' Again, in September 1953 he brusquely told General Alexandros Papagos, the Greek prime minister, that there would never be a Cyprus question and he refused to discuss it. Anthony Nutting's version of this incident is that Eden felt the Greek prime minister was trying to trap him into a meeting to discuss Cyprus and to take advantage of the fact that Eden was unprepared for a discussion. He had been ill for some time and away from the office. He had not been briefed, had no officials with him, was recuperating after major surgery and simply wished to 'spend a lot of time doing nothing and lying in the sun'. The meeting between the two had been suggested and arranged by the British ambassador, Peake, whose wife recalled that when Papagos asked Eden, '*Et maintenant, premier ministre, la question de Chypre?*', Eden replied, '*Ah, non, mon cher, on ne discute pas ça.*' Lady Peake thought that Papagos felt 'he had been rather told to go to the nursery and play with the children'. Papagos's attitude hardened significantly after what he saw as this second rebuff: 'relations between the two were pretty strained thereafter' and the ambassador and his family, who had been quite popular when they first arrived in Athens, now found themselves very unpopular there.[36]

The British cabinet had discussed Cyprus on 26 July and had reached a number of decisions. For security reasons full sovereignty over Cyprus must be retained for the foreseeable future. No statement should be attempted that Britain might in the future be able to contemplate self-determination for Cyprus and, on the contrary, it should be reaffirmed that they could not contemplate any change in sovereignty. The 1948 offer of a constitution should be withdrawn and a more limited type of self-governing institution should instead be imposed at the earliest practical date. Because the British government was not prepared to risk a majority of communists, the new constitution should be in the form of a legislature with a majority of official and nominated members. An early statement should be made in parliament. The governor should be authorized to take the necessary steps to enforce existing laws. And, finally, the leader of the United Kingdom delegation to the UN should threaten to withdraw from the discussion if Cyprus were inscribed on the agenda, but the threat should not to be carried out without prior reference to London.[37] Two days later, when Hopkinson made his statement about no further withdrawal from Cyprus, he also told the Commons that he had instructed Armitage to introduce the new constitution. None the less, his speech, which included seven references to there being no question of any change of British rule, altered the whole political situation in Cyprus and greatly complicated Armitage's task: 'British intransigence epitomized by Hopkinson's "never" made any progress towards a political solution impossible.'[38]

Armitage ensured that Hopkinson's statement on the constitution was quoted in full in the Cyprus broadcasting service's English, Greek and Turkish news that evening and he immediately followed with a broadcast message, which was repeated in Greek and Turkish. During the night he had pamphlets, in all three languages, containing the statement and the text of his broadcast 'taken by despatch rider all over the island'. He was keen to do this to allow people a reasonable time to digest the development 'before the Greek Church, press and politicians reacted to it'. He also expressed his message, on which he had worked carefully for several days, in a somewhat 'sentimental' tone in contrast with 'the stark form of the statement'.[39]

> The Turks were at once relieved there was to be no enosis and the constitution proposed was obviously safe. The Greek Cypriots reacted more slowly but the two principle impressions gained [were, first,] genuine disappointment and surprise that the constitution outlined was less liberal than the 1948 offer or even the pre-1931 arrangement. [Second,] the feeling that the whole thing ha[d] been ill-timed and that the correct moment to say 'No enosis' and to introduce the constitution would have been after the Cyprus question ha[d] foundered at the United Nations.... Everyone would then be saying that the widely advertised reference having failed, it was time to have a change of policy and the public would have been less inclined to feel that something was being imposed on the people by force.[40]

Armitage's broadcast message was designed also to avoid demonstrations, to seek support for the constitution, to hold out the prospect of further advance and, while avoiding the word 'never', to reinforce the point that there was to be no change of sovereignty. He was anxious that moderate opinion should not be submerged by intimidatory opinion.

The chances of support, peace and calm were, however, slim and even the anticipation of an announcement of constitutional proposals was met by the ethnarchy with a blunt rejection: 'We will fight any form of constitution, without even considering it, immediately it is offered or imposed.... Acceptance of a constitution would mean stopping the fight while the battle is being won, a retreat while we make progress towards the enosis goal.'[41]

Armitage's announcement of the proposals was followed by demonstrations by thousands of schoolchildren and others. This decided him to state, on 2 August, that the sedition laws – until now liberally interpreted – would be enforced and be interpreted to include references to enosis. His aim was to reduce the level and strength of anti-constitution pronouncements so as to encourage more moderate, pro-constitution opinion. His statement, taken by opponents in Britain and Cyprus as an attack on press freedom, was followed immediately by a week's newspaper strike in Cyprus. He had to explain that the law had not been changed and, provided it was not broken, there was no question of curtailing press freedom. Two days later, under continuing attack, Criton Tornaritis, the attorney-general, explained that, because of the intimidatory mass of enosis propaganda, people were afraid to try to operate the constitution and moderate opinion had no chance to 'crystallize' in the face of such sedition. In response, Makarios defiantly preached a number of seditious sermons one after the other.[42]

The early responses to the constitutional statement and worries about sedition – particularly the strength of feeling in Britain – led the Colonial Office to propose that Alan Lennox-Boyd, the new secretary of state, pay an early visit to the island.[43] Armitage strongly opposed this:

> In fact the island is remarkably quiet. Reports from the rural areas indicate that the proposals for the constitution have been accepted with indifference or faint interest. The people of Cyprus have got used to the idea of enosis.... If the secretary of state should come here it is clear that people will ask in their own minds at any rate why is he coming? and [they will believe] he considers that the policy announced in parliament should be modified and the only way that it could be modified could of course be to weaken it. [They would also think he was going to climb down on enforcing the sedition law]. That is another reason why I feel that a visit now would be inopportune.[44]

He believed the Greeks would feel Britain was making a last-minute attempt to prevent the Greek government taking the Cyprus question to the UN. The Turks could not be guaranteed to remain inactive in the face of probable Greek demonstrations, and provocation between them might lead to otherwise preventable breaches of the peace. In the light of this advice, the secretary of state, after consulting the prime minister, decided not to visit Cyprus at that juncture but to pay a short visit later in the recess.[45]

A number of functions Armitage attended were boycotted by many Cypriots and, as he feared, there was a general strike. This was accompanied by demonstrations on 12 August in which stones, bottles and tear gas were thrown – to reject the new constitution because the ethnarchy, the nationalists and communists all insisted on union with Greece. The trouble was widespread, and in Limasol soldiers shot three students. Eight days later the Greek government asked the UN – in the event unsuccessfully – to place the question of Cyprus's right to self-determination on its agenda.[46]

Hopkinson's restatement of Eden's 'never' had turned the question from being simply a British colonial problem into an international matter – events 'dragged Cyprus into the stock market of world affairs'. It also obliged the Foreign Office to take a closer interest in what formerly had been primarily a Colonial Office matter. They argued that retained sovereignty over Cyprus was essential for Britain to discharge its treaty obligations to the Arab states, NATO, Iraq, Libya, Turkey and Persia. The matter was further internationalized by the World Council of Churches publicly recognizing 'the right and fitness of the people of Cyprus to determine for themselves their future status'.[47]

Towards the end of August, the minister of state reported to cabinet on the current position in Cyprus, based on Armitage's recent reports. The Greek public were disappointed in the illiberality of the proposed constitution and were awaiting the outcome of the Greek approach to the UN. The Turkish public were prepared to accept the constitution with adequate safeguards. All communities, however, were 'puzzled at the Archbishop being allowed to make seditious statement without prosecution'. Despite the contrary impression that might have been gained from the British press, the island had remained reasonably quiet during the past week or so. There had been some slight increase in tension. This reached its peak when the Greek government handed its request to the UN and lifted its ban on enosis demonstrations in Greece and the Greek islands. In contrast with Greece, there had been 'no violence, no clashes, no arrests and no bloodshed'.[48]

A fortnight later, Armitage summed up the situation from his point of view:

> We are heavily criticized for having made the 28 July statement [as being] ill-timed, for having offered an illiberal constitution and for the form of the Attorney-General's statement [on sedition]. Against that we have weathered the storm with mild sedition from [Makarios], a general

strike regarded as a holiday, much greater sedition from [Bishop] Kyrenia, some poor attempts at it from other prelates. There is a falling off between Greeks and British.... A rash of writing has appeared on walls and streets. Nationalists and communists seem to have combined to keep the situation free from violence. Their case has certainly been going well, the Labour Party in the House of Commons, the British press formerly and still the liberal and labour sections of it all support enosis. The Greek government is working things up to fever pitch in demonstrations. The Americans are obviously in a fix. [Their] desire for the principle of self-determination pulls them one way and fear of communism and support for NATO another. The Arab states may be more pro-British. Recent cuttings from British press are more critical of Greece. Here in Cyprus, no one certainly would stir a finger for a constitution now, they all expect HMG and the Greek government to compromise.[49]

As demonstrations increased and Makarios's public statements became more and more seditious, Armitage became convinced that there should be a firm policy statement. He also felt that the law should be enforced and that Makarios should be prosecuted, together with the Greek Cypriot newspapers, which repeatedly championed enosis.[50] Although he had been contemplating this since May, his executive council strongly advised him to announce that they were going to enforce the law more strictly, but only to do so during the summer 'when everyone is averse from taking strenuous exercise or decisions'. He felt that they should tell the world that:

In order to get the problem properly studied in Cyprus we can't have sedition openly practised and with impunity. When the country has settled down to constitutional government and learnt how to practise it, it can reach gradual degrees of self-determination.... The present laxity cannot continue if [the] UK proposes to keep control and you cannot introduce a constitution unless there is control.

He was not convinced, however, that they should wait to make this announcement because if the UN supported enosis, enforcing the law would become more difficult and be 'billed as repression'. He advised the Colonial Office that they should 'go for curbing sedition at once'. The secretary of state made it clear that he would not refuse to 'contemplate prosecution of a church leader on the clearest grounds of incitement to violence', but hoped it would not be considered necessary to prosecute the archbishop for anything less. The Colonial Office felt sure it would be 'a great mistake to put any obstacle in the way of the

Archbishop going to New York for the general assembly of the United Nations'.

Armitage soon began to regret his announcement about strictly enforcing the sedition laws. A prosecution could easily fail because of the need to prove incitement to violence, and a successful prosecution would raise the archbishop to the status of hero and martyr. If he were not prosecuted, how could lesser Cypriots be prosecuted? As was later remarked: 'The clumsy attempt to make the Sedition Law effective, far from facilitating the introduction of a constitution, made the authorities look foolish.'[51] The British government, fearful of the repercussions of prosecuting Makarios, summoned Armitage to London in October to report to the cabinet. Churchill – who 'looked white and tired and limp' and who became 'very annoyed' when the governor argued for censorship – said 'he could have as many soldiers as he needed to put down trouble, but he must not interfere with the freedom of the press.'

Churchill 'would have preferred an emergency to be imminent or to occur and to be suppressed rather than to threaten the press and enosists with penalties'. Armitage urged the government to repeat that enosis was ruled out. This was to encourage moderates to support the proposed constitution and to persuade Makarios of the hopelessness of his opposition and his demands for enosis. Indeed, he was quite concerned that the Colonial Office hoped they and the Foreign Office could 'present a united front' and offer 'two alternatives to cabinet: a statement of no change in sovereignty, with no self-determination in sight or with ultimate self-determination'. He was 'annoyed at this turn round [on self-determination] and so pressed strongly for no mention of [it]', on the grounds that if one conceded ultimate self-determination now, since self-determination meant enosis, one acknowledged the rightness of enosis and one would thereby encourage the enosists to redouble their efforts to secure it immediately rather than later.[52]

He had a number of discussions at the Colonial Office about his constitutional proposals. They agreed the governor should be able to act against the advice of executive council. They discussed whether it would be possible to prevent the legislature discussing a change in sovereignty but thought this would be difficult and instead they should rely on the government majority to vote it down if it ever came up. He thought, and they agreed, it would be better if he had no Speaker in the early stages because he himself had experience of legislative assembly work and because of the difficulty of finding a qualified person. He reported that the reorganization of the secretariat into shadow ministries was almost complete. His ideas on the composition of the legislative assembly were that there should be three officials, 15 nominated non-officials, 12 elected Greeks and three elected Turks. He agreed to consider having a majority of elected members, for example 15 elected – 12 Greek, three Turk – with 10 nominated and three officials, relying on the three elected Turks to support the official side on major questions.[53] While in London he spoke to 100 MPs and the press, answered their questions and appeared in a television programme in which he hoped to debunk the archbishop.[54]

Back on the island, Armitage found himself in a 'state of suspended animation': 'The prevailing attitude is one of wait and see.' The view of officials was that no real progress could be made till the UN had made a decision on the Cyprus reference. 'Once that has happened there is reasonable hope that moderate men will turn to consider how they can play their part in creating self-government in Cyprus.'[55]

On his way to the UN in September, Makarios gave Grivas 'the green light' to return secretly to Cyprus to begin to organize resistance, expand the organization, recruit more members and have everything ready but not to start action until he gave the order to do so.[56] Grivas landed other caïque loads of arms in October, after his supporters had watched the proposed landing site and observed police movements for two weeks. On the evening of 11 November, he landed and immediately began to set up the nucleus of his organization and to train saboteurs and guerrillas with the arms landed in March and October. He organized the youth, including schoolchildren, by appointing leaders in every school. He wished to have a display of force at the time of the UN debate to show, especially the Americans, that the Cypriots were serious in their demands.

In the event, he was dissuaded by Makarios – who also originally thought of starting violence during the UN debate. It was agreed the archbishop should decide the date of rebel activity depending on progress at the UN. It appears that the Cyprus police knew in general terms by 16 November about 'thugs from the Greek isles', and by 24 November that Grivas – although not by name – had landed on the island earlier in the month. Certainly, they received reports during October of the secret shipping of weapons from Athens and of intended infiltration of Greek saboteurs. Peake had warned Armitage as early as 16 September that he might 'expect some Crete brigands . . . if UNO rejects the Cyprus question'. The government took these reports as 'an indication, if nothing else, of the Greek thinking in the event of a failure in the Cyprus case at the UN'. They did not discount 'possible attempts to organize armed resistance' and were watching the situation closely. It was at this time, too, that the first slogan saying 'Armitage must die' appeared in the villages. By early December he was discussing with the service chiefs and the commissioner of police 'the problem presented by gunrunning and desperados'.

In December, the UN debated Cyprus but a US-backed resolution ensured that no action was taken.[57] The only result in Armitage's view was 'widening the rift between Greece and Britain'. Relationships between Greece and Turkey also worsened because during the debate they had seriously clashed over Cyprus for the first time publicly, and the debate had significantly decreased the prospects of a settlement. The rejection of Greece's case on the grounds that it was 'not the appropriate time' was greeted in Cyprus by strikes and demonstrations during which the army wounded three schoolboys.[58] Armitage had organized an 'island-wide exercise for internal security' for the day of the UN decision, presumably as a precaution against disturbances and as a show of strength, but in the event he called it off 'as real incidents might have occurred!'

Unlike the strike on 12 August, which was 'a completely peaceful affair' because the schools were on holiday and no one was prepared to risk a seditious demonstration, by December 'the church leaders, the press and the schools had been allowed so much rope that fear of the consequences had been dissipated.' Consequently, the strike and riots were more violent. Those who favoured the introduction of constitutional advances were still finding excuses for making no effort to achieve them. The most common excuse was that the tension aroused by the appeal to the UN and the ensuing riots must be given time to simmer down. Armitage found depressing the 'complete lack of any initiative or determination among many people who were fully aware that the consequences of enosis would be disastrous to themselves'.[59]

Makarios and Papagos now fully supported Grivas's activities.[60] Neither the British government nor Armitage at this time foresaw serious trouble, or difficulty in controlling any that might occur, despite the recent violence:[61]

> We [in the Colonial Office] can, I think, assume that Sir Robert Armitage is satisfied that the police and military available in the island are sufficient to quell any riots on a scale that can at present be considered even remotely possible. He would, I am sure, let us know at once if he had any doubt on that score.[62]

Early in January 1955, Lawrence Durrell, the director of information services, who was in close touch with Greek Cypriot opinion, suggested to Armitage that the governor should meet Makarios unofficially. Durrell, with Maurice Cardiff, director of the British Council, believed Britain should offer Cyprus self-government with a promise of self-determination at some unspecified future time. It may well be that Armitage particularly consulted Durrell and Cardiff, both fluent Greek speakers, because he felt the lack of day-to-day information. Few of his senior officials spoke modern Greek or had much direct contact with local people. He also thought they might 'infiltrate' Greek Cypriot society, influence it and keep him apprised of their feelings. When he consulted them in January 1955, they were particularly worried about the archbishop's return from the UN and violence during a state of tension. The governor phoned Peake in Athens to find out what the archbishop's plans were and to 'propose a possible meeting at which things in general would be discussed, on neutral ground'.[63]

It is unclear how initial contact was effected, but two approaches were made by Makarios in February. First, the secretary of state received a letter from I. Araouzo – a member of a much travelled wealthy shipping family, Anglicized and pro-British – saying that Makarios had expressed a desire to meet Lennox-Boyd if he visited Cyprus in the near future. The governor was asked for his comments and possible forms of reply; it might be possible for Lennox-Boyd to arrive in Cyprus towards the end of March.[64] Second, the archbishop's political secretary, Nicos Kranidiotis, approached Durrell about meeting Armitage. Durrell was told that Makarios was keen on a meeting. He gained the impression that this was largely due to concern about the drift towards local violence and to the Greek government's move towards moderation, which was creating difficulty with extreme nationalists in Cyprus.

Armitage thought the meeting might have beneficial effects on local opinion. He instructed Durrell to reply that he was interested, but could not agree to any communiqué being issued afterwards that mentioned self-determination.[65] Colonial Office officials thought the archbishop was 'anxious somehow to get himself dissociated from the possibly awkward evidence' that might emerge in the imminent trial of a number of men charged with smuggling explosives.[66] Foreign Office officials felt there might be 'some loss of face for the Governor in the rather hole and corner method' of the proposed meeting and 'perhaps the Governor need not be too precipitate about the date of the meeting'.[67]

Durrell learned from Kranidiotis that the archbishop was prepared to meet the governor at 8.00 p.m. on 28 February at Kykko monastery. The meeting was to be secret and no communiqué was to be issued. If by chance news of the meeting became known, they would issue an agreed communiqué.[68] Lennox-Boyd was unhappy about the proposed venue:

> I accept that an initiative coming from the archbishop for a private talk with you should not be rebuffed. I realize there is no possibility of getting

him to come to Government House but I fear that a secret meeting at night on his ground (once it became known as it surely speedily will) is very likely to be misinterpreted as indicating readiness and even anxiety on your part to seek an accommodation over self-determination.... I should greatly prefer your meeting to be arranged for a convenient date on some more neutral ground.[69]

Armitage had been 'well received' when he visited the monastery six months earlier and he was quite happy with the proposed venue. He argued that Kykko, although ecclesiastical property, would not be regarded in Cyprus as Makarios's ground, since the Abbot of Kykko had a great degree of independence. It was far more secure than a private neutral house. Other alternative places and times had been exhaustively considered and rejected. 'Surely meeting if it takes place can be explained as signal of triumph in starting to break down the barriers of this intransigent prelate and we hope we can get to the end of boycott imposed by the church for the last 20 years.'[70]

The secretary of state still had considerable doubts about the meeting being at Kykko, doubts shared by colleagues whom he consulted. Consequently, he felt he must submit the matter to the cabinet, but could not do so for several days.[71] In the meantime, Armitage had worked on a communiqué wording, but Makarios, to whom it was put, thought it 'merely reiterated the present impasse' and he would be criticized for breaking the boycott on meeting the governor to no object. He thereupon withdrew his offer, but if at any time there was a change in the government's attitude he would be willing to meet. Armitage said that, since contact had merely been broken off and not completely severed, it was possible that a meeting would be profitable at some future time.[72] Lennox-Boyd told Armitage:

> I am sure that the Archbishop's initiative for a talk with you and the suggested arrangements for it are still giving you anxious thoughts as they did me. Like you, I welcome any reasonable prospect of breaking down the barriers and I appreciate your willingness not to insist too rigidly on formalities to achieve that end. On the other hand, I could not but feel doubtful of circumstances of the first meeting in secrecy after dark at a place which would have been regarded here as church ground. [I assume] you are content to let matters rest [for the present] and I concur in this view.[73]

It is possible that the governor and secretary of state were at cross-purposes over the Kykko venue. Certainly, the monastery itself, 'one of the richest and most powerful in the Orthodox world', would have been most inappropriate. Makarios had received his early training for the priesthood and had been ordained there. It was also the venue for the only meeting Makarios had with Grivas during the subsequent state of emergency and Grivas was 'in close contact with the Kykko monastery, around which he built his organization' after 1 April 1955. In fact, Armitage had in mind not the monastery itself but the Kykko annexe, which was close to Government House and the secretariat, whereas the monastery was high up in the western part of the Troodos range, remote and dangerous.[74]

Armitage had a long talk with Patrick Maitland, a visiting MP who had been to Athens and had met the King of Greece, the foreign minister, S. Stephanopoulos, 'and many others including pro-enosists'. He felt the Greek government was 'fed up with the Archbishop'. The King and probably Papagos had told the Archbishop they were prepared to support a constitution in Cyprus with an elected majority in the legislature. Since Makarios had made it clear he did not support a constitution, Armitage correctly concluded he was not to be swayed by Greek government wishes. There was a feeling in Greece that Makarios would stir up violence as the only alternative to a constitution acceptable to Greece with no agreement on self-determination, but the governor's view – mistakenly – was that the archbishop's return to Cyprus from Athens would 'be on a peaceful basis and that he will not advocate violence'. Maitland thought the current Greek mood for accepting a constitution with a majority of elected members would last a few months and then wear off as they prepared for the UN debate.[75]

Makarios's return on 10 January – via Athens where Papagos told him he wanted rebellious action taken in Cyprus[76] – was warmly received by 'many thousands at airport and cathedral' and he made 'his most pugnacious speech ... welcoming the demonstrations and bloodshed and talking more of strife and sacrifices. He looks as though he is out to get as much support for violence as he can and he is not accepting the Greek Government's advice to work through a constitution.'[77] He said that 'although Mother Greece [was] standing by their side, Cypriots should not expect everything from Greece, but should themselves intensify their struggle, sacrifice themselves for it, and stop at nothing.'[78]

Officials expected the archbishop to exercise care in his speeches in view of the December disturbances, but in violent language he urged his adherents to intensify their efforts, congratulated those who had taken part in riots and shed blood for the cause and declared that the struggle would 'continue until death'. While he was outspoken in church, he omitted from press releases those parts of his speech too obviously in conflict with his publicized policy of a peaceful struggle.[79] The day after his return he secretly discussed the date for starting a revolution: Grivas wanted to start straight away, but the archbishop preferred 25 March, Greece's independence day.[80] Shortly, Grivas decided on 31 March. Armitage felt that he himself was 'getting up against a stone wall' and would 'have to consider strategic plans, a frontal attack, enflanking movement or a period of static defence.' He had been correct that the archbishop would not follow the Greek government's advice but wrong about not advocating violence.

Early in January 1955, Churchill asked 'for a firm and realistic policy for the future of Cyprus' to be drafted.[81] Because it was important for the governor not to leave the island at that particular time, Lennox-Boyd asked John Fletcher-Cooke, the chief secretary, to go to London.[82] When he returned on 13 January, he told Armitage he had found the Foreign and Colonial Offices 'at pretty good loggerheads over future policy' in Cyprus. There seemed to be a move in the Foreign Office that 'one should mention self-determination as the ultimate objective and bully the Greek Government to keep quiet' about it and not push for its early implementation. Armitage's steps to meet Makarios had not been well received; the Foreign Office, especially Eden who was 'very angry' and 'reacted very hostilely' to the proposal, were against all compromise or discussion with the Greeks, and were prepared to prosecute the archbishop.[83] As a result of his meetings with Fletcher-Cooke and correspondence with Armitage, Lennox-Boyd wrote an interim reply to the prime minister:

> [Although] the United Nations resolution on Cyprus rejected all discussion for the time being at least, most Cypriots feel that the question is bound to come up there again at the end of this year. . . . Accordingly, the Governor reports that it will almost certainly not be possible this year to find sufficient middle-of-the-road Cypriots to accept nominations as members of the proposed legislative council [and] it will be virtually impossible to introduce a constitution as long as the Greek Government goes on actively supporting the Archbishop in the international sphere and by broadcasts etc. I have been thinking whether there might not be basis for some form of long-term agreement with Greece and Turkey which would satisfy for the time being and buy us time to introduce the constitution and popularize the British connection. The Governor believes that any suggestion of talks with the Greeks will be interpreted as weakness in Cyprus and I understand that the Foreign Secretary does not believe that this line of thought would be fruitful.[84]

Armitage recommended that the July 1954 proposals be altered by adding three more Cypriot members to his executive council, making six in all, and giving three of them responsibilities for departments as 'members'. He believed he could get Cypriots to come forward for this. He also recommended that the constitution provide for a legislature with a small elected majority – but not a majority of elected Greeks – and that it be announced in parliament that the goal was self-government and ultimately Cyprus would be allowed self-determination. He referred to these changes as 'the new look policy'. Colonial Office officials recommended that the secretary of state endorse his conclusions.

> By introducing a constitution of the kind now recommended (accompanied or rather preceded by the proposed statement) we shall be accepting obvious dangers and difficulties but the present position is intolerable and the alternatives are even less attractive. Further, we shall be providing the Greek Government with a pretext for abandoning their active support of the enosis campaign which will satisfy large sections of public opinion in the United Kingdom and internationally . . . and there will be a hope that we shall at least to some extent 'turn the eyes of Cypriots inward to running their own affairs and distract their attention from the attractions of Greece'.[85]

The minister of state read Armitage's proposals 'with great interest – and sympathy', adding, 'The whole situation is fraught with risk but I think he is right in coming down in favour of a more liberal form of constitution.'[86] A little later in February, the secretary of state presented a memorandum to the cabinet. In it he said that their aims were to keep effective control in Cyprus and to persuade the Cypriots that Britain was not going to be bundled out by the enosis campaign; to introduce a constitution; to strengthen Britain's position internationally so as to defeat the Greeks if they raised Cyprus again at the UN; to keep the support and cooperation of Turkey; and to induce the Greek government to revert to its earlier policy of not actively prosecuting its Cyprus claim. It would be necessary to keep a firm hand both on internal order in Cyprus and on the actions of the Greek government and take every chance to dissuade them from interfering in Britain's domestic affairs in Cyprus. He had no doubt about Britain's ability to keep order but the constitutional deadlock, coupled with incitements from Greece, might lead to extra violence partly to create conditions for a new appeal to the UN.[87]

Armitage firmly believed that the most important elements in the situation were Makarios and the Greek government. Acting together they were impossible to crack, but if they were not acting in unison and if he could get the Greek government to support a new constitution, they might leave Makarios 'in the heat'. It was now clear to him that 'never' was out of the question, that progress towards self-determination would have to be conceded and that its pace would be for politicians to argue.[88]

He was extremely anxious to make progress. He had been in Cyprus a year and had made little, if any, advance in fulfilling his instructions to introduce a new constitution. When he discussed this with Fletcher-Cooke and Tornaritis on 14 February, they agreed that 'no constitutional advance can be made without some formula by Her Majesty's Government for Self-determination or at least Self-government and that the Greek Government must acquiesce. If these are not done then we have to maintain the status quo and face the possibility of a gradual increase in exhortation by [Makarios] and provocation to acts of violence.'[89] This recognition that conceding the principle of self-determination was essential followed Durrell's advice given a month earlier, but was in direct conflict with the British government's oft repeated adamant position, although there were signs that officials were beginning to question this stance.

The next day, executive council confirmed the view that the basis for advance must be a formula granting internal self-government followed by the opportunity at an unspecified later stage to decide the country's future status. The Greek government should be asked to acquiesce in this. Given these steps, they should be able to get reasonable men to nominate to legislative assembly and they should be nominated before an election '*pour encourager* the election candidates'. They accepted the 'obvious danger' that elected Greeks, with some non-Greeks, would support a motion for self-determination. The governor noted at this time, 'we are now moving to [a] formula of [a] constitution with Self-government leading to Self-determination.' Armitage was well aware that acceptance of his ideas would involve a volte-face by the British government, but he could see no alternative if any constitutional progress was to be achieved.[90]

Although Makarios continued to make speeches during church services condemning the idea of a constitution and labelling all those who took part as traitors, William Clark of the *Observer*, in an interview with the archbishop, of which he told the governor, found him 'most moderate, so different from the tone of his speeches' and very willing to meet Armitage. He added that there would have to be a compromise, although he would not indicate its nature. Presumably, it would revolve around conceding ultimate self-determination – a point with which the governor, but not the British government, now agreed. Makarios recognized, Clark said, that there would have to be a constitution and – unlike the governor – insisted that a time limit must be fixed for self-determination. Clark believed enosis could no longer be laughed off: it now had 'a dangerous edge' and he would say so in his press reports.[91]

Clear evidence that violent political activity was indeed in the offing was received when the caïque *Aghios Georghios*, laden with arms and ammunition was seized at night at Khlorakas on 25 January.[92] Five of the crew with eight members of the reception party were arrested, including Socrates Loizides. The caïque had sailed from Greece, financed by Makarios, on 13 January and, two days later, the archbishop warned Grivas that their plans had been betrayed and that the British were watching the western half of the island. Already Eoka had infiltrated even the higher ranks of the Greek Cypriot members of the police and the 'tip-off' almost certainly came from this source. Makarios and Grivas had no means of warning the caïque and they spent 'two agonizing weeks' awaiting its arrival. Armitage also waited anxiously for 'the long awaited news' that the caïque was approaching Paphos and he was playing bridge when it arrived. The police seized the shore party and the men of HMS *Comet* captured the caïque. The caïque captain cursed and said he was carrying explosives, which would blow the British into the sea.[93]

Armitage's intelligence was good; this became clear later from the prosecution evidence. Six weeks earlier he had asked the admiral whether, if there were a ship in Cyprus waters it could be used 'in a gunrunning episode'. The admiral said this could always be done, including getting a ship from the Canal Zone, if he had enough warning. Even so, he could see that it would be difficult to use naval ships actually to capture the gunrunners. During the week preceding the capture he knew of the caïque's mission and was able to have his men lay in wait, and with Alexi Ionnu's excellent planning to build up his communications 'into a fine art'. There was, however, a feeling among some senior members of the district administration that 'there was virtually no intelligence-gathering organization in Cyprus at the time' and that the capture followed the receipt of chance information by government. The evidence, a good deal from outside Cyprus, was collected by 'a young and upcoming' Greek Cypriot police officer, Kyriacos Aristotelus, who looked upon Eoka activists as criminals. He was later murdered by Eoka. He knew the landing area and precise details of the cargo. The success of the seizure operation – 'the neatest and most dramatic capture... in the long history of Cypriot smuggling' – planned and executed by the new commissioner of police, G. H. Robins, pleased the governor who found it 'very exciting', called it 'the great smuggling event', stayed up until 2.00 a.m. to be in touch with events, and told his parents elatedly: 'We do not have many dull moments in Cyprus and a little explosive running just keeps us tuned up.' As one senior administrative officer remarked, 'Sir Robert would have been pleased at the apparent Police success as any sort of success was pretty rare at that time.' A great deal had been done during the previous six months to introduce and train a special branch. Senior officials from MI5, including the director, had visited Cyprus to help. The need was particularly great because there had been no confirmatory evidence from the island of intelligence reports from Greece.[94]

The news of the seizure and the arrest of people connected with the leading right-wing organization, together with its one-time general secretary, Socrates Loizides, came as a shock to many people in the colony. The archbishop was placed in an embarrassing position to explain the incident away and in fact made no attempt to do so. Grivas had a narrow escape because he had originally intended to be on the beach personally to supervise operations when the caïque arrived, and the seizure and arrests — which he described as 'a staggering blow' — forced him to delay his sabotage plans. The Greek Cypriot press suggested that the explosives had been landed for the perfectly innocent purpose of dynamite fishing. Armitage asserted that 'no Cypriot would ever believe that such a quantity of dynamite could be intended for fishing purposes but in the absence of a better explanation it was made to sound [as convincing as possible] both in Cyprus and in Greece.'[95]

Armitage was particularly pleased with the hard and successful work done by Robins who had worked very long hours since his arrival on 27 November.[96] He had had to face riots and demonstrations, reorganize police riot procedures, discreetly carry out riot training, establish radio communications, develop the special branch, establish a corps of special constables, 'assemble fat dossiers' on the bishops, businessmen and members of the ethnarch council who travelled frequently between Cyprus and Greece, begin to intercept phone calls, orders and letters from Eoka, and organize operations leading to seizing the caïque: 'he has really done remarkably well'.

The monthly political situation reports from Cyprus had, until Robins arrived, a somewhat parochial, carefree, light-hearted, almost jovial tone about them, a tone which from time to time implied that whatever was going wrong politically was not within the government's power — or even responsibility — to alter. Armitage, and the Colonial Office must have found the early reports less helpful than they could have been. Robins was gradually building up his intelligence system, despite having been told at the Colonial Office that 'nothing will ever happen without you getting to know about it because the Greek Cypriots can't keep their mouths shut.' Nothing, Robins was to discover, was further from the truth. 'Their ability to keep a secret was absolutely fantastic and this was true even before they became frightened by Eoka.'

The British policy, implemented by Wright for five years, of keeping Cyprus quiet had led to 'grave gaps in the machinery of efficient government', especially in the police, and 'an air of *laissez-faire* about the security situation which ... had seriously affected police morale'. As Robins remarked, it had become 'a very happy-go-lucky place'. Another officer remembered Robins's predecessor as a 'happy-go-lucky fellow' and he 'had the reputation of being very much a peacetime police chief in a sleepy Mediterranean island and quite happy to carry on as if nothing would ever happen'. Grivas commented that the police 'were of low standard, thanks to poor pay and conditions; they were unarmed, short of transport, without radio, while many village police stations did not even have a telephone'.

Soon after his arrival, Robins had been asked by the governor to draw up an operations order, which he code-named 'Operation Pursenet', and had an RAF flight of Meteors and a naval frigate, HMS *Charity*, placed at his disposal. Working closely with MI5 and MI6, Robins learned of the *Aghios Georghios* voyage.

> We flew under the operation order dawn and dusk Meteor patrols to pick up the caïque and see where it was, and *Charity* was on duty beyond the horizon ready for whatever task it was asked to do ... we got a report from the Meteor patrols that a caïque answering to *Aghios Georghios* looked as though it was on its way. So *Charity* was put on the alert but nothing happened that night.... Another frigate [*Comet*] came on duty and that next night we got information that the caïque was approaching. She was shadowed by the frigate and by this time we'd set up a very Heath Robinson communications system because of the lack of communications. We had a set down in my headquarters in Nicosia. I had to put an officer ... on top of Olympus. He received on one frequency, transmitted down to Paphos on another frequency – so there was a time delay – and at an appropriate time I said 'Right. Tell the police party to go.' ... The police party left and captured the whole of the reception committee, all the arms and explosives but the caïque got away with the captain on board and was immediately arrested by the frigate.[97]

It appears from Armitage's instructions to Robins, from the deployment of the Meteors and the naval frigate and from the involvement of MI5 and MI6, that the governor was very well aware of the fast increasing unlawful activity and threats to peaceful government, but it is possible the awareness was confined to the threat of smuggling of arms, ammunition and personnel and did not yet extend to a full realization of the future violence the smuggling portended. What is certain is that he did not know of the existence of Eoka until February 1955:

> Investigations into the arms smuggling ... have brought to light evidence of a highly dangerous criminal organization both in this country and in Greece whose existence had hitherto not been suspected and whose leaders are apparently prepared to resort to desperate and violent measures to further the enosis cause. Such a spirit of recklessness is more characteristic of Greek than Cypriot.[98]

A note in Armitage's personal diary summarizing the month of February 1955 simply says 'Frustration'. Part of this frustration stemmed from Makarios's persistent uncompromising stance in his public utterances 'and so it makes it more and more difficult for those who want to follow a moderate line to produce their support'. This was a possibility he had foreseen and had tried to foretell in his broadcast in July the previous year.[99]

During a visit to the Middle East in February 1955, Sir Kenneth Grubb, chairman of the World Council of Churches' commission on international affairs, held a number of interviews, the records of which indicate the stance being taken by several important participants in Cyprus affairs with whom Armitage had to deal.[100] The council had paid for Makarios to study in Boston, USA, from 1946 to 1948.

In Greece, the King deplored the passion roused over the Cyprus question and emphasized that the Church and the nation were historically so closely identified that it was not possible to separate their interests. He was 'clearly well informed' and valued personal contacts in the pursuit of reconciliatory policies in international questions. Former Prime Minister Georgios Papandreou was worried about the danger of Cyprus dividing the British and Greek people. The issue would not remain 'merely an affair of the politicians punctuated by occasional student riots', but would involve the people of both countries, Britain and Greece.

The US ambassador gave Grubb 'a clear account' of US policy on Cyprus. The USA was disinclined to overpublicize the issue. It wished either to abstain from voting, to vote for a compromise at the UN, or for deferring or face-saving measures. It emphasized the importance of Britain declaring 'the undisputed right of self-determination'. It was convinced conceding self-determination would somewhat satisfy psychological demands and that the timing and methods of self-determination 'could be the subject of prolonged talk'. It stressed the importance of harmony of interests between the USA, Britain and Greece within NATO, 'which was a main element in holding the Turks to Europe'.

The archbishop of Athens — 'this tough old warrior' — firmly believed that union was not merely political but essentially moral; he trusted the issue would not divide the Church of England and the Greek Church. The royal chaplain stressed the danger of communism gaining ground unless reasonable ambitions were satisfied.

The prime minister — 'a cultured and somewhat austere man' — spoke of the dangers to Anglo-Greek friendship in the enosis question not being resolved, which he attributed to Britain's intransigence forcing him to overcome his reluctance to take the matter to the UN. All political parties in Greece were united on this issue. The solution was an immediate liberal constitution for Cyprus followed 'in a few years' time' by a plebiscite. The prime minister defended Makarios's activities. The question of Cyprus being a base was not an issue because 'not only Cyprus but all Greece and the islands were open to the UK or USA for the establishment of bases'.

The British ambassador, Peake, commended the US attitudes and drew attention to the strength of Turkish feeling, the willingness of apparently strongly pro-enosis Greeks to accept favours from the British, the 'somewhat worldly' attitudes and conduct of Makarios, and many Cypriot ecclesiastics' suspicions of those in Athens. Peake believed some experience of self-government in Cyprus without formal connection with Greece might lead to 'an extensive revision of opinions' — a view that Armitage shared.

Grubb also had a number of interviews in Cyprus itself. First, he spoke to Armitage, who believed that the very widespread desire in Cyprus was not for enosis but for self-determination, but not under conditions that would mean the island falling forthwith into the arms of Greece. This desire came partly from a feeling that Greek politicians were insincere and simply wanted Cyprus so that Greeks needing jobs could occupy public offices and the relative wealth of Cyprus could boost the relative poverty of Greece. The feeling that the majority — but not all — in Cyprus were essentially Greek by history and tradition did not mean they desired more than a cultural association with Greece, whose expansion had not improved conditions in the islands. The Communist Party in Cyprus could probably get 40 per cent support in a vote. It held many influential offices and one could not be sure if the Greek government was sufficiently in control to ensure safety from communism. 'It was notorious that the Church was completely neglecting the people and concentrating on politics.' He concluded:

> Politically [progress] towards self-determination must be maintained by HMG and successive constitutional steps taken to fulfil it, until the Cypriots [are] in a position to judge their future for themselves. At

present both HMG and the Ethnarchy [are] completely inflexible, and in such conditions no progress [can] be made. If some gesture could be given it would probably be found that the Greeks themselves were not so intransigent as they might seem. The Greeks [are] not too pleased with the results of their adventures at the UN, and the general effect of this international showdown has been to make the situation more rigid. It [is] probable that the Greeks [are] looking for some means to climb down without losing face.

Later, the governor told Grubb that he feared that with Cyprus, as so often, the Colonial Office would do too little too late. In reply to Grubb's suggestion, he said it would be a mistake to invite Makarios to London unless Britain and Greece had reached an agreement and it was hoped to press it on him. Even so, one could not be sure the archbishop would fall in with any such agreement because 'he had interests of his own quite distinct from his beloved enosis.'

Immediately after speaking with Armitage, Grubb had an interview with Makarios who said the Communist Party's influence over votes was much exaggerated and that it was precisely the refusal to concede self-determination that provided fuel for the communists. The strategic aspects had been much exaggerated and if enosis were granted Britain could readily negotiate satisfactory arrangements. The whole connection of Cyprus, historically, was with the Greek world. The Turks were a minority and their presence must not be overstated. There was no reason to suppose they would not secure effective constitutional guarantees: having achieved freedom, the Church would not deny it to others.

Finally, Grubb interviewed Fletcher-Cooke who had concluded that enosis was in the blood of the Cypriots and one way or other they would have it. They had been talking about it for too long ever to give up the demand. He spoke of the difficulty of getting the Colonial Office to see things in a more flexible way, and he gave a number of 'vivid illustrations' of the Church's neglect of its pastoral mission.

Right at the end of his visit, Grubb met the governor again and generally reviewed the impressions he had gained. In his view, the British government should recognize the right of self-determination, as did the World Council, which the Greek Orthodox Church had now pressed into supporting enosis. He suggested talks between the British, Greek and Turkish governments and supported a constitutional approach to political development. Armitage found Grubb's communiqué at the end of his visit 'verbose' and unlikely to please anyone. Many years later Cardiff recalled that, like many visitors at the time, Grubb had already made up his mind about the situation before arriving in Cyprus and was reluctant to modify it: 'He had a strong anti-colonial bias.'[101] Even so, his interviews give a good picture of the views of a number of major individuals in the politics of Cyprus with which the governor had to contend. Armitage and Fletcher-Cooke spoke frankly about the need to concede the principle of self-determination, a view they knew to be contrary to British government policy.

At the beginning of March Armitage wrote to Lennox-Boyd. He reiterated his firmly held view of the importance of Britain conceding self-determination and commented on a draft policy statement the Colonial Office had prepared because the July 1954 proposals were making no progress.[102]

> I must reaffirm that the prospects of introducing a constitution here are dependent on [a] statement conceding ultimate self-determination however phrased [and] such statement being acquiesced in by the Greek Government.... Draft statement must disarm the Greek Government in order that it informs the Archbishop to accept HMG's proposals, curbs Athens radio and ... declares that it will not have further recourse to the United Nations.... If HMG is prepared to [concede] internal self-government and an ultimate change of status, then let the statement freely and generously concede it. If HMG is prepared to go thus far then remember the slogan of too little and too late. Draft statement should be turned round to emphasize the 'new look' policy and refer in passing only to constitutional proposals.

Then, in an innovative shift in thinking, he wondered whether they were focusing too much on introducing a constitution. The idea had entered his mind that they had become 'completely bogged down by stressing a constitution':

> What about announcing that in view of the prime minister's statement about the hydrogen bomb it is clear that for five years the strategic situation will be fluid and during the following five years some clarification will be achieved. At the end of ten years therefore HMG will consult with the Greek Government as to the future of Cyprus. In the meanwhile there will be no further move towards a constitution for Cyprus.

He felt this would be popular and warmly accepted in Greece, would please Greek Cypriots – except those wanting immediate enosis and those genuinely wanting a constitution – and would compel those who wanted one to ask for it. The idea of a constitution at present was rejected by everyone. He conceded that this proposal might in fact lead to enosis in ten years.

The secretary of state read Armitage's letter 'with much interest' and asked him to fly to London to discuss it further, almost immediately because Eden, the foreign secretary, was soon leaving for Turkey.[103] As Armitage remarked, 'There are now so many complications in the Cyprus problem, one cannot deal with affairs here freely.'[104] In telling his parents about this visit he said:

> I have had the most intense talks at the Colonial Office. Today we started with the Secretary of State... Nutting of the Foreign Office and Hopkinson... and rows of officials. There was general agreement for the first part and then I reacted badly to Foreign Office proposals and so we went on! However, basically the talks have gone as I expected and would have wished. It is in the methods of approach that I differ from the Foreign Office and I am impertinent to do it I suppose as they should be all-knowing. We will see.[105]

The Foreign Office proposed that Britain should consult only Turkey about the policy statement and not Greece, except perhaps 12 hours before to say that they 'had a formula referring to a chance of ultimately considering a change of status'. Armitage must have been pleased that the principle of self-determination might be becoming acceptable, but he 'argued furiously' with Nutting against consulting only Turkey. He was aware he was putting himself at odds with the Foreign Office – whose current and next secretaries of state were to become prime minister – but he stood his ground. His 'We will see' suggests he thought his own view might ultimately prevail, as indeed his view on self-determination was showing some signs of gaining ground. In Cyprus itself, the general opinion of the press was that Britain was going to make a statement conceding the right of self-determination in general, vague terms with no specific time attached and probably with new constitutional proposals. Armitage pressed the British government to publish its proposals before parliament rose on 7 April and the Colonial Office hoped they could be published during the Cyprus schools' Easter holidays so as to minimize trouble from schoolchildren.[106]

At his meeting with Lennox-Boyd on 14 March, Armitage reported considerable uncertainty in Cyprus. The archbishop and other ethnarchy leaders were outwardly intractably in favour of self-determination. However, Makarios had privately put forward a proposal to the ethnarchy for a constitution, on condition there was a guarantee of self-determination after a limited number of years. This had been opposed by extreme enosists and Athens radio was maintaining its propaganda against a constitution. It was impossible to make a move on the constitution until the Greek government had been persuaded by a statement to remove its backing from the archbishop. If a constitution were introduced without a statement and elections were held, the communists and Turks – but not the Greek nationalists – might take part and the communist members might move resolutions on enosis.[107]

Armitage worked with Lennox-Boyd on a revised statement. It was a difficult piece of drafting. They needed to reassure the Turks and the Foreign Office that self-determination was neither imminent nor guaranteed, and the Greeks that it was a possibility. They needed to satisfy international opinion that Britain genuinely wished to advance Cyprus to internal self-government. They needed to reassure the government's supporters and military allies that the island would, for the foreseeable future, remain in Britain's strategic control. They also needed to get the Cypriots to accept a constitution involving elections. These conflicting requirements obliged them to couch their draft in cautious phraseology and to hedge the whole with qualifying and unspecific words.

> HMG have given further consideration to their plans for political advance in Cyprus and have decided that the new legislature shall from the first have a majority of elected members.... This will be a first stage in the closer association of the people of Cyprus with the administration of the island and it will, if successful, be followed by further advances in the same direction leading finally to full internal self-government subject, of course, to satisfactory safeguards for minorities. For strategic and political reasons HMG cannot at present foresee when a change in the status of Cyprus could be contemplated. They would, however, be glad to consult with elected representatives of the people on that question as soon as the system of full self-government has proved to be working successfully and provided that the international situation then permits.[108]

His time in London was very rushed and he anticipated 'many tense moments and anxious problems to solve' on his return to Cyprus. Less than two weeks later and following 'nothing but interviews all week talking politics',[109] sabotage on a wide scale took place in the early morning of 1 April on the orders of Grivas with Makarios's agreement. Bombs exploded at strategic points in all the main towns. The Cyprus broadcasting station, the secretariat and the barracks were wrecked at Nicosia, as were the courthouse, commissioner's office and police station at Larnaca, a generator at Famagusta, and the power plant and two police stations at Limasol. In the broadcasting station the 'charges were well placed in the hall and the transmitters were blown all over the place' by a four-man group led by Markos Drakos. Paraffin was poured over the studios so that areas not wrecked by the explosions were burned out.[110]

Harold Macmillan, then minister of defence, saw the attacks as 'very bad news': 'In spite of the confidence of the governor and the Colonial Office that there would be no trouble, there have been serious bomb outrages including the destruction of the new wireless station (which has cost HMG an immense sum).'[111] Armitage too was particularly upset by the damage to the broadcasting station which he had hoped to use for propaganda.[112]

The government had no warning that the attacks were to take place or indeed were likely. Some senior officers initially thought the reports that they had taken place were an April Fools' Day joke. In the days that followed these initial outrages there were numerous further grenade and small bomb attacks – designed by Grivas 'to make it plain that [they] were fighting a deliberate and systematic war' – one of which took place just after Armitage had left the hotel where he had been dining.[113]

Armitage reported the government's lack of knowledge and preparedness to London: 'Owing to lack of information regarding originators of these acts it is debatable whether they are independent or connected with ethnarchy nationalists ... or some other organization. ... No special steps had been taken to post armed guards at buildings attacked as there was no indication that sabotage would be attempted.'[114] He just did not think the Cypriots would resort to violence. This was surprising because he should have heeded the warning inherent in the caïque landing of arms and explosives. Robins had already much improved the intelligence-gathering system and he had known for several weeks of the existence of 'a highly dangerous criminal organization' prepared to resort to 'desperate and violent measures' to further the enosis cause.

He must have assumed the caïque incident was an isolated attempt to land explosives, arms and ammunition, and it is unclear how much the incident impressed itself on his mind as a portent of trouble ahead. Clark had already warned him that enosis now had 'a dangerous edge'. Others later believed that the relative ease with which the caïque plot was discovered and those immediately involved brought to trial 'may well have induced a sense of false security in British official circles'.[115] It is possible that the success of the capture and Robins's improvements blinded him and his advisers to the possibility that it was not isolated and that other, undetected, landings might have been made.

It was also surprising, as Cardiff later emphasized, when 'Athens radio had programmes inciting the Cypriots to violence beamed at the island twenty-four hours a day. The Greeks put the Cypriots on their metal to show that they had the guts to throw out the British as they had themselves thrown out the Turks.'[116] The district commissioners – who chaired district security committee meetings of which army commanders and police officers were members – kept him informed daily of security, intelligence and other political developments. 'There was no doubt,' in the view of one of the commissioners, 'that Sir Robert was well aware of the current developments all over the island.'[117] It appears, however, that on 1 April 1955 he was insufficiently aware and that Macmillan believed 'the intelligence and security system was certainly inadequate'.[118]

Shortly after this outbreak of violence, heads of departments were addressed by a senior special branch officer who did his best to impress upon them that it was no passing crisis. He dwelt especially on the oath Eoka members were required to take, which was bound 'to have a compelling hold over the youth in a country where religion and family ties mean so much'.[119]

A month after the violence broke out, Armitage privately summed up the results:

There is an undercurrent of satisfaction at the violence, no real condemnation of it in private circles, a general holding back from contact with the British and an anti-British feeling in a lot of places. The children are getting very impudent with shouts of union and enosis and naturally everyone says the Government has no control, this especially said by civil servants.... The stock of [Makarios] seems to be high.... Everyone seems to think he knows of terrorist acts.[120]

There was a lull in the violence during the latter part of April – on Makarios's instructions – as Grivas 'regrouped [his] forces for heavier attack' and as security was stepped up. The governor had an escort wherever he went, and night patrols and road checks by the army, police and special constables made it difficult for the terrorists to plan easily and to move explosives without very careful precautions. The official view on the bombings was one of contempt. Armitage hoped morale would recover, but doubted whether the terrorists would allow the tension to slacken. In the meantime, Grivas was pleased his success 'had electrified the island, and young men pressed forward to join Eoka's ranks'; he concentrated on mobilizing young people to distribute leaflets, watch agents and police and take part in mass demonstrations. Armitage was not much helped by the public statement of Dr Fazil Kütchük, the Turkish Cypriot leader, that the Cyprus government did nothing to maintain law and order, although he was comforted when Soublis Kanaan, a Turkish member of executive council, said the Turkish community generally disapproved of the statement.[121]

The caïque trial opened on 3 May, but suddenly ended when the accused pleaded guilty to one of the charges.[122] The likelihood of guilty pleas grew as the evidence accumulated, and they were secured as part of a deal to which Armitage must have agreed. This was that two men who had been caught, but not on the beach, would be discharged and two professional sailors on the caïque would get light sentences. Loizides was sentenced to 12 years' imprisonment, and others to between four and six years.

The evidence during the trial included the recovery by frogmen of the rifles and ammunition thrown overboard from the caïque. These had Greek army insignia on them and were embarrassing proof of Greek government involvement. One reason for the deal, apart from the Greek Cypriot officials' wish for leniency, was the desire of Eoka and their Greek Cypriot sympathizers to prevent evidence harmful to Eoka emerging. The deal not to press the case and to accept lesser pleas, was made in the hope that Britain would be 'buying' the sympathy of Greece to abandon its complicity in underground activities in Cyprus. The Greek Cypriots were pleased with the discharges, light sentences and suppression of damaging evidence, and the Turkish Cypriots and British, while disappointed on these scores, were none the less pleased with the capture and convictions. Few people were surprised at the outcome of the trial. There was a feeling, shared by Tornaritis, that maybe they would now 'remain in a stage of pamphlet war only'. This mistaken view reinforces the probability that the governor was not as fully alive as he should have been to the possibility that the caïque landing was not an isolated incident.

Armitage was concerned about 'the unfortunate position taken up by each side ... from which it was getting more and more difficult to retreat'. He realized the importance of withdrawing from the totality of Hopkinson's 'never', and when Britain was prepared to discuss self-government he added privately: 'If only they could have gone further and said there would be a time when we would talk about the future status of the island.'[123] He remained convinced that without conceding self-determination at some, if necessary unspecified, time in the future, it would be impossible to secure Greek and Greek Cypriot support for the working of even an interim constitution.

He feared the British government would do nothing positive before the forthcoming general election and there was a feeling that the lull in violence would continue 'until the election is over, as if Labour gets in there will be no need for more violence'. The Labour Party said it would have a plebiscite in Cyprus, and this would almost inevitably lead to enosis. In the meantime, Armitage would 'just have to sit and hope for the best after the election', and he confessed, 'we have no firm policy to pursue except that of preserving law and order.'[124]

When Greece complained to the UN about affairs in Cyprus, Armitage was privately critical of Britain's delay in moving forward with policy: 'They are going to put themselves in the position of having to talk to the Greek Government at a stage when their demands are going to be pitched far higher than they need have been three months ago.'[125] He felt that 'doors [were] being firmer slammed than ever and while the election progresses, no policy can be announced by HMG'.[126]

Despite the lull and in the absence of being able to take any constitutional steps forward, because he anticipated further trouble, he continued to concentrate on preserving law and order and keeping security high. He engaged a company to advise him on internal security and they were much occupied with precautions against further landings of arms and personnel from the sea. A land radar system would have been too expensive, but they planned to have radar equipment on motor launches. He realized that the judges, especially Greek Cypriot judges, were in a difficult position 'as popular feeling among the Greeks is largely on the side of the accused'. He was privately critical of one judge who imposed very low fines for demonstrations on the grounds that he had to take into account local sentiment.[127]

He was pleased the Conservatives were returned with a reasonable majority at the general election towards the end of May – though he doubted a good turnout on Derby Day! – since they would now 'be able to plan for the future'. 'The first problem they will have to tackle will be Cyprus.'[128]

He was also concerned about the Cyprus broadcasting service. He considered that several of its staff were 'no good' or 'unsuitable in more ways than one', despite the appointment of a new director after the former head suffered a breakdown and resigned. 'So for many months there was no efficient direction of these ... services, when the approach to the Greek Cypriots had to be to their minds and not just as exercised by the police against their bodies.' To get support for the government's anti-enosis efforts, he took steps to improve its information and publicity services. 'I am now all for publicity. It looks as if the enosis campaign will be won by the word, spoken and written, and the Special Branch.' Even so, some British journalists felt 'there was no close contact with the Press at that time', and that he was 'painfully shy of the press'. Cardiff's view was that 'Armitage did not handle the press well. He was not overanxious to meet them and was not impressive when interviewed.'[129]

Armitage continued to seek views from all shades of opinion and, naturally, these frequently conflicted.[130] Durrell's assistant, Achilles Papadopoulos, believed that one could not reason with the people and that hard-line action similar to that taken in 1931 should be taken. This would have ruled out any constitutional advance and have incurred even greater problems with Greece. On the other hand, to M. N. Munir, the solicitor-general, the circumstances of 1931 were very different and the remedies could not be the same. Dr George Spanopoulos – who had a close relationship with the security liaison office – advocated tough methods: deport Makarios and others, suppress the press, 'give castor oil' and 'spend more money to get one's way'. Armitage, however, believed him to be a moral coward and one who 'would be the first to raise the Greek flag on enosis'.

Sir Panayiotis Cacoyiannis, a leading lawyer and a member of executive council until 1946 – a pro-British, wise and trusted adviser to a succession of governors – believed a recent speech by Makarios was concerted with the Greek government. He ascribed its militancy to the advice given by Richard Crossman, a visiting Labour parliamentarian, that violence should be used. Crossman had also told the archbishop that Armitage believed that the Cypriots would not use violence. He felt that since Makarios could do nothing without Greek government support, Britain should make an agreement with the Greek government and then a liberal constitution would be able to get going.

Paul Pavlides was also of the firm opinion that British policy had to be agreed with the Greek government. He suggested five years for a limited constitution, followed by five years of self-government and then a plebiscite to decide the future. Underestimating the effects of the growing intimidation to which officials were being subjected, he believed sufficient government officers and *muktar*s would vote against enosis to form nearly 50 per cent of the voters. It was vital to get the civil service 'back on our side'. Others who had seen Makarios said there was little point in anyone from the British government meeting Makarios. Rather, progress should be made through the Greek government, which could influence the archbishop and help him to restrain his more extreme nationalists.

Araouzo, who had seen both Lennox-Boyd and Makarios, told Armitage that the archbishop would be pleased to see the secretary of state on neutral ground when he visited the island in five to six weeks' time. Provided the principle of self-determination was conceded, the British would find him 'much more prepared to concede things than we expected'. When Araouzo saw Makarios the following day, the archbishop said the Greek government would accept any agreement he himself made, and he would make an announcement against violence once the secretary of state came to Cyprus and conceded self-determination.

Armitage also received interesting views from Durrell, who believed the police had neither the resources nor the penetration to keep control. He suggested a liberal constitution with an overall Greek majority, which would 'put the Ethnarchy in a dilemma', and in which the communists would come in and probably get a majority.[131] If they then took action the government disliked, a nominated majority could be appointed. The ethnarchy would be bound to come in at some stage because 'people like Dervis want power not enosis' and the communists would fragment, since many, in Durrell's view, were only different degrees of liberals. 'Psychologically, then, the whole Ethnarchy case is based on refusal of a constitution because they recognize that means the end of enosis. Once you get a constitution the power of Ethnarchy and [Makarios] is shattered, that driving force is removed from the nationalists, and personal power will become the driving force.'

The 'great point' behind these views was to divide the Greek government and Makarios and then possibly Greece would withdraw support for enosis if Britain agreed that Cyprus could decide its own future in 20 years' time. In the meantime, Cyprus would have a constitution and spend more time on local affairs than on debating enosis. Without a liberal constitution and the Greek government retracting, they neither avoided an approach to the UN nor got support in Cyprus itself.

Armitage recorded Durrell's views at some length in his private diary; he seemed to think they had some validity. In essence, they involved conceding self-determination, hoping it would not lead to enosis, at least not for a long time, and getting the Greek government to accept a constitution in Cyprus. In the meantime, this might deprive Makarios of Greek government support and give leadership primarily to the communists rather than the ethnarchy. In any event, it was hoped that whoever the self-government leaders were, they might become so enamoured of exercising power as not to surrender it to Greece.

Life was made more difficult by the Greek government, which Armitage described as 'pretty impudent' – engineering or exploiting an embarrassing and provocative situation. On 19 May, given 30 minutes' notice that five Greek air force planes from Korea were due to land in Cyprus and wanted to stay the night, Armitage decided they could stay for refuelling only. This was interpreted as an insult by the Greek consul who said he wanted to entertain them to a meal in town. The governor, fearing unruly demonstrations, refused this request also. He was then told that the Greek airmen were suffering from flight fatigue and was cornered into letting them stay the night. However, he insisted on them being kept in RAF control, commenting that 'international relationships will presumably be further jarred.' They left the following morning, but the Greek government protested to the UN about the

Cyprus government's behaviour. As Armitage remarked, 'We do not get many periods when we are not kept on our toes!'[132]

Armitage was indeed kept on his toes, and his worries were much increased from 24 May, Empire Day, which he described as a 'restless day'.[133] It started with 700 schoolchildren, mostly girls, demonstrating, shouting slogans and throwing stones in Nicosia 'with such determination', Grivas recorded, 'that the police bolted before them, pursued by a hail of stones, and the army had to be called out'. Later, 500 schoolboys stoned Government House. The police did not disperse them and the governor remarked that this must start soon and he considered using dye to stain clothes and identify culprits. It ended with Armitage taking a party to the film *Forbidden Cargo* – an inauspicious title – at the cinema in aid of the British Legion.

There were very few Greeks in the audience 'as they are not keen to be associated with such things at present', but seconds before the governor's party arrived, a municipal worker planted a time bomb under a seat on the balcony, where the Armitages were to sit. The bomb had been made by Markos Drakos – a 22-year-old clerk of a mining company and, in Grivas's view, 'one of Eoka's greatest heroes'. The time pencil burned slowly for two hours only a few feet from Armitage. Since, however, there was no interval and no bar, the governor with his party were able to leave a little earlier than normally. Just after they left, the bomb exploded, blew out seven rows of seats and wrecked the gallery. Many other cinema-goers were still in the foyer or on the pavement outside when the bomb exploded.

Until this time, it seems as if Armitage had believed that the capture of the caïque and his concentration on suppressing the smuggling of arms and ammunition had meant that the Cypriots would not turn to violence: these beliefs dimmed his perception of the possibility of sabotage. Now he realized that explosives and men with the knowledge of how to use them existed on the island. The commissioner of police coolly announced – with no great degree of perspicacity – that it looked very much as if the explosion 'had been calculated to take place in the presence of His Excellency'. Others phlegmatically thought that an attempt on the governor's life 'seemed to be going rather far'. An army spokesman 'thought we were among friends. What a pity.'[134] In a letter written only four days earlier agreeing to provide a message for the jubilee anniversary of All Saints' Church, Ealing, built as a memorial to the assassinated Spencer Perceval, Armitage said 'events here have been disturbing and time-consuming, in fact somewhat too reminiscent for my liking of the fate that overtook my great-great-grandfather.'[135]

He was particularly worried about schoolchildren being used for political purposes: they were 'being suborned by masters to be nationalist and by Eoka to be seditious and saboteurs'. Grivas recalled that after 24 May 'nothing could hold the schools back.' Armitage commented on the support students gave the bombings and felt that, while a lot of this was 'patriotic fervour kept at a high pitch by teachers and parents', the greater part was the result of intimidation. 'The spirit of intimidation is so much about that I feel none of these people will have the moral courage to make a stand.' Grivas warned Cypriots against interfering in his activities with schoolchildren and his 'threat was carried out in the case of some incorrigible teachers'. Armitage tried expelling the worst offenders and closing down the worst schools, but this failed because the boys were either loose on the streets or taken on elsewhere.[136]

Some of Armitage's senior officials were beginning to feel the strain of events and he worried about the effects of this on their performance.[137] Fletcher-Cooke, who had been unwell for some time, went on leave 'undoubtedly tired and perhaps [he had] not given all the consideration he should have to some of our problems'. Armitage noted that Tornaritis 'does not really get to the points and seems on many occasions too overworked [and is] too impetuous perhaps'. Robins noted that 'the Attorney-General showed a great deal of strain ... he was very nervous.' General Keightley remarked that he found J. W. Sykes, deputy colonial secretary, 'so slow and frustrating', to which Armitage responded, 'it may well be that he is the symbol of a creaking government machine which we would like to activate but which he finds very difficult.'

The director of the Cyprus broadcasting service had had a breakdown and been replaced. The governor's aide-de-camp was depressed and took time off. Durrell was 'most depressed'. The police were unsettled and resigning in worrying numbers. The secretary of state's police adviser, considering them 'underpaid and overworked', warned there would be trouble if they got nothing for the extra hours they were now working. Armitage himself stood up to the strain very well and his wife told his parents that 'he takes it all so calmly and says he could go on forever on the enosis question.' Their social engagements fell off a great deal and they felt confined by the floodlights, barbed wire, guards and other precautions at Government House.

The strain on the police force was particularly worrying. The force comprised 60 per cent Greek Cypriots and 40 per cent Turkish Cypriots. In the past they had worked harmoniously together, but now Grivas distributed large numbers of notices advocating 'Death to Police', and Eoka began to 'go hard for all the Greek Cypriot Police'.[138] The threats gravely affected morale and loyalty:

> Murders in the street, in broad daylight, were the most terrifying new aspect of the situation. The police were the killers' chief target ... the Police Commissioner, was soon at his wits' end to stop Greek resignation from the Force. ... Robins revealed no secret when he said that things were virtually out of control. ... Years of stagnation had sapped the spirit of his men long ago. ... The bravest and most stubborn went down first and all that Robins could do for them was to walk behind their coffins, listening to the wail of the widow and the orphan. 'If my men can't rely on the public,' he said, 'I can't rely on them.'[139]

The governor was also having trouble with the civil service association over the vigilance squads he wanted to introduce. The proposal had not been discussed with the joint consultative council and the attorney-general advised that the measure could be justified only in an emergency, 'which we can't say we have actually at present'. Armitage doubted whether Lennox-Boyd would back him if he forced the issue. He consequently decided to drop the proposal and have 'proper paid watchmen'. A very high proportion of the civil service was Greek Cypriot and fearful of the threats Eoka was making about 'collaborators' and of 'anonymous telephone calls ... warning them what would happen to them soon'. The governor's confidence in their commitment and loyalty was not high and he found 'the Civil Service very unsettled; they do not know whether enosis is near or not'.[140]

Traditionally, and until violence erupted early in 1955, relations between Greek Cypriot and Turkish Cypriot civil servants were good, especially on an individual basis. They became strained, however, when Greek Cypriot officials started being intimidated by Eoka and when they actually became Eoka members. The situation was aggravated when Turkish Cypriot officials also were subjected to Eoka violence, as well as the Greek Cypriots and the British. In defence, the Turkish Cypriots established resistance movements and attack brought retaliation and a further deterioration of relationships. The deterioration was noticeably more acute in departments that were intimately concerned with security, such as the police, the administration and the attorney-general's office. In these 'front line' departments, 'the Greek Cypriot members were terrorized into virtual inaction and the Turkish Cypriot civil servants had to manage as best they could.'[141]

A widespread series of bomb, incendiary and grenade attacks — forecast for some time by Armitage's intelligence sources — took place on 19, 20 and 21 June. Directed mainly against army personnel and their houses and against police stations, they formed part of Grivas's 'second full-scale attack' designed to terrorize the police and cripple the administration throughout the island. This time Eoka used 'powerful and deadly bombs filled with shrapnel placed so as to cause maximum damage'. Two policemen were killed and many others wounded. The main door of the police headquarters in Nicosia was blown in, killing a Greek passer-by and injuring a number of Turks. Another explosion smashed windows at the house of Sir John Sterndale-Bennett, political adviser to Middle East headquarters. During the trial of the men accused of the 1 April sabotage, a large crowd quickly turned into a riot, which was met with tear gas and baton charges from the police. The accused were convicted and given long terms of imprisonment. The judge said that in some countries they would have been shot.[142]

Although the commissioner of police advised against it on security grounds and others thought it 'a grave error of judgement', Armitage initially insisted on the usual seasonal move of the government from Nicosia to Troodos.[143] This was mainly to keep up morale and partly not to damage the tourist trade, but the Colonial Office was extremely worried about this intention. The secretary of state's police adviser urged strongly that the move should not take place. Besides the governor and his personal staff, it involved the colonial secretary, the attorney-general, the solicitor-general and the financial secretary. It would mean placing guards at Troodos as well as at the empty Government House in Nicosia, and would subject the commissioner of police and other officials to frequent five-hour round journeys to Troodos. There were additional risks, including the inadequacy of secure telephone facilities between Nicosia and Troodos. Cyprus was 'near emergency' and the police and army were being encouraged to treat their work as if such a situation actually existed. Sir Thomas Lloyd, the permanent secretary, was reluctant to interfere: 'If a man is worthy of the trust of managing the affairs of a difficult colony it should not be necessary to question his judgement on these personal issues.' He thought, however, that if Lennox-Boyd wished to intervene, it should be done by a personal letter and this he did:

> The matter is essentially one for your discretion but I should like to be assured that you are satisfied there is no undue risk in the separation of not only yourself but part of the central machinery of government ... with whom you would have to consult urgently in an emergency. If the need arose how quickly would it be possible to re-establish the essentials of central government in Nicosia?

The new attacks – much more serious than the 1 April bombings – and the views of the Colonial Office persuaded Armitage to change his mind over removing his office to Troodos for the hot season. Instead, he and his officials stayed in Nicosia. This was as well, because only two weeks later Grivas moved to the Troodos area to supervise terrorist training and the expansion of guerrilla units.

The governor was finding it extremely difficult to get clear guidance from executive council or from his other senior officials. This was an unfortunate change because, in the past, 'he could fully rely for advice on his executive council.' Now, 'you can ask a dozen people for their views on what should be done and you will get a dozen different replies.' When he asked council's opinion on whether the secretary of state should come to Cyprus, whether he himself should deal with Makarios, or whether the first approach should be through the Greek government, 'all they would agree was that an early announcement by Her Majesty's Government on some policy would be beneficial and break the tension.' He found a 'distinct split' between top officials who thought Makarios should be approached because he was currently showing willing and those who regarded the Greek government as more important: at least the latter could withdraw its case from the UN and its support of terrorists; it could stop the attacks by Athens radio and it could discourage Makarios from being too severe. Even in the judiciary no consistent view was forthcoming. When the chief justice discussed with his judges sentencing for illegal assemblies, he found one group were fearless, another said each case had to be judged on its merits and the third were 'virtually in favour of enosis'. They would not agree to the scales of sentences being adjusted. The governor, recognizing the serious deterioration in the security situation, commented privately: 'Emergency powers may have to be used and then we go on to the bitter end.'[144]

When the Conservatives were returned to power on 26 May 1955 (with a majority increased from 16 to 59) and Eden became prime minister, one of his first actions was to ask Macmillan (now foreign secretary) and Lennox-Boyd (still at the Colonial Office) to work out with him 'the most promising means of establishing Self-government' in Cyprus. It was urgent that a fresh political move should be taken to halt the deterioration in security. They proposed to have a new constitution with an elected majority in the legislative assembly. This would be led by a Cypriot chief minister, with full ministerial powers over everything except defence, foreign affairs and security, which would remain the governor's responsibility. Some seats in the legislature would be reserved for the Turkish minority. These proposals were based on Armitage's advice and agreed with him. What was not agreed with the governor, however, was how they were to be announced. This was because the British government now believed that, to secure Cypriot cooperation in implementing the constitution, there had to be some goodwill from both Greece and Turkey. The British were anxious, too, to secure the support of these governments because their continued collaboration was important to NATO, of which they were members.[145]

With these considerations in mind, Eden and Macmillan, with Lennox-Boyd's acquiescence but without consulting Armitage, broke a long-standing rule that Britain would not tolerate foreign interference in domestic issues in colonial territories.[146] They decided to invite representatives of Greece and Turkey to London to discuss 'the common interests of the three Governments in the political and defence problems of the Eastern Mediterranean as a whole' and to discuss Cyprus in this broader context. During a Commons debate on 5 May, the opposition had suggested – as had Grubb – a meeting of Britain, Greece and Turkey to try and reach a solution. Turkey was a strongly anti-communist state whose government now welcomed being involved in Cyprus, both as a diversion from its own deteriorating economy and as a lever to secure further financial support from the USA.

Turkey made its adamant position clear on 24 June when its government cabled the UN to say that if the British left Cyprus it would step in. This was because enosis with Greece would mean war in the Middle East and, ultimately, lead to the triumph of communism. This did not come as a surprise to Armitage because a year earlier he had been told by a Swedish journalist that when he was in Turkey it had been made clear to him that: 'If HMG pulled out [of Cyprus] Turks would come in; volunteers if the army would not do so. They reckoned a battalion would hold Cyprus.'

The British government, like Turkey, wanted to secure the support of other nations, especially the USA, in excluding UN intervention in Cyprus affairs. Consequently, it wished to demonstrate the sincerity of British policy by initiating tripartite talks and constitutional progress. Peake saw Macmillan in June and implored him not to hold the conference if he was going to consider the Turkish view only: and the archbishop sent Kranidiotis to Athens to try and persuade Papagos not to accept the invitation to the conference. Continuing disorder throughout June virtually forced the British cabinet to choose between a 'policy of repression and the offer of a conference'. As Nutting, minister of state in the Foreign Office, recalled:

> Macmillan called [the] conference ... because we had reached a situation where we had to get off the hook. Too many people in the world [had] the impression that here were the stuffy British simply trying to hang onto a colony which desperately wanted independence and here were we horrible imperialists who were denying the people their freedom.... This was not really the nub of the problem. True, we needed Cyprus for strategic reasons ... to back up our forward bases in the Middle East at

the time, but we were also holding the rein between the Greeks and the Turks, between Greece and Turkey and between the Greek Cypriots and the Turkish Cypriots, because we knew that if we just packed up and moved out we would bring on probably a blood bath in Cyprus and maybe a war between Greece and Turkey who were the two southern members of Nato and this would have been a disastrous situation for Nato and indeed for the whole western world. So we had to take some initiative and although Anthony Eden, when foreign secretary, had set his face rigidly against any ... international discussion of Cyprus, holding firmly to the view that it was a colonial matter and therefore not within the purview of any international conference or discussion, when Macmillan became foreign secretary ... he took a rather different attitude personally to the attitude that had been taken by Anthony. And he, goaded by me, needed a conference. I knew that a conference would not resolve the issue but at least it would give me some ammunition for the United Nations to keep the subject off the agenda. ... It was of crucial importance ... if we were able to get off the hook internationally we should expose just what the true nature of the Cyprus problem was for all three countries that were involved. So for those reasons and with that argument, Macmillan was able to persuade Eden, against his own nature, to allow a conference to be called, and by doing so to internationalize the Cyprus problem.

Armitage was extremely irritated when, after years of insistence that Cyprus was exclusively a British matter and after 'months of waiting and protesting and niggling', he was told on 29 June that the prime minister was to announce the following day that the Greek and Turkish governments would be invited to London to a conference on Middle East affairs including Cyprus: 'the one line of action [he had] been repeatedly told could never be approved'. 'So all the toils and moils of weeks and months are brought to an abrupt end in a manner which we have been repeatedly told could never be contemplated. What a difference if they had done this last year. No Eoka, no tension, no loss of friendliness.'[147] The Greek government also felt that if Britain had taken this initiative earlier 'many unfortunate occurrences would have been avoided in relations between [the two] countries.' Eden thought this Greek point was arrived at 'by a curious process of logic'.[148]

Armitage hoped the announcement would ease tension. However, he feared that the Greeks would be annoyed that the Turks were invited, for they 'could never understand that Turkey would express any views on the Cyprus question'.[149] He was also afraid because an intelligence report had revealed Eoka plans to kill a Greek Cypriot member of the special branch and other selected police officers. Indeed, he was aware that these officers had been shadowed for a long time and that their movements were known, adding 'So we have to act fast' to secure detention of persons legislation. He found this intelligence report 'rather grotesque on the same day as the announcement which should have eased all the tension'.

Colin Legum of the *Observer* told him that Eoka proposed to call off the current phase three of their campaign. This was because it had been successful in intimidating civil servants, warning 'traitors' and securing the support of the Greek Cypriots without rousing the Turkish Cypriots and popular opinion against the attacks. Phase four would be of greater intensity and be directed against very selected individuals, including, later intelligence reports confirmed, very senior army officers.

Lennox-Boyd made a 'flying visit' to Cyprus in advance of the London conference. He wished to discuss the meeting, a state of emergency, and strengthening security and intelligence arrangements – publicly referred to simply as 'internal administration'. This was the first visit of a Secretary of State for the Colonies since the British took over from the Turks in 1878. He arrived on 9 July amid strong security arrangements. Police radio vans and military police jeeps patrolled the road to the airport; the guard at Government House was increased and special squads of military and civil police guarded his aircraft. His visit was welcomed by both Turks and Greeks. The Turkish press said that the Turkish minority would be 'delighted' to tell Lennox-Boyd that they would never accept a constitution that gave Greek Cypriots a majority in a local legislature. The Greek Cypriot press said that the visit would be a 'precious opportunity for Cypriots to acquaint the secretary of state [with their] unshakable will to achieve self-determination'.

Almost immediately on arrival, he joined executive council in a meeting that 'endorsed all the proposals for a constitution which [executive council] had already agreed and sent to the Colonial Office'. Kanaan made the Turkish Cypriot position very clear: no enosis but a constitution safeguarding minorities and with adequate representation for the Turks in both executive council and legislative assembly. All members emphasized that there should be no resident ministers from Greece and Turkey. The only significant point of disagreement was whether they should impose a constitution if the Greek government did not accept the proposals. Pavlides and Tornaritis said to wait and Clerides and Kanaan said to go ahead. It seems that at this meeting of executive council 'a promise was given to the Greek members that left them with the impression [that] the British Government would recognize the Cypriots' right to self-determination at the three-power conference', and that Armitage promised 'he would make every possible effort for the recognition – even vague – of the Cyprus people's right to self-determination' during the visit to London.[150]

Late in the afternoon there was a two-hour meeting at the Ledra Palace Hotel with the archbishop – the first between the governor and the ethnarch since 1931 – arranged over the preceding 48 hours by a number of intermediaries.[151] It was significant that Makarios had agreed to this meeting – on neutral ground – without, as he had repeatedly insisted, Britain first conceding self-determination. It is possible he knew of the impression gained in executive council that the concession would be made at the London conference. Six people were present: Lennox-Boyd, Sir John Martin, Armitage, Makarios, Kranidiotis and Paschalis Paschalides, a secretary. The secretary of state found the archbishop 'entirely non-committal' but the governor recorded in his private diary:

> The significant point that I took was that if Self-determination was conceded in principle then that was a basis of discussion for a constitution.... The Secretary of State could not get any satisfactory explanation from [Makarios] for why they did not regard a constitutional approach to the problem as reasonable. He hedged as usual on why [there was] no condemnation of terrorism. He made it clear [that there was] no anti-British feeling.... I agreed with [Makarios] that this matter had to be settled by the Cypriots in Cyprus. [Makarios] made it clear that if the Greek Government made an arrangement with Her Majesty's Government which he does not accept, he will oppose it.[152]

When Makarios said 'Britain gives freedom everywhere, even to the Gold Coast' and Cyprus should not be treated 'less progressively', Lennox-Boyd replied:

> It may seem strange that an ancient civilization like yours might have something to learn from the Gold Coast. Is it not possible that this is so? They set up representative institutions which have enabled us to consult with the people of the Gold Coast about their own affairs. If Cyprus had done so, we should have had a body now properly representative of the people with whom we could discuss problems of the island.[153]

Makarios smiled at this and made no comment. Armitage, who thought it was 'a most useful meeting', told his parents that the archbishop was 'very smooth and affable': 'He is handsome and has poise and eyes that light up when he wants and he must be a competent rabble-rouser. If his speech does not betray him he is not a fanatic.'[154] On two major points Armitage agreed with the archbishop but differed from the

British government: the need to accept the principle of self-determination and the need for Cypriots, and not Greece or Turkey, to decide their future.

Makarios was not enamoured of the London conference initiative, and immediately after meeting Lennox-Boyd went to Athens to press the Greek government to force action through the UN, saying, 'the people of Cyprus will never accept any decisions of the London conference which do not accord with their rights and aspirations even if these decisions are endorsed by the Greek Government.' He also sent a message to Grivas: 'I congratulate you. Eoka has contributed infinitely more to the Cyprus struggle than 75 years of paper war.'[155] At a press conference a week later he said:

> [The] conference constitutes a trap and a means of delay with the purpose of undermining Greece's appeal to the United Nations, and of entangling the matter in complicated patterns, whence it will not be easy for it to be extricated. The Cyprus question does not constitute a political issue between Britain on the one hand and Greece and Turkey on the other. [It] is purely a question of self-determination and concerns the British Government and the Cypriot people only, and it can be extended so as to concern the Greek Government whenever the latter, in interpreting the feelings of the Greek and especially the Cypriot people, acts as the people's mandatary for the safeguarding of the island's right of self-determination.[156]

During Lennox-Boyd's second day in Cyprus, in the course of several meetings, he was given a good picture of the numerous factions and their greatly differing views with which Armitage regularly had to deal. 'Several Greeks told the Secretary of State they did not want to be administered by Greece.'[157] The meetings were interrupted by a time-bomb explosion in the Nicosia tax office half a mile away.[158] The day ended with Lennox-Boyd giving a press conference:

> Lennox-Boyd took off his coat to a job he understood. With flawless technique ... he held a straight bat to the trickier deliveries of foreign correspondents ... allowed one or two fast ones to go by, and smacked incautious balls from Cypriot journalists to the boundary. The Minister would not admit that the conference might lead to a change in sovereignty in Cyprus; but he could not be said to deny it. When someone asked him about Mr Hopkinson's 'never', he sharply advised the questioner to check his reference, implying that there had never been a 'never' after all.[159]

Armitage felt the meetings 'did not take the matter much further as he would not commit himself on any agreement over the future policy for Cyprus'. The secretary of state's own view of the visit was that, 'on balance it did good', although his private secretary 'gathered it was quite unproductive'. In a handwritten note at the foot of his letter thanking the governor 'for all that [he] did to make it all pass off so agreeably', Lennox-Boyd wrote, 'I and my colleagues value and trust so much your calm and efficient handling at this difficult time.'[160] There was some rowdiness at the airport on his departure. As he climbed into the plane, several hundred Cypriot Greeks in the spectators' enclosure shouted 'Enosis' and 'Down with the Constitution'.[161] The chief of the imperial general staff, Field Marshal Sir John Harding, who had been officially visiting Turkey, was in Cyprus at the same time as Lennox-Boyd. It was carefully explained that he was in the island on leave and there was no connection with the secretary of state's visit.[162]

To avoid declaring a state of emergency, which would be embarrassing so close to the London conference and which was less pressing during a period of relative calm following the announcement of the conference, but still to have the necessary legal powers to deal with violence and subversion, Armitage – prior to Lennox-Boyd's visit – secured the secretary of state's provisional approval to enact a detention of persons law. He realized he would be heavily criticized for it, but felt he must have the powers. He would have preferred power to declare a state of emergency, for he did not believe that Eoka would 'depart from their policy of assassination and bombs in offices, unless we can break them wide open'. On his return to Britain, Lennox-Boyd formally agreed to the detention of people suspected of being members of terrorist organizations. There were two purposes behind the enactment: first to control those 'high up in Eoka' – the decision makers – and second to pick up a large number of others concerned with the execution of Eoka decisions. In practice, Armitage had to postpone the second of these because the police were not ready. He thought they were pushed prematurely into arresting nine men who were 'high up in Eoka' because of known attacks to be made on Kyriacon of the special branch 'without whom the Special Branch would not exist'. He feared the result would be to make Eoka merely tighten its security and 'drive deep people who were still on the surface'. Shortly, he sent Robins to the Canal Zone to vet applications from police officers there to be used in the special branch and in communications as part of the general expansion of the force. The police 'were bearing a dangerous burden and needed the reinforcement of experienced officers'.[163]

The leaders of the Turkish community discussed the safety of their people with the governor and asked for them to be armed, a request Armitage and Robins immediately dismissed. Kütchük was in the process of reorganizing the Turkish-Cypriots' political party, renaming it the 'Cyprus is Turkish Party', and forming a sister party in Turkey itself ready to support them and regain the island for Turkey if Britain abdicated in Cyprus. All this, he claimed, was with the Turkish government's approval.[164]

Keen to combat inroads by the Greek press and radio, which 'keeps telling the Cypriots to throw bombs', in the middle of July Armitage held a meeting with officials to decide the broadcasting service's policy on enosis. They agreed that Eoka must be 'hit as hard as possible' and that they should 'go for' Athens radio whenever it was inaccurate. Athens radio beamed on Cyprus a programme, *Voice of the Fatherland*, 'which daily lashed the air with denunciations of British atrocities'.[165] He also discussed political propaganda – a matter that had 'exercised [him] for some time' – and concluded that it needed coordination to achieve maximum effort. 'It seems essential to get one man in charge who can coordinate the radio word, the written word and the spoken word and even black propaganda through fake pamphlets etc.'[166] He and his advisers concluded that John Reddaway was the only man who could effect this coordination as 'he has the temperament and knows the Greek and Turkish mind quite well', although Armitage, in discussing politics in Cyprus with Colonial Office officials some 16 months earlier, had spoken about 'employing him elsewhere'.[167]

It was not only coordination of political propaganda that worried Armitage. He had also long been concerned about the control and coordination of sea, air and land operations. Indeed, only three weeks after he arrived in Cyprus, he remarked: 'There is a lack of coordination between the forces and government.' At that stage, however, he attributed it to the move of the Middle East headquarters from Egypt to the island. He held numerous meetings about the control of operations and the need to overcome differences of view between armed services chiefs and civilian officers. He was especially concerned about one 'who has never taken to civilian control of these affairs and is often behind trouble of this sort'; another who 'does not like having initiative removed from his men but is prepared to do things our way if we insist'; a third who said that in air–sea operations the navy should run affairs, being fed with intelligence from the civil side; and the commissioner of police 'who likes things done his way and does not drive with a loose rein'.[168]

In one very senior police officer's view, the problem of coordination was never completely resolved. Some military commanders at various levels did not really trust the reliability of the mainly Greek Cypriot police in dealing with incidents. Some senior police officers felt they had good reason for not sharing intelligence. There had been incidents of the army taking precipitate action on intelligence supplied from police sources that had cost lives and cut off valuable links established with much patience, expense and, often, personal danger. The military desire for quick and spectacular success sometimes conflicted with the long-term benefits of maintaining the security of reliable sources of intelligence. In particular, Robinson, 'a tough, determined man' brought in by Armitage to head the special branch, 'did not take kindly to military indiscretions in dealing with intelligence'.[169]

Armitage was 'most annoyed' when the date of the London conference was fixed for 29 August. Lennox-Boyd would be away for the whole of August in the Far East and it was provocative to the Greeks, who had to have any application in to the UN to discuss Cyprus by 20 August. Stephanos Stephanopoulos, the Greek foreign minister, explained to Macmillan that the Greek government was under extreme pressure. It was 'having a tremendous battle against the extremists' and Makarios was stirring up trouble in Athens, where he had had 'a bitter dispute' with Papagos. If the conference could not meet until 29 August, they would have to insist on Cyprus being placed on the UN agenda. Macmillan simply told him that this would be a 'serious error' and an affront to Britain. A member of a wealthy pro-British shipping family asked to see the governor. He told him that Stephanopoulos had agreed with him in Athens that the request to discuss Cyprus should not be made to the UN, but then had to give in to Makarios 'who had made such progress with the opposition parties'. He had quarrelled with Makarios over this and been told it had to be done 'to keep the Communists down'.[170]

Armitage hoped for a few weeks of quiet before the conference. He was encouraged that the archbishop was 'going for a rest into the country, telling no one where he was going'. Trouble, however, continued. Athens radio stepped up its campaign still further, exhorting that the murder of 'traitor' police officers should 'be a lesson to those who forsake their most holy duty'. In the meanwhile, Grivas stepped up the terrorist campaign and two special branch officers, one Greek, one Turk, and a special constable were shot on the street in broad daylight. Armitage placed a week's curfew on Agros and, on 17 August, arrested the 'first large batch of people to be declared as Eoka'. His intelligence reports were sufficiently accurate for the principal Eoka men to be identified and many of them arrested.[171]

Armitage was becoming increasingly worried about the courts: 'Greek magistrates who were affected by nationalist sentiments and did not give adequate sentences and used courts as a forum for nationalism, the great procrastination in disposing of cases... and the demands made... for military courts if things could not improve.'[172] He was concerned too to get a new deputy for Robins and to push ahead with recruiting extra police from Britain to strengthen the force and to counter the low morale of local officers.[173] 'The Commissioner of Police is not happy that he has the resolute leadership which will put police morale high and keep the public in a state of healthy respect for the police.'[174]

On 24 August, following one of the worst weeks he had ever had for hard work, Armitage flew to London. The next day he had talks with Hopkinson and lunch with Macmillan. They discussed the possibilities of a formula about self-determination, but Macmillan insisted that 'the Tory Party and Great British Public' would not stand for anything that could lead to enosis. Armitage did his best to explain that Britain now had no friends they could rely on in Cyprus 'except 80,000 terrified Turks'. He saw Oliver Woods, 'but could not give him the obvious lead to push a formula on self-determination because it is unlikely to get Cabinet backing'.[175]

On 29 August the conference opened at Lancaster House. Britain was represented by Macmillan, Hopkinson, Armitage (who had spent the morning at Lords watching South Africa play Middlesex), Bowker (a Foreign Office official), Peter Carrington (parliamentary secretary, Ministry of Defence) and Peake. Macmillan 'ran' the conference and Lennox-Boyd 'tragically' was absent until the last day. This first meeting was purely procedural and they agreed to issue no reports save for the official communiqués. At dinner that evening, Armitage sat between Muharrem Nuri Birgi, head of the Turkish Foreign Office, and a Greek general, Dovas. After dinner, he talked with Stephanopoulos and all they could agree was that they had to find a solution and keep talking, and that Makarios was not an extremist.[176]

On the second day of the conference, they 'began the real business', and Macmillan 'made a portentous speech, lasting nearly an hour, setting out the whole military, historical, economic and geographical complex of the Eastern Mediterranean and the island of Cyprus. (Everything was included, except a tribute to Aphrodite.)'[177] Armitage – and no doubt others – must have found this an aeolian rather than a meaningfully practical introduction. Turkish delegates acknowledged that it was 'a learned speech... but non-committal in so far as the solution to the problem was concerned'. In it, Macmillan criticized those responsible for terrorism in Cyprus and said that the reason why no Cypriots were present was their refusal over a long period to accept internal self-government.[178]

The British government was keen that, following Macmillan's introduction, Greece and Turkey should set out their positions clearly and publicly because 'the world' did not appreciate how wide the difference of opinion between them was. 'Too many thought our troubles due to old-fashioned British colonialism.' By securing a precise definition of these differences, he 'hoped to show the true nature of the problem'. The exact terms of Britain's proposals for the future could then be presented.[179]

On 31 August the conference met again and Stephanopoulos argued for self-determination, largely on the grounds that it would produce a contented population for a military base he recognized as essential. He denied that his government sought enosis. He would concede three years of democratic government before self-determination was established. 'Although he disowned enosis as a policy, he went on to detail the safeguards which the Greek government would give the Turkish minority in Cyprus.' He believed that neither Greece nor Turkey had the right to decide the future status of Cyprus: only Cypriots should have that right. Kranidiotis had been sent to London by Makarios and was still trying 'to persuade Stephanopoulos not to participate [in the conference] and not to recognize any right to the Turkish government for the future of Cyprus.'[180]

Later that day in the Colonial Office, Hopkinson discussed 'endlessly' a plan for a more liberal constitution to which Armitage reacted privately with exasperation: 'As if anyone yet cares what the constitution will be: the Turks don't want one and the Greeks won't accept one unless you recognize Self-determination.'[181] This exasperation continued into the next day, when the conference was addressed by Turkish Foreign Minister Fatim Zorlu, who rejected self-determination. He insisted on Cyprus remaining British for strategic reasons and if this was not the case then Turkey would consider completely reviewing the treaty of Lausanne, resuming control over the island and opening the way to Turkish counterclaims against Greece in Thrace and the Dodecanese. Eden was convinced that Turkey would never let Greece have Cyprus and he was anxious, and now gratified, that they should say so publicly.[182] It was after this formal session that Armitage's exasperation surfaced:

> At 3.30 p.m. we all met Macmillan and discussed a paper about a liberal constitution that Hopkinson is putting to cabinet and a paper about agreeing to differ and a tripartite committee to consider our draft constitution sitting in London, even a Greek and Turkish High Commission in Cyprus to see that the terms of the agreement are maintained, to be put by Macmillan. I could not agree with any of it and said so; I can only accept some formula about Self-determination.[183]

Macmillan also was somewhat exasperated – both with the Colonial Office and its 'almost Byzantine incompetence' and with Armitage, who he concluded 'seems ineffective even for a Wykehamist, and without any faith in the sacredness of his mission'.[184]

After lunch the following day, Zorlu and Birgi took Armitage to one side and told him he had not taken strong enough measures. They said that the nationalist leaders should be dealt with and that, with 'the heads of the tallest poppies cut off', all would be well. The governor suggested this was bound to provoke damaging retaliations against the Turks, who were in a minority, often very scattered and vulnerable. Zorlu disagreed and implied that the Greeks would collapse under pressure. Apparently, Zorlu had already told others he had no thought for the Turkish families in Cyprus and was concerned only to safeguard the approaches to southern Turkey and their ports and defences there. To Armitage, 'this very firm attitude seems to have made everyone here consider we can accept the idea of disagreement and therefore the Turkish position.' Privately, Zorlu suggested to Macmillan that they might move ahead with a degree of self-government if they could secure an 'armistice' for five years on the question of sovereignty. 'He seemed genuinely alarmed at the prospect of a serious deterioration in relations between Turkey and Greece.'[185]

Two days later, Armitage and Lennox-Boyd went through the Foreign Office paper setting out the ideas Macmillan proposed to place before the conference. They also discussed the recent telegrams from Cyprus, which indicated a seriously deteriorating security situation. Armitage's exasperation surfaced again:

> I made the point as strongly as possible that we met here to discuss self-determination and we must put forward a formula on that first. We all knew that this was the only point for the meeting. If we can't find a formula then we can fall back on some resolution of agreeing to disagree and self-government only, which even if the Greek Government accepts the Ethnarchy and Eoka will not.

Lennox-Boyd accepted the force of these arguments and took them to the Foreign Office, but unsuccessfully. Armitage was told at luncheon that only when self-government was working would Britain consider the future status of Cyprus. 'I just do not know how HMG expects me to turn the Greeks in Cyprus in our favour with self-government only and lots of British troops.' Later that day he was told that the cabinet had agreed with Macmillan's proposals.[186]

Armitage's words that 'we met here to discuss self-determination' and 'we all knew that this was the only point for the meeting', reinforce the probability that during his 9 July executive council meeting Lennox-Boyd had either stated or had allowed members to be left with the impression that Britain would recognize the right of Cypriots to self-determination. As far as Armitage was concerned, this probability approached convinced certainty. It seems likely that the 'agreement' in Nicosia was to push hard for conceding self-determination and that Armitage had promised to make every possible effort towards achieving this end. Only if this failed, that is, presumably, if it were unacceptable to Turkey, would they take up the fall-back position of agreeing to disagree. In the event, however, much to Armitage's exasperation, the British government did not attempt to concede self-determination and the fall-back position assumed dominance.

Armitage was incorrect to claim they all knew that 'the only point for the meeting' was to discuss and put forward a formula on self-determination. Eden and Macmillan made their points within the context of 'the vitally important defence considerations which ... demonstrated [their] thinking on the future of the Island'. They wished to show the world how great was the gap between the Greeks and the Turks. They wanted to get Turkey positively, publicly and firmly to discountenance enosis. They also wanted to persuade the UN of Britain's good faith. If the UN could be dissuaded from intervening in the affairs of Cyprus, this would give Britain the opportunity and the time to move forward with internal constitutional progress while delaying further discussion on self-determination.

Armitage was probably not clearly informed that these were the British government's real objectives. He did not, it seems, consider the very distinct – almost inevitable – possibility that if a formula on self-determination were put forward, the Turkish delegates would walk out. Britain would consequently have achieved little and probably have placed itself in a worse position than formerly. Basically, Eden had a strong aversion to appeasement, viewed Papagos as a budding dictator and was irritated by Greece's 'cordial treatment of a disaffected British subject', Makarios.[187] Simply put, he disliked the Greeks, preferring Britain's traditional allies, the Turks, while Armitage's views on the need to concede the principle of self-determination – which ran the high probability, though not inevitability, of enosis – favoured Greece and were as a result anti-Turkey.

They all knew that a new constitution was essential if Cyprus was to progress and if Greece and the UN were to be kept at bay and prevented from interfering in the country's affairs. Similarly, they all knew that Turkey would never accept the union of Cyprus with Greece. Consequently, Eden and Macmillan decided not to pursue the question of self-determination. They believed that some constitutional progress could be made without it. They tried to weaken Makarios's position by getting Greece on their side and by excluding the archbishop from the conference, thinking either that he could be ignored with reasonable safety or that he would follow the Greek government's line and advice.

Armitage, on the other hand, was convinced that no progress at all could be made internally without Makarios's agreement. It had long been abundantly clear that this could be secured only by conceding the principle of self-determination, hopefully with its implementation being many years ahead. He was convinced too that the archbishop would not follow the Greek government's line and advice unless he fully agreed with it. It is unlikely that Armitage believed Makarios could be safely ignored.

Armitage sought acceptance for a formula that would buy off Greece and Makarios and get a constitution. It would do this by conceding self-determination in principle, but making it clear that its implementation in practice might, and probably would, be a long way off. He wanted this formula to make it reassuringly clear to Turkey that self-determination and enosis were not necessarily the same thing. No one, however, put sufficient thought and ingenuity into convincing Turkey of this. Once self-determination was agreed in principle, its practice could be delayed. Armitage had already received advice, for example from Spandopoulos, on possible ways of avoiding self-determination and enosis being the same thing. Britain might have got away with this by adopting the high moral position that no one, including Greece, Makarios, Turkey or Britain, was entitled in any way to prejudge what the Cypriots might decide their ultimate future should be. Stephanopoulos had already expressed this view on behalf of Greece and Makarios had made the same point.

On 6 September the conference held its final session.[188] Macmillan, asking the conference to agree to differ over the ultimate status of Cyprus but in the meantime to accept self-government, announced the British government's plan. This was an elected majority in the legislative assembly with reserved seats for the Turks; Cypriot ministers responsible to the assembly for all departments except defence, security and foreign affairs; a proportion of ministers to be Turkish; the new administration to be headed by a Cypriot chief minister; a tripartite committee to examine the draft constitution, to consider safeguards for various communities and to stay in being for further self-government; and Greek and Turkish government representatives residing in Cyprus with direct access to the governor — which Armitage's executive council had unanimously rejected. British sovereignty was to remain unaffected. The Greeks objected, peculiarly on the grounds that no other governments should be concerned in the affairs of a democratic government in Cyprus. Stephanopoulos merely said he was disappointed and would refer the plan to his government.[189] In reply to a question from Zorlu, Macmillan foresaw no change in Britain's attitude towards sovereignty 'in the foreseeable future', adding: 'We do not accept the principle of self-determination as one of universal application.'[190]

Even so, the Turks were most bitter towards the British government, Zorlu shortly saying there should be no self-government for Cyprus while Greece supported self-determination. Birgi found the conference 'very frustrating because the same ideas were repeated and repeated on every side'. Later, Armitage said, 'all that was achieved by Macmillan's proposals was alienating both sides.'[191] A Cypriot civil servant much later recalled the general view among his Greek Cypriot colleagues: 'As was expected, nothing came of that conference. It only caused much grief to the Greek Cypriots because Turkey was brought in as an interested party without any legal or moral right, and left a bitter feeling in their hearts and minds. The situation in Cyprus grew progressively worse.'[192] The conference made the impossibility of an acceptable solution abundantly clear. Britain wanted immediate self-government with the question of self-determination indefinitely postponed; Greece also wanted immediate self-government but for only a brief period prior to early self-determination; Turkey would consider self-government only; Makarios shared – or maybe determined – Greece's view.

In Turkey itself, the end of the conference coincided with rioting by Cyprus Turkish Association members and destruction of Greek property in Istanbul, Isinger and Smyrna following a bomb attack on the Turkish consulate in Salonica next to Atatürk's birthplace, which was damaged.[193] Grivas claimed that the Turks themselves threw the bomb in order to 'engineer a bloodthirsty pogrom against the Greek minorities in Turkey'. The main targets of the rioting were Greek traders and the Orthodox Church. In Istanbul 29 of the 80 Greek churches, 4000 shops and 2000 homes were completely destroyed. Those killed included two bishops and many priests. A British journalist recorded of this 'incredible pogrom':

> At a score of points in Istanbul trouble had been prepared.... Churches went up in flames, tombstones were uprooted, coffins torn open and thrown into the streets. In the mile-long Independence Avenue few shops were left unlooted. Americans and Jews as well as Greeks were dragged from their beds and murdered, and the Turkish Government's purpose – which was to make Turkey's interest in Cyprus seem more impressive – was lost in the orgy of violence.[194]

The Turkish view of these events was very different. A senior diplomat claimed that no blood was shed, there were no casualties and, although shops were raided and furs and jewellery were thrown into the streets, 'nobody touched anything.' The disturbances were, in their view, 'a little more than a peaceful demonstration [but] much less than atrocities'. The demonstration got out of hand and, they believed, was not simply anti-Greek but a 'revolt of the have-nots against the haves, indiscriminately'. In Eden's words, 'the strength of the Turkish feeling was beginning to declare itself.' To the Turks, 'this was the flame that ignited the keg of powder in public opinion in Turkey.' Substantial military reinforcements were sent immediately to Cyprus.

It is likely that the Turkish government at least connived at these retaliations against the Greeks. Little effort was made by the police to protect the churches and shops, although Bergi believed that the rioting was the work of *agents provocateurs*. Another official claimed that 'the government took very stern measures immediately to stop' the damage being caused. It is likely too that not only Turkey, but Eden also, hoped this violent outburst would convince Greece that enosis was unacceptable to them. It could thus bring about an impasse between the Greek and Turkish positions, which might allow Britain to move towards self-government without self-determination in Cyprus. Kranidiotis tried to persuade Stephanopoulos to use the riots in Turkey as an excuse for leaving the conference and taking no more part in it.[195]

Early in the morning of the day upon which the final steps were taken at the conference, Armitage's father died.[196]

On 9 September, Armitage discussed further policy with Lennox-Boyd and Hopkinson. He advised that if the British proposals were rejected they should wait for the foreign secretary's official reply, which should emphasize their determination to maintain law and order. The proposals for maintaining law and order included declaring a state of emergency, but telling the secretary of state in time to warn the prime minister; detaining nationalists and not only terrorists; deporting Makarios, bishops, some others and 'all Greek nationalists against whom there is suspicion' to Cameroon, the Seychelles or Kenya; evacuating British families to safe areas; and replacing local government authorities if they broke down.

They also included censorship and closing down the press; the death penalty for possessing arms; creating new offences such as being a member of Eoka; generally increasing penalties for offences; military courts; and buying interests in Greek newspapers in Cyprus and in Greece – for which private money was available. The governor's advice to jam Athens radio was not rejected, but they decided to await the Greek attitude to the proposals. Plans were made to send a battalion of commandos from Malta to Cyprus and to bring in other military reserves from Britain.[197]

Over lunch with Lennox-Boyd, Armitage's exasperation surfaced yet again: 'I emphasized how stupid it had been to hold the conference and not to attempt to discuss self-determination and how it was a tragedy that Lennox-Boyd had been away during the first week.' He was given general approval for a 'get tough' policy in due course and was asked for a report on the Bishop of Kyrenia's sermons and the need to deport him: 'So things look as if they are moving at last.' He was fully aware of the violent trouble now facing him and was not afraid to deal with it firmly. He had 'a long and satisfactory luncheon' with the secretary of state and they looked forward to 'keeping Cyprus affairs back on the colonial plane and out of international politics'. Lennox-Boyd's parting words were to ask him if he was happy to remain in Cyprus as there was 'a more important governorship going', to which Armitage replied that he had taken on the job and would like to finish it.[198]

Makarios was furious that no Cypriot had been invited to attend the conference and that Turkey had been invited to debate the island's future. In a sermon, he defiantly urged Cypriots to fight for self-determination 'unto death'.[199] The security situation quickly deteriorated and on the day of the governor's return to Cyprus, 12 September, commandos and Royal Engineers had to be used to clear the streets. Eoka banners now became commonplace and the police were jeered and stoned as they went to take them down. The broadcasting station and an RAF station were bombed. A number of Cypriot police were murdered by Eoka urban execution squads as part of the deliberate drive against the police. 'Resignations began pouring into Force Headquarters and those who continued to work for the British hardly dared to show their faces.'[200]

Armitage reported to executive council on his return to Cyprus, and his attitude was 'one of great disappointment and frustration' and a realization of the intractability of the problem, which was shared by other members.[201] He must have begun to feel himself isolated. Fletcher-Cooke had been away on leave, and Tornaritis, frequently denounced by Athens radio as a traitor, went on indefinite secondment to the Colonial Office: 'Seldom can [anyone] have been so pleased to leave.'

The support of the non-official members of executive council began to ebb away.[202] Kanaan had died recently and Pavlides and Clerides both spoke with great feeling of having been let down by the British government since self-determination was not mentioned and 'never' was reinforced. Somewhat to the governor's surprise, H. E. Chudleigh,

A. F. Bates (officials) and Munir supported them. Pavlides, also frequently denounced by Athens radio as a traitor, privately handed Armitage a draft letter of resignation from executive council, his reason being Britain's refusal to accept self-determination at the conference. The governor hoped he would stay until November. A little later Clerides told the press that he also was contemplating resignation if Britain would not accept self-determination and he could not persuade them to change their mind. At this Pavlides decided to resign immediately.

None of them expected Britain to call a conference and then not discuss self-determination, especially since in June, as far as the officials were concerned, she had been prepared to discuss it. Clerides's public announcement, designed he claimed to help the governor, in fact put him at odds with Pavlides and embarrassed Armitage because it was now clear how much at variance the local and the British governments were. Armitage felt the resignations, or threats of resignation if no amendment to British policy could be secured, were 'a bad thing' and he would have great difficulty in getting anyone to take their places.

Worse, however, was to follow. During the evening of Saturday 17 September, two days after Eoka was proscribed, there was a riot in Nicosia – 'a nasty shemozzel' as the commissioner of police recalled – which was to have serious and swift consequences for Armitage.[203] It was an incident 'which finally impressed upon sceptics what a serious situation was developing'. Ralph Izzard of the *Daily Mail* reported that 'for three hours [he] witnessed one of the most shaming scenes in the history of British rule in [Cyprus].' Under headlines that read '*Daily Mail* man sees handful of boys take control of the heart of Cyprus', 'I'd sack the Governor for this', and 'Nobody acted for three hours', Izzard wrote of a 2000-strong mob, by no means ill-natured, which gathered in Metaxis Square when Eoka placards and Greek flags were displayed on the steps of the civic hall. No attempt was made to disperse the crowds, nine-tenths of whom were 'cheering and jeering' onlookers and the remainder were 'hysterical schoolboys who... became emboldened by their own audacity'.

First, they stopped, overturned and burned a British military police Land-Rover, without interference despite it taking them 40 minutes to accomplish. Then, they 'systematically and methodically battered their way into the British Institute, set it ablaze and destroyed its large and valuable library': 'not the slightest organized attempt was made to stop this act of vandalism', despite it taking half an hour to accomplish. Three hours of this hooliganism passed before riot squads of the South Staffordshire Regiment were introduced. 'It took them less than one minute to clear the entire Metaxis Square.' 'This lamentable and deplorable incident need never have occurred ... the lack of coordination at top level is ridiculous.... But unless considerable changes in personnel are made, there is no guarantee that it will not occur again.'[204]

It was clearly important for the Cyprus authorities to confine the damage that these and many similar newspaper reports were certain to cause, and the military officials were quick off the mark. Early in the morning after the riot, Colonel 'Tiger' White, the army's senior public relations officer, called a press conference for that afternoon[205] without letting Armitage or Fletcher-Cooke know.[206] Durrell did know, but did not tell Fletcher-Cooke and did not himself attend the conference: many years later John Walters, who had reported the riot for the *Daily Mirror*, said:

> It would have been characteristic of Durrell to leave explanations to his assistant [Achilles Papadopoulos]. Durrell concealed his affection for those Greeks who were struggling for independence. ... I had no prejudice against Durrell as a superb writer, but as Press Officer he was hopeless in his general indifference to daily happenings. He loved his home and young Greek companions.[207]

Walters also referred to the markedly 'pro-independence attitude of the British Press Relations Officer who lived with male friends in a lovely villa outside town and who never talked to the Press until late in the day'.[208]

White was accompanied by Durrell's assistant and neither of them felt able to speak on behalf of the police who were therefore unrepresented. Later that afternoon the press was told that Robins was unable to see them. White gave a precise account of what had happened from the army's point of view, with detailed timings and said that although army officers had asked the Nicosia police if they wanted help four times between 10.20 and 11.20 p.m., each time the offer was refused. These discussions took place 'at a junior level in the absence of anyone more exalted'.[209] Eventually, at 11.45 p.m. the police, supported by an army platoon and company, used tear gas and batons to disperse the crowd. By 11.50 p.m. Metaxis Square was cleared. Asked why the police had not cleared the area much earlier, White said he understood the police felt that if the crowds were not provoked the troubles would 'fizzle out on their own' to which the reporters replied that several times since December similar situations had not 'fizzled out and that the same pattern of police inactivity had been followed each time'.

White tried to be objective and not to attribute blame to anyone, but he did defend the army and since the police and administration were not represented they, by default or implication, took the blame. Clemens's excuse for not being present to meet the press, despite being asked by White, was that he 'had officers to take to the races and so was not able to attend!' The governor felt that the 'real trouble here' was this interview given by White, and he blamed Ricketts, the army commander, for permitting it, Durrell for not telling either Fletcher-Cooke or Robins, and Clemens for not being present.[210]

Armitage found the burning of the British Institute a severe 'moral and psychological blow'. It revealed that there was 'no proper tie-up between military and police', despite all the steps he had taken to get effective coordination of operations.[211]

Embarrassed and angry, he held an urgent meeting of his senior security advisers the day following the riot and ordered an investigation into what had gone wrong.[212] Robins asked 'Do you think I should resign? 'No', replied Armitage. 'Governors are expendable but not Commissioners of Police.' Robins was deeply grateful for this support and he remembered it until the end of his life. A few days later a government press release said: 'Special steps have been taken to ensure that the plans for closer cooperation between the military and police forces which were worked out some time ago and which have been under constant revision, will be implemented in future with the least possible risk of failure.'

During the day on which the Metaxis Square riot later took place, Armitage wrote his usual fortnightly letter to his mother and said: 'This next week is going to be an interesting one.'[213] Little did he realize just how interesting it was to be.

By the same Viscount aircraft that brought his son Jeremy on holiday to Cyprus on 23 September, at almost precisely the moment when Eden told Macmillan he was moving him from the Foreign Office to the treasury,[214] and the day upon which the UN decided not to put the Greek resolution on Cyprus on its agenda,[215] there arrived a letter from Lennox-Boyd saying he had the prime minister's agreement to replace Armitage as governor, almost immediately, and offering him the governorship of Nyasaland, which was shortly to become vacant.[216] Despite Lennox-Boyd's hint only two weeks earlier and his own view expressed to Robins only a few days earlier that governors are expendable, the letter came as 'a bitter blow'[217] to Armitage notwithstanding the secretary of state's kind attempts to soften the impact:

> You will not be surprised to hear that I have been giving a great deal of thought to the problems of the Government of Cyprus. Whatever the difficulties in Cyprus itself may have been, brought about by the failure of the recent talks to reach agreement, the Conference did bring out very

clearly the vitally important defence considerations which have dominated our thinking on the future of the Island; and it now seems inevitable that we are in for a period of sustained activity by the security forces to restore law and order.[218]

For these reasons he had come to the conclusion that it was desirable to have a military governor. Earlier in the day, Eden and he had seen Sir John Harding, who was shortly giving up his job as chief of the imperial general staff, and asked him if he would undertake the task. He had promised to let them have a very early answer. Lennox-Boyd intended that Harding should be supported by 'a civilian Deputy Governor of high standing in the Overseas Service from outside Cyprus'.

> I hope you will realize that this is in no sense a reflection on your own administration as Governor. You have had an extraordinarily difficult task, which would have been hard enough anyhow but which has been immensely complicated by international considerations to which Her Majesty's Government has been bound to pay regard, and which from time to time have led to your being prevented from carrying out a number of things that you as Governor have felt would have improved the situation. Under these trying circumstances you have done your task very well. I am making this change not because of any inadequacy on your part, but solely because the present situation calls, as it did in Malaya a few years ago, for a Governor with military standing and experience.
> You have, I hope you know, my own personal confidence and that of your many friends and colleagues here. I should like, if you agree, to submit your name to Her Majesty The Queen for the forthcoming vacancy in Nyasaland. I very much hope that you will be ready to accept this.
> I think you will agree that once a difficult decision of this kind has been made it should be carried out as soon as possible. I expect to hear definitely from John Harding tomorrow, but I think it is almost certain that he will accept. I will, of course, let you know immediately I hear from him.
> I should like to be able to make an announcement as soon as I can, indeed next Monday if this is possible, and the change would take place as soon afterwards as it could be arranged.

Armitage accepted the Nyasaland post – where he hoped to be able to resume his 'natural task of economic and political development' – and commented privately: 'At least we shall not have barbed wire in the garden and an armed bodyguard and escort and be prisoners in our own house.'[219] Although he had only a week in which to pack and to tie up affairs, he tried to keep 'some control over policy', which was not an easy task, not helped by the lack of confidence between Fletcher-Cooke and Robins. The commissioner of police found the colonial secretary 'a very ambivalent character; he would say one thing to you and then do something else. He was never absolutely straight. He was basically a politician.' Others saw Fletcher-Cooke as 'mediocre' and Lennox-Boyd had decided to replace him with a senior officer from outside Cyprus.[220]

Armitage tried to get 'some of the main mistakes of [17 September] sorted out to work towards a new and tighter coordination of police and army'. The UN's refusal, contrary to his own expectations, to place the Cyprus question on its agenda was, as Armitage saw it, the 'first real victory' against Makarios who was bound now to take further disruptive action.[221] On the night the UN decision was announced, 16 of the worst detainees, 16 of Grivas's best men, including Markos Drakos, broke out of Kyrenia castle where they had been moved because they had been making too much noise in the central prison. They escaped through ineffectively repaired windows by knotted sheets in the full glare of floodlights and lowered themselves to the beach of the country club. When a young officer at the castle reported to the club that he had seen something moving, it is said he received the reply: 'People on the Country Club beach? You'd better ask them if they're members, old boy.' The police continued to use tear gas to break up unruly crowds in Nicosia and Limasol, even on the day of the governor's departure. Soldiers in civilian clothes were stoned. There was a general strike. A curfew was imposed and troops opened fire, killing a youth. Some 216 arrests were made.[222]

None the less, in the few days remaining to him in Cyprus, Armitage had time to reflect, to ask himself questions and to be comforted by the kind things a number of people said about him.

> There were references I am told on Athens radio that I had been a moderate governor. Mantovani told me that the talk in the cabarets and coffee houses was that I could have got a 15 years acceptance of self-government before self-determination. I think there is a general feeling that I was advocating a moderate approach to the Cyprus question. At least it was a political one. Force surely can't be the end all and means. At some stage, the removal of [Makarios] with detention of the Ethnarchy Council and other extreme nationalists, [together with] the closing of the press for a short period, the bullying and bribing of the secondary schools, [and] perhaps jam[ming] Athens radio would I think have led to information about Eoka. But they have missed all the

psychological moments, have allowed [Makarios] to promulgate passive resistance, have not even removed the menace of Kyrenia from him.[223]

He wondered if Pavlides linked up with Makarios when he saw him before Armitage went to London, and he had worrying doubts about Clemens's behaviour on the night the British Institute was burned down. But he was philosophical: 'The 17th was a night of the most incredible mishaps and blunders and could not happen again. I feel it was predestined because it was all so incompetent and inexplicable, also that the [ship] is sailing on Thursday and so we can catch it.'[224]

The Armitages had the heads of department and other senior officers for a final drink, and received the farewells of many people. They went for a last walk around their beloved garden in which they had spent many deeply happy hours over the preceding 19 months, taking a walk through the grounds each afternoon after tea and cutting flowers for the house. Decades later, the staff still recalled the way in which Lyona always had vases of lovely flowers in most of the rooms. They left Government House – surrounded by barbed wire, floodlights and guards – on 29 September.[225]

It was an emotional departure for the Armitages and for the Government House staff, including a very junior member, Neophytos Sofocleous.[226] He had been engaged as a 20-year-old private servant by the Armitages in May 1955 and he got on well with them. One of his special tasks was to look after their two cats of whom he became very fond: 'Benji and Pooh were two lovely kittens. It was my duty to look after them and, believe me, it was the most pleasant duty I ever had.' Shortly after the Armitages left Cyprus, Neophytos approached Eoka and was enlisted as a member of the hard core. In March 1956, he attempted to murder Harding, the governor, by placing a time bomb under his bed. Subsequently, he became an area commander in Eoka and then, from 1961 to 1993, he was a member of the Cyprus police force, ending his career as assistant chief of police. A few years after retiring, he recalled the Armitages' departure in September 1955:

> On that particular day the staff was gathered at the main entrance to say goodbye to the couple. . . . It was a very touching moment. All of us were sorry because they were leaving, and the girls were crying. Then the couple shook hands and said a few words to each of us. Sir Robert said to me, 'Goodbye, my son, and thank you for everything.' I said, 'Goodbye Your Excellency and God bless you.' Lady Armitage said to me, 'Goodbye, Neophytos, and do continue to look after the cats, please.' I replied, 'I will do, my Lady, I like the cats, you should know that.' Then she said, 'Yes, I know that and thank you, Neophytos.' Finally, I said

'Goodbye, my Lady, and I shall think of you very often.' After that they got into the car and they left. We were ready to go back to work when we saw them returning. They went up to the telephone operators' room to say goodbye to the blind boys. It was a very touching moment, which I will never forget. And I shall remember for ever that both of them treated us, not only as servants, but as human beings too.

They drove, through virtually deserted streets, since there was another general strike, to Larnaca where the governor inspected a guard of honour of the Green Howards. All members of executive council, Clerides 'in great emotion', were there. A crowd of youths on the seafront were held back at some distance by the army and police and 'made play with enosis'.[227] They boarded the ship late in the morning and sailed at noon. As a British journalist wrote – perhaps not realizing that even in less hurried transfers of authority very few colonial governors ever met their successors or predecessors:

> Sir Robert Armitage was bundled out of the island even before his successor arrived, as if to underline that his advice was worthless. There was a pathetic and shabby scene on the quay at Larnaca, where a launch waited to carry him out to his ship. The crowd on the waterfront were roughly elbowed back by the police and they took their revenge with boos, jeers and whistles as the former Governor shook hands with the line of officials who had come to see him off. It seemed an ironic ending, for Armitage had done his best to get some political action from Whitehall; now the process would have to start all over again.[228]

Although the sudden removal came as a shock to Armitage, other government officers were not surprised. A Turkish Cypriot civil servant, a great admirer of Armitage, later said: 'There was no shock when Sir Robert was suddenly replaced. It was expected. The civil service was sorry to lose such an efficient [person and a] real gentleman. But his weakness with the security forces was a common secret. Sir Robert's departure was a sudden and sad occasion.'[229] Another officer recalled: 'He was a nice man, but governors do not usually survive the sort of situation he was exposed to.'[230]

As Nancy Crawshaw said, 'Sir Robert Armitage, the patient, imperturbable Wykehamist, was released from his thankless task and left the island, eventually to become Governor of Nyasaland.'[231] In departing, he looked for some comfort: 'When one looks into the rolls of barbed wire in the garden, the bodyguard and armed vehicles which follow me whenever I go out, the virtual boycott of unofficial Greeks which prevents us asking any of them there, it is not altogether unwelcome that one should move to another atmosphere.'[232] And he would have been comforted had he known that Eden later referred to his 'intelligent and faithful' service to 'Cyprus [which] had not been easy to govern'.[233]

Just over two months after Armitage left the island, a major debate on Cyprus took place in the House of Commons.[234] It was opened by Macmillan who paid tribute to Harding for his 'high sense of duty' in undertaking the task of governor, and felt that it was 'right that public expression should be made of our gratitude'. He did not mention Armitage but when Lennox-Boyd rose to speak later he made very early reference to Armitage and thereby remedied Macmillan's omission.[235] He spoke of the former governor's 'courage and patience which he showed throughout' and said it was 'beyond praise'. He spoke also of the many Cypriots who joined in paying tribute to his 'amazing accessibility ... to anyone who wished to see him'.

> I would say that, in the view of the Government, he discharged his work in Cyprus in an exemplary fashion. The only reason for the change was ... that the position in Cyprus had reached a point where the interests involved were much wider than those of the administration of an overseas territory. They extended to Her Majesty's Government's whole defence and political interests in the Middle East, and it seemed clear to us that Sir John Harding ... was uniquely qualified to take the post of Governor at that time.

Lennox-Boyd went on to say that if anyone thought vigorous action should have been taken earlier, he or she should reflect that much of the positive action since taken by Harding 'was obviously planned when Sir Robert Armitage was Governor'. If there was delay in taking action 'these are matters in which the final responsibility rests, not with the Governor, but with Her Majesty's Government and I, as Colonial Secretary, take full responsibility for any action that was or was not taken.'

This statement by Lennox-Boyd, in conjunction with other factors, makes it virtually certain that Armitage advocated tough measures to the British government but had them turned down. The other factors include his belief, recorded in his private diary, that the removal of Makarios, detention of the Ethnarchy Council and of other extreme nationalists, closing the press, 'bullying and bribing' the secondary schools and jamming Athens radio would have led to more information about Eoka, but 'they' – presumably the British government – had missed all the psychological moments. Another factor was Lennox-Boyd's reference to Armitage being prevented from carrying out a number of things he as governor felt would have improved the situation.

Lennox-Boyd's statement in the Commons was a fulsome, supportive and fitting tribute for which Armitage must have been grateful. Right at the end of his speech, at the close of the debate, the secretary of state repeated the words the British government shortly before had presented to the Greek and Turkish governments and to Makarios:[236] 'It is not our view that the principle of self-determination can never be applied to Cyprus.'[237] This concession of the principle, the abandonment of Eden and Hopkinson's 'never' (and of Macmillan's 'not of universal application', which implies 'never' somewhere or other, most obviously Cyprus) so soon after Armitage's departure, was the single most important political move he had consistently advocated – one he thought had been agreed before the London conference and a step Macmillan had resolutely refused to take at that conference only three months earlier.

It is difficult to imagine a more complete volte-face than from 'never' to 'not never', but Armitage was to experience and suffer from an equally complete change of mind under Macmillan five years later. For the present, however, he was glad to be able to relax and prepare himself for his new post back in Africa. No doubt he was happy to say to Harding, as Othello – with a different emphasis and meaning – had said to Lodovico, 'You are welcome, sir, to Cyprus.'[238]

5

Nyasaland I

This country has certainly entered a new phase. The new order is certain to require a new look. Let us hope we have more success in presenting it than we had in Cyprus.

From Larnaca the Armitages sailed for Genoa.[1] The ship's staff 'could not have been more attentive', their travel companions were congenial and they began to relax a little. During their three-hour stop at Athens, Peake took them to breakfast, looked after them and 'commiserated' with them. They stopped at Naples and visited Pompeii, and they passed close to Stromboli at night, seeing and enjoying the volcano's pink glow. All the way along the Italian Riviera they sailed close to the shore; 'it was all enchanting and ravishing.'

At Genoa their troubles restarted when they could not get a sleeping compartment on the train to Paris, having had no time to book. The British consul general looked after them, drove them round the town, gave them tea and then secured a first-class compartment to themselves to Paris. At Paris there were no porters and they had to 'hump nine pieces of baggage' some distance into the *Golden Arrow*. They were relieved and grateful that at Calais and Dover porters carried all their luggage for them. The channel crossing was quick though choppy. At London their troubles re-emerged: there had been a muddle over their bookings at the Royal Empire Society and there was no space for them. London's hotels were 'absolutely full', so Lyona went to stay with relatives and Armitage stayed at the Oxford and Cambridge Club. It was 9.15 p.m. before he got there – having reached Victoria three hours earlier – and remarked 'You can imagine how I slept.'

They spent their first few days with Armitage's cousin at Lypiatt in 'the peace of the Cotswolds'[2] and the next three months, partly at a Wivelscombe farmhouse near Lyona's aunt and partly at Bournemouth. He enjoyed a day watching stag hunting on the Somerset moors and called on Grigg, now Lord Altrincham, who talked cheerfully but tired quickly and was not well: he died six weeks later at the age of 77. They called on Armitage's aunts at Dadnor, stayed with the Haworths, long-standing family friends, in Cheshire and went to the Cheltenham and Wincanton races.

They had Charles Footman, chief secretary of Nyasaland, to lunch, who told them that Government House in Zomba and its gardens had 'been made marvellous by Lady Colby'. He found Footman pleasant but old-fashioned. He was comforted by a 'nice letter' from Harding in Cyprus and by a kind reference welcoming them back to Africa at a dinner given by the Central African Federation's high commissioner. At this dinner he sat at the high table and met Gilbert Rennie, high commissioner; Lord Malvern, federal prime minister; Donald MacIntyre, federal minister of finance; Munro, Southern Rhodesia MP; Lord Selbourne, and other leading figures from, or interested in, central Africa. In this way, he began to develop his knowledge of Nyasaland and he extended this by speaking with others at the Colonial Office, including Lennox-Boyd soon after his arrival, and by reading about the country.

Lennox-Boyd and Armitage were fortunate the Nyasaland governorship was shortly to become vacant and available for Armitage – but only just! Wyn-Harris recalled:

> When I was home on leave in 1955, Sir Thomas Lloyd, then Under-Secretary [at the Colonial Office], asked me if I would like to be considered for the Governorship of Nyasaland and I replied that I would. Possibly mistakenly I considered the appointment settled and I was somewhat disappointed to see in *The Times* that when ... Armitage was removed from Cyprus to make way for Lord Harding, he had been appointed Governor [of Nyasaland]. Fresh information came to me a few days later when Sir Thomas Lloyd wrote me a letter explaining that he had been on holiday in Majorca and it had come to him as a complete surprise [to learn] first of ... a change in Cyprus and a few days later of Armitage's new appointment.[3]

It is unlikely that Lennox-Boyd knew of the arrangement between Lloyd and Wyn-Harris.

Once he had recovered from the initial trauma of leaving Cyprus and had settled down to enjoying his leave, he found time to learn about Nyasaland: the incumbent governor, Sir Geoffrey Colby, was not due to leave until March 1956. Armitage was familiar with East Africa from his Kenya days, and with West Africa from his Gold Coast days, but he needed to learn afresh about central Africa, especially Nyasaland and its part in the Federation of Rhodesia and Nyasaland.

The country, which is 130 miles from the Indian Ocean, is long and narrow. It is 560 miles north to south and 30 to 100 miles west to east.[4] A quarter of its 46,000 square miles is covered with lakes. The northern two-thirds of the country is split between Lake Malawi (formerly Lake Nyasa) to the east – this occupies the southern extremities of the great Rift Valley – and plateau country to the west. This is 4000 feet above sea level, but rises to 8000 feet in the Nyika Highlands. The southern third is comprised of the Shire River valley, descending from 1500 feet to about 100 feet, also in the great Rift Valley, with the Shire Highlands to the east, at 3000 feet but rising to over 10,000 feet in the Mlanje mountains, and the Kirk Range to the west at 3500 feet. It is a country of varied landscapes and great natural beauty.

The monsoonal climate has a hot main rainy season from November to March, followed by two months of late rains and a cooler dry season from June to October. Mean temperatures vary with season and altitude from quite hot to pleasantly cool. Nearly all the rainfall occurs between November and March and varies from over 80 inches in the far north, the Nkata Bay area, Zomba and Mlanje mountains, to less than 30 inches in the Mzimba and Kasungu plains and the Shire valley.

In 1956, the African population was 2,600,000. In addition, there were 6500 Asians, 3500 Europeans and 2000 Euro- or Indo-Africans. The vast majority of the Africans were subsistence farmers. The Asians were overwhelmingly traders and storekeepers. The Europeans were more or less evenly spread between government service, mission work, agriculture and commerce. And the Euro- and Indo-Africans were primarily occupied in trading, transport and agriculture. The country's population density was one of the highest in Africa and growing at a rate that doubled it every 25 years.[5]

At the time of Armitage's arrival, the Nyasaland executive council had five official and two non-official members, all of whom were European. The legislative council had 11 official (all European) and 11 elected non-official members (six non-African and five African). The governor presided. At the central government level, the civil service had 8344 members allocated to 23 territorial departments, the largest of which were public works, the police and agriculture. Eight departments with 2351 civil servants had been transferred to federal responsibility in 1954, the largest being health and posts and telecommunications. Administration at the local level was conducted through the provincial and district administration and the native authorities. There were three provinces – northern, central and southern – each in the charge of a provincial commissioner, and 18 districts, each in the charge of a district commissioner. The provincial and district commissioners were responsible for the native authority councils, which exercised local executive, legislative, judicial and financial functions. In 11 districts, statutory multiracial district councils had been established. There were African provincial councils and a protectorate council to encourage 'the representative expression of African opinion and to obtain equal opportunity of representation by hereditary dignitaries and others, whilst retaining as far as possible the indigenous tribal structure of administration at Native Authority level'.

The work of Armitage's immediate predecessor as governor was important, for it was this that Armitage inherited. Colby had been governor for eight years, which was significantly longer than the average of his ten predecessors, and his influence had been considerable. The most important issue Armitage had to face was federation, which he systematically approached from three angles: he looked at the history of closer association between the Rhodesias and Nyasaland; he found out what his predecessor's stance and actions had been since the federation came into being three years earlier; and he worked out what he should try to accomplish during his own term of office.

First, on the history of closer association,[6] a number of conferences and commissions held in the 1920s and 1930s to explore the possibilities had come to naught, principally because of African opposition in Northern Rhodesia and Nyasaland. The 1945 British general election then brought the Labour Party to power, which had pledged to prevent amalgamation unless it was what the Africans desired. Rhodesian Europeans, however, strengthened by the growing power of the South African National Party with its commitment to apartheid, continued to press for closer association. It was felt by the British government that a more liberal state in central Africa would act as a bulwark against apartheid and the spread of communism. In 1949, at an unofficial conference of European politicians from the three territories at the Victoria Falls, amalgamation was abandoned and replaced by a proposal to form a federation.

The following year James Griffiths, the secretary of state, set up a conference of officials to consider whether the territories could profitably form a federation. He visited central Africa himself and ended that visit with another Victoria Falls conference. The conference's report highlighted the economic interdependence of the three territories and the importance of integrating economic policy. It recommended that closer association should be by federation rather than amalgamation and that substantial safeguards for African interests should be included. It concluded by saying that the need for action was urgent. Griffiths increased African suspicions by instructing officials neither to advocate nor criticize federal proposals.

In August 1951, Griffiths visited Nyasaland, where members of the

European chamber of commerce and convention of associations alerted him to the totality of African opposition to federation. He also met leaders of the African protectorate and provincial councils and of the Nyasaland African Congress; and again the Africans' strong opposition was made abundantly clear. Their opposition was based on fear of Nyasaland's absorption into Southern Rhodesia, of more European immigration and, consequently, of the loss of African land. Griffiths's visit concluded with another Victoria Falls conference. This time Nyasaland African representatives attended and uncompromisingly opposed federation. The conference's final communiqué, despite strong African dissent, favoured federation in principle, but further discussions would be necessary.

In November 1951, the Conservatives came to power and Oliver Lyttelton, the new secretary of state, endorsed the communiqué and hoped the Africans would accept the assurances contained in the report of the officials' conference. Notwithstanding this, Colby sent a secret telegram to Cohen at the Colonial Office saying it was his considered opinion that there is no possibility in the next 12 months of getting Africans to change their attitude towards federation and he felt very strongly that they should 'take the initiative and pull out'. Cohen doubted it was 'politically practicable to abandon [the] campaign of persuasion now and in our judgement it would have disastrous consequences if Nyasaland were to pull out at this stage'. He hoped the governor would soon 'take a less gloomy view'.

The *Nyasaland Times* at this time published a long article on African opposition to federation. 'They are 100 per cent against it, and that fact is well known to the imperial Government.'

At this stage, then, not only the Labour Party in Britain, but also the governor and the press in Nyasaland, were convinced of the Nyasaland Africans' total opposition to federation. None the less, the British government reconvened the Victoria Falls conference in London in April. This conference compiled a draft federal scheme and appointed commissions to recommend solutions to outstanding judicial, fiscal and staffing problems. Following the publication of the draft scheme, Hopkinson, minister of state, visited Nyasaland where the African Congress and provincial councils again emphasized the Africans' great opposition.

A further London conference in January 1953 produced a draft federal constitution. On 9 April, the Southern Rhodesia electorate overwhelmingly accepted the federal proposals and, 11 days later, the Nyasaland legislative council debated a motion favouring 'the Federation of Southern Rhodesia, Northern Rhodesia and Nyasaland'. Every member of council spoke, the chief secretary replied, Colby reread the motion and asked, 'Would those in favour of the motion rise?' E. K. Mposa and E. A. Muwamba walked out, all nine officials and all European non-officials rose save A. B. Doig who, with P. Dayaram, remained seated in dissent. Colby cast his deliberative vote in favour of the motion and declared it carried.

Two principle concerns occupied Colby and his officials in the following six months: finance and security. Hard and careful work secured very favourable financial arrangements – further Colonial Development and Welfare Fund allocations and a significant share of federal loan expenditure. The security situation now became one that could deteriorate dangerously. Over the next four months a number of relatively minor incidents and provocative breaches of the law were handled without injury. From mid-August, however, the disturbances spread as labourers on the tea estates and the railways went on strike. Telephone lines were cut, stones were thrown at vehicles and roadblocks were erected. Intimidation and looting occurred.

The police and King's African Rifles (KAR) carried out widespread patrols to disperse crowds and to clear roadblocks. Crowds attempted to 'depose' chiefs loyal to government, and roadblocks, unlawful assemblies, patrols, tear gas, baton charges, village searches, arrests, seizure of arms and weapons, prosecutions and widespread disruption continued. Some 11 Africans were killed and many more were injured. Colby told the secretary of state that he did not intend to declare a state of emergency. However, the danger of unrest remained and Colby asked permission to introduce legislation enabling the government to detain persons, as proposed in the draft emergency regulations he had prepared in case of need. No further violence occurred and by early November things had quietened down. In the meantime, federation had become a legal *fait accompli*.

The steps taken to achieve closer association between the three British territories in central Africa had been hesitant and protracted. They were pushed by Southern Rhodesia and, with the exception of the missionaries, by the non-official Europeans of Northern Rhodesia and Nyasaland. They were resisted by the Labour Party, by the Nyasaland governor and, overwhelmingly and unequivocally, by Nyasaland Africans. The turning point had come with the officials' conference report in June 1951, and the point of no return with Lyttelton's decision in November 1951 to pursue federation. Thereafter, things were driven fast and the federation came into existence on 1 August 1953.

This was what Armitage found when he studied the background of federation. If any one factor stuck in his mind it must have been the Nyasaland Africans' consistent, extraordinarily strong and virtually unanimous opposition to federation and to an association with Southern

Rhodesia. He would also have become aware of his predecessor's strong advice against introducing federation. What, however, had been Colby's stance once federation had been imposed?

From the outset, Colby was particularly concerned about Southern Rhodesia's attitude towards Africans. There had been a hardening of anti-African opinion, a growth in racial intolerance (fuelled by unwise and provocative public statements by European federal MPs) and opposition to any progressive racial policy. He wrote a long and carefully considered letter to Roy Welensky, who was shortly to become federal premier. He told Welensky that he had advised against including Nyasaland in the federation, but that once it had been instituted he had done, and would continue to do, all in his power to ensure that it worked – a claim Welensky fully accepted and about which he 'never had any doubts'. He then dealt with a number of issues: the need for African advancement, particularly in the civil service – 'without doubt the greatest single political problem which faces the Federal Government'; the continued immigration (especially from South Africa) and employment of Europeans in jobs Africans could readily do, which had both economic and political dangers; the futility of believing that African advancement could be avoided by force; and the need to give Africans more say in the government of their country. He was convinced that in five or ten years' time, Africans and not Europeans would be the arbiters and deciding factor in what happened in Nyasaland and elsewhere in Africa. 'We must therefore do everything we can in the meantime to get [them] on our side and in favour of federation. I feel bound to say that we have not made much progress in that direction so far.'

Having stated his views so clearly, Colby set himself two sets of guidelines for his remaining three years in Nyasaland. First, he consistently advocated publicly to the federal government, Nyasaland Europeans, politicians and others that their 'primary object in the next few years' should be by their actions to dispel the Africans' fears of federation and convince them that federation was in everyone's best interests. His other guideline, which he did not admit to publicly, was to hold the federal line where it had been drawn in 1953 and, while doing nothing to hinder progress in what had already become the federal sphere, to do nothing to extend it. He preferred to seize every benefit to Nyasaland he could in the federal sphere and to push ahead independently with Nyasaland developments outside that sphere. He resisted attempts to create a federal police force and to federalize public works and non-African agriculture in Nyasaland. In all these he successfully resisted expansion of the federal sphere and held the federal line where it had been drawn in 1953.

With his knowledge of the history of attempts to secure closer association – and the African reaction to them – and with his understanding of the stance adopted by Colby during the previous three years, Armitage was much better placed to work out what he should try to accomplish in respect of federation during his own term of office from 1956 onwards. He did not, however, rush immediately into this. Wisely, he waited until he could reach Nyasaland, see conditions on the ground and gather the views and feelings of others, of all races, before deciding his plan of action.

The Armitages spent the first few days of January 1956 packing, getting their luggage ready for the ship and making a number of last-minute visits. They lunched and dined out a good deal in London, and met a number of 'useful' people: Colonel William Codrington of the Nyasaland Railways; the journalists John Grigg and Oliver Woods; Alan Burns, former governor of British Honduras and of the Gold Coast; Margery Perham; and the Reverend Michael Scott, whom he thought was trying to curry favour with him. They enjoyed a concert at the Albert Hall, and went to the theatre and the cinema, squeezed in a few race meetings at Windsor and did a little last-minute shopping, including ordering a radiogram, which the Crown Agents had agreed they could buy for Government House. Armitage made a last call to the Colonial Office, where he learned 'nothing new'.[7]

On 10 January, Rennie collected them and drove them to the London docks where they boarded the *City of York*. This was to be their first – and only – sea voyage down the whole western coast of Africa. The rough seas prevented them enjoying the first few days. Later, although finding the 'people on board not of great interest', they enjoyed the fancy-dress night, played bridge most evenings, entered and did well in the deck game competitions and generally enjoyed the relaxation of a leisurely voyage.[8]

They landed in Cape Town late in the afternoon of 26 January, surviving the rolling of the ship and the cold, dull weather during their last day on board. They spent the next two months in the Cape. Although Lyona was not always well and Armitage found 'this lazy life' suited him but tended to be irksome and would make it hard to get back to work again, their time was fully occupied. They went to the races every week – losing money but eventually recovering nearly all of it. They also went to the theatre and cinema, enjoyed looking at Dutch paintings in the museum and visited various places of scenic interest, including farms, orchards and vineyards. They met many interesting people: the governor-general, ambassadors, the chief justice, ministers, parliamentarians, bankers, stockbrokers, the admiral at Simon's Town and people who had known Lyona's father. They were entertained a great deal and scarcely took any meals in their own hotel. They played a good deal of bridge and golf, Armitage taking lessons from a professional and completely altering – he hoped for the better – his swing. He attended sittings of parliament when the constitution amendment bill and the budget were debated and he spoke to the Institute of International Affairs about Cyprus.

He learned a good deal about race relations and politics in South Africa and in his private diary he revealed some of his own thinking:

> The Nationalists are certainly the dominant force; they have a policy of apartheid and a policy of up with the Afrikaner and they pursue each through legislation and administratively as hard as they can. They don't give any, or very little, appearance of appreciating that apartheid is in practice impossible to the degree that they require in order to satisfy their emotions and the extreme Nationalists. This blind surge to increase apartheid is coinciding with a liberal sentiment throughout the world which more and more forces the white races to tolerate and respect the coloured races. ... The thinking men among the Nationalists realize that they cannot isolate themselves from the world at the tip of Africa and that means recognizing coloured government and eventually having diplomatic contacts with them and this will lead to social contacts. But they have got political power on apartheid policy and they can't modify it without jeopardizing their political position, and they are too pleased and arrogant with power to face that situation yet.

He then turned to the National Party's second policy, that of 'building up the Nationalists'. He believed that this conflicted with the long-term policy for whites in South Africa, their need to close their ranks and not split them. With their separate schools for English and Afrikaans and their insistence on Afrikaans for candidates to government service and promotion in it, their refusal to attract outside capital and labour, especially non-nationalist labour, they were driving a wedge between the two white sections and slowing down the country's economic advancement. 'This jeopardizes the white position as it restricts the increase of white population and the build-up of further white positions in industry and commerce. The result is that the coloureds are being used to do the jobs that many whites would otherwise be doing. So total apartheid becomes more impossible.'

Other entries in his diary give insights into what he was observing about race relations and attitudes, and about politics in South Africa. One 'elder statesman adviser' who represented moderate opinion with whom he discussed politics was anxious that South Africa should recognize the emerging African states. The president of the reserve bank said that it was a rule of 'the club of reserve bank chairmen' to have no restraints in dealing with any other member: 'He had shaken hands with Indian, Pakistani and Ceylon chairmen and he supposed he would be able to with the Gold Coast and Nigeria when they came up!' Armitage was very clear in his own mind that total apartheid was impossible and that at some stage even Nationalist supporters would acknowledge that South Africa had to recognize further non-white countries. He listened to Johannes Strijdom's hour-and-a-half speech on the Constitution Amendment Bill, which was accompanied by 'the gesticulations and intonation of the mob orator'. He felt that too much attention was being placed on 'the legal aspect, when really it is the moral that counts. It may be the coloureds today but will it be the English tomorrow?'

Armitage also had a meeting with the minister for external affairs, E. H. Louw, who asked first about Cyprus and Makarios.

> He then asked me about the Gold Coast and Nkrumah [and] was obviously anxious to find out what the position and prospects were. ... He had decided to set up an African Affairs department on a bigger basis in his department as they had agreed that they would recognize non-white countries in Africa. He talked a good deal of the changing aspect of the Commonwealth, with the possibility of the Gold Coast, Nigeria, Malaya joining the already non-white members. ... He drew the distinction between these purely native states like the Gold Coast and the multiracial, and obviously justified the new South Africa look to them on the grounds that they were purely native and in fact in conformity with the Nationalist policy [of separate racial development] here.

To Armitage, it was clear that no one had any alternatives to the policy of segregation that would win votes. Things would go on as they were unless there was a coalescence of splinter groups opposed to the National Party, or, eventually, a violent revolution. This could not happen yet because 'there is too much prosperity and the powers of the police and machine guns are all powerful'. The police, he felt, were of poor quality, regarded as enemies by the Africans and coloureds and as of hardly any help to the whites.

> The theory that Rhodes' soul still animates this land is no longer correct. There is no equal opportunity for all civilized men. It may well be that with the admission that they are to have relationships with the non-white countries of Africa – that implies social contact with non-whites – the repercussions will lead them back to Rhodes' identity.

It is clear from these entries in his private diary early in 1956 that Armitage grasped the inconsistencies in the nationalist policies of separate racial development and Afrikaner superiority among the whites, and the inevitability of their eventual failure. He detected, too, that a number of leading politicians accepted, albeit reluctantly, the need for South Africa to have dealings with emerging black states in Africa, rationalizing this as consistent with their policy of separate development. He could not see an early change to this state of affairs and, although he foresaw an eventual violent revolution, he did not think this was likely to happen for some time. The country currently was too prosperous and 'the machine guns too powerful'. He thought that diplomatic recognition would lead to social contact and that South Africa would then have to adjust its attitudes.

The Armitages left Cape Town on 26 March – paying part of their hotel bill with £50 he had won on the Grand National two days earlier – and sailed on the *City of Exeter*. They called at Port Elizabeth, East London and Durban before reaching Lourenço Marques on Sunday 8 April. Here he was met by the federal consul general and taken by the aide-de-camp to call on the governor-general of Mozambique.[9]

He had originally planned to arrive in Nyasaland on 30 March, but while he was in Cape Town he learned that this would be inconvenient. 'Heard that Nyasaland do not want us on the 30th as it is Good Friday. Most annoying but we are the first people to realize how unpopular we would be to spoil all the high-ups' Easter holidays!'

A severe hurricane, codenamed 'Edith', struck Mozambique early in April and caused a good deal of damage to the coast and adjacent inland areas, including washing away part of the embankment leading to the railway bridge over the Shire River at Chiromo in southern Nyasaland. They had planned to leave the ship at Beira and travel by rail – as had most of his predecessors – to Limbe to be met there by an official reception party and taken by car to Zomba. With the Chiromo flood, however, this became certainly unwise and probably impossible. Instead, Lord Llewellin, the governor-general of the federation, arranged for them to disembark at Lourenço Marques, and for a VIP Dakota of the Royal Rhodesia Air Force (RRAF) to take them to Chileka airport in Nyasaland on 9 April.[10]

It was a cloudy, rainy day, but from their Dakota they could see quite well. They were impressed by the amount of water in the Shire and Ruo rivers and in the swamps, and by the greenness of the countryside.[11] The pilot circled Blantyre so that they could see the largest – although quite small – township in Nyasaland and the main commercial centre of the country in which they were to spend the next few years. They landed at Chileka, where they were formally met by senior members of the government and leading non-officials. They were then driven the 50 miles to Zomba, where they arrived in the late afternoon.

> Next day [he] dressed in [his] blue uniform and went to the Legislative Council room in the secretariat at 10.00 a.m. and was sworn in by the acting Chief Justice. [He] met members of Executive Council who only were present. Then [he] went out and inspected a guard of honour of the 1st KAR [King's African Rifles] and then back to Government House, changed into a morning suit and [they] had 110 to a drinks party, mostly Zomba officials, farmers, KAR, etc.

The party was also attended by the African federal MPs, W. M. Chirwa and C. R. Kumbikano, and two of the African members of legislative council (MLCs), H. B. M. Chipembere and J. R. N. Chinyama. Shortly, both Chirwa and J. F. Sangala, president-general of Congress, sent him friendly letters of welcome.

On the day of his arrival he was handed a letter left for him by Colby.[12] Colby started by saying he did not propose to inflict a lot of handing over notes on Armitage, for he would find his views 'plastered over secretariat files' if he wanted to read them, but added that after eight years in the country it would be 'somewhat unusual' if he had not formed strong views on certain subjects. He mentioned only three subjects: relations with the Colonial Office, land and federation. He feared he had been at loggerheads with the Colonial Office for the last year or so and did not think Nyasaland was well served there. In his view, William Gorell Barnes had no real understanding of the problems, Lloyd appeared to take no interest and Lennox-Boyd 'had no time as he always has a series of crises on his hands elsewhere'. In a letter to Armitage late in 1955, Colby said: 'It will not be necessary for me to tell you that the heaviest cross a Governor must bear is the conglomeration of smart alecks in Church House.' On the question of resettling Africans on formerly private land acquired by the government, Colby simply said that it needed very close watching and 'may well become a trouble spot again'. The main thrust of his letter was concerned with federation:

> The real problems arise from federation.... I advised originally against the inclusion of Nyasaland not because I objected so much to the idea of federation but rather because I was convinced that there was no goodwill towards us or understanding of our problems in Salisbury. I fear I have to say that this has been borne out in practice. I do not believe that federation can succeed unless there is a complete change of heart in Salisbury – at present I see no sign of this. The fundamental fact to my

mind is this — in a country where there are 550 Africans to every one European, what the Africans say will go: it is just a question of time and I don't think there is very much time left and in that interim the Federal Government must get the Africans on their side by making substantial gestures — if they don't this country will inevitably become an African-dominated state and break away from the federation and this in my view would be a disaster. . . . Politically I am afraid the tempo is beginning to simmer again and the new African members of Legislative Council are not going to help much.

Armitage recognized the importance of Colby's eight-year experience: 'His views would clearly be of immense help to me.'[13] He quickly realized that federation was the most pressing and vital of all the problems likely to confront him. He read Colby's letter — and a copy of one Colby had written to the secretary of state on 24 January — carefully and with gratitude: 'So, not only did I learn, on the day of my arrival in Zomba, that I had to find the means to persuade the Africans in Nyasaland to accept the Federation, but I also had to persuade the Federal Government to win over these same Africans.' These twin tracks of persuasion immediately became the new governor's top priority. He set about tackling them straight away and they occupied the centre of his thoughts and activities over the next two years.

Armitage first started with the official members of his executive council.[15] These were the chief secretary, Footman; the financial secretary, Kenneth Simmonds, who had also worked with him in Kenya; the attorney-general, Basil Hobson; the secretary for African affairs, John Ingham; and the director of agriculture, Richard Kettlewell.[14] They met on 13 April.

Ingham claimed to have been 'most frustrated under the old regime' and wanted to be active in selling the federation and in promoting African advancement. He also wanted his own position regularized so that he was responsible for the provincial and district administration. If this were done it would help the administration, which felt it had no influence in Zomba and its views were not sought.

Simmonds was perturbed about the lack of financial assistance forthcoming from the federal government and felt Nyasaland was getting no more than it would get without federation. Armitage found it 'a sterile argument' as to whether Nyasaland was better off or not. 'The short point is we are in the Federation for keeps and have to sell the Federation idea as a counter to the Congress plan to get out of it.' He formed the view that Colby 'evidently had an obsession about the lack of benefits of federal finance' and he later said that with him, Armitage, 'it only occurred in passing'.

On the whole, Armitage found these executive councillors 'a dispirited group', largely because little, if anything, had been done to explain the merits of federation to the Africans of Nyasaland. The federal government, including ministers, heads of department and civil servants, made no attempt to understand the protectorate's special problems and were not promoting African advancement sufficiently to have an impact on African views. The governor's plan was that the way to sell the federation was through propaganda, which would require material from Salisbury and they would have to send material to the British press 'especially to defeat the *Observer* and the Scots', that is the Church of Scotland missionaries.

Footman acquiesced in this plan, Simmonds saw no alternative to it and Ingham was delighted because he could now put some spirit into the provincial and district administration. Within a week of his arrival, Armitage approved a letter to all district commissioners 'to get on with selling the idea of federation to the Africans'. In addition to the official members of executive council, Armitage saw the heads of most departments, including some federal departments, during his first week or so in Nyasaland.

Ten days after arriving in Nyasaland, he travelled to Salisbury, flying in an RRAF Dakota sent by the governor-general. Here, in the course of the next four days he met and had talks with Llewellin; Malvern (formerly Godfrey Huggins); Peveril William-Powlett, governor of Southern Rhodesia; Robert Tredgold, federal chief justice; General Garlake, head of the federal army; R. E. F. Paget, the Anglican archbishop of central Africa; Garfield Todd, prime minister of Southern Rhodesia; the editor of the *Rhodesian Herald*; W. Adams, principal of the University College; and several senior civil servants and representatives of commerce and industry. Todd

> regarded Nyasaland as the danger point of the Federation because unless the Africans in the Federation were persuaded to accept Federation, he could not see Federation being a success. [Armitage] said that the white Rhodesian was regarded as public enemy number one by the Nyasaland African Congress and that attitude had to be changed to get success. [Armitage] told him [he was] prepared to operate on a two-way basis.

The Armitages returned to Zomba on 23 April – with a deep freeze, curtain material, meat and fruit.

He was keen to make himself as familiar as possible with conditions and views in Nyasaland 'and establish, if possible, a working relationship' with people who were running industry, commerce, farming and estates.[16] 'So [he] embarked on an endless series of visits and tours of inspection.' He opened the tobacco auctions and made a speech there. He toured Blantyre and Limbe, including the new African township of Soche. He visited the cement factory. He called on a pilot who was in hospital after a recent plane crash. He visited two estates and he saw M. H. Blackwood, who accepted an invitation to become a member of executive council. He did all this in one day and there were many similarly full days. He need not have worried, as he had while in South Africa, that he would find it difficult to get back to work.

There were, of course, many other days spent at Zomba. He quickly set about reading the more important files and attended some of the meetings Ingham chaired of the provincial commissioners, who met periodically in Zomba. They spent a good deal of time discussing the enforcement of agricultural legislation, soil conservation and the early planting of crops. During his predecessor's time, these had been enforced coercively and made the government, especially the agricultural department, extremely unpopular and 'a very easy target for agitation'. The provincial commissioners believed that the enforcement had 'in places degenerated into an indiscriminate fining of people [and] it is almost like another tax'. In fact, the coercive approach had been relaxed a year or two earlier, but this had not gone far enough and was still causing a good deal of opposition from the Africans and apprehension in the administration. 'There is growing resentment which is made use of by the Congress. So [the provincial commissioners] are to try and use better persuasion and go to court only in last instance. Very difficult.' In this way, the provincial commissioners made the governor aware of a problem that could – indeed did – provide a stick with which Congress could beat the government in future.

Another important early meeting was with the European non-official members of legislative council.[17] These were A. C. W. Dixon, Blackwood, F. G. Collins, H. P. Coombes, V. G. Milward and L. A. Little – the last three being recently elected, the first three having also been members of the old council. Dixon had asked to see the governor very shortly after his arrival and to meet, privately, the European non-official members. Armitage saw them very early in May and the main thrust of their worries was that under Colby they had been insufficiently consulted and involved in government decision making, and they wished this to change.

They also used the occasion to raise perennial complaints they felt had received inadequate attention in the past. These concerned: the produce marketing boards and the chairmanship of the director of agriculture; salary levels and length of leave for expatriate civil servants; the need for industrial development; the lack of dynamic leadership in many government departments; the cost of the public works department; African cultivation; soil conservation practices; and the general enforcement of law.

The meeting enabled Armitage to meet the expatriate non-official members of legislative council, to get to know the nature of their worries and to assess the relationships between them. It also enabled the members to get a number of complaints 'off their chests' and, in so doing, to have a 'dig' at Colby, with whom they had not got on particularly well, and at Kettlewell, his loyal and energetic director of agriculture and successful chairman of the marketing boards.

Early in July, Armitage called for a review to be prepared of Nyasaland in the federation.[18] He wished to add to his knowledge and understanding of Nyasaland's political problems and build on Colby's experience and advice, the views of others to whom he had spoken and his own observations. It began by tracing the history of closer association and African responses to it after the introduction of the new territorial constitution in 1956 and the election of African members to legislative council by the three provincial councils. Since all the African members were either Congress leaders or strong supporters, Congress received a new lease of life. 'This has encouraged the formation of a strong African Congress party caucus consisting of the central office-bearers of the Congress, the African members of Legislative Council, and the African Members of the Federal Assembly. This central body is dominated and directed by the strong personality of Manoah Chirwa, one of the Nyasaland Federal Members of Parliament.'

There was only one effective African political party and it had the clear central aim of removing Nyasaland from the federation and securing an African state within the Commonwealth with political power in African hands. These objectives were shared by most native authorities, by 'nearly all such Africans as have given thought to the matter' and would be accepted by those in the urban areas and workers on European-owned estates, 'unquestioned ... if the African political leaders wanted at any time militant support'.

> The emotional appeal of African nationalism is supported by a fear that continued participation in the Federation spells not only the end of African hopes of political domination, but also of African hopes of unfettered economic and social advancement. Clearly the only hope of turning the African of this country from the course which he has set himself lies in dispelling those fears.

The review went on to point out that the policies of the federal government so far had been directed at economic development, although there were very noticeable inequalities in its tempo between the three territories.

These policies carried European and, to a lesser extent, Asian support, but 'the underlying tone of the utterances of the new African Members of the Nyasaland Legislature has consistently indicated their fears of an extension of a South African form of apartheid to the Federation and the possibility of land alienation, both of which they ... believe would result from a greatly increased tempo of industrial development.' The Africans also feared a slowing down or reversal of the Nyasaland government's more liberal policies of maximum advancement of Africans in all spheres of life. This was very marked among African civil servants who felt that immigration of 'cheap Europeans' might block their own progress.

On the economic side, the review acknowledged the federal government's substantial capital investment in Nyasaland, particularly in the fields of communication and public health. However, they feared a general falling off, after the first three years, of the level of federal capital works in the protectorate.

> All these trends serve to indicate the essential conflict which exists between the Federal Government policies and the aims and aspirations of the comparatively small educated section of the Nyasaland African population. For whereas the Federal Government preaches the principle that social and political advancement can stem only from economic development, the Nyasaland African intelligentsia ... is concerned that neither of these two aims should be in any way retarded or influenced by colour prejudice or economic barriers.

To offset African fears of the effect of federal policies on their aims and aspirations, the Nyasaland government had 'consistently pursued a policy of opening up new avenues for advancement to Africans in the civil service and was progressively alleviating the distinctions between the European and African civil service'. Furthermore, they were implementing a substantial housing programme with improved services so as to encourage the African to settle permanently in the urban areas 'and take his place as a member of the industrial and commercial communities'. But the long-term economic advantages provided a 'very poor counterweight' to the 'emotional appeal of African nationalism and the glittering prospect of political power'.

The review detected recent signs that the federal cabinet wished to liberalize its policies gradually, but the difficulties were great because it was unlikely to carry the electorate along with these ideas since many

'European settlers ... have not yet been able to acclimatize themselves to either the principle or the spirit of partnership.'

> If the time comes when the majority of the European population is prepared to give the African a full place in the sun and if, by that time, African nationalism has not proceeded too far along its narrow road, it may not be too late to persuade the Nyasaland African that there is a substantial future for him in the Federal organization.

The review concluded that only an 'immediate and patently obvious' material advantage to the Nyasaland Africans would have any effect on influencing their views towards federation and even then only if it were accompanied by 'a clear-cut and irrevocable change of heart' on the part of those holding power in the federation concerning the Africans' political, social and economic advancement.

The review gave an overall picture of past events but Armitage had to deal with the future. Somehow, he was convinced, he had to get himself trusted by Africans so that he could put forward his arguments that they would prosper in the federation and that their advancement in Nyasaland would not be retarded. He had to try and persuade the Europeans in Nyasaland too that if the country was to remain in the federation, they must not hinder African advancement but actively promote it. He had also to try and persuade the federal politicians that Nyasaland must be developed and Africans in the civil service and armed forces must be trained for promotion to officer status and not merely as clerks, unskilled or semi-skilled labourers and soldiers. These were his three targets: Africans, Europeans and federal politicians.

In a letter to Lennox-Boyd written early in July 1956[19] he made it clear it was not merely the Nyasaland Africans who had cause to criticize federal policies but also the European politicians because of federal reluctance to develop the protectorate, and European federal civil servants because of the 'quite incompetent way' in which the interim public services commission was handling civil service affairs.

> We need a breathing space to try and show such African opinion here as is prepared to listen to reason that Nyasaland has a far greater future within the Federation than outside it. But we are getting no breathing space and everything that is done in the constitutional field by the Federal Party politicians makes it more difficult for me to have any influence with our African politicians.

He hoped that the secretary of state would not think he was writing in a depressed state of mind – he had not, he said, been in office long enough to be depressed – but rather he was beginning to realize 'the tremendous sense of frustration' that had already built up.

There were other worrying portents. Doig, a church minister now nominated to represent African interests in the federal assembly and a member of its African affairs board, called on him and said that although there had been no personal antipathy between Africans and Europeans it was beginning to grow. The 'most serious aspect' was the refusal of Congress to start or continue any multiracial activities, even cultural ones. This opposition was soon made clear when at the first sitting of the new legislative council the African members 'rejected the policy of a multiracial government and interracial cooperation' because, Armitage believed, they thought it would curtail their own political power.[20]

His task was one of extraordinarily great difficulty and was made worse by a number of factors. First, correspondence in the Southern Rhodesia press continued to be blatantly racist. The governor particularly noticed letters containing provocative statements, such as that from a European settler in July 1956: 'Let us make it quite clear ... that there is no such thing as equality between Europeans with a thousand years of noble tradition behind them and the black man in Africa who has only touched the fringe of our civilization during the past 60 years.'[21]

Second, Nyasaland African Congress leaders, especially those recently elected to legislative council, stepped up their public opposition to federation and their demands for secession and independence. They used Hansard as 'the Congress mouthpiece'. As they saw it, almost everything the party wanted said they said in legislative council under parliamentary privilege and then had it published widely and cheaply by government itself. They 'left no method unexploited to get publicity for the Congress' through the council. They even planned to create scenes so that they would 'be carried out on the shoulder of the sergeant-at-arms for refusing to obey an order to withdraw', though this strategy was never put into operation. After accepting Armitage's invitation to lunch on the day of the first sitting of the new legislative council – an invitation designed, they believed, to 'take the wind out of their sails' and soften them up – they refused to attend future luncheons.[22] Within a week of his arrival in Nyasaland, Armitage wrote to Oliver Woods: 'With this new Leg. Co. and semi-democratically elected Africans, this country has certainly entered a new phase. The new order is certain to require a new look. Let us hope we have more success in presenting it than we had in Cyprus.'[23]

Third, the confidence of Lord Malvern – and more importantly Welensky, his imminent successor as prime minister – in the governors of the northern territories was badly shaken by Sir Arthur Benson, the governor of Northern Rhodesia. Benson had written a long and severe dispatch to the secretary of state, which had been highly critical of the federation and its leaders. Welensky was – and remained – incensed because Benson was a governor of one of the three territories and a participant in the 1951 conference of officials, which had recommended federation. Unfortunately for Benson, he wrote unguardedly, not knowing that the Colonial Office would pass the dispatch to Sir Alec Douglas-Home, the Commonwealth relations secretary, who would transmit it to Malvern and later to Welensky. As Welensky recalled eight years later:

> From beginning to end it was a bitter indictment of the Federal Government, who had never had the faintest intention, Sir Arthur alleged, of making Federation a success; all our policies in his opinion had been directed towards converting Federation into amalgamation, and as soon as we took office we had begun a set campaign of taking over control of as much as possible, paying scant regard even to restrictions of staff or finance.[24]

Welensky's disgust at Benson's disloyalty, discourtesy, lack of propriety and secrecy in failing to tell the federal government about the dispatch, was confined to Benson and remained with Welensky throughout his life. He never suggested or possibly thought that Armitage would act in a similar way and he did not attach any of Benson's ills to Armitage, but none the less his faith in the relationship with colonial governors generally had been dented and increased the difficulty of Armitage's task.

Fourth, at about the time of Armitage's arrival, Malvern made his first bid for federal independence. On 12 March 1956, he wrote to Home and warned that, unless the federation's status was raised to match that shortly to be granted to the Gold Coast, Nigeria and Malaya, 'grave political consequences would ensue and stability could well be lost'.[25] Although the British government stood firm in not agreeing to the federation's independence, the knowledge of Malvern's proposals and advocacy seriously disturbed African opinion in Nyasaland and made Armitage's task more difficult:

> Far from demonstrating to the Nyasaland African [the required] change of heart, action is constantly being taken by the Federal political leaders which makes clear their intention of establishing a barrier beyond which African advancement in all spheres cannot proceed. Furthermore, such measures as pursuance of Dominion status for the Federation, as

proposed by Lord Malvern, and hints of the transference of further responsibilities from the territorial to the Federal sphere have stimulated African fears that the one guarantee of the attainment of their aspirations, namely, the influence and protection of Her Majesty's Government, will be removed.[26]

Fifth was the question of federalizing non-African agriculture. This was an irritating problem that was to continue as a dangerous issue, separating still further the races in Nyasaland, throughout virtually the whole of Armitage's governorship.

To avoid the conflict with critical members of the legislative council (which would almost inevitably arise so long as the governor, the head of the executive, also presided over the legislature), Armitage decided to appoint a Speaker of legislative council so that he himself no longer presided.[27] It may also have been the case that he wished to avoid the personal abuse that the new, more vociferous, African councillors were likely to aim at him. He did, however, preside over the first few meetings of the new council.

Armitage found the legislative council chamber small and cramped. This was hardly surprising given that council only had seven members when it was built, whereas by 1956 there were 23 members and a few members of the public were admitted. He was pleased that a new council building with a very much larger chamber was being built and would soon be ready for use.[28]

After their experiences in Kenya (a large and fairly well-developed country), the Gold Coast (a wealthy and also fairly well-developed country) and Cyprus (a small country but of very great strategic importance), the Armitages found many things in Nyasaland (which he saw as 'still a complete backwater'), small, primitive and inadequate.[29] This applied both to the legislative council chamber and – save for its size – to their residence. Government House in Zomba was an old and not particularly soundly constructed building. It had been modified largely piecemeal over the years and furnished, often frugally, to suit the tastes of the various and changing incumbents. On the day of their arrival, Armitage recorded in his diary:

> We got to Government House at 4.50 [p.m.] and then looked round the house. It is large, with big rooms, upstairs most inconveniently arranged. Our suite is rough and ready and tolerable but all needs refurbishing. It is essential to remember this place only came out of the bush in about 1950, that is its attraction for many, not us after Cyprus.

They were very disappointed with the interior of the house. Exactly a week after their arrival, he summoned the director of public works, N. F. Richards, to Government House, ostensibly to 'learn about public works department form in Nyasaland'. However, he took the opportunity to discuss the house with him. Richards said it was built of half burnt bricks and mud, the tower had cracked during the last earth tremor and he could not recommend any structural alterations for fear that they would 'find the place unsafe'. To pull down the house and rebuild it would be prohibitively costly.

Two days after his arrival he recorded his worries about the professional operational – as opposed to domestic – side of affairs in Government House: 'all the arrangements [were] most antiquated' in his own and his private secretary's office.[30] He was disturbed that the private secretary and the stenographer between them had to do all the cipher work and the inward codes. He discovered that Colby would not have the mechanical methods used in Northern and Southern Rhodesia and the federation 'because he said they could break down'. This reason sounds unlike Colby and it may be that he managed with somewhat old-fashioned methods partly because he had fewer secret communications with the Colonial Office than Armitage anticipated after his experience in Cyprus, partly because he sometimes found it convenient not to be able to respond immediately to Colonial Office communications, and partly because his wife was skilled at deciphering and coding – which she had learned during the war in Nigeria – and was able to help when necessary. In any case, the new governor gave immediate instructions to acquire mechanized means and 'to get the thing installed at once'.

An internal telephone exchange was also to be installed with all the lines independent of the others. By early September, although things were much better, he was still worried about a number of difficulties. The volume of daily telegrams both open and in cipher was increasing and, although the 'typex' machine was in 'reasonable use', the telephones were not yet working properly: 'They can't get the hang of this Dutch machine!' He now had three stenographers who were 'all being kept pretty well flat out' and he wondered what they would have done without the 'typex' and the extra staff.

Armitage inherited most of his Government House staff.[31] Beryl Freeman had worked as a stenographer in the Nyasaland civil service since February 1952 and in Government House since November 1955. She was stenographer to the last three governors of the protectorate. Of the domestic staff, three were particularly important: Wilfred the Government House driver; Douglas the head cook; and Wilson the head gardener. Wilfred was a former KAR sergeant-major, was chauffeur to the last three Nyasaland governors and was awarded the

British Empire Medal. Of Douglas, Armitage said that he was 'the best African "chef" I ever knew. He had a second cook to assist him [which] was fortunate. As in the case of all the best chefs, he very occasionally relaxed with a bottle and did not appear. But in our five years he never let us down on a really important occasion.' And of Wilson he said:

> At Government House I was lucky, as I had a head gardener, an African called Wilson. He had a staff of about six, whom he directed. He was responsible for the vegetables and fruit and flowers. He was a competent gardener in his own right, educated, and was able to plan and carry out the monthly programme and think up new plans. I ordered the seeds, plants, shrubs and trees. We discussed the garden endlessly. Often I would walk round in the evening and would meet him. Everyone else had gone home, and when asked what he was doing, he would reply 'rounding', that is looking and thinking and deciding how things were going and what to do next.

But Armitage's aide-de-camp and private secretary was new. Major Russell Rowan, retired from the Grenadier Guards, was introduced through his ex-commanding officer to Oliver Woods, colonial editor of *The Times* who was a friend of Armitage. They met in London during Armitage's leave after departing from Cyprus. The governor considered himself fortunate:

> We were extremely fortunate to have Russell Rowan as my Private Secretary and Aide de Camp. His service with the Grenadier Guards, also having been adjutant, helped greatly. So he kept us, and everyone else, in order and good order at that. He was a great organizer of ceremonial.
>
> [He] rapidly had everyone, except Lyona, from the Chief Secretary to the Officer Commanding King's African Rifles, under complete control. That we were able to rely on our visitors being properly received, our visits within and without the territory correctly planned, and our daily life organized with the least trouble or anxiety to ourselves, was entirely due to him.

Armitage's first impression of Government House grounds[32] was favourable: 'The gardens here are pleasant, mostly terraces and flowering shrubs and lots of trees and some beds of cannas and dahlias, but rain [after the recent cyclone] has spoilt most vegetables and lots of flowers. The grass here, which requires no upkeep, is a great feature.' Lady Armitage also was pleased with the grounds and wrote to her mother-in-law saying that the garden was 'really very lovely' with 'beautiful trees' and a very fast stream 'dashing through a wilder part of the garden'. By mid-May the gardeners were 'very busy getting seedlings out, phlox, antirrhinum, stocks'.

Armitage wrote to his mother with his first impressions of their new home:

> This house is on the slope of Zomba mountain ... in most extensive own grounds.... It is calm, peaceful and very green; we feel almost like being at Tambach again. In fact for the last three days we have had nearly as much isolation! The house is a great disappointment. High, dark barrack-rooms, none except our suite with their own bathroom. Furniture would not even be found in a junk store it is so antiquated and depressing. No taste, no convenience anywhere. All fabric and arrangements need modernizing and practically every room needs refurbishing entirely. Our own suite is tolerable, no more. Good view. We shall no doubt deal with things as we always have but at present we are somewhat depressed.[33]

Zomba was widely considered a really lovely and peaceful place and had been so considered from its very earliest days as the seat of government. It brought out the best of Reginald Maugham's powers of description. Widely travelled, he came to Zomba as secretary to the administration in 1894 and in a strikingly beautiful passage wrote that of the many attractive spots he had seen in Africa,

> Zomba is the loveliest of all.... The view, bounded in the extreme distance by the gigantic Mlanje mountains sixty miles away, roamed over a wide and fertile plain, wooded as far as the eye could reach, save away to the northeast, where the faraway flash of sun on water plucked your eyes to the glossy sheet of Lake Chilwa half hidden behind the curiously curved peak of Mpiupiu. In the middle distance, a fascinating confusion of billowy tree-clad kopjes extended for many miles, struck out of the right of the picture by the broken, craggy hill, Usiene throwing up its glittering granite peaks to a height of 4000 feet. Beyond this, Chanda ... with an horizon of distant purple mountains beyond.[34]

Although small details of the landscape had changed in the ensuing half century, particularly as the area became more heavily populated, Zomba remained a beautiful, in many ways serene spot and the Armitages enjoyed living there.

In mid-April there were traces of loneliness: they did not yet know anyone sufficiently well to invite them to dinner on Lyona's birthday. Instead, she made lampshades and the two of them were quite happy on their own. Even the private secretary went out to dinner elsewhere. By the end of April, however, with rather more sunshine and with the arrival of their pet cats from Cyprus, Lyona was recovering from her earlier depression. She was busy with the alterations to the house and with new furniture and carpets, the cost of which had not yet been agreed by finance committee, though Armitage hoped 'to bully people into agreeing'.[35] There were now highly political Africans on this committee whose cooperation could not be assumed. By the beginning of June they recorded: 'The plans for altering the house are going ahead well and work should start next Monday. The trouble is, the more time we give to it, the more ideas we have! At least a lot of the rooms should look more civilized when we are finished.'[36]

Although they had 'a very restricted circle of people in and around Zomba', guests were now beginning to travel over from Blantyre; officials such as provincial commissioners came to stay with them. They were improving the red earth tennis court and found just enough space for a croquet lawn on one of the terraces, both of which attracted social guests. They found the annual Zomba race meeting 'great fun'. They liked the small red-brick St George's Anglican church, with its 'nice carved stone altar', the good organist and the visiting priest who, though 'very high church by persuasion ... was not in the least unctuous'.[37]

Notwithstanding the difficulties of settling in to their new environment and the exacerbating effects of letters to the Southern Rhodesian press, the irritations of the new African members of legislative council, the damage of the secret Benson dispatch, Malvern's boat-rocking bid for independence and the attempts to federalize non-African agriculture, Armitage devoted much of his time and energy to the tasks of building good relationships with the various sections of the community. This was important if he was to persuade, first, the Africans of the benefits of federation and win them over to accepting it; second, federal politicians to make significant gestures towards a more liberal approach to Africans and to Nyasaland generally; third, the Europeans of Nyasaland to accept the desirability and inevitability of African political progress; and fourth, businessmen to invest further in the protectorate.

In his tours of the three provinces and on his visits to districts close to Zomba he met many of the chiefs and established good relationships with them. Of Zomba district, for example, he recorded 'the chiefs seemed pleased and asked me to keep going round the districts.'[38] He entertained Chirwa and Kumbikano on a number of occasions, usually with Europeans, but not Chipembere or M. W. K. Chiume after the first legislative council meeting lunch. It is unlikely that he did not wish to invite them and more likely that he soon learned they would not accept social invitations from him. Later, Chiume explained:

[Just before] the first session of the Legislative Council, the MLCs were guests at... Government House and the youngest Nyasaland African Congress MLCs put in a prominent position on the high table.... Not only did he try to understand these, whom he was meeting for the first time, but also to... mellow the African MLCs from the twin objectives of secession and independence. [However, he] was left in no doubt that he could not succeed in his policies and that he was dealing with a new group of African militants that could not be contained by traditional methods of being nice to the Africans.... From that day, the relations became sour and there was very little official or unofficial contact between us and the Governor.[39]

Chiume and Chipembere were convinced that Armitage, with his reputation for having worked so well for the Gold Coast government under Nkrumah, was sent to Nyasaland to 'soften' them and win them over to federation. But as Chiume recalled, they 'did not intend to be softened so easily'.

On a number of occasions Armitage deliberately arranged social functions at which leading members of the various racial groups could meet informally and in pleasant conditions.[40] While most of these gatherings were social, not all were. For example, on 30 November 1956 he had at lunch Chirwa, N. D. Kwenje, D. W. Chijozi and Ingham at which the Africans spoke of the need to revive the protectorate council and to order chiefs to permit Congress meetings and be allowed to attend them. Ingham, a few weeks earlier, had visited the central and northern provinces and Armitage recorded: 'He is depressed at the apparent deliberate opposition of the MLCs and their influence on the chiefs, opposition to things on political and racial grounds or because they are government.' With such feelings and different viewpoints it was natural that he should wish to get his secretary for African affairs and the more restrained African politicians together to discuss the problem.

As for the other African MLCs, while Chipembere and Chiume usually acted in concert, were anti-government and deliberately embarrassed the governor, it may be that Chiume took the lead in this behaviour. Armitage was eager to create a branch of the St John's Ambulance in Nyasaland – he later became a Knight of St John – and felt this would be a useful, non-political association that would bring people from various communities together. He needed, however, active African political support for his ideas, but it was not forthcoming. Even so, Chipembere was good enough to reply to the governor and explain why he could not help him: 'I have had letters from Chipembere and Kwenje, both in [the] same vein that while they think that St John's is good, as it is connected with Southern Rhodesia they can't do anything to support it actively. Shows how strong this anti-Southern Rhodesia fixation is.'

Armitage himself had cause to be irritated by the Southern Rhodesian government, which had recently declared as prohibited persons the Nyasaland Congress president-general and secretary-general. Two things annoyed him about this. First, it had been done without the Nyasaland government being told anything about it and, consequently, they had no idea why they had been banned. Second, these were both quite moderate politicians. In any case, as the two principal leaders of Congress, their prohibition would do nothing to wean Congress members from their intense dislike of Southern Rhodesia and move them towards accepting federation. Southern Rhodesia's action would further alienate African opinion against them, would insult Congress and would be proof to the Nyasaland Africans that federation was in no way a real partnership.

An indication of how Armitage's mind was working is given by his heavily sidelining part of an article by Margery Perham, which was published in *East Africa and Rhodesia* on 11 October 1955. It was an article he filed and kept in his private papers:

> But there comes a moment when Britain can no longer effectively govern a subject people against the will of the educated minority. Once that position is reached we have to go with and not against their ambitions. There should therefore come first a period of vigorous preparation for self-government and then another period, the longer the better for them, though difficult enough for us, when we begin transferring power while still supplying trained staff and retaining ultimate powers of security.[41]

In his contacts with European politicians[42] he had a long talk with Milward and was pleased to find him 'more pro-African than many here and keeps his feet on the ground'. Armitage also had talks with John Foot, a federal MP from Nyasaland and junior minister in charge of information. Like Milward, Foot recognized African aspirations and he professed to accept that one day Africans would be in political control. Not all his meetings with European politicians, however, were happy. When he had R. Bucquet, Nyasaland federal MP, to dinner with Chirwa and Kumbikano, he recorded: 'Bucquet ... obviously can't stand Chirwa but is the sort who merely provokes him to worse things.'

Although his relations with Welensky were cordial, he got a mixed response from him when the federal prime minister stayed at Government House in November 1956. The governor tried to draw him on improving race relations through blacks and whites meeting at sports, arts and drama functions. Welensky responded by saying he disliked pushing such contacts, though Armitage felt he agreed in principle with such mixing. He was surprised that Welensky did not agree that the role of the white man in central Africa was generally speaking to keep just in front of the bulk of the Africans, letting only selected and qualified Africans compete with the whites on equal terms. '[Welensky] said that he envisaged the day when black and white would do the same jobs, on equal terms, even blacks and whites both driving lorries.' Armitage did not expect him to have this view.

In his discussions with European non-politicians,[43] Armitage had a long talk with Doig about the future franchise and representation. Doig did not support a universal franchise, but wanted a low qualification level – 'a broad-based affair' – and in particular that village headmen should have the vote.

> The snag is that they are not going to be literate in English. He seems convinced that European representatives of native interests will not be required after this first assembly. Thinks they are welcomed by Africans for the approach they have to ministers, but more often now their views are said by the African MPs to be based on factors European rather than African.

In his attempts to gain the confidence of Europeans in Nyasaland, Armitage naturally had frequent talks with the two non-official members of executive council, Dixon and Blackwood. He found that Blackwood was 'most affable' when Dixon was not present and, on at least one occasion, he found him 'grumpy' when other guests were at lunch. Blackwood told the governor that he thought the future of Nyasaland must be as a black state, 'which was not a popular thought at present'. But first, he argued, non-African agriculture and the police must be put under federal control, the former because he thought there would be an African director of agriculture in four to six years – Armitage thought it would be a generation; in fact it was 18 years. Dixon said the Europeans in Nyasaland had no clear policy regarding federalizing non-African agriculture and, while there was no technical justification for it, they felt generally they should be treated the same as Southern and Northern Rhodesia.

> Dixon wants dominion status [for the federation] as soon as possible in the hope of keeping out a Labour government from pushing our Africans into self-government here at earliest possible date. He strongly opposed [having] an African on Executive Council from security and secrecy

angle. [He] felt that in a few years there would be an African majority over Europeans in legislative council.

As a consequence of all these discussions and seekings of views, Armitage began to formulate in his mind a means of reconciling the conflicting wishes of the Europeans and the British government to retain and develop the federation, and of the Africans to secure self-government. His idea was that Nyasaland should advance to self-government within the federation.[44] Strangely, this seemed a new idea, and one he first mooted at the end of August 1956: 'Had a preliminary talk with Chief Secretary, Attorney-General, Financial Secretary and Secretary for African Affairs on subject of our attitude to Congress. [I] put over my idea of self-government for Nyasaland within the federation, if the federal government would agree to such a thing.' They were unanimous on two things: within 25 years Nyasaland would have an African-controlled government, and force, whether federal or territorial, would not keep the Nyasaland Africans permanently subjugated.

In mid-October he had Dixon and Blackwood to lunch after the meeting of executive council, as was his custom, 'loosed a theory that we should go for self-government within the federation' and asked what was to be the ultimate state of Nyasaland.

> Blackwood said that the Europeans would not mind having an African majority over the Europeans in Legislative Council provided there was an overall official majority and that first non-African agriculture was federalized. He said all had set their hearts on this whatever, if any, the benefits ... to prevent [an African-controlled] government saying what they could or could not do with their land which by and large could not be conceded.

A week later the governor spoke with Foot on the same subject. He 'cautiously tried out on him [his] idea of independence for Nyasaland within the Federation' and asked whether the Federal Party accepted Malvern's statement that federation did not mean amalgamation. This somewhat embarrassed Foot who replied that one member in Northern Rhodesia and one in Nyasaland did not accept it, but the trouble would come from Southern Rhodesia. Foot agreed in general with Armitage's ideas on independence within the federation, but asked him how he would reach it. 'I said parity between Africans and non-Africans in legislative council in 1960, an African on executive council before that, and parity between Africans and non-Africans on executive council by 1970, all the time an official majority holding sway.' Another week later the governor also tried out his idea on Desmond Lewis – former commandant of the KAR, now a tobacco planter near Zomba, a moderate and confidential adviser to a succession of governors – who agreed and thought the present African politicians would not be interested, although the idea would be a basis for producing an opposition to Congress.

It was not only with European and African politicians – all near Zomba and Blantyre – that Armitage had dealings during his first few months in Nyasaland. As he set about learning as much as he could about the country and various people's views, he undertook numerous tours in the rural areas, including all provinces and most districts. He met chiefs, village headmen and civil servants and visited development projects, schools, hospitals, missions, estates and factories.[45]

He had looked forward to a meeting arranged early in October 1956 so that the four central Africa heads of government could discuss issues of common importance.[46] In the event, they discussed only a few economic matters and a federal government proposal that the federal assembly should be doubled in size. They left it to their law officers to examine what legislation was available in each territory to handle public security: in particular – ominously – they wished to avoid using the expression 'declaring a state of emergency'. Clearly, the other heads of government were not as actively interested in African political advancement as was Armitage. Nyasaland's governor had hoped for more progressive discussions and was disappointed that 'the really important matters, which are the future political and constitutional development of each of the Governments and the attitude of the Federal Government towards the territorial Governments, were not mentioned.'

He saw the meeting as an exercise to enable the Southern Rhodesian government to put forward its views and for the federal government to get the support of the northern territories to turn them down – which they did 'fairly consistently'. Malvern told him in the strictest confidence that he proposed to retire within the month. Armitage felt this brought 'rapidly to the foreground' the question of future constitutional and political development in Nyasaland and he lost no time in having a long discussion about it with Welensky. He particularly urged the necessity for the federal government to make an early and convincing announcement following up Malvern's recent statement that federation did not mean amalgamation and that within the general cover of the federation each territory could develop on its own lines. Armitage regarded this necessity as being 'of the greatest importance'. Malvern had presented them with an excellent opening. 'In the course of our discussions Sir Roy did not appear antagonistic to the further development of African politics provided that it was done on constitutional lines. He even suggested that we should make friends with Congress and not ignore them.'

Armitage made the point that to counter the Congress cry of 'withdraw from the federation' they must give the African politicians 'some political horizon'. This, he felt, could well be further constitutional progress within the federation 'rather than within a position of independence in the Commonwealth', the status to which they currently aspired. Although Welensky recognized African political advancement in Nyasaland had to come, he stressed the extreme difficulties he would have with his own electorate to try and get support for such a policy. In particular, he reacted 'somewhat violently' when Armitage suggested they should have an African on executive council – a proposal he had already put to Lennox-Boyd three months earlier.[47] Welensky – like Dixon – objected that 'secrecy would never be observed'; Armitage's experience was that Africans on council were no more liable to break their oath of secrecy than were Europeans.

They ended their discussions 'on a very cordial note'. Armitage felt he had convinced Welensky of the need for the four heads of government to try and agree on a common policy towards constitutional development before any steps were taken, for example, to double the size of the federal assembly. In reporting this discussion to Lennox-Boyd, Armitage said Welensky was clear that federation did not mean amalgamation and he hoped Welensky would soon make a public statement to that effect – a step the governor believed would be 'the most valuable thing we could do in the immediate future', especially if the statement repeated Malvern's view that each territory could advance constitutionally within the federation.

Much of Armitage's second year in Nyasaland was devoted to the same sort of activities on which he was engaged during the first, and with the same objectives and hopes. He continued to tour extensively various parts of the country and he paid visits to Southern Rhodesia – to attend meetings of the four heads of government – and Northern Rhodesia where, as with Southern Rhodesia, many Nyasas worked. He was, in any case, keen to show close relationships with the two other countries in the federation. He persisted in arranging and encouraging others to arrange and attend functions to which people from the various racial groups were invited. He inspected and formally opened a number of industrial and business concerns and took what opportunities he could to encourage economic development.

In the case of a number of important individuals, Armitage was now working with new people. Welensky succeeded Malvern as the second prime minister of the federation in November, though Armitage had been in close contact with him before that date. On 24 January 1957 Lord Llewellin died and, after two acting appointments (Tredgold and Sir William Murphy), Lord Dalhousie succeeded him. In Nyasaland, Simmonds left the country in September 1956 and was succeeded by H. E. I. Phillips as financial secretary. In July 1957, Donald King succeeded Hobson as attorney-general and George Hodgson, the most senior provincial commissioner, was seconded to the federal government.[48]

Armitage entertained three important official visitors during 1957: Lennox-Boyd, secretary of state for the Colonies, Home, secretary of state for commonwealth relations, and Queen Elizabeth, the Queen Mother.

Lennox-Boyd spent a week in Nyasaland in the middle of January.[49] Although he had spent 55 of the previous 75 hours in an aircraft, the secretary of state greatly impressed the governor with his 'vitality and intense desire to see as many people as he could'. He spent virtually the whole of each day in meetings. He attended a dinner for 'old timers' – Europeans – and a formal dinner for officials at Zomba. He attended cocktail parties in Zomba, Blantyre and Lilongwe. He lunched with the chief justice and with the Rotary Club. He dined with and addressed the Nyasaland Association – the only European political party in the country. He stayed a night with the provincial commissioner of the central province and spent an evening being entertained by the African directors and members of the Ndirande Club in Blantyre. The Ndirande Club party impressed and encouraged Armitage:

> I had opened the Club in October 1956 [and] congratulated them on their building representing a spirit of self-help. They had built it themselves, with little outside assistance. So the Club and building was a real community effort. This party showed one that there were Africans who were genuinely prepared to cooperate with Europeans, if only their extreme politicians would let them.

Armitage found the secretary of state 'a friendly and genuine man, who listened to frank talk and spoke frankly in return'. He was 'an extrovert who worked at great pressure and pushed himself to the limit. He always wanted to see what was going on for himself.' Despite the nonstop activity, Lennox-Boyd showed no sign of flagging – save that he 'could not face' a dance at Zomba Club for Hungarian relief. The Armitages had 'a very busy and exhausting time' and it took them two days to recover after the visit. The main thrust of Lennox-Boyd's visit was to reinforce Britain's policy:

He told the whites that the Federation was here to stay, but they must improve their social and other contacts with the blacks. He told the blacks that they could not take Nyasaland out of the Federation, but there could be local political and constitutional progress in which they would take a large part. So his theme was that Federation was a good thing and it was to the benefit of all races to make it work. He stressed that Federation was not a device to enable one race to rule over the others. A multiracial society, with everyone working together was the goal. . . . The British Government had a special role to play in the Northern Territories and to retain the confidence and loyalties of the Africans. He hoped that these loyalties would be eventually transferred to the Federal Government.

He was, however, given a very clear impression of the strength of African opposition to federation. They wanted African self-government and secession as soon as possible and they considered a multiracial government simply a European device to keep the Africans down. The secretary of state did his best to answer African fears and to be reassuring. He said that federation was to the advantage of all the people in Nyasaland because they would be partners in a wider complex and their conditions would improve. The white man would not dominate the black. African land would not be alienated. 'Federation is here to stay and must be made to work.' He hoped that in time the opponents would change their view. Federation would not prejudice the orderly constitutional progress of the constituent territories. Britain was as opposed to amalgamation as it was to secession, and had no intention of withdrawing protection from Nyasaland 'unless and until that protection is no longer needed'.

Although the secretary of state said nothing new, he quite firmly reinforced what the governor was saying and doing to reassure both the Africans and the Europeans. It is, however, likely that he was more comfort to and was better believed by the Europeans than the Africans. Armitage was pleased that his 'ideas and endeavours [were] fully endorsed at the highest level'.

Home spent four days in Nyasaland in the middle of October 1957.[50] Again it was a very full time, but less exhausting than the earlier visit. He attended a civic luncheon and met members of the Federal Party, federal MPs and African members of legislative council. He was entertained to tea at the Ndirande Club: 'a very sociable occasion'. He had meetings with the Euro-Africans, the Interracial Association and the Indian Association – 'all rather tedious' as the governor saw them; they raised mainly racial problems and wanted legislation to deal with them. In Blantyre, Home publicly made it clear that federation was there to stay and that it would be sensible for everyone to concentrate on making it work. He publicly expressed his confidence in winning African support for it 'with patience and understanding'. He said the 1960 federal review would reassure all races that nothing would be done to prejudice their interests. Finally, he had a discussion on franchise with the governor and his officials. His visit was in some ways a courtesy visit to Nyasaland as part of a longer visit to the federation. Armitage concluded that it was a success and enabled him to 'clarify a number of points about the political future' in Nyasaland.

Half way between the visits of the secretaries of state, Queen Elizabeth, the Queen Mother, visited Nyasaland – from 12 to 15 July.[51] She stayed at Government House and her visit was a great joy to the Armitages. Planning the visit, and then the visit itself, took up a great deal of their time during the first half of the year. As Armitage recalled:

> This was to be the first visit ever to Nyasaland of a royal personage. Her tour covered the whole Federation, so she had engagements in each of the territories. But naturally we were preoccupied only with the Protectorate. We had instructions from London for her preferences in food and drink etc. We were visited by the officials of the Federation, who were coordinating her tour. We had our own planning team. I was particularly involved as I had to ensure that all the alterations to, and redecorating and refurnishing of, Government House were completed in time. I was treated very well by the Finance Committee and allowed money for what we estimated the refurnishing would cost.

The result was that Government House and its grounds had a great deal of work done to them, which was of lasting benefit to the governor and his wife. A new Rolls-Royce car was ordered for use during the visit – and remained for the governor's use thereafter. While all this work was going on, detailed planning and preparations for the visit were taking place and rehearsals were held for many of the public events: 'Factors making for success were many – we rehearsed and organized to the last degree so that the risk of errors was remote and few appeared and they were negligible really – there was never a cloud in the sky for the 72 hours Her Majesty was in Nyasaland.'

> She was in most sparkling form, fell in love early with the country, put everyone at ease immediately, was delighted with the welcomes she got everywhere. Her evident enjoyment and ease made everyone that little bit better in performance, whether it was a right wheel on the parade ground in slow time, or a deep curtsey in a chiffon dress.

Armitage was particularly delighted that at a large daytime meeting of African chiefs and others, the Queen Mother at his suggestion wore evening dress with tiara, full decorations and her Garter jewels. She had never done this before and kept her decision to be so attired a secret until the last moment. The effect on the waiting crowd was extraordinary and, as Armitage drove with her to the parade ground, his 'heart sang'. Her visit was a delightful relief from his normal official life and the politics that went with it.

Politically, in addition to the ongoing tasks of gathering views and attempting to formulate a way forward constitutionally, two principal matters occupied Armitage's attention during his first two years. These were developments in Congress and continued arguments over federalizing non-African agriculture.

During this period, the nature of Congress changed, although it was to change even more thereafter. Of the five new African members of legislative council, all of whom were strong Congress supporters, two were young, vigorous, radical and more extreme than the others: Chipembere and Chiume, both new to active Nyasaland politics. The others were of an older school and Chinyama and Chijozi had been leading Congress officials for some years. Furthermore, the Nyasaland African representatives in the federal assembly – Chirwa and Kumbikano – were also of an older school and incurred the displeasure of other members of Congress by accepting and then retaining seats in the assembly. The president-general and secretary-general of Congress, Sangala and T. D. T. Banda, too, were of an older school. In effect, then, Chipembere and Chiume were the only young and dynamic nationalist politicians in a much larger group of more mature, more moderate, more old-fashioned leading Congress politicians.

At its annual conferences in 1955 and 1956, resolutions were proposed demanding the resignation of the Nyasaland representatives from the federal assembly. Chirwa and Kumbikano felt that they could better oppose federation from within the assembly, but Congress took the view that their continued presence there was inconsistent with opposition to federation. They were expelled from Congress in August 1957 for refusing to resign.[52]

In June 1958 a Congress delegation saw Lennox-Boyd in London. Its members reiterated the proposals already given to Armitage and emphasized, now more clearly even than before, their strong wish for early constitutional reform. This was to enable the Nyasaland African viewpoint to be made strongly at the 1960 federal review conference. Lennox-Boyd assured them he understood their anxieties and added that he expected Armitage's recommendations after his return to Nyasaland in August.[53]

Although federalizing non-African agriculture in Nyasaland – the other major issue to occupy him in 1957 and early 1958 – was presented as a technical matter, it had extremely deep political implications. The European farmers in Nyasaland felt they had every cause to push for federalization because, they claimed, when federation was introduced it was acknowledged that 'to secure non-African agriculture on a stable and prosperous footing, responsibility for European agriculture should be transferred to the Federal Government' and the constitution provided power to do so. They also claimed that, although Colby opposed the transfer on the grounds that the financial implications were obscure, he promised that as soon as Northern Rhodesian non-African agriculture was transferred, Nyasaland would follow suit. Also, in May 1954 the secretary of state advised the European non-official members of legislative council to 'scramble the federal egg' and he instanced the federalization of non-African agriculture as 'the main factor in stabilizing Nyasaland'. When, on 1 January 1956, non-African agriculture was federalized in Northern Rhodesia, Nyasaland did not follow suit.[54]

The question was debated in legislative council in February and May 1957.[55] In December, John Caldicott, federal minister of agriculture, and Malcolm Barrow, federal deputy prime minister, discussed the issue with Armitage in Blantyre – they had flown specially from Salisbury. On 4 December, the whole question was discussed 'fully and at length' in executive council. Here it was decided that the matter should be left for consideration at the 1960 federal review conference. Armitage felt that, with his steps to try and make federation work rather better and with a number of things that could well bring African opposition even more to the fore – changes in federal franchise and proposals to increase Nyasaland African tax – this was no time to rock the boat by pursuing federalization of non-African agriculture. It was in any case an explosive issue. It was linked in the African mind with the danger of alienating their land to Rhodesian immigrant farmers.

> Dixon and Blackwood, of course, bitterly opposed the decision and are bound to feel most hurt as they reckon they can interpret European feelings to us and we have for once gone against them. They threaten that the Europeans will do all they can to make Government unworkable. I discussed with them the question of getting European views on constitutional progress and they said [it was] quite impossible in present circumstances.

On 9 December 1957 Armitage told the European farmers that, while he accepted a prima-facie case had been established on agricultural and economic grounds for transfer to the federal government, he intended to postpone the issue 'lest it should antagonize extremist opinion'. Because of political repercussions the postponement was to be excused on the pretext of financial stringency. The farmers were 'most disappointed' with his statement.[56]

In a further attempt to calm the situation, Armitage spent a good deal of time very early in 1958 working on a speech on citizenship, which he delivered to the Rotary Club on 6 January. He wished to use the occasion to say to both Africans and Europeans that they belonged to Nyasaland whatever their race and should collaborate to improve conditions in the country. He was encouraging a common loyalty.[57] A month later, Barrow addressed a public meeting in Limbe. Speaking from material prepared for him by the Nyasaland government, he read a joint statement by the federal and Nyasaland governments announcing their decision to defer further consideration of federalizing non-African agriculture for 12 months, 'when it will be considered afresh by the Nyasaland Government in the light of circumstances then obtaining'. Armitage felt that, with this statement, 'we had won another round'.[58] This is where the matter rested until much later in 1958.

For a while, the pressure died down. However, people were sensitive about the issue and there were fears that the federal subsidy to northeastern Rhodesia's tobacco industry would revive the arguments.[59] The stirrings continued and Armitage discovered that both the Nyasaland farmers' union and the tea association had written to Welensky wanting the question reopened 'at once': 'They are trying to bully all of us into agreeing to federalize non-African agriculture, and threatening [the] stick of getting the federal government to take over marketing and so [the agricultural produce and marketing board, which] spends £100,000 a year on the production side of government agriculture.' Blackwood had raised this matter at Barrow's public meeting and, although he believed the federal government was unlikely to take over the board during the present slump, he felt that Armitage was 'in serious trouble still with the Europeans over non-African agriculture'.

At this point, the six European non-official members of legislative council – no doubt led by Dixon and Blackwood who had already made the threat to Armitage – turned the screw on the governor by saying they could put forward no proposals for constitutional reform until the question of federalizing non-African agriculture was satisfactorily settled. As Armitage said, he was 'certainly up against the vocal European community' over the matter, but soon after arriving on leave, he got Lennox-Boyd to agree that they should 'wait a bit before deciding what to do'. Later during his leave he discussed the matter again at the Colonial Office and concluded that they could not do much about it until he got back to Nyasaland, had more talks with the Europeans and saw what the federal elections brought.

Armitage continued to canvas opinion in Nyasaland. The boat was well and truly rocked on 1 October when Caldicott threatened the Nyasaland government in a speech at Blantyre. He said that if they did not federalize non-African agriculture, the federal government would take over tobacco marketing if the United Federal Party (UFP) were returned to power.[60] 'We have gone far enough in this matter. If we can't persuade the Nyasaland Government to see our point of view, then we'll take action.' Caldicott criticized the Nyasaland government for its policy of 'masterly inactivity in regard to the transfer'. On reflection, Armitage said Caldicott was right to accuse him of masterly inactivity 'because that is what our policy was'; he added that he and Lennox-Boyd were 'experts in stalling' when it was their policy. He knew that he had a strong hand relative to the federal government because transfer required a resolution of his legislative council before it could take place.

Caldicott argued that if transfer did not occur, the Nyasaland tobacco industry would simply decline until it was of no interest to anyone. Barrow supported him by saying that there was no possible reason for leaving non-African agriculture 'out on a limb' in Nyasaland when the other two territories had passed their responsibility to the federal government. He also dismissed the claim that the Africans feared they would lose their land, by pointing out that the first five years of federation had demonstrated there were no dangers to African land rights. When Armitage looked into reports of Caldicott's statement it appeared that there was nothing very definite about it and it was unclear whether the threat was to take over the marketing of all tobacco or only non-African-grown tobacco, or whether it was a move to take over all produce marketing. The governor found the statement embarrassing as: 'If we should want to federalize non-African agriculture, we would now appear to do so under threat of the federal government. This would set all the opposition and anti-federation tongues and pens active. Caldicott's speech is also clearly against all courteous dealings and undertakings. We await full texts.'

When Armitage read the texts he decided to 'go cautiously' to Welensky with a 'more in sorrow than anger' tone. He also decided to write to the secretary of state asking whether in the face of the threat they could now really federalize non-African agriculture and, if so, could they get some useful *quid pro quo* from the federal government after the election. He would dearly love to tie the matter up with the review of the Nyasaland constitution but, as he remarked, time was against him. If, as the non-official European members of the legislature were insisting, the only way to get them to come forward with constitutional proposals was to agree to federalize non-African agriculture, Armitage was, it seems, prepared to pay that price.

At a meeting of the Nyasaland intelligence committee held on 7 October 1958, Peter Youens, the acting chief secretary, assessed the security situation – which was deteriorating – and indicated the ways in which they might handle it.

> Government considered it advisable to hit Congress with all possible provocation measures in order to force [Congress leaders] into taking some unconstitutional action. In this respect it was being contemplated whether to announce the federalization of non-African agriculture, should the Government decide to accept the federal government's proposals, at the same time as [the governor] announced his constitutional revision.[61]

Armitage was still finding Caldicott's speech an embarrassment when, towards the end of November, Barrow telephoned to ask if he would meet with himself and Caldicott to discuss a motion in the legislative council the following week to federalize non-African agriculture. The governor refused because Lennox-Boyd had telephoned him to say that Welensky – with whom he was discussing the matter in Britain – agreed that Barrow should not do anything until he returned to the federation, when he would talk about it with the governor. Armitage forthwith told Dixon of this and consequently no motion was put down for debate in the legislature. Dixon said he had never been in favour of federalizing non-African agriculture. This surprised the governor because Dixon's evidence on behalf of the tea association to a select committee of the legislature seemed in favour; it now read 'funny' to the governor.

Barrow again asked Armitage – at Welensky's request – to speak with him and Caldicott. The governor said he planned to visit Salisbury in about two weeks' time and could not do so earlier because of legislative council sittings. It was the case, too, that fewer than ten months before, Barrow had said publicly that the matter was to rest for 12 months. Armitage realized that Barrow had hoped for an earlier meeting, but Armitage was playing for time: 'I would like to see who the new minister of agriculture is to be.' In fact, Caldicott moved to economic affairs after the 1958 election and J. C. Graylin took over the agriculture portfolio.[62]

For some time the tea association had been so anxious to get out of federalizing non-African agriculture that they wanted to take over the tea research station and run it independently of all governments.[63] They now decided to do this. 'Why,' the governor asked himself, 'could not they have done this two years ago?' For Armitage, it made 'the problem on the ground ... no longer so difficult as regards non-African agriculture'. On 7 January 1959, executive council discussed the matter and the governor recorded in his diary: 'I am now assured that all European [members of legislative council] are behind it ... and we can go ahead cautiously, hoping to announce when everything is tied up and ready for a Bill in Legislative Council in March.'

It is unclear how this decision of the tea industry helped Armitage to move towards accepting that non-African agriculture should be federalized. It is likely the pressure of European politicians was a greater influence. They had refused to bring forward constitutional proposals until the question of federalization had been settled to their satisfaction. Without these proposals, Armitage felt unable to make constitutional recommendations to the secretary of state. Yet the price he would have to pay for getting them was to risk violent African reaction. Blackwood and Dixon wanted both – using federalization to provoke unlawful acts by Congress. Armitage seems to have considered for a while that if he announced both constitutional and federalization proposals at the same time, the former might make the latter more acceptable or perhaps would divert attention from it. Further discussions, however, reinforced his caution and he was uncertain whether to announce the federalization of non-African agriculture and a new constitution at the same time or to announce federalization at a later date. There were 'so many views on which will be the most aggravating to violence', and, recognizing that 'one can go on arguing for ever on all these', he concluded they would have to decide the constitutional changes first.

Even so, his uncertainty continued because some ten days later he wrote to Gorell Barnes at the Colonial Office about the action he might take if, as he believed, 'disorders and trouble' occurred in the coming few months when they announced the federalization of non-African agriculture and the proposed constitutional changes.[64] It might be that a simultaneous announcement of the two sets of proposals would provoke Congress leaders to take unlawful steps as Dixon and Blackwood intended. At a meeting of the national farmers' union early in January they said:

> There is going to be a showdown with Congress. This has got to come.
> ... The issue of federalization of non-African agriculture will precipitate trouble.... We will log the issue in legislative council at a time which seems to us appropriate ... and trouble will probably ensue but it will be at a time when we want it.[65]

In a private conversation a month later Blackwood repeated the need for a showdown with Congress and emphasized that it would come when he and Dixon wanted it.[66] At the farmers' union meeting they told the members, 'on behalf of government', they understood that the transfer would take place in April or May shortly before violent troubles were expected to occur: the trouble could then be blamed on the transfer.

Kettlewell recorded:

> The Nyasaland Government havered on this explosive issue, under fire from black and white. But, finally – and rightly – they rejected the Europeans' demands because nothing could have exacerbated African feeling towards federation more than the belief (however erroneous) that European land, which they regarded as synonymous with agriculture, was being lost to local control.[67]

Kettlewell – who even on technical grounds was not in favour of transfer – believed that it was Ingham who, after a long discussion with Kettlewell, influenced Armitage with their 'decisive opinions' that nothing was more likely to strengthen African hostility to the federal government than to federalize non-African agriculture.[68]

These two political matters – changes in Congress and especially the federalization of non-African agriculture – took up a great deal of Armitage's time, thought and energy during 1957 and the early part of 1958 before he went on leave to Britain. Behind it all, and throughout this period, he was seeking views on, and trying to develop an acceptable way forward with, constitutional advancement. He had 'intense political talks' and found that between these talks playing golf helped him to keep a clear mind.[69]

In September 1957, T. D. T. Banda, D. K. Chisiza, Chiume and Chipembere formed a Congress delegation to see the governor to seek constitutional reform. They wanted a legislative council of 40 – 32 Africans, six non-Africans elected on universal suffrage and two ex-officio members and an executive council of two officials with the remainder elected by the legislature. Armitage felt these proposals were too advanced and impracticable, although he neither accepted nor rejected them. When the delegation pressed him for his own proposals, he refused, saying he needed first to consult other communities and it would be better – as Lennox-Boyd had asked in 1955 – if Congress met with European political leaders and tried to reach agreement between them.[70]

At the very beginning of 1958[71] he spent time 'trying to get [his] ideas clear on what progress [he could] make in getting a climate of opinion in which [he could] announce future constitutional changes, when [he could] think up what they should be!' It was known that Armitage was planning to go on leave to Britain in April 1958 and would undoubtedly have important talks with the secretary of state. Congress activities and pressures in the few months before his departure were stepped up and very early in January they held an emergency meeting 'to decide what to do in 1958'. As the governor recorded privately: 'They have put forward their ideas for an African-controlled government and think that when I go to [the] UK in April they will send a delegation and this will all be fixed up with the secretary of state.'

Kwenje, with whom he had a long talk on 6 January 1958, wanted an elected African member of legislative council from each of the administrative districts and six Europeans, while on the official side there should be nine officials, two of the elected Africans and nominated chiefs to give an official majority. As Armitage noted, 'so he did not want African government yet.'[72]

When a delegation of Asians saw the governor on 30 January 1958, Sattar Sacranie – whom he saw as 'a very clever and determined man' – did nearly all the talking:

> Sacranie is very opposed to federation. He developed usual theme of one reserved seat for Asians elected on a common roll. [He] did not want to oust Europeans from their supremacy but stressed that each of the communities went its own way and only by a common roll would they have to be dependent on each other and so develop a nonracial outlook. He said expand unofficials on executive council but keep official majority, but the delegation seemed to agree that nominated members for legislative council would be possible if the right men were chosen![73]

Charles Matinga's Progressive Party met Armitage on 20 February. The governor felt privately that they 'had sense in that they admit the African is not yet ready to run a government', but he did not see any political appeal in that view. They thought there had to be nominated members of the government, for no elected members would work with the government. Armitage later said it was clear they did not want to be members of a party dominated by 'extreme and forceful' members and they favoured a gradual approach. In those conditions, they thought they would be listened to. 'In other words they wanted a lot of friendly Africans and Europeans to collaborate with friendly officials. But, of course, politics cannot be this easily organized.'[74]

The coloured community delegation told Armitage when they met him on 26 February that they represented the Indo-Africans, but also many others of mixed race. They would naturally like a representative in the legislature, but realized there was no hope of that. Armitage gained the impression that they were asking him to tell them what to do. The following day he met a Euro-African delegation that had broken away from the Indo-Africans. As Armitage saw it, they wanted a 'glorified debating society' for legislative council with communal representatives on a common roll, and no official side but with a large executive council of representatives of all races and members of legislative council deciding all matters in the best interests of the country. The governor saw these proposals as 'quite unreal'.[75]

Of the European members of legislative council, Armitage met only Coombes, whom he thought had little contact with his fellow European members largely because he had always advocated their meeting with African members and thereby had attracted European criticism. The governor did, however, receive a memorandum from the six European members. It said they could put forward no proposals for constitutional reform until the question of federalizing non-African agriculture had been settled satisfactorily – presumably to their own satisfaction. This was a stubborn, indeed somewhat 'dog in the manger', potentially extremely dangerous and certainly unhelpful response. He also received a letter from Foot, who pleaded with him not to leave the country during the coming crucial six months. He believed that they would be 'the most important Nyasaland will have to face, and from these months a future of great misery could develop'. Armitage present in the country would ensure that 'the struggle to retain the goodwill of the African moderates' would not let up and 'a reasonably happy future for our country may develop.' He was convinced that Armitage's leadership 'here in Nyasaland' was essential over the coming half year.[76]

When Chirwa asked on 1 April about constitutional reform, Armitage told him they must have an official majority in executive council and asked how that was to be achieved in legislative council. He got the impression that Chirwa was prepared to accept an interim government before full African control, but again the federation was the stumbling block. Chirwa said no African would accept it and 'so one makes no progress'.[77]

When Armitage asked the five African members of legislative council whether they wanted to see him before he went on leave, Chipembere and Chiume wrote to say that since he knew their views and they knew his, they would not (and they did not) come.[78] The other three – Kwenje, Chinyama and Chijozi – did see the governor on the day he left for Britain. They proposed a legislature comprised of 22 Africans elected by African adult suffrage, ten non-African members elected by non-Africans and four ex-officio members: a council of 36.

They also proposed equal numbers of Africans and non-Africans in executive council, with the governor as president and all members having ministerial responsibilities. 'In discussion it was clear that they wanted to preserve Colonial Office control, to get Africans and non-Africans collaborating in executive council and legislature, rather a debating house, but had no clear view of how you built up a government and opposition side.' There were to be no parties, but communal voting was essential. As Armitage remarked: 'A very woolly conception as one would imagine from those three, but friendly withal.'

Kwenje, Chinyama and Chijozi did not share the demands made by Chipembere, Chiume and other members of the Congress delegation. Armitage was clear that their views were 'nothing like as extreme' as Chipembere's and Chiume's. Armitage feared that 'Congress are putting up such extravagant demands for constitutional development that white opinion is recoiling sharply.' He was fully aware that 'no moderate party has yet successfully emerged in the present state of nationalism in Africa.' He was despondent after the meeting with Matinga, who represented the 'slow, moderate approach to political maturity for the African'. He saw them as lacking leadership, enthusiasm and following. Nor was he particularly heartened by Geoffrey Burden, the Nyasaland government representative in Southern Rhodesia telling him that there was a good deal of feeling among 'respectable Nyasas in Salisbury' against the extravagant demands and rudeness of the African members of legislative council in Nyasaland. Blackwood and Dixon were convinced that Southern Rhodesia was going to try and remove Nyasaland from the federation in 1960 because Congress was 'such a menace'. Armitage found the uncertainty 'depressing', especially since he could not 'make these people see much sense'.

A few days before he left to go on leave in April, Armitage received a delegation from Congress. This was to protest that he had neither produced constitutional plans nor got the Europeans to submit proposals to him before he went to Britain.[79] He explained he was aiming for changes in 1960 only and, although they might be disappointed, 'that was a fact.'

> They can't tolerate that. As the majority, that is Africans, want an immediate change, that must come about. We spent an hour round this one theme. They can't take no. They can't see their proposals are wrong.... Our main stumbling block is federation, no Africans will accept it and no Europeans will negotiate with any who do not.

They were annoyed because he would not move on constitution-making before he went on leave. Congress may have been additionally impatient because it had just dismissed its president-general and he was refusing to go. Armitage's own impatience may have been increased by the delegation appearing before him 'rather bedraggled in their green clothes and grass skirts, aping Ghana'.

The governor, naturally, also discussed possible new constitutional patterns with his officials. On 3 February he had a meeting with the chief secretary, attorney-general and acting secretary for African affairs.[80] Although they found it difficult to get the points clear in their minds, they were able to come up with a number of guidelines. There should be no ministers in executive council because they 'really would not have the Europeans of calibre and no Africans [had] been on executive council at all yet'. In the legislature they should preserve an official majority and to do this it appeared 'virtually necessary' to preserve an ex-officio majority.

In view of the intense dislike of all communities – except possibly some Asians – of a system of nomination, their scope to increase membership was limited and they could see only two alternatives. Either they could have six non-Africans, eight Africans and 15 officials – the absolute limit of officials they could use – or six non-Africans, 12 Africans and up to 14 officials with a chance of up to four non-officials who would be in executive council and on the official side. There would, they recognized, have to be voting safeguards. In reflecting on this in later years Armitage said:

> These deliberations show what a restricted field we considered we could operate in. We were all obsessed with the need to have an official majority in both Councils. This again reflects how influenced we were by conditions in the other territories. We could not envisage having party government. That would have led to Government control by Congress. We could not contemplate this, especially as Northern Rhodesia would not have supported us, and in any case we could not see many members of Congress being capable of forming a Government.

By early April he had got no further: 'We are quite at sea on [the] political future here unless we can force someone to break through this barrier of take Nyasaland out of federation.' He later wondered what they would have proposed if they had not been in the federation and having to take account of the views of the federal and the other territorial governments. He reflected, however, that at that stage no conservative government in Britain would have contemplated an African-controlled government in east or central Africa.

As Armitage pondered his first two years as governor of Nyasaland, just before going on leave, it was clear to him that he had made no progress with getting any support for the type of constitutional changes he could put to the Colonial Office. A reasonable amount of progress had been made with economic development schemes, but these were all departmental affairs: all he had to do, he said, was to discuss with the heads of the departments concerned and 'try and keep everyone keyed up and enthusiastic'. But political progress was different:

> I had had many hours of discussion with Europeans and Africans on political matters. I had toured the whole Protectorate and met all the important chiefs. I had visited many places, seldom, if ever, visited before. I had showed my presence and done my best to get interracial harmony and collaboration going.... I left behind a Government House well furnished, efficient and well equipped. The garden had been greatly improved, both for flower growing, vegetables and fruit. The old, leaking swimming pool was now becoming a rose garden for one hundred roses.[81]

His problem, of course, was that the swimming pool of politics was still leaking badly – and getting worse – and there were no signs of anything like roses appearing.

6

Nyasaland II

Act or abdicate.

Armitage did not get any guidance on constitutional development when he visited the Colonial Office on leave: there were 'no conclusions reached'.[1] 'Can't do much yet about new constitution... until I get back and have more talks with the Europeans and see what the federal elections bring. No sign of any cooperation from any African politicians in Nyasaland.'[2] It was, of course, the case that the Africans had come forward with proposals and the Europeans had refused to do so.

On his return from leave he announced he had no statement to make on constitutional changes, but wished to complete his discussions with all political parties and then come forward with proposals. Congress was disappointed: encouraged by overseas press reports, it had assumed that when Lennox-Boyd said he expected the governor to produce proposals on his return from leave, this meant immediately on his return.

A month before Armitage arrived back from leave, Dr Hastings Kamuzu Banda returned to his home country, Nyasaland, after more than 40 years' absence. Congress had asked him to return to lead its members in their struggle to secure independence and secession from the federation. At its annual conference on 1 August 1958, Congress elected him president-general with exclusive power to appoint officers and executive committee members. He chose Chipembere as treasurer, Chiume as publicity secretary and Dunduzu Chisiza as secretary-general. In doing this, he ignored the older, more moderate elements in Congress in favour of the younger, more vigorous and extreme elements.[3]

In the following three months Banda had a number of meetings with the governor, the secretary for African affairs, the acting chief secretary and heads of department.[4] He also toured and made speeches all over the country, and his very large audiences 'hung on his every word'. Armitage quickly became aware of the effect of his return, his reorganization of Congress and his speeches, some of which were followed by demonstrations, including stone-throwing by Africans against

Europeans. Many observed that 'the rallies caused an immediate sense of expectation and excitement among ordinary Nyasalanders. Civil disturbances and aggressive bloody-mindedness became the norm.'

The rallies and speeches caused great alarm in the non-African communities, where Armitage was criticized for not taking more effective action against the demonstrators. In fact, he was not inactive as the local press alleged, but taking the early steps needed for more effective action later. As early as August, in his monthly intelligence report to the secretary of state, he warned that 'disorders are virtually certain in or before 1960.' When Lennox-Boyd inquired about this 'disturbing document', Armitage explained:

> We are watching the situation caused by Dr Banda's boosting of Congress here and it is clear that at some time we shall have a show-down with Congress. He is giving the impression that there are going to be a whole number of changes of a widespread character, even approaching self-government, so it is clear that when we do publish our territorial constitutional changes [which will not contain anything like self-government] reactions by Congress will be sharp.

Also, in November, Philip Finney, head of special branch, revised the lists of those to be arrested in the event of disturbances. This was because the intelligence committee contemplated trouble in May or June 1959. For the first three weeks in December, Banda attended the All-African People's Conference held at Accra, Ghana. During his absence, legislative council granted additional powers to the government to control crowds and to punish those who stoned vehicles. Armitage authorized special branch to tap Banda's telephone, and called for a report on emergency prison and detention accommodation. After Banda's return, violence and law-breaking became extensive.

Just before Banda left for Accra, he was interviewed by Oliver Woods who told Armitage:

> I don't think he is negotiable. I don't think he thinks in those terms. He seems to be a fanatic and probably not a politician at all. . . . I think he's just out for the martyr's crown of gold, or thorns. Although I don't think he's much political sense, others of course advise him and may advise craftily. I believe in the long run you could smoke him out but I don't suppose there'll be a long run the way things are going.[5]

On 5 January 1959 Banda met Youens, who shrewdly detected the dilemma in which he found himself. The doctor had stomped the country raising his followers to a fever pitch of anticipation, but

Armitage was not coming forward with the statement on constitutional advance, which had been expected on his return from leave.[6]

Armitage's general feeling was that the government was 'going to have [its] work cut out to avoid trouble'. He was particularly concerned about the increasing violence over the past few months. His immediate priorities were, first, to 'clean up the trouble spots and then prevent disorder' and, second, to hold talks on a new constitution and 'have it in force by May 1960'. He wrote to Gorell Barnes about the possible action he might take if, as he believed, 'disorders and trouble' occurred in the coming few months. First, he could declare Congress an unlawful society, a solution he would have to consider 'in the light of the circumstances then prevailing'. Next, he could place restriction orders on the Congress leaders, but Nyasaland was not a large country and did not have well-defined inaccessible areas, which ruled out restriction orders. These difficulties could be overcome by the third possibility, detention, but introducing detention legislation 'would give advance notice of [his] intentions, and action under its provisions would carry its own complications'. Although he asked Gorell Barnes's views on introducing a detention bill 'if and when trouble seems imminent', detention was not his preferred option, which was deportation. He did not at this stage suggest handling matters by declaring a state of emergency. By the end of January, however, declaring a state of emergency had become an important part of his thinking: the necessary regulations were prepared and ready for use, and the chief secretary was 'going hard on getting the emergency prepared for'.[7]

A little earlier, an emergency meeting of chairmen and Congress branch secretaries was called for the weekend of 24–5 January. On the Sunday, 140 delegates were taken to an open site, selected at very short notice, in the bush just outside Limbe. Although most other Congress leaders were there and Armitage believed it was held at his direction, Banda did not attend. All present were required to preserve the secrecy of the proceedings – special branch believed they were sworn to secrecy under threat of death – and so effective was this requirement that it took some time before Armitage could learn much about what had taken place.[8]

It took Finney time fully to receive, check, collate and analyse the reports from his sources, but by 13 February this task was sufficiently advanced for him to report that a three-part strategy had been agreed. First, until the proposals were announced 'there should be illegal meetings and processions'. Second, if Banda rejected the proposals there should be a general strike. Third, if as a result Banda was arrested 'there should be a widespread campaign of assassination of Government officials, murder of European men, women and children and wholesale sabotage.' Colonial Office officials were concerned about the reports from Nyasaland, and a senior officer was sent to the protectorate to assess the position. On his return, he reported to the secretary of state that 'there was evidence for the plot coming from secret sources which could not be quoted', but he was 'not entirely happy about the handling of the situation in the field' and felt the government was somewhat 'distant' from the African people.[9]

Discussions on constitutional advance continued alongside the rising lawlessness and Armitage's attempts to deal with it.[10] Late in November 1958, James Morgan of the Colonial Office visited Nyasaland. He came to discuss what attitude Britain should adopt at the 1960 federal review on federal and Southern Rhodesian demands for dominion status and African nationalist demands for secession from the federation. He found virtual unanimity among officials that Nyasaland should remain part of the federation for economic reasons and that protectorate status should not be ended until Nyasalanders desired it. This view was based on grounds partly that good faith demanded it and partly that if protectorate status were withdrawn and dominion status granted to the federation, 'there would be a really serious internal security situation.'

Officials were less of one mind on the internal political future. Some believed that a constitution not based on racial distinctions would be desirable, while others looked forward 'to a situation in which political influence would belong predominantly to the Africans' because of their overwhelming numbers. All, however, thought it incumbent upon the British government to 'find a formula' that would advance Nyasaland towards self-government within the federation, retain protectorate status and reject or delay dominion status for the federation. Consequently, they accepted the suggestion being considered in London that they have 'some kind of commission' come up with a formula before the 1960 conference. Morgan believed Britain should make up its mind about the Nyasaland territorial constitution 'and get our local constitution fixed' regardless of what the federal review might propose, but Welensky wanted the federal future settled first. Privately, Morgan expressed the view that Banda was 'a nasty little man' and added – one knows not with what degree of seriousness – that they ought to get someone to get rid of him: 'Shall we get a friend to do it?'

Armitage invited 'all groups in Nyasaland' to put forward suggestions for a new constitution and received three widely divergent major results. Banda stuck to the proposals given over a year earlier: a legislature of 40 of whom 32 would be Africans, six European non-officials and two officials. The Asian Convention suggested equal representation for Asians, Africans and Europeans on both councils. The third set of suggestions came from 'moderate groups of the European, African,

Asian and Coloured communities' who worked together at the invitation of the United Federal Party. These groups suggested an equal number of Europeans and Africans on legislative council with an official majority; they saw no objection to Africans being members of executive council nor to non-official members holding portfolios.[11] The *Manchester Guardian*, noting that the chances of compromise between the widely varying suggestions were negligible, thought Armitage would now have to come forward with his own proposals – as Congress had asked him 18 months earlier and as Banda was expecting – and see what support they could win.[12]

Armitage described his general approach to Banda during these negotiations: 'I had to give him as much time as I could to make up his mind to see in fact whether he differed from the original Congress proposals put up by quite different people ... hence my view that this was something which one had continually to plug on and on until time was running out.'[13] Banda himself, at least up to October 1958, 'did not want to hurry [the governor] or embarrass him' by asking for a meeting to discuss constitutional advance.[14]

Armitage's strategy with the doctor was one of delay and persistence: 'We kept going at him ... and we were able to keep talks on constitutional matters going for several months'.[15] His idea was to 'go on and on and on' trying to get the various interests to agree proposals and, if this did not come about, to produce his own, but at the very latest time that would enable the new constitution to be in operation before the 1960 federal review. He knew his proposals would not be to Banda's liking, but at such a late stage he might acquiesce in them as something gained and the best offered. Banda, on his side, may have recognized Armitage's strategy, planned to let it take its course and hope to negotiate a somewhat better deal out of the last-minute offer. With so many conflicting political interests and proposals, Armitage was in 'somewhat of a flap', and unclear of the way ahead: 'The fancy franchises involved and completely irreconcilable views put forward, leave us in rather a muddle.'[16]

The great variety and quantity of views were indicated in a summary of proposals made to him, which Armitage prepared towards the end of February.[17] In this, as well as his own proposals, he gave details of proposals by the Nyasaland African Congress, African Progressive Association, Asian Convention, Euro-African Association, Coloured Community Welfare Association, non-party Africans, Chirwa, Nyasaland Association, Blackwood and Dixon, Congress Liberation Party (CLP), United Federal Party and 'certain elected non-African members of legislative council'. Some of the proposals were exceedingly complex. The governor's difficulties were exacerbated by two factors.

First, Dixon and Blackwood were taking the firm and unhelpful position that so long as Banda was allowed to stir up the crowds and the police took little action against them and 'so long as the present temper of the Europeans and Asians exists, against Government and the African, there [was] very little chance of [their] being able to get any proposal approved by the European and Asian electors.' Second, the Colonial Office was not formulating and expressing views of its own. As he recalled: 'I found that Her Majesty's Government in London had no idea what constitutional advance would be suitable for Nyasaland ... the officials in the Colonial Office were unable to agree to present a unanimous picture to the Secretary of State, for which he could get cabinet approval.'[18]

On 12 January he wrote to the Colonial Office suggesting that constitutional advance could best be handled by a personal visit from Lennox-Boyd. The secretary of state agreed and said he proposed to arrive on 21 February. However, he told the prime minister on 4 February that he wished Lord Perth, his minister of state, to make an early visit to East Africa during the first three weeks of March, and thought 'it would be a good idea if Perth went a little earlier than he would otherwise have to and spent a week in Nyasaland and Southern Rhodesia' in his stead.[19]

While arrangements were being made for the visit, Armitage met Dixon and Banda at Government House on 20 January. He hoped very much that Banda would meet European politicians, but the only way he could get this done was to be present himself. The doctor was surprised when the governor opened by saying that he had called the meeting to get the doctor's views on constitutional reform, for he had already told him what his views were. He was surprised too that Armitage was still having to consult the Europeans and thought he had finished these consultations. When, a few days later, Banda appealed in a speech for patience, he was hoping, that having discussed matters and come to no agreement, the governor would now make his own recommendations.[20]

Armitage made fairly definite proposals to the Colonial Office late in January 1959 as the alternative to mutually agreed proposals.[21] He envisaged a legislature of 29 made up of 14 elected and 15 ex-officio and appointed members. Of the 14 elected members, eight were to be elected on a general roll and in effect would be African; and six were to be elected on a selective roll and in effect would be European. Among the 15 on the 'government' side, he would consider some non-official nominated members if the need for this emerged during negotiations. He envisaged an executive council – over which he would preside – of five officials and four appointed, elected non-officials, two of whom would be non-Africans and two Africans. The non-official members of executive council would be advisory only and there would be no ministerial system. Beyond this, although he did not say so, he could not go without prejudicing the work of the commission being considered in the Colonial Office to produce a formula before the 1960 conference. His plan was to go as far as he could now and indicate that his proposals would be in operation by May 1960. In the meantime, the commission would come up with suggestions for further territorial advance within a framework dealing with the longer term future of the federation as a whole.

By mid-February, unrest was even more widespread. There were disturbances in schools, strikes in hospitals, post offices and other government offices, malicious damage to an airfield putting it out of operation, assaults on government officers, stonings, forceful release of prisoners, arson, looting, widespread breaking of soil conservation laws, arrests, and police use of teargas and firearms. For some time, Armitage had believed trouble would erupt in 1959 but not early in the year. He planned that his constitutional talks would be concluded in February and his precautions to handle disorders were in the anticipation that they would be needed after his proposals were announced and, presumably, rejected by Banda.[22]

On 19 February Armitage concluded that conditions in the north were so bad that he must send for the first battalion of the KAR from Lusaka and two platoons of the Northern Rhodesia police mobile force (PMF). The following day he travelled to Salisbury and met the governor-general, Benson, Welensky, Barrow and the premier of Southern Rhodesia, Edgar Whitehead. Armitage reported on the severe and increasingly disturbing situation in Nyasaland, and 'it was decided to send federal troops to Nyasaland to keep the peace'. He was convinced he would have to take 'rapid executive action' and declare a state of emergency 'unless there could be some miracle on the constitutional issue with the arrival of Lord Perth'.[23]

In reporting the Salisbury meeting to the Colonial Office, Armitage said Welensky, Whitehead and Benson had all agreed to assist to the limit of their police or military capacity. Everyone at the meeting was aware of his difficulty in immediately dealing with Congress more forcefully when he had inadequate forces and when Perth was about to arrive for talks. When these restraints were removed he hoped to 'take complete control of the situation', but he was aware that in the meantime others would think him inactive.[24]

Violence continued and police and military forces killed two Africans when dispersing rioting crowds. In these troubled circumstances, Armitage concluded on 25 February that Perth's visit should be postponed. The Colonial Office accepted this advice.[25]

When Armitage now told Perth he would probably declare a state of emergency at midnight on 2–3 March, Perth replied: 'Your plans have our fullest support. Good luck. Hope the birds won't have flown'. A little later, on his return from Aden, Lennox-Boyd also cabled, saying he had been brought up to date and adding 'All good wishes'.[26]

On 27 February, Armitage told the Colonial Office it was inevitable he would have to declare an emergency within the next few days. Looking to the future, and drawing on his Cyprus experience, he added: 'I must have a bill ready for enactment before that state of emergency is terminated. I naturally hope that such determination will take place within a relatively short time and this factor increases the urgency of the enactment of a bill [dealing with detention outside a state of emergency].'[27] The previous day Whitehead declared a state of emergency in Southern Rhodesia to control any disturbance while he freed troops and police to go to Nyasaland. He proscribed Congress in Southern Rhodesia and detained its leaders.[28]

Conditions remained peaceful in Southern Rhodesia, but not in Nyasaland, where Armitage believed the 'Government was in serious danger of losing control'. Riots, disorders and personal attacks on Europeans, Asians and African court staff continued; another African was shot dead by the army in dispersing rioters. Welensky mobilized all territorial reservists in Northern and Southern Rhodesia. Over 1000 troops were airlifted to Nyasaland. The additional forces now in Nyasaland were the first battalion of the Rhodesia African Rifles (RAR) less one company, the first Mashonaland and first Matabeleland battalions and two supporting companies of the Royal Rhodesia Regiment (RRR), the first battalion of the KAR, the Northern Rhodesia Rifles (NRR), two depot companies of the Royal Rhodesia Air Force and a contingent of British South Africa Police (BSAP). The NRR and both KAR battalions were African soldiers under European officers; and the RRR were young European territorials.[29]

On 2 March, Armitage signed documents to bring the state of emergency into force just after midnight. During the preceding few days his intelligence sources reported widespread activity by Congress branch officials encouraging disturbances to 'prepare for the general plan of violence'. He had recorded a broadcast message about the declaration and the reasons for it, and had pamphlets ready to be air-dropped with a message to chiefs and African civil servants. Just after midnight, on 3 March, he declared a state of emergency and proscribed Congress and its affiliated bodies. In an operation named 'Sunrise', leaders, including Banda, were arrested and placed in detention. By 5 March, 263 had been arrested and 72 of them flown to Southern Rhodesia.[30]

Operation Sunrise was on the whole efficiently conducted. District pick-up teams effected their arrests with the minimum of trouble and difficulty. In the actual pick-up arrests, 120 people were detained within the first 12 hours and only five were injured; none was killed. Although in a few cases excessive restraint — in the sense that more restraint than proved necessary in the event — was probably used, generally the arrests were made peacefully and with the cooperation of those arrested. Fairly large numbers gave themselves up. The worst problems were encountered not in effecting the pick-up arrests but in dealing with the crowds that gathered as a result of those arrests. Although in five cases resistance was such that five detainees were injured, in two other incidents 21 others who were not being arrested but demonstrating against the arrests were killed and 29 injured. Of these, 20 were killed and 28 injured at Nkata Bay in by far the most serious encounter of the whole emergency.[31]

Armitage was now working very long hours. He arrived in his office at 7.30 a.m., worked all day and, after vespers attended by senior civil servants, police, army and air force officers at 9.00 p.m., he left at about 11.00 p.m. He rarely got to bed before midnight. He set up the Nyasaland Operations Committee comprised of General Robert Long, the officer commanding the army in Nyasaland, John Mullin, commissioner of police and Kettlewell, whom he appointed because of his intimate knowledge of the protectorate and his close contacts with district commissioners and chiefs.[32]

The day the emergency was declared, Lennox-Boyd reported it to the House of Commons, emphasizing that Armitage had taken action himself, freely and at his exclusive discretion, without any outside pressures from, for example, the federal government, but with the full support of the British government. He added that once order had been restored the governor would 'consider what constitutional reforms may be appropriate'.[33]

In an adjournment debate later that day,[34] and replying to taunts about the influence of the federal government on the British government to press Armitage into declaring a state of emergency, Lennox-Boyd said: 'Some days ago information ... made it clear that plans had been made by Congress to carry out widespread violence and murder of Europeans, Asians and moderate African leaders: that, in fact, a massacre was being planned.' Colonial Office officials were 'somewhat taken aback' when the secretary of state mentioned murder and a planned massacre 'not because [they] were uncertain about the intelligence' but because they feared they might be unable to satisfy the House without revealing the source and this they could not do. Lennox-Boyd conceded to his officials that he had 'overstepped his brief'. This was the first time the plans for murder had been mentioned in public and Armitage, who had tried desperately hard not to give them publicity, was 'staggered' when he learned what Lennox-Boyd had said.[35]

Closing for the government, Julian Amery, minister of state, dealt with the four main opposition charges: the major cause of the crisis was delay over constitutional discussions; there were no real grounds for declaring the state of emergency; it was wrong to introduce federal forces into Nyasaland; and what had happened was the result of 'a conspiracy or machination' on the part of the federal government.

At this point, to support what the secretary of state had said earlier under pressure, Amery dealt with 'a still more sinister feature': 'There was a conspiracy of murder... if we had not taken appropriate action at the right moment there may well have been a massacre of Africans, Asians and Europeans on a Kenyan scale.' Colonial Office officials seem not to have been sufficiently 'taken aback' by Lennox-Boyd's statement on this matter to have persuaded Amery in the meantime to 'go easy' and not repeat it.

When the House divided, the government received 259 votes, the opposition 201.

Once the immediate Sunrise phase was over, Armitage embarked upon the second phase which included a 'campaign of harassment'.[36]

> It was decided that there should next be a vigorous policy of harassing and breaking up Congress organizers, supporters and hoodlums at a lower level, an aggressive policy being needed to break up the existing pattern of intimidation, threats and truculence and to demonstrate the Government's determination to break the Congress organization.... The objectives of the new operation were to arrest leaders still at large, to make propaganda, to give firm but friendly displays of force in quiescent areas and to take tough, punitive action in areas where lawlessness and acts of violence were being perpetrated or planned.[37]

In most districts these field operations took the form not of harassment but of mopping-up and 'showing the flag'. They were a politically dangerous exercise. There could be little objection to flag-showing if it merely demonstrated the presence and authority of government and its support of the chiefs, especially if this simply meant the security forces, accompanied by members of the administration, spending time in the rural areas. Nor could there be much objection to mopping-up if this meant ensuring that those supposed to be arrested earlier were now apprehended and that Congress cells were no longer operating. The danger of flag-showing and mopping-up was that they could so readily assume some of the less acceptable attributes of harassment exercises. It was the campaign of harassment that was not entirely wise. Even the expression was open to criticism, smacking of vindictiveness and a determination to inflict punishment, including, in troublesome areas, punishment of the innocent as well as the guilty.

A good deal of the criticism levelled at Armitage about security force activities arose from the harassment campaign. Despite the tough action the governor was prepared to take, he was far from happy at having to take it. The governor-general was clear that Armitage felt the presence of federal troops in Nyasaland, while necessary for security purposes, would only increase the unpopularity of federation in African eyes. He was also clear that Armitage 'did not think the use of force in any way was a solution to civil disorder'. Another indication of Armitage's views on the efficacy of force was given at a press conference the day before the state of emergency was declared, when, in answer to a question 'Do you feel that troops would be able to hold Nyasaland against the wishes of three million Africans?', he replied promptly, 'I doubt it.'[38]

The criticisms of his actions by parliament and much of the British press – which he saw as a 'campaign' – concerned Armitage.[39] This was partly because he felt that a 'personal witch-hunt [was] clearly on', but more importantly because he feared a 'very serious deterioration' in the relations between a large number of people in Britain and the federation. He felt that he would never persuade those bent on injuring the federation that his actions were justified. Any attempt at forthright statements would only strengthen the belief among government's opponents that 'a dastardly Federal plot is being covered up.' The assassination plot was something 'almost outside the ken of the man in the street in Great Britain and therefore viewed by him with suspicion'.

Armitage concluded that the most effective way to 'support the action' taken was for him to issue a statement setting out in a 'completely straightforward manner' what the Congress policies were, the evidence for knowing that these were their policies, and the action taken by Congress to pursue those policies. Consequently, he proposed to write a dispatch along these lines, which he hoped Lennox-Boyd would publish immediately. He was trying to divert prime attention away from the murder plot, which he saw as simply a part of Congress policy, and to publicize the whole spectrum of their opposition and lawlessness.

He spent 'a ghastly week' preparing the dispatch. The 'flurry' involved a great deal of work and contact between London and Zomba, including many telephone calls over poor lines, which caused him to 'strain to hear and yell to be heard, [with] intelligent conversation ... impossible'. It was written in great haste, under pressure from the

British government, without all the documents being available. A few slips that were made in proof-reading were later exploited by others. He supported his dispatch by sending with it a 161-page document elaborating every page and almost every paragraph in it. Armitage sent his dispatch to the Colonial Office on 18 March and it was published in a white paper five days later. In it, he reviewed the events and Congress actions that finally led to his declaring a state of emergency. He also described the position that had developed since 3 March.[40]

Within three weeks of declaring the state of emergency, Armitage reported to Lennox-Boyd that all three provinces were 'generally quiet': 'Very active sweeping and patrolling of last fortnight has had an excellent calming effect and restored order widely.' Consequently, he felt it was time to withdraw the RRR and, although there would 'inevitably be eruptions in some areas', he was confident the remaining military forces and the police would contain them.[41]

Immediately after the emergency was declared Lennox-Boyd decided that Perth, in East Africa at the time, should be asked to travel to central Africa. The secretary of state told his Colonial Office colleagues:

> It is not for the purpose of formal constitutional talks that Lord Perth is going – the fact that so many of the leaders are in detention would make this impossible – but in order to get first-hand information and to report to HMG. The real purpose, of course, would be to make sure that there is proper coordination machinery between the two Northern Governments and the Federation, to see that the views of the Northern governors carry proper weight, that prejudices pro and anti the Federation are not interfering with security needs, and generally to knock all their heads together.[42]

Perth stayed with Armitage from 12 to 17 March. He spent a day each in the northern and central provinces and Blantyre, and two days in Zomba. He met a wide variety of people: provincial and district commissioners, African, European and Asian politicians, African civil servants, schoolteachers, detainees, villagers, African businessmen, missionaries and many others. He also visited a number of places where trouble had occurred. On his return to Britain, his report to the cabinet dealt with security, constitutional progress and African fear of federation. On all these issues Perth was extremely supportive of Armitage and the Nyasaland government. In dealing with the fears of federation, which he found to be almost universal among Nyasaland Africans and particularly in the civil service where it was 'a specially grave problem', he said:

The fear of Federation, and of Sir Roy Welensky in particular, is held passionately, unreasoningly and apparently with an unshakeable tenacity.
... There is a widespread belief that HMG will fail to stand by their pledges and will sacrifice the Africans to the ambitions of the Federal Government. At the same time there exists an equally strong, if less irrational, fear among Europeans that we are going to sell out to the Africans too quickly.

Perth's visit was very full and thorough. He gave the British government a first-hand, up-to-date and perceptive appreciation of the situation in Nyasaland.[43]

Within two days of the declaration of a state of emergency, the British cabinet decided to set up a commission of inquiry into the disturbances.[44] Officials expressed doubts – shared by Lennox-Boyd – about the wisdom of an inquiry specifically related to the disturbances. At an interdepartmental meeting on 12 March, Gorell Barnes said one of the findings would almost certainly be that the Nyasaland Africans' distrust of federation was among the causes of the disturbances, and that this would prejudice the 1960 review. He thought it best to decide on a wider inquiry into the problems that would arise. This could be done by a commission which could also make an interim report on Nyasaland.

Armitage too 'was opposed to having the Commission [of inquiry into the disturbances] at all and foretold adverse consequences'. He was 'very concerned' about the possibility of appointing MPs on the grounds that this would defeat the political advantages of a completely parliamentary inquiry and the objectivity of a completely independent inquiry, and would make the commission 'unnecessarily unwieldy'. The British government accepted his advice that parliamentarians should not be members and, on 17 March, decided that the inquiry should be carried out by 'a Commission of three persons presided over by a judge'.

Attempts to secure others having failed, Sir Patrick Devlin was appointed chairman and Sir Percy Wyn-Harris, Sir John Primrose and Edgar Williams were appointed members, with Anthony Fairclough as secretary. Their terms of reference were short and undetailed: to inquire into the recent disturbances in Nyasaland and the events leading up to them, and to report thereon.[45]

Although Armitage could see that the early appointment of the commission had advantages, he could also see disadvantages, primarily that his and his colleagues' efforts were concentrated on preparing the case for the commission – 'what a sweat it is going to be to get all the documents and correspondence for them!' Consequently, they were not yet ready to commence any major prosecutions; and the kind of evidence so far available made such prosecutions unlikely.[46]

From the beginning, Armitage argued that if the commission had power to subpoena witnesses, this 'would have a disastrous effect on the special branch', whose 'agents should not in any circumstances appear before [the] Commission since, if they did, [the] whole ... Intelligence Service would collapse'. Lennox-Boyd accepted this view and excluded the power from the commission's warrant.[47]

At a very early date Devlin made it clear he wished to examine 'all (repeat all) documentary evidence on all (repeat all) matters referred to in the White Paper including the complete relevant files of the Administration, the Police and the military'. These wishes suggest he intended to place considerable emphasis on Armitage's dispatch and harboured doubts whether the governor intended or was willing to produce all the documentary evidence on every matter referred to in it. Armitage had, of course, submitted 161 pages of supporting documentation covering virtually every paragraph in the dispatch. While he could not let the commission see the government's working files, he had new files made up containing all the relevant material from the main files, including secret and top secret documents, but went through the material with the 'greatest care'. If any problems arose he would consult the secretary of state. He was particularly keen that potential difficulties should be ironed out before Devlin left Britain.[48]

The commission arrived in Nyasaland on 11 April.[49] Footman met them and gave them lunch,[50] and Armitage noted wryly: 'They are being wary of approaching me. I suppose they want to make certain that no one can accuse them later of having been influenced or intimidated by me!'[51]

With the problem of government contact with the commission in mind, soon after the commission was appointed Armitage discussed with the secretary of state the accommodation to be provided for them: 'In regard to nature of enquiry could it be criticized if accommodation is arranged either in Government House or in houses of senior officials in Zomba? ... I would be delighted to accommodate at Government House if appropriate.'[52] Devlin's response to this seeking of advice and sensitive offer of hospitality was that 'the Commission should be seen as clearly as possible to be independent of Government and therefore it would be a mistake for Commission to stay at Government House or with officials.' On their arrival, Armitage invited the commissioners to dine with him. They saw even this invitation as insensitive, were deeply embarrassed and sent Fairclough – who had suggested it in the first place – to get the invitation withdrawn so as to avoid declining it formally. They felt this incident revealed Armitage's unawareness of the commission's role and his part in it.[53]

They started their inquiry on 11 April, spent five weeks in the protectorate, travelled extensively and received evidence in all three provinces. They also sat for a week in Southern Rhodesia, and four days in London. They finished their hearings on 26 June.[54]

Armitage gave evidence for an hour on 15 April.[55] They asked him almost exclusively about the talks he had had and the arrangements he had made with Welensky and Whitehead to get reinforcements to Nyasaland. They quite quickly concluded that he had acted independently in declaring and conducting the emergency. Earlier that day he had replied to a letter from Devlin helpfully asking if there were points into which he felt the commission should inquire. Armitage believed there were five points. He suggested they inquire into the ways in which the Africans had suffered from federation since he would be supplying a good deal of evidence showing its benefits. He also thought it would be valuable if Devlin ascertained what effects the presence of Rhodesian troops had on the African population since he had been criticized for bringing them in. Next he thought that 'it would be desirable if [the] Commission could clarify the position of the Church of Scotland Mission ... as regards Congress and the influence of Congress on the Mission [because Devlin] will have received evidence of the damage caused by schoolchildren, at times accompanied by their teachers, in the vicinity of schools in the Mission areas.' He believed another material point would be to determine how Congress got its following, whether by intimidation and spurious promises, 'or whether it depends on personalities or other factors not easily apparent'. Armitage's final suggestion was that Devlin try to discover the extent to which the numerical weakness of the administration and the police contributed to the support given to Congress and the extent to which its members resorted to violence. At his interview Armitage was asked briefly about these points, and Wyn-Harris then asked if he intended to make a reappraisal of the 'murder plot'. This surprised him, but he turned the question to his advantage by clearly giving his view of the part the murder played in the multifaceted Congress plan.

> As I see it they took it into their heads that they could disrupt government here. Now how were they going to do it? They strung together a whole variety of things: disorders everywhere; release of prisoners; disruption of communications ... and as part of that pattern the murder of a variety of people. I just regard that plan to murder as part of an overall plan ... I regard the murder part of this as part of a phase in a plan which they never got to – they were never allowed to get there.

On 21 May, two days before the commission left Nyasaland, Armitage spent two hours with them.[56] The purpose of the meeting was for the commission to put to him various criticisms they had received. First, Devlin dealt with a number of paragraphs in the 18 March dispatch, which, it was alleged, were incorrect. In most cases, the commission simply made the point and noted Armitage's reply: they did not inquire into the reply or seek further elucidation. They spent a good deal of time on the allegations of illegal action by the army and police, including excessive force in making arrests, meting out punishment for uncooperative attitudes, burning houses and indiscriminately confiscating weapons, including agricultural implements. On this last point, Armitage's view, stated many years later, was:

> Devlin... did not pay any attention to the fact that in a state of emergency, when lives are being threatened, property is being destroyed [and] tempers are being raised, my administrative officers had to deal with each situation as it arose in the way that they could best handle it to protect lives and property. Now you can't approach an incident of this sort having regard entirely to the legalistic and judicial aspect of what you are doing. [Devlin] took no account whatever of the administrative side of the situation and in my mind the whole emergency was an administrative episode requiring administrative action.[57]

Basically, his point – which Devlin rejected out of hand – was that unlawful administrative action might be justified if it prevented far more damaging breaches of the law and injury to life and property.

Devlin recognized that 'his relationship to the Governor was essentially awkward', but told Perth his purpose was to assist Armitage rather than inquire into him.[58] It is clear, however, that from the outset Devlin and, except for Wyn-Harris, his colleagues – probably under the judge's influence – were gravely ill-disposed towards Armitage. Devlin's own impression of him was: 'He was not impressive as a witness but he was of course in a very difficult position – a Governor in the days when Governors expected to be treated as royalty summoned to give evidence in his own bailiwick.'[59] His impression of the governor was shared by Williams: 'Armitage was an ineffectual witness and seemed quite unprepared for a Devlin-style cross-examination.' Devlin's impression seems also to have been shared by Primrose: when two missionaries at Livingstonia 'tried to put in a good word for the Governor, Sir John only grunted'.[60]

There were signs during his inquiry that Devlin's report might not be favourable to the government and they might wish to reject parts of it. Only ten days after Devlin arrived in Nyasaland, Gorell Barnes sent

Armitage a copy of the secretary of state's 1950 circular dispatch on 'the principles to be followed when a Governor wishes to dissent from the findings or opinions contained in the report of a Commission of Inquiry'.[61] When he replied, Armitage said he and Lennox-Boyd ought to 'see and if necessary comment on' the report while still in draft.[62] Again, on 13 June, he told Morgan he had 'been doing some speculation on the possible findings [and] trying to assess the probable local reactions to them'. He thought it 'highly important from an internal security angle' that he should know the gist of the main findings as far in advance of publication as possible, so that they could 'prepare [them]selves against the effects of publication'.[63] Armitage and his Colonial Office colleagues, including ministers, therefore took a close interest in how and when Devlin would submit his report.

Perth had a long talk with Devlin on about 22 June. He explained the government's anxiety to have the report so that it could be debated in parliament before the recess and to give all parties time to study it before the debate. Also, the government and Armitage should be able to examine it before publication in case the governor needed to take security measures in Nyasaland.[64]

When, about mid-June, Lennox-Boyd was told Devlin's report would probably not be ready until 17 July, Gorell Barnes's view was that if the report reached them that late they would 'be placed in a quite impossible position unless [they had] seen a copy first in draft'. Since Lennox-Boyd was 'quite firm' the final document should not be printed until at least he himself had read it and this might cause further delay, publication could not be expected before 23 July, only a week before the recess.[65]

The Colonial Office considered delaying the report and the debate until after the recess. Although the advantage of this would be that the session did not end on a sour note, the chief whip's anxiety was 'not so much the Labour Party but being unable to answer the strictures if any in the Devlin Report in a convenient forum in order to satisfy moderate opinion and the party supporters'.[66] Furthermore, an autumn general election was a distinct possibility: they could not risk delaying the report and the debate on it until after the recess and incurring dissent among their own ranks or violent attack from the opposition on the eve of an election.

Devlin was somewhat delayed in completing his report by the need radically to alter the final part at a very late stage. On the evening of 9 July, he and Wyn-Harris had a long discussion about the report, which was all but completed. Wyn-Harris was worried about the closing paragraphs and proposed to dissent from the findings of the commission and submit a 'separate expression of his own'. The final part of the report as Devlin had drafted it – and that to which Wyn-Harris took grave exception – was a hard-hitting condemnation, a devastating indictment, of the Nyasaland government for abuse of power. Wyn-Harris argued in a 'passionate manner' that the report as drafted was unfair. He admitted to being 'very disturbed' and to making a number of 'intemperate remarks'.[67]

The result of the evening's discussion was that Devlin removed the paragraphs that offended Wyn-Harris and replaced them with a shorter section covering, factually, four matters that 'might be the subject of criticism': burning houses, confiscating implements, using unnecessary force in arrests and using force in villages. He did, however add, as 'a fact': 'The Government has not at any time, either before us or, so far as we are aware, to anyone else, expressed any regret for or disapproval of what has been done under these heads.'[68] This profoundly puzzling and undoubtedly calculated accusation – since he had the evidence before him as he wrote – was unfair and untrue. Devlin himself asked Armitage: 'If... we find cases where... people have been struck, not only with fists but with rifle butts, what... do we say about it? Do we say the Government approves, or do we say the Government disapproves and regrets, or what?' Armitage's reply was immediate and clear: 'I would have to say that there can only be an answer that the Government disapproves and regrets.'[69]

The Colonial Office had been working on the practicalities of getting the report, in whatever form, to Armitage as soon as possible and arranged for an administrative officer, who would soon be returning from leave, to take copies of the report to Nyasaland.[70] He flew from London on 13 July and arrived at Chileka the following day, carrying two copies of page proofs of the report, not fully amended, so that Armitage and his 'closest advisers only' could study them. In a formal letter accompanying the copies of the report, the secretary of state particularly stressed: 'The Report has yet to be completed and signed by Mr Justice Devlin and... in its present form should therefore be treated as secret.' In a personal letter he told Armitage, 'I know you expected a bad report and so did I, and I'm afraid it confirms our expectations.'

> There are one or two redeeming features in it, notably the endorsement of the action you took in declaring a state of emergency as being the only possible one you could have taken, and the exoneration of the security forces from some of the charges against them. Otherwise it is almost uniformly bad – hostile, tendentious and grossly unfair.
>
> We are giving urgent consideration to our next moves... but I hope you will... come to London.... Meanwhile I would like you to know how much I sympathise with you in this further ordeal and how

admirably I think you have handled everything. We are all in this together.

Armitage and his colleagues were now plunged 'into a maelstrom of activity'. For three days they analysed in great detail Devlin's account of events, the conclusions he had drawn, his references to evidence given and the ways he had interpreted it. He asked special branch officers to go through the report 'with a fine-tooth comb to see where [the commission] had gone wrong, what clear errors they had made, and where there were discrepancies which [they could] later take up'. They worked without break for many hours to produce 'a very full brief' for him to take to London.[71]

The British government quickly decided that a very high level working party should spend the coming weekend at Chequers, drafting a dispatch from the governor to accompany the publication of Devlin's report.[72] The matter was now one of the greatest importance to the Conservative government. They had been badly mauled during the 3 March debate; the Hola prison killings in Kenya were still an acute embarrassment to them; many of their own supporters were uneasy about the handling of affairs in Africa, particularly Nyasaland. The full five years of the current parliament would end in June 1960 and there was talk of an autumn 1959 election.

The composition of the Chequers working party shows the seriousness with which their task was being taken. On the British side were the lord chancellor, the attorney-general, the secretaries of state for the Colonies and commonwealth relations, two Colonial Office ministers of state and the chancellor of the duchy of Lancaster. They were supported by a number of very senior officials, including security advisers. From Nyasaland, Armitage, Denys Roberts – acting solicitor-general – and Finney also spent the weekend at Chequers helping with the drafting.[73]

Armitage arrived in London on Saturday 18 July and carried with him a first draft of the dispatch providing a 'framework examining the main paragraphs of the Report and commenting on them'. A draft had also been prepared by the Colonial Office. Together they worked on the full draft, which was 'considered most carefully and amended'. Lennox-Boyd, 'cheerful and expansive', had Macmillan's encouragement 'to handle the report robustly'. He and Reginald Manningham-Buller, the attorney-general, were the dominant personalities. Colonial Office officials thought Armitage 'played a rather passive part in the proceedings': he had, of course, put a great deal of work into the draft he brought from Nyasaland. In two days they tried to cover four months of the commission's work. He was 'most heartened' by the

British government making 'an all out effort ... to defend [the Nyasaland government] where the Report criticized [it]'. He spent the whole of Monday 20 July at the Colonial Office, the dispatch was finalized and a guide to the contents, with cross-referencing to the report, was prepared for issue as a white paper and the Cabinet approved it. It was published at the same time as the Devlin Report. When Macmillan read the press comments on it the following morning he asked for his congratulations to be sent 'to all those who had taken part in "a well-conducted exercise"'. Armitage also received the personal congratulations of Dalhousie and Welensky on his 'excellent despatch'. Its preparation was a rehearsal of the government's case in the subsequent Commons debate.[74]

The Commons debated the Devlin Report on 28 July on a motion by Manningham-Buller, taking note of the report, thanking the commission and endorsing its conclusions that a policy of violence had been adopted by Congress leaders, 'the Government had either to act or to abdicate' and the declaration of a state of emergency was fully justified.[75] The motion regretted the loss of life but acknowledged that the governor's action prevented more serious losses. It expressed gratitude to the administration and security forces, and looked forward to normality returning and to continued constitutional and economic progress based on respect for law and order. James Callaghan, for the opposition, moved an amendment that the House accept the report *in toto* and alleged that the government had winnowed through the report, 'sieving out and dredging up everything that would support their case and averting their eyes from anything that might in the slightest degree be embarrassing to them'. Six major speeches were then made on each side by leading members specially interested in Africa, each supporting the motion proposed by their party's spokesman. Closing for the government, Lennox-Boyd said it was not only open to a government to reject a commission's findings but it was its duty to do so where it disagreed with them. He emphasized there was no option but to declare the state of emergency and he put as favourable a light as possible on the criticisms covering unlawful activities, while denying that any of the illegalities was authorized by higher authority. He concluded: 'The test was – was there a real threat to the lives of Europeans and Africans as a result of the adoption by Congress of a policy of violence? From the Commission's report it was clear that there was.' When the House divided, the opposition amendment was defeated by a majority of 63, and the government motion was carried by a majority of 62.

After the Commons debate, which Armitage attended in the gallery – as did, among others, Chiume[76] – he spent a further day in London and discussed with Footman, by telephone, the arrangements for his arrival back in Nyasaland. Footman proposed a formal airport reception with a guard of honour, executive council and 'other dignitaries' and a press conference. Armitage did not like the proposed publicity and feared his reception might be 'described as an ovation by whites and a boycott by blacks'. Consequently, there should be no official reception unless it was nonracial. As things turned out, his arrival at Chileka on 31 July was accompanied by a guard of honour and 'close on 1000 people who had gathered spontaneously to ... give a rousing reception'. Those present were indeed from all races and a number of chiefs joined the official reception party. Two aircraft from a local flying club flew overhead in a close formation salute. So much for an absence of publicity![77]

Armitage found the cheering and waving and the dozens of congratulatory letters he received 'staggering and bewildering'.[78] He was both pleased and embarrassed by his welcome at Chileka. He used the press conference 'to bring together in one comprehensive statement some decisions of importance that [had] been taken ... during [his] absence'. His first point was that Devlin had found the declaration of the emergency justified, and he added there was no intention to lift it at present, although its application could be relaxed. Detainees would continue in detention although he would review their cases from time to time. His second point was a very limited constitutional advance: in the absence of holding elections under existing conditions he proposed to increase the number of African members of the legislature by nomination – matching them with an increase in official members – and appoint two Africans to executive council. He hoped that by these means – which privately he described as 'rather meagre' – African members of the legislature would feel more intimately associated with the formation of government policy. His third point was that the advisory commission preparatory to the 1960 federal review would comprise 26 members: 13 from the United Kingdom or the Commonwealth, and 13 from the federation, including three from Nyasaland of whom two would be Africans. He thought it very important to announce this proposal at this stage, even before details had been worked out. In his fourth point he said that during the discussion on the limited constitutional advance,

> the Prime Minister ... said that the British Government would not withdraw its protection from Nyasaland in the short run, and in the long run the object is to advance the territory to fully responsible government [and] able to dispense with HMG's protection and stand entirely on its own feet as a component of Federation. ... When all the units are in a position to agree and are agreed that British protection is no longer

needed, then and only then can the whole Federation go forward to full independence and full Commonwealth membership.

If Macmillan had made this statement six months earlier he would have given the African politicians the 'political horizon' Armitage advocated and would have calmed their fears about dominion status for the federation – the factor that triggered violent opposition to the government and gave urgency to the African struggle against federation – and may have saved lives. Next, Armitage announced his decision to postpone federalizing non-African agriculture. In this way he disposed of an issue that was a constant threat to political calm in Nyasaland and at the same time he gave a 'categorical denial' to those who saw in this a desire to work for Nyasaland's secession or to belittle its part in the federation. Finally, he spoke of the 'many things to keep us busy', including forming a local, nonracial, civil service and increasing the number of Nyasalanders in responsible positions in the service.

The enthusiasm with which Armitage had been greeted by Europeans at Chileka was repeated when shortly he attended a function at the Zomba gymkhana club, where he was 'cheered to the rafters', and in Limbe where a performance of *HMS Pinafore*, which he had missed while in London, was specially repeated for him. It was also evident in Southern Rhodesia when he was embarrassed by many Europeans telling him he 'had saved them by his firm stand' against Devlin.[79]

Early in October, just before the general election in Britain, Armitage wrote a long confidential letter to Lennox-Boyd.[80] He felt it was time to review the political situation, assess trends and bring the departing and a possibly new government up to date with affairs in the protectorate. His general view of conditions was: 'We are in a state of surface normality, but in many places we find the undercurrent of African opinion is very aloof.'

He wrote first of the continuing need for detention. Some 500 Africans were still detained and he could see 'little likelihood of a flood of releases'. Although there was a steady flow, 'there remains a hard core of Congress adherents who, given the slightest encouragement, would not hesitate to come out into the open and undo everything we have achieved. We just cannot afford to let this happen.'

He dealt at length with Banda, whom he saw as 'a major problem'. The influence of Congress was so great and the 'messiah-like concept of its leader' still so alive that the vast majority of Africans, especially potential politicians, continuously saw 'the shadow of Dr Banda over their shoulder', and were consequently reluctant to voice any views not conforming to his. He did, however, hold out 'one redeeming feature', albeit 'but a straw in the wind'. They had an interim constitution and had rearranged the machinery of government to prepare, by 'natural evolution', for a form of ministerial government. There were signs too of some Africans appearing prepared to follow political parties with aims very different from those of Congress and to cooperate with Europeans and Asians. He thought it 'possible if not probable', however, that only by eliminating the opposition of the 'most forceful and indeed able' Congress leaders, and the proscription of public meetings, that they would have the chance of fostering a nonracial and liberal approach to politics. He concluded with the words: 'We must not give too little too late but if we give too much too soon we could wreck the whole future of the Protectorate.'

Although Lennox-Boyd did not find the dispatch as depressing as did others and thought there were 'chinks of light showing', Perth read it 'with interest and depression'. Macmillan found it a 'pretty depressing picture' although he did say that the paragraph on the 'one redeeming feature', the 'straw in the wind', was 'interesting'.[81]

At the 20 October 1959 general election the Conservatives were returned to power with an increased majority, of 100, with 'the right wing ... less in evidence'.[82]

For some time Macmillan had realized Africa would demand a great deal of his urgent attention. On the basic issues in Nyasaland, little had changed: the crisis continued, the governments were no further forward and Banda – content to bide his time – also was no further forward. An impasse had been created by the emergency, which in many ways had made it more difficult to resolve the dilemma than before. Someone needed to do something to resolve it.

With the confidence his more secure position in the Commons brought him, Macmillan determined to act positively and quickly. On 1 November – the day after he read Armitage's 'pretty depressing' letter – he wrote a note to Sir Norman Brook, secretary of the cabinet.[83] He first reflected on the Commonwealth tour he had undertaken the previous year and then turned to Africa, 'the biggest problem looming up for us here at home'. In effect, casting his mind back to events in recent months in Nyasaland, he was relieved his government's Africa policy had not resulted in his defeat at the general election, but he realized how vulnerable that policy had made him. He did not propose to run that risk again and he determined on two things: there should be a change in the policy or at least in its application and he would try to 'lift Africa onto ... a plane above that of narrow party politics'. To accomplish these things he decided to do what he 'had long determined': to visit Africa. He also appointed a new type of secretary of state for the Colonies: Iain Macleod.

Very soon after taking office Macleod asked Armitage to London for consultations. At their first meeting, on 9 November, Macleod asked him to survey developments in Nyasaland since his dispatch of 6 October.[84] Armitage said the election had a 'sobering effect' on the Nyasaland Africans who were disappointed by the result. Whereas earlier they had been reconciled to Banda staying in detention for a year, they now thought it would be much longer. He spent some time discussing Banda, in Gwelo gaol with the 'four main extremists'. He did not think the relationship was 'altogether happy'. The doctor was working hard, reading and writing but was 'doubtless being worked on by the other four'.

> The question was at what stage we might use him. The time could not possibly be right until after the Advisory Commission since if Dr Banda were released earlier, that would inhibit *all* other Africans from expressing their views before the Commission. On the other hand, once other politicians got going strongly enough, his release would need to be considered. The idea of release was anathema to the Federal Government. Much would depend upon the ability to keep the core of extremists in detention with arrangements short of a state of emergency. It was quite essential to be able to assure both the Africans who were cooperating with Government and other Africans that the situation could still be controlled if the state of emergency was lifted.

He felt 'the first essential' was to discover how Banda himself was thinking, particularly whether he would dissociate himself from his colleagues. He did not accept the view that Banda was the only person with whom he could treat. In fact, he had the gravest doubts whether one could ever negotiate with him as a man who would keep his side of a bargain.

Macleod wanted to distinguish between Banda on the one hand and Chipembere on the other – as had Devlin whom he consulted just after taking office – and hoped they could make it clear that, whatever Banda's future, the extremists 'were likely to be out of circulation for a very long time'.

Armitage's first impressions of Macleod were favourable: 'My new Minister appears very reasonable and I did not have to give anything away.'[85]

It is clear that as early as November, Armitage felt he might need to treat Banda specially in order to distinguish him from the extremists and thereby be able to release him and use him in the advancement of the country. However, he was very unsure of how to do this in his quest for constitutional advance within the federation. His attitude towards the release of detainees generally was: 'There were a number of hard-core detainees who could not be released in the foreseeable future.... There was a controlled and steady release of persons and we saw no possibility of accelerating this. But we aimed at ending the state of emergency.'[86]

On his return to Nyasaland, Armitage called a meeting of executive council and explained what had happened in London: 'no new policies or plans', which provoked 'no particular comments'.[87] He and his colleagues were not anticipating any particular or swift changes from the new secretary of state. Armitage was much concerned with what was still the basic problem, introducing a new constitution for Nyasaland, and he had already privately worked out his 'own plan for the future'.[88] The differences in what he was now prepared to recommend in a new constitution, compared with his proposals ten months earlier, were considerable. He was no longer hampered by the conflicting and unrealistic demands of numerous political parties and sectional interests, and the emergency had introduced a significant air of realism and progress into his thinking. His legislature of 29 members would now be reduced to 25 of whom only three would be ex-officio as against 15 ex-officio and nominees earlier; the non-African non-officials remained at six; and definite African non-officials would in effect increase from eight to 16. His executive council would increase from 10 to 11, including himself as president; his official members decreased from five to three; non-Africans remained at two; and Africans increased from two to five. Whereas no non-officials would have been ministers, now the five Africans would all be ministers. There would be a clear African majority in legislative council and, excluding the president, parity – of a sort – in executive council, the number of African ministers matching the combined total of official and non-African members. Yet the air of realism and progress, which the emergency had introduced, still fell short of envisaging Banda playing a part in the proposals the governor felt able to recommend: for this the air needed to be stirred into something more like a wind, maybe a gale.

Early in December Macleod wrote a note to Macmillan setting out his thinking on Nyasaland: 'probably the most difficult single problem' they had in the field of colonial policy.[89] There were then 470 people still in detention, 90 of them in Southern Rhodesia. The early 'fairly swift' release of detainees had recently slowed down and, disappointingly, the numbers had started to rise again. He was convinced they had to achieve a 'substantial reduction very swiftly' and bring the emergency to an early end. He also wanted to treat Banda differently from the other detainees, improve his conditions, and then at an appropriate moment order his release. Indeed, Macleod 'was really determined to release him from the moment [he] became colonial secretary'.⁹⁰ He believed the best chance lay in a swift reduction of detainees to the hard core before Walter Monckton arrived; receiving in due course 'imaginative proposals' from him which would allay African fears; the promise of early constitutional advance for Nyasaland; and a period of stability after the 1960 federal review 'during which we must try by every means in our power to see that federation works'. This policy involved risks, but he was certain it presented 'the most hopeful possibility of advance'. He had not discussed the rapid reduction of detainees with the governor. He proposed to ask Armitage to meet him in Dar es Salaam during his imminent visit, to discuss it.

On 18 December, Armitage flew to Dar es Salaam where he had a number of interviews with Macleod and quickly learned that his initial impression of 'no new policies or plans' was gravely mistaken. The secretary of state opened by saying the state of emergency was no longer justified and he could not defend it. He expressed his strong view that they should have a very rapid rundown of all detainees and deal with Banda separately. Armitage, 'staggered by the approach', in response 'argued vehemently' that there was a serious security risk in Macleod's proposals. He felt strongly that to release the detainees quickly in the absence of any indication of future policy would be to release them into a vacuum, which would result in further and worse disturbances necessitating calling in federal troops. Armitage felt strongly about the need to give the Africans a 'political horizon', an indication of Britain's intentions, and about the dangers of releasing detainees into a 'vacuum'. It was a point he frequently made. Furthermore, he argued, Banda's release 'might well jeopardize the whole tour of the Monckton Commission'. The governor insisted he would 'run down detainees in order so as not to have troubles in [the] districts'. Eventually they agreed to an accelerated release of detainees with Banda being treated as any other detainee. Macleod undertook to take this proposition to the cabinet. It was a compromise, Armitage giving way over the pace of release, Macleod giving way over treating Banda as a special case. The following day, after much arguing and straight talk, they agreed on 100 releases in January, 80 in February, 70 in March, 41 in April, 38 in May and 38 in June, leaving only 49 detainees in July. Of these 49 hard-core detainees, 'it would be impossible to say when they could be released.' They also discussed a successor as chief secretary when Footman reached retirement age, and agreed that the change should take place on 30 June 1960.⁹¹

Armitage also had a long meeting with his provincial commissioners, the chief secretary and other senior advisers, on 29 December. They believed the programme agreed with Macleod for releasing detainees — which they accepted — was not likely to be a security risk for a few months. If Banda were released to Nyasaland this would be 'the beginning of the end' and the chiefs and others would all follow him. Consequently, on release he should be sent to the United Kingdom, and negotiations with him should be delayed until the advisory commission had reported and the federal review had taken place. Thereafter, once the Nyasaland constitution had been arranged, he could return to Nyasaland. In later years, Armitage recalled how nervous they were that conditions would deteriorate into another emergency and, in retrospect, he felt they placed too much weight on this fear. At the time, they 'were too close to the emergency to recognize that it was by providing a chance for further constitutional change that [they] would enable the hard-core element to come back into political life'.[92]

Reporting this meeting to the Colonial Office,[93] Armitage said his provincial commissioners were taking a very serious view of the security situation if Banda's release were combined with accelerated releases generally. He advised that releases be decelerated and the possibility of a large hard core accepted if Banda were released before 1 April. In any case, the doctor should not be let out unless Macleod himself visited Nyasaland and unless Banda expressed a clear willingness to enter discussions on the basis of self-government within the federation. He pointed out that release could be to Britain and discussions could take place there; if Banda objected to this, for example because he could not properly consult his people, they 'might just have to send him there'.

At the close of 1959, Armitage was feeling somewhat dejected and helpless: 'I find life most depressing and see myself with no room to manœuvre, only sit on a boiling pot getting more steam!' 'I am not sorry to see the end of 1959, but 1960 opens with the prospect of being much worse.'[94]

Although the agreement Macleod had reached with Armitage was, as he had also agreed, submitted to the cabinet, the secretary of state accompanied it with a covering note when it went to the cabinet on 4 January:[95]

> Attached paper on Nyasaland is the result of discussions with Armitage at Dar es Salaam and represents the highest common factors of agreement. Firstly, I feel that programme is too slow, although release rate represents twice the rate Armitage first suggested. There are no rehabilitation problems in the Kenya sense and rate of release is simply judgement of security risk and can be increased or decreased as the situation requires.

No serious problems had so far arisen following releases, and intelligence reports were not alarming. He hoped, therefore, to step up the February and March releases and reach the hard-core position by the end of April, when the state of emergency might be ended. 'Secondly, I feel that 50 hard core is much too high and doubt if we could justify more than about 20, if that. Thirdly ... Armitage now agrees that we must discuss, some time, constitutional matters with Banda.'

In another note to the cabinet, Macleod said he was anxious to ensure the emergency was ended as soon as possible and meanwhile the release of detainees should be accelerated and the conditions of Banda's detention relaxed.[96] Three days before the cabinet met on 4 January, and subsequent to the two notes being written, Macleod had 'a little discussion' with Macmillan and Home, in which he had 'produced the ideas' about the increased rate of release. However, rather than risk their rejection at that stage he said he wished to think more about them before making definite recommendations. Having introduced his ideas in this indirect and apparently tentative way, and possibly taking advantage of the prime minister's mind being significantly occupied with his imminent departure for Africa, he very shortly came forward with quite definite proposals, which the cabinet accepted.

Macmillan was feeling very tired and was taking sleeping pills. He had spent the previous day at Sandringham and had flown back that morning just before the cabinet meeting, which dealt with 'a lot of tricky questions [including] Nyasaland and Dr Banda'. There were also a number of absentees from the meeting, including Duncan Sandys and Ernest Marples. Armitage was not told about either of Macleod's notes to the cabinet, even though they significantly altered the agreement reached with him. He later expressed the view that Macleod 'was utterly ruthless so that he just bulldozed his way through any views ... which were put up to him'.[97]

On 4 January 1960, the day before Macmillan left Britain to start his tour, Armitage received a cable from Macleod immediately after the cabinet meeting. It said that they had just agreed, subject to the security situation and Macmillan's discussion with Welensky, that Banda should be released after Macmillan left the federation on the last day of January. There was to be accelerated release of detainees – at least 120 a month with immediate effect so as to leave only 50 by the end of March and 12 by the end of April – but there was no question of constitutional talks being held.[98] He did not reveal that it was on his advice that the cabinet reached these decisions. Armitage was 'absolutely astonished to receive this telegram' and to see the extent to which his agreement with Macleod had not been adhered to.[99] Home told Welensky of the cabinet's decision greatly to accelerate releases and said that Macmillan looked forward to discussing the emergency and Banda's release with him later in the month.[100]

Armitage told executive council on 6 January that, in Macleod's view, virtually all detainees should be released by April and that, with the permanent detention legislation in place, the state of emergency would then be ended. Council's reaction was that this would be proceeding too fast to gauge the possible effects and, in any event, those who were a threat to security should remain in detention.[101]

The next day, Armitage wrote to Macleod about the security aspects of the accelerated release of detainees, especially Banda. All the advice he was receiving was that if Banda went willingly to Britain the danger of disturbances would be greatly reduced, especially if it could be announced that he was discussing matters with the secretary of state. On his present assessment, he felt it unlikely that Banda would go to Britain willingly. In any case, the doctor never had controlled, or could control, the hooligans among his followers. He told Macleod that he would need three companies of RAR, two of first battalion KAR, three of second battalion KAR, nine PMF platoons, air transport, reconnaissance aircraft and the services of his special constables. He concluded, however: 'If situation seriously deteriorates it is anybody's guess [what forces would be required].'[102]

The position, then, by the middle of January 1960 may be summarized. In Britain, Macleod and Macmillan were intent on faster progress towards self-determination in Africa generally and Nyasaland in particular. They felt unable to justify continuing the state of emergency. They were anxious to reduce the number of detainees speedily and were prepared to release even many of the hard core, whom they felt could be dealt with by enacting preservation of public order legislation. They recognized Banda as the only real leader of Nyasaland Africans and the person who could most readily – and quite easily – command virtually total African support. To retain the federation, they envisaged a self-governing Nyasaland within it, but knew that to stand any chance of succeeding in this aim, they needed to make substantial and very early advances in the Nyasaland constitution. Such advances could not be made while Banda was in detention: he had to be an active party to them and he ought to be released to Nyasaland before Monckton arrived there so that he could give evidence to him. They acknowledged that releasing Banda was a security risk. They believed Armitage's attitudes were hampering the breaking of a political deadlock, and early and radical changes were essential.

In Nyasaland, Armitage's non-official advisers were much more certain deteriorating security and violence would accompany Banda's release. Blackwood felt his early release would cause Southern and

Northern Rhodesia to withdraw from the federation and then 'there would be no federation to contain Nyasaland.' Dixon believed his release would involve 'the gravest disorders'. Both, unlike the governor, considered Banda to be one of 250 or so hard-core detainees. They advocated he should not be released until the pattern of the federation had been decided and he should be kept out of Nyasaland for two further years: if he then returned 'the new constitution would be working and he would be deflated'.[103]

Notwithstanding the non-official members' hard-line opinions, Armitage, with his official advisers, had moved towards agreeing with most of the British government's views. No doubt they had recognized the direction in which Macleod was going and his determination not to be thwarted and were adopting a 'more forthcoming attitude'.[104] They, too, wanted an early end to the emergency, with permanent legislation to cover detention and public order. They, too, wanted to run down the number of non-hard-core detainees as soon as possible, although they had in mind a significantly slower rate of releases than had the British government. They, too, recognized Banda as the only real leader of Nyasaland Africans – 'we could only improve the situation by dealing with him.'[105] Earlier, however, they had gravely doubted whether Banda was the sort of man with whom they could deal. Fearing that he might not negotiate, they had toyed with the idea of supporting and using Wellington and Orton Chirwa. They had hoped that by keeping Banda in detention other, more moderate, leaders would be encouraged to emerge. They, too, agreed they could deal with Banda only if he were released from detention. They, too, aimed at a self-governing Nyasaland within the federation and recognized that very early and substantial territorial constitutional advance was essential if they were to stand a chance of succeeding in this aim. They, too, believed there was a security risk in releasing Banda but felt – provided they were allowed to draw on sufficient reinforcements – they could, at least for a while, contain any violent trouble.

The Nyasaland government, however, differed from the British in two respects.[106] First, and most important, it believed territorial constitutional discussions could proceed without Banda being in Nyasaland, and it would be much safer if he were sent to Britain when released. In effect, Armitage wanted to attach conditions to Banda's release, whereas Macleod was convinced it should be unconditional. The governor's fears about an unconditional release were shared by Evelyn Hone and Arden-Clarke – a member of the Monckton Commission: 'In a letter of 18 January 1960, Hone made the point to me that we were letting Banda out of detention with nothing to go on and with no indication that he intends to follow a more reasonable line – precisely what Arden-Clarke said to me in March was the distinguishing fact between Nkrumah's release and Banda's.'

Second, the Nyasaland government placed greater emphasis on the inevitability, scale and risk of violence accompanying Banda's release to Nyasaland, especially if it coincided with an accelerated general release of detainees. Armitage wanted to release Banda as soon as possible but was held back because he had nothing, as yet, to offer him that he would accept. 'To have let him out without offering some constitutional advance and some indication that secession was not entirely ruled out would have been catastrophic. Armitage wanted HMG to concede the principle of secession but it was not until [much later] that anyone from HMG said it was possible.'

Armitage was already feeling distinctly uneasy about Conservative Party thinking on colonial issues, especially that revealed by Macleod's views. The October 1959 election had brought into parliament a number of new, young, liberal-minded members whose seats were safe for several years to come and who, therefore, could afford to express their views openly, maybe brashly, even when these did not coincide with more established party philosophy. He was deeply irritated by one of these new Conservative MPs who visited Nyasaland early in 1960 – Peter Tapsell.

Tapsell, then aged 29 years, arrived at Government House on 7 January and Armitage's account of part of the visit was:

> An interesting visitor was Peter Tapsell [in another version he is referred to as 'a peculiar visitor'] a Tory who had just become Member of Parliament.... He seems to have extreme views that the African must always be right; anyway, Africans have enormous support from Labour and the left wing and we had better give them control fairly soon. He knew all the answers and did very little listening. At luncheon and dinner he argued hard and was most provocative. I should have thought he would have been better in the Labour Party. I brought the evening rather abruptly to a close by saying I could not really stand the Labour tail wagging the Tory dog.... He is obviously a great admirer of Macleod. He talked about the unanimous opposition to Tory policies in Central Africa in the Universities and [claimed] that Macleod said that in ten years' time those people would destroy the Tory party, if I understood him aright. There will be no British influence in Africa to destroy then at any rate.[107]

Although Armitage had little choice but to tolerate Macleod's views since he was secretary of state, he did not have to tolerate Macleod-like views when expressed by a young and inexperienced admirer of Macleod, even if he were an MP.[108]

Many years later Tapsell recalled the occasion and particularly the way in which the governor brought the evening to a close by throwing his napkin on the dining room table and saying he would not be spoken to in his own house in the way in which Tapsell was addressing him, and retired for the night. The following morning Armitage apologized, saying he had been feeling rather tired. Tapsell also felt badly about the altercation, believing he himself may have appeared arrogant and bumptious. It is possible Armitage made his disapproval of Tapsell's attitude known because, on his return to London, Tapsell was tackled about the incident by the chief whip.[109]

Another new Conservative MP whom Armitage entertained was Humphry Berkeley, who recalled:

> I first visited ... Nyasaland in January 1960. Many of my contemporaries believed that Iain Macleod would hasten the pace of granting Independence to British Colonies or Protectorates in Africa. Sir Robert Armitage believed that Nyasaland should remain in the Federation. He was opposed to ending the Emergency and to the release of Dr Banda. ... I believed that the Federation should be broken up and that, as a result, Nyasaland should be able to secede. ... When I returned [from Nyasaland,] I recommended to Iain Macleod [before parliament reconvened on 26 January 1960[110]] that Sir Robert Armitage should be replaced. *Macleod said he had himself already come to that conclusion.*[111]

Armitage fared somewhat better with another Conservative parliamentarian who stayed with him at this time, Reginald Bennett.[112] When told about Banda's release, Bennett considered 'there were definite risks in letting Banda out in Nyasaland, risks one could not clearly forecast. If Banda went to the United Kingdom [they would] get time locally and perhaps he would lose some of his influence.' Bennett was Macleod's *fidus Achates*, and his parliamentary private secretary. He expressly avoided being briefed by Macleod or any of his experts in the Colonial Office in order that he might 'so to speak, carry *tabulae rasae*' with him. He visited all three territories and made 'a death-defying journey to the man-eating missionaries of the Scottish Reformed Church at Livingstonia'. As he said later, 'a Parliamentary Private Secretary was deemed expendable.' His primary concerns were with the 'organized opposition seemingly backed by Jock Campbell of Booker Brothers' and 'a remote nest of religious vipers at the end of the line in Livingstonia':

> They were convinced of some desperately tyrannical attitudes and actions which the Tory government was going to inflict on them. This

was the simplest socialist party propaganda, and I told them so. I added what I knew Iain's attitudes were, though not in detail. They were good enough to accept all this and the atmosphere relaxed completely.... I think I had drawn the venom. At least what little I could tell them came to pass.... I knew that Armitage and Iain were at loggerheads, and I was ... inclined to share his [Armitage's] misgivings about the release of Banda locally.

Macleod told Bennett, in principle before his visit and in detail on his return, his feelings about the necessity for releasing Banda and the importance of dealing with him as the leader in respect of political advancement for Nyasaland. On his return – about the middle of February – Bennett was also told by Macleod that he felt progress could not be made so long as Armitage retained his current attitudes and remained in office. Bennett's own reaction following his visit was that Armitage, and his government, was 'timid and overcautious and would solve nothing'.

On 5 January 1960, the prime minister and his party had set off for Africa. He visited Ghana and Nigeria and then flew to Salisbury, arriving early on 18 January. During talks with the federal and Southern Rhodesian prime ministers he said the main objective in Nyasaland must be to end the emergency and make a start with constitutional progress. Welensky expressed displeasure over not being consulted about Banda's release, which, he said, had apparently already been decided by Britain. 'If this were true, [he] warned Macmillan, an early release would simply increase the risk to Nyasaland's security.' He also warned that 'the result would be bloodshed for which the British Government had to accept responsibility.' Macmillan agreed to discuss Banda's release and the general security situation with Armitage and 'undertook to consult further' with Welensky after his visit to Nyasaland.[113]

In Northern Rhodesia, Macmillan met the governor and executive council, including two African ministers. The resident commissioner of Barotseland recalled that at the evening reception:

The prime minister had a drink in his hand and said, 'I don't know what to do about all this business of the Federation.' I had never before seen a man so unprepared, so unknowledgeable about affairs, poorly briefed, taking very little interest in matters, not knowing what was going on or taking any interest in it either. He didn't seem to care about matters – as if he just did not care and was not interested.[114]

The weekend was spent privately at the Victoria Falls and early on

Monday 25 January he left for Nyasaland, was met by the governor and lunched with members of executive council.

The agreed programme[115] included a period from 4.30 p.m. to 7.30 p.m. for 'United Kingdom business', but Macmillan had told Welensky he would discuss Banda's release with the governor, and the period after 4.30 p.m. was in fact taken up in a discussion between Macmillan and Armitage. So important was the discussion that, after a break from 7.00 p.m. – when they changed for dinner, taken in the governor's study, and attended a reception – they resumed from 10.50 p.m. until 12.30 a.m. Macmillan then retired but Armitage continued discussions with his officials for another two hours.[116]

Of the remaining differences between the British and Nyasaland governments, the single most crucial one was over Banda's release. Its timing was particularly important, but the place to which he should go was even more so. Should it be Nyasaland, as Macleod wished (so as to place no restraints on him), or Britain, as Armitage wished (mainly to reduce the likelihood, scale and severity of violence)?

Of the two parts of the discussion, the one following the reception was the more acrimonious and controversial. No conclusion was reached during the earlier part, although Macmillan agreed about the possible dangers following Banda's release before concrete constitutional plans had been approved by the British government. The prime minister changed his mind on this during the break in the meeting, almost certainly as a result of conversations during the reception. The only points argued, and strongly so, were the date of Banda's release and the place to which he should go when released.

As to the date of Banda's release, the British cabinet had already decided on a number of early dates and was currently considering 3 March, the anniversary of his arrest. Although Armitage was reluctantly prepared to release him before then, he was not prepared to do so on that date. A cabinet decision was an immensely difficult obstacle to move, but Armitage was prepared to defy Macmillan. He said that he, the governor, was responsible for law and order and that Banda would not be released on that date. Macmillan, cornered by this response – because his ministers had made great play in parliament that the governor was exclusively responsible for ordering detention and release from detention – started to leave the room, but changed his mind and did not leave.

The differences between the two men were even more pronounced over the place to which Banda should be released. Armitage was trying to do a deal: release at an early date, if necessary before, but not on, 3 March, in exchange for exile to Britain. Macmillan wanted both release on 3 March and return to Nyasaland. Both dug their toes in deeply and neither gave way. Both were tired and stressed and neither, especially following the reception, was in the best mood for polite conversation and compromise. The Nyasaland officials present found Macmillan's behaviour 'rude and gross', while the British officials found Armitage 'deliberately offensive' and 'stubborn to the point of insubordination'. Armitage accused Macmillan of being prepared to risk lives in the colonies for the sake of votes in Britain. 'Governor,' objected Macmillan, 'that was a most offensive remark.' 'Prime Minister,' retorted Armitage, 'it was intended to be.'

These discussions were neither happy nor — with one possible exception from Macmillan's viewpoint — fruitful. The exception concerned Banda's lawyer, Dingle Foot, who had discussions with Chiume, Macleod and Monckton in Britain before he left, and long conversations with Banda, Chipembere and Chisiza in Gwelo prison on arrival in central Africa.[117] Foot got in touch with the British prime minister in Nyasaland and Macmillan arranged for him to be invited to the evening reception at Government House on 25 January.[118] Shortly, he took Foot to one side and was told Banda would 'never under any circumstances' change his opposition to federation. Banda would not agree to be released from detention unless his friends were also released, or a definite early date fixed for their release. He would be pleased to join in discussions on Nyasaland's constitutional future, could be trusted to keep his word, was opposed to violence, would be 'very susceptible to a personal approach at a high level', and would want to be released to Nyasaland and nowhere else. Macmillan was, therefore, briefed, almost up to the minute on the stance being adopted by Banda. Armitage also knew at least the broad outline of what Foot said to Macmillan.[119]

The next day the prime minister told the governor that Banda would not be sent to Britain and that the date of his release would be fixed with Macleod.[120] At Blantyre he met the acting provincial commissioner to whom he 'made it clear that though most of the detainees ought to be let out shortly, Banda and two or three of the principal Congress leaders (such as Chiume and Chipembere) would continue under some sort of restraint for a considerable time: there was no question of independence for Nyasaland or the Federation being dissolved.'[121]

Macmillan then attended a civic luncheon at Ryall's Hotel during the course of which a demonstration took place outside the hotel.[122] This demonstration, mild and small in scale as it was, was seized upon by a hungry press with little else of great interest to report during the Africa tour and the incident was given high prominence in Britain. The reporters were 'heard in the press plane that took them to Salisbury that afternoon encouraging each other to give the affair a sensational turn'.[123] When the prime minister left Ryall's Hotel he drove to Chileka airport and flew to Salisbury. Of the prime minister's arrival at Chileka, a senior police officer recalled: 'Macmillan sat in the Rolls-Royce and said in my hearing to one of his aides, "Where is this Governor fellow?" in a most demeaning and petulant manner. He refused to leave the car until Sir Robert was there to accompany him.'[124] The following day, Macmillan flew to South Africa.

When Macmillan left Nyasaland on 26 January 1960, he dined with Welensky, Malvern and Whitehead in Salisbury.[125] According to the federal prime minister, he (Welensky) was especially anxious to discuss Banda's release, but every time he attempted to raise the question Macmillan evaded it and talked about something else. The same thing happened at the airport the next morning. The governor of Southern Rhodesia was even clearer. He told Home: 'Your Prime Minister when here would not discuss the subject with Welensky at all.' According to the British prime minister, the evening was a social affair and his hosts 'were not anxious to talk business'. Armitage's understanding was that Macmillan had 'funked it' and had refused to discuss Banda's release with Welensky and Whitehead, who were 'most upset' by it.

Macmillan had, however, prepared notes for his talk with Welensky in which he said that Armitage and he had agreed that constitutional talks must take place as soon as possible and that these must be with Banda, but that his release might prejudice Monckton's work. Armitage proposed that Banda should be released, sent to Britain immediately and kept there until the end of the summer. Macmillan's objection to this was that the legal basis was dubious. Also, it would not satisfy demands for his release without restraint and talks would be unsatisfactory. Indeed, agitation would be whipped up, which would harm Monckton's inquiry. The choice was between keeping Banda in gaol throughout 1960 or releasing him fairly soon without conditions. They must take the second choice, but Macmillan was 'ready to contemplate' constitutional talks in London.

Perhaps they could manage a sequence of meetings in London and Nyasaland. If they could keep Banda on the move for a few months, this would reduce the likelihood of his stirring up serious disorder. He proposed to tell Welensky that these were his tentative thoughts, that his conversations with Armitage were 'inconclusive' and that he had delayed consulting his colleagues in London until he had spoken with Welensky. But Macmillan's plans for handling the question of Banda's release with Welensky had gone awry. His meeting with Armitage the previous evening had prevented him from reaching a clear decision on Banda's release that he could put to Welensky. He was able, however, to tell him that, although he was clear the doctor could not be held in detention for much longer, he would carefully consider the Nyasaland security situation and would keep him informed about Banda's future.

In respect of Armitage's advice, Macmillan had already told Macleod that he was 'rather staggered' by the turn events had taken when he arrived in Nyasaland and by Armitage's 'entirely new proposal' to remove Banda to London under restraint. As a result, he said, he had a lot of new ground to cover and was unable in the available time to bring Armitage to a definite decision.[126] If Armitage's proposal that Banda should be released to Britain was 'entirely new' to the prime minister, this can have been only because Macleod had concealed from him the fact that it had been discussed for more than six months in the Colonial Office. Macmillan suspected – correctly – that Armitage had been persuaded against his better judgement to accept Macleod's plan in Dar es Salaam and – incorrectly – that on his return to Zomba had been reproached by his advisers and was now trying to find a course they would accept.

> But however that may be we must take it as a fact that the Governor and his Council now consider it an unacceptable security risk to have Banda at large in Nyasaland when the Monckton Commission is there. And we must take account of Hone's anxieties about the reactions in Northern Rhodesia. If both Northern Rhodesia and Nyasaland explode together we should be in trouble. It looks as though we should then have to bring United Kingdom troops from Kenya.[127]

On the other hand, Macmillan could see the obvious risks in 'hanging on without any positive policy' – a point Armitage had frequently made – and suggested a 'middle course' by which they would appear to be taking a positive step towards constitutional advance. 'If we could get Banda to London as a free man we should be seen to be making an advance in that direction while at the same time meeting the Governor's fears about the security position in Nyasaland.'[128]

On the first day of February Armitage received a long telegram in which Macleod restated the area of agreement between them: constitutional talks should start as soon as possible and must be with Banda.[129] Macleod pointed out, however, that Armitage, his advisers, Welensky, his cabinet and Hone had concluded that the security risks in releasing Banda to Nyasaland ought not to be accepted. Macleod was convinced that Armitage's alternative proposal of releasing Banda to London was not feasible, even though Macmillan was inclined to consider it. Macleod went on to say that, having considered the problem very carefully, he, Macmillan and Home had reached 'agreed and firm conclusions': 'All this boils down to the straight proposition that the only choice lies between releasing Banda unconditionally in Nyasaland as soon as possible, or keeping him in detention and the emergency in force throughout 1960. We have concluded that on every ground the arguments for the first course are overriding.'

This meant accepting, with their eyes open, the security risks as assessed by Armitage, Welensky and Hone. There were no means of avoiding them, but there might be ways of reducing them. Armitage – as he had suggested – was to be allowed to 'predispose additional security forces within Nyasaland' to contain from the outset any local demonstrations. Macleod agreed that detainee releases should immediately be decelerated – but not to fewer than 50 a month – until they could judge the effects of Banda's release and his own visit. Macleod then added, in response to the governor's repeated urging that they have something fairly clear to offer Banda, that:

> If preliminary talks with Banda went well and appeared to establish a basis for further discussions, it might at that point be useful to pursue the idea of a conference in London, to be timed after Monckton's visit to Nyasaland. This would help to keep Banda in play, and [induce] him to cooperate with [the] Monckton Commission in [the] interval, and meanwhile to keep his followers in order.

Macleod assured Armitage they had reached their decisions after 'the most anxious thought' and in full recognition of Armitage's own views on 'the difficult dilemma' they faced, and of the 'heavy responsibility' it placed upon the governor. They were sure it was the 'proper, logical and courageous course'.

Four days earlier, Macmillan had cabled Macleod and said he agreed there were only two alternatives – unconditional early release for Banda or indefinite detention – and that the first was preferable. This view was the opposite of what Macmillan had himself told the acting provincial commissioner in Blantyre only three days previously.[130] He made it plain, however, that in taking this course they would be acting contrary to the view of the security position taken by the governor, Welensky and Hone. He was, therefore, 'somewhat concerned' about the way in which the Nyasaland administration might deal with any disturbances following Banda's release.

> To be frank I was not favourably impressed with the administration there. Even now they seem very quick to take repressive measures against demonstrators etc. The recent incident [outside Ryall's Hotel] during my visit to Blantyre is significant. If they are now ordered to take a course which they believe will lead to disorder they may well be predisposed to

take a somewhat exaggerated view of such troubles as arise and to react to them too strongly. In other words I think we must be prepared for a repetition of what Devlin thought they did last time.

These considerations should not deflect them from what they believed to be the right course, but he would feel very much happier if Macleod were able to take immediate steps to strengthen the administration in Nyasaland. 'I understand for example that Footman is due to retire in a few months' time. Could you not send a good man there to replace him now? You may think that this would not be enough. If you would prefer to find a new Governor you could count on my full support.'

Armitage had gravely offended Macmillan by defying him and standing firm on what he saw as his duty to preserve law and order. Macmillan's retribution was swift. Initially, the prime minister's officials thought Armitage would be dismissed at a very early date. The prime minister 'thought very poorly of Armitage, rejected his views and was determined to replace him'. He told the Queen that 'the Administration struck [him] as tired – from the Governor downwards'. From early November the previous year Macmillan had felt that the inability to find Nyasaland Africans to serve on the Monckton Commission was the fault of the Nyasaland government's 'lack of energy (and perhaps actually ca'canny tactics)'. Now, early in February 1960, the prime minister thought that it was Armitage's fault that the central Africa ministers were uncooperative. 'The real truth is the weakness of the Nyasaland administration. If Armitage were a man like Sir James Robertson (for instance) he would soon deal with Whitehead and Welensky.'[131]

Armitage himself thought that he might be sacked or induced to resign.[132] Macleod had already concluded that Armitage should be replaced. But the task of disposing of the governor was not to be taken lightly, no matter how ruthless or vindictive one might be prepared to be. The government had robustly defended and supported him over the emergency and the Devlin Report; there were many pressing political and security issues to be settled in the coming months; Welensky's grave wrath would be incurred; and many of Macmillan's own party would be dangerously offended – already there was the imminent risk of one or other of the Commonwealth or colonial secretaries of state resigning over differences of opinion about Banda's release.[133] Given these difficulties, it would be dangerous to dispose of the governor. Indeed, provided new blood and new thinking could be injected into the higher levels of the Nyasaland administration, it was not strictly necessary to do so – at least not immediately.

On 2 February, a week after the Government House row, Armitage received a cable from Macleod.[134] The cable had been delayed in its transmission and did not reach Armitage until 23 hours after it was dispatched from the Colonial Office. As he began to read it, with trepidation, it must have reminded him chillingly of the cable he had received from Lennox-Boyd telling him he was to be replaced in Cyprus:

> We are entering a new phase in constitutional and other developments in Nyasaland and there will be great advantage in having continuity from now on for some time in the higher posts in the Nyasaland Administration. I have, therefore, come to the conclusion after consulting with the Prime Minister that [Glyn] Jones [minister for African affairs in Northern Rhodesia] must take Footman's place at a much earlier date than we had in mind when we discussed in Dar es Salaam. I hope that Hone will be able to agree that Jones can take over immediately.

Macleod said the decision had been made by Macmillan, Home and himself after 'the most careful thought' and after a personal appreciation of the situation by the prime minister. He was certain it was 'by far the quickest way to dispose of this small affair'. He admitted this was 'a drastic step' and one which 'only the interest of the Service' would induce him to take and he felt 'sure that with his public spirit [Footman would] recognize the overriding needs of the situation.' Armitage 'thought back to Macmillan's visit and what Footman could have said or done to bring about the early change' in the date of the chief secretary's departure. He thought Brook took a dislike to Footman.[135] It may well be that, while the blow struck Footman, the damage was aimed at Armitage, although Macmillan's criticisms were more frequently — but by no means exclusively — of 'the Nyasaland administration' than of the governor himself.

Footman was born in 1905 and joined the colonial administrative service in 1930. He served in Zanzibar until 1947, when he was transferred to Nyasaland as financial secretary. In 1951 he was promoted to be chief secretary of the protectorate.[136] In January 1958, some seven months before going on leave, he wrote to the governor saying that the time had come when he hoped his future position in Nyasaland as chief secretary could be considered as he wished 'to plan ahead for family reasons'. He explained that he would reach the normal retiring age of 55 years on 3 September 1960 and, with the accumulated leave then due to him, he would be required to serve only some 15 or 16 months during his next tour. He was anxious to continue earning for at least two or three years beyond that date. Having been in Nyasaland since 1947, he felt that any further service could probably be most effectively given 'in this part of the world', particularly since he recalled Welensky asking him some time previously if he intended to remain in the federation where 'there was a need for people of experience in public affairs and indeed, probably, opportunities for them'.

Footman thought that, with the federal constitutional review taking place in 1960 or 1961, it might be desirable to have someone who 'knew the ropes to undertake the representation of Nyasaland's views and to devote himself more or less whole time' to the preparation of Nyasaland's case. He also hinted at the possibility that, by then, they might 'also require something in the nature of a Chairman of Committees'. Later, he suggested to Colonial Office officials that he might be considered suitable for the post of Speaker of legislative council in Nyasaland when the present incumbent's contract expired. This was ruled out, as a potential embarrassment to his successor as chief secretary and because it would appear as if the post had been specially created for him on his retirement. 'Either of these would, [they felt] sure, be very damaging to the prospects of such an appointment being successful.' The Colonial Office felt 'very strongly' that such posts in Nyasaland should be filled from outside. More specifically, Footman recalled that Armitage was prepared to second Hodgson, senior provincial commissioner, to the federal prime minister's office of race relations for two years and that he, Footman, 'might well be qualified to succeed him'. Indeed, he added, the timing would be most appropriate.

Soon after he returned from leave in August 1958, Armitage discussed Footman's future with him.[137] The governor, as he reported to Morgan, favoured extending Footman's service by two extra years in a special capacity to 'see us through ... the awkward period of 1960 to 1962'. One way of doing this would be for Footman to be seconded internally for special duties and to head the official Nyasaland team for the federal review conference. Alternatively, he suggested, Footman could be seconded to the Colonial Office early in 1960 to lead the Nyasaland team preparing for the conference. He made it clear to Footman and the Colonial Office that he would want a new chief secretary early in 1960 who 'could be well into the saddle before the conference starts', and he anticipated that the new person would act as governor during his own absence at the conference.

Morgan suggested that someone from the Colonial Office should be seconded to Nyasaland as chief secretary for a two-year period, but Armitage was opposed to this because 'it would mean someone who had no experience of executive action being Chief Secretary and at times Acting Governor during a period when there is certain to be considerable unrest here if not actual trouble.' He concluded his letter to Morgan by saying: 'I think that unless an extension of his period of service can be arranged for Charles Footman, it would be better to get someone from the Colonial Service for appointment as Chief Secretary here early in 1960.'

Soon after he arrived in England on leave, on 25 September, Footman discussed his future with officials at the Colonial Office and made it clear – as he had to Armitage – that the ideal arrangement from his own point of view would be to do two additional short tours, with leaves, which would extend his service to at least 1963.[138] Alternatively, he would like to take one further, long, tour until late in 1961 or early 1962 and then take leave. In any event, he wished formally to retire in 1960 – when he reached the maximum pension – take his retirement gratuity and pension and then continue on a contract basis.

The Colonial Office, however, had serious objections to this. To extend his service as chief secretary beyond the nine years he would already have held the post, at a time of general contraction of senior posts and promotion difficulties in the service, would be to deny the opportunity to deserving officers. They thought that it would be the secretary of state's view that Footman's appointment should not be extended beyond his fifty-fifth birthday. They noted Armitage's wish to have a new chief secretary in place early in 1960 and, although they recognized that Footman's retirement then, some months before his fifty-fifth birthday, would not be welcome to him, they accepted that 'it may be necessary to make a change at that stage.'

With Armitage's agreement, they told Footman that his service as chief secretary would not be extended, that the precise date of his departure was not yet clear but that he ought to envisage as one possibility – but 'no more than one possibility which [they] felt bound to put into his mind in fairness to himself' – that it might be decided in the public interest that his successor should be in post 'in the early part of 1960'. When he enquired 'about retirement jobs in the Colonial Office itself', officials there quickly told him that he should not regard such appointments as at all likely. They hoped these conclusions would not come as too great a disappointment to him. They had been reached 'with very great reluctance and ... on general Service grounds which [they] knew that [he] would be the first to appreciate'. They wrote to Footman to this effect on 6 November and repeated their conclusions at a meeting with him on 19 November, when he was 'rather sore' about the possibility of having to leave early in 1960. In telling Armitage this in a letter of 28 November 1958, A. R. Thomas sympathetically said:

> It would be very nice if we could see a way round this difficulty which, without granting him any major extension or envisaging an additional

tour, could enable him to defer his retirement until the early part of 1961. It seems to us too early, however, to attempt to reach any conclusion about this and we are accordingly proposing to give no further thought to it at present but to review the position in about six months' time.

Six months later, Gorell Barnes asked Armitage precisely when he anticipated Footman would retire and the chief secretaryship become vacant. He thought that if they brought in a newcomer to replace him, there might be an argument for doing so in advance of Footman's departure, possibly 'in such a role as Special Commissioner (Planning) or something of that sort'. This sounds as if Gorell Barnes wanted to find a way of giving Armitage a new man with whom to work from early 1960, yet retain Footman as chief secretary until somewhat later in the year. Alternatively, if the post were to be filled from within Nyasaland, then Ingham 'would seem a possible choice' and, if that were agreed, they would need to give some thought to who might succeed him. Ingham's was the first name to be suggested as a possible successor to Footman – in May 1959.[139]

In reply, Armitage repeated his concern about having a new chief secretary in post early in 1960 and said that he was pleased Gorell Barnes had mentioned Ingham. He was sure that 'the greatest consideration' must be given to this and hoped Gorell Barnes would survey the field as early as possible and let him know if there were any alternative candidates. If Ingham succeeded Footman, then Hodgson, who had considerable experience both in the field and in the secretariat, should become the new secretary for African affairs.[140]

In mid-August 1959, Leslie Monson, assistant under-secretary, wrote from the Colonial Office to tell Armitage that Ingham's case had been 'most carefully considered', but at present he thought it likely that the secretary of state would consider R. S. Foster of Northern Rhodesia 'an even stronger candidate'.[141] It was the view of all those at the Colonial Office who were 'in a position to compare their respective merits that Foster [was] a superior candidate to Ingham, good though the latter [was]'. He now thought that Footman should retire on or soon after his fifty-fifth birthday and that, in view of this and out of consideration for the successor (probably Foster), perhaps Armitage would reconsider and advise on the precise timing of the handover.

When he replied, the governor compared the records of Ingham and Foster and concluded that the former was the stronger candidate. Ingham had served in more than one territory and had been promoted to be secretary for agriculture and natural resources and then administrative secretary in Kenya – as Armitage himself had been – before Foster had even been made senior district officer in Northern Rhodesia.

In addition, he pointed out, Ingham's service since 1947 had been in ministries and secretariats, 'which is the normal training ground for a chief secretary'. Also, he had been a member of executive and legislative councils since 1955, while Foster had never held a permanent post in a secretariat or ministry, or been a member of either council. Ingham had been senior secretary to the East African Royal Commission and his services had been recognized by the award of the MBE in 1947 and the CMG in 1956. Foster, after 23 years in the administration, had not yet been decorated. So far as the timing of the handover was concerned, much depended on when he himself would go on leave. He said that since his appointment came to an end in April 1961, he would prefer to go on leave in June 1960 and return in October in time for the federal review conference. Footman should stay on until the governor returned from leave.

The matter was now taken up by Sir Hilton Poynton, permanent secretary at the Colonial Office, who wrote to Armitage on 21 September. He said that it was the express wish of the secretary of state – Lennox-Boyd – that Footman should retire on or as soon as possible after his fifty-fifth birthday. As for his successor, they had borne in mind matters other than those brought out by a comparison of the two candidates from their record on paper. He thought that Foster was the stronger on grounds of leadership, that there was advantage in bringing in new blood from outside Nyasaland and in doing so 'from the sister territory of Northern Rhodesia'. He proposed therefore to consult Foster's governor, Hone. In a private note written on his copy of Poynton's letter, Armitage asked what the effect would be on those senior to Foster in Northern Rhodesia where he was second from the bottom of the list of provincial commissioners. He wondered, too, whether the secretary of state personally had seen the papers. He also made the point that it would not necessarily be advantageous to bring in someone from Northern Rhodesia with its anti-federation reputation, 'while we, with [the] secretary of state, are pro-federation'.[142]

It is relevant to this point of Armitage's, although no one pointed it out, that there was at least symbolic significance in the fact that in the Northern Rhodesia government, as in Southern Rhodesia, the term 'native affairs' was officially still widely and consistently used, whereas in Nyasaland it had for some considerable time been replaced by the term 'African affairs', for this was considered less offensive. When he sought Hone's opinion, Poynton wrote:

> The local candidate is of course Ingham and he is a strong candidate having had a distinguished career with all the right experience. The outside field has also been examined and the strongest outside candidate

who emerged from this exercise is Robin Foster. I should make it clear from the start that we ourselves think that he has the edge on Ingham from the point of view of leadership qualities and we also think that it would be a good thing to bring in new blood from outside Nyasaland and there might be advantage in bringing in someone from the sister territory of Northern Rhodesia.... We should be most grateful for your views on how you regard Foster as a candidate for this difficult and important post and, if you agree with us that he is the man for the job, when you can spare him.... We want to avoid so far as possible an interregnum between Footman's departure and the appointment of his successor, and indeed, ideally we should like to see some overlap.[143]

Hone found it difficult to make valid comparisons. However, he pointed out that Foster did in fact have some experience in secretariat work – albeit in a temporary acting capacity. He also said that he intended to give Foster a spell as secretary to the Ministry for Native Affairs before his appointment as minister of native affairs on Jones's retirement or promotion. He gave so well-balanced a view of the two candidates that he could only conclude that all depended on what the Colonial Office was looking for and on whether the importance attached to bringing in new blood outweighed the passing over of the strong local candidate.[144] Armitage still felt that Ingham had the edge over Foster because of the latter's lack of legislative and executive council experience, which Hone also thought 'might prove a bit of a difficulty for him in the early stages'. Although he did not say so, Armitage was worried about Northern Rhodesia's anti-federation reputation, for he now asked Poynton, 'is there no one from East Africa for instance who has this top secretariat experience and whom we could consider in this short list?'[145] At this stage, late September 1959, Ingham was still Armitage's preference and Foster was the 'strongest outside candidate'.

Despite the outside field having already been examined, the names of J. V. Wild of Uganda and, for the first time on about 15 November, G. S. Jones of Northern Rhodesia, were shortly suggested. However, Armitage asked that they be 'discarded', in Jones's case because he was too old.[146] It is strange that Jones's name came forward so late in the day, especially since the outside field had been examined for at least six months and Foster had consistently been considered to be the strongest candidate in that field. Armitage was still keen that if the next chief secretary was to come from within central Africa, he should come from Nyasaland, where the government was pro-federation, rather than from Northern Rhodesia with its known anti-federation attitudes. Consequently, he now suggested that Phillips, the financial secretary, and

Hugh Norman-Walker, the development secretary, of the Nyasaland service should be considered, although he felt both were 'rather young'. They were highly regarded by Welensky and had worked closely with the federal government. Although he did not mention it, these facts would have been important to Armitage in his appointed task of trying to make the federation work well and be accepted by Nyasaland Africans as being to their advantage.[147]

Once Macleod became secretary of state for the Colonies the matter moved forward rapidly. On 20 November Poynton cabled Armitage:

[The] Secretary of State is considering whether to offer transfer to G. S. Jones despite his present high office. At 51 we do not think him too old. In fact his appointment would maintain the advantage of introducing new blood and leadership and at the same time bring in a distinguished officer older [by two years] and senior to Ingham.[148]

The word 'despite' is puzzling. High office, short of a chief secretaryship, was, one would have thought, precisely the sort of qualification being sought. It is likely that the Colonial Office felt that Armitage's insistence on the superiority of Ingham over Foster could be overcome only by appointing an officer older – Jones would be 52 in less than two months' time – and more senior than Ingham. It is also likely that, during Macleod's talk with Devlin soon after taking office, the judge had made his views of the Nyasaland administration clear and that this would have included his unfavourable view of Ingham, the secretary for African affairs. It is also possible that Macleod saw the Northern Rhodesia service's anti-federation beliefs as an advantage to him in the British government's dealings with the federal government and a support to him in any conflict between the Colonial and Commonwealth Offices over central African affairs. It seems that the secretary of state was keen to secure Jones's services as chief secretary of Nyasaland because in his cable of 20 November Poynton asked if there was any prospect of improving the salary of the post so as to make it 'more attractive to Jones'. The salary was not improved.

The secretary of state's consideration of Jones as Footman's successor did not dissuade Armitage from continuing to press his own views. On 9 December, he restated his opinion that Jones was too old for the job and added: 'Unless further candidates have been found from West Africa, the choice appears to lie between C. A. L. Richards, Foster and Ingham.' Richards had served in the administrations of Uganda and Tanganyika, was currently Resident of Buganda and was shortly to become minister of local government in Uganda. Born in 1911, he was younger than Jones and Ingham and older than Foster.[149]

Macleod was now fast becoming impatient with the discussions over who should be the new chief secretary of Nyasaland and he brought the matter to a brisk conclusion.[150] When Armitage met him in Dar es Salaam on 19 December, Macleod told him he had decided that Jones should fill the post. They agreed that he should arrive at the end of June, after the secretary of state had paid a visit to the protectorate, and Footman should leave on 30 June 1960. When Armitage wrote to Monson on 21 December about the Dar es Salaam meeting, he presumed that Monson would now be offering the post to Jones and that they would soon learn whether or not he had accepted it.

Jones was on a skiing holiday with his family in Zurich from 1 to 15 January 1960. During this period, on 6 January, Poynton wrote to him offering him the post of chief secretary of Nyasaland, adding that if he accepted it they would wish him to arrive in Nyasaland 'towards the end of June'. Poynton said that he was sure Jones would find this offer 'a little puzzling' given that his views on Foster as a suitable candidate for the post had been sought sometime earlier. This seems to be the first indication to Jones that he was himself being considered. At the permanent secretary's invitation, Jones spent 18 and 19 January with Poynton and Monson at the Colonial Office. It is likely that it was subsequent to these meetings that he accepted the post.

In these ways, Armitage had inadvertently helped to lay the foundations for Footman's early departure, primarily in making it clear that he would like a new chief secretary in post early in 1960. He had tried to find other ways of extending his service and had agreed that Footman's departure should be delayed until the end of June when Jones would take over. Had he not been so insistent on Ingham's claims to promotion, on not wanting someone from Northern Rhodesia and on effectively forcing the decision up to secretary of state level, the matter would have been concluded before Lennox-Boyd left office and it is virtually certain that Foster and not Jones – who entered the lists very late in the day – would have been appointed chief secretary of Nyasaland early in 1960.

Armitage received the cable from Macleod saying Jones should take over immediately, at 3.45 p.m. on 2 February. He then discussed the legal aspects with King at 6.00 p.m. and told Footman an hour later.[151] Early the following day he sent a personal telegram to Macleod:

> Your decision has come as an extreme shock to me. I realize the exigencies of the service must always prevail but I would not be carrying out my duty to keep you informed of all aspects of life here if I did not tell you that I have never had such a distasteful task as telling Footman that Jones should take over from him immediately. I realize that you have

taken all considerations into account and I know that you are aware that Footman has been responsible for organizing the security planning for this Government and we are faced with the security risk of the release of Dr Banda at the end of February. Our task is already somewhat complicated but the foregoing is not going to simplify it.[152]

He proposed that he second Footman for special duties, especially internal security, until Jones 'is settled in, has made himself acquainted with the country and the problems which crowd in on us. This period may well last into mid-March.' Macleod welcomed this proposal of an overlap, which he recognized would reduce the inconvenience for Footman and would help Jones. He made it clear, however, that it was the purpose of the early change that Jones should 'as soon as possible get his grip upon both the political and the security aspects of [Nyasaland's] affairs which are completely interlocked'. He wished Jones 'to carry the full responsibility falling upon the Chief Secretary in security matters particularly'.[153]

Footman, naturally, was devastated by the news of his immediate removal from office.[154] Having discussed the matter with King and Phillips, he wrote to the governor giving the essence of his concerns the following day. 'It is a great shock to me after 30 years' service, and a matter of the deepest regret that my employment should be terminated in this way.' He had received no offers of re-employment after his retirement and he was expecting to have four or five more months in which to find a new job and a house. The early retirement would be a financial loss he could ill afford: he was married with three young children whose names he had entered at schools in Southern Rhodesia and Britain. He was convinced that 'being removed from office in a hurry' could have only one interpretation placed upon it and that since the secretary of state's reasons could not be made public, he stood to suffer and would have his chances of finding employment prejudiced.

He asked that there should be an immediate announcement of his successor, an indication that he, Footman, was very shortly to retire and that the date of his successor's arrival would be announced as soon as possible. He also asked that, under the circumstances, he should be compensated. Armitage immediately drafted a cable to the secretary of state telling him of these points that Footman had made, adding, save for the point about compensation, that he agreed with them. The cable was not in fact sent because only six hours after Footman was given the news of his early departure, Macleod telegraphed to say that he was offering him a four-year contract as chairman of the public services commission in Tanganyika, a post which, 'much relieved and heartened', he gratefully accepted. The annual salary was only £50 less than that of the chief secretary of Nyasaland.

Armitage thought it 'most desirable', and the secretary of state also was keen, that the announcement of Jones's appointment and early arrival should be accompanied by an announcement of Footman's new appointment. The governor was anxious that, in the announcement, 'Footman's good name should not suffer because of his early departure and that [the] civil service generally should not feel that there is something wrong.' He hoped that Macleod would feel able to 'make some appreciative remarks concerning his service'. The press statement announcing both appointments was made on 10 February, but Macleod was advised by his press officer that it would be 'contra-productive' for him to make special reference to Footman's service. He would, he said, have liked to have done so, but it would be unusual and 'the press would undoubtedly draw the inference that Footman's services were unsatisfactory.' He had, consequently, decided not to make the remarks Armitage had sought, but had instructed his information officers to take the opportunity to tell press enquirers that he 'was particularly glad that an officer of Footman's experience and ability [was] available for this important post in Tanganyika'.[155]

Jones was due to sail back to Africa from leave on 3 February, the day after Armitage received Macleod's cable about Footman being replaced immediately. The sea passage was cancelled and Jones left London by air on 7 February, arriving in Lusaka two days later. By agreement between Hone and Armitage, the new chief secretary arrived in Nyasaland on 19 February. On the same day Footman was seconded to 'special duties' for two months. Armitage must have heaved a sigh of relief that this long and troublesome matter was settled, but not before he had dealt with an unexpected and worrying issue.

Armitage now found himself with two chief secretary salaries to pay for a while and provision for only one.[156] This would not normally have presented a problem. The governor signed a special warrant, which then needed covering approval from legislative council. The usual way of handling this was for the matter to be agreed by the standing finance committee, primarily so as to avoid public debate in the legislature. In this case, however, the committee, led by Blackwood, refused to agree and instead asked for a full report of the circumstances. It hoped to expose and make political capital out of the way Macleod was handling Nyasaland affairs. Blackwood's action was 'extremely embarrassing' for the government. Phillips, the chairman of the committee – who felt that without Blackwood's intervention 'there would have been no difficulty at all – suspended discussion. He told Armitage about it and suggested that he, the governor, should speak personally to Blackwood.

To make the matter more acceptable to the committee, Phillips suggested that Armitage seek to have the provision paid for by the British government as part of its contribution towards paying for expenditure arising from the emergency. 'It would not', Phillips said, 'be unreasonable to say that what has occurred is of itself a result of the Emergency.' He believed that if this were agreed, he would stand a better chance of being able to talk the committee out of the stance it was taking. British treasury officials did not agree to this request because they felt that to do so 'would give rise to [the] danger that unofficials might think they could at any time swing expenditure on to HMG by threatening embarrassing debate in Legislative Council'.

When the standing finance committee shortly took up the matter again, Phillips found that Blackwood 'was in no better frame of mind. In fact he once again displayed his inner knowledge of events [as a member of executive council] and indeed [Phillips] had to pull him up sharply for so doing.' After some ten minutes of 'sharp exchanges', Phillips decided to call the discussion to a halt and put to the vote the ratification of the governor's special warrant. By first asking the less dominant members of the committee their view, and leaving Blackwood till the last, he was able to secure a vote of four to two in favour of ratification. It had been an unhelpful and deliberate irritant, which Armitage could have done without.

While all these developments about Footman's departure and Jones's arrival were unfolding, Home cabled Welensky, on 2 February, to say that Macleod would arrive in Zomba on 29 February and that Banda would be released just before or just after that. Welensky's and Whitehead's reaction was 'very sharp'. They felt that Banda's release meant taking uncalculated risks and insisted that either Home visit central Africa or they go to London. Macmillan was worried that 'new trouble is developing with Welensky and Whitehead ... sending intemperate telegrams, threatening secession and the break-up of the Federation all because of HMG's wish to release Banda and get on with some constitutional advance in Nyasaland.' He expected some reaction, 'but not as bad as this'.[157] Armitage had not yet given up hope that Banda would not be returned to Nyasaland: 'I still do not think the release of Dr Banda to [the] UK has been finally thought out. He can't be the security risk there that he could be here and we should get a better chance to assess the risks.'[158]

The Nyasaland intelligence committee considered the security position if Banda were released in February. It believed the release would produce 'overwhelming emotional reactions followed by mass demonstrations, disorderly and large illegal meetings and processions' causing breaches of the peace and riots. Having received this assessment,

Armitage told Macleod that it was extremely important for the government to decide what its maximum concessions to Banda would be and to embody these in a clear plan for constitutional advance. Macleod, however, wanted room to manœuvre in response to Banda's reactions, whatever they might be. He did not therefore think it necessary before Banda was released to have 'a firm and final plan', agreed in advance with Welensky, for how far Britain was prepared to go on constitutional advance. He would, of course, have to have 'some pretty firm ideas' of the limits within which they might operate, and 'enough of a political carrot' to secure Banda's cooperation. He thought it sufficient for immediate purposes if he were to give the doctor a general indication of the kind of political progress that might be made, together with a clear indication that he and some of his colleagues could expect, subject to good behaviour in the meantime, to be part of the Nyasaland representation at the review conference. He hoped this would be enough to keep Banda 'in play' and out of serious mischief, at least until they could hold further discussions in London, perhaps in May or June. Armitage was taking some comfort from the fact that 'the date of the release of Banda was being set back a little' but still he 'was obsessed with the plan to get [him] to the UK somehow'. In discussing the release with Dixon and Blackwood, he said it would have to take place at the latest in June, but he still preferred it to be to Britain and 'that had not been fully explored in [his] opinion'.[159]

The press at this time reported rumours that Armitage had threatened to resign if Banda were released. When he enquired into this, Macmillan was told: 'The Colonial Office ... feel quite certain that there have been no public utterances by Sir Robert Armitage on these lines.' Against this minute Macmillan wrote, 'I am not so sure!'[160] It is more likely that Armitage was beginning to accept the problems with a degree of resignation. 'As [Macleod] is doing all the driving from the back seat, one wonders if it is not time to let him come out and try his hand on the steering wheel. He obviously fancies that he is a good negotiator and if he can establish confidence with Banda well and good.'[161] In any event, the resignation rumours died down fairly quickly.

Since the federal government refused to alter the dates of Monckton's arrival in Nyasaland to take place after Banda's release, the British cabinet agreed that as long as he was released in March it could be on the last day. Armitage wanted to avoid the doctor's release while the commission was in Northern Rhodesia because he would not be able to call on security reinforcements, which would be needed there at the same time.[162]

Home visited the federation from 19 to 26 February to try and 'resolve the question of Banda's release and security in Nyasaland and the Rhodesias'.[163] In discussions, the federal ministers were very anxious that Banda should not to be released to Nyasaland, but that he should be 'either kept permanently in detention or banished to the UK or elsewhere'. If this were not practicable, he certainly should not be released before Monckton left the federation. They would, however, agree to Banda's release immediately after Monckton had left and, if Macleod wished, constitutional talks could follow. If the British government would not accept this, Welensky would immediately hold a general election and go to the country on a platform of independence from Britain. Whitehead would be forced to follow suit. They would denounce Britain's actions and demand the commission's withdrawal from the federation.

When Home reported this to Macmillan, the prime minister telephoned Macleod and asked whether he would like the dilemma discussed in cabinet or in a small group. Macleod preferred the cabinet and said that ministers were in no doubt: they disliked giving in to pressure. Macmillan's view, with which Macleod agreed, was that they could face disintegration of Rhodesia's relationships with Britain simply by not waiting three weeks longer to release Banda. The Boston Tea Party was a constant reminder to them of what British settlers overseas could do when they became angry. So the cabinet decided to delay Banda's release until Monckton had left Nyasaland. Then, as Macmillan recorded in his private diary:

> Suddenly – and to everyone's amazement – [the] Colonial Secretary announced at [the] end of Cabinet that although he thought we had taken the only possible decision, he could not possibly be associated with it and must resign. He stayed a few minutes after Cabinet and (although remaining firm about his intention) agreed to take a little time. [The] Home Secretary came to luncheon alone with me. We were both puzzled. Is it a plot? (*à la* Thorneycroft) Is it nervous strain? (It's Iain's first post which entails real strain) Is it 'Bridge' (or perhaps Poker) or is it emotion? It seems hardly worthwhile resigning (and putting in jeopardy all that we have won for the Party and the country by Iain's own successes and my African tour) over a question as to whether this African (who has already been eleven months in prison) is to be released three weeks earlier under one plan than under another.

Macmillan did not know what to do about his colonial secretary. Some of Macleod's colleagues talked with him but he seemed 'merely to repeat that his honour was involved'. Macmillan was relieved that nothing had leaked out to the press: 'This comforts me a little. Iain's contacts with the Press (especially [the] popular Press like the *Daily Mirror*) are very intimate. If he were playing a hand against me he would have used the Press.' The prime minister feared that Macleod had got himself into 'an emotional Celtic position'. After another talk with him, Macmillan recorded:

> I am now pretty sure that he has said (or perhaps, worse still, written) some foolish things to some of these Africans. He is very clever and very keen and enthusiastic. But he is also quite inexperienced in this sort of thing. His 'honour' cannot really be involved in this question of three weeks less or more before Banda is let out. But it may well be engaged if he has said (or let it be known) that Banda will be let out in Nyasaland in time to give evidence to Monckton. This is the very point at issue between us and the Rhodesian ministers. Anyway, I asked if it would make a difference to his attitude if Banda were released three days before Monckton left Nyasaland instead of three days after. He was quite excited by this and said it would solve the problem.

Macmillan immediately telephoned Home in Salisbury and, in guarded language, they agreed that Home would try to secure Banda's release three or four days before 'the Moncktonians' left Nyasaland. This was to give him the chance to give evidence, if he wished to do so, as a free man and in his own country. The prime minister was 'much relieved' – 'Alec Home is a really splendid fellow.'

Home argued with Welensky that if Banda were not released to give evidence and take part in constitutional talks as a free man, it might well be that, after the constitutional review, the British parliament would find it impossible to continue federation in the face of implacable Nyasaland African hostility. Mainly by using this point and 'every device of patience and argument', he was able to secure agreement that Banda should be released on 1 April. This would be several days after Monckton arrived – so that moderate African opinion could be put – but several days before they left – so that Banda could give evidence as a free man. The federal government's acquiescence, Home reported, was 'utterly against all their feelings, which are deeply, however wrongly, held'.[164]

When Home told Whitehead what the British government wished to do in Nyasaland, the Southern Rhodesia prime minister promptly retorted: 'I tell you straight, that if you release Banda in Nyasaland, Southern Rhodesia will blow up and I shan't be able to stop them.' Only two of his supporters had to cross the floor to put the Dominion Party in power and Britain then, by its own act, would have achieved not only the secession of Southern Rhodesia but also union with South

Africa. At this point Home asked if European confidence could be restored if, as part of a comprehensive plan, restraints on Southern Rhodesia's constitution were removed. Whitehead's response was immediate: 'That would make all the difference in the world, but it must be done quickly and completely.'[165] As Armitage recorded:

> This could have been arranged long ago ... if we had not been faced by Macleod saying that the Cabinet decision on 4 January had been to release Banda on 29 January. The new date nearly reaches my first day of compromise, mid-April ... I can't imagine I can get any further advance on this except that I would like to release him on a Monday, i.e. 4 April.[166]

He felt crowds were less likely to gather on a working day than at a weekend. Release this particular weekend, following the end of month pay-day, 'would inevitably increase one hundred fold [the] risk of disorders accompanied by drunkenness'.

Armitage was aware that if Home's agreements with Welensky and Whitehead had not been reached, and if Macleod had not budged over Banda's release, one or other of them would have resigned and a cabinet split have resulted.[167] It may be that it was Macleod's uncertainty of the outcome of his trial of strength that dissuaded him from replacing Armitage, as he was inclined and for which he had Macmillan's support. The governor found

> All [this is] so unnecessary. Macleod had agreed with me in Dar es Salaam to put the accelerated release of detainees only, and Banda not treated differently to the others, to the Cabinet. He obviously got the Cabinet on 4 January, on the eve of Macmillan's departure, to agree to extra accelerated release of detainees and Banda out at the end of January, all without consulting Welensky, a thing ... he would not think of doing in Dar es Salaam.

Contemplating these affairs, Armitage wrote, 'What a worrying life!' Looking back over what had happened since early January: 'I find it clear how determined Macleod was to get his way, bullying his Cabinet and trying to ride roughshod over Welensky and Whitehead. This course of action provoked Welensky into making the extravagant claims of breaking with Her Majesty's Government and going it alone with the Federal Government.'

When Home returned to London on 27 February and discussed his trip with the prime minister, he confirmed Macmillan's suspicions that the federal secret service 'knew all about Macleod's "commitments" to

Banda etc.' They knew the proposed time schedule for Macleod's visit to Africa and for Banda's release before the British government could even consult them. This was the cause of their anger and Macmillan attributed it to 'a certain naïveté which the Colonial Secretary has'. These worries about Macleod's 'emotion', 'inexperience', 'naïveté', failure to tell the prime minister the 'whole truth', 'strain', possible plotting, bridge or poker tactics and saying or writing 'foolish things' to African leaders, drained Macmillan's strength: 'I feel very tired. Since I got back from Africa the work has been really overwhelming. I begin to wonder how long I can stand the strain.'[168]

At the beginning of March Armitage wrote: 'So we start the great move to see whether we can contain the Monckton Commission, Macleod's visit and Banda's release all at the same time! The Federal Government reckon we can't and I suspect Her Majesty's Government feel we shall fall down on all this.'[169] He was right. Macmillan was 'somewhat concerned' about the way the Nyasaland administration might handle disturbances following Banda's release.

On 2 March Macleod announced he would visit the federation from 13 March to 9 April; and he made it clear to Armitage that he expected to meet Banda soon after his release. Throughout March, Armitage devoted much of his time and thought to considering Banda's release, when and how it was to be done and its security implications. He wished to keep the release secret: prior notification would only enable Congress to stage demonstrations, which would be widespread and thus disperse the security forces. For similar reasons in the Gold Coast Arden-Clarke had given Gbedemah and two of his colleagues only three hours' notice of Nkrumah's release from gaol.[170]

He was clear that a 'very elaborate programme [would] have to be organized' and detailed work on this began after the secretary of state's arrival plans were telegraphed to Armitage on 9 March.[171] Macleod thought that it 'would give him too much kudos' if Banda met him and the governor at Government House. Armitage, however, did not think so. The secretary of state may have felt that a meeting at Government House would also have given the governor too much kudos. Macleod proposed the chief secretary's office as an alternative, but Armitage again disagreed, pointing to its exposed position and the large number of people working there who would immediately recognize the doctor. Excited crowds would quickly gather, 'which would be unlikely to make for profitable and balanced discussion'. The governor may have felt that a meeting at the secretariat would have given the chief secretary too much kudos. When Armitage strongly advised against the secretariat, Macleod accepted his arguments and then suggested police headquarters. Once more Armitage disagreed. He argued that, since

NYASALAND II   271

Banda must be a free man when he met the secretary of state, to do so at police headquarters would be 'psychologically wrong', for it would suggest some sort of continued restraint. He told Macleod:

> The point as we see it is that kudos accruing to Banda will stem from the fact of his coming straight from prison to meet with you and the Governor. I feel that his being summoned to meet with you and me at Government House will be accepted by Banda in the right spirit and be accepted by all as being the proper line to take. A meeting anywhere else might in fact confer additional kudos upon him in that it will be interpreted as the mountain going to Mohammed.

Macleod eventually agreed the meeting should be at Government House. Armitage would have recalled that when Nkrumah was released from prison it was to the governor's residence in Accra that he was summoned by Arden-Clarke. Also, while Footman, Youens and Jones had all been to see Banda, Armitage never had, and it is almost certain that the doctor would have considered it entirely proper for him to go to Government House — as he had on each previous occasion — rather than the governor meet him elsewhere.

The Monckton Commission arrived in Nyasaland on 21 and Macleod on 29 March.[172]

The scene was now set for Banda's release. Armitage had postponed the date as much as he could and had moved it gradually from late January to 1 April. He was still very concerned about the possibility of violence, and his non-official advisers and Welensky were convinced that there would be bloodshed. The combination of the Monckton Commission's presence, the arrival of the secretary of state for constitutional talks and Banda's release could be an explosive, difficult to control mixture. Armitage was pleased that Northern Rhodesia had agreed to let him have police reinforcements. Irrespective of the fears of others, Macleod was determined to take the risks involved and try to persuade Banda to keep the African population peaceful. Although Welensky made it clear that his government dissociated itself from the decision to release Banda and accepted no responsibility for it, the federal government cooperated fully in the mechanics of the release.[173]

On 30 March the governor and the secretary of state held a meeting at Government House, attended by the provincial commissioners and the most senior provincial police officers. For at least one of these officers it was

> a disagreeable experience.... Macleod was gratuitously offensive to the Governor in front of the six of us. Macleod also criticized [the provincial

commissioner of the Central Province] about some incident and was not prepared to listen to [his] reply. [Another provincial commissioner] was not personally an object of Macleod's venom but ... took a strong dislike to him. ... I do not forgive Macleod's treatment of the Governor on that occasion nor his treatment of [the provincial commissioner].[174]

The following day, Armitage and Macleod had a meeting with Dixon and Blackwood. Macleod's attitude towards them throughout was aggressive and boorish. Halfway through the meeting Blackwood said that things would be better in Nyasaland if the Conservative Party were not divided over what policy to adopt. This remark touched Macleod on a raw nerve – sensitivity over the possibility of a cabinet split he himself had induced – and he lost control of himself, shouting at Blackwood, 'What the blazes are you talking about, Blackwood? You mind your own bloody business.' There was a long silence while he cooled down. Blackwood did not respond – just turned a bit pink. Armitage was embarrassed but said nothing.[175]

The task of bringing Banda back to Nyasaland fell to Youens. His instructions were that Banda was to be removed from Gwelo and produced in Zomba without anybody, particularly the press, getting at him first, and there was 'a very complicated exercise' mounted with the Royal Rhodesia Air Force.[176]

Armitage recorded what happened on the day of Banda's release in his private diary for 1 April 1960:

> A bright morning and so no danger to the aircraft, which landed at Zomba.... Banda was brought to Government House by Youens.... Then shortly after 10.00 a.m. he came down to see Macleod and me in my office. We exchanged a lot of pleasantries and then broached the subject of constitutional talks.... Banda seemed to bear no resentment against any of us and said he had been well treated in Gwelo, was pleased that Youens met him. [Macleod] asked Banda whether he would like to broadcast a message of peace, which he had stressed throughout. This he agreed to do.[177]

Banda's message, which he was 'persuaded' to record before he left at 11.45 a.m. for broadcasting later, was short and helpful. Armitage was 'surprised' that he agreed to give it.[178]

Macleod was 'very obviously relieved when it became clear that the release had not led to widespread disorder – he was unusually flushed and talkative at dinner that night', and told Macmillan that it was 'a great relief now to have the little man out of gaol'. The secretary of state's private secretary had 'a clear memory of Macleod being in a high state of what might be called relieved tension on the evening of the release when it became clear that there would not be any ... major disturbance'. They finished the day noisily at Government House with Macleod 'hurling cushions across the room in the style of a rugby scrum-half', with the governor – less enthusiastically – retrieving them.[179]

Macleod spent the next few days in a fast succession of visits. On 6 April Banda flew from Chileka to visit London and the United States.[180]

Banda was away from Nyasaland for a month and during this time, on 29 April, Armitage lifted the ban on public meetings, imposed when the emergency was declared. On 10 May, the attorney-general introduced into legislative council bills that enabled the governor to end the emergency but to continue the detention of certain people already detained. The way was now clear for Armitage to end the state of emergency, and this he did on 16 June. The previous day he had brought the new legislation into force and this enabled him to continue to incarcerate the 20 people still in detention, including Chipembere and the Chisiza brothers.[181]

As a result of his discussions with Banda in the first few days of April, the secretary of state concluded that there were just sufficient grounds to justify holding a constitutional conference during the summer.[182] On 25 May he asked the governor to submit nominations of the various groups to attend the conference, but at this stage the secretary of state was not particularly sanguine about its outcome: '[It] looks in one sense as if it will have very little chance of success. It would have none if Banda alone was not in charge.'[183] It was also Armitage's view that there would be no chance of success if the remaining few hard-core detainees were allowed to attend the conference. Macleod believed that the chances would be improved if they could talk to Banda through a third person who had influence with him. There were a number of possibilities. Oliver Woods of *The Times* knew Banda well, saw a lot of him, and would 'wholeheartedly support' the sort of constitutional advance Macleod had in mind. Sir Jock Campbell also had considerable influence over Banda and for a while he was considered a possibility. Macleod ruled out Dingle Foot because he did not regard him as 'either trustworthy or efficient'. He thought that Chipembere's and Chisiza's absence from the conference might conceivably wreck it, but that it probably would not. Of his general approach, he told Welensky:

> In all my thinking about Nyasaland I have been concentrating on what I call the realities of power as against the appearance of power: and I am sure that in Nyasaland that means firm retention of official control of the

executive at the present stage. In other words, if you will allow a comparison with the railways, I would like to be in the position with the Governor of Nyasaland of driving the train on its next journey; I don't mind who blows the whistle or waves the flags.[184]

On 5 July, Armitage received a cable from Macleod asking him to assure Banda that, although he would have 'certain ideas to put before the conference as a pattern for future constitutional development', he would not be bringing a closed mind to the conference and hoped others would not do so either. 'Any prospect of the success of the conference depends on the readiness of all concerned to move towards each other in a spirit of responsibility and moderation from the widely divergent viewpoints I found during my visit. Please tell [Banda] how much I am looking forward to seeing him here.' Armitage viewed this message as Macleod trying to be 'all things to all men', and he was very suspicious of this approach, 'knowing it was not in his nature to come to a meeting without his mind made up as to what he wanted to achieve'.[185]

Two days later the governor had a long talk with Banda at Government House, in which he said he was pleased to be able to talk with him before the conference and hoped things would go well in London. On his side, the doctor said he was prepared to reach agreement with others who were prepared to compromise and he hoped he would find that spirit there. In his view, it was necessary for the African majority in Nyasaland to be recognized and to take part in any constitutional decisions. Armitage was unable to draw him any further than this. They discussed the continuing intimidation in the country – which Banda denied. They also discussed the effect of the doctor's speeches, particularly the feeling of disquiet they gave to civil servants. To this the doctor replied that if he were given responsibility, they would find his speeches very different. Armitage found this interesting. Banda had not previously said so categorically that he would be prepared to act responsibly once he was given responsibility. Banda feared that Macleod had already made up his mind on what was to happen at the conference and had agreed this with Welensky. He did not, it seems, fully trust the secretary of state. It was a constructive and friendly meeting and already the two men were establishing a very fair relationship. The governor concluded from this meeting:

> It was clear that he has made up his mind that he is coming out on top and that he will ensure that ... all ... people involved in government will work against Federation. Its destruction is his main target. I am sure that when he has met Macleod he has been assured that he will get his way.

Therefore the first task that he has set himself is to get control of Nyasaland. Again I am virtually certain that he was promised that by Macleod. His manner left me in no doubt that he was approaching the winning of that battle. His party organization meant that no African in Nyasaland could effectively oppose him.[186]

Armitage was now in a mood of despondent resignation:

I was already approaching the view that the Government, through civil servants, chiefs and local authorities, would not be able to stand up against a well-drilled African nationalist party machine.... Without declaring another state of emergency and bringing in the federal army, we could not impose any policy which Banda refused to support. No one in Nyasaland ever contemplated another state of emergency and using the federal army. I suspect that the only condition on which Welensky would send his troops here would be to take over the country. We could not contemplate that and there was talk at times from London that they would send over British troops to prevent it, if necessary.[187]

In this mood he left Chileka on 20 July for London.

There were fears by the British, federal and Nyasaland governments that if the London talks broke down there would be an outburst of violence in Nyasaland; and discussions were held to handle this. Welensky's forces would be fully stretched because he needed to arm the Northern Rhodesia border with the Congo, where severe disorders had broken out. Armitage was opposed to reinforcements by federal troops because they might affect negotiations with Banda. Macmillan offered British military assistance, but Welensky was opposed to bringing in British troops until all local troops were fully committed – and there were large numbers of them.[188]

During a stopover in Salisbury, Armitage had discussions with Welensky – whom he found 'in a thoroughly bad mood' – particularly about their security force response should the London conference break down. 'Substantial military reinforcements' had already been alerted. Armitage stressed the extreme danger of white, territorial troops shooting Nyasas. He added that, if the London talks broke down, maximum reinforcements would be needed in Nyasaland. They would need to stay for a long time and this was a job for regular, not territorial, troops. The federal regular army was of African soldiers under white officers.[189]

When he arrived in London he went straight to the Colonial Office for a meeting with Macleod and his senior officials: 'Discussed programme for the conference which is completely conditioned by the need to spin out the proceedings until Parliament rises on Friday and there can be no more pressures from that quarter!'[190]

The conference – to advise Macleod on the next stage of constitutional advance – opened at Lancaster House on 25 July, five years almost to the day after the Cyprus conference had been held there. Questions affecting Nyasaland's relationships with the federation were outside its scope. Macleod opened with a sentence in Cinyanja[191] – which went down well – and by saying that the task before them was:

> to seek a pattern for the orderly evolution of Nyasaland's political institutions on a democratic basis, in a form which would meet the aspirations and apprehensions of the peoples of Nyasaland; which would provide for the continuance of stable government and progressive administration; and which would enable Her Majesty's Government effectively to discharge their political responsibilities towards Nyasaland for as long as its peoples so desired.[192]

Philip Short, Banda's biographer, described this as 'a typical piece of Macmillanish ambiguity, enough to give some comfort to both sides of the table, but which carefully obscured the basic dilemma with which the conference was concerned'.[193] The dilemma facing Macleod and Armitage was how to reach a compromise short of immediate self-government and yet avoid the alternative, as Banda saw it, of 'another March 1959'.[194] Replying to this opening speech, Banda spoke highly of Macleod's intentions and restated his own willingness to give and take, but went on to say:

> My people expect great things from this conference. If under the pretext of securing a stable government a scheme is hammered out here which does not satisfy my people, I will not be a party to it. Nyasaland is an African country. The time has come when Africans must govern ... we have had many dirty deals in the past. It is about time we had a fair deal.[195]

The nature of the next three days' discussions, and the input of each of the 12 non-official representatives, was summed up by Armitage:

> Banda ... threatened the chiefs that if they interfered with the constitutional pattern to be arranged (presumably to the Malawi Congress Party liking) they would be for it. ... Chinyama followed and attacked Banda and the Malawi Congress Party [MCP] for intimidation, and said chiefs should be rulers. Rather a brave effort. Dixon was hopeful of ordered progress. ... Chiefs Chinde and Ntaja were for the Malawi Congress

Party and self-government. [Chiefs] Masula and Makanjiri were against. These attacks on Banda and retorts by his followers are laborious.... Chikumbula also attacked Banda. Dr Antao supported the Malawi Congress Party; Chinyama and M. Phiri attacked it. Finally, Chiume came along and made a smooth speech in favour of one man, one vote democracy and rule by the majority.... Blackwood ... hit Banda and company ... especially by quoting from speeches made previously.[196]

The talks at this point reached deadlock and, on 29 July, Macleod summed up and put forward the British government's views. Armitage recognized that Banda was worried by the opposition demonstrated against him, including that by Africans, and was embarrassed that he could not display the massive support he could in Nyasaland.[197] Macleod's proposals, announced just before the weekend break, were presented in the form of four guiding principles.[198]

First, Nyasaland was destined to become an African state and the time had come for a clear African non-official majority in the legislature, but other non-official representation should be retained. Second, non-officials should be elected but for the present the franchise should be qualitative and broad based, not universal. Third, executive council should be advisory to the governor and be neither entirely responsible to the legislature, as Banda wanted, nor totally unconnected with it, as the United Federal Party wanted. Fourth, some official representation on executive council should be retained, with non-official members drawn mainly, maybe entirely, from those elected to the legislature. Also, it might be appropriate to introduce some form of ministerial system. As Armitage recorded:

> We adjourn to Monday, when we start the real issue, which is whether Banda and company can accept these very watered down ideas. They seemed stupefied when they heard them. It will be interesting to see whether Macleod is like a boa constrictor who can mesmerize his victims while they are in front of him. Will Banda repeat all the very confident things he has said about him? Or has he been taken for such an almighty ride that he cannot get by and must rebel.... So far Macleod has played the game superbly. We have so many chiefs etc., Banda could not earlier have walked out or it would have left the field wide open. Can he now? Does he want more suffering?[199]

Over the weekend, Banda visited Macleod and told him that his colleagues had wanted to walk out of the conference, but that he had restrained them. The secretary of state said that there was still a great deal to be discussed, but made it clear that he would not yet accept one man one vote. Armitage was spending the weekend with Jeremy in Kent, but Macleod called him back to discuss what they thought the two sides would accept.[200]

The conference resumed on Monday and after a few speeches they broke up into smaller groups with Macleod and Armitage discussing proposals with each of the opposing groups.[201] When the secretary of state was away on the Tuesday, Armitage noted: 'The lack of progress and precision when Macleod is not there is quite remarkable.'[202] The secretary of state, however, felt progress was being made and told Macmillan:

> This strange conference continues. We are now in the extremely odd position that if it was not for the fact that we know Monckton is going to report, I believe I stand a very good chance of getting an agreement from every single delegate to the conference. Certainly all extreme attitudes on both sides have been abandoned and people have been talking within a very narrow compass. . . . I am very puzzled to know how to end the conference whilst still keeping a line open for Walter [Monckton] but I am trying to devise a formula which will do this and I will speak to him this evening.[203]

On 4 August the conference ended with all delegates agreeing to the final report.[204] Armitage must have felt that the boa constrictor had indeed mesmerized its victims. But, as Macmillan confessed in congratulating Macleod on the conference's success: 'With all our troubles and difficulties it is rather encouraging when something goes right.' In essence, this agreement was that the executive council should be advisory and number ten: three non-official members of the legislature elected on the lower roll – effectively Africans – and two on the higher roll – probably Europeans – and there should be five officials including the governor as president.

This composition of the executive council was precisely what Macleod sought as his 'opening bid'. It contained more officials – five as against three – and fewer Africans – three as against five – than Armitage had in mind seven months earlier. All members should have ministerial status. Also, the legislature should have five official members, 20 lower roll and eight upper roll non-officials. This composition of legislative council had rather more African and rather fewer non-African seats than Macleod had in mind, and had no government nominees, which he had in mind as his 'opening bid'. It contained rather more in each category than Armitage had been prepared to accept seven months earlier – 20 as against 16 Africans; eight as against six Europeans; and five as against three officials. There were also agreed safeguards for, or agreements on, the judiciary, fundamental rights, the civil service, local government and the chiefs. All delegates stated their intention to make the new constitution work and their recognition that a reasonable trial period was necessary for stability upon which economic, social and constitutional progress could be based. In his concluding remarks, Macleod said:

> When first in Central Africa I announced that this conference would take place, and even when we assembled here in London ten days ago, practically no one in Nyasaland, or the Federation, or here, thought there was any chance of agreement. Yet we have shown that men of different races, African, European and Asian, can come together round the table and reach agreement, even though they started from widely differing points of view.[205]

Although Armitage and his colleagues 'had no overt role to play' in the conference, Macleod did consult him frequently and the governor 'basically agreed with his ideas'. He thought that this contributed to the success of the conference. The outcome had not gone as far as he himself, unknown to others, would have been prepared to go. Macleod also kept Welensky informed by sending him daily telegrams.[206] Privately, Armitage summed up by saying:

> Banda and the Malawi Congress Party got the prospect of achieving power in due course, but had to be content with very slow progress. Dixon and Blackwood disagreed with the pace of change, slow though it was. They could not have expected more... the field was left clear for [Macleod] to get his policies across. He did this immensely well, without provoking anyone to walk out, though no doubt they often wanted to. Banda equally had the Malawi Congress Party under complete control. He now knew it was only a question of time before he was supreme in Nyasaland.

On the second day of the conference Armitage had lunched with Macleod at White's Club and was told that the secretary of state did not propose to recommend an extension of his tour. Macleod said Jones would take over as governor and he wanted him to attend the federal review conference, which would start in the autumn 'so as to keep Dixon and Blackwood in play, amongst other things'. Armitage would stay in office until that conference was over. He could go on leave during the current year and Macleod preferred him to take a shorter leave than he had planned so as to be back in Nyasaland before the conference started. They were looking for a new chief secretary to fill

Jones's place. On the day the conference ended, he received a letter from the Colonial Office confirming that his term of office would not be extended. This was 31 years to the day after he had landed at Mombasa to take up his first appointment.[207]

On 4 August, also, Armitage went to see the Queen Mother – it was her birthday. 'What a calm, serene creature and how understanding. Her rooms were full of flowers. We talked for over twenty minutes.' She displayed an 'intense interest' in Nyasaland and the conference. He then went on to Lord Perth's 'for the celebration cocktail party' for the delegates, spent some time talking with Banda and commented on how 'tired and yellow-grey' he looked: 'Banda was either overcome by exhaustion or emotion and could hardly stand. At times he focused and spoke with difficulty. He had a very exhausting time physically, can't be strong, may have to pep or tranquillize himself.'[208] The following day Armitage called at the Colonial Office, mainly to discuss recruitment to the civil service. In the evening, he flew back to Nyasaland.[209]

7

Nyasaland III

It is quite impossible to think that when I came back from leave, I should have been able to depart in these very changed circumstances.

A week after the conference ended the Armitages went on leave and Jones took over as acting governor. They had made plans for some considerable time to coincide their leave with the federal review, but Macleod preferred him to take a shorter leave now and save the remainder due to him until he retired. They were seen off by the general manager of the railways, the chief justice, the European non-official members of executive council, the mayor of Blantyre–Limbe and the provincial and district commissioners. They enjoyed the train journey down the Rift Valley escarpment, the lower Shire valley and the Zambezi plain to the coast, despite the bumpiness of parts of it. They travelled in the general-manager's coach, where the service was excellent. They were amused that they could now say they had taken a bath on a train! At Beira, they were received by the federal consul general, railway officials and business people. The Portuguese governor called on them at their hotel and Armitage returned the call.[1]

They boarded the *Africa* on 13 August and, although they found their cabin small, they appreciated the air conditioning, the good public rooms and the 'very attentive' staff. Their son, Richard, and Susan Haworth, his fiancée and daughter of one of the Armitages' oldest friends, who had been staying with them in Zomba since July, travelled with them. At Dar es Salaam they were entertained by Footman – now chairman of the public service commissions there – who seemed to be 'well settled' after his abrupt departure from Nyasaland. They called at Zanzibar. At Mombasa they were looked after by John Pinney, the district commissioner, who had visited Nyasaland on security matters early during the emergency. Simmonds, a former financial secretary in Nyasaland, looked after them in Aden. Here he learned that troops at Nairobi had just been placed on four days' stand-by instead of the 24 hours on which they had been placed in case they were needed in Nyasaland. They called at Suez and Port Said, stopped at Brindisi and arrived in Venice on 30 August. At last Armitage 'was recovering [his] stamina and no longer sleep[ing] most of the day and night' and he felt that for a while he could 'forget Africa and enjoy sightseeing'. They spent a few days in Venice and, although Lyona was unwell, Armitage, Richard and Susan enjoyed the many sights – notwithstanding that 'the public conveniences are difficult to find here!' They then travelled overland to Britain.

Almost as soon as he left, the *Nyasaland Times* published a leading article headed 'Sir Robert is needed'.[2] The editor felt that he should 'remain as Governor of Nyasaland for some time yet'. He paid tribute to Armitage's 'firm yet tolerant attitude' in guiding the country. He had earned the respect and gratitude of thousands of all races for his 'firm attitude towards those who seek to ruin the country through underhand political tricks'. The main argument for extending his term of office was that he was a man of honour and principle whom people trusted. 'When things looked blackest for Nyasaland, Sir Robert Armitage provided the leadership that restored our faith and we want him to remain Governor, at least until the new constitution is in being and the country shows that it is settling down to prepare itself for further advance.' Armitage was grateful for this support and expression of confidence, but realized that it came from a paper owned, edited and read by Europeans.

They rented a flat near Poole Harbour – where they had a number of 'marvellous' days with Jeremy and his wife, Phoebe, staying with them – and a flat in London.[3] They had a very happy time at Richard and Susan's wedding. They went to the cinema, enjoyed the Olympic Games and horse racing on television, looked at houses in Dorchester they might buy for their retirement, and bought a new car. They spent some time also with his mother. It 'needed special activities' to get them to London, but towards the middle of October they went. One purpose was to buy fabrics at Peter Jones – where they had a 'happy time' – for the governor's lodge at Blantyre. The other was for Armitage to visit the Colonial Office, which he did on 13, 27 and 31 October.

On the first of these occasions, Watson brought him up to date on Nyasaland and Monckton Commission affairs, although Jones had written to him quite extensively and his new private secretary, Nicholas Maxwell-Lawford, kept him informed of social events. On the second visit, he went with Hone. Macleod was ill, so instead they talked with officials and 'needled them on whether HMG was prepared to break up the federation'. They got the impression that 'if Banda and [Kenneth]

Kaunda would not accept any compromise they would be prepared to do so.' On 31 October, Armitage spent half an hour with Macleod:

> We talked about Banda coming to the federal review and he was clearly very self satisfied about the state of Nyasaland now as compared with what he had inherited a year ago; the success of the release of Banda and later of all the detainees and the inescapable task of negotiating only with Banda until he proved himself one way or the other. To my question whether he would hold a federal review if Banda or Kaunda or both would not come, he said he supposed it would have to be held, otherwise the criticism of giving in to African nationalism would be immense.... He said that Welensky would be no factor in this conference [because he would not accept a looser form of federation and even if he did the Africans would not accept him in it] and asked me who would replace him in power. He was *persona non grata* to all Africans. So therefore little could be achieved while he was around. I said that Whitehead would have to be a force to be reckoned with and might take over from Welensky in the federal sphere if Welensky left it for any reason. Anyway, Welensky was a sick man. I got the clear impression that the secretary of state was only interested in the African aspect of all this, that he will let European interests go hang if they interfere with Africans and that he is firmly in control and in power.... As I left he said when would I be back and I said in June and he seemed to mutter that he would see me before then which I did not quite understand. No mention of any affairs in Nyasaland.

Armitage never saw Macleod again, nor did any senior official from the Colonial Office ever again get in touch with him. He later concluded that, having spent so many months arguing with Macleod and at times 'making him change his [mind]', no doubt the orders were that he was not to be involved in any future Colonial Office activities.

Later that day, after visiting MI5, he was driven in a federal high commission car to London airport where he remarked: 'Last time we shall ever use the VIP lounge.'[4] They flew back to Nyasaland via Salisbury where they lunched with the governor-general:

> Simon [Dalhousie] said the bitterness between Welensky and Her Majesty's Government was terrific and coloured all thought and action now. He had nearly persuaded Welensky of the need to make some dramatic gesture to the Africans, but he had failed. All Welensky would think of was being let down by Macmillan. Simon was most depressed by Southern Rhodesian reactions and obviously could see no future.

After lunch they flew to Nyasaland by RRAF Dakota. Armitage was apprehensive about his remaining months in Nyasaland. His private secretary told him that the Europeans were 'very depressed'. Armitage confided: 'We are not going to have a very happy final five months I am afraid: antagonisms, latent or flaring, all round us. But later perhaps we will return to a more tranquil existence.'

While he had been away a number of developments had taken place. On 25 August, Jones, who kept him informed of what was happening, wrote of the several acts of intimidation made by Congress members against UFP members and others, and especially against Kwenje and Mattheus Phiri, vice-president of the UFP in Nyasaland.[5] The district headquarters, files and papers of the CLP in Luchenza had been destroyed by fire. The Phiri incident was very unpleasant: he was heavily stoned by '200 shouting and chanting Africans', was forced to take refuge in a nearby shop and would have been seriously injured but for the help given by a number of Europeans and the 'prompt and vigorous action' of the police who, with the courts, had gone a long way to reassure the public.

> Dixon ... became hysterical and made a press statement and sent to the secretary of state a cable, both intimating that the Nyasaland UFP were thinking in terms of repudiating the Lancaster House agreement. I have had a long talk with Dixon since then and he is on an even keel again and will not repudiate the agreement, at any rate without seeing me first. I think it is the usual line of keeping things in a state of tension on the off-chance that the Lancaster House agreement may come to naught because of actions and statements made by Banda.

Jones had also seen Banda and told him that incidents such as the Phiri one stemmed from his 'contemptuous references to such people in his speeches', and cautioned him to avoid 'extravagant vilification of political opponents which may be perfectly legitimate in England but is dangerous in Africa'. Banda had raised the question of coming on to the legislative and executive councils, but Jones thought he was trying to make a deal so that the four 'nominated stooges' could be removed from legislative council to make way for Chipembere and Chiume – who would resume their former seats, which they had forfeited because they were not in the country and able to attend meetings – and Banda with one of the Chisizas. In Jones's view, such trading involved not only 'kicking out people who have done well for us according to their lights during the last eighteen months', but also releasing the hard core from detention. He was not agreeing to this and was confident that the secretary of state would back him up.

When Jones wrote on 12 September, he hoped that by the time

Armitage returned to Nyasaland some of the current problems might have been solved, although 'at the moment uncertainty and tension prevail'.[6] Just before he went on leave, Armitage had discussed with him and Youens how to handle the query already raised by Macleod about those still in detention: 'We want to play the game as slowly as possible, not easy as Macleod hates nothing so much as to defend in the House of Commons a policy of this sort, where he gets political blame rather than kudos. We don't yet know what Banda really wants.' In the short interim, however, it seems that the doctor had made it known to Jones what he wanted. Banda was pressing him very hard indeed about releasing the detainees and he thought they might have to do something about it, otherwise the doctor would break off contact and they would be in danger of 'drifting back to March 1959'.

Jones, with the support of his official advisers, had proposed to the secretary of state that they 'wipe the slate clean both as regards detainees and also restrictees' to try and get Banda in a reasonable frame of mind to study the Monckton Report. If they did not do this, they might be accused of weakness and be subjected to further pressure – both by Banda – to give way on other points such as bringing Chipembere on to the legislative and executive councils.

> If we do not meet him over the detainees the signs are that we shall have fairly serious trouble – he is being driven against the wall himself over this matter and is having difficulty restraining his hotheads. If we are going to wipe the slate clean at all there is a strong argument for doing it while Banda is pleading with us. Once he begins to threaten we shall be in a difficult position. As you see the situation has hardened a bit since you left.

It could, of course, have been argued that 'meeting him over the detainees' would lay Jones open to accusations of weakness – by Europeans – and subject him to further pressure – by Banda – rather than the contrary, as he argued.

At this time, Jones was told that he would succeed Armitage as governor. Shortly afterwards he told Armitage that he had accepted the appointment 'with somewhat mixed feelings', for he already knew enough about the job to know that it was no sinecure: 'the kicks come from all sides and the situation is as difficult as any I have had to face and will, it seems to me, remain so for some considerable time.'[7] Banda may also have learned that Jones was to become governor and was taking an early opportunity to put pressure on the man most likely to be in a position to accede to his demands.

On 18 September, Armitage replied to Jones's letter and, in congratulating him on the announcement that he was to be appointed governor, said it had been difficult at times to conceal that he had known of the decision to do so.[8] He was pleased Jones was reversing the trend of fortunes of his previous chief secretaries who had left their posts rather hurriedly — Fletcher-Cooke, who was removed from Cyprus at the same time as Armitage, and Footman. He supported him in his proposal to release the detainees, but asked whether Banda could control his people and whether Jones could make a deal with him. In replying to these crucial questions on 28 September, Jones thought no one could answer the first. Concerning the second, however, he had made a deal in which the doctor would publicly denounce violence and intimidation and would give an undertaking to control his lieutenants, particularly the Chisizas and Chipembere, and let him know 'immediately they begin to get out of hand'.

> My dilemma has been that continued detentions and restrictions were leading to the point when we would lose contact with Banda completely and he would say that his position was impossible because government was not giving him a fair chance to show his people that the Lancaster House agreement meant a new start for all. There was a distinct danger that Banda would give up any pretence of holding his extreme elements in check and let things take their course — which in his view meant a return to Gwelo and all that. On the other hand, one could make the gesture of wiping the slate clean and have at one's back the argument that government had done all in its power to create a cordial atmosphere in which the preparations for the elections could take place. If the ex-detainees cause trouble, government might have to take firm action again and could do so with a clear conscience.[9]

At Jones's request, Banda issued a statement denouncing violence. He said that he had been having discussions with Jones about the Lancaster House agreement and had made clear to him his policy that the elections and the preparations for them should be conducted on their part in a true democratic spirit. Although they would strive by all lawful means to obtain as many seats as possible, they would not deny the right of other parties to do the same. He added:

> I believe in the maintenance of law and order in the country. Such incidents as have appeared in the newspapers and are heard on the radio are not sweet music to my ears... where they are proved to be true, let the law deal with them as it does with any other criminal act. I denounce violence and intimidation just as anyone else and all members of my party are aware of my views on this point.[10]

This statement enabled Jones to announce the release of the remaining detainees and the revocation of all restriction orders. He explained that he had taken this step so that no further cause for bitterness should remain and in the hope and trust that it would bring about an atmosphere of peace in which the introduction of the new constitution agreed to at Lancaster House could go forward.

While Jones felt the general situation justified these steps, Nyasaland was passing through a difficult period of change, bringing its own tensions. On the one hand, the government was castigated for its apparent inactivity in dealing with lawlessness: on the other hand, it was strongly criticized for measures taken where defiance of lawful authority had been blatant. The truth, he explained, was that, while taking firm action where the need had arisen, the government had, in an effort to permit peaceful and ordered planning for the future, exercised tolerance, forbearance and patience. There was, however, clear evidence that 'numbers of people have little regard for law and order' and nobody should be in any doubt that, if it became necessary, the government would take 'resolute measures to preserve law and order'. He wanted to see peace in Nyasaland so that people could make the most of the opportunities provided by the constitution agreed at Lancaster House.[11]

Jones told Armitage, in his letter of 28 September, that he took full responsibility for announcing the decision to release the remaining detainees. He had considered mentioning Armitage's name, but finally decided not to because it would be unfair on Armitage if things then went wrong. If they did go wrong, Jones accepted that the blame must be his. It was not said, but alternatively, if things went well, the credit would also be his. He expected to be criticized severely for releasing the detainees, particularly by some Europeans who would feel that this was yet another sign of giving way to Banda. He expected most Africans would welcome the move. Jones ended this letter by saying that his great anxiety was that he might have done something that would make things more difficult for Armitage. 'That I would avoid at all costs for it seems to me you have had more than your fair share of difficulties and deserve to be given a good canter home.'[12]

Immediately on his return from leave, Armitage held a meeting of executive council, on 3 November 1960, at which they discussed the forthcoming federal review conference, the holding of elections in Nyasaland and the intimidation, which had become widespread.[13]

He had a long discussion with Dixon and Blackwood, who were 'quite tempestuous about affairs'. They envisaged the federal review delegates would get to London and speeches would be made in which there would be a very firm refusal by Welensky and Whitehead to vary the main ingredients of the present constitution. They would sit tight on this and, when the British ministers made proposals for varying them, they would refuse to agree and the conference would then come to an end. The delegates would depart, everything would go on as at present, there would be no provision for further constitutional review, the constitution would remain in being, and the future to that extent would be clear. The federal prime minister would do nothing himself to break up the constitution.

Armitage thought Welensky would be much readier to go on talking than they thought. When he asked how Welensky would then maintain the federation in being, they replied he would not hesitate to use force and would put his army into position on the airfields and at other strategic points. It would then be necessary for the British government to make a military attack if it wanted to recapture the situation. Opinion in Britain would be so much against a Tory government doing this that they would never make such a move, but would give way, climb down and leave Welensky in physical control of the federation's territories.

Armitage then asked them to consider the situation from a tactical point of view. It would not be easy for federal forces to hold all the airfields in the two northern territories without spreading their strength so thinly that invading forces would have no difficulty in overrunning the defenders. Blackwood and Dixon discarded this suggestion, saying the British government 'would not have the guts to make a physical attack of this nature'. The discussion went 'round and round in circles'. There was a great deal of repetition and, throughout, Blackwood and Dixon revealed Welensky's and his followers' obsession about what they described as the British government 'letting down' the federal government. They said that, since the British government's good faith had disappeared, there was no longer any desire to maintain even a commonwealth relationship, hence the thinking behind keeping control through military force and breaking all links with the Commonwealth.

Armitage suspected that the thinking of his non-official advisers had been conditioned by an exaggerated view of the weakness of the British government, the unpopularity of some ministers in it, and the allegedly right-wing feeling of the British public preventing action being taken against the Europeans in the federation to support African interests. He countered by saying that, in his estimation of the feeling in government circles and among the British public, first, maintaining the federation would not be supported if it meant using force and, second, any likelihood of federal armed forces being used against Britain would be met by military retaliation. Blackwood and Dixon did not accept this opinion and suggested that, at a very early stage in the conference, there would be such conflict of views between the federal or Southern

Rhodesian government and the British government that the conference might well come to an end after two or three days. When Armitage reminded them of the skill with which British ministers conducted these conferences and their ability to keep delegates talking for days or weeks on end, they replied that, while this had happened at other conferences, it would not happen at the federal review.

Armitage was concerned about the general feeling in the country. He found there was 'low morale, uncertainty on all sides, tension at the high degree of intimidation being practised by the MCP and the feeling that HMG, Whitehead and Welensky are on such bad terms that anything could happen'. A fortnight later, Armitage had another discussion with Dixon and Blackwood in which he tried to probe further their views on the federal review. Welensky, they said, would take the view, so often repeated by Britain, that the federation was there to stay, but would concede a number of practical and procedural items where changes were reasonable. He would also support 'somewhat extraneous suggestions', such as a bill of rights and a council of state. Having made this tactical position clear, he would sit back and wait for Britain to propose any drastic changes that might be contemplated.

At this stage, Welensky would reject the proposals and, having tidied up other parts of the order in council and included a bill of rights and a council of state, the review would be drawn to an end with no new federal association. To Armitage, all this indicated was that if Britain wished to press for major alterations to the present constitution, it would have to force the issue. Dixon and Blackwood believed the British government would have given way to Whitehead on all the points of Southern Rhodesia's constitutional subordination to Britain by the time the review conference opened. On the other hand, as Armitage pointed out, it might be a question of some bargaining over those points and certain federal adjustments.

> I think there is some wishful thinking that HMG is going to agree to the perpetuation of a federal constitution much closer to the present constitution than anything that we have contemplated HMG could possibly accept. Dixon and Blackwood certainly consider that some form of virtually imposed federal constitution will come out of all this and they will be surprised if a state of emergency and the arrest of a few [about thirty] MCP leaders is not required. In their view that should be the end of all opposition and everything would thereafter be peace and quiet.

Armitage believed the outcome of the conference was bound to be 'obscure'. Conceivably, there could be 'nothing but negatives and frustrations', but he thought not, for basically Banda did not want to go back to Gwelo. He thought Macleod had such 'an intense influence over these people' that he would almost certainly make them accept a compromise, if Whitehead could be brought that far. Whether Macleod could do this would depend on Welensky.

While Armitage was on leave, Poynton consulted Jones about who should succeed him as chief secretary when he became governor.[14] Jones said that Youens was the best local candidate. However, when Poynton asked his opinion of Foster, he 'had to say in all frankness that [he] thought Foster was the better man but [that] his coming might create difficulties'. He was particularly worried that if Foster were made chief secretary, Youens might become 'despondent' and suggested that 'some prospect of promotion in another territory in the foreseeable future should be held out' to him. On 9 November, Hone told Armitage that Foster had declined the recently made offer of the chief secretaryship. No reason was given and Armitage assumed that Youens – whom Jones said was 'not well regarded in the Colonial Office' – would be passed over again in favour of Peter Stallard, who was having to leave Nigeria because of the demand there for Nigerians to fill key posts.

Armitage robustly defended his deputy chief secretary against the Colonial Office's criticisms and was quickly able to show they were unfounded. A little later, Jones told Armitage that Banda expected Youens to be the next chief secretary and welcomed this. Foster had in fact declined because he did not expect there to be eight years work left for him in Nyasaland before he retired. Others also thought that there was little future – or pleasure – in a career in Nyasaland. The Colonial Office was experiencing great difficulty in filling the solicitor-general's post – which at least three people had turned down – and Jones persuaded it to make a further attempt to get Foster to accept the chief secretaryship. Armitage's view was: 'How ignominious all this hawking round of senior posts is.' He learned that Phillips was unlikely to get the financial secretaryship of Northern Rhodesia when shortly it became vacant, and he feared that his own unpopularity at the Colonial Office had prejudiced the promotion prospects of his senior colleagues.

The Nyasaland government received a good deal of criticism, especially from the local European press, for dealing with Banda and, as it was seen, capitulating to Congress. Some Europeans, however, were showing early signs of recognizing that they must accustom themselves to dealing with Africans, 'but not, of course, that man Banda!' Internal security was still much in Armitage's mind and he spoke about this with Jones and other advisers, who said that some progress was being made with prosecutions. Executive council shortly discussed whether they should take powers to prosecute newspapers, such as

Congress's *Malawi News*, and the attorney-general came under fire for not prosecuting Chipembere and others for sedition.[15]

In the meantime, Banda went to Nigeria for its independence celebrations and Armitage waited 'rather uneasily' to see what would happen during his absence. 'He has been making less venomous speeches of late, although the effects of his earlier ones get worse. ... But we are continually arresting people for intimidation, assault and so on and a great number are punished. Where we lack success is getting support for such crimes not to be committed.'[16]

On 30 November, Jones, Ingham and Phillips left for London to attend the federal review conference. Phillips went to see Armitage to say goodbye because he was going on leave after the conference and would not be back before Armitage left the country on retirement. Phillips told him of a letter the standing finance committee wished to send to him deploring his retirement. Armitage was sorry about this: 'The position of Jones and myself is awkward enough anyway!'

> He is going to the Federal Review when I would normally have gone, but Macleod made it clear he wanted him there as he would have to carry out the terms of various agreements which the Review decided on. As Macleod had said he would not recommend an extension to my appointment, I did not really care. I would have liked to see the whole situation carried through to its conclusion, but as I was not considered suitable to do this, I accepted that I could, hopefully, have a quiet time holding the fort in Nyasaland, clearing things up and saying goodbye to our friends. I imagined that Macleod would control the Review and shrug off all the complaints that would come from Welensky, Whitehead and others. I was quite happy in being able to keep out of any controversies that arose.[17]

> I suppose I ought to regret that I am not going to the Conference, but I have always taken a fatalistic view that my main activities are governed by a higher authority. I am resigned to not going. That is the way it has been ordained for me presumably and I assume I have some other role to play in all this.[18]

Some three months later, he again referred privately to the difficult situation in which Jones and he found themselves. When he was told by the chairman of the Nyasaland Railways that many thought he, the governor, had been very badly treated, he recorded: 'It boils down to the selection of Jones while I am still here. Events have actually minimized the difficulties, tragically for them [because they had to stay in Britain with their very ill son,] but I am afraid it has meant Jones has started off on the wrong foot with many.'[19] A little later still, when the Nyasaland government representative in Salisbury spoke to him about the rift between him and Jones, Armitage told him it was untrue, but that 'there was a section determined to do Jones down as Macleod's man'.

In a private letter to Armitage written several years later, Welensky told him that he had 'always felt very resentful' of the way Armitage had been treated.[20] Indeed, he 'had a stand up go with Macmillan over the fact of them appointing Glyn Jones while [Armitage] was still Governor'. Armitage's view that Jones had unfortunately got off to a bad start was exacerbated in the eyes of a number of civil servants and others by the unusual nature of the knighthood conferred on him early in November. It was unusual for a governor-designate to be knighted and even more unusual for this to be done other than in the New Year or Birthday honours' lists. It was felt to be particularly insensitive, and possibly a deliberate snub, while Armitage was still governor and administering the protectorate.

Others will have detected a snub, too, in the fact that when Macleod left Nyasaland after the release of Banda, the secretary of state took the unprecedented step of writing, not to the governor but directly and personally to Jones, asking him to pass on to other civil servants his thanks for arranging both Banda's release and his own visit. Although privately they almost certainly both felt that the position in which they found themselves was 'awkward', Armitage and Jones seem unfailingly to have treated each other with courtesy, professionalism and respect. When one or the other was out of the protectorate, they wrote frequent personal letters – full, helpful and designed to keep the other up to date – which in tone and content were precisely the sort of letters one would expect between a governor and his chief secretary and successor designate.

Although Armitage had hoped to 'have a quiet time holding the fort' while Banda, Jones and others were away in London, this was not to be. In the first place, he was virtually without executive council advice: three of his five official members – Jones, Phillips and Ingham – were at the conference and another – King – was seconded for special duties, while both Dixon and Blackwood were also at the conference, leaving only Kettlewell. In the second place, for the first time in two years Banda's radical lieutenants were out of detention and free in Nyasaland at the same time as the doctor was out of the country. In particular, Chiume had returned in May and Chipembere had been released from detention in September 1960; together they now embarked upon a speaking tour. The first dangerous incident was at Port Herald on 1 December. The League of Malawi Youth (LMY) attacked the police recording van; stones were thrown, teargas had to be used and riot squad reinforcements had to be called in. Chipembere and Chiume were 'making a lot of rabid speeches condemning ... government and stooges' and threatening to deal with them severely once Congress got into power.[21]

For a while, Armitage felt that the government 'would be able to coast along', but by early December 'the security situation had become worse'. Finney reported on how very active LMY members were being and how they were causing trouble in Nkata Bay and Karonga, where they were very anti-police, government and Europeans. He advised that action could be taken against them and contained within those districts without sparking off too much trouble elsewhere. He also believed that Chipembere's and Chiume's tactics were to keep up 'the task of frightening the government', for they were confident that Macleod would not permit force to be used against them again.[22]

It was after one of Chipembere's speeches at a Congress meeting that the Ndirande house of Chester Katsonga, founder and leader of the newly formed Christian Democratic Party (CDP), was burned down. The meeting was followed by stoning the police and two constables were injured. After the crowd was dispersed by teargas, a mob of about eighty stormed the house and burned it to the ground. Katsonga, his wife, father and three children were only just able to escape from it. The Christian Democrats, who were opposed to Banda, were backed by the Roman Catholic Church and, as a consequence, that church and others were being vilified by Congress. Armitage wondered why Chipembere and Chiume were behaving in this way and whether they had been instructed, presumably by Banda, to do so. He thought it more likely that, fearing Banda might compromise in London and cooperate with the Europeans, they were trying to undermine him and show him and others where the real power lay. Armitage noted that the situation had suddenly deteriorated since 21 November when Banda decided not to return to Nyasaland from West Africa, but to go direct to London.[23]

Others, from outside central Africa, also witnessed and became fearful of the deteriorated law and order conditions in Nyasaland. Armitage gave lunch to six visiting British MPs:

At Blantyre they had seen Chester Katsonga's burnt house and talked to him ... while the League of Malawi Youth watched, jeered and picketed. They were very emotional and windy [and] said they had never been so frightened. They obviously did not want to start off another incident. I told them of the tightrope act we were executing in order to give the Review Conference a chance to produce a political solution. I think they saw the problem.[24]

On 4 December, Jones had a meeting in London with Macleod and Perth about the security deterioration in Nyasaland, as a consequence of which the secretary of state saw Banda in the evening and the doctor agreed to make 'a firm statement' denouncing violence and calling on his followers to behave themselves.[25] He said he would send the statement to Nyasaland that day and publish it in London the following day. His followers seem to have paid little attention to his statement two months earlier denouncing violence. A 'soothing' telegram sent by Banda had the opposite effect: intimidation of Africans who were not Congress members continued apace and Europeans were shouted and jeered at. On specific steps the governor contemplated, Jones told him:

> It is accepted here that you will have to withhold permits to speak at public meetings from Chiume and Chipembere and that this might lead to their becoming liable to prosecution if they defy the law. It is also accepted that you may have to proceed against Chipembere for his Rumpi speech.... The issuing of a control order against Chiume is regarded here as being more serious than the proposal to prosecute Chipembere. The reason for this is that Banda had said – at the time of Chipembere's release – 'Let the law take its course when people break it.'

The Colonial Office hoped the governor would stay his hand until the results of Banda's statement and an approach by Youens to Chipembere and Chiume were known. Chipembere's arrest at that particular point might lead to Banda's precipitate departure for Nyasaland to take control of Congress – as he said he wanted to – and this would 'embarrass the Conference'. They agreed that if Chipembere continued to defy Armitage and to utter violent statements, he would have to be prosecuted and, for this, the governor would get the secretary of state's backing. Macleod would, however, like to be given warning of any action before it was actually taken by Armitage. The governor was disturbed that Jones did not take Ingham or Phillips into his discussions with Macleod, although Jones wrote to him saying that 'the secretary of state did not tell him much'.

Armitage was becoming so concerned with Chipembere's and Chiume's activities that he advised district commissioners to be careful in granting them permission to hold meetings.[26] The district commissioner at Port Herald asked him for a control order to get them out of his district, but the governor refused. He did so on the grounds, not that it would be provocative, but that if he granted it, 'every district would want one.' Armitage believed that this district commissioner and his even 'more reactionary' wife were 'quite unprepared to move with the times' The governor was being very restrained and cautious. A little later he was annoyed to receive letters from Dixon and Blackwood complaining that Banda had addressed a crowd gathered in Blantyre without a permit: 'They can't allow the police to use discretion, they want everything broken up.'

Although the attorney-general had a prima-facie case against Chipembere for sedition in a speech made at Rumpi, and wished to arrest him, Armitage felt that he 'must hold back and report to the secretary of state'. He then cabled Macleod. It was, as Armitage pointed out, ironic that the attorney-general should have been under fire from all quarters – both Congress and the Europeans were talking of a vote of no confidence in him – and yet was not now allowed to proceed. Macleod replied that he had seen Banda who had agreed to send a message to Chipembere and Chiume to keep calm. Armitage did not think they had received this message because they had gone to the north to continue their speaking tour. Even so:

> We decided that if a case for prosecution lay against them it should be pressed but could be delayed to settle the timing and so avoid Banda walking out of the Conference and busting it or coming back here. None of us have any time for Chiume and Chipembere and if we could split them from Banda or put them away for a bit, so much the better. [The attorney-general] is getting quite belligerent against them.

Armitage – who felt they were 'all on a tightrope' – was very keen to stay his hand and was playing a 'rearguard action on a very difficult terrain' in trying to hold things stable so that the review conference could meet and enable 'a political situation to be solved by a political solution in London'.

The progress of the conference in London was causing great tension, both there and in Nyasaland. Armitage travelled to Salisbury to confer with Barrow – acting prime minister in Welensky's absence – and gave him Nyasaland's most recent intelligence assessment and his analysis of why the position was now worse than it had been in July: there was less room for Banda to manœuvre over secession than over self-government. Also, whereas in July Banda had been in effect the sole negotiator from Congress, now his lieutenants were out of detention and were stirring up trouble and putting pressure on him. Graylin, the federal minister of agriculture, who 'seemed friendly and reasonable', told Armitage that, in the federal government's view, 'if Nyasaland seceded, all would secede; if Nyasaland went, all went.'

The distinct possibility of the London talks breaking down and of Banda's reaction inducing grave disturbances in Nyasaland, persuaded Armitage to ask for reinforcements. Barrow personally agreed that they should bring in British troops, but he knew Welensky would oppose such a move. He contacted Welensky about this and Armitage cabled the Colonial Office asking that British troops in Kenya be moved from seven to two days' preparedness. The federal government agreed that a company of KAR be moved to Lilongwe to release the PMF platoon there to go to the northern province where the provincial commissioner expected trouble. Part of Welensky's objection to the use of British troops in Nyasaland was that they would be answerable to Armitage rather than to himself. Indeed, Brook had advised Macmillan in clear and strong terms that responsibility for security in Nyasaland rested with the governor and the colonial secretary and that decisions about it ought not to be sought through talks between the federal government and the commonwealth secretary.

Finney also was being restrained: he thought that to prosecute Chipembere 'would ignite a powder train' and he advised – so as not to offend Banda – that Chipembere should be warned in the hope that he would then behave himself. They considered arresting him and letting him out on bail, but feared he would then tour the country, even if conditions were imposed on his movements and talking. They could remand him in prison but felt this 'might set the country alight'. They wondered, too, what they should do about Chiume and concluded that he had done nothing to merit prosecution. In any case, he came from the northern province where his position was strong and the LMY predominant; reaction to proceeding against him would consequently be acute. This was why the Colonial Office regarded a control order against him as more serious than prosecuting Chipembere.[27]

While Armitage was still in Salisbury, Banda – with Kaunda and Joshua Nkomo – walked out of the London conference, and Macleod cabled to say the talks had been postponed 'to try and drive a wedge between the three African leaders'.[28] Armitage thought the next 48 hours would be crucial. When he telephoned Youens in Zomba, he was relieved to hear that all was quiet: there had been no reaction other than MCP and LMY leaders saying they must be ready for some positive action at an unspecified time. Later, he learned that Congress considered the walkout a victory for Banda. Its supporters were, however, 'very irritated' that the doctor had gone to church with Welensky: 'They say they are told not to collaborate with the white man but what is this?'

The governor spoke again, this time about Banda's return, to Barrow, who had got 'the usual violent reaction' from Welensky about alerting British troops. Barrow thought the British government itself might be having second thoughts about using British troops, though it had agreed to reduce the stand-by time – probably without Welensky's agreement. A little later, Armitage was told that the British government was prepared 'to play' on the possibility of reinforcements from Kenya coming to Nyasaland, although naturally their use would be a political decision and Welensky was making no concessions.

Concerned about the sporadic disorders caused by discontented members of Congress and the distinct possibility of escalation, Armitage had a review made of the security forces available and of those he might try to obtain.

> We realized considerable forces would have to be deployed. We had thirteen platoons of the Police Mobile Force and could call up the reserve. We could use Special Constables again. We would hope to get Army battalions from Rhodesia and we had our own. We even considered armoured cars and aircraft.... It was surprising how quickly the situation had deteriorated. The Commissioner of Police considered all the Native Authorities had been won over [to Congress] or neutralized. This made the security situation graver as there was no restraining influence on the Federal issue from the Native Authorities. This was aggravated with the accent on the future of the Conference. On the other hand, Chiume and Chipembere were clearly angry at not having been taken to London and they were accusing Banda of going pro-European. They did not trust Banda not to compromise.[29]

Again the governor telephoned Macleod, saying that he was considering prosecuting Chipembere for his Rumpi speech and possibly also Chiume for speeches at Zomba and Ndirande.[30] He gave three reasons for prosecution: they had experience of the damage such speeches could cause to the type of audiences addressed; they had been waiting for a strong and suitable opportunity and this had now occurred; and they were being accused of enforcing the law against lesser persons while the leaders of Congress were immune. He added that, whatever Banda might now say to calm his followers, what they had already done could not be undone. He emphasized that if prosecutions were not to be instituted, it must be because he, the governor, had decided it was not in the public interest.

He did in fact arrest the Karonga district leader of Congress and four members of the executive committee of the LMY in Blantyre. He was anxious about the probable reaction to the arrests when Banda returned two days later; and he was generally concerned about the effects of intimidation on the forthcoming registration of voters and the elections. He discussed this with his senior officials and they concluded that they could do nothing about 'the Africans' propensity to being intimidated which makes those who want to use it so powerful. But they themselves are cowards if physically threatened or resolutely opposed, as we have many instances to show.' They decided to 'deploy the police, reservists and specials' at the time of registration and the elections, if this became necessary.

On 16 December, Jones wrote to Armitage, having spoken with Macleod, saying:[31]

> It would not be possible to avoid taking action against Chipembere and probably others... and we could be in real trouble. Macleod said he appreciated all this and promised to have a final word with Banda on Saturday afternoon before the latter leaves England. You have been asked to hold your hand on issuing a summons to Chipembere for the time being.... I said that, depending on your reply, there could be no harm done this end if you issued summons against Chipembere on Saturday 17th.... That would ensure that it was issued before Banda's return.

Macleod saw Banda again on Saturday afternoon, 17 December, just before he left and told him he hoped the doctor and his followers would keep the peace and eschew intimidation. He also told him that Armitage would be prosecuting Chipembere. Banda was in a good mood and gave Macleod the assurances he was seeking about keeping the peace and rejecting intimidation. He said that so far as prosecuting Chipembere was concerned, the law should take its course.

Just before Banda arrived back in Nyasaland, the Nyasaland police issued a summons against Chipembere on charges of making a seditious speech and of proposing violence. On this day, too, Finney reported to Armitage that there was a great deal of confusion in Congress, arising from Banda's attendance at Chequers and his association with Welensky, and that the LMY were 'raring to go and beat people up'. When the summons was served on him, Chipembere accused the police of being afraid to arrest him. Armitage – who at one stage had hoped that by being arrested Chipembere would be unable to address the crowds awaiting Banda's arrival – was relieved that they had not arrested him. This was because he felt the police would have difficulty in opposing bail successfully.

Banda's return to Nyasaland did not cause the disturbances Armitage had feared:[32]

> Dr Banda duly came back from London and behaved as he had told the Secretary of State. But his idol is now Macmillan, not Macleod! Snobbery I think! He can now tell his people that although Federation is not yet buried, he is on such terms with Macmillan that it is only a

question of time. If he can play it that way and keep everyone quiet, it won't worry me. He has started all right.

No longer was Armitage able to prevent the doctor's return on a Sunday, nor did it rain as he had often hoped in the past. There were 5000 at Chileka to greet him, hundreds in Blantyre and thousands at Congress headquarters. Banda 'made a most conciliatory speech and appeared most relaxed'. Armitage almost detected a willingness to concede some sort of federal concept if only Welensky and Whitehead would accept a looser form. Indeed, Banda was 'in a most convivial mood, relaxed, only screamed twice'.

When he moved into his new house in Blantyre on 21 December, Banda had a ceremony at which he received the keys and made a speech attacking the police and the judiciary.[33] He told his audience of 2000 that the police automatically arrested Congress members and the magistrates automatically convicted them without evidence. The governor said: 'This is clearly sedition and a more or less cast iron case. The Chief Justice is very angry and it is all very awkward.' He had expected some sort of outburst from Banda 'because he must have some direction in which to let off steam'. The following day Youens went to see the doctor at his new house and he

> found him a very tired tiger ... looking that yellowy-grey that I saw him in London in August. He said he was indispensable to the government, implying *après moi le déluge*. He said he is not being let alone by his boys and seemed to discuss things more in sorrow than anger. Somewhat disturbing as if [he] goes then we have no stabilizing influence that one can see.

On Christmas Eve, Armitage had his usual Saturday morning meeting with Finney, who reported that there had been criticism of Banda for some time in Karonga and there now seemed to be a more widespread feeling that, since Banda had not achieved secession, a more militant leader should be sought. The governor commented: 'We shall be in a jam if he can't last the pace.' There had been more burnings and beatings and a killing at Nkata Bay. The magistrates were 'giving out useful sentences', but the Europeans were still complaining about the government not supporting the police. They admitted, however, that there was less tension and fewer people were being molested. At their meeting the following Saturday, Finney reported a growing split between Orton Chirwa and Aleke Banda, who together had founded the Malawi Congress Party during the emergency, and Dr Banda on the one hand and Chipembere and Chiume on the other, 'with

Chisiza as yet uncommitted'. Banda's moderation and lack of success in breaking up the federation was 'not appreciated by many' and Armitage thought 'Banda will need good health and [to] keep a jump ahead of these extremists if he is to hold them.' He felt too that the LMY would be a thorn in the doctor's side. Karonga was more peaceful now that some of the Congress leaders there had been imprisoned, and Port Herald was in the doldrums with only one top Congress leader left there. Even so, 'violence [was] everywhere', in Nkata Bay in particular, and intimidation was giving Congress control in so many places that it could not be opposed.[34]

On 28 December, Armitage had an all-morning discussion with the attorney-general contemplating prosecuting Banda for sedition.[35] He recognized there was 'every reason' to do so in principle, but he wondered if the doctor had really meant to say precisely what he did say about the police and the judiciary when he took over his new house. He also believed there were signs of hope on the federation issue: the *Malawi News* was 'the mildest ever', even saying federation was not dead, having previously said that it was, and Chiume was saying the slogan should be 'secession in 1961 or never'. Armitage felt that even if Banda were prosecuted and convicted, he would be sentenced only to a fine or less than a year's imprisonment.

> This would rally all support round him at a time when he is supposed to be losing support to extremists.... Welensky says he is the UFP's best friend! It would also finally kill any prospect of a negotiated federal concept. We should lose the one man we have made contact with and would find it difficult ever to make contact with MCP leaders and we have still to govern and will have to do so even after the next general election. There is also the possibility that Banda might call the MCP to arms and we should then have a major security situation on our hands. On balance today I feel that we should not prosecute.

The attorney-general was 'very angry' with Armitage's conclusion because this was the opportunity for which he had been waiting and he thought that Banda would always let them down. Armitage felt that King had 'always held liberal views', but was finding it 'difficult to reconcile the actual behaviour of Banda and company with his own ideas of what they are justified in doing'.

The governor then sent off a telegram to the secretary of state setting out the pros and cons of proceeding against Banda for his speeches against the judiciary and the police. This was discussed by Macleod, Jones and Colonial Office officials. They agreed to cable Armitage that 'the Secretary of State accepts [Armitage's advice] that there is a strong political case for not prosecuting Banda at present.' Macleod did, however, ask him to rebuke the doctor. Before he did this, the governor had the chief justice and his wife to lunch and, after the meal, told him that Macleod had agreed it was undesirable to prosecute the doctor, but rather that he should be rebuked. The chief justice accepted that if a prosecution risked starting a security situation leading to a renewal of the emergency, then obviously this should not be done, and he accepted the alternative of a rebuke.

That afternoon, 30 December, Banda went to see Armitage who found him 'very relaxed and dapper'.[36] This was their first meeting since August. For an hour and a half Banda talked, with 'obvious delight', about his reception and tour of Nigeria and then the London conference. He had also been to Ghana, 'but was very reticent about that'. He was most impressed with having received the personal attention of Macmillan, but he hardly mentioned Macleod. Banda had deliberately seen and been entertained by only Conservative MPs 'because they were the government and it was important for him to know how they were feeling towards federation'. He reckoned that the majority felt it had to be changed, and Armitage gathered they had pointed out the economic and other dangers of breaking up the federation. Banda seemed to appreciate these points and Armitage thought he was beginning to realize what a mess they might be in if the federal ties were completely snapped.

Armitage intervened only once in this conversation to say that Orton Chirwa's speech at the conference was most unpleasant. Banda replied that other people had already drawn his attention to it and he had told them to listen to what he, Banda, said and not to others. Having created this opening, the governor then delivered the rebuke Macleod had requested:

> Then I had to give him the rebuke about the attack on the judiciary and he seemed taken aback and asked me to tell the Secretary of State he was very sorry to have used those words, although he said they were true. We argued a bit about police action and convictions against the evidence and extreme sentences but he did not seem to take these much to heart. He may have been putting on a great act for me but I think that partly he is beginning to understand the problems he is up against.

The day following this interview, Armitage learned that Chipembere had issued a Congress circular appealing for funds to engage defence counsel from Britain for his trial—attempts were made to secure the services of Gerald Gardiner and Frank Soskice—and repeating the words Banda had used on 21 December against the police and the judiciary, to which the government had taken exception and had considered prosecution for sedition.[37] As the governor exclaimed: 'So more fat in the fire!' At a meeting with the attorney-general, solicitor-general, acting chief secretary and commissioner of police to discuss this worrying development, they decided they could not just ignore the matter. They could ask Banda to issue a statement contradicting the allegations of police and judicial prejudice; failing that they should prosecute Chipembere. The attorney-general 'was not at all happy about this', but they decided they must break the chain of not prosecuting anyone who repeated or made similar allegations.

Youens spent some time with Banda – who claimed he had never seen the circular or knew anything about it – and, partly by saying that failure to issue a statement was 'letting the secretary of state down', eventually got him to agree to issue one, though he insisted on discussing its contents with Aleke Banda and using his own words. Shortly afterwards, he withdrew all copies of Chipembere's circular. Armitage was worried about reports from Youens that Banda was isolating himself with padlocked gates and a high wall round his house and was spending nearly all his time in his medical practice without any planned public programme. The governor's fears were that: 'There are clear dangers in this isolation that all the civil servants will go their own way and commit him to things that he does not know of until too late. Then we get 1958–9 all over again.'

As usual, the Armitages spent the Christmas break in their cottage on Zomba plateau, coming down on Christmas morning to go to church and to give presents to the children of Government House staff. This time they had a message of thanks for what they had done over the past five years read out by the senior chauffeur. They went to the African hospital and listened to carols sung by the African nurses in training. For the first time, they saw the wards cheerfully decorated for Christmas and attributed this to the 'peculiar combination' of a white South African matron and a fully qualified African sister. They went to the service of carols and lessons where the place was 'packed with children and adults', and they returned to the peace and solitude of the plateau cottage. As 1960 came to a close, he wrote the final words in his private diary: 'A year ends of mixed benefits and a great deal of frustration and hard work.'[38]

In the new year 1961, the Armitages began to prepare for their departure. The governor said goodbye to officials as they went on leave, for he would have left before their return. It saddened him to play his last game of squash with Kettlewell – the governor winning two games against him 'for the first time ever!' Kettlewell had been a sound and experienced adviser, 'fully justifying the faith [Armitage] had placed' in him. Mrs Kettlewell shared Armitage's love of gardening and she supervised the botanical gardens set out below the old Residency. He said goodbye, too, to King, who was leaving Nyasaland at the age of 50 because he had a young family and wished to find further employment for several years to come. Armitage was sure King was 'not sorry to be getting out of all this'. He went to a sherry party to say goodbye to H. W. Wilson, the Speaker of legislative council, who was retiring, much to Armitage's relief! He also attended a conference of assistant scout commissioners to take his leave of them. Phillips and Finney, the latter of whom was retiring, had already said goodbye. Ingham and Kettlewell knew that their days in Nyasaland were short, Dixon was very unsure about his future and Bishop Frank Thorne was retiring in April, depressed and worried about 'all the omissions in his life!' A little later, one of his provincial commissioners, much disillusioned, left to go on leave and the governor was saddened that his wife had not said goodbye to Lady Armitage.[39]

They paid a farewell visit to Mzuzu in mid-January to bid farewell to people in the northern province.[40] The pilot who flew their plane alarmed them somewhat because he wore a number of US medal ribbons and 'did not seem to be very sure of his way'. A cocktail party was given for them and he spent a morning in discussions with the district commissioners, all of whom had travelled to Mzuzu:

> They have a difficult time getting the locals to cooperate in the ordinary affairs of administration as the MCP likes to attack the government and its officers on most occasions. But a lot of the extremists have now been convicted for assaults etc., others are subdued, and others have left for pastures new where they think they can make more trouble. The call by Banda for peace and quiet has had a good effect and things are less tense than they have been for some time. He certainly is in full control up there.

The provincial commissioner entertained the governor, Lady Armitage, the district commissioners and their wives to dinner. Armitage recorded that it was 'an excellent farewell trip, as we shall not go back there again if all goes well'. Because the chiefs in the north were so unanimously and strongly pro-Congress and anti-government, he did not meet any of them.

Back in the south, he faced events that illustrated the sensitive political atmosphere, the attempts by some of Banda's leaders to handle difficulties in a calm fashion, and the moves by some European leaders to provoke trouble.[41] Banda had summoned a 'peace and calm' conference of some 200 MCP delegates. However, failures in the public address system, the arrival of the police recording van – which was blamed for the prosecutions for seditious speeches – and a 'rather silly' policeman, who pointed an empty teargas ejector in the direction of Banda, led to a riot in which 'the PMF were called in and everything was broken up rather roughly. Aleke Banda rang [Youens] in a frenzy and [Youens] went over to Blantyre to see [Dr] Banda [who was] very surly and looked ghastly. Said he had been witness of fearful attacks on his people and this was all against the agreement with government.'

Youens explained the government's version of what had happened, namely that the LMY had deliberately provoked the incident. He observed that Chipembere was the only Congress leader present who did nothing to help. Banda and his other lieutenants had a number of meetings with the delegates in which they emphasized the need for peace and calm. Chisiza 'even said the people were to ignore the riot as if it was nothing!' At the same time, Armitage was convinced that Blackwood and Dixon, who threatened to resign from executive council, were being deliberately difficult. 'I think they pin all their hopes on an emergency and so postponement or cancellation of everything. They may try and get this here by needling the MCP or government and create disorders or take a stand on Northern Rhodesia or federation matters and so provoke Banda.'

He also thought that 'they reckon Macleod is on the way out and like jackals want to be in at the kill and to claim that they helped to pull him down.' A little later Dixon and Blackwood tried to introduce a motion for debate in legislative council expressing no confidence in Macleod and this was taken sufficiently seriously for the secretary of state to say that if they did this they would be removed from executive council. Armitage thought this was 'pretty stupid as they are safer in than out'. In the event, the debates 'went reasonably' and were 'a damp squib'.

The Armitages made their farewell tour of the central province early in February. They visited the chiefs in Fort Manning, Lilongwe, Visanza, Dedza and Ncheu and had tea with them in each district. He visited all the district commissioners and had long talks with the provincial commissioner 'about the present and the future': 'Apart from sporadic incidents there is no trouble and no particular trouble-makers.' He thought the provincial commissioner was fully aware of the need for change and was telling this to his district commissioners and chiefs. There was 'excellent cooperation between the administration and the police'. He visited African and Asian schools, the forestry school at Dedza, the Lilongwe municipal council, European and African farmers, community centres, health centres, mission stations and met over 300 people at various cocktail parties. He had always got on well with people in the central province and he thought they were sorry his 'time was up, two years of which were completely wasted'. He found the central province 'so peaceful'.[42]

On his return to Zomba, he was relieved to learn that Chipembere had been convicted and sentenced to three years' imprisonment.[43] Jones, still in England, 'was also very glad to know that Chip[embere] ha[d] been sent down for three years and hope[d] that [the sentence would] stick'. Given this success in prosecuting Chipembere, Armitage discussed with his senior colleagues whether they should also prosecute Chiume for sedition. Although they had a very good case, they decided not to proceed because they considered him to be of 'not much account' and not popular, principally because he had not been detained and was not a 'prison graduate'.

Two months earlier, they had been reluctant to prosecute Chiume because they believed that he was popular in the north and that his prosecution would lead to strong reactions from the LMY. In the meantime, it seems, Armitage's cautious but firm tactics had weakened Chiume's position. Banda had recently sent him to West Africa and England and D. K. Chisiza to India. Armitage recognized that they wanted to make an impression in the Afro-Asian countries, which could prove useful to them in setting all African nations free. Although he did not comment on it, it was also the case that they were out of the country and less able to cause trouble during Chipembere's trial.

There followed a period of relative quietness.[44] The country was calmer than it had been for many months. In federal matters, attention was being focused on Northern Rhodesia, which gave Nyasaland a breathing space. The possibility of a breakdown in the negotiations over Northern Rhodesia's future and Welensky's threat that he might declare independence for the federation caused Armitage to discuss with Youens what they might need to do 'if he took over our airfields and put us all in house arrest. Maybe extravagant thoughts but Benson raised this two years ago and I did one year ago with the Colonial Office! ... If trouble came they presumably must tell us what forces they move here and what we are to do!'

In the middle of February, the army commander in Zomba was instructed by his superiors in Salisbury to move troops to Lilongwe and Fort Hill, but the order was countermanded half an hour later. The chiefs of staff in Britain prepared a scheme to defend Nyasaland and Northern Rhodesia should the federal government turn hostile. On the other hand, Armitage was shortly told by a Colonial Office official that Britain would not use troops if Welensky tried to take over the northern territories, but that there would be 'some form of paper handing-over of officials, police, government etc.' Although the army commander in

Nyasaland told the governor that he was 'aware of no specific activities being contemplated' by the federal government, Armitage received several cables 'about the federal government going to South Africa for military help and also about their amendment to the Defence Act to enable them to mobilize manpower for internal security as well as defence in war'. The matter was extremely complex:

> Spent some time discussing what would happen if federal government declared independence with or without bringing in federal troops. Decided that Banda and MCP would eventually resist and as a government we would have to suppress disorders whether we were under federal control or not. To suppress them we would require reinforcements and if it was an African revolt, the loyalty of the police would be doubtful.

There was a widespread belief among the leaders and members of the UFP that Welensky would declare independence during the first week of March. Banda thought that if Welensky tried to take over Nyasaland, the British government would move in to protect the Nyasalanders. At the end of February, Armitage was very unsure 'whether Welensky is merely rattling a sabre singing "Halleluiah, here we come" with a male voice chorus clad in battledress, or will announce a D-Day when his planes, guns and troops will take over *à la* Castro'. Even as late as mid-March, executive council discussed the possibilities and concluded:

> [First,] Welensky says I declare independence and HMG flies troops in: confusion all round. [Second,] Welensky says I declare independence and HMG does nothing: holocaust all round. [Third,] Welensky says I declare independence and HMG agrees Nyasaland government should assist: shambles all round with British civil servants going and LMY [taking action]. But Blackwood says Welensky would come up and do a deal with Banda. A most hopeful sign!

Armitage thought that Welensky was coming round to the view that 'nearly all want to get rid of Nyasaland to HMG.'

Voter registration began in mid-February and went smoothly. Congress was fully occupied in getting as many as it could on the register and not worrying about other things. On 12 February, Macleod told Armitage that Foster, having been offered the post of chief secretary again, had accepted it. The governor was working very hard — including working out the details of the ministerial system of government to be introduced after the elections. He and Lyona were 'too weary to celebrate' their thirty-first wedding anniversary. He was, however, able to play a little golf and some 'hilarious bridge' with the bishop, the head of special branch and an eccentric retired army major. He was mock-serious, although actually amused, about an 'invasion' at Government House. A party of young KAR subalterns decided to steal the stuffed leopard – the symbol of Nyasaland – from its stand at the end of the dining room. They found an unlocked door and, in entering, attracted the attention of the guard who engaged them and 'quite a battle ensued'. Some of the governor's domestic staff joined in. Eventually, the private secretary was awakened and 'the defence became too strong and so the marauders made off', leaving the leopard to be safely recovered from the driveway. The following day, the culprits were marched before the governor, who gave them a dressing down – for having been caught.[45]

The period of quiet extended into March – 'more quiet in recent weeks than for many, many months'. The courts caught up on the large arrears of intimidation and violence cases from the previous year and Armitage privately commented wryly, 'they should be clear with luck in time for the next outbreak!' Banda was more relaxed and self-confident. At a large dinner given for him by Sacranie – with Youens and Ingham present – he made a speech in which he said that independence was only the first mile in a 10,000 mile journey, which the governor thought had a salutary effect. He also said that he was relying on the British government 'not to let Nyasaland down and to deal with Welensky'. This led Armitage to believe that, unless the federal government made some overt unconstitutional act against Britain, he need expect no trouble from the doctor or the MCP. In a tour of the central and northern provinces, Banda held no large meetings and everything remained peaceful. Jones remained in London with his still extremely sick son and Armitage was pleased that peaceful conditions in Nyasaland enabled him to stay there.[46]

The focus of political attention outside Nyasaland remained on Northern Rhodesia and this lent something of an air of unreality to Armitage's last few weeks in the country.[47] On 10 March, he wrote privately:

> A month today the type of life I have lived in progressive stages for nearly 32 years comes to an end. It is all rather remarkable. One is in a peculiar, unreal atmosphere at present. As all our intelligence reports show, the conditions in Nyasaland are more peaceful and the tension is less than it has been for nearly three years, since before Banda came back in fact.

Everyone's thoughts were, he continued, on getting onto the voters' rolls all the people who were qualified and this had been helped by Congress fully cooperating with government officials.

> Yet outside our borders the atmosphere sizzles, lashing speeches are made in the House of Lords, the press makes attacks and defences, the politicians of all races do the same and threaten anything from Mau Mau downwards. I am most apprehensive that out of all this will come decisions and actions that may affect this little place disastrously. One can only hope and pray.

The lull in events gave Armitage the opportunity to get on with his sorting and packing and he was grateful for 'our last peaceful weekend before we go into three weeks' hard labour with [our final] farewell visits and entertaining'.

They visited all districts in the southern province. He called on the chiefs at Zomba, Kasupe and Fort Johnston – 'this pleasant hot place' – and had tea with them.[48] The European Zomba Club gave him a farewell sundowner party – 'they have been very loyal to us' – and he went to his last meeting at the multiracial Zomba turf club. At Cholo he attended a farewell reception, had tea with the chiefs, lunched with a number of planters long resident in the country and visited the Bvumbwe experimental station. At Mlanje they visited tea estates, had tea with the chiefs, looked in at a number of mission stations and again visited an experimental station. They stayed for a week at the new government lodge in Blantyre to say goodbye to various people there and drove over 'pretty poor' roads to visit Chikwawa and Port Herald in the far south where, again, there were sundowner parties for chiefs and residents. They visited Chiradzulu district headquarters on their way back to Zomba and arrived 'pretty weary'. In Blantyre he attended a Rotary Club luncheon, had a golf sundowner at Limbe, dined with 90 of his European and Asian friends and said goodbye to the chiefs.

The chiefs of the Blantyre district gave him an address in which they said that he was one of the few governors who had visited the headquarters of all the chiefs in the district. They added: 'You had to take drastic steps at one time, but the fact remains that during your term of office great changes for the better have taken place.' Everywhere people were 'exceedingly kind' and gave them many farewell presents. This brought him a quiet pleasure because he felt it indicated that quite a lot of people appreciated what he and his wife had tried to do for them. They each chaired annual general meetings of a number of bodies of which they were chairpersons or patrons. He presented medals at a farewell parade and beating the retreat at Zomba police headquarters. The mayor of Blantyre gave a civic luncheon in their honour.

> More speeches of course and I am running out of words! At least I told them I thought we were off the knife edge and that there was a chance to keep Nyasaland in the federation . . . all these people are being very kind and of course really associating me still with dealing with the emergency and not with the problem of winning the peace!

He made as many as four speeches a day and each time told his audience that the tide had turned and they 'were beyond the worst'.

Luck was on his side.[49] In the middle of one of his speeches he sent his private secretary out to listen to the Grand National on the radio: of the four horses on which he had placed bets one came first and another second and he had backed both for win and place! He even risked having a pre-lunch sherry party on Palm Sunday and he wrote to his mother:

> I know it was wrong on Palm Sunday but I managed to get Dr Banda and leaders of his party and all the political parties, plus officials and others of all races to meet and mix happily. Politics were joked over and there were only the 5 per cent of each colour who could never approve who criticized. I felt the Lord would condone a good deed done on his day?

The question mark is interesting. Perhaps Mrs Armitage would not condone so readily. Armitage felt it was important to invite Banda and his senior colleagues to this party and was uncertain whether the invitations would be accepted.

> The day started dull and drizzly, then the sun came out as we waited for the experiment regarded as dubious by very many I suspect of inviting Banda and some MCP here. O. E. Chirwa had accepted and D. K. Chisiza actually telephoned yesterday to say he would be away. I wonder who will come. In the event Banda arrived at 11.15 on the dot in his red convertible, accompanied by his nurse, Miss Kadzamira, and Y. Chisiza. All his people came too as did the UFP and CDP but CLP [Congress Liberation Party] did not. Chester Katsonga told me they had merged with CLP and T. D. T. Banda had a large meeting which kept him away. We had nearly 300 of all races and political foes and all colours mingled amicably.

Undoubtedly, bringing people of such diverse and opposing views together was a triumph and, probably more than anything else, in its simple way, marked the vast changes that had taken place in the past 12 months: a year earlier Banda had still been in gaol and Armitage had been anxious to keep him there. Even more important, with Armitage's general amicable and sensitive dealings with Banda in the meantime, it laid the basis of goodwill at the close of his term of office upon which his successor could work.

An equally significant occasion followed when the doctor gave the Armitages a farewell party for 150 guests of all colours.[50] It was a 'very sociable evening'; 'It was all very pleasant and friendly and no rancour or venom.' Banda and Armitage gave speeches and 'skated over the thinnest ice' successfully. They had agreed in advance that neither would mention politics. It was an extremely generous gesture by Banda and Armitage was moved by it: 'So now the ice is truly thawed and people of goodwill will have to launch the crafts to keep cooperation going. It was quite impossible to think that on the 1st November when I came back from leave, that I should have been able to depart in these very changed circumstances.' He was conscious of the importance of the steps he and Banda were taking and, in his private diary, he wrote: 'So I can leave having cleared the decks with Banda and the MCP, they can be kept committed to nonracial social affairs and others can now build on the foundation laid.'

Jones came back the same day, with his family, including his still very sick son, and Armitage had a number of meetings with him, bringing him up to date and ready to take over.[51] Jones had said that he wanted to return a little earlier in order to take part in the legislative council meeting, but Armitage said he would not be needed until a few days before he himself left. Jones made it clear, too, that he did not want to resume his duties as chief secretary, but preferred to take over directly as governor. Armitage therefore seconded him for unspecified 'special duties' for the next six days. In handing over, Armitage thought that everything was in as good order as possible: 'I went over the present situation. Not really much from the security or political angle, election regulations now ready... administration set up for a ministerial system being geared to start in June when I say they should have their final legislative council meeting and get the budget through.' Jones bought Armitage's blue gubernatorial uniform, which was a financial relief to the retiring latter if not a sartorial blessing to the more diminutive former. When the Jones family called on them for drinks on the day before their departure, Armitage confided in his private diary, 'We can never get on the same waveband as Nancy but at least we had no arguments.'

On 6 April, Armitage attended a farewell parade by the second KAR with the whole battalion on parade. The battalion gave him double three cheers followed by the African shouted salute, *Sokole*, an awe-inspiring and impressive roar, which, strangely, he had never heard before. He found the parade 'Most moving and memorable. My last salute. So we are through.' *Sokole* was repeated at the officers' mess during an informal cocktail party after the parade at the conclusion of which the officers surrounded their car to push them off, but 'with the Rolls' automatic gears one can't start like that'. He had received 'many tributes from a vast number of people' and, although they were mostly whites, he was gratified there was 'no unfriendliness from the blacks' and indeed he received many gifts from the chiefs.[52]

When the day of their departure dawned Lyona had developed malaria – possibly caught in the Lower River – for the first time since they lived in Kericho in the early 1930s, and they were almost unable to leave Zomba. An early morning visit from the doctor and fairly heavy medication reduced the shivering and the temperature and they were able to leave Government House on time at 8.30 a.m. They said goodbye to the domestic and office staff and received farewell gifts from them. As they passed through Zomba, they stopped at the district commissioner's office where a large number of people had gathered to say goodbye. On their way to Chileka airport, schoolchildren – European and coloured – were by the roadside, also to say goodbye. At Chileka, he spoke with members of the press, inspected his last guard of honour and said goodbye individually to the 150 'top people' who were there to see them off. The upstairs verandas of the airport were packed with people who sang lustily and loudly, if rhetorically, 'Will ye no come back again?' followed by 'For they are jolly good fellows'. At 10.15 a.m. they walked with the Joneses and the chief justice and his wife, said their final farewells at the foot of the aircraft steps and boarded the waiting RRAF Dakota, provided by Welensky, which immediately took off for Salisbury.[53] They were much touched by a telegram received in flight from Jones, wishing them Godspeed and a happy retirement.[54] Shortly, Jones was to write to him and say: 'I found it to be a fine experience working for you. I admired your clear thinking and your courage.' In thanking Jones for these kindnesses, Armitage wrote:

> I wish you all joy in Nyasaland, good luck and final success in reaching the best solution. The people are basically too nice and the country too pleasant to be subjected to strife and bitterness.[55]

8

Retirement

The autumn tints are wonderful, there has not been so much wind lately and the leaves have not all come off.

In Rhodesia they did a good deal of travelling – to the Eastern Highlands, Kariba and the Victoria Falls – calling on various people they knew, including Welensky and Whitehead.[1] They borrowed Dalhousie's Bentley and found it very comfortable on the tarmac strip roads. Three weeks later they left to catch the ship, boarding the train at Umtali for its 12-hour overnight journey to the coast.

At Beira they were met by the federal and British consuls and called on the new Portuguese governor. They sensed a distinct unease in the European population there, fearful of the spread of nationalism and violence in Africa and uncertain of their own future. Welensky and Whitehead had expressed similar fears to them.

They boarded the *Kenya*, called at Nacala; stayed with Turnbull, now governor of Tanganyika, at Dar es Salaam; and called at Zanzibar, where the chief secretary entertained them. At Mombasa they stayed with the Pinneys and then flew to Nairobi to stay with the governor, Sir Gilbert Renison.[2] Renison had the Aga Khan to dinner, so Armitage was able to talk with him about race horses. At Aden, the governor came on board to collect and entertain them. They passed through the Suez Canal – in a convoy of 32 ships including 15 tankers – 'for the last time, a very different Egypt from when [they] first went through it'. They went ashore briefly at Port Said to buy newspapers and Turkish delight, sailed close to the desolate, precipitous coast of Crete, passed through the Straits of Messina, close round Stromboli and on to Barcelona, Marseilles and Gibraltar before landing at Tilbury.

Life on board was relaxing. Armitage played deck tennis each evening – reaching the semi-finals – played quoits, and went 'horse racing' with toy horses pulled on strings by passengers on the deck, played bridge and entered the fancy-dress competition. Younger passengers travelling on the same ship recalled the couple: 'She was very sweet.' 'He was unassuming and nice, enjoyed himself and was relaxed.'³

Soon after boarding the *Kenya*, Armitage wrote to his successor in Zomba:

> With the peace and ease of life on board ship I must write and wish you well in Nyasaland. The turmoil and problems of leaving did not give me the chance of doing this properly. I am very grateful to you for all the help you have given me over more than a year and I am only sorry that your anxieties over [your son] did not permit you to be in Nyasaland during recent months.... I feel very conscious that there must have been many things which I have not explained to you, especially about the house and garden. If there are any, please don't hesitate to write and ask me.... It must be 'Bob' and 'Lyona' in future, all formalities passed!⁴

Jones continued to write to him from time to time and, in an early letter, passed on complimentary remarks Banda had made. Indeed, Banda wrote himself to Armitage a friendly letter saying he hoped to see him in Britain when on a visit. The Colonial Office sent an official to meet them with a car at Tilbury when they arrived.⁵ In this they were fortunate: Grigg commented on his arrival when he retired from Kenya:

> No official to meet me; not a soul. Governors get accustomed to being met; and I realized with a start that whether I came or went was now a matter of indifference to a world preoccupied with other things. It is, I soon found, quite hard to lay aside the Governor point of view, and I admit finding that my sudden insignificance gave me a sense of depression and chill.⁶

In London, during their first few days they 'got acquainted with Katherine', Phoebe and Jeremy's daughter and their first grandchild, born on 27 January 1961. Their second grandchild, Richard and Susan's son, Stephen, was born on 24 August 1961. Armitage called at the Colonial Office about his pension and to say goodbye to a number of officials there, and visited Robinson, the new federal high commissioner, learned of what was happening in central Africa and was relieved that Nyasaland was peaceful. They called also on a number of people they had known in Nyasaland and then went to Bourton for Katherine's baptism.⁷

They drove, early in June, to Cheltenham, spending their mornings looking for houses and visiting estate agents.⁸ They wanted a furnished cottage or flat to start with, since they felt they would take a long time to find the house they wanted. This would be the first home of their own, for they had always lived in government accommodation. They had planned to buy a house during their last leave from Nyasaland, but when this was shorter than they had expected they did not have time to do so. Later in June they moved into a converted house at Uploaders near Bridport in Dorset while they looked for their permanent home. This was a lengthy and frequently disappointing experience:

> On Friday we went to see three houses near Taunton, one too large and too expensive, one obviously often flooded ... and the third all right and price too, but faced wrong [direction] and [had] only tiny garden. So one goes on.... On Saturday we went to look at a house near Axminster; faced right, price right but the garden was on three steep terraces ... and it had a perennial spring flowing almost underneath it. View of battery henhouses.

They hired a television set, but it would not work, then when it was fixed they could get only one channel: 'Why does one have the things?'

They were frequently invited out to lunch, dinner or drinks – usually with ex-colonials, admirals, mayors, knights, former governors and the parson. They attended church regularly and Armitage timed each sermon, considering 20 minutes 'too long' and 22 minutes 'disgraceful'. In Nyasaland, he had spoken with the bishop and this had resulted in one of the parsons reducing his sermons to ten minutes each.

Early in July they stayed in London because Armitage had a number of engagements there. He addressed the Rhodesia Club on Nyasaland and the federation and tried to concentrate on past events and give his views and impressions in a 'very guarded' way. This was because the BBC was recording it and he did not wish to say anything that would be unhelpful in Nyasaland. He 'had put a lot of time into' preparing this lecture and thought it worth the effort. They attended the Club dinner in the evening and he was later disappointed his speech had not been reported in *East Africa and Rhodesia*. They also called at the Country Gentleman's Association to see what it could do for them in the way of advice about, and discounts on, the numerous purchases they needed to make for their home. The next day he lunched with the Nyasaland Railways board. Each day Lyona met Jeremy in the city and lunched with him. They then drove back to Dorset. The unaccustomed driving placed a considerable strain on his leg and an orthopaedic surgeon, diagnosing housemaid's knee, advised that he should have heat treatment for it. He found cleaning the windows a tiring job and washing the car 'a labour of love', but they were fortunate in being able to employ local women to help clean the house, cook some of the meals and do some of the washing up.

Their house-hunting continued. For a while, they were very interested in a cowshed that was being converted, but eventually their surveyors examined it and said it was not a good proposition. Five different sets of people were doing the plumbing, electricity, walls and so forth, all on a day-to-day basis, with no qualifications and not properly supervised: 'So that project will be off and we have to start again.'

By mid-August they had become a little unsettled: 'We don't want to lead this rather aimless life for too long' and they were relieved to find the sort of house they were looking for at Marnhull near Sturminster Newton in Dorset. It was built in 1827 and the stable block was over 200 years old. 'On the outskirts, up Caraway Lane, a cul-de-sac. Called Elm Tree Cottage (no elms survive), an old cottage added to. Faces south-southeast, has two and three-quarter acres of land, orchards and garden, central heating, pleasant rooms, 4 bed and 2 bath and an attic with a playroom and two more tiny bedrooms.' They visited a number of sales, bought furniture and equipment for the house, purchased wallpaper, carpets and soft furnishings and started on the repairs and refurbishing of the house, including wrestling with a badly smoking fireplace. They also attended lectures on local geography and geology to learn more about the area in which they were to live.

Very early in New Year 1962, they moved into their new home, which they named South Well, having studied the local tithe maps and discovered that this was the name of an adjacent field in 1840.[9] They experienced, to them, the new traumas of moving into fresh property. The day was one of heavy rain, the removal men arrived well over an hour late, the van could not get into the yard, the driver 'was not very clever, everything had to be carried out from the house onto the road and the whole operation took an hour longer than it needed'. Then, at South Well the van arrived an hour after the Armitages, and less than two hours later it departed: 'The house was full of workmen and nothing quite finished so we left ... coming back [the next day] after an early breakfast. Things were better then.'

Within a very short time they had some carpets down and some curtains up, unpacked their winter clothes, leaving the rest in boxes, and hired another television set. There was still a lot of work to be done in the house and a good many of their effects were still in boxes in the dining room, hall and stable, but at least they had moved in and were fairly warm and comfortable, although they were pleased to get away for the weekend for Katherine's first birthday and the Lingfield Park races. They were away for a week during which the cooker, washing machine and refrigerator arrived safely and the painters, paperers and carpenters worked well. Shortly, they had a telephone installed and their new notepaper printed – he was disturbed by the inclusion of commas in the address: 'No doubt correct but somehow it upsets the balance.' For seven years he had used Government House notepaper. By the end of January, the hyacinths in the garden had given way to snowdrops and crocuses in the grass outside the yard wall and in the garden; and their first callers had visited them and invited them to lunch.

It took them some months after they moved into their Marnhull home gradually to find a place to sit in the church that suited them. It was a big church, with large pillars 'and remote unheated areas'. People of longer standing in the community had laid claim to some of the pews, so newcomers like the Armitages had to 'hunt around to find some place to sit regularly'.[10] This, too, was a new experience. As governor of Cyprus and of Nyasaland and the Queen's personal representative he had not had to bother about finding a good seat in church.[11] Soon, he was reading the lesson at matins: 'Luckily my early training and education included a lot of bible reading so I know most of the passages I read.'

At the end of January, just after they moved into South Well, he travelled to Scotland, by train, and gave lunchtime lectures on central Africa in Aberdeen, Edinburgh and Glasgow for the Institute of International Affairs. The audiences asked sensible questions and included a number of people from the colonies, some of whom he knew. Willie Chokani, whom he had detained three years earlier in Nyasaland, was present at one of the lectures. He had been to the USA and was on his way back to Nyasaland; he was staying with Revd Tom Colvin, whom Armitage had declared a prohibited immigrant from Nyasaland – so he 'had to be careful'.[12]

On their return to Marnhull, they were pleased with the progress made in laying new floors in some of the rooms.[13] They began to unpack the nine boxes of glass and china, most of which they had not seen since leaving Accra – governors used crested Government House glass, china and silver. He found this unpacking 'fairly wearying', but was relieved there were very few breakages. By early February, they had nearly all the curtains up and there were covers on the sofa and chairs.

A month later, he was pleased to learn that Ingham, who had left Nyasaland, had been appointed secretary to the Beit Trust. He felt sure he 'must be pleased to be out of the shambles now prevailing in the country he started his work in and loved so much'. A little later, the Kettlewells visited them; he also had recently retired from Nyasaland. Ingham and Kettlewell were the first Nyasaland 'constitutional casualties', their posts being taken over by African ministers. Bishop Thorne stayed with them in the summer and they took him to see Lord Fisher, former Archbishop of Canterbury, who had retired nearby. They called on the Fox-Strangways: he had been secretary for African affairs in Nyasaland and she had been at school with Lyona. Soon they could say they were 'able to mix all sorts of activities, and [were] meeting quite a lot of people'. There were few of the 'indigenous families' left and most were newcomers to the area 'and a lot like us, looking for warmth and a central position. At least it makes for getting to know people!'

By early May he had made a good deal of progress in the garden, trying his hand at glazing the cold frame his predecessor's children had broken, raking out the moss from the lawn – in 20-minute stints: 'what muscles these regular gardeners must develop' – and mowing the lawns and tennis court with his new electric lawnmower.[14] The kitchen garden was now 'certainly a very different place from a few months ago' with lots of vegetable seedlings showing through and 'the whole pretty clean'. They enjoyed rhubarb and asparagus from the garden, and planted out carnations, salvia, phlox, aubretia, delphiniums and polyanthuses, buying some of the seedlings with a gift voucher given to them by the Zomba garden club before they left: the Hoyles – he was chairman of the club – were shortly to visit them and they were anxious to show how the garden was progressing!

By the summer they were enjoying the roses, peonies and lupins and home-grown peas, carrots, turnips, potatoes, beans, lettuces and strawberries. He was having difficulty eliminating nettles, docks, buttercups, conch and ground elder from parts of the property, but hoped herbicide sprayings would eventually work. He made two new beds out of old mounds of rubbish outside the kitchen window, and cleaned out a brickwork trough, which ran the whole length of the house, and planted it with dianthus. He employed local men to repair the badly deteriorated stone walls round the property and to grub out some old cider apple trees ready to plant new pears, apples and peaches.

A neighbour was keen to remove unwanted stone from his old walls, so Armitage took it, three to five barrow loads a day, to repair his own walls. He disposed of a good deal of his rubble by giving it to the local school, which needed it for building new classrooms and a playground. He sold two and a half tons of fallen cider apples locally. He was delighted with a tractor load of manure – 'fresh of course' – from a local farmer, but heaping it all at the back of the kitchen garden exacerbated the trouble he was already having in his shoulder and arm muscles and his tennis elbow, and he now blistered his hands: 'I suppose my body was not trained to take all this.' At least his housemaid's knee seemed to have recovered and the doctor said he had no arthritis, which was a family susceptibility.

They had already been back in Britain for a year. Their house and garden were in good order, they were beginning to have a few friends staying with them, they had made a fairly large number of friends locally and they were generally settling well. Armitage began to expand his outside activities: the Conservative Association, Joint East and Central Africa Board, St John's, the local church, lecturing at NATO and addressing a number of groups and – most important, interesting and fulfilling – work as a Beit trustee.

They joined the Marnhull Conservative Association and he was appointed to the committee: 'There is a fête arranged for 9 June and of course we shall have to be active.' In the event, the fête was 'exhausting but not an outstanding success' and he was disappointed his bottle stall made only half that made the previous year. He declined to get more involved in events for a while, especially the projected bingo drive in November – 'a social occasion of some status in the village' – although he regularly attended committee meetings.[15]

In June, he attended his first meeting of the Joint East and Central Africa Board as the representative of the Nyasaland chamber of commerce.[16] He had been asked before he left Nyasaland if he would be its representative, but the Colonial Office felt 'that it would be better not to proceed' with the invitation until he had been retired from Nyasaland for a year. The board, which met in the House of Lords, 'promoted the interests and welfare of all people in these areas' and most of the members were businessmen, although a few were politicians:

> [Rab] Butler [secretary of state for central Africa] spoke for 25 minutes, very interesting, he takes a human view of the problems out there and does recognize that there are human values, in all colours involved. He has set up working parties to assess the effect of Nyasaland leaving the federation and of the various new forms of association which the Rhodesias could have.

He gathered from people recently returned from central Africa that Welensky and Whitehead were pleased with the Butler approach. He also met a number of old friends from Kenya. At the July meeting of the board, Patrick Wall, who had recently visited central Africa addressed them: 'Butler seems to be playing the game well and slowly and all are becoming reconciled to the disappearance of Nyasaland from the Federation as it now is. There is apparently still a blank refusal from Banda to discuss the economics and financial effects of isolation.' The Armitages went to the dinner of the Rhodesia and

Nyasaland Club during their visit to London and met Julian Amery, who still said how correctly he and Armitage 'had thought in 1959 when [they] agreed [they] should never let Banda out'.

In March 1962, the federal government asked Armitage if he would accept an appointment as a paid director on the boards of the Nyasaland, Central African and Trans Zambesian railways. He was unable to accept this invitation because of the general rule that, save in exceptional circumstances, a former governor is not allowed to take up a directorship of a company connected with his territory, for three years, and because 'Jones did see certain problems from the political point of view, although of course he had no objection personally to [Armitage's] appointment.'[17]

Also in March 1962, Armitage was invited to become a member of the Council for the Order of St John for Dorset. He had taken a keen personal part in getting St John's established in Nyasaland and he had been made a knight of the order at an investiture the previous October. He was appointed chairman in 1965, a post he occupied until he resigned ten years later. He specialized in the council's financial work and reorganized its investments, putting to good use the knowledge and skills he had developed in Kenya and the Gold Coast. He had the task also of absorbing Bournemouth into Dorset, a tricky task but, as his successor as chairman remarked, 'as a diplomat this was done with ease'. He attended the quarterly meetings of the council at Dorchester: 'Rather a lot of hot air but the problem is always lack of money!' He found the work worthwhile and interesting.[18]

For their first Christmas at Marnhull the Armitages had their two sons, two daughters-in-law and two grandchildren staying with them.[19] They enjoyed family quizzes and 'writing games' and went to church on Christmas day. Lyona's mother joined them for lunch. They all went to a drinks and supper party at the house of a nearby Old Wykehamist and met several other Old Wykehamists there. Lady Harding, wife of Armitage's successor in Cyprus, was there and they confessed to a common dislike of Harding's successor, Sir Hugh Foot.

Over the new year it was bitterly cold, there was snow and hail and the roads were icy – they reminded Armitage of driving in the mud in Kenya. He spent hours trying to clear the snow away and was glad of the moleskin coat lining and gloves Lyona had given him for Christmas. 'We have done nothing except exist and I find it takes me all my time to deal with drawing room fire, dustbins, birds, dogs and generally see the house keeps going.' The cold weather lasted till the end of February, pipes froze and he kept his hands warm with 'ointment, gloves and short periods of strenuous work'. Shortly thereafter, he went into hospital for a few days to have an operation on his right wrist and palm.

In April 1963, he was made a member of the church council of St Gregory, Marnhull, but since there were 29 members he would have no qualms if he missed a meeting. 'It is almost impossible to get the non-gentry to take any interest although quite a lot of them go to church. Can't be bothered, so we have to, the relics of the ruling classes!'[20]

In his retirement, especially during the first ten years or so, he addressed a great variety of groups.[21] In October 1962, he spoke on current affairs at Scarborough to a course for 130 army officers, including three generals and 11 brigadiers. 'My talk was not altered by the Cuba affair. I think it was well received. There is a great interest in Africa. The questions asked were for information and not trying to secure a political point as usually happens with a civilian audience.' A month later he flew to Paris to lecture on Africa to a group of participants on a NATO course, all of about colonel rank from all services and from 11 nations.

Soon after becoming a member of the parish church council he was asked to speak and advise on missions and he decided to talk about the Jairos Jere Association as a result of a recent visit to central Africa. He also persuaded the church to adopt the Jairos Jere centre in Bulawayo, Rhodesia, a centre for rehabilitating African disabled and blind. For the next 11 years he spoke annually in church, telling the congregation about the centre and giving them up-to-date news. He prepared his talks with care, calling on his long experience in Africa for illustration and inspiration, and spoke with feeling, saying he saw no solution to the violence and fatalism in Africa but Christian teaching. The work of missionaries in medicine and education was bound to produce a change in attitudes eventually. He kept his notes from year to year so that he could refer to earlier talks, but not repeat himself, and he nearly always started with a question to catch his audience's attention: 'Have you ever thought how you would teach a deaf and blind boy how to speak?' And he was able to retain attention with his first-hand knowledge of such matters as leprosy, which were known to most of his listeners only from the bible.[22]

He was also invited to speak on current affairs in Africa, at Bryanston School, Blandford.[23] He did this for a number of years in the 1970s. Since his audience, 100 boys and girls in the upper sixth form, changed annually, he was able to keep the same structure of his talk, although the detail differed and was brought up to date each year. He took a broad geographical and historical perspective of Africa and then narrowed it down to the current situation. In speaking of Rhodesia, still in the grip of civil and guerrilla war, he raised many imponderables, was very uncertain of what would happen and concluded his talk by saying that the answers would be clear to them before they were five years older. Just before he gave this particular talk he altered his draft from 'middle aged' to 'five years older' – he had learned from experience how time horizons lessened with alarming speed in Africa. On another occasion at the school he spoke bluntly of Malawi. Some 15 years after retiring, he no longer felt constrained by the requirements of official discretion:

> An example of a British colony now controlled by a dictator and one party rule is Malawi. Dr Banda... is in supreme control. The Malawi Congress Party is the government, no other parties are allowed. He chooses the MPs and Ministers. I suspect he also decides on changes. When I was there recently the minister of justice, who is also the attorney-general, was expelled from the Party and all his offices taken from him. Dr Banda decides on social behaviour [clothing, censorship, morality]. The only newspaper is a government one, and any imported are sold only after censorship.... Five years ago [Ian] Smith [in Rhodesia] and Banda could have looked to continue in power indefinitely, with the patterns of government around them unaltered. But where will they be in five years' time?

Perhaps his use again of a quinquennial time horizon was subconsciously a reflection of the enormous changes he had seen in his five years in the Gold Coast and, even more so, his five years in Nyasaland. In the course of one of these addresses, he advised the students: 'Work hard and keep your mouth shut and you will do well.' Perhaps, and again subconsciously, he had learned that it was not sufficient to work hard but there were also occasions when one needed to keep one's mouth shut – especially, he may have thought, when speaking with the prime minister and the secretary of state for the colonies.

Other groups he addressed were the English Speaking Union at Exeter, Salisbury and Bournemouth; the Sturminster Newton Probus Club; King's College Junior House sports and prize giving at Taunton; the local Mothers' Union; the Bournemouth and Poole Round Tables; the local branch of the National Farmers' Union; Bournemouth Rotary Club; London University; and the University of Hull Committee for Education in the Forces.[24]

Towards the end of July 1963 Armitage was invited by Sir Alfred Beit to become a Beit trustee. The previous winter he had sat next to Lady Beit, herself a trustee, at a dinner at the Savoy and it had crossed her mind that he might be interested. She felt it would be a great advantage to the trustees to have someone with his experience of Africa and it would be nice for him to have a reason to visit the countries he knew so well and to carry on some interesting work there. In extending the invitation – which Armitage readily accepted – Beit said that notwithstanding the demise of the federation, the trustees were continuing their charitable and public activities in the three territories; the work was 'not exacting' and the trustees met twice a year, at the Mayfair Hotel in London, and made visits to central Africa from time to time.[25]

In the 23 years he spent as a trustee, he made six visits to central Africa and, in all but one – the first and the only one when Lady Armitage accompanied him – he visited Malawi, formerly Nyasaland. His first visit, from 21 January to 12 February 1965, was an extremely arduous one in which he travelled 2500 miles in Rhodesia and Zambia. The visit was organized by the secretary, Ingham. He visited a large number of schools, colleges and training centres – including the Jairos Jere centre – mission stations, social service organizations and hospitals, and had meetings with ministers and senior civil servants.[26]

Four years later, in 1969, he visited Rhodesia and Malawi, spending a week in the former and two weeks in the latter.[27] Again his visit was arranged by Ingham, who accompanied him throughout. In Rhodesia, he stayed at Government House as the guest of Sir Humphrey Gibbs and visited educational and social work institutions and mission stations. He noted the attempts being made to improve the lot of Africans but there were still aspects of racial practice that puzzled him.

Though he no doubt looked forward to his visit to Malawi, he must have anticipated it with mixed emotions. The country was nearly five years into independence and a few leading Congress members he had known from the past were now ministers. There were not many, however, because, some six weeks after independence day in July 1964, Banda's cabinet had, almost to a man, rebelled against him and, consequently, either resigned or been dismissed. All these dissidents had now left the country. Chipembere had led an armed revolt against Banda in 1965 and been surreptitiously evacuated to the USA later that year. Yatuta Chisiza had also led an armed revolt against Banda and had been shot dead in doing so in 1967. Most of the 'second eleven' whom Armitage had detained in 1959 were in exile. In a private conversation, Armitage spoke of the friendliness of the Malawian politicians and he spoke well of the former Congress leaders, disliking – and intensely so – only Chiume: 'He always was a poisonous type.'

He arrived at Chileka on 11 March, just a few days beyond the tenth anniversary of having declared a state of emergency. 'We ... were welcomed by Mr G. Mkumtumanji, Minister for Health, Education, Local Government and the Regional Minister ... and stayed at Nyambadwe House [formerly the provincial commissioner's residence] as guest of the Malawi Government.' The following evening Mkumtumanji – whom he had also detained in 1959 – hosted a dinner for him and Ingham. Five other ministers, a number of Europeans playing a prominent part in public life in Malawi, and 'some old friends' were present. He 'was very touched by this very friendly and pleasant entertainment'.

A little later, he had 'a very friendly audience' with Banda, now the president – Malawi having become a republic in 1966 – at State House which, as Government House, had been his own home in Zomba for five years: 'He was looking extremely well which he attributed to hard work, and talked of the many developments in hand.' He had discussions with the permanent secretaries for health and education – both African – works and finance – both European – and with the vice-chancellor, registrar and development advisor of the University of Malawi. This had not even been a proposal when he left, but now had 1100 students in four colleges. The vice-chancellor got the impression that Armitage 'was pretty lofty and did not suggest any strong interest in the university'. In this view – which was not shared by all others present – he was probably mistaken because, following the visit, the trust gave the university 'a very fair grant'.

He travelled in all three regions – formerly provinces – which now had no civil servant commissioners, but a regional minister to whom the district commissioners – now all Malawians – reported on political matters. He visited numerous secondary schools and colleges, hospitals, leprosaria, mission stations – where many of the schools and hospitals were located – and the Malawi museum. He had discussions with the Anglican bishop of Malawi and the Roman Catholic bishop in the central and northern regions. At Mua mission, they slept in the fathers' house built in 1902 'and were excellently fed by the sisters'. He was much touched at one secondary school where he was accompanied by the minister of education who formally opened a new dining hall and insisted that Armitage take part in the tape-cutting ceremony.

He saw the *Chauncey Maples*, now used as a water bus, tied up alongside the jetty at Nkata Bay and his mind must have gone back ten years to the shooting tragedy there on the day he declared the emergency. He was interested to learn of the Lengwe game reserve project, especially of how conservation practices were greatly increasing the number of nyala there, and also in other game reserves being developed in the central and northern regions. He admired the excellent medical and health work being done by various missions, particularly in the more remote areas of the country, and was concerned at the grave shortage of doctors and the difficulty of getting any to work in the more isolated areas. Everywhere he found pressure on schools to add further streams to their work, and in many places there were worries about water supplies, particularly to hospitals and health units.

Armitage's second Beit Trust visit to Malawi was for ten days at the beginning of March 1972.[28] In his report he outlined his main impressions:

> My impressions of the country are primarily of a few major improvements since I was here three years ago. The most useful of these is the modern tarmacadam highway between Zomba and Lilongwe. The railway to Nacala is now complete and in operation and ... congestion is already building up at Nacala because of the use being made of the new rail link. The power line from the Tedzani Falls runs all along the highway to Lilongwe and power should be flowing through it in August. The other road improved is the stretch between Karonga and Mlowe ... a tourist road.

Although his primary impressions were of 'a few major improvements', he in fact saw many changes and it was clear to him that there was a great deal of new development in the country from which he sensed 'a tremendous air of activity'. He was especially impressed with the land development project near Lilongwe and there were similar projects in the lower Shire valley for cotton and at Karonga for rice. If these schemes continued their current progress, there would be 'a tremendous increase' in African incomes in those areas.

Armitage made an early call on Banda and spent half an hour with him: 'It was a most relaxed informal talk about various development projects that he had in mind.' He gathered Banda's next road project would be to extend the main highway from Lilongwe northwards and to build a new one from Salima on the lake shore through Moatise in Mozambique to Rhodesia. In speaking with the shortly to retire secretary to the cabinet, Bryan Roberts, he got a sense of 'the general state of feeling in the country', particularly concerning the cases of some Europeans who had been asked to leave at short notice. He was pleased to meet George Jaffu, the secretary to the treasury, who was about to succeed Roberts and become the first Malawian secretary to the president and cabinet and head of the civil service. He also met John Msonthi, minister of education – one of the 1959 detainees and the only leading politician from those days to have been a minister before the 1964 ministerial revolt and to remain in office thereafter – a matter that was not raised, still less discussed! He had discussions with the permanent secretaries to the cabinet office, treasury, agriculture and natural resources, education and health.

After visiting a mission hospital and a girls' secondary school in the south, he travelled to the central region. 'The 3rd March [the anniversary of the declaration of the emergency] was "Martyrs' Day" and a public holiday, and every activity throughout the country was closed down. We took the opportunity to motor to Lilongwe.' In the central region he visited a number of health centres and hospitals – mainly run by Catholic nuns – met several people he had seen on his previous visit, and was able to compare progress. Water supplies were still often a worry. He was shown over the new capital city site and commented on the large number of houses being built and roads being installed: 'At present one can certainly see considerable development in some areas, and nothing at all in others. But it would appear that the determination to succeed is there, and therefore gradually more development will take place ... a lot of thought is being given to artistic planning.'

A few days later he flew to Mzuzu, so once again visited all three regions. In the north he visited a number of schools and the pressure to add more streams continued. He flew to Karonga with the Roman Catholic bishop in the bishop's Cessna aircraft and found 'this much more comfortable and certainly faster' than the Beavers to which he had been accustomed in the past. They landed on the new airstrip at Karonga and then flew on to Chitipa, formerly Fort Hill, where the airfield had been taken over by rioters in 1959 and the government had lost control. He was enthusiastically welcomed by Chief Nyondu, who said how much he appreciated his visit and the help the trust was giving in setting up a new hospital. Armitage was presented with a live chicken, which he promptly but discreetly passed on to the sister in charge of the local homecraft centre. He returned via Zomba and then left for a visit to Rhodesia.

Armitage's third visit to Malawi as a Beit trustee was for a week at the end of February and beginning of March 1976.[29] He paid an early call on the president: 'He was in excellent form; he said he was too busy to get ill or to grow old.' Banda spoke about his railway projects. The extension from Salima to Lilongwe was already under construction and he hoped to extend it to the Zambia border to join up with an extension from the Tanzam railway, which Kaunda had agreed to build. The doctor also told him about other developments, including major roads and the Lilongwe land development scheme. Over a million acres were now included in this scheme with World Bank financing, but 'it is admitted that they cannot get roads, water courses and soil erosion works maintained by the farmers, and this problem is just being left to solve itself.'

On this visit he again visited all three regions, having meetings at institutions for the deaf and blind, secondary schools, vocational training centres and teacher training colleges. He visited the new capital city at Lilongwe, where most of the ministry headquarters were now located and a number of diplomatic headquarters and residences had already been built. He had meetings with the permanent secretaries for education and health, the bishop of Lilongwe, and the principals of the university's Chancellor College and Bunda Agricultural College – all Malawians. In Zomba, the houses previously occupied by civil servants were now occupied by university staff, the former having moved to the new capital city. At the various secondary schools, water supplies were still a problem and there was still pressure to add yet more classes and streams.

African refugees, fleeing from guerrilla warfare in Mozambique, were moving into the Mlanje, Kirk Range and Dedza areas and Armitage could see that some of these areas were becoming so densely populated that people were having to move elsewhere. He could also foresee 'an endless demand' for rural health centres in these and other areas as the population increased.

The one feature that impressed him more than any other on this trip was the immense expansion of reading and the use made of libraries, wherever located, by Africans: 'Everywhere we went the library was in constant use', not simply for leisure purposes but for education. Finally, 'On 3rd March, Martyrs' Day and therefore a public holiday, as no-one was allowed to work throughout Malawi, we flew to Salisbury.'

The fourth visit Armitage made to Malawi as a Beit trustee was for a fortnight in the second half of March 1980, as usual with Ingham, and again they saw Banda who, six months earlier, had visited Britain.[30] The Armitages on that occasion had been invited to a luncheon at 10 Downing Street given by the prime minister in the president's honour.[31] On this 1980 visit he recalled: 'We had a telephone message to say the President would like to see us. We found him as ebullient as ever on the developments in hand and planned ... the President talked enthusiastically about the Queen's [recent] visit, which was a tremendous success.'

The railway was pushing forward towards Zambia – but still President Kaundu had not indicated when and where it would link up with his railway. The main road was pushing north and was already beyond Kasungu. A few days later Banda invited Armitage to a formal dinner in honour of the prime minister of the Republic of China. They visited the Church of Scotland church at Blantyre, now the Cathedral of St Michael and All Angels, where major help was required to preserve the building, and they spent some time with the Anglican archbishop and his wife – 'his clerk of works', the 'forceful' Jane – and was impressed by the 'vigorous policy of expansion' on which they were embarking.

At St Andrew's School in Blantyre, he commented on the considerable expansion now to over 600 pupils, 80 per cent of them the children of diplomats and expatriates serving on contract in Malawi. The headmaster filled the remaining places with children from any country:

'Every colour, creed and race, girls and boys. Apparently it is a great success.' He met the new vice-chancellor, David Kimble, whom Armitage had known in the Gold Coast, and they discussed the prospects and difficulties of training doctors in Malawi, for currently they had to be trained overseas, mainly at Manchester: 'Few qualify and even fewer return to Malawi.' They visited a number of mission hospitals and schools, and noticed the very greatly increased number of deliveries in the maternity sections of the former and the great expansion of classes and streams in the latter.

Armitage was pleased that the St John's Ambulance he had founded when governor was 'flourishing'. It, like the Red Cross, but unlike the Boy Scouts and Girl Guides, had not been closed down by the government after independence. He met the permanent secretaries of the ministries of health and education and of the former he said that he was 'one of the most charming and competent permanent secretaries [he had] ever met'.

In his report to the trustees, there were signs of a sense of a fond 'belonging' to the country: he said how delighted he was at Lilongwe 'to meet several old friends whom I had virtually forgotten', and he referred to Bishop Jobidon as 'an old friend from Mzuzu'. On this occasion a few Beit advisers from Zambia and Zimbabwe accompanied him. He felt this was an excellent idea and the advisers were often impressed with what they saw: 'They remarked on the courtesy with which we were met at each Ministry and the efficiency of the staff. We entertained and were entertained extensively. A great number of high ranking Africans were met socially. In fact it was an admirable public relations exercise in my opinion.'

Armitage's final visit to Malawi was from 28 March to 5 April 1984.[32] He flew out on what he described as the 'lollipop plane' because it was carrying 'hundreds of [expatriate] schoolchildren returning from the United Kingdom for the holidays', and he landed at the new international airport at Lilongwe, opened the previous year. The new capital city 'was looking lovely, with cassia avenues in full flower and areas of mown grass'. The Capital Hotel was packed with visitors and its accommodation was being extended. He stayed with the British high commissioner with whom he spoke freely of the past, particularly of Cyprus and Nyasaland.

He visited the Kasungu nature park where a game ranger had recently been killed by ivory and rhino horn poachers, and learned that the Lengwe reserve was fast becoming overstocked: 3000 nyala had to be culled in one year. He was pleased with the success of the 1000 wildlife clubs in primary schools – where ecology was a compulsory subject – whose monthly newsletter the Beit Trust had supported. Other visits were to the national library service, British Council, Seventh Day Adventists mission and hospital, the private health association, council for the handicapped, the university and St John's Ambulance.

Probably the most remarkable aspect of this final visit — and possibly of all his visits — was his meeting with Banda. On two of his previous visits he had been in Malawi on 3 March, the anniversary of his having imprisoned the doctor and more than a hundred of his leading followers. In 1984, he avoided this date but was there on 1 April, the twenty-fourth anniversary of Banda's release from Gwelo gaol. Armitage had been scheduled to visit the Lengwe game reserve that day, but instead, in response to an invitation from the president, he attended a packed celebration at the national stadium to mark the anniversary of the doctor's release from detention.

Armitage was an honoured guest and sat on the platform with the president who asked him to rise and shake his hand publicly before the 10,000 crowd, which cheered loudly. Photographs of this remarkable hand-shaking scene were published in local newspapers the following day.[33] Banda — now well over eighty years of age — danced for at least ten minutes with each of the seven groups of women dancers which, to Armitage, showed his physical fitness. The doctor arrived from Zomba and returned there by helicopter, which he now always used for travelling in Malawi except when he went to the north and travelled by plane. Armitage also had an audience with the president at State House.

> He was very gracious and welcoming. As usual I tried to find out what developments he had planned but there was clearly nothing especial. I think times are somewhat hard. He had been offered loans, but had no money to secure them. ... Having given us a brief lesson in Latin, his favourite language, and Greek, he took us into the garden. ... Miss Kadzamira [his official hostess, whom Armitage had first met when she accompanied the doctor to the Palm Sunday sherry party at Government House in 1961] joined us and I congratulated her on the beauty of the garden.

He was pleased that the garden, which had been his pride and joy and where he had relaxed many late afternoons during even his most troubled days as governor, had been looked after so well.

In conversation with Banda, Armitage learned that the most serious matter for the economy was the disruption to rail facilities. The Beira–Harare railway scarcely functioned because of 'the activities of brigands and the revolutionaries' in Mozambique. The port of Beira was run down and, although some goods were shipped through Nacala where the 'chaos in handling' was less, there were tens of thousands of tons of sugar and tea waiting to be moved. Some of it went by road to Lusaka and Tanzania and 40 tons of tea were flown out each week by a French airline. On the positive side, there was an adequate maize crop and part of it was being sold to the EEC. Trade, too, seemed reasonable and the shops were well stocked. 'The place [had] an air of tidiness.' The railway had been extended to the Zambian border, but there was still no link with Zambia railways. Armitage compared Malawi favourably with the other two countries in the former federation: 'Zambia gives the impression of being run down'; in Zimbabwe industry was starved of foreign exchange and the government had forbidden all dismissals from work – 'if owing to the drought, a farmer wanted to reduce his labour force he was forbidden to do so.' 'Of the three countries I would choose Malawi to live in, and be circumspect.'

Armitage's work as a Beit trustee was an important part of his life. It extended for a quarter of a century his contact with, and contribution to, Africa and particularly Nyasaland-Malawi. Over this long period, by five personal visits and by reading the trust papers and reports, he gained an insight into the changes taking place in Malawi probably more fully than any other person from outside the country. During this period of early independence, he sensed the mood of the country and of its leaders and the changes in those moods.

In 1972, he spoke of the 'tremendous air of activity' and 'the determination to succeed'. In 1984, he detected that 'times are somewhat hard', but 'the place [still has] an air of tidiness' about it. He was able, too, to compare Malawi with its former federal partners. Zambia gave 'the impression of being run down'. Zimbabwe was starved of foreign exchange and the socialist government forbade employers to dismiss their workers. In observing and recording the changes in Malawi, he spoke openly in 1976 at Bryanston School about Banda being a dictator, the MCP being the government and the regime being repressive.

Over these years he catalogued the major developments taking place in the country: the new capital city; new international airport; the creation of the university; the extension and improvement of highways, the railways and the electric grid system; game conservation; the large land development projects; the development role of the churches; and the extension of education and health facilities. On the other hand, he noted demands for improved water supplies not being fully met and the demand for additional streams and classes in schools being accelerated. He observed the very large number of African refugees who poured into Malawi from Mozambique, and noted the pressures this put on the Malawi government. In the race relations field he spoke frequently of the courtesy and kindness of his Malawian hosts, including several for whose imprisonment in 1959 he had been responsible.

He detected no sign of bitterness or resentment about the past. Indeed, Banda was keen to have Armitage call on him during each of his visits and he publicly fêted him on the twenty-fourth anniversary of his release from detention. Most of the more violent and extreme of Banda's early lieutenants had left the scene, not always peacefully, and many of the ministers during Armitage's visits were relative newcomers. He recorded with approval the success of the multiracial – albeit élitist – St Andrew's School in Blantyre. He did, however, detect that a number of expatriates who were critical of Banda's methods, were forced to leave the country often at very short notice. He did not comment on what many may have seen as the slow rate of Africanization and presumably he approved of the slow but sure pace.

As governor, he had taken the first significant steps towards Africanization by appointing Yaw Adu, former head of the Ghana civil service, to make recommendations on localizing the Nyasaland civil service. There was a manifest pleasure in witnessing the advancement of Malawians to the top of the civil service – in one case meeting 'one of the most charming and competent permanent secretaries [he had] ever met'. He noted, how, over the years, an increasing number of permanent secretaryships were filled by Malawians, including the headship of the civil service and secretaryship to the president and cabinet. He no doubt derived great satisfaction from observing Malawians catching up with Ghanaians, behind whom he had earlier felt they had lagged. He enjoyed visiting all three regions of the country, retreading ground he had so diligently trodden while governor. He enjoyed, too, his visits to State House, formerly Government House, and its gardens and never once in his letters, diaries or other papers did he refer to it as the place where he had formerly resided.

One detects from his reports and other papers an expanding fondness of the country and a quiet satisfying feeling of 'belonging'. Towards the end of his series of visits he referred quite frequently to meeting his 'old friends' and by this he did not mean those from his gubernatorial days but rather those from his earlier Beit visits. There was, too, a largely unspoken pride in the country and its achievements: he was keen that Beit advisers from Zambia and Zimbabwe should see Malawi's developments and that 'a good public relations image' should be projected. Of the three countries he would choose Malawi to live in – 'and be circumspect'. He did not himself comment on it, but through his work as a Beit trustee he was instrumental in channelling a significant number of development grants to projects in Malawi, and this, too, must have given him a good deal of satisfaction. He may even have felt that he was, in retirement, able to make the sort of contribution to Malawi's social and economic welfare he had been unable to make earlier when politics so consumed his time and attention, and to do so in an atmosphere of friendliness.

On 5 November 1986 – now aged 80 years, Armitage wrote to Sir Alfred Beit to say that he wished to resign as trustee. Beit accepted this with regret and said how much he and his wife had enjoyed and valued his advice at meetings, and far from considering him – as he had suggested – too outspoken, Beit appreciated his 'definite views and criticism'. He hoped that Armitage would 'enjoy a peaceful retirement' – this, 25 years after he had retired from the colonial service.[34]

When not engaged on these other activities – the Conservative Association, Joint East and Central Africa Board, the St John's Ambulance, the local church, the Beit Trust, lecturing and giving talks – Armitage derived much enjoyment from his two great passions: horse racing and gardening.

During his long retirement, he indulged his passion for horse races and betting on them. This life-long enthusiasm arose initially from his contacts as a schoolboy with the Astor family. Even at school, he wrote to his father asking for money with which to place bets. When he first met his future wife, while still at New College and aged only 21, she frequently accompanied him to the races. In the Gold Coast their house was very near the race course – too close for Lady Armitage's liking – and he was a regular attender. One of his closest African friends was Thomas Hutton-Mills, 'a delightful creature', who 'bought beautiful horses from Nigeria [which often won on the] very good race track' in Accra, and upon which their owner would bet very large sums. Hutton-Mills, a fellow cabinet minister in the Gold Coast, later became high commissioner in London 'and if he wasn't in his office you could always find him at Newmarket'.[35] In Cyprus, too, he was regularly at the races and donated the Armitage Cup to the racing club. In Nyasaland:

> Armitage was very interested in horse racing. . . . He was not as sound an expert on form as he and others believed and lost as much money as he gained, although he mentioned only the wins and seldom the losses. He bet a good deal, up to £50 at a time and had an arrangement whereby he would call his private secretary into a meeting in which he was engaged, and pass him a slip of paper. This was to tell the private secretary to place bets of certain values on certain horses, and the private secretary, using a code, would then telephone and place the bets. He was [however] not a compulsive gambler.[36]

In retirement, betting seemed to become almost an obsession and Lady Armitage would hear the 'clicks' on the telephone just before the races and would know that he was ringing his bookmaker. He lost heavily and eventually had to realize some of his investments to pay his betting debts. One of the reasons why he got on so well with the Queen Mother and Lord Dalhousie was their shared profound interest in horse racing. He kept all the race cards from previous meetings, studied them and 'form' very carefully. During his retirement he not only attended numerous race meetings, but also watched many others on the television. He seemed unperturbed about losing and always spoke of his winnings, but rarely of his losses save in his private diary. Jeremy discovered that towards the end of his retirement his father was betting fairly heavily on the horses and that he had an open account with his bookmakers. He was able to have a weekly limit placed on the account, but this figure was never reached.[37]

Gardening also meant a great deal to him and he derived enormous pleasure from it throughout his life and well into retirement. 'Bob's other great love was gardening. He may have got this from his father who, when he retired from India in the 1920s, at Whitchurch, made a lovely garden and took great interest in it. He made gardens wherever he lived. Gardening was his great hobby and he found it both relaxing and creative.'[38] Very soon after his arrival in Cyprus he told the people of the island of his deep interest in gardening: 'I come from a family one of whose main pursuits is horticulture.' Frequently, especially in Cyprus and Nyasaland, he would touchingly end the day's entry in his private diary with references to the garden – 'the roses look grand,' 'lovely rain this afternoon' – and he would do this at the conclusion of even the most ghastly days in the office. He was able to switch quickly from the anxieties of violence and political intransigence to the peaceful and refreshing haven of Government House garden, sometimes with Lyona or the head gardener, but often by himself. It was a remarkable gift. This fondness for gardening was reflected in a love of nature and an appreciation of beautiful scenery. In Kenya, he described the hills as 'breathtaking in their blueness and greens' at Kakamega and the 'marvellous view' from his camp sites at Tambach, and in his retirement at Marnhull he wrote: 'The autumn tints are wonderful, there has not been so much wind lately and the leaves have not all come off. We have some fine elms, oaks and sycamores we look at and they shine gold and bronze with the sun on them.'[39]

In the early 1980s, Granada television set about producing a series of programmes entitled *End of Empire*, which were broadcast in the summer of 1985, the year in which the producer, Brian Lapping, published his book of the same title.

> The motive behind both this book and the television series... was the desire to seize an opportunity. Many of the people who had crucial

responsibilities aboard the Empire as it sank live quietly in retirement. To film them and record their contrasting versions of events that concluded with the lowering of the British flag seemed a worthwhile task of historical evidence-gathering.[40]

In selecting the ten cases he felt were the 'most important and exciting', he chose four in which Armitage had played an important role as a senior official – in two cases the most senior. These were Kenya, the Gold Coast, Cyprus and Nyasaland. He asked Armitage to take part and he agreed. It involved a good deal of hard and careful preparation and the recollection of events that had taken place between 21 and 32 years previously. Many of the events and their details were, however, indelibly etched on his mind, and he had his diaries and letters to his parents with which to refresh his memory as to dates and finer details.

One of the first steps was to help the researchers and interviewers to prepare chronologies of the main events.[41] In the case of Nyasaland, this was done by Norma Percy. Then, a list of points for discussion was drawn up. On 6 April 1982, this was followed by a 'first conversation' with Norma and Lapping and a transcript of this conversation was produced. Only in one case did Armitage seem to become impatient: 'When asked if he considered what Southern Rhodesia troops in Nyasaland would do to his efforts to sell the Federation, he got very angry – what would you do if you had a rebellion?' Lapping promptly felt that 'it would be nice to capture this anger on film', but it did not appear in the final version. Armitage must have felt sensitive to criticism on this point because he knew better than anyone else the effect European federal troops had on Nyasalanders' reactions to federation and had done all he could to minimize their involvement in the protectorate. Other comments were made privately by the interviewers, such as: 'When he talks about Iain Macleod he makes the phrases "chess player" and "bridge player" sound like a curse.'

The 'second conversation', two weeks later, was based on replies to points agreed after the first. Finally, the interview, based on the earlier papers and especially on the replies given in the second meeting, was recorded on camera on 1 August 1982 and later, shortly before the series was finalized, in December 1984. Peter Connors interviewed him for these recorded sessions. The questions were short, the interviewer rarely intervened and the answers were fairly full. Maxine Baker produced the Gold Coast and central Africa programmes and, after they had been transmitted, Armitage wrote to her to say that, especially in respect of the latter programme, she had 'got the story right' and had asked all the questions he would himself have asked. He added that he wished Maxine had produced the Cyprus programme, which he disliked. She felt this was an interesting comment and a reflection on how he, 'reflecting on his career in tranquillity', saw events.

He was shortly able to see the Granada television series, *End of Empire,* and to read Lapping's book. These, together with his own contacts and visits to central Africa, no doubt helped him reflect on events in the former colonies since he had left and since Britain's retreat from empire in Africa had been completed. He would have been encouraged by Kenya and saddened by Ghana, Cyprus and Malawi.[42]

In December 1963, Kenya – the first colony in which Armitage served – became independent with Jomo Kenyatta as prime minister. He remained head of government until his death in 1978. Thereafter, as Lapping remarked:

> The general air of Kenya remained that of a modernizing, free-enterprise state, successfully overcoming both its lack of ... significant natural resources and the general backwardness of its people. In this Kenya followed, in the first 20 years after independence, the path the British hoped for. [By] the standards of ex-British colonies in Africa, Kenya was the big success.

On 6 March 1957, the Gold Coast – the second colony in which Armitage served – became independent as Ghana with Nkrumah as prime minister. He remained head of government until deposed by a military coup in February 1966. 'In nine years he had turned the model colony into an economic and political disaster area, which, under a succession of military and civilian rulers it has remained.'

> What went wrong in Ghana was simple. Nkrumah insisted on spending huge sums of money on spectacular projects which would confirm Ghana's position as the leader of independent Africa. ... To bring Ghana and then Africa into the twentieth century, industry had to replace agriculture as the main source of wealth. He thought the economists and bankers who had told him that this objective had to be approached slowly were either neo-colonialists or lacking in courage. He ignored their advice and ... tried to keep Ghana orderly by repression ... as the economy of [the country] declined. ... In the end he became a megalomaniac dictator out of touch with the real world, surrounded by a corrupt and harsh security force. ... Nkrumah's great expenditures overtook the income from cocoa – declining but still enormous – and the country fell into debt.

Cyprus – the third colony in which Armitage served and the first of which he was governor – became an independent republic in August

1960 with Makarios as president and Kütchük as vice-president. The constitution made it illegal to campaign for enosis or partition, prohibited political or economic union with any other state and none of its 48 basic articles could ever be changed. Its main purpose 'was not to secure good government in Cyprus but to avoid war between Greece and Turkey'.

> If Cyprus was a violent place in the five years before independence it was much more so in the fifteen years after.... In December 1963 Makarios and his cabinet sanctioned a major campaign of violence by Greeks against Turks in Nicosia.... A Turkish intervention to protect their people was forestalled only by the setting up of the British [military] 'green line' in Nicosia and Larnaca. This soon proved ineffective at protecting the Turkish Cypriots [and] was taken over by the United Nations, but it still could not protect the Turks [who] retreated into the enclaves where they took over complete military and administrative control.... The island remained thus divided, with the Greeks trying to blockade the Turkish areas amidst sporadic outbursts of violence, from 1964 till 1967, when a bloodless coup d'état overthrew the elected government in Greece and [Grivas] created a new organization ... whose target was no longer the British Government or the Turks but Makarios himself ... in July 1974 they had him overthrown. Turkey invaded Cyprus [and] seized much more of Cyprus than was necessary merely to protect the Turkish enclaves, continuing to pour in Turkish troops and civilians until the Cyprus problem was, so far as Turkey was concerned, settled.... The Cyprus Republic, to which Makarios was soon restored as President, was restricted to the southern half of the island.

Nyasaland – the fourth and last colony in which Armitage served – became independent as Malawi on 6 July 1964, with Banda as prime minister. Within a few weeks, a ministerial revolt led to the whole of his cabinet either resigning or being dismissed. Banda rallied other Congress leaders and the bulk of the party around him and a ruthless purge of dissenters resulted in his personal dominance being massively enhanced. In the 1970s, at Bryanston School, Armitage described the way in which Malawi had become a one-party state and Banda, its life president, a dictator. By the end of that decade:

> The president had established a network of comprehensive and highly personal control that had the full power of the law and yet was completely arbitrary. He had the power to determine unilaterally who might or might not be a member of the party and of parliament; the power to determine

whether or not people might hold title to land and whether or not they might engage in business; he could arraign people before courts of his own choosing in circumstances that gave them little chance of acquittal and even if, in spite of this, they were acquitted, he had the power to disregard the verdict and insist that they either be retried immediately or be held in custody awaiting another trial, which would be held at his convenience and in circumstances he deemed appropriate. To supplement this vast range of powers, he had virtual monopoly of the means of communication and the power to inflict severe penalties on anyone who uttered anything displeasing to him.[43]

During the 1980s, the country became even more harshly and oppressively ruled. Many of its citizens were incarcerated without trial for indefinite and often very long periods in severe conditions, frequently in solitary confinement. All opposition, real, imagined or simply concocted, was brutally suppressed and Banda was widely feared and despised.

For some time, Armitage had intended to write his memoirs.[44] It seems that initially he kept documents covering his career simply because 'they should make some sort of record of one's life.' When he first sorted out his 'all jumbled up' Nyasaland papers, in December 1961, he did so 'largely because racing was cancelled at Hurst Park'. Later, he decided to write an account of his Nyasaland – but not other – days. Throughout his career he had kept many papers, both professional and personal. He had also written diaries from an early date and his parents had kept, and handed back to him, virtually all his letters to them over a very long period. Until he left Africa, he had little spare time to devote to writing and then, for the first 20 years, he was too fully occupied domestically and otherwise to get down to it.

In March 1963, the Institute of Commonwealth Studies at Oxford asked him if he would deposit his private papers with them. He replied that he would go through the material he had 'in the next couple of years and then decide'. A year later, the institute asked again and this time he replied, 'Bring [it] up in five years.' It may have been that the enquiries made by Granada and the preparation for its programmes, together with a realization that the years were passing quickly, provided the stimulus to begin writing. In any event, in January 1980, he agreed to cooperate with the Oxford Development Research Project – which had taken over from the institute, collected manuscripts and tape-recorded memoirs from former colonial service officers – on gathering Nyasaland material. In reply, they referred to his 'proposed book' and, towards the end of January 1981, he wrote to say that he had started to write his recollections.

Whether this was in response to the project request – made a year earlier – or whether he then had a book in mind is uncertain, but by May 1981 other members of the project, including Kettlewell, felt 'great satisfaction' that he had started to write his 'experiences of those far off difficult days in Zomba'. Two years later he told Kettlewell his 'winter task' of writing had gone well and he had almost finished his 'stint of writing' about Nyasaland, but he was then transferring his enthusiasm and time to his annual summer gardening and would not be able to complete the Nyasaland story until November. It is likely, however, that he did some work on the story during the summer because, by the end of October 1983, he had sent Kettlewell an account of his first three years as governor of Nyasaland. There remained the final years of his governorship and since these were immensely full and vastly important, writing about them took some time. In November 1985, Kettlewell wrote to say he hoped to be able to see the 1958–60 part.

The Armitages had already moved from Dorset to Kent in 1979, wanting to be nearer to Jeremy. In 1988, they moved to Amesbury Abbey in Hampshire because they felt they were getting older and not so well able to look after a garden and house.[45] Jeremy, too, no longer had an office in Kent and was spending his weekends in Hampshire, so they could continue to see him. He hoped to have more leisure at Amesbury to complete the Nyasaland writing, and indeed by June the following year, 1989, he was able to send to Oxford an extensive typescript account covering the period in Nyasaland up to November 1960.

This was based on his diaries to which he added other material and commentaries. Armitage hoped that the account of his Nyasaland days could be published and, before the typescript was formally lodged in Rhodes House Library as part of the development research project, advice on this was sought. The publisher to whom a copy was sent felt it was too long, would need considerable pruning, many of the names mentioned would need explanation and much of the detail about visitors, personalities and letters quoted would need to be removed. This would be a substantial, indeed formidable, task and, in addition, the part after November 1960 – which, although it was not then fully appreciated, was in fact an extremely important part – had not been written.

In the autumn of 1989 Armitage fell and broke his leg, which led to a spell in hospital and in a nursing home. By the end of November 1989, he was back at Amesbury trying to recover his strength in order to be able to send the final part of his memoirs to Oxford. In a very shaky and distressingly jumbled letter written on 30 November 1989 he wrote:

I am quite incapable of writing the final section of my book and so I am sending it to Jeremy to send it on to you for you to do the best you can. I ... can do nothing more. So I am leaving it all to you and any others you can find useful to finish it off and do what you can and in any way you can.

When they first arrived at Amesbury, Armitage was still quite active. He would daily walk the half mile or so into the village, but after a few months the neuralgia, from which he had suffered since returning to Britain, worsened. The painkillers he was prescribed were powerful, but left him in a drugged state. As a consequence, he took them at night so as to get a good night's sleep, but this put him in severe pain during the day, a pain from which he secured relief by drinking whisky in the evenings. He deteriorated noticeably during 1989. He stopped driving and gave Jeremy power of attorney over his affairs. On 18 February 1990, the Armitages celebrated their sixtieth wedding anniversary and were delightedly surprised when a chauffeur from Clarence House arrived with a large and beautiful basket of flowers and 'a lovely letter' from the Queen Mother. They had a celebration party at which their sons and grandchildren were present. It was a very happy occasion.[46]

Less than four months later, on 7 June 1990, Armitage died. His death was unexpected and, although he had a chest infection, the end – due to acute cardiac failure – was sudden. A funeral service was held a week later at the church of Saint Mary and Saint Melor at the entrance to Amesbury Abbey grounds. He was cremated at Salisbury the following day and his ashes were later interred near the family home, at Bridstow church in Herefordshire. Eight years earlier he had made the necessary arrangements with the vicar: that the urn containing his ashes should be placed beneath a stone – the design and inscription of which he gave – in the churchyard next to the grave of his aunts Nora and Cecilia.[47]

The address at the funeral service at Amesbury was given by Donald Goldie with whom he had been a close friend since his days in Cyprus.[48] It was an address both factual and deeply moving, an address that briefly recalled Armitage's career and that gave thanks for his 'life of distinguished public service'. Goldie described him as 'one of the last of that great company of gifted, intelligent and dedicated men who gave their lives in the service of the Empire'. He recalled his early days in Kenya and particularly his work at Isiolo where he 'enthusiastically set about' facing the challenge of the large influx of refugees from Abyssinia, and he commented on his energy, his compassion and his determination.

Of Armitage's Gold Coast contribution, Goldie remarked on the success with which he won Nkrumah and his colleagues' confidence, which 'undoubtedly played an important part in achieving a peaceful transition'. Turning to Cyprus and then Nyasaland, Goldie said that in neither case was time on his side: 'It was his great misfortune to achieve eminence in the Colonial Service just as the famous winds of change began to blow with mounting ferocity.' In Cyprus, he 'set about the task of reassuring the Turks and calming the Greeks' and Goldie felt that if Armitage had arrived two or three years earlier he might have been able to forestall the events that eventually led to the island's partition.

In Nyasaland, he truly believed a multiracial federation was an actual possibility, which 'could have become a model for the peaceful development of the whole of southern Africa'. 'But, as in Cyprus, the time needed for bridge building and the development of trust was lacking. The winds of change had become an uncontrollable hurricane.' Throughout all his appointments, Goldie continued, Armitage had a confidently relaxed and benign manner and he was wholly without pomposity and assertion. He 'carried his distinctions with a most persuasive modesty'. He spoke of him as 'a gifted administrator, with his calm, irenical and relaxed manner, and total transparent integrity'. Finally, he spoke of Armitage's devoted membership of the Church and his clear faith, which added much to his service in Africa and Cyprus:

[In] discharging his high office, it was clear that he was not just doing a job – he was quite simply faithfully fulfilling his vocation.

9

Missions Impossible

You were dealt an impossible hand.

Robert Armitage came from a classic colonial service background. His family served the Crown overseas. He was sent to a preparatory boarding school in England at a tender age while his parents remained in India. He went to a major public school – as had his father and uncles, and as did his sons. He did reasonably well both academically and athletically, but more importantly, from the Colonial Office point of view, he became headboy of both schools. He went on to Oxford – following a well-trodden path from Winchester to New College – and stayed an extra year to attend the colonial service course.

He was the great-great-grandson of a British prime minister. While only a schoolboy he met the Prince of Wales and Lloyd-George. Through his uncle, the prime minister's private secretary, he stayed with the Astors and met Britain's first two women MPs; his uncle became an MP, governor of Kenya and a peer. These connections put him at ease in the company of distinguished people and political leaders: later he was to work closely with Nkrumah, Makarios, Banda, Malvern, Dalhousie, Whitehead and Welensky, and to have important dealings with Churchill, Eden, Macmillan, Lyttelton, Lennox-Boyd, Macleod, Perth and Amery. He got on superbly well with the Queen Mother.

His career development and preparation for gubernatorial office was thorough – much more complete than that of any of his predecessors or his successor in Nyasaland. The early professional years were not unusual in being spent in the district administration, although he did become a district commissioner after six years, a relatively short time. His experience in field administration – learning at first hand the way of life, needs and problems of the African people he was administering – was wide and covered a range of environments and conditions. His work at Isiolo, in particular organizing and running the huge refugee camp, was an important step in his career. What he undertook and achieved there would astonish – in many cases daunt – those who much later in the twentieth century seek to relieve the hardships of refugees in Africa, backed as they are with massive – albeit inadequate – international aid and the resources of the UN High Commission for Refugees. After fewer than ten years in the field he was posted to the secretariat – again a significant, but not unusual, step although its timing was helpful. Here his experience was important for his future work: 'A stint in the Secretariat was essential for the ambitious, and gave officers a wide view of policy-making.'[1]

As clerk to legislative and executive councils and secretary of finance committee he was closely involved with Kenya's highest decision-making bodies. He was able to observe at close quarters the ways in which senior officials, leading expatriate non-officials and the governor operated; to learn, in effect, albeit vicariously, how governors govern. For a while, towards the end of his time in Kenya, he was himself a member of legislative council. The preparation of the annual estimates, gruellingly onerous work though it was, enabled – indeed forced – him to become intimately acquainted with the country's economy and the government's finances. It also gave him early experience – either directly himself or by observing others – of hard-nosed negotiation, during the discussions between the finance branch and heads of department and between the official and non-official members of finance committee.

In the secretariat, too, he had direct experience of an evolving ministerial system of government – an important constitutional development as Britain began to loosen its imperial hold – during the lead up to, and the very early days of, the 'member' system. This particular experience was valuable to him in the Gold Coast and Nyasaland and potentially valuable in Cyprus. His work in the secretariat brought him and his abilities to the attention of very senior officials and the governor. He became administrative secretary of Kenya shortly before leaving the country.

In the Gold Coast, his work was important from the point of view both of the country's peaceful and constructive advance to independence and of his own career. As a member of executive council and later of the cabinet, he was part of the top executive decision-making team, involved in all the major decisions made both in running the country and in guiding it peacefully to independence as the first black colony in Africa to become sovereign. As financial secretary and later minister of finance his knowledge of economic development and public finances and their management became profound. He was in many ways fortunate in the booming cocoa market and, as a consequence, some thought 'perhaps he was not fully extended'.[2] While this enabled him to finance many and expensive projects and to expand government services, two things need to be said.

First, the revenue to be derived from cocoa did not automatically drop into the treasury coffers. It, like the cocoa itself, needed to be harvested and managed. Under Armitage, cocoa added vast sums to the government's revenue because he taxed cocoa exports, taxed imports purchased with money earned by those growing and transporting cocoa, and taxed the income of those engaged in the cocoa industry. Managing the revenue once collected also tested his financial skills, for he successfully balanced exploiting the wealth of the cocoa industry with giving the Gold Coast people a feeling of economic wellbeing and confidence in the future. He successfully balanced, too, the use of revenue to expand current services with its use for longer term development, especially infrastructural and alternative income projects.

Second, being relatively flush with money did not automatically make his task of distributing the revenue any easier. Ministers of finance frequently have to make harsh and difficult decisions. Whereas in times of penury the decisions are inevitably harsher, they are not necessarily more difficult to make, for the solutions are often clear: one concentrates on the relatively few basics and rejects the rest. In times of plenty, the decisions once made may be less harsh but making them is often more difficult because the options are more numerous and the expectations – and therefore pressures to fulfil them – greater.

Armitage's contribution to the Gold Coast included teaching his successors the rudiments and then the finer details of public finance and its management. He bequeathed to them very substantial revenues and reserves with which to start the nation's life of independence on a sound footing. As a member of the governor's executive and legislative councils and the cabinet, and also as acting chief secretary, he learned at first hand more about how governors govern.

In his funeral oration, Goldie suggested that Armitage had been unfortunate in not reaching the top of his profession – the governorships of Cyprus and Nyasaland – a few years sooner. The timing was indeed crucial. In the late 1940s and early 1950s, under both socialist and conservative governments, economic development in the colonies was the prime consideration in the minds of the colonial powers and their officials. Political advancement could wait, first, because there seemed to be no need to hurry and, second, because a sound and well-managed economy was seen as an essential precondition to political autonomy. Given these circumstances, those governing the colonies needed experience, skill and flair in the field of economics and finance. Colby, appointed to Nyasaland as governor in 1948, had these attributes and put them to very great advantage during his period of office, especially during his first five years, but by 1954 economics had begun to give way to politics as the most important objective of colonial policy, certainly in the minds of the colonial peoples and increasingly in the minds of the colonial powers.

It was precisely at this time that Armitage was appointed a governor. The change in British attitudes and colonial policy was not sudden. Indeed, it was scarcely perceptible at the time, but, although he did not comment on it, for Armitage it was marked. His preparation for high office was thorough and, while it encompassed considerable political experience, it was particularly strong in the economic sphere. For him, the change was marked because, first, he moved from the Gold Coast, where economic development was still a major consideration, to Cyprus, where it was not nearly so important but where international political implications were pre-eminent. Then he moved to Nyasaland, where major economic development and most financial responsibilities had been removed from the protectorate to the federal government and where economic development was already sinking below the surface of the political pool, a surface already disturbed by ripples and occasionally waves of African opposition.

The problem, however, was not that the important environment was changing from one in which economic development was paramount to one where political development became supreme, nor that Armitage was solely prepared for the former – since his political experience and skills were considerable. The problem was that the tasks he was given were impossible to perform and the British government, in its retreat from imperialism, changed its policies determining those tasks without making it clear to him in advance that they were going to change or, indeed for some time in Nyasaland, that they had changed.

In Cyprus, he was told to introduce a constitution and was assured that, if the Cypriots did not accept it, it would none the less be imposed. Even an imposed constitution must be workable if it is to have practical significance. This means it must be sufficiently acceptable, because a government can not force people to become active members of the executive or legislature: enough have to be willing to be elected or nominated. It was clear to Armitage, as it must have been to the British government, that neither Turks, fearing Greek enosis, nor Greeks, yearning for enosis, wanted or would accept the sort of constitution Britain was prepared to grant. It was similarly clear that the only way to gain sufficient acceptance was to concede the principle of self-determination. This would readily win over the Greek Cypriots, and the Turks would have to suffer its imposition. This was a fairly sound Colonial Office way of looking at things, but the Foreign Office saw things differently and would not jettison Britain's traditional allies, the

Turks, for the Greeks whom Eden, the foreign secretary and then prime minister, thoroughly disliked.

In essence, Armitage was asked to perform a task – to introduce a constitution – and was then debarred from applying the only operable solution. Benson saw the task given to Armitage in Cyprus as 'one of the foulest that any man could be sent to tackle'.[3] William Teeling, an MP who visited Cyprus in April 1955, 'went away from the island feeling that [Armitage] had an absolutely hopeless task and [was] almost certain to be made a scapegoat'.[4] Even Altrincham felt that 'Cyprus was a cow (as the Australians say) to be saddled with.'[5] Armitage's mission was made impossible by those who gave it to him. It was not helped by the British government changing its mind over the fundamental point of permitting – indeed it encouraged – Greece and Turkey to be party to Britain's deliberations over the future status of Cyprus. Some three months after Armitage left Cyprus, General Keightley wrote to him about affairs on the island: 'We are all expecting HMG to agree to something [presumably a formula on self-determination] which if they had given to you to negotiate with six months ago would have avoided everything [that went wrong].'[6]

In Nyasaland he was instructed to win over the Africans to accept federation – which had been imposed on them. Again he was given an assurance – consistently voiced publicly by ministers – that federation was a permanent institution and would not be abolished. An imposed constitution would not have worked in Cyprus and an imposed federation was, from the Africans' point of view, not working in Nyasaland. It was not working politically and there were grave doubts about its economic benefits. Just as in Cyprus, where decades of pro-enosis stubbornness by the Greek majority had made it clear that self-determination was the only way forward acceptable to them, so in Nyasaland decades of anti-federation stubbornness by the African majority had made it clear that independence, with secession from the federation, was the only way forward acceptable to them.

As in Cyprus, where he came up with a solution – conceding the principle of self-determination – so he came up with a solution in Nyasaland. This fell well short of conceding the principle of secession because, rather than try to persuade the British government to give up its apparently firmly held principle – as he had, he thought unsuccessfully, in Cyprus – he proposed what now appears elementary yet which, surprisingly, was novel at the time: self-government within the federation, a form of regional autonomy. To gain a degree of African acceptance, even for this, would require him to keep out of the way those violently opposed to any idea of staying in the federation – Banda and his lieutenants – sufficiently long for more moderate leaders to emerge. Again, his mission was impossible and again the British government changed its mind, over negotiating with Banda and over the fundamental point of secession. As Gorell Barnes expressed it to him shortly before he retired: 'In the end it seems that you were dealt an impossible hand.'[7]

In both Cyprus and Nyasaland, he faced leaders commanding an overwhelming majority who were ruthless, immovable and would not negotiate or concede. Both, too, were men with strong church connections, which gave them a form of practical immunity and a good deal of external support, and both later proved themselves to be men of violence. He did not advise in Cyprus that self-determination should be granted, but merely that the possibility of ultimately conceding the principle of self-determination should be indicated. In Nyasaland, he did not go even this far, and for two reasons. First, to have advised any solution that involved the, even ultimate, concession of the principle of secession would have been utterly contrary to the task given to him: one can not win acceptance of something by abolishing it. Second, his current experience and belief was that the British government would not give way on the principle of secession in Nyasaland because it had not given way on the principle of self-determination in Cyprus. It is unlikely that he knew at this time that only a month after he left Cyprus Britain offered to concede the principle of self-determination. In both cases he needed time to wean the countries away from their demands and towards accepting the British principles: no enosis, no secession.

Did his previous experience in Kenya, the Gold Coast and Cyprus affect the way he reacted in Nyasaland?

In Kenya, he had become accustomed to the influence, in many respects the dominance, of European interests and European politicians over African interests and African politicians – of whom, at the time, there were very few and none had reached prominence. There were similarities between Kenya and central Africa in this respect, but it is unlikely he was influenced by them. While there was European dominance in central Africa – in Southern Rhodesia and the federation – this was not the case in Nyasaland, where the expatriate population was small and African interests had long been paramount.

In the intervening years, too, powerful African politicians had emerged in Nyasaland, as they had in Kenya, and Armitage had served in the Gold Coast where African interests and African politicians were overwhelmingly dominant. His views on race relations in Africa and on the effect of South African policies on the future of the Commonwealth, which he recorded privately on his way to Nyasaland, are revealing. Three years before Macmillan's 'wind of change' speech in Cape Town, Armitage was clear that maintaining apartheid was impossible, that the 'blind surge to increase apartheid' was coinciding with a 'liberal sentiment throughout the world', which was increasingly forcing the white races to tolerate the coloured races. He believed that at some stage even the nationalists in South Africa would acknowledge that they had to come to terms with the non-white countries.

Armitage must have been struck by some of the similarities between what happened in the Gold Coast and what happened in Nyasaland. For example, in the Accra riots there were intelligence reports that revolutionary plans included assassination and terrorism. The emergency declared by Arden-Clarke kept Nkrumah out of the way for several months and enabled the government to restore law and order fairly quickly. In the meantime, CPP branches were organized on a nationwide basis and Nkrumah – more clearly now than ever the leader of the African masses – achieved self-government very soon after his release from prison. In each of these cases there were close parallels in Nyasaland.

Banda modelled himself on Nkrumah and wanted for Nyasaland what Nkrumah had achieved for the Gold Coast. One might expect Armitage's Gold Coast experience substantially to affect his reaction in Nyasaland. In West Africa he had worked hard, dedicatedly, amicably and successfully with leading African politicians, helping them to achieve statehood, and Britain to withdraw, at a relatively fast pace. Why did he not do the same in Nyasaland? The reasons are threefold.

First, the Gold Coast's future, in Armitage's early days there, was determined by a Labour government in Britain, which was committed to rapid advance to independence in the colonies. Nyasaland's future, however, was determined by a Conservative government, which was less convinced, in Armitage's early days there, of the wisdom of such speedy progress.

Second, Nyasaland, unlike the Gold Coast, was confined within a federation. This meant that whereas Arden-Clarke had externally to deal with (and take into consideration the views of) only the British government, Armitage in Nyasaland had to deal with (and take into consideration the views of) not only the British government but also the federal and Southern and Northern Rhodesia governments. It was this factor that prevented Armitage from moving forward with working out Nyasaland's constitutional advance, as Arden-Clarke had done while Nkrumah was in prison. In addition, the federal and Southern Rhodesia governments were European dominated and the Northern Rhodesia government had a powerful European element in its executive and legislative councils. The less powerful Europeans in his own legislative council in Nyasaland were of little help to him. They played an extremely dangerous game in refusing to produce constitutional proposals and using this refusal as a lever to try and secure the federalization of non-African agriculture. Indeed, it could be claimed that their tactics, which caused considerable delay in Armitage's ability to produce his own proposals, were a major cause of the African political unrest, feeling of exasperation and violence, which resulted in the declaration of the state of emergency and the deaths and other hardships that followed from it. It has been argued that Armitage paid too close attention to the wishes of Welensky, but this ignores the fact that his task was to help make the federation work and he could hardly do so by taking an independent line and ignoring the wishes of the federal prime minister. The task given to him required that he work closely with the heads of the other governments in central Africa and these included Welensky and Whitehead.

Third, whereas there were many well-educated Africans in the Gold Coast, of whom a significant number had experience in administration in the civil service, Nyasaland lacked a similar group. The general feeling in government was that this prevented an early move along the path to self-government and the loosening of imperial control. Preparing the African civil service for higher-level administration was hampered by a large proportion of Nyasaland African civil servants, especially the more skilled ones, being in the federal service and thus outside Armitage's control. He pressed Welensky – as had Colby – to train and promote Africans in the federal civil service and army.

Towards the end of his term of office, he himself appointed Adu, with whom he had worked in West Africa, to advise on methods of localizing the Nyasaland service. It had been on Armitage's advice that a localization office had been created in the Gold Coast. Adu's view, expressed privately to Armitage, was that the MCP was 'very inexperienced and [had] no idea how they [would] run a government and [had] no people to get promoted in [the] civil service except with considerable risks'.[8]

Briefly, the progressive elements of the Gold Coast experience covered matters that Armitage's successor in Nyasaland, rather than he himself – unless his term of office had been extended – could, if he had similar experience, have put to good use. This included the experience of encouraging, teaching and working with African ministers, of training and promoting African civil servants while retaining the services and maintaining the morale of expatriates, and of organizing the required machinery of government as the country moved speedily towards independence. In this sense, Armitage reached the top of his profession and arrived in Nyasaland a few years too early rather than too late.

What was the effect of his Cyprus experience on the way in which

Armitage reacted in Nyasaland? Both countries had a strategic significance for Britain. In Cyprus, the significance was military and diplomatic, involving a number of Britain's allies and the security of the Middle East. In central Africa, the significance was ideological: creating a bulwark against apartheid from the south and communism from the north, and the opportunity, it was hoped, to build a genuine nonracial state – a state from which Britain could withdraw with a clearer conscience.

It is not surprising that the strategy in the Middle East was seen as more important than that in central Africa. Immediate military, naval and air bases in the Mediterranean, on the vulnerable southern flank of Europe, may well have seemed more important than eventual nonracial political, economic and social institutions the other side of the equator especially if, as Macmillan's Cape Town speech was designed to assist, South Africa took a less racially discriminating stance in the future. Also, while Britain could readily retreat from its immediate responsibilities in Africa, it could not safely withdraw from them in like manner in the Middle East.

The immediate fate of Cyprus during Armitage's time was decided by Macmillan as foreign secretary, that of Nyasaland by Macmillan as prime minister. In both cases, because responsibilities were divided between different cabinet ministers and separate departments of state, British policy was less well-balanced, less coordinated, less stable and less clear than it could have been. Cyprus was the responsibility of the Colonial Office, but the Foreign Office had a major, indeed overriding, interest in it. Nyasaland was the responsibility of the Colonial Office, but the federation was the responsibility of the Commonwealth Relations Office.[9] Compared with both Cyprus and Nyasaland, the Gold Coast's governor had a much simpler set of external government departments with which to deal.

Armitage has been criticized for acting too slowly and too gently in Cyprus and too quickly and too firmly in Nyasaland in dealing with violence.[10] One could argue that this was indeed the case and that he learned from his Cyprus experience that ruthless terrorism could rapidly escalate and include murder and must be stamped on vigorously. Again, two things need to be said. First, there is a great deal of evidence that he was not personally intimidated by events in Cyprus, including attempts on his life. He resented rather than welcomed the security arrangements made to safeguard him. Indeed, he was quite fearless, though not foolishly so. Second, whereas in Cyprus he had no doubt about murder being committed and increasingly so – because it actually happened – in Nyasaland he had considerable doubt about it and was able to pre-empt any that might have been planned.

Would, as Goldie suggested, more time have made a difference? Certainly time was exceedingly short. Armitage – who frequently said that a 'breathing space' was necessary – inherited decades of opposition to Britain's colonial policy both in Cyprus and in Nyasaland, and his time in which to accomplish anything was very limited. Britain's imperial retreat – though sounded on muted trumpets and effected by a series of ad hoc tactical withdrawals – was already under way. Britain was in the process of pulling out of Egypt and needed Cyprus for its bases. In central Africa the federal review was due in 1960 and Malvern was already bidding for dominion status. Yet it was not just a question of time. The wind blowing through Africa was not simply a wind that drove things faster, it was primarily a wind of *change*.

What was being done as well as how fast it was being done both changed dramatically. Only a month after Armitage left Cyprus, his successor, Harding, handed Makarios a document in which the British government conceded the Cypriots' right to self-determination – exactly what Armitage had recommended so strongly but Britain had adamantly and consistently rejected. During his final months in Nyasaland – and after his retirement had been announced – the Monckton Commission acknowledged that 'there should be an opportunity [for Nyasaland] to withdraw from the [federation]' – precisely what the British government had instructed Armitage to avoid. Nyasaland seceded and the federation was abolished three years later.

What was Armitage's approach to change and the pace of change? His guiding philosophy in administration was to decide what was the right thing to do and then accept as little alteration to it on political grounds as possible.[11] This is a praiseworthy amalgam of the ethical and the pragmatic but it frequently puts the public servant holder of the philosophy in the position of appearing to resist the will of the politician who places the pragmatic above the ethical or who simply does not share the same view as to what is right. It frequently puts the holder of the philosophy, too, in the position of appearing to fight a rearguard action, giving ground only when forced to do so by politicians.

In Cyprus, Armitage believed that the British government should concede the principle of eventual self-determination – even though this risked enosis at some stage – and he strongly recommended this course of action to the government. Since the Foreign Office, especially the secretary of state, Macmillan, and the prime minister, Eden, did not at the time share the same view, Armitage was at odds with them. In Nyasaland, he believed that the Congress leaders should be kept in gaol or out of the country while more moderate leaders emerged with whom he could negotiate constitutional advance within the federation and with whom there could be built a more peaceful, democratic and prosperous future than he believed would otherwise be the case. He strongly recommended this course. Since, however, the Colonial Office, especially the secretary of state, Macleod, and the prime minister, now Macmillan, did not share the same view after the October 1959 general election, Armitage was at odds with them – with Macmillan for the second time.

Once events reached the point in Nyasaland at which it was no longer possible to argue that the same course of action was right – that Banda and the remainder of the non-hard-core detainees should be kept in gaol, for they had been released – Armitage changed the approach to his task. Now, to continue to pursue his mission – winning the Africans over to accepting federation, even if it was a different form of federal association – he needed to do it in cooperation with Banda. This was less a question of bending with the political wind than it was of deciding on the right thing to do to accomplish his mission. Although he could recognize as well as any, and a good deal better than most, which way the wind was blowing, no one had altered the task given to him. His mission remained the same as previously, though his means of accomplishing it had changed.

In many ways, this change led to Armitage's greatest contribution to Nyasaland. Quickly and firmly, but in an unflustered manner – almost as a matter of course – he laid the foundations of the road upon which his successor could take Nyasaland relatively peacefully and amicably to independence. He accomplished this during the final five months of his service. He felt that two years of his governorship had been wasted, and the remaining months were important. Others in Armitage's position would have reacted differently.

He already knew that he would not stay on as governor and that he would leave in April 1961.[12] He had not been treated as honestly by Macleod as he could have been. Indeed, he later confessed that Macleod had made his existence 'a misery' by his ruthlessness, his forcefulness, his failure to listen to arguments, his bulldozing manner, his deviousness, his manipulations and his treatment of people as chess pieces or playing cards rather than as human beings. Armitage did 'not have much time' for Macleod. He would have had less had he known, for example, that the secretary of state had shown discourtesy and lack of loyalty in conversation with at least one expatriate non-official in the country at a particularly sensitive time.

On the afternoon of Banda's release from detention Macleod asked a pro-Congress businessman to see him at Government House. When the businessman explained his reluctance on the grounds that he was not welcome in Government House because the governor did not approve of him, Macleod replied, 'Bugger Armitage; I've sent him up the mountain with a picnic basket.' Armitage believed that Macleod's trouble was that 'he had no human approach to the people he was meeting.' The most important thing about Armitage himself, which the subsequently hard-core Eoka terrorist, Neophytos Sofocleous, recalled decades later, was his treatment of everyone as human beings. In Nyasaland, there was a growing feeling at the end of 1960 and beginning of 1961 that Macleod had overplayed his hand within the Conservative government. Armitage was approaching the end of a long and frequently arduous career. He had little to lose.

The period between Armitage's return from leave in November 1960 and his departure in April 1961 is a fascinating one. For critical parts of this period he was virtually on his own at the top of government, all but one of his executive councillor officials – and fortunately a very good one, Kettlewell – were away, and for all but a few days he was without the services of his chief secretary, the person who was to succeed him. The men of violence, Banda's radical lieutenants, were out of detention, free to roam the country at will and stir up what trouble they wished, and for crucial parts of the time Banda was not there to attempt to restrain them. The Europeans were anxious about the future. The politically active Africans, especially the MCP and LMY, were feeling triumphant. The appointment of a new and possibly more malleable governor, who had quickly released the remaining and very hard-core detainees soon after Armitage went on leave, had been announced, internal self-government was theirs and secession could not be far behind. Macleod was unlikely to stop them. Seen from Government House it could have been an awesome prospect.

On his return to Nyasaland from leave, Armitage discussed the London conference with his senior officials and said that 'Banda seemed to be the leader at present. So whatever else happened, we must so regard him and never let these people get at arms' length again.'[13] This was the first step, a most important recognition and instruction, which marked a vital turning point in the way he wished to proceed. He then had to ensure that his relationships with Banda were good. They had always got on fairly well, although naturally they had treated each other circumspectly. He had made a particular point of asking Banda to meet him in June 1958 before the doctor's return to Nyasaland. He had ensured that he met him immediately he was released from detention and that the meeting took place at Government House. He had a long discussion with him just before the July 1960 conference, said he was pleased they could have a talk and hoped that all would go well. He had gone out of his way to talk amicably with him at Perth's reception after the conference.

Their next meeting three months later was an interesting one. Banda was clearly very much at ease and Armitage let him speak at length about his visits to West Africa and London before gently moving the conversation round to the point where he could deliver the rebuke Macleod had requested. Then, clearly, firmly but without rancour, Armitage gave the doctor a ticking off. This very much took Banda aback and there were several moments of guilty shock before he could recover and apologize for his attacks on the judiciary and the police – although he said they were true. The effect, no doubt intended, was to show Banda that Armitage was not a pushover, that he was still in charge, that Macleod was prepared to accept his view in finding fault in the doctor and have him deliver a rebuke, but he did it in a way that Banda accepted and of which he did not take advantage.

Armitage deliberately used Youens – although the secretary for African affairs was available – to see and have talks with Banda because he knew that they got on well together. He was worried about the doctor not having a programme of public activities (he was concentrating too much on his medical practice) mainly because he felt that this was denying senior civil servants any guidance on the policies he would shortly wish to pursue. He may also have had in mind that the lack of a public programme weakened Banda's influence on the populace at large both to enhance personal support and to restrain law breakers, as well as providing a partial vacuum into which Chipembere and Chiume could move.

Armitage may well have realized, too, that by remaining firmly in charge and clamping down on violence, he was in fact supporting Banda and giving him as good a start on the road to self-government as he could. He had spoken on a number of occasions about the need to separate Banda from his more extreme lieutenants and followers, and he prosecuted Chipembere and Congress leaders from Karonga and Port Herald. They were all convicted and kept out of the way for some years. Banda did not demur. The governor was pleased that the country was sufficiently quiet for the courts to catch up on the backlog of cases, many of them involving intimidation and violence. In all this, Armitage was careful not to rock the boat unnecessarily. He contemplated prosecuting Chiume, but did not do so, initially because he thought this might stir up trouble but later because he felt Chiume was not a man of much consequence.

He even discussed prosecuting Banda, but this was never a real possibility and he advised against it. Presumably, he had to go through the motions so as not to alienate, for example, his attorney-general. Constitutionally, of course, it was the attorney-general's responsibility to decide on prosecutions, but the extent to which Armitage made the decisions shows how much he really was in charge. He was careful, too, to discuss with the chief justice his reprimand of Banda before he delivered it. He resisted the pressure Dixon and Blackwood put on him to prosecute Banda and others for doubtful or minor breaches of the law; and he resisted the district commissioner at Port Herald's pressure to ban political meetings in his district. He was keen that the police should use their discretion on such occasions. He was particularly anxious that there should be no provocation that could damage the proceedings at the federal review conference.

Throughout all of this, he tried to bring the expatriate civil service round to accepting the changes and to working cooperatively with the law-abiding elements of the MCP. This was especially clear during the registration of voters for Nyasaland's first general election, when there was gratifying cooperation between the administration and the party. He used his farewell visits, which covered the whole of the country and involved many arduous days and much hard travelling, to rally the civil servants, expatriates generally and, where he could, the chiefs to accept the changes and to show them that the government still cared about them. He also used his time energetically to prepare for events after his departure so that as much as possible would be ready for his successor. In particular, he ensured that the registration of voters proceeded efficiently apace and he worked out the details of the ministerial system of government, which was shortly to be introduced. In the former case, he – and only he – had first-hand top level experience of general elections from his days in the Gold Coast. In the latter case, he – and only he – had first-hand top level experience of ministerial government from his days in Kenya and the Gold Coast.

On his return from Armitage's funeral service, John Grigg, who had been pageboy at the Armitages' wedding 60 years previously, a distinguished journalist, wrote to Jeremy about his father: 'He had rotten luck in the latter part of his career, but the early part was a great success story. Even Cyprus and Nyasaland were successes in the fundamental sense that his reputation for decency and integrity wasn't tarnished by either.'[14] This was true, but the closing months of his career in Nyasaland were also a great practical success. In these last five months of his governorship, Armitage was able to call on, and put to good use, the experience he had gained and the skills he had developed over the preceding three decades. He cleared the ground and smoothed the road for his successor in a way that made this part in many respects the most successful of his whole career.

When he resigned as secretary of state in October 1959, Lennox-Boyd wrote to Robert Armitage and thanked him for his 'stalwart and courageous work and for [his] constant help and support'.[15] Paradoxically, however, the most telling appreciation of his service to the crown and to the colonies came from the person whom in the whole of his service he least admired: the man who succeeded Lennox-Boyd. It was an appreciation that succinctly covered his contribution to the four colonies in which he had served. Just before the end of Armitage's retirement leave, Macleod wrote to him a personal letter in which he thanked him for all he had done throughout his 'long and distinguished career in the Colonial Service':

> I have been glad to learn of the many tributes paid to the exceptional administrative ability which marked the 19 years of your service in Kenya and to your great success when in charge of financial matters in the Gold Coast. In looking at the difficult and arduous period of your governorship of Cyprus, I recall the praise of your qualities and of your administration there which my predecessor expressed in the House of Commons on 5 December 1955. You accepted its termination in very exceptional circumstances with characteristic public spirit and were then called upon to serve in Nyasaland, where you were soon faced with a situation of great and mounting difficulty. You won the respect and affection of those who served under you in these testing times and I gladly take this opportunity to express my appreciation of the leadership you gave them in facing the many problems which arose.[16]

Biographical Notes

AMERY, Julian, b. 1919; war correspondent, Spanish Civil War, 1938–9; served Second World War in RAF and Army; MP, 1950–66 and 1969–92; Parliamentary Under-Secretary of State and Financial Secretary, War Office, 1957–8; Parliamentary Under-Secretary of State, Colonial Office, 1958–60; Secretary of State for Air, 1960–2; Minister of Aviation, 1962–4; Minister of Public Buildings and Works, 1970; Minister for Housing and Construction, 1970–2; Minister of State, Foreign and Commonwealth Office, 1972–4; created Baron AMERY of LUSTLEIGH, PRESTON and BRIGHTON, 1992.

ARDEN-CLARKE, Charles Noble, b. 1898; served in First World War, 1917; Colonial Administrative Service, Nigeria, 1920; Principal Assistant Secretary, 1934; Secretary to the Government of Bechuanaland, 1936; Resident Commissioner, Bechuanaland, 1937–42; Resident Commissioner, Basutoland, 1942–6; Governor of Sarawak, 1946–9; Governor of the Gold Coast, 1949–57; Governor-General of the Gold Coast, 1957; member of the Monckton Commission, 1960; CMG, 1941; Kt., 1946; KCMG, 1948; GCMG, 1952; d. 1962.

BANDA, Aleke, b. 1939; educated Southern Rhodesia; arrested 1959 and briefly detained; deported to Nyasaland; co-founder, with Orton Chirwa, of Malawi Congress Party; founder of *Malawi News*; secretary-general Malawi Congress Party, 1966; held various ministerial posts; dismissed 1973 and subsequently detained.

BANDA, Hastings Kamuzu, b. probably 1898; medical practitioner and politician; worked in Southern Rhodesia and South Africa as a young man; educated USA and Scotland; practised medicine Liverpool, Tyneside and London, 1939–53 and Ghana 1953–8; returned to Nyasaland 1958 and took over leadership of Nyasaland African Congress; detained 1959 in Gwelo gaol, Southern Rhodesia; released 1960; Minister of Natural Resources and Local Government, 1961–3; Prime Minister of Nyasaland and then Malawi, 1963–6; President of Malawi, 1966–94.

BANDA, Thamar Dillon Thomas; politician; President-General, Nyasaland African Congress, 1957; dismissed from office, 1958; founded Congress Liberation Party 1960.

BARROW, Michael Palliser, b. 1900; planter and politician, Nyasaland; Member of Legislative Council, 1943–53; of Executive Council, 1943–53; Deputy Prime Minister, Defence, Economic Affairs and Power, Federation of Rhodesia and Nyasaland, 1953–63; CBE, 1948; Kt., 1953; d. 1973.

BENSON, Arthur Edward Trevor, b. 1907; Colonial Administrative Service, Northern Rhodesia, 1932; Colonial Office, 1939; Prime Minister's Office,

1940–2; Cabinet Office, 1942–3; Colonial Office 1943–4; Northern Rhodesia, 1944–6; Administrative Secretary, Uganda, 1946–9; Chief Secretary, Central Africa Council, 1949–51; Chief Secretary, Nigeria, 1951–4; Governor, Northern Rhodesia, 1954–9; CMG, 1952; KCMG, 1954; GCMG, 1959; d. 1987.

BIRGI, Muharrem Nuri, b. 1908; diplomat; entered Turkish Foreign Ministry, 1932; 3rd, 2nd and then 1st Secretary, Turkish embassy, Warsaw, 1935–9; Ministry of Foreign Affairs, 1939–41; 1st Secretary, Turkish embassy, Paris-Vichy, 1941, then transferred to Madrid; various posts in Ministry of Foreign Affairs, 1945–57; Turkish ambassador to the Court of Saint James's, 1957–60; Turkish permanent representative to NATO, 1960–71; retired 1972; d. 1986.

BLACKWOOD, Michael Hill, b. 1917; lawyer and politician; Member of Legislative Council, Nyasaland, 1954; Member of Executive Council, 1956; CBE, 1963.

BRANIGAN, Patrick Francis, b. 1906; called to Irish Bar 1928; Colonial Administrative Service, Kenya, 1931; Crown Counsel, Tanganyika, 1934; Solicitor-General, Northern Rhodesia, 1938; Legal Secretary to Government of Malta, 1946–8; Minister of Justice and Attorney-General, the Gold Coast, 1948–54; Kt., 1954.

BROOKE-POPHAM, Henry Robert Moore, b. 1878; commissioned into Oxfordshire Light Infantry, 1898; Royal Flying Corps, 1912; Director of Research, Air Ministry, 1919; various senior posts in RAF, 1921–36; Principal ADC to the King, 1933; Governor of Kenya, 1937–9; DSO, 1915; AFC, 1918; CMG, 1918; CB, 1919; KCB, 1927; GCVO, 1935; d. 1953.

CALDICOTT, John Moore, b. 1900; farmer, Southern Rhodesia; MP 1948; Federal Minister of Agriculture and Lands, 1951; Minister of Agriculture, Health and Public Services, 1953, Economic Affairs, 1958–63; CMG, 1955; KBE, 1963; d. 1986.

CHIPEMBERE, Henry Blasius Masauko, b. 1930; politician; graduated Fort Hare University College, South Africa; District Assistant, Nyasaland civil service; Member of Legislative Council, Nyasaland, 1956; Treasurer of Nyasaland African Congress 1958; detained during state of emergency, 1959–60; released 1960; convicted of sedition 1961; released 1963; Minister of Local Government 1963–4; Minister of Education 1964; resigned from office 1964; led unsuccessful armed rebellion 1965; evacuated to live in USA, 1966–75, with temporary return to Tanzania, 1966–9; d. 1975.

CHIRWA, Orton Edgar Chingoli, b. 1920; teacher, lawyer and politician; educated Zambia; schoolteacher; Fort Hare University College, South Africa, 1947–51 where he graduated BA and B.Ed. with a diploma in Education; returned to Nyasaland in 1951 and taught at teacher training college; London, studying law, 1955–8; called to Bar 1958; returned again to Nyasaland and became legal adviser to Nyasaland African Congress, 1958; briefly detained in emergency, 1959; founded Malawi Congress Party 1959; various ministerial posts – Parliamentary Secretary, Minister of Justice, Attorney-General 1961–4; dismissed from office September 1964; lived in exile in East Africa; returned to Malawi; detained in prison where he died in early 1990s.

CHIRWA, Wellington Manoah, b. 1916; schoolteacher and politician; trained as a teacher; headmaster, Nkata Bay, 1936: Clerk to Tonga Tribal Council; Secretary local Teachers' Association; Chairman, West Nyasa Native Association; 1938–47 taught in Southern Rhodesia; Principal, Gloag Ranch mission school; 1945–6 journalist, Southern Rhodesia; returned to teaching; Fort Hare University College, South Africa, 1948–52; Chairman of Nyasaland Students' Association and of Students' Representative Council; BA 1951; teacher's diploma, 1952; returned to Nyasaland and briefly resumed schoolteaching, 1952; elected as Nyasaland African Provincial Councils' representative to National Assembly of the Federation of Rhodesia and Nyasaland, 1953; Member of African Affairs Board; expelled from Nyasaland African Congress, 1958; member of Monckton Commission 1960; voluntary exile in England from 1960, teaching and engaged in charity and human rights work.

CHISIZA, Dunduzu, b. 1930; worked in Southern Rhodesia; Secretary-General Nyasaland African Congress, 1958–9; detained during state of emergency, 1959–60; Parliamentary Secretary, Ministry of Finance, 1961; d. 1962.

CHIUME, Murray William Kanyama, b. 1929; teacher and politician; educated Tanganyika and Uganda; taught in Tanganyika; returned to Nyasaland; Member of Legislative Council, Nyasaland 1956; Publicity Secretary, Nyasaland African Congress, 1958; overseas during state of emergency, 1959–60; Minister of Education 1961–4; Minister of External Affairs, 1964; dismissed from office September, 1964; lived in exile in East Africa, 1964–94.

COHEN, Andrew Benjamin, b. 1909; Home Civil Service, 1932, Inland Revenue; transferred to Colonial Office, 1933; seconded to Malta, 1940; Assistant Secretary, Colonial Office, 1943; Assistant Under-Secretary, Africa Division, 1947; Governor of Uganda, 1952; Permanent Representative, UN Trusteeship Council, 1957; Director-General, Department of Technical Cooperation, 1961; Permanent Secretary, Ministry of Overseas Development, 1964; OBE, 1942; CMG, 1948; KCMG, 1952; KCVO, 1954; d. 1968.

COLBY, Geoffrey Francis Taylor, b. 1901; Colonial Administrative Service, Nigeria, 1925; Principal Assistant Secretary, 1939; Director of Supplies, 1943; Administrative Secretary, 1945; Governor of Nyasaland, 1948–56; CMG, 1947; KCMG, 1949; d. 1958.

CREASEY, Gerald Hallen, b. 1897; served in First World War, 1916–18; Home Civil Service, Colonial Office, 1920–45; Chief Secretary, West Africa Council, 1945; Governor of the Gold Coast, 1948–9; Governor of Malta, 1949–54; OBE, 1937; CMG, 1943; KCMG, 1946; KCVO, 1954; d. 1983.

DURRELL, Lawrence George, b. 1912; poet, journalist and novelist; early journalism and press work in Middle East and Mediterranean; Director of Public Relations, Cyprus, 1954–6; d. 1990.

EDEN, Robert Anthony, b. 1897; served First World War, 1915–19; Member of Parliament, 1923–57; Parliamentary Private Secretary to Secretary of State for Foreign Affairs, 1926–9; Parliamentary Under-Secretary, Foreign Office, 1931–3; Lord Privy Seal, 1934–5; Minister without Portfolio, 1935; Secretary of State for Foreign Affairs, 1935–8; Secretary of State for Dominion Affairs, 1939–40; Secretary of State for War, 1940; Secretary of State for Foreign Affairs, 1940–5; Leader of House of Commons, 1942–5;

Deputy Leader of the Opposition, 1945–51; Secretary of State for Foreign Affairs and Deputy Prime Minister, 1951–5; Prime Minister and First Lord of the Treasury, 1955–7; KG, 1954; created first EARL of AVON, 1961; d. 1977.

FINNEY, Philip Edmund Stanley, b. 1904; Indian Police, 1924–47; commerce 1948–59; head of Special Branch, Nyasaland Police, 1959–64; OBE, 1947; CPM, 1960.

FLETCHER-COOKE, John, b. 1911; Colonial Office, Assistant Principal, 1937; Private Secretary to successive permanent under-secretaries of state for the Colonies, 1937; Malayan civil service, 1937–40; Under-Secretary Government of Palestine, 1946–8; Member of Executive Council, 1947; duties with United Nations, 1948–50; Colonial Secretary, Cyprus, 1951–5; CMG, 1952; Kt., 1962; d. 1989.

FOOTMAN, Charles Worthington Fowden, b. 1905; Colonial Administrative Service, Zanzibar, 1930; seconded to East African Governors' Conference, 1942; seconded to Colonial Office, 1943–6; Financial Secretary, Nyasaland, 1947; Chief Secretary, Nyasaland, 1950–60; Chairman, Public Service Commissions, Tanganyika and Zanzibar, 1960–1; Commonwealth Relations Office, 1962–4; Ministry of Overseas Development, 1964–70; CMG, 1952; d. 1996.

GLENDAY, Vincent Goncalves, b. 1891; Colonial Administrative Service, Kenya, 1913; Senior DC and DO in charge Northern Frontiers, 1934; PC 1934; Governor and Commander-in-Chief, Somaliland, 1939–42; Colonial Office, 1942–3; British Agent, East Aden, 1944; OBE, 1929; KCMG, 1942; d. 1970.

GORELL BARNES, William Lethbridge, b. 1909; Diplomatic Service, 1932–9; offices of the War Cabinet, 1939–45; Personal Assistant to Lord President of the Council, 1942–5; Personal Assistant to the Prime Minister, 1946–8; seconded to Colonial Office, 1948; Assistant Under-Secretary of State, 1948–59; d. 1987.

GRIGG, Edward William Macleay, b. 1879; editorial staff, *The Times*, 1903; assistant editor, *Outlook*, 1905; head of colonial department, *The Times*, 1908; joint editor, *Round Table*, 1913; served with Grenadier Guards in First World War; military secretary to Prince of Wales in Canada, Australia and New Zealand, 1919; Private Secretary to Prime Minister, 1921; elected Member of Parliament, 1922; Secretary of Rhodes Trust, Oxford, 1923; Governor of Kenya, 1925–31; MC, 1917; DSO, 1918; CVO, 1919; CMG, 1919; KCVO, 1920; KCMG, 1928; PC, 1944; created first Baron ALTRINCHAM of TORMARTON, 1945; d. 1955.

GRUBB, Kenneth George, b. 1900; Chairman, Council of Churches on International Affairs 1946–68; Chairman, House of Laity, Church Assembly, 1959–70; d. 1980.

HONE, Evelyn Dennison, b. 1911; Colonial Administrative Service, Tanganyika, 1935; Secretary to the Government of Seychelles, 1944; Assistant Secretary, Palestine, 1946; Colonial Secretary, British Honduras, 1948; Chief Secretary, Aden, 1953; Chief Secretary, Northern Rhodesia, 1957; Governor of Northern Rhodesia, 1959–64; OBE, 1946; CMG, 1953; CVO, 1954; KCMG, 1959; GCMG, 1965; d. 1979.

JONES, Glyn Smallwood, b. 1908; Colonial Administrative Service, Northern Rhodesia, 1931; Commissioner, Native Development, 1951; Provincial Commissioner, 1955; Secretary for Native Affairs, 1958; Minister for Native Affairs, 1959; Chief Secretary, Nyasaland, 1960; Governor of Nyasaland, 1961–4; Governor-General of Malawi, 1964–6; d. 1992.

KETTLEWELL, Richard Wildman, b. 1910; Colonial Agricultural Service, 1934; served in Army in East Africa, Middle East and Ceylon, 1939–43; Director of Agriculture, 1951; Secretary for Natural Resources, 1959; retired 1962; CMG, 1955; d. 1994.

KING, Ralph Malcolm MacDonald, b. 1911; solicitor, Hong Kong, 1936–41; prisoner of war 1941–5; Colonial Legal Service, Somaliland, 1947–50; Solicitor-General, Nyasaland, 1953; Attorney-General, Nyasaland, 1957–61; Legal Draftsman, Northern Nigeria, 1963–7; OBE, 1968; d. 1997.

LENNOX-BOYD, Alan Tindal, b. 1904; President, Oxford Union, 1926; MP, 1931–60; Parliamentary Secretary, Ministry of Labour, 1938–9; Ministry of Home Security, 1939; Ministry of Food, 1939–40; RNVR, 1940–3; Ministry of Aircraft Production, 1943–5; Minister of State for Colonial Affairs, 1951–2; Minister for Transport and Civil Aviation, 1952–4; Secretary of State for the Colonies, 1954–9; joined family firm of Arthur Guinness, 1960; CH and created first Viscount BOYD of MERTON, 1960; d. 1983.

LLOYD, Thomas Ingram Kynaston, b. 1896; Assistant Principal, Ministry of Health, 1920; transferred to Colonial Office, 1921; Principal, 1929; Assistant Secretary, 1939; Assistant Under-Secretary of State, 1943; Permanent Under-Secretary of State, 1947–56; CMG, 1943; KCMG, 1947; KCB, 1949; GCMG 1951; d. 1968.

LYTTELTON, Oliver, b. 1893; MP, Aldershot, 1940–54; President Board of Trade, 1940–1; various ministerial posts 1940–5; Secretary of State for the Colonies, 1951–4; PC, 1940; created first Viscount CHANDOS of ALDERSHOT, 1954; KG, 1970; d. 1972.

MACLEOD, Iain Norman, b. 1913; with De La Rue's, 1935–8; student, Inner Temple, 1938–9; war service, 1939–45; Conservative parliamentary secretariat, 1946; head of home affairs research department of Conservative Party, 1948–50; MP, 1950; Minister of Health, 1952–5; Minister of Labour and National Service, 1955–9; Secretary of State for the Colonies, 1959–61; Chancellor of the Duchy of Lancaster and Leader of the House of Commons 1961–3; d. 1970.

MACMILLAN, Maurice Harold, b. 1894; served in First World War, 1914–18; ADC to Governor-General of Canada, 1919–20; MP, 1924–9 and 1931–64; Parliamentary Secretary, Ministry of Supply, 1940–2; Parliamentary Under-Secretary of State for the Colonies, 1942; Minister Resident at Allied Head-quarters, North West Africa, 1942–5; Secretary for Air, 1945; Minister of Housing and Local Government, 1951–4; Minister of Defence, 1954–5; Secretary of State for Foreign Affairs, 1955; Chancellor of the Exchequer, 1955–7; Prime Minister and First Lord of the Treasury, 1957–63; FRS, 1962; OM, 1976; created first Earl STOCKTON, 1984; d. 1986.

MAKARIOS III, b. Michael Mouskos, 1913; Greek Cypriot ecclesiastic and politician; deacon, 1938; priest, 1946; Bishop of Kitium, 1948; Archbishop and Ethnarch, 1950; exiled to the Seychelles 1956; returned, to Athens, 1957;

returned to Cyprus, 1959; elected President of Cyprus, 1959, re-elected 1968 and 1973; d. 1977.

MANNINGHAM-BULLER, Reginald Edward, b. 1905; called to the Bar, 1927; MP, 1943–62; Parliamentary Secretary to the Minister of Works, 1945; Solicitor-General, 1951–4; Attorney-General, 1954–62; Lord High Chancellor, 1962–4; Kt., 1951; created Baron 1963; created first Viscount DILHORNE of GREEN'S NORTON, 1964; Lord of Appeal in Ordinary, 1969–80; d. 1980.

MITCHELL, Philip Euen, b. 1890; Colonial Administrative Service, Nyasaland, 1912; KAR, 1915–18; ADC and Private Secretary to the Governor of Nyasaland, 1918; transferred to Tanganyika, Assistant Political Officer, 1919; Assistant Secretary for Native Affairs, 1926; Provincial Commissioner, 1928; Chief Secretary, 1934; Governor of Uganda, 1935; Political Adviser to General Wavell, 1941; British Plenipotentiary in Ethiopia and Chief Political Officer to GOC East Africa, 1942; Governor of Fiji, 1942–4; Governor of Kenya, 1944–52; MC, 1917; CMG, 1933; KCMG, 1937; GCMG, 1947; d. 1964.

MOORE, Henry Monck-Mason, b. 1887; joined Ceylon civil service, 1910; Assistant Colonial Secretary, 1914; Colonial Secretary, Bermuda, 1922; Principal Assistant Secretary, Nigeria, 1924; Deputy Chief Secretary, Nigeria, 1927; Colonial Secretary, Kenya, 1929; Governor of Sierra Leone, 1934; Assistant Under-Secretary, Colonial Office, 1937; Governor of Kenya, 1940–4; Governor of Ceylon, 1944–8; Governor-General of Ceylon, 1948–9; CMG, 1930; KCMG, 1935; GCMG, 1943; d. 1964.

MORGAN, James Conwy, b. 1910; Colonial Administrative Service, Tanganyika, 1934; KAR, 1939; British Military Administration, Somaliland, 1941; Home Civil Service, 1947; Colonial Office, Principal, 1947; Assistant Secretary, 1955; attached to Monckton Commission, 1960; CMG, 1966; d. 1977.

NKRUMAH, Kwame, b. 1909; Gold Coast/Ghana politician; schoolmaster, 1931–4; General Secretary, West African National Secretariat; Joint Secretary, Pan African Congress, London and Manchester; editor, *New Africa*, London, 1945–7; first General Secretary, UGCC 1947; Formed CPP 1949; elected to Legislative Council, 1950; Leader of Government Business in Assembly, 1951; Prime Minister, 1952–7; Minister of External Affairs, 1957–8; Minister of the Interior, 1958–9; first President of the Republic of Ghana, Head of State and Supreme Commander of the Armed Forces, 1960–6; deposed by military coup, February 1966; d. 1972.

PAVLIDES, Paul George, b. 1897; financier and company director, Cyprus; member Advisory Council, 1933–6 and 1940–2; Member Executive Council, 1948–55; CBE, 1949; Kt., 1955; d. 1977.

PERTH, 17th Earl, b. John David Drummond Perth, 1907; Intelligence Corps, 1940; War Cabinet Office, 1942–3; Ministry of Production, 1944–5; Minister of State for Colonial Affairs, 1957–62.

PHILLIPS, Henry Ellis Isidore, b. 1914; Institute of Historical Research, University of London, 1936–9; served in war, 1939–45, prisoner of war 1942; Colonial Administrative Service, Nyasaland, 1946; Development Secretary, 1942; seconded to Federal Treasury of Rhodesia and Nyasaland,

1953–7; Deputy Secretary, 1956; Financial Secretary, Nyasaland, 1957–64 and Minister of Finance 1961–4; MBE, 1946; CMG, 1960; Kt., 1964.

RENNIE, Gilbert McCall, b. 1895; joined Ceylon civil service, 1920; Police Magistrate, 1923; Secretary to the Governor, 1934; Financial Secretary, Gold Coast, 1937; Chief Secretary, Kenya, 1939; Governor of Northern Rhodesia, 1948–54; Federation of Rhodesia and Nyasaland High Commissioner to London, 1954–61; CMG, 1941; Kt., 1946; KCMG, 1949; GBE, 1954; d. 1981.

ROBERTS, Denys Tudor Emil, b. 1923; novelist and lawyer; served Royal Artillery, 1943–6; Colonial Legal Service, 1953; Crown Counsel, Nyasaland, 1953–9; Acting Solicitor-General, representing Nyasaland Government at Devlin Commission, 1959; Attorney-General, Gibraltar, 1960–2; Solicitor-General, Hong Kong, 1962–6; Attorney-General, Hong Kong, 1966–73; Chief Secretary, Hong Kong, 1973–8; Chief Justice, Hong Kong, 1979–88; OBE, 1960; CBE, 1970; KBE, 1971.

ROBINS, George Herbert, b. 1908; Ceylon Police, 1930; Tanganyika Police, 1948; Director of Colonial Police Studies, UK Police College, 1950; Tanganyika Police, 1953; Commissioner of Police, Cyprus, 1954–6; Nigeria Police, 1956; Commissioner of Police, Bermuda, until retirement in 1969; MBE, 1948; KPM, 1953; CBE, 1965; d. 1993.

SALOWAY, Reginald Harry, b. 1905; entered Indian Civil Service, 1928; Secretary, Board of Revenue and Finance Ministry, Rampur State, 1937–46; Director-General, Resettlement and Employment, Government of India, 1946; transferred to Gold Coast, 1947; Secretary for Rural Development, 1947–50; Colonial Secretary, 1950; Chief Secretary and Minister of Defence and External Affairs, 1951–4; d. 1959.

TURNBULL, Richard Gordon, b. 1909; Colonial Administrative Service, Kenya, 1931; Provincial Commissioner in charge of the Northern Frontier District, 1948; Minister for Internal Security and Defence, 1954; Chief Secretary, 1955; Governor of Tanganyika, 1958–61; Governor-General of Tanganyika, 1961–2; Governor of Aden, 1965–7; CMG, 1953; KCMG, 1958; GCMG, 1962.

WELENSKY, Roy, b. Southern Rhodesia, 1907; started work at age 14, became a railway engine driver and heavyweight boxer; transferred to Northern Rhodesia; became leader of railway workers' union; Member of Legislative Council of Northern Rhodesia, 1938; Director of Manpower, 1941; member of War Committee, Northern Rhodesia, 1941; leader of Northern Rhodesia unofficial members, 1946; Federation of Rhodesia and Nyasaland Minister of Transport, 1954; Deputy Prime Minister, 1955; Prime Minister, Minister of Defence, Minister of External Affairs 1956–63; KCMG, 1953; d. 1991.

WHITEHEAD, Edgar Cuthbert Fremantle, b. 1905; educated Oxford; served in Second World War 1939–45 in West Africa and Britain; Member Legislative Assembly, Southern Rhodesia, 1939–40, 1946–53, 1958–63; Acting High Commissioner, Southern Rhodesia, to UK, 1945–6; Minister, 1946–53; Minister for Federation of Rhodesia and Nyasaland, Washington, 1957–8; MP, 1958; Minister, 1958–60; Prime Minister, 1958–62; retired England, 1968; OBE, 1944; CMG; 1952; KCMG, 1954; d. 1971.

WILLIAM-POWLETT, Peveril Barton Reiby Wallop, b. 1894; Royal Navy,

1914–53; retired as Vice Admiral and Commander-in-Chief South Atlantic, 1953; Governor of Southern Rhodesia, 1954–9; CBE, 1945; KCB, 1953; KCMG, 1959; d. 1985.

WYN-HARRIS, Percy, b. 1903; Colonial Administrative Service, Kenya, 1926; Commissioner for Labour, 1944; Provincial Commissioner, 1945; Chief Native Commissioner, 1947; Governor of the Gambia, 1949–58; climbed Mount Kenya with E. E. Shipton, 1929; member of Everest expeditions, 1933 and 1936; member of Devlin Commission of Inquiry into Nyasaland Disturbances, 1959; MBE, 1941; CMG, 1949; KCMG, 1952; d. 1979.

YOUENS, Peter William, b. 1916; Colonial Administrative Service, 1939; naval service, 1939–40; Sierra Leone, Assistant DC, 1942; DC, 1948; Colony Commissioner and MLC, 1950; Assistant Secretary, Nyasaland, 1951; Deputy Chief Secretary, 1953–63; MLC, 1954–61; Secretary to Prime Minister and Cabinet, Malawi, 1964–6; company director, London, 1966–94; OBE, 1960; CMG, 1962; Kt. 1965.

Notes

1. Early Years

1. Material in this and the following paragraph is from C. Canry, *Encyclopaedia of Historic Places* (London: Mansell Publishing, 1984), vol. II, pp. 547–8; *Madras Mail*, 21 December 1906 and *passim*.
2. Material in this and the following paragraph is from B. I. Anson, *The History of the Armytage or Armitage Family* (London: Hazell, Watson & Viney, n.d.); Marquis of Ruvigny and Raineval, *The Plantagenet Roll of the Blood Royal* (London: Jack, 1905); D. Gray, *Spencer Perceval: The Evangelical Prime Minister* (Manchester: Manchester University Press, 1963); *Ross Gazette*, 8 September 1955; *The Times*, 7 September 1955; *Who Was Who 1951–1960*, p. 35; Obituary, R. P. Armitage, *Daily Telegraph*, 13 June 1990.
3. Material in this and the following paragraphs dealing with Highfield School is from M. Gedge to author, March 1991, and *The Highfield School Magazine*, Lent term 1917, vol. VI to Christmas term 1923, vol. XIV, *passim*.
4. J. Sabben-Clare, *Winchester College: After 600 Years, 1382–1982* (Southampton: Paul Cave, 1981), p. 1. Material in this and the following paragraphs dealing with Winchester College, except where otherwise stated, is from this source, from J. D'E. Firth, *Rendall of Winchester: The Life and Witness of a Teacher* (London: Oxford University Press, 1954) and from H. Alexander to author, 20 April and 7 May 1991.
5. Jeremy Armitage, interviews with author, 20–22 November 1996.
6. *The Wykehamist*, vol. 589, 30 October 1920, *passim*.
7. See, for example, *The Wykehamist*, vol. 589, 30 October 1920, p. 516.
8. R. G. Wickham to author, 15 April 1991.
9. A. Bates to author, 18 April 1991; D. Sturch to author, 26 January 1992; and B. V. Gibbs to author, 21 November 1991.
10. Armitage Papers (hereafter Papers), Winchester College, Middle Part, Junior Division, Report, March 1921, IV.X.NA.
11. Papers, Armitage's letters to his parents (hereafter Letters), 26 June and 21 September 1921. Letters to correspondents other than his parents indicate the name of the addressee.
12. Letters, 11 and 25 April 1922.
13. Letters, 17 June 1922.
14. Letters, 18 June 1922. Passing the tests is evidenced in Papers, Army form B.2075, dated August 1925.
15. *The Wykehamist*, vol. 621, 30 June 1922, p. 214.
16. Letters, 25 June 1922; *The Wykehamist*, vol. 622, 26 July 1922, p. 228, and vol. 632, 3 April 1923, p. 329.
17. Letters, 27 August, 24 September and 22 October 1922.

18. Letters, 24 September 1922.
19. Letters, 22 October and 3 December 1922.
20. Papers, Winchester College, Senior Part, Middle Division, Report, November 1922.
21. Letters, 22 and 29 December 1922. See also Letters, 3 December 1922. For Grigg's relationships with the Astors, see D. Wilson, *The Astors: The Life and Times of the Astor Dynasty, 1793–1992* (London, Weidenfeld & Nicolson, 1993), pp. 155, 184, 232.
22. Wickham to author, 15 April 1991.
23. Papers, Winchester College, Senior Part, Middle Division, Report, April 1923.
24. Winchester College Calendar, August 1923, p. 50.
25. Letters, 11 November 1922; *The Wykehamist*, vol. 640, 23 November 1923, pp. 417–18 and Supplement.
26. *Winchester College Calendar*, August 1924, pp. 50, 54.
27. Alexander to author, 7 May 1991.
28. Letters, 16 December 1924.
29. *The Wykehamist*, vol. 600, 30 November 1920, p. 531.
30. Letters, 28 July 1925.
31. Ibid.
32. Material in the remainder of this paragraph is from *The Wykehamist*, vol. 602, 7 February 1921, p. 18; vol. 604, 31 March 1921, p. 35; vol. 605, 18 May 1921, p. 54; vol. 607, 22 June 1921, p. 67; vol. 618, 4 April 1922, p. 179; vol. 629, 17 October 1923, p. 290; vol. 645, 19 March 1924.
33. Firth, op. cit., p. 128.
34. Ibid., p. 129.
35. J. S. Furley to M. J. Rendall, 21 July 1924, cited in Firth, op. cit., p. 170.
36. The judge was Richard Wilberforce and the ministers were Richard Crossman and Douglas Jay. Hugh Gaitskell was a year ahead of them at Winchester.
37. *The Wykehamist*, vol. 653, 21 November 1924, p. 29.
38. Papers, photograph of the New College and Magdalen beagles, including Armitage.
39. Papers, Lyona Meyler to Armitage, 31 August to 22 December 1927, *passim*; Jeremy Armitage to author, 10 September 1996.
40. Letters, 11 March 1922.
41. Letters, 11 April 1922.
42. Ibid.
43. Material in this paragraph is from Rhodes House Library, Oxford (hereafter RHL), Mss. Afr. s.2204, Box 4, folder 2 (hereafter 4/2, *mutatis mutandis*).
44. RHL Mss. Afr. s.2204, 4/2, Parkinson to Armitage, 16 August 1928.
45. RHL Mss. Afr. s.2204, 4/2, Fisher to Armitage, 11 November 1928.
46. Letters, 3 August 1929.
47. C. Atkins to author, 10 September 1994.
48. W. H. Hale to author, 4 August 1994.
49. Jeremy Armitage to author, 10 September 1996.

2. Kenya

1. Material in this and the following three paragraphs is from *The Dominions Office and Colonial Office List, 1929* (London: Waterlow & Sons, 1929), pp. 330 *et seq.*; A. H. M. Kirk-Greene, 'The Thin White Line: the Size of the

NOTES TO CHAPTER 2

British Colonial Service in Africa', *African Affairs*, vol. 79, 1980, pp. 25–44. Throughout this book, place names – in Kenya, the Gold Coast, Cyprus and Nyasaland – are those used at the relevant time: they have not been rendered into their present-day form.
2. J. L. H. Webster to author, 1 August 1994.
3. Material in this and the following two paragraphs is from Papers, Armitage's personal diary (hereafter Diary), 6 July to 9 August 1929.
4. Webster to author, 1 August 1994. See also C. C. Trench, *Men Who Ruled Kenya* (London: The Radcliffe Press, 1993), pp. 99 *et seq.*
5. Diary, 10 and 14 August 1929; Atkins to author, 10 September 1994.
6. Material in this and the following paragraphs covering Armitage's early days in Kakamega, except where otherwise stated, is from Diary, 15, 19, 21, 22, 24 and 29 August, 1, 4, 5, 6, 10, 12, 16, 17, 18, 20, 23, 24, 26 and 27 September, 1, 2, 3, 5, 16 and 30 October, and 8 and 13 November 1929; Letters, 15 August, 22 September, 5, 12 and 19 October, 12 and 16 November, and 1 December 1929.
7. Trench, op. cit., p. 99.
8. Diary, 23 August, 27, 28 September, 11 October, 20 December 1929; Letters, 28 September 1929.
9. Colonial Office, September 1926, Pamphlet African No. 973, 15th edition, *Regulations for the employment of officers in the East African dependencies*, copy in RHL Mss. Afr. s.2204, 5/2.
10. Government of Kenya, *Life and Duties of an Administrative Officer in Kenya Colony* (Nairobi: Government Printer, 1929), p. 2: copy in RHL Mss. Afr. s.2204, 5/2.
11. Material in the remainder of this and the following two paragraphs, except where otherwise stated, is from Diary, 1, 14 and 19 October, 2, 3, 8, 11 and 15 November, and 8 December 1929; Letters, 7 September, 19 and 28 October, 3 and 16 November, and 24 December 1929.
12. RHL Mss. Afr. s.2204, 4/2, Colonial Secretary to PC Kisumu, 23 October 1929 and PC Nyanza to DC North Kavirondo, 2 November 1920.
13. Material in this paragraph is from Letters, 24 December 1929.
14. Diary, undated pages following 31 December 1929.
15. Material in this and the following two paragraphs is from Diary, 1, 10 and 13 January 1930; Letters, 1 December 1929, and 5 and 12 January 1930.
16. Diary, 12, 21, 24 and 25 January 1930; Atkins to author, 10 September 1994. The reason why not many people would – or did – attend the wedding ceremony was that the vast majority of non-officials thoroughly disliked the governor, Sir Edward Grigg, and declined his invitation: Letters, 3 August 1929, 12 and 28 January and 23 February 1930.
17. Diary, 1 October 1929, 1 and 7–12 February 1930; Letters, 9 February 1930.
18. Diary, 12–15 February 1930; Letters, 12 January 1930.
19. Material in this paragraph concerning Armitage's marriage is from RHL Mss. Afr. s.2204, 4/4; Letters, 23 February 1930; Diary, 18 and 25 February 1930.
20. Diary, 8 and 11 April, 10 October and 28 November 1930; Letters, 21 April 1930; RHL Mss. Afr. s.2204, 4/2, Chief Native Commissioner to Armitage, 11 November 1930.
21. Diary, 25 October 1930; Letters, 16 November 1930; Trench, op. cit., p. 105.

NOTES TO CHAPTER 2

22. R. Turnbull to author, 3 April 1991. See also Webster to author, 1 August 1994; Letters, 3 November 1930.
23. Material in this and the following six paragraphs, except where otherwise stated, is from Turnbull to author, 22 January and 1 April 1991; Papers, Turnbull to Armitage, February 1980.
24. Diary, 14 September 1931.
25. Diary, 31 October and 13 November 1930, 25 and 26 September 1931, and 7 January 1932; Letters, 10 November 1930; Trench, op. cit., p. 106.
26. Turnbull to author, 1 April 1991; Diary, 1 April and 27 December 1931.
27. Material in this paragraph is from Diary, 15 November 1930, 27 April, and 8, 27 and 28 May 1931, and 4 June and 3 July 1931.
28. Diary, 3 August and 27 December 1931; Letters, 23 March 1931.
29. Turnbull to author, 1 April 1991.
30. Diary, 11 January to 2 February 1932.
31. Diary, 6 February to 10 July 1932, *passim*.
32. Diary, 18–22 July and 8–13 August 1932.
33. Material in this paragraph is from Diary, 15 and 25 August, 13 and 16 September, 14 October, and 23 October–11 December 1932, *passim*, and 5 January, 3 and 22 March, 15 May and 6 July 1933.
34. Material in this paragraph and the following paragraphs dealing with Kisumu is from Webster to author, 1 August 1994; Diary, 3, 28 and 30 September, 11 October and 27 November 1932.
35. Diary, 13 November 1933 and 10, 12 and 14 March 1934; RHL Mss. Afr. s.2204, 4/2, Wade to Armitage, 22 April 1936; Diary, 23 November 1935.
36. RHL Mss. Afr. s.2204, 4/3, Lambert to Armitage, 29 February 1936; Diary, 23 November 1935.
37. Diary, 13 and 14 July 1934.
38. Diary, 23 January, 30 November and 14 December 1935.
39. Diary, 17 January, 7 and 28 March and 4 April to 23 October 1936, *passim*; Papers, correspondence with the Middle Temple, 1928 and 1936.
40. Diary, 13 to 19 November 1936; Trench, op. cit., p. 142.
41. Diary, 21 and 22 November 1936; F. J. Wright, *A Tenth Child's Family History*, unpublished memoirs, p. 67, privately held.
42. Diary, 23 November 1936.
43. E. Huxley, *Out in the Midday Sun* (London: Chatto & Windus, 1985), p. 162.
44. Wright, op. cit., p. 69; RHL Mss. Afr. s.2204, 4/1, Annual Report, 1936, Wajir and Handing Over Notes, Low to Armitage; Webster to author, 1 August 1994. For details of administrative work in the Northern Frontier Districts see Trench, op. cit., Chapters 4, 11, 12 and 15.
45. Government of Kenya, op. cit., pp. 18–19.
46. Turnbull to author, 20 and 25 January 1992; Webster to author, 1 August 1994; RHL Mss. Afr. s.2204, 4/1, Handing Over Notes, Low to Armitage; RHL Mss. Afr. s.2204, 4/3, Glenday to Armitage, 22 December 1936.
47. Turnbull to author, 20 and 25 January 1992; Trench, op. cit., p. 144.
48. Material in this and the following three paragraphs is from Diary, 4, 25 and 28 December 1936, 1 and 22 January, 4 and 15 February, 16, 27, 30 and 31 March, 1, 7 and 14 April, 11, 12, 14 and 31 May, 18 and 21 June, 29 July, and 10 August 1937.
49. Wright, op. cit., p. 64; Diary, 25 January and 1 February 1937.

50. Diary, 18 January 1937. See also Huxley, op. cit., p. 166 and Trench, op. cit., pp. 143–4.
51. RHL Mss. Afr. s.2204, 4/3, Glenday to Armitage, 20 August 1937; Diary, 20 August 1937.
52. *East Africa Standard*, 26 August 1937.
53. Diary, 1–3 September 1937. See also Trench, op. cit., pp. 91–2, 145.
54. Huxley, op. cit., p. 152.
55. Material in this and the following paragraphs covering Armitage's time in Isiolo, except where otherwise stated, is from RHL Mss. Afr. s.2204, 4/3, Rimmington to Armitage, 5 September 1937; Diary, 30 August to 3 November 1937.
56. RHL Mss. Afr. s.2204, 4/3, Glenday to Armitage, 9 September 1937.
57. RHL Mss. Afr. s.2204, 4/3, Glenday to Armitage, 22 September 1937.
58. RHL Mss. Afr. s.2204, 4/3, Turnbull to Armitage, 26 December 1937.
59. RHL Mss. Afr. s.2204, 4/3, Harris to Armitage, 21 August 1937.
60. RHL Mss. Afr. s.2204, 4/3, Armitage to, Glenday, 24 October 1937.
61. Huxley, op. cit., p. 154; Trench, op. cit., p. 147.
62. Huxley, op. cit., pp. 153–4; Turnbull to author, 3 April 1991.
63. *Mombasa Times*, 22 October 1937, p. 2.
64. Diary, 3 November 1937.
65. Diary, 4 and 9 November, and 12 December 1937.
66. Material in this paragraph is from Diary, 8–17 November 1937.
67. Material in this and the following paragraphs covering the first part of Armitage's time at Tambach, except where otherwise stated, is from Diary, 14 November 1937 to 16 August 1938.
68. RHL Mss. Afr. s.2204, 4/1, Annual Report, Elgeyo, 1938.
69. Ibid.
70. Material in this and the following two paragraphs dealing with the theft case at Tambach, except where otherwise stated, is from Diary, 26 May to 6 June 1938.
71. Webster to author, 1 August 1994; Lady Armitage, interview with author, 24 November 1991.
72. Webster to author, 14 July 1994.
73. RHL Mss. Afr. s.2204, 4/3, Hodge to Armitage, 7 June 1938.
74. Material in this and the following paragraph is from Diary, 23 and 26 February, 25 March, 2 and 16 April, and 22 October 1938.
75. Diary, 8 and 20 January, and 2 and 12 December 1938.
76. Material in this paragraph is from Diary, 22 February, 17 and 18 March and 1 July 1938, and 18 and 27 January 1939. For other examples of the governor's interference in district matters, see Trench, op. cit., p. 147.
77. Diary, 27 January 1939.
78. Diary, 9, 10, 11, 17 and 21 February, and 6 and 11 March 1939; W. H. Hale to author, 4 August 1994.
79. For example, 26 June to 2 July 1939, December 1941, March 1942, October 1942, December 1943 and August 1945.
80. Diary, 28 February, 11 and 18 March and 26 July 1939, and 16 September 1940.
81. Webster to author, 14 July 1994.
82. Diary, 12 June, 17 and 21 July, 27–30 August and 2 October 1939, and 2 April 1940.

NOTES TO CHAPTER 2

83. Diary, 4, 19 and 26 April, 1 and 9 May, 1 June and 22 August 1939.
84. Diary, 31 August and 3 September 1939.
85. Material on the secretariat fire is from the *East Africa Standard*, 13 and 15 September 1939; Diary, 12 and 13 September 1939; Webster to author, 14 July 1994.
86. Diary, 10 October 1939. Material in the remainder of this and the following two paragraphs is from Diary, 27 October, 14 November, 19 and 20 December 1939 and 6 January, 16, 23, 24 February, 28 March, 2 and 29 April 1940.
87. Diary, 31 May, 1, 3, 5, 20 and 22 June, 12, 22 and 29 August and 4 September 1940 and 18 April, 25 May and 15 August 1942.
88. Diary, 24 June 1940; Webster to author, 14 July 1994.
89. Diary, 2, 8, 9 and 29 July, and 5 and 24 August 1940.
90. Diary, 12–19 December 1940.
91. Diary, 20–24 December 1940.
92. Diary, 28 February and 4–5 December 1941; RHL Mss. Afr. s.2204, 4/7, Lyona Armitage to Frank Armitage, 16 December 1941.
93. Diary, 14 December 1941.
94. RHL Mss. Afr. s.2204, 4/7, Lyona Armitage to Frank Armitage, 16 December 1941.
95. Material in this paragraph, except where otherwise stated, is from Diary, 9 July and 14 September 1940, 7 March and 9 and 30 May 1941, and 23 January, 17 April, 14 May, 9 July and 10 September 1942.
96. Letters, 1 February 1942.
97. Diary, 28 December 1940, and 7 August 1942.
98. Material in this paragraph is from Diary, 20 and 26 March, 14 April, and 5 and 19 June 1942.
99. Diary, 15 May 1942.
100. Diary, 14 July 1942.
101. Material in this paragraph is from Diary, 6 and 8 July, 28 September, 8, 11, 12 and 29 October, 17, 23, 24, 26 and 30 November, 1 and 3 December 1942, 4 January, 1 and 14 February, 5 March and 3 April 1943.
102. Material in this paragraph is from Diary, 8 March, 3, 22 and 24 May, 7 and 8 June 1943.
103. Diary, 1 and 23 July 1943.
104. Material in this paragraph is from Diary, 16 June, 6, 7, 30 and 31 October, 1, 4 and 11 November 1943.
105. *Daily Telegraph*, 13 June 1990, p. 21, obituary.
106. Material in this paragraph is from Diary, 8 October 1943, 3, 7 January 1944.
107. Diary, 17 February 1944. See also Diary, 14 June 1943.
108. Material in the remainder of this paragraph, except where otherwise stated, is from Jeremy Armitage to author, 10 September 1996; Diary, 21 March, 17, 21 April, 16 May 1944.
109. Jeremy Armitage to author, 10 September 1996.
110. Huxley, op. cit., p. 88.
111. Material in this and the following paragraph is from Diary, 28 July, 1 August 1945.
112. Diary, 17 September, 2 October, 4 December 1945, 26 March 1946.
113. Diary, 20 September, 6 November 1945.
114. Diary, 30 April 1945, 3, 4 January 1946.

115. Turnbull to author, 20 January 1992; RHL Mss. Afr. s.2204, 4/3, Colonial Secretary to Armitage, 28 October 1937 and Glenday to Armitage, 13 October 1937; Letters, 1 December 1929 and 8 March 1944.
116. Diary, 25 February, 9 and 25 March 1942, 1 January, 20 May, 23 September 1943, 10 January 1945 and 10 January 1946.
117. RHL Mss. Afr. s.2204, 4/2, Chief Secretary to Armitage, 25 June 1946. Material in the remainder of this paragraph is from Diary, 22 September, 12, 31 December 1943, 21 November 1945, 19 February 1946.
118. Unreferenced newspaper cutting dated March 1947, in RHL Mss. Afr. s.2204, 5/1; Webster to author, 14 July and 1 August 1994.
119. RHL Mss. Afr. s.2204, 4/7, Armitage to Haworth, 6 April 1947.
120. RHL Mss. Afr. s.2204, 4/2, Cohen to Armitage, 2 September 1947.

3. The Gold Coast

1. Material in this and the following three paragraphs, unless otherwise stated, is from the *Colonial Office List, 1955* (London: HMSO, 1955), pp. 93–100.
2. For a compact account of the Gold Coast's history from 1475 to 1947, see B. Lapping, *End of Empire* (London: Paladin Grafton, 1989), pp. 423 *et seq.*
3. D. Tripp to author, 28 April 1991.
4. D. Rooney, *Sir Charles Arden-Clarke* (London: Rex Collings, 1982), pp. 82–93; H. MacGiffin to author, 13 July 1991.
5. S. R. Kingston to author, 17 April 1991.
6. Lapping, op. cit., pp. 436–8; Rooney, op. cit., p. 87; A. J. Willing to author, 20 March 1992.
7. RHL Mss. Brit. Emp. 527/5(1), Codrington, p. 140; N. Goldie-Scott to author, 23 April 1991; Tripp to author, 28 April 1991.
8. Material in this and the following paragraph is from Lapping, op. cit., pp. 438, 441–2; RHL Mss. Brit. Emp. 527/5(1), Robinson, pp. 153 *et seq.*, and Thomson, pp. 191, 196.
9. RHL Mss. Brit. Emp. 527/5(1), Armitage, p. 35.
10. Lapping, op. cit., p. 442; RHL Mss. Brit. Emp. 527/5(1), Armitage, p. 36.
11. Papers, *Gold Coast Bulletin*, vol. iv, no. 11, 16 March 1949; C. Arden-Clarke, 'Eight Years' Transition in Ghana', *African Affairs*, January 1958, p. 31; Rooney, op. cit., p. 88; Lapping, op. cit., p. 444.
12. Rooney, op. cit., p. 103; *Who's Who*, 1995; RHL Mss. Brit. Emp. 527/5(1), Branigan, p. 109.
13. RHL Mss. Brit. Emp. 527/5(1), Armitage, p. 42.
14. Arden-Clarke, op. cit., p. 29.
15. R. Saloway, 'The New Gold Coast', *International Affairs*, October 1955, pp. 469–70.
16. RHL Mss. Brit. Emp. 527/5(1), Armitage, pp. 26–7, 48; Arden-Clarke, op. cit., p. 32; Rooney, op. cit., p. 94, 100; Lapping, op. cit., pp. 445–7.
17. Arden-Clarke, op. cit., p. 32. See also Rooney, op. cit., p. 105 and Saloway, op. cit., p. 471.
18. Material in this paragraph is from Arden-Clarke, op. cit., p. 33; Rooney, op. cit., pp. 117–19; Lapping, op. cit., pp. 449–50; RHL Mss. Brit. Emp. 527/5(1), Armitage, pp. 27–8, 39, 45, and Branigan, pp. 109 *et seq.* See also H. K. Akyeampong, *Tributes to Dr J. B. Danquah* (Accra: State Publishing Corporation, 1967), p. 13.

19. Arden-Clarke, op. cit., pp. 34–5; Saloway, op. cit., pp. 471–3.
20. D. Austin, *Politics in Ghana, 1946–1960* (London: Oxford University Press, 1970), p. 153.
21. RHL Mss. Brit. Emp. 527/5(1), Armitage, p. 26.
22. T. J. Nurser to author, 3 December 1991.
23. Material in the remainder of this paragraph is from L. M. Davies to author, 30 June 1991; RHL Mss. Brit. Emp. 527/5(1), Russell, pp. 164 *et seq.* and E. Powell to author, November 1996.
24. E. B. S. Alton to author, 5 May 1991; RHL Mss. Brit. Emp. 527/5(1), Gbedemah, pp. 169, 181.
25. N. Goldie-Scott to author, 23 February 1991; A. Bullwinkle to author, 26 May 1991.
26. Davies to author, 30 June 1991; RHL Mss. Brit. Emp. 527/5(1), Armitage, p. 45.
27. Goldie-Scott to author, 23 April 1991.
28. H. Brind to author, 18 April 1991.
29. G. Haddow to author, 17 April 1991.
30. Tripp to author, 28 April 1991.
31. Davies to author, 30 June 1991. Material in the remainder of this and the following five paragraphs, except where otherwise stated, is from this source.
32. T. A. Mead to author, 29 April 1991.
33. Davies to author 30 June 1991.
34. *Accra Evening News*, vol. 4, no. 31, 24 November 1949.
35. Lapping, op. cit., p. 454.
36. Material in this and the following two paragraphs, except where otherwise stated, is from RHL Mss. Brit. Emp. 527/5(1), Armitage, pp. 45–9; Davies to author, 30 June 1991.
37. T. J. Nurser to author, 3 December 1991.
38. Kingston to author, 17 April 1991.
39. Kingston to author, 17 April 1991.
40. P. Lindsell to author, 24 June 1991. See also Rooney, op. cit., pp. 110–11; Austin, op. cit., p. 158; and Saloway, op. cit., p. 473.
41. M. Ensor to author, 16 April 1991.
42. Davies to author, 30 June 1991. Material in the remainder of this and the following two paragraphs, except where otherwise stated, is from this source.
43. Austin, op. cit., p. 158.
44. Saloway, op. cit., p. 476.
45. RHL Mss. Brit. Emp. 527/5(1), Gbedemah, p. 192; and A. Cohen, *British Policy in Changing Africa* (London: Routledge & Kegan Paul, 1959), pp. 31 *et seq.*
46. See Austin, op. cit., p. 157.
47. Davies to author, 30 June 1991.
48. Kingston to author, 17 April 1991.
49. Willing to author, 20 March 1992.
50. Davies to author, 30 June 1991.
51. Willing to author, 20 March 1992; Davies to author, 30 June 1991.
52. Willing to author, 20 March 1992.
53. Davies to author, 30 June 1991.
54. Tripp to author, 28 April 1991.

55. Davies to author, 30 June 1991.
56. Ibid.
57. Papers, Budget Speech, 1949–50.
58. Papers, Budget Speech, 1950–51.
59. Papers, Armitage to Saloway, 30 April, 1 May and 23 June 1950 and Armitage to Arden-Clarke, 1 July 1950.
60. Papers, Chancellor of the Order of Saint Michael and Saint George to Armitage, 1 January 1950.
61. Papers, Budget Speech, 1951–2; RHL Mss. Brit. Emp. 527/5(1), Armitage, p. 45.
62. Papers, J. H. Levey to Armitage, 20 April 1951; Papers, Armitage to Levey, 23 April 1951.
63. Papers, Budget Speech, 1952–3; RHL Mss. Brit. Emp. 527/5(1), Armitage, p. 32.
64. Papers, Budget Speech, 1953–4.
65. *Gold Coast Weekly Review*, vol. iii, no. 10, 11 March 1953.
66. Tripp to author, 28 April 1991.
67. *Gold Coast Weekly Review*, vol. iii, no. 10, 11 March 1953.
68. *Colonial Office List, 1955* (London: HMSO, 1955), pp. 93 *et seq.*
69. A. Forbes to author, 28 April and 7 May 1991. Material in the remainder of this and the following four paragraphs, except where otherwise stated, is from RHL Mss. Brit. Emp. 527/5(1), Armitage, p. 34, and Papers, Armitage's notes for Granada *End of Empire* series.
70. Davies to author, 30 June 1991.
71. W. Sabine to author, 22 March 1991 and 29 February 1992.
72. Davies to author, 30 June 1991.
73. Papers, Lloyd to Armitage, 1 August 1953; *Daily Express*, 19 August 1953; Papers, unreferenced newspaper cutting, n.d., probably 31 July 1953. The other appointments were Scott to Mauritius, Turnbull to North Borneo, Pike to Somaliland, Addis to Seychelles and Harford to St Helena.
74. RHL Mss. Brit. Emp. 527/5(1), Armitage, p. 49.

4. Cyprus

1. Material in this and the following seven paragraphs, except where otherwise stated, is from *The Colonial Office List, 1955* (London: HMSO, 1955).
2. C. Foley, *Legacy of Strife: Cyprus from Rebellion to Civil War* (London: Penguin, 1964) (hereafter *Legacy*), p. 23.
3. For brief outline political histories to 1945, see S. Kyriakides, *Cyprus: Constitutionalism and Crisis Government* (Philadelphia: University of Pittsburg Press, 1968), Chapter 1; K. Kyle, *Cyprus* (Minority Rights Group, Report No. 30, 1984), pp. 4–6; Chatham House Memorandum, *Cyprus, Background to Enosis* (London: Royal Institute of International Affairs, 1958), p. 1. Material in this paragraph is from these sources and from C. Foley, *The Memoirs of General Grivas* (London: Longman, 1964) (hereafter *Grivas Memoirs*), p. 1; Chatham House, op. cit., pp. 2–9; D. Barker, *Grivas: Portrait of a Terrorist* (London: Harcourt Brace, 1960), p. 54.
4. CO 926/209, Report for May 1954.
5. Material in this and the following paragraph is from Foley, *Memoirs*, p. 2; Chatham House, op. cit., pp. 5–9; Foley, *Legacy*, pp. 13–14; Meikle to author, 23 November 1992; Papers, Armitage's Notes on Chronology for the Granada *End of Empire* series, 1985 (hereafter *Chronology*); Kyriakides, op. cit., pp.

30–4; G. H. Kelling, *Countdown to Rebellion. British Policy in Cyprus, 1939–1955* (London: Greenwood Press, 1990), p. 127; R. Stephens, *Cyprus: A Place of Arms* (London: Pall Mall, 1966), pp. 127–8; Glavcos Clerides, RHL Mss. Brit. Emp. s.527/3(1), p. 152.

6. N. Crawshaw, *The Cyprus Revolt: An Account of the Struggle for Union with Greece* (London: George Allen & Unwin, 1978), p. 62; Chatham House, op. cit., p. 9; Kyriakides, op. cit., p. 36; Stephens, op. cit., p. 133.
7. Material in this and the following three paragraphs is from Foley, *Grivas Memoirs*, pp. 13–21; Barker, op. cit., pp. 55, 61, 64; Crawshaw, op. cit., pp. 93–6; Lapping, op. cit., p. 386; Stephens, op. cit., p. 134; Nicos Kranidiotis, RHL Mss. Brit Emp. s.527/3(1), p. 201.
8. CO 926/209, Report for December 1953.
9. CO 926/209, Report for January 1954.
10. CO 926/209, Report for February 1954.
11. Letters, 5, 12 and 17 February 1954; Papers, Lyona Armitage to Mrs Armitage, 22 February 1954; Papers, Armitage to Haworth, 7 February 1954; *Chronology*; Papers, Armitage's Notes for Granada *End of Empire* series.
12. Diary, 18, 19 and 20 February 1954. For a description of Government House and its grounds, see Foley, *Legacy*, p. 13.
13. Diary, 20 and 21 February 1954.
14. B. J. Weston to author, 15 February 1993.
15. Papers, unreferenced newspaper cutting, Cyprus, 31 July 1953.
16. Ibid. and Diary, 21 February 1954.
17. Diary, 21 February 1954; Letters, 27 February, 27 March, 10, 17 and 24 April, 1954; Papers, Armitage to Haworth, 7 February 1954; CO 926/209, Report for February 1954.
18. Letters, 27 February 1954.
19. CO 926/209, Report for February 1954; Diary, 8–12 March and 21 May 1954.
20. Material in this and the following five paragraphs is from Diary, 10, 11, 20, 23, 27 and 30 March and 9–10 April 1954; and W. Byford-Jones, *Grivas and the Story of Eoka* (London: Robert Hale, 1959), pp. 85–6.
21. Letters, 6 March 1954.
22. Letters, 27 March 1954, 3 and 24 April 1954.
23. Material in this and the following paragraph is from Papers, Armitage's Notes for Granada *End of Empire* series; *Cyprus Mail*, 29 July 1954; Letters, 3 and 10 April, 1, 15 and 29 May, 5 and 12 June; J. Reddaway, RHL Mss. Brit. Emp. s.527/3(1), p. 167.
24. *Chronology*, p. 2. See also Letters, 5 June 1954.
25. O. F. Muftizade to author, September 1992.
26. CO 926/209, Report for April 1954.
27. Material in this and the following paragraph is from Papers, Armitage's Notes for Granada *End of Empire* series; Crawshaw, op. cit., p. 73; Letters, 15 May, 19 June and 16 July 1954; CO 926/209, Report for May 1954; Diary, 16 June 1954.
28. Letters, 29 May 1954.
29. Papers, Armitage to Haworth, 11 May 1954.
30. CO 926/209, Report for June 1954.
31. Crawshaw, op. cit., p. 75; Letters, 26 June 1954; Papers, Lyona Armitage to Mrs Armitage, 26 June 1954; Lapping, op. cit., p. 391; Kelling, op. cit., p. 145; Diary, 27 June, 1954.

NOTES TO CHAPTER 4   373

32. Letters, 12 June and 2 July 1954; Diary, 1 July 1954.
33. Letters, 16 and 23 July 1954.
34. Lapping, op. cit., pp. 388–9.
35. Crawshaw, op. cit., p. 75; Stephens, op. cit., pp. 136–7; *Chronology*, p. 4; Letters, 12 June 1954.
36. Crawshaw, op. cit., pp. 70–1; Kelling, op. cit., p. 129; Lapping, op. cit., p. 388; Stephens, op. cit., pp. 133–5; Kyriakides, op. cit., p. 37; Barker, op. cit., p. 68; Hansard, Commons, vol. 531, cols. 504–6; RHL Mss. Brit. Emp. s.527/3(3), Lady Peake, pp. 153–5.
37. CO 926/256, Note by Minister of State, for the Cabinet: Cyprus, n.d. but late August 1954, Annex, Cyprus: the Cabinet Decision of 26 July, Parliamentary Statement of 28 July and Attorney-General's Warning of 2 August (hereafter Note for Cabinet, August 1954).
38. Crawshaw, op. cit., p. 75; *Cyprus Mail*, 29 July 1954; Foley, *Legacy*, p. 16; M. Cardiff to author, August 1992.
39. CO 926/209, Report for 1 July–10 August 1954; Diary, 26, 27 and 29 July 1954; *Cyprus Mail*, 29 July 1954. See also Crawshaw, op. cit., pp. 80–1.
40. CO 926/209, Report for 1 July–10 August 1954.
41. Markides, editor-in-chief, *Ethnos*, cited in *Cyprus Mail*, 29 July 1954.
42. Diary, 2 August 1954; Chatham House, op. cit., p. 10; Crawshaw, op. cit., pp. 80–1.
43. CO 926/256, Note for Cabinet, August 1954.
44. CO 926/256, Armitage to Lloyd, 6 July 1954.
45. CO 926/256, Note for Cabinet, August 1954.
46. Diary, 7, 12 and 14 August 1954; Foley, *Legacy*, pp. 16–17. For details of the UN proceedings, see Crawshaw, op. cit., pp. 82–8.
47. L. Durrell, *Bitter Lemons* (London: Faber & Faber, 1959), p. 101; Letters, 13 August 1954; Chatham House, op. cit., p. 11.
48. CO 926/256, Note for Cabinet, August 1954.
49. Diary, 11 September 1954.
50. *Chronology*, p. 3; CO 926/256, Lloyd to Armitage, 23 August 1954; Diary, 28 and 30 May, 25 June and 15 July 1954.
51. Crawshaw, op. cit., p. 81; Dr H. M. Necati Munir Ertekun (hereafter Munir) to author, 4 September 1992.
52. Lapping, op. cit., p. 393.
53. CO 926/256, Meeting of 21 October 1954, Note for the Record.
54. Diary, 13–23 October 1954; Letters, 21 October 1954; Papers, Armitage to Haworth, 21 October 1954.
55. Letters, 27 November 1954.
56. Material in this and the following paragraph is from Andreas Azinas, RHL Mss. Brit. Emp. s.527/3(1), p. 7; Nicos Kranitiotis, RHL Mss. Brit. Emp. s.527/3(1), pp. 175 *et seq.* and 201; Diary, 16 September, 10 and 16 November and 10 December 1954; Foley, *Grivas Memoirs*, pp. 24 *et seq.*; Crawshaw, op. cit., pp. 100–5; Byford-Jones, op. cit., pp. 50–1, 61; Barker, op. cit., pp. 71–3; Stephens, op. cit., pp. 135–6; CO 926/209, Report for October 1954.
57. *Chronology*, p. 1.
58. Diary, 18–19 December 1954; Crawshaw, op. cit., p. 89; Foley, *Grivas Memoirs*, p. 29.
59. Diary, 16 December 1954; CO 926/209, Report for December 1954.

NOTES TO CHAPTER 4

60. Crawshaw, op. cit., p. 105; Foley, *Grivas Memoirs*, p. 29.
61. G. Robins, interview with author, 13 June 1992.
62. CO 926/209, Minute, Lloyd to Minister of State, 25 January 1955.
63. Diary, 25 September 1954 and 3 January 1955; Crawshaw, op. cit., p. 75; Weston to author, 15 February 1993; Cardiff to author, August 1992 and 13 January 1993.
64. CO 926/256, Note of meeting in Secretary of State's room on 9 February 1955 to discuss Cyprus policy.
65. CO 926/256, Armitage to Secretary of State, 24 February 1955.
66. CO 926/256, Minute, Morris to Martin, 25 February 1955.
67. Ibid.
68. CO 926/257, Armitage to Secretary of State, 25 February 1955.
69. CO 926/256, Secretary of State to Armitage, 25 February 1955.
70. Diary, 11 August 1954; CO 926/257, Armitage to Secretary of State, 26 February 1955.
71. CO 926/257, Secretary of State to Armitage, 27 February 1955.
72. CO 926/257, Armitage to Secretary of State, 27 February 1955.
73. CO 926/257, Secretary of State to Armitage, 28 February 1955.
74. Foley, *Legacy*, p. 25; Lapping op. cit., p. 384; Kyriakides, op. cit., p. 29; Barker, op. cit., p. 97.
75. Diary, 8 and 9 January 1955.
76. Barker, op. cit., p. 83.
77. Diary, 11 January 1955; CO 926/209, Report for January 1955.
78. Kelling, op. cit., p. 151.
79. CO 926/209, Report for January 1955.
80. Stephens, op. cit., p. 141; Foley, *Grivas Memoirs*, p. 29.
81. CO 926/256, Minute, Secretary of State to Prime Minister, n.d. but early January 1955.
82. Ibid.
83. Diary, 13 and 14 January 1955; Papers, Armitage's Notes for the Granada *End of Empire* series.
84. CO 926/256, Minute, Secretary of State to Prime Minister, n.d. but early January 1955.
85. CO 926/256, Minute, Martin to Lloyd, 4 February 1955.
86. CO 926/256, Minute by Minister of State, 7 February 1955.
87. CO 926/256, A Cabinet Paper on Cyprus: Memorandum by the Secretary of State for the Colonies, February 1955.
88. Diary, 15 January 1955.
89. Diary, 14 February 1955.
90. Diary, 15 February 1955.
91. Diary, 16 and 17 January 1955.
92. For Grivas's account, see Foley, *Grivas Memoirs*, pp. 29–30. See also Barker, op. cit., pp. 83–7; Crawshaw, op. cit., pp. 105–7; Stephens, op. cit., p. 141; Byford-Jones, op. cit., pp. 64–7.
93. Diary, 25 January 1955; Munir to author, 4 September 1992.
94. Diary, 23 August, 18 October, 13, 14 December 1954, 25 January 1955; Weston to author, 15 February 1993; Munir to author, 4 September 1992; Meikle to author, 23 November 1992; Kelling, op. cit., p. 151; *Chronology*, p. 5; Byford-Jones, op. cit., p. 65.

NOTES TO CHAPTER 4

95. CO 926/209, Report for January 1955; Crawshaw, op. cit., pp. 106–7; Byford-Jones, op. cit., pp. 65–7; Foley, *Grivas Memoirs*, p. 30; Weston to author, 15 February 1993.
96. Material in this and the following two paragraphs is from Robins, interview with author, 13 June 1992; Meikle to author, 27 April and 23 November 1992; Munir to author, 4 September 1992; Byford-Jones, op. cit., p. 53; CO 926/209, Report for March 1954 and other monthly political situation reports, 1953–4, *passim*; Papers, Armitage's Notes for the Granada *End of Empire* series; Foley, *Grivas Memoirs*, p. 31. By May 1955 there were over 800 special constables, mostly Turkish (Diary, 8 May 1955).
97. Robins, interview with author, 13 June 1992.
98. CO 926/209, Report for February 1955.
99. Diary, 28 February 1955, insert; Letters, 12 February 1955.
100. Material in this and the following paragraphs on Grubb's visit, unless otherwise stated, is from Report on visit to Cyprus by Sir Kenneth Grubb, Chairman of the World Council of Churches' International Affairs Commission, Precis of the Interviews held 13–18 February 1955 (probably compiled by O. F. Noldie), Travel Diary of K. Grubb, in the library of the Council, Geneva, copies privately held.
101. Cardiff to author, August 1992.
102. Material in this paragraph is from CO 926/257, Armitage to Secretary of State, 6 March 1955. See also CO 926/257, Armitage to Martin, 7 March 1955.
103. CO 926/257, Secretary of State to Armitage, 9 March 1955.
104. Diary, 13 March 1955.
105. Letters, 18 March 1955.
106. CO 926/209, Martin to Armitage, 25 March 1955.
107. CO 926/257, Note of meetings on future of Cyprus on 14 March 1955.
108. CO 926/257, Statement as revised on 14 March 1955.
109. Diary, 1 April 1955.
110. Foley, *Grivas Memoirs*, p. 33; Crawshaw, op. cit., pp. 113–15; Lapping, op. cit., p. 393; Letters, 2 April 1955.
111. H. Macmillan, *Tides of Fortune* (London: Macmillan, 1969) (hereafter *Tides*), p. 664.
112. Robins, interview with author, 13 June 1992.
113. Ibid.; Rauf Denktas, RHL Mss. Brit. Emp. s.527/3(1), p. 194; Foley, *Grivas Memoirs*, p. 34; Barker, op. cit., p. 95.
114. Messages, Cyprus to CO, No. 190, 2 April 1955, RG 1081/222, FO 371/117628, and Cyprus to CO, No. 187, 1 April 1955, RG 1081/216, FO 371/117628, cited in Kelling, op. cit., p. 152.
115. Crawshaw, op. cit., p. 112.
116. Cardiff to author, 13 January 1993.
117. Muftizade to author, September 1992; Letters, 29 May, 31 December 1954.
118. Macmillan, *Tides*, p. 664.
119. Meikle to author, 23 November 1992.
120. Diary, 1 May 1955.
121. Foley, *Grivas Memoirs*, p. 34; Foley, *Legacy*, p. 24; Crawshaw, op. cit., p. 115; Diary, 3 May 1955.
122. Material in this and the following paragraph is from Robins, interview with author, 13 June 1992; Weston to author, 15 February 1993; Diary, 9 May

NOTES TO CHAPTER 4

1955. The deal was probably made by Tornaritis and Fletcher-Cooke with the defence lawyers (Munir to author, 4 September 1992).
123. Diary, 6 May 1955.
124. Diary, 8, 11 and 18 May 1955; Meikle to author, 23 November 1992.
125. Diary, 10 May 1955.
126. Papers, Armitage to Haworth, 21 May 1955.
127. Ibid.
128. Ibid.; Diary, 17 May 1955.
129. Diary, 29 April, 17 May 1955; Papers, Armitage's Notes for the Granada *End of Empire* series; J. Walters to author, 25 June 1992; Cardiff to author, 13 January 1993; Foley, *Legacy*, p. 32.
130. Material in this and the following three paragraphs is from Diary, 18 and 31 May and 16, 18, 22 and 23 June 1955; Meikle to author, 16 January 1993.
131. Diary, 20 May 1955.
132. Diary, 19, 21 and 24 May 1955.
133. Material in this and the following paragraph is from Diary, 24 May 1955; Foley, *Grivas Memoirs*, pp. 26, 34, 36. See also Crawshaw, op. cit., p. 121.
134. Foley, *Legacy*, p. 22.
135. Papers, Armitage to Revd M. C. Humphrey, 20 May 1955.
136. Diary, 27 May 1955; Foley, *Grivas Memoirs*, pp. 34–5.
137. Material in this and the following paragraph is from Diary, 5 April 1954, and 20 and 30 May, 1 and 2 June and 19 July 1955; Letters, 30 April and 7 May 1955; Robins, interview with author, 13 June 1992.
138. Robins, interview with author, 13 June 1992.
139. Foley, *Legacy*, pp. 33–4.
140. Diary, 4 June 1955; Byford-Jones, op. cit., p. 54; Letters, 3 June 1955.
141. Munir to author, 4 September 1992; Meikle to author, 23 November 1992; Skettos to author, 28 July 1992 and Weston to author, 15 February 1993.
142. Diary, 19, 20, 21 June 1955; Foley, *Grivas Memoirs*, pp. 36–7; Foley, *Legacy*, p. 28. See also Crawshaw, op. cit., p. 122; Barker, op. cit., p. 104.
143. Material in this and the following paragraph, except where otherwise stated, is from Diary, 13 May 1955; Robins, interview with author, 13 June 1992; Cardiff to author, 13 January 1993; CO 926/141, Minute, Smith to Martin, 10 June 1955; CO 926/141, Minute, Lloyd to Secretary of State, 18 June 1955; CO 926/141, Lennox-Boyd to Armitage, 20 June 1955; Crawshaw, op. cit., p. 127; Foley, *Grivas Memoirs*, p. 40.
144. Muftizade to author, September 1992; Diary, 13, 24 and 25 June 1955.
145. A. Eden, *Full Circle: The Memoirs of the Rt Hon Sir Anthony Eden* (London: Cassell, 1960), p. 397; Lapping, op. cit., p. 394.
146. Material in this and the following two paragraphs is from Chatham House, op. cit., pp. 13–14; Diary, 1 October 1955; Macmillan, *Tides*, p. 665; Nicos Kranidiotis, RHL Mss. Brit. Emp. s.527/3(1), pp. 175 *et seq.*; Anthony Nutting, RHL Mss. Brit. Emp. s.527/3(1), pp. 69, 83.
147. Diary, 29 June 1955.
148. Lapping, op. cit., p. 398.
149. Material in this and the following paragraph is from Papers, Armitage to Haworth, 12 July 1955; Diary, 30 June and 1 July 1955.
150. CO 926/190, Reuter cable, Nicosia, 8 and 9 July 1955; Crawshaw, op. cit.,

NOTES TO CHAPTER 4   377

p. 124; Foley, *Legacy*, p. 312; Lapping op. cit., p. 399; Diary, 9 July 1955; *Kypriaki*, cited in *Times of Cyprus*, 20 September 1955.
151. Diary, 7 and 8 July 1955. The intermediaries included Clemens, Palias, Andreas Araouzo and finally, at Makarios's request, Reddaway. See also Foley, *Legacy*, pp. 30–1 and Crawshaw, op. cit., p. 124.
152. Diary, 9 July 1955.
153. CO 926/190, Lennox-Boyd to Martin, 12 July 1955.
154. Letters, 16 July 1955.
155. Foley, *Grivas Memoirs*, p. 39; Lapping, op. cit., pp. 400–1; R. S. Churchill, *The Rise and Fall of Sir Anthony Eden* (London: MacGibbon & Kee, 1959), p. 205.
156. Eden, op. cit., pp. 399–400.
157. Diary, 10 July 1955.
158. CO 926/190, Reuter cable, Nicosia, 11 July 1955.
159. Foley, *Legacy*, p. 31.
160. Diary, 11 July 1955; Papers, Lennox-Boyd to Armitage, 15 July 1955; J. Johnston to author, 22 July 1992.
161. CO 926/190, Reuter cable, Nicosia, n.d., probably 11 July 1955.
162. CO 926/190, Reuter cable, n.d., probably 8 July 1955.
163. Lapping, op. cit., p. 399; Macmillan, *Tides*, p. 666; Eden, op. cit., p. 399; Diary, 6, 13 and 15 July 1955; Papers, Armitage to Haworth, 12 July 1955; Robins, interview with author, 13 June 1992.
164. Robins, interview with author, 13 June 1992; Foley, *Legacy*, p. 29.
165. Foley, *Legacy*, pp. 27–8; Diary, 21 July 1955.
166. Diary, 28 July 1955.
167. Ibid.; Diary, 30 March 1954.
168. Diary, 15 March 1954 and 22, 25, 27 and 29 July 1955.
169. Meikle to author, 23 November 1992 and 16 January 1993.
170. Letters, 5 August 1955; CO 926/190, Reuter cable, Nicosia, 7 July 1955; Macmillan, *Tides*, p. 666; Diary, 3 August 1955.
171. Foley, *Legacy*, p. 33; Letters, 12 August 1955; Diary, 17 August 1955.
172. Letters, 5 August 1955.
173. Robins, interview with author, 13 June 1992; Diary, 4 August 1955.
174. Letters, 5 August 1955. See also Robins, interview with author, 13 June 1992.
175. Letters, 19 August 1955; Diary, 24 and 25 August 1955.
176. Diary, 29 August 1955. See also Crawshaw, op. cit., pp. 129 *et seq.*; Kyriakides, op. cit., pp. 38–42; Stephens, op. cit., pp. 141–2; Kelling, op. cit., p. 30; Chatham House, op. cit., pp. 14–16; Foley, *Legacy*, p. 35.
177. Macmillan, *Tides*, p. 668.
178. Orhan Erlap, RHL Mss. Brit. Emp. s.527/3(1), p. 42; Crawshaw, op. cit., p. 130.
179. Eden, op. cit., p. 400.
180. Diary, 31 August 1955; Eden, op. cit., pp. 400–2; Macmillan, *Tides*, p. 668; Crawshaw, op. cit., p. 131; Nicos Kranidiotis, RHL Mss. Brit. Emp. s.527/3(1), p. 181.
181. Diary, 31 August 1955.
182. Diary, 1 September 1955; Macmillan, *Tides*, p. 669; Stephens, op. cit., p. 142; Lapping, op. cit., p. 394.
183. Diary, 1 September 1955.

184. A. Horne, *Harold Macmillan, Volume I, 1894–1956* (London: Viking, 1989), p. 365.
185. Diary, 2 September 1955; Macmillan, *Tides*, p. 669.
186. Diary, 5 September 1955.
187. Kelling, op. cit., p. 129.
188. Diary, 6 September 1955; Crawshaw, op. cit., p. 133; Stephens, op. cit., p. 142; Macmillan, *Tides*, p. 671.
189. Diary, 7 September 1955.
190. *Chronology*, p. 5.
191. Nuri Birgi, Mss. Brit. Emp. s.527/3(1), p. 120; Diary, 7 September 1955.
192. Skettos to author, 6 February 1992.
193. Foley, *Grivas Memoirs*, p. 44. See also Crawshaw, op. cit., pp. 136–7; Chatham House, op. cit., p. 16; Stephens, op. cit., pp. 142–3; Kyle, op. cit., p. 7.
194. Foley, *Legacy*, p. 36.
195. Orhan Erlap, RHL Mss. Brit. Emp. s.527/3(1), p. 42; Nuri Birgi, RHL Mss. Brit. Emp. s.527/3(1), p. 120; Nicos Kranidiotis, RHL Mss. Brit. Emp. s.527/3(1), p. 181; Lapping, op. cit., p. 394; Macmillan, *Tides*, p. 671; Eden, op. cit., p. 401.
196. Diary, 6 September 1955. Frank Armitage had been ailing for some time: Diary, 27 August and 3 September 1955.
197. Diary, 9 September 1955; Papers, My Appreciation for Secretary of State – Notes.
198. Diary, 9 September 1955.
199. Lapping, op. cit., p. 395.
200. Diary, 12 September 1955; Lapping, op. cit., p. 395; Crawshaw, op. cit., p. 138; Foley, *Grivas Memoirs*, p. 42.
201. Munir to author, 4 September 1992.
202. Material in this and the following paragraph is from Diary, 14, 15 and 17 September 1955. See also Crawshaw, op. cit., p. 139.
203. Material in this and the following paragraph, unless otherwise stated, is from Chatham House, op. cit., p. 12; Robins, interview with author, 13 June 1992; Meikle to author, 23 November 1992.
204. *Daily Mail*, 19 September 1955. See also *Daily Mirror*, 19 September 1955; *Times of Cyprus*, 19 and 24 September 1955; Foley, *Legacy*, pp. 37 et seq.
205. *Times of Cyprus*, 19 September 1955. Details in the remainder of this paragraph, unless otherwise stated, are from this source.
206. Foley claimed that the press conference followed a meeting at Government House, in which case Armitage would have known about it (Foley, *Legacy*, p. 38).
207. Walters to author, 17 August 1992.
208. Walters to author, 25 June 1992.
209. Foley, *Legacy*, p. 38.
210. Diary, 19 September and 2 October 1955; *Times of Cyprus*, 24 September 1955.
211. Diary, 18 September 1955.
212. Material in this paragraph is from Diary 18 September 1955; Robins, interview with author, 13 June 1992.
213. Letters, 17 September 1955.
214. Macmillan, *Tides*, p. 688.

215. Chatham House, op. cit., p. 16.
216. Diary, 23 September 1955.
217. Diary, 23 September 1955; Letters, 24 September 1955.
218. Papers, Lennox-Boyd to Armitage, 22 September 1955. Details in the remainder of this paragraph are from this source.
219. Diary, 24 September 1955.
220. Diary, 28 September 1955; Robins, interview with author, 13 June 1992; Munir to author, 4 September 1992.
221. Letters, 17 and 24 September 1955.
222. Diary, 24 September 1955; Foley, *Grivas Memoirs*, pp. 44–5; Foley, *Legacy*, p. 38; Diary, 29 September and 1 October 1955.
223. Diary, 24 September 1955.
224. Diary, 26 and 28 September 1955.
225. Diary, 28 and 29 September 1955; Neophytos Sophocleos, RHL Mss. Brit. Emp. s527/3(1), pp. 190 *et seq.*
226. Neophytus Sophocleos to author, March 1997.
227. CO 926/141, Acting Governor, Cyprus, to Secretary of State, 29 September 1955.
228. Foley, *Legacy*, p. 39.
229. Muftizade to author, September 1992.
230. Weston to author, 15 February 1993.
231. Crawshaw, op. cit., p. 140.
232. Letters, 24 September 1955.
233. Eden, op. cit., pp. 395, 402.
234. Hansard, Commons, 5 December 1955, Vol. 547, No. 68, col. 31.
235. Ibid., cols. 143–7.
236. Macmillan, *Tides*, p. 674 and App. 3; Eden, op. cit., p. 408.
237. Hansard, Commons, 5 December 1955, Vol. 547, No. 68, col. 155.
238. Shakespeare, *Othello*, Act IV, Scene I, Line 274.

5. Nyasaland I

1. Material in the first four paragraphs of this chapter, except where otherwise stated, is from Letters, 6, 14, 15 and 29 October 1955.
2. Papers, unreferenced Stroud newspaper cutting, 14 October 1955.
3. Wyn-Harris to Devlin, 5 April 1959, RHL, Devlin Papers (hereafter DP).
4. For a general account of the geography of Nyasaland see J. G. Pike and G. T. Rimmington, *Malawi: A Geographical Study* (London: Oxford University Press, 1965).
5. Material in this and the following paragraph is from *Nyasaland: Report for the Year 1956* (London: HMSO, 1957), pp. 17, 133–41.
6. For an outline of the history of closer association, see Colin Baker, *Development Governor: A Biography of Sir Geoffrey Colby* (London: British Academic Press, 1994), Chapter 13. The following account is a condensation from that source.
7. Material in this and the following paragraphs covering the period up to Armitage's arrival in Nyasaland, except where otherwise stated, is from Diary, 1–10 and 26 January 1956, 2, 5, 6, 9, 13, 15, 20 and 22 February, and 26 and 27 March 1956.
8. Papers, Armitage to Haworth, 11 February 1956.

NOTES TO CHAPTER 5

9. Diary, 26 March 1956; Papers, Armitage to Haworth, 26 March 1956.
10. Papers, Armitage *Memoirs* (hereafter *Memoirs*), 1956, pp. 1–2; Letters, 13 April 1956.
11. Material in this paragraph is from Diary, 9, 10 and 15 April 1956; Letters, 13 April 1956. Where the context does not make it clear, W. M. Chirwa and O. E. C. Chirwa are referred to by their initials preceding their surnames.
12. Armitage to author, 9 May 1982, enclosing Colby to Armitage, 20 March 1956.
13. Material in this paragraph is from *Memoirs*, 1956, pp. 3–4; Colby to Lennox-Boyd, 24 January 1956, enclosed with Armitage to author, 9 May 1982.
14. Diary, 13 April 1956.
15. Material in this and the following two paragraphs is from Armitage to author, 9 May 1982; Diary, 14–21 April 1956; *Memoirs*, 1956, pp. 5, 23–5.
16. Material in this and the following paragraph is from *Memoirs*, 1956, p. 25; Diary, 5 May 1956.
17. Material in this paragraph is from Dixon to Armitage, 21 April 1956, enclosed with Armitage to author, 9 May 1982.
18. Material in this and the following paragraphs dealing with the review of the federation is from *Memoirs*, 1956, pp. 32–51.
19. Papers, Armitage to Lennox-Boyd, 4 July 1956.
20. Diary, 28 May 1956; *Memoirs*, 1956, p. 49.
21. *Rhodesia Herald*, 25 July 1956, cited in *Memoirs*, 1956, p. 48.
22. M. W. K. Chiume, *Kwacha: An Autobiography* (Nairobi: East African Publishing House, 1975), p. 83; A. J. Wills, *The History of Central Africa* (London: Oxford University Press, 1964), p. 338; Chiume to author, 19 August 1994.
23. Armitage to Woods, 15 April 1956, Woods Papers, Macmaster University Library, Hamilton, Ontario, Canada.
24. R. Welensky, *Welensky's 4000 Days: The Life and Death of the Federation of Rhodesia and Nyasaland* (London: Collins, 1964), p. 70. See also J. R. T. Wood, *The Welensky Papers: A History of the Federation of Rhodesia and Nyasaland* (Durban: Graham Publishing, 1983), p. 473.
25. Wood, op. cit., pp. 466–83.
26. *Memoirs*, 1956, p. 50.
27. *Memoirs*, 1957, p. 7.
28. *Memoirs*, 1957, pp. 16–17.
29. Material in this paragraph is from Letters, 5 July 1956; *Memoirs*, 1956, pp. 22, 52; Diary, 9 April 1956. See also A. Mell, *Government House and the Old Residency, Zomba* (Zomba: The Government Printer, 1960), pp. 7–8.
30. Material in this and the following paragraph is from Diary, 11 April and 6 September 1956.
31. Material in this paragraph dealing with Government House staff is from Mrs Beryl Leeds (née Freeman) to author, 14 March, 13 April and 31 May 1995; R. Rowan to author, 8 November 1991; Papers, P. A. S. Robertson to Woods, 6 December 1955; *Memoirs*, 1957, pp. 22, 38, 39, 58.
32. Material in this paragraph dealing with Government House grounds is from Diary, 11 April 1956; Papers, Lady Armitage to Mrs Armitage, 11 May 1956; Letters, 10 May 1956.
33. Letters, 10 May 1956.

34. R. C. F. Maugham, *Africa As I Have Known It* (London: John Murray, 1929), p. 93.
35. Papers, Lady Armitage to Mrs Armitage, 11 May 1956; Armitage to Haworth, 30 April 1956.
36. Letters, 3 June 1956.
37. Letters, 10 May 1956; Papers, Armitage to Haworth, 15 May 1956.
38. Diary, 26 October 1956.
39. Chiume to author, 19 August 1994; Chiume, op. cit., p. 83.
40. Material in this and the following two paragraphs is from Diary, 25 and 27 August, 7 and 21 September, 14 and 27 October, and 2, 11 and 30 November 1956.
41. RHL Mss. Afr. s.2204, 5/1.
42. Material in this and the following paragraph is from Diary, 9 July, 25 August, 25 October, and 14–16 November 1956. For relations with other federal and Southern Rhodesian politicians, see *Memoirs*, 1956, pp. 58, 69, 75, 76, 80, 83; Letters, 10 May, 12 October, 1 November, and 5 and 13 December 1956. In cases where the context does not make it clear whether John Foot or Dingle Foot is being referred to, their initials are used.
43. For relations with other Europeans, see *Memoirs*, 1956, pp. 68, 73, 74, 77, 81, 82, 83; Diary, 14 June, 8 and 28 August, 16, 17 and 31 October, and 1 November 1956. For relations with businessmen and industrialists, see *Memoirs*, 1956, pp. 65–8, 85, 87, 88; Letters, 1 November and 5 December 1956; Diary, 2 June 1956.
44. Material in this paragraph dealing with Nyasaland's advance within the federation is from Diary, 30 August, 17 and 25 October, and 1 November 1956.
45. For Armitage's tours, see Diary, 21–9 June, 30–31 July, 14–16 August, and 19 November 1956. For his visits to industry, see Diary, 16, 18 and 20 July and 26 November 1956. For his visits to development projects, see Diary, 18 July, 20–1 September, 5 November, and 29–30 December 1956. For his visits to missions, see Diary, 17 July, 1 August, and 11–12 September 1956.
46. Material in this and the following three paragraphs, except where otherwise stated, is from Papers, Armitage to Lennox-Boyd, 11 October 1956.
47. Diary, 20 July 1956.
48. Wood, op. cit., pp. 30, 536; Nyasaland Government Staff Lists, 1956 and 1957.
49. Material in this and the following paragraphs dealing with Lennox-Boyd's visit is from *Nyasaland: Report for the Year 1957* (London: HMSO, 1958), p. 1; *Memoirs*, 1957, pp. 1–8.
50. Material in this paragraph dealing with Home's visit is from *Nyasaland: Report for the Year 1957* (London: HMSO, 1958), p. 3; Letters, 13 and 17 October 1957; Wood, op. cit., pp. 561, 558, 562–3.
51. Material in this paragraph dealing with the Queen Mother's visit is from *Nyasaland: Report for the Year 1957* (London: HMSO, 1958), p. 2; *Memoirs*, 1957, pp. 37–47.
52. Chiume, op. cit., p. 86; W. M. Chirwa, interviews with author, 23 February 1996 and 11 February 1997.
53. *Report of the Nyasaland Commission of Inquiry*, Cmnd. 814 (London: HMSO, 1959), para. 30.

54. J. Ness to unnamed addressee, n.d. but early 1961, enclosed with R. Howard to author, 3 February 1983.
55. Material in this paragraph is from Letters, 15 February and 10 December 1957; *Memoirs*, 1957, p. 1 and 1958, p. 4; Diary, 4 December 1957.
56. *Memoirs*, 1958, p. 4.
57. Diary, 1 and 6 January 1958; Letters, 2 and 9 January 1958. For text of Armitage's Rotary Club speech, see *Memoirs*, 1958, pp. 12–17.
58. *Memoirs*, 1958, pp. 4–5.
59. Material in this and the following paragraph is from Diary, 9 and 21 January, 14 February, 21 and 27 March, 16 April, and 11 and 24 July 1958.
60. Material in this and the following two paragraphs is from Diary, 28 August, and 2, 3 and 5 October 1958; Letters, 3 October 1958; *Memoirs*, 1958, pp. 5–6.
61. R. Wade to de Quehen, 13 October 1958, enclosed with Wade to author, 6 January 1995.
62. Diary, 21, 24, 26 and 27 November 1958.
63. Material in this and the following paragraph is from Diary, 24 November 1958, and 6, 7 and 10 January 1959.
64. CO 1015/1519, Armitage to Gorell Barnes, 20 January 1959.
65. Moxon, evidence, 22 April 1959, DP Box 15, transcripts file, vol. 2.
66. Moxon, evidence, 22 April 1959, DP Box 15, transcripts file, vol. 2.
67. Kettlewell, memoirs, p. 83; Kettlewell to author, 23 May 1992; Letters, 2 April 1958.
68. Kettlewell to author, 23 May 1992.
69. Letters, 2 April 1959.
70. Cmnd. 814., para. 28. To distinguish him from Dr H. K. Banda, T. D. T. Banda is always referred to by his initials. D. K. Chisiza's brother, Y. K. Chisiza, is also always referred to by his initials.
71. Material in this paragraph is from Diary, 3 January 1958; Letters, 2 January 1958.
72. Diary, 6 January 1958; *Memoirs*, 1958, p. 23.
73. Diary, 30 January 1958; *Memoirs*, 1958, p. 9.
74. Diary, 20 February 1958; *Memoirs*, 1958, p. 38.
75. Diary, 26 and 27 February 1958; *Memoirs*, 1958, pp. 38–9.
76. Diary, 20 and 27 February 1958; Papers, J. Foot to Armitage, 5 April 1958.
77. Diary, 1 April 1958.
78. Material in this and the following paragraph is from Diary, 14, 19 and 20 March 1958; *Memoirs*, 1958, p. 23; Letters, 6 and 20 February, and 20 March 1958; Papers, Armitage to Haworth, 17 March 1958.
79. Material in this paragraph is from Diary, 2 April 1958.
80. Material in this and the following paragraph is from Diary, 3 February 1958; *Memoirs*, 1958, pp. 9–11.
81. *Memoirs*, 1958, p. 46.

6. Nyasaland II

1. Diary, 24 July 1958.
2. Diary, 1 July 1958.
3. Chisiza, evidence 18 May 1959, DP, Box 12A, pp. 2001–36; Welensky, op. cit., p. 98; Philip Short, *Banda* (London and Boston: Routledge & Kegan Paul, 1974), p. 90; Cmnd. 815, *Despatch from the Governor of Nyasaland* (London: HMSO, 1959), para. 48.

NOTES TO CHAPTER 6   383

4. Material in this and the following paragraph is from Short, op. cit., pp. 91–2; Wood, op. cit., p. 633; Papers, 12 August 1959 and 22 August; Bill Jackson, *Memoirs* (hereafter Jackson), pp. 47–51, privately held; Youens, interview with K. Bradley, 26 November 1970, p. 6, ODRP; *Nyasaland Times*, 28 October 1958; Cmnd. 814, para. 54; Late Question, No. 36, Preparation of Sunrise Lists, response prepared by Finney, 4 June 1959, DP, Box 24; Finney, evidence 12 May 1959, DP, Box 14, pp. 1403–4; Letters, 1 November 1958; Theunissen, interview with author, 26 June 1994.
5. Papers, Woods to Armitage, 10 December 1958.
6. Youens to Armitage, 5 January 1959, DP, Box 5, pp. 71 *et seq*.
7. Letters, 9 and 30 January, and 13 February 1959; *Nyasaland State of Emergency*, Cmnd. 707 (London: HMSO, 1959), paras 15 and 23; CO 1015/1519, Armitage to Gorell Barnes, 20 January 1959; Diary, 31 January and 1 February 1959.
8. Chisiza, evidence 18 May 1959, DP, Box 12A, pp. 2001–36; Chipembere, evidence 16 May 1959, DP, Box 12A, p. 1945; Cmnd. 707, para. 24; Cmnd. 814, para. 98; Diary, 24 and 25 January 1959.
9. Finney to Mullin, 18 February 1959, attached to Mullin to Footman, 18 January 1959, DP, Box 1, also Box 9; R. Posnett to author, 14 September 1993 and 15 March 1994.
10. Material in this and the following paragraph is from Letters, 28 November 1958; *Memoirs*, 1958, p. 98; Youens interview with author, 4 January 1995; Foreign and Commonwealth Office, Research and Analysis Department (hereafter FCO), Report by Morgan, January 1959 (the commission mentioned was eventually the Monckton Commission).
11. Letters, 7 February 1959; CO 1015/1976, Summary of Proposals made on Revision of Nyasaland Constitution, February 1959.
12. *Manchester Guardian*, 30 January 1959.
13. Armitage, evidence 21 May 1959, DP, Box 14, p. 1609.
14. Banda, evidence 16 May 1959, DP, Box 14, p. 1727.
15. Armitage, evidence 21 May 1959, DP, Box 14, pp. 1609–10.
16. Letters, 7 February 1959.
17. CO 1015/1976, Summary of Proposals made on Revision of Nyasaland Constitution, February 1959.
18. RHL Mss. Brit. Emp. s.527/1, Armitage, pp. 66–7.
19. CO 1017/1977, Armitage to Lennox-Boyd, 12 January 1959; Secretary of State to Armitage, 28 January 1959; Lennox-Boyd to Prime Minister, 4 February 1959.
20. *Memoirs*, 1959, pp. 4–5; Letters, 22 January 1959; Armitage, evidence 21 May 1959, DP, Box 14; Banda, evidence 16 May 1959, DP, Box 14, pp. 1737, 1742.
21. Details of Armitage's proposals are from Commonwealth Relations Office to High Commissioner Salisbury, 30 January 1959 (FCO).
22. Letters, 7 and 13 February 1959; Cmnd. 707, para. 26; Armitage, evidence 15 April 1959, DP, Box (NYC) 15, p. 2.
23. *Memoirs*, 1959, p. 14; Diary, 19 and 20 February 1959; Welensky, op. cit., p. 120; CO 1015/1515, Armitage to Morgan, 24 February 1959.
24. CO 1015/1515, Armitage to Morgan, 24 February 1959.
25. CO 1015/1538, Armitage to Secretary of State, 25 February 1959. See also Papers, Armitage to Haworth, 23 February 1959; CO 1015/1535, Perth to Manningham-Buller, 15 May 1959.

26. CO 1015/1515, Minister of State, Colonial Office to Governor Nyasaland, 27 February 1959; Secretary of State to Armitage, 1 March 1959.
27. CO 1015/1518, Armitage to Morgan, 27 February 1959.
28. Wood, op. cit., p. 643; Welensky, op. cit., p. 123.
29. CO 1015/1839, Armitage to Lennox-Boyd, 6 October 1959, para. 5; Cmnd. 814, paras. 133–6; W. A. Brent, *Rhodesian Air Force: A Brief History, 1947–1980* (Kwambona, RSA: Freeworld Press, 1987), p. 8; V. Flintman to author, 2 August 1995; Franklin to author, 30 January and March 1995; Edwards to author, 1 September 1995; *Evening Standard*, Salisbury, 3 March 1959, p. 1.
30. CO 1015/1515, Armitage to Secretary of State, 2 March 1959; Armitage to Lennox-Boyd, 2 March 1959. Armitage to Secretary of State, numerous telegrams 3 March 1959; Armitage to Secretary of State, 5 March 1959; *Memoirs*, 1959, p. 27; Colin Baker, *State of Emergency: Crisis in Central Africa, Nyasaland, 1959–1960* (London: Tauris Academic Studies, I.B.Tauris, 1997); Colin Baker, 'Dr Banda's Arrest and Resease from Detention', *Society of Malawi Journal*, vol. 49, no. 3, 1996, pp. 1–14.
31. F. Seaton, 'One Man's Emergency', *Outpost*, May 1959, pp. 19–22. More than 40 people from Fort Manning surrendered voluntarily. The other death was at Fort Manning. The Nkata Bay tragedy is dealt with in Cmnd. 814, paras. 226–39; Brock, evidence 7 April 1959, DP, Box 13, pp. 1161–85; Van Oppen, evidence 20 May 1959, DP, Box 13, pp. 1827–39; Nhlane, Munthali and Chunga, evidence 2 May 1959, DP, Box 13, pp. 976–83; inquest proceedings, DP, Box 17.
32. Letters, 5 March 1959; Papers, Lady Armitage to Mrs Armitage, 5 March 1959; *Memoirs*, 1959, p. 34.
33. Hansard, Commons, 3 March 1959, cols. 216–23.
34. Hansard, Commons, 3 March 1959, cols. 279–342. Details of the debate are from this source.
35. Posnett to author, 15 March 1994; RHL Mss. Brit. Emp. s. 527/1, Armitage.
36. *Memoirs*, 1959, p. 41.
37. Cmnd. 814, para. 258.
38. Cmnd. 814, *passim*; Lord Dalhousie to author, 24 December 1991; CO 1015/1515, Transcription of a shorthand note on a press conference by His Excellency the Governor to members of the press at 2.45 p.m. on Monday 2 March 1959.
39. Material in this and the following paragraph is from CO 1015/1517, Armitage to Welensky, 14 March 1959.
40. Letters, 27 March 1959; Armitage to Lennox-Boyd, 18 March 1959, DP, Box 5; Cmnd. 707, p. 3.
41. DO 35/7476, Armitage to Secretary of State, 23 March 1959; Letters, 20 March 1959.
42. CO 1015/1517, Minute by the Secretary of State, 9 March 1959.
43. CO 1015/1977, Report by the Minister of State for Colonial Office on a visit to the Territories of the Federation of Rhodesia and Nyasaland from 12 to 21 March 1959; CO 1015/1976, Notes on Nyasaland visit, 12 to 17 March 1959.
44. Material in this and the following paragraph is from A. Horne, *Macmillan, 1957–1986, Vol. II of the Official Biography* (London: Macmillan, 1988), p. 179; DO 35/7478, Meeting of interdepartmental central Africa committee, 12 March 1959; CO 1015/1544, Morgan to Macpherson, 6 July 1959; CO

NOTES TO CHAPTER 6

1015/1535, Lennox-Boyd to Armitage, 17 March 1959; CO 1015/1535, Armitage to Secretary of State, 20 and 22 March 1959.
45. Cmnd. 814, p. iii and para. l.
46. Letters, 27 March 1959. The Commission also asked Armitage a number of 'late questions' on points that had not previously been fully covered. There were at least 64 such 'late questions' (DP, Box 7).
47. CO 1015/1539, Note of Meeting between Secretary of State and Members of the Nyasaland Commission of Inquiry, 2 April 1959.
48. CO 1015/1535, Secretary of State to Armitage, 26 March 1959; Armitage to Lennox-Boyd, 31 March 1959, DP, Box l, p. 25.
49. Cmnd. 814, para. 1
50. *Memoirs*, 1959, p. 56.
51. Letters, 12 April 1959.
52. Armitage to Lennox-Boyd, 25 March 1959, DP, Box 7.
53. Wilks to Armitage, 26 March 1959, DP, Box 7; CO 1015/1539, Note of Meeting between Secretary of State and members of Nyasaland Commission of Inquiry, 2 April 1959; Williams, interview with author, 8 October 1993.
54. Cmnd. 814, para. 1.
55. Material in this paragraph is from Armitage, evidence 15 April 1959, DP, Box (NYC) 15, pp. 1–12. See, also Letters, 12 April 1958 (*sic*, must be 1959); Armitage to Devlin, 15 April 1959, DP, Box 16.
56. Armitage, evidence 21 May 1959, DP, Box 14, pp. 1601–23; Points for consideration by the Nyasaland Government, 27 May 1959, DP, Box 16.
57. RHL Mss. Brit. Emp. s.527/1, Armitage, p. 43.
58. CO 1015/1540, Notes on Lord Perth's talk with Devlin, 23 June 1959.
59. Devlin to author, 3 January 1992.
60. Williams, interview with author, 8 October 1993; Moreton to author, 28 September 1993; Jackson, p. 105.
61. CO 1015/1535, Confidential Circular Despatch from Secretary of State James Griffiths to Officer Administering the Government of Nyasaland, 12 August 1950.
62. CO 1015/1535, Armitage to Gorell Barnes, 30 April 1959.
63. CO 1015/1540, Armitage to Morgan, 13 June 1959.
64. CO 1015/1540, Notes on Lord Perth's talk with Devlin, 23 June 1959.
65. CO 1015/1540, Secretary of State to Gorell Barnes, 17 June 1959; CO 1015/1538, Gorell Barnes to Moreton, 18 June 1959; CO 1015/1540, Morgan to Gorell Barnes, 24 June 1959.
66. CO 1015/1540, Perth to Secretary of State, 6 July 1959.
67. Information on the meeting comes from Wyn-Harris to Devlin, 12 July 1959, DP, Box 26; Devlin to Primrose, 10 July 1959, DP, Box 20, p. 48; Proof of paras. 288–98 of draft report, DP, Box 18; Williams, interview with author, 8 October 1993.
68. Cmnd. 814, paras 285–6.
69. Armitage, evidence 21 May 1959, DP, Box 14, p. 1615. Roberts says that 'other witnesses, District Commissioners, said how sorry they were that deaths and injury resulted from the necessity for them to maintain and restore law and order' (Roberts, interview with author, 1 July 1993). It is possible that the word 'an' in Armitage's reply was a shorthand mistranscription of the word 'one'.
70. Material in this paragraph is from CO 1015/1540, Secretary of State to

Armitage, 24 June and 13 July 1959; Wilks to Morgan, n.d., probably early July 1959; Secretary of State to Armitage, 13 July 1959; Papers, Lennox-Boyd to Armitage, 13 July 1959, cited in *Memoirs*, 1959, p. 78.

71. CO 1015/1540, Armitage to Secretary of State, 16 July 1959; *Memoirs*, 1959, p. 79.
72. CO 1015/1540, Morgan to Macpherson, 14 July 1959.
73. Letters, 20 July 1959; Posnett to author, 15 March 1994.
74. *Memoirs*, 1959, p. 81; Posnett to author, 15 March 1994; Letters, 20 July 1959; CO 1015/1537, Guide to contents of dispatch from Governor of Nyasaland, n.d.; *Nyasaland: Despatch by the Governor Relating to the Report of the Nyasaland Commission of Inquiry*, Cmnd. 815 (London: HMSO, 1959); CO 1015/1540, Armitage to Footman, 19 July 1959.
75. Hansard, Commons, 28 July 1959, cols. 317–454. Details of the debate are from this source.
76. Letters, 29 July 1959. See also Chiume, op. cit., p. 126.
77. *Memoirs*, 1959, p. 98.
78. Material in this paragraph is from Papers, various letters of congratulation; Letters, 4 and 27 August 1959; Papers, Statement by Armitage, 30 July 1959. See also CO 1015/1544, Armitage to Secretary of State, 15 July 1959.
79. Pegg to author, 17 July 1995; Papers, Lady Armitage to Haworth, 8 September 1959; Muir to author, 28 March 1995.
80. CO 1015/1839, Armitage to Lennox-Boyd, 6 October 1959. See also Letters, 9 October 1959.
81. CO 1015/1838, Minute by Lennox-Boyd, 14 October 1959; CO 1015/1839, Minute by Perth, 13 October 1959; CO 1015/1839, de Zeuluta to Howard-Drake, 2 November 1959.
82. Sampson, op. cit., p. 183.
83. CAB 21/3155, Macmillan to Brook, 1 November 1959.
84. Material in this and the following paragraph is from Diary, 7 November 1959; CO 1015/1984, Note of a meeting in the Secretary of State's room, 10 November 1959. Details in the following two paragraphs are from this latter source.
85. *Memoirs*, 1959, p. 137; Letters, 10 and 12 November 1959 and Papers, Armitage to Haworth, 29 November 1959.
86. *Memoirs*, 1959, p. 135.
87. Diary, 16 November 1959.
88. *Memoirs*, 1959, p. 136.
89. Material in this paragraph, except where otherwise stated, is from PREM 11/3075 and DO 35/7564, Macleod to Macmillan, 3 December 1959.
90. Shepherd, op. cit., p. 188.
91. Diary, 18 and 19 December 1959; CO 1015/1518, Macleod to Perth, 20 December 1959; Theunissen, interview with author, 26 June 1994.
92. Diary, 29 and 31 December 1959; *Memoirs*, 1959, p. 147.
93. Papers, Armitage to Secretary of State, 30 December 1959.
94. Diary, 28 December 1959; Letters, 31 December 1959.
95. CO 1015/1518, Macleod to Perth, 20 December 1959; Note by Secretary of State on Nyasaland Emergency, 24 December 1959.
96. DO 35/7476, Minute, unsigned, dated 24 December 1959; DO 35/7476, Minute by Shannon, 29 December 1959. Material on the cabinet meeting is

from Macmillan's diaries, held in the Bodleian Library, Oxford, Ms. Macmillan, dep. d. 37, diaries for 3 and 4 January 1960.
97. RHL Mss. Brit. Emp. s.527/1, Armitage, p. 36.
98. DO 35/7476, Macleod to Armitage, 4 January 1960.
99. RHL Mss. Brit. Emp. s.527/1, Armitage, p. 85.
100. DO 35/7476, Commonwealth Relations Office to Welensky, 5 January 1960.
101. Diary, 6 January 1960.
102. Papers, Armitage to Macleod, 7 January 1960.
103. *Memoirs*, 1960, pp. 5–6.
104. DO 35/7564, Macleod to Macmillan, 16 January 1960.
105. *Memoirs*, 1960, p. 6.
106. Material in this and the following paragraph is from Papers, Armitage's manuscript note on Secretary of State to Armitage, 4 February 1960 and Theunissen, interview with author, 26 June 1994.
107. *Memoirs*, 1959, pp. 4–5. See also Diary, 7 January 1960.
108. For Tapsell's admiration and support of Macleod, see Shepherd, op. cit., pp. 362, 364.
109. P. Tapsell, interview with author, 7 January 1994, and Tapsell to author, 18 October 1995.
110. Wellman (House of Commons Library) to author, 21 October 1994.
111. H. Berkeley to author, 17 May 1994.
112. Material in this paragraph is from R. Bennett to author, 6 January and 16 August 1992. See also Diary, 21 January 1960.
113. PREM 11/3075, Note of meeting of ministers held at Salisbury on 19 January 1960. For Welensky's account of meeting, see Welensky, op. cit., pp. 171 *et seq.*; see also Wood, op. cit., pp. 731–4. Macmillan found that 'Ghana and Nigeria were the easiest intellectually; the Federation (especially with Welensky and Whitehead on one side and the Governors of Northern Rhodesia and Nyasaland on the other) was the trickiest' (Macmillan's diaries, Bodleian Library, Oxford, Ms. Macmillan, dep. d. 38, diary for 7 February 1960).
114. G. Clay, interview with author, 26 October 1994.
115. Papers, *Official Programme*, op. cit. The published programme followed precisely that proposed by Armitage (CAB 21/3155, Armitage to Secretary of State, 30 November 1959).
116. Details of meeting are drawn from Diary, 25–26 January 1960; *Memoirs*, 1959, pp. 12–13; Rowan to author, 5 July 1993; Maxwell-Lawford to author, 26 May 1994, and interview with author, 26 April 1994; King to author, 6 and 27 November 1991; Ingham to author, 19 November 1991; Hunt to author, October and 26 December 1991; Hunt, op. cit., pp. 107–8; Robertson to author, 11 March and 7 October 1992; H. Macmillan, *Pointing the Way* (London: Macmillan, 1972) (hereafter *Pointing*), pp. 148–9; Wade to author, 6 January 1995. Thus, of those who were present, only the accounts of Brook and Footman – the heads of the two civil services – are not available. Wade was a federal intelligence officer.
117. Fisher, op. cit., p. 158; DO 35/7477, Macmillan to Macleod, 26 January 1960; Welensky, op. cit., pp. 175–8.
118. CAB 21/3157, Minute, Brook to Macmillan, 24 January 1960; PREM 11/3075, Note, Brook to Macmillan, 24 January 1960; PREM 11/3075, Blight to Macmillan, 26 January 1960; Diary, 25 January 1960.

119. PREM 11/3075, Note of meeting between Macmillan and Foot at Government House, Zomba, 25 January 1960; Diary, 25 January 1960.
120. Diary, 26 January 1960.
121. Watson to author, 20 January, 1994.
122. *The Southworth Commission Report* (Zomba: The Government Printer, 1960).
123. Hunt to author, 26 December 1991; see also Diary, 15 March 1960; and *Memoirs*, 1960, p. 16.
124. R. H. Martin to author, 21 January 1995.
125. Material in this and the following two paragraphs is from Welensky, op. cit., p. 179; PREM 11/3085, Gibbs to Home, 6 February 1960; DO 35/4564, Macmillan to Home and Macleod, 28 February 1960; Macmillan, *Pointing*, p. 149.
126. DO 35/7564, Macmillan to Macleod, 28 January 1960.
127. DO 35/7564, Macmillan to Home, 28 January 1960.
128. Ibid.
129. Material in this and the following paragraph is from DO 35/7477 and DO 35/7574, Macleod to Armitage, 1 February, 1960. Material in this paragraph is from this source. See also Diary, 2 February 1960.
130. DO 35/7564, Macmillan to Macleod, 28 January 1960.
131. Hunt to author, 26 December 1991; Macmillan to the Queen, 30 January 1960, cited in Macmillan, *Pointing*, Appendix 2, p. 485; Macmillan's diaries, held in the Bodleian Library, Oxford, Ms. Macmillan, dep. d. 37, diary for 11 November 1959 and dep. d. 38, diary for 7 February 1960.
132. Diary, 29 January 1960.
133. See Sampson, op. cit., pp. 189–90.
134. DO 35/7564, Macleod to Armitage, 2 February 1960.
135. Diary, 2 February 1960.
136. Material in this and the following paragraph is from Papers, Footman to Armitage, 23 January 1958.
137. Material in this and the following paragraph is from Papers, Armitage to Morgan, 13 August 1958.
138. Material in this and the following two paragraphs is from Papers, A. R. Thomas to Armitage, 13 October, 12 and 28 November 1958; Thomas to Footman, 6 November 1958; Armitage to Secretary of State, 27 October 1958; Footman to Armitage, 7 November 1958.
139. Papers, Gorell Barnes to Armitage, 20 May 1959.
140. Papers, Armitage to Gorell Barnes, 9 June 1959.
141. Material in this and the following paragraph is from Papers, Monson to Armitage, 13 August 1959; Armitage to Monson, 19 August 1959.
142. Papers, Poynton to Armitage, 21 September 1959; and Armitage's manuscript note thereon.
143. Papers, Poynton to Hone, 21 September 1959.
144. Papers, Hone to Poynton, 30 September 1959, and Hone to Armitage, 30 September 1959.
145. Papers, Armitage to Poynton, 2 October 1959.
146. Material in this paragraph, except where otherwise stated, is from Papers, Armitage to Secretary of State, 16 November 1959; Monson to Armitage, 3 December 1959.
147. Welensky, interview with author, 12 June 1982.

148. Papers, Poynton to Armitage, 20 November 1959.
149. Papers, Armitage to Poynton, 9 December 1959.
150. Material in this and the following paragraph is from Papers, Armitage to Monson, 21 December 1959 and Armitage to Secretary of State, 11 January 1960; Jones Papers, personal diary, 1–19 January 1960; Poynton to Jones, 6 January 1960 and Chambers to Jones 6 January 1960.
151. Papers, Secretary of State to Armitage, 1 February 1960 (dispatched at 16.43 hours on 1 February and received at 15.45 hours on 2 February) and Armitage's manuscript note thereon.
152. Papers, Armitage to Macleod, 3 February 1960.
153. Ibid.; Papers, Macleod to Armitage, 4 February 1960.
154. Material in this and the following paragraph is from Papers, Footman to Armitage, 3 and 5 February 1960; draft telegram, Armitage to Secretary of State, 4 February 1960; Macleod to Armitage, 4 February 1960.
155. Papers, Macleod to Armitage, 4, 8 and 10 February 1960; Armitage to Macleod, 6 February 1960.
156. Material in this and the following two paragraphs is from Papers, Macleod to Armitage, 1 and 4 February 1960; Armitage's manuscript note on Secretary of State to Armitage, 11 February 1960; minutes, Phillips to Armitage, 1 March and 9 April 1960; Armitage to Monson 3 March 1960; Monson to Armitage, 5 April 1960.
157. Welensky, op. cit., pp. 179–81; Wood, op. cit., pp. 743–5; *Memoirs*, 1960, p. 27; DO 35/7564, Welensky to Macmillan, 3 February 1960; Macmillan's diaries, held in the Bodleian Library, Oxford, Ms. Macmillan, dep. d. 38, diary for 7 February 1960.
158. Diary, 2 February 1960.
159. DO 35/7564, Armitage to Macleod, 10 February 1960; DO 53/7564, Macleod to Armitage, 12 February 1960; *Memoirs*, 1960, pp. 31–2; Diary, 17 February 1960.
160. *Daily Express*, 19 February, 1960; *News Chronicle*, 19 February 1960; PREM 11/3081, Evans to Macmillan, 20 February 1960; PREM 11/3081, Macmillan note, 21 February 1960.
161. Diary, 16 February 1960; *Memoirs*, 1960, p. 31.
162. Diary, 23 and 24 February 1960, *Memoirs*, 1960, p. 33.
163. Material in this and the following paragraph is from Macmillan's diaries held in the Bodleian Library, Oxford, Ms. Macmillan, dep. d. 38, diaries for 23 and 25 February 1960.
164. DO 35/7565, draft Cabinet paper on the release of Banda: discussions in Salisbury, memorandum by Secretary of State for Commonwealth Relations, n.d., probably late February 1960; PREM 11/3076, Home to Macmillan, 22 February 1960. For Welensky's account of Home's visit, see Welensky, op. cit., pp. 183 *et seq.*; Wood, op. cit., pp. 751 *et seq.*
165. DO 35/7564, Home to Macmillan, 21 February 1960; Diary, 26 February 1960.
166. Diary, 27 February 1960.
167. Material in this paragraph is from Diary, 27 February 1960; *Memoirs*, 1960, p. 35.
168. Macmillan's diaries, held in the Bodleian Library, Oxford, Ms. Macmillan, dep. d. 38, diary for 27 February 1960.

169. Diary, 2 March 1960.
170. *Memoirs*, 1960, p. 37; RHL ss.Brit. Emp. s.527/5, p. 167, Gbedemah.
171. Material in this paragraph is from Diary, 5, 7, 9 and 14 March 1960; DO 35/7564, Macleod to Armitage, 9 March 1960; DO 35/7564, Commonwealth Relations Office to High Commissioner Salisbury, n.d., probably 9 or 10 March 1960; DO 35/7566, Macleod to Armitage, 12 March 1960; DO 35/7566, Armitage to Macleod, 14 March 1960.
172. *Nyasaland: Report for the Year 1960* (London: HMSO, 1961), p. 3.
173. Diary, 27 March 1960.
174. Haskard to author, 27 February 1994.
175. Codrington to author, 12 February 1994.
176. Youens, interview with Bradley, 26 November 1970, Oxford Colonial Records Project (Youens's privately held copy); interview with author, 4 January 1995. See also Colin Baker, 'Dr Banda's Arrest and Release from Detention, 1959–1950', *Society of Malawi Journal*, vol. 49, no. 3, 1996, pp. 1–14.
177. Diary, 1 April 1960.
178. DO 35/7566, Watson to Morris, 1 April 1960; *Memoirs*, 1960, pp. 44–5.
179. Howard-Drake to author, 7 October 1993 and 1 February 1994; see also PREM 11/3070, Macleod to Macmillan, 3 April 1960; Fisher, op. cit., p. 160; Shepherd, op. cit., p. 203, citing Monson.
180. DO 35/7566, Macleod to Dalhousie, 4 April 1960; Short, op. cit., p. 131.
181. *Memoirs*, 1960, pp. 54, 62, 66; Proceedings of Nyasaland Legislative Council, 3rd Meeting, 74th Session, 10–12 May 1960, p. 281; *Nyasaland: Report for the Year 1960* (London: HMSO, 1961), pp. 4, 115–16; DO 35/7477, Text of announcement by Armitage, 15 June 1960; see also PREM 11/3077, Macleod to Macmillan, 2 June 1960, and PREM 11/3077, Minute, Macmillan, 3 June 1960.
182. *Report of the Nyasaland Constitutional Conference*, Cmnd. 1132 (London: HMSO, 1960).
183. PREM 11/3082, Macleod to Welensky, 30 May 1960, Annex 2.
184. Ibid.
185. Macleod to Armitage, 5 July 1960, cited in *Memoirs*, 1960/2, p. 15.
186. *Memoirs*, 1960/2, pp. 16–20.
187. Ibid., pp. 20–1.
188. Wood, op. cit., pp. 799–801; PREM 11/3075, Brook to Macmillan, 10 February 1960; PREM 11/3076, Watson to Monson, 23 February 1960.
189. *Memoirs*, 1960/2, p. 23.
190. Ibid., p. 24.
191. Wood, op. cit., p. 804.
192. *Report of the Nyasaland Constitutional Conference*, Cmnd. 1132 (London: HMSO, 1960), p. 5.
193. Short, op. cit., p. 135.
194. *Guardian*, 26 July 1960.
195. Short, op. cit., p. 135.
196. *Memoirs*, 1960/2 pp. 24–6.
197. *Memoirs*, 1960/2, p. 26.
198. Short, op. cit., pp. 135–6, citing *The Times*, 30 July 1960.
199. *Memoirs*, 1960/2, p. 27.

200. Diary, 31 July 1960; *Memoirs*, 1960/2, pp. 27–8.
201. Diary, 1 August 1960.
202. *Memoirs*, 1960/2, p. 28.
203. PREM 11/3077, Macleod to Macmillan, 2 August 1960. But see Wood, op. cit., p. 806. Both Dixon and Blackwood thought the conference would break down on 2 August 1960.
204. Material in this and the following paragraph, except where otherwise stated, is from Cmnd. 1132, pp. 5–9; PREM 11/3077, Macmillan to Macleod, 6 August 1960; Macleod to Welensky, 30 May 1960, cited in Wood, op. cit., pp. 787, 792.
205. Cmnd. 1132, pp. 9–10.
206. *Memoirs*, 1960/2, pp. 31–2; PREM 11/3077, Macleod to Macmillan, 2 August 1960; Welensky, op. cit., p. 205. Indeed, Macleod's first report to Welensky was made within an hour of his opening speech (Wood, op. cit., p. 804).
207. *Memoirs*, 1960/2, p. 25; Diary, 26 July and 4 August 1960.
208. Diary, 4 August 1960.
209. Diary, 5 August 1960.

7. Nyasaland III

1. Material in this and the following paragraph is from Diary, 10–31 August 1960; *Memoirs*, 1960/2, pp. 38, 41. Armitage's *Memoirs* covering 1960 are bound in two volumes: 1960/2 denotes the second volume.
2. Cited in *Memoirs*, 1960/2, pp. 39 *et seq.*
3. Material in this and the following paragraph is from Diary, 8–13, 27 and 31 October 1960; *Memoirs*, 1960/2, pp. 42 *et seq.*, 54–6.
4. Material in this paragraph is from Diary, 31 October and 1 November 1960; *Memoirs*, 1960/2, pp. 56–7.
5. Papers, Jones to Armitage, 25 August 1960.
6. Papers, Jones to Armitage, 12 September 1960.
7. Papers, Jones to Armitage, 28 September 1960.
8. Jones Papers, Armitage to Jones, 18 September 1960.
9. Papers, Jones to Armitage, 28 September 1960.
10. Cited in *Memoirs*, 1960/2, pp. 43–4.
11. *Memoirs*, 1960/2, pp. 44–5.
12. Papers, Jones to Armitage, 28 September 1960.
13. Material in this and the following six paragraphs is from Papers, Minute, Armitage to Jones, 3 November 1960; Diary 30 November 1960.
14. Material in this and the following paragraph is from Papers, Jones to Armitage, 28 September and 29 December 1960; Diary, 9 November 1960; Foster, interview with author, 20 April 1995.
15. Diary, 23 November 1960; *Memoirs*, 1960/2, pp. 83–4, 94.
16. Letters, 11 November 1960.
17. *Memoirs*, 1960/2, pp. 97–8.
18. Diary, 30 November 1960.
19. Diary, 4 March 1961.
20. Material in this and the following paragraph is from Diary, 27 April 1961; Papers, Welensky to Armitage, 24 February 1964; Welensky, interview with author, 12 June 1982; Jones Papers, RHL, Macleod to Jones, 7 April 1960. Welensky asked Macmillan to recognize Armitage's services as governor –

392   NOTES TO CHAPTER 7

presumably by the award of the GCMG – but this, vindictively in Welensky's view, was not done.
21. Diary, 1 to 4 December 1960; *Memoirs*, 1960/2, p. 102.
22. Diary, 3 December 1960; *Memoirs*, 1960/2, pp. 102, 129.
23. Diary, 6 December 1960; Letters, 9 December 1960; *Memoirs*, 1960/2, p. 104.
24. Diary, 6 December 1960.
25. Material in this paragraph is from Papers, Jones to Armitage, 5 December 1960; *Memoirs*, 1960/2, pp. 131–2.
26. Material in this and the following three paragraphs is from Diary, 5–12 December 1960 and 21 January 1961; Letters, 17 December 1960; *Memoirs*, 1960/2, pp. 105–6, 119–21; PREM 11/3075, Brook to Macmillan, 10 February 1960.
27. *Memoirs*, 1960/2, pp. 129–30.
28. Material in this and the following paragraph is from Diary, 12, 14 and 18 December 1960.
29. *Memoirs*, 1960/2, p. 130.
30. Material in this and the following paragraph is from *Memoirs*, 1960/2, pp. 130–1; Letters, 17 December 1960.
31. Material in this and the following paragraph is from Papers, Jones to Armitage, 16 December 1960; Letters, 19 December 1960; Diary, 16–17 December 1960; *Memoirs*, 1960/2, pp. 135–6.
32. Material in this paragraph is from Letters, 19 December 1960; Diary, 18, 21 and 22 December 1960.
33. Material in this paragraph is from Diary, 22, 23 and 25 December 1960.
34. Diary, 24 and 31 December 1960.
35. Material in this and the following paragraph is from Diary, 28 and 30 December 1960; *Memoirs*, 1960/2, p. 140.
36. Material in this and the following paragraph is from Diary, 30 December 1960; Letters, 6 January 1961.
37. Material in this and the following paragraph is from Diary, 31 December 1960.
38. Letters, 30 December 1960; Diary, 25 and 31 December 1960.
39. Letters, 6 and 13 January 1961.
40. Letters, 13 and 21 January 1961; Diary, 18–20 January 1961.
41. Material in this and the following two paragraphs is from Diary, 22–5 January 1961.
42. Letters, 11 February 1961.
43. Material in this and the following paragraph is from Letters, 18 February 1961.
44. Material in this and the following paragraph is from Letters, 24 February 1961; Diary, 13, 21, 23, 24 and 26 February, and 4, 7, 9 and 10 March 1961; Papers, Armitage to Haworth, 26 February 1961.
45. Diary, 12, 16, 18 February, and 11 March 1961; Letters, 17 February 1961.
46. Letters, 3 March 1961.
47. Material in this paragraph is from Letters, 10 March 1961.
48. Material in this and the following paragraph is from Letters, 17, 23 and 31 March 1961.
49. Material in this paragraph is from Letters, 23 and 31 March 1961; Diary, 26 March 1961.

50. Material in this paragraph is from Letters, 4 and 7 April 1961; Diary, 4 April 1961.
51. Material in this paragraph is from Diary, 4, 6 and 9 April 1961; Letters, 7 April 1961.
52. Diary, 6 April 1961; Letters, 7 and 15 April 1961.
53. Letters, 15 April 1961.
54. Referred to in Armitage to Jones, n.d., Jones Papers.
55. Armitage to Jones, n.d., Jones Papers.

8. Retirement

1. Material in this and the following five paragraphs, unless otherwise stated, is from Letters, 15 April to 23 May 1961.
2. RHL Mss. Afr. s.2204, 4/2, Renison to Armitage, 4 March 1961; Armitage to Renison, 9 March 1961.
3. D. and S. Ould, interview with author, 22 August 1991.
4. Armitage to Jones, 1 May 1961, Jones Papers.
5. Armitage to Jones, 10 June 1961, Jones Papers.
6. Lord Altrincham, *Kenya's Opportunity* (London: Faber & Faber, 1955), p. 90.
7. Papers, Phoebe Armitage to Mrs Armitage, 29 June 1961.
8. Material in this and the following four paragraphs is from Letters, 6 June to 15 October 1961 and 24 March 1963.
9. Material in this and the following two paragraphs, except where otherwise stated, is from Letters, 21 and 28 January 1962.
10. Letters, 27 May and 2 September 1962.
11. Foley, *Legacy*, p. 21.
12. Letters, 4 February 1962.
13. Material in this and the following paragraph is from Letters, 4 February, 25 March, 1 April, 8 July and 12 August 1962.
14. Material in this and the following two paragraphs is from Letters, 1 April, 4 and 27 May, 5 and 26 August, 23 September and 11 November 1962.
15. Letters, 4 May 1962.
16. Material in this paragraph is from Letters, 3 and 21 June and 15 July 1962.
17. Papers, Colonial Office to Armitage, 20 March 1962.
18. J. Wilson to author, February 1992; J. Weld to author, 17 January 1992; Letters, 17 September 1962.
19. Material in this and the following paragraph is from Letters, 27 December 1962, and 3 and 20 January 1963.
20. Letters, 13 March, and 13 and 28 April 1963.
21. Material in this paragraph is from Letters, 20 October and 2 December 1962; and Papers, Lady Armitage to Mrs Armitage, 21 October 1962.
22. Papers, Notes for talks to parish church council on Jairos Jere Centre.
23. Material in this paragraph is from Papers, Notes for talks at Bryanston School, Blandford.
24. Letters, 1962–5, *passim*.
25. Papers, A. Beit to Armitage, 22 July 1963 and Lady Beit to Armitage, 8 August 1963.
26. Papers, unpublished Report to Beit Trust on visit to central Africa, January–February 1965.

27. Papers, unpublished Report to Beit Trust on visit to central Africa, March 1969.
28. Papers, unpublished Report to Beit Trust on visit to central Africa, March 1972.
29. Papers, unpublished Report to Beit Trust on visit to central Africa, March 1976.
30. Papers, unpublished Report to Beit Trust on visit to central Africa, March 1980.
31. Papers, Invitation, 11 September 1973, and seating plan. See also *Daily Telegraph*, 12 September 1973.
32. Papers, unpublished Report to Beit Trust on visit to central Africa, March–April 1984.
33. *Daily Times*, 2 April 1984, pp. 1, 2.
34. Papers, Armitage to Beit, 5 November 1986, cited in Beit to Armitage, 12 November 1986.
35. RHL Mss. Brit. Emp. s.527/5(1), p. 49.
36. Maxwell-Lawford, interview with author, 24 April 1994. Material in the remainder of this paragraph is from this source.
37. J. Armitage, interview with author, 24 November 1991.
38. Lady Armitage, interview with author, 24 November 1991.
39. Letters, 11 November 1962.
40. Lapping, op. cit., p. 21.
41. Maxine Baker to author, 30 May 1991, and enclosures. Other details about the Granada series preparation are from Papers and RHL Mss. Brit. Emp. 527.
42. The following quotations on Kenya, Ghana and Cyprus are from Lapping, op. cit., pp. 419–22, 466–8, 522.
43. T. D. Williams, *Malawi: The Politics of Despair* (London: Cornell University Press, 1978), p. 260.
44. Material in this and the following two paragraphs is from Papers, Tawney to Armitage, 4 March 1963 and 15 April 1964; Thomas to Armitage, 22 January 1980 and 29 January 1981; Kettlewell to Armitage, 15 May 1981, 30 October 1983 and 10 November 1985; Armitage to Kettlewell, 19 May 1983.
45. Material in this and the following two paragraphs is from Lady Armitage, interview with author, 24 November 1991; Papers, Kirk-Greene to Armitage, 2 June, 29 July, 1989; Kirk-Greene to Armitage, 21 August 1989 and Armitage to Kirk-Greene, 30 November 1989, both enclosed with Kirk-Greene to author, 26 February 1990.
46. Lady Armitage, interview with author, 24 November 1991; Jeremy Armitage, interviews with author, 20–22 November 1996.
47. Papers, Armitage to the Vicar of Bridstow church, 28 August 1982; Papers, death certificate, 11 June 1990; Jeremy Armitage, interviews with author, 20–22 November 1996.
48. Address by Canon Donald Goldie at funeral service, 14 June 1990, privately held.

9. Missions impossible

1. Trench, op. cit., p. 198.
2. Davies to author, 30 June 1991.
3. Papers, Benson to Armitage, 26 September 1955.

4. Papers, Teeling to Armitage, 29 September 1955.
5. Papers, Altrincham to Armitage, 27 September 1955.
6. Papers, Keightley to Armitage, 3 January 1956.
7. Papers, Gorell Barnes to Armitage, 4 February 1961.
8. Diary, 4 November 1960.
9. The Colonial Office and the Commonwealth Relations Office were merged in 1966 and then amalgamated with the Foreign Office in 1968 to form the Foreign and Commonwealth Office. See, G. K. Fry, *The Administrative Revolution in Whitehall* (London: Croom Helm, 1981), p. 45.
10. *Daily Telegraph*, 13 June 1960.
11. Jeremy Armitage, interviews with author, 20–22 November 1996.
12. RHL Mss. Brit. Emp. s.527/1, Armitage, p. 36; P. Howard, interview with author, 30 July 1994.
13. Diary, 3 November 1960; Kettlewell, interview with author, 24 March 1994.
14. Papers, J. Grigg to Jeremy Armitage, n.d. but mid-June 1990.
15. Papers, Lennox-Boyd to Armitage, 25 October 1959.
16. Papers, Macleod to Armitage, 7 July 1961.

Sources

Primary sources

1. The Armitage Papers. There are two collections of these. His private papers covering the years 1929–47, i.e. his years in Kenya, are deposited in Rhodes House Library, Oxford: Mss. Afr. s.2204. Those covering subsequent years, i.e. his service in the Gold Coast, Cyprus and Nyasaland and his retirement, together with miscellaneous papers concerning mainly his family, have been lent to the author by Armitage's elder son, Jeremy, and will, in due course, be deposited with the other papers in Rhodes House Library. These private papers include Armitage's personal diaries and letters from 1929 to 1961 and his draft memoirs for the years 1956 to 1960. The Armitage papers are referred to as Papers; the Armitage Diaries as Diary; the Armitage letters as Letters; and the Armitage draft memoirs as *Memoirs*.
2. The Glyn Jones Papers in the possession of his daughter, Elisabeth.
3. The Colby Papers deposited in Rhodes House Library.
4. The Devlin Papers deposited in Rhodes House Library. In 1994–6, when the research for this book was undertaken, the Devlin Papers had not yet been catalogued. Reference to them, therefore, is made by Box number.
5. The Granada *End of Empire* Television Series documents in Rhodes House Library: Mss. Brit. Emp. s.527/1, s.527/2, s.527/3, and s.527/5.
6. The Kellock Papers deposited in the Borthwick Institute of Historical Studies, University of York.
7. Sir Edgar Williams's Papers, privately held.
8. Anthony Fairclough's Papers, privately held.
9. The Rhodes House Library collection of transcripts of interviews carried out by the Oxford Development Research Project and its predecessor projects.
10. Documents in the Foreign and Commonwealth Research and Analysis Department library.
11. Private memoirs:
    W. Jackson, *Send Us Friends*, privately held. These memoirs have since been published privately by Jackson under the same title.
    R. W. Kettlewell, *Memories of a Colonial Officer*, privately held.
    R. H. Martin, *My Middle Years, Palestine to Nyasaland, 1949–1964*, privately held.
    F. J. Wright, *A Tenth Child's Family History*, privately held.
12. Private correspondence with more than 300 people who knew or worked with Sir Robert Armitage from his early preparatory school days (1917) until his death (1990), in the possession of the author.
13. Interviews conducted by the author with:

SOURCES 397

Jeremy Armitage, Lady Armitage, Humphry Berkeley, John Codrington, Sir Robert Foster, Michael Harris, Sir David Hunt, Bryn Jones-Walters, Richard Kettlewell, Paul Lewis, Alan Lodge, Nicholas Maxwell-Lawford, Albert McAdam, Roddy Meyler, Sir John Moreton, Lord Perth, Sir Henry Phillips, Nigel Ramage, George Robins, John Sheriff, Sir George Sinclair, Sir Peter Tapsell, Julian Theunissen, Martin Van Oppen, Richard Van Oppen, Sir Roy Welensky, Sir Edgar Williams, Sir Peter Youens.

14. The Colonial Office (CO), Commonwealth Relations Office (DO), Cabinet Office (CAB) and Prime Minister's Office (PREM) records in the Public Record Office, Kew:

CO 926/141	Administration of the Government of Cyprus.
CO 926/190	Political Situation in Cyprus, Visits by Secretary of State and Minister of State.
CO 926/209	Political Situation Reports, Cyprus.
CO 926/256	Policy on New Constitution in Cyprus.
CO 926/257	Policy on New Constitution in Cyprus.
CO 1015/1515	1959, Disturbances in Nyasaland.
CO 1015/1517	1959, Disturbances in Nyasaland.
CO 1015/1518	1959, Disturbances in Nyasaland.
CO 1015/1519	1959, Measures against civil unrest in Nyasaland.
CO 1015/1535	1959, Commission of Inquiry into civil unrest in Nyasaland, appointment of members.
CO 1015/1537	1959, Commission of Inquiry into civil unrest in Nyasaland, Order in Council authorizing commencement of work.
CO 1015/1538	1959, Commission of Inquiry into civil unrest in Nyasaland, rules for access to documents by Commission.
CO 1015/1539	1959, Commission of Inquiry into civil unrest in Nyasaland, rules for evidence for witnesses attending Commission.
CO 1015/1540	1959, Commission of Inquiry into civil unrest in Nyasaland, publication of reports.
CO 1015/1544	1959, Commission of Inquiry into civil unrest in Nyasaland, action on report.
CO 1015/1839	1959, Reports by Governor on internal situation in Nyasaland.
CO 1015/1976	1959, Visit by Minister of State in the Colonial Office to central Africa.
CO 1015/1977	1959, Possible visit by Lord Perth, Minister of State in the Colonial Office to Nyasaland.
CO 1015/1984	1959, Record of meetings in the Colonial Office with the governors of Northern Rhodesia and Nyasaland.
DO 35/7476	1959–60, Rioting in Nyasaland: reports and situation: position of detainees; ending of state of emergency.
DO 35/7477	1960, Rioting in Nyasaland: reports and situation: position of Nyasaland detainees; ending of state of emergency.
DO 35/7478	1959, Rioting in Nyasaland; interdepartmental Central Africa Committee.
DO 35/7564	1959–60, Constitutional development in Nyasaland: visits of Lord Home to Salisbury and of Mr Macleod to Nyasaland; release of Dr Banda.
DO 35/7565	1960, Constitutional development in Nyasaland: visits of Lord

	Home to Salisbury and of Mr Macleod to Nyasaland; release of Dr Banda.
DO 35/7566	1960, Constitutional development in Nyasaland: visits of Lord Home to Salisbury and of Mr Macleod to Nyasaland; release of Dr Banda.
CAB 21/3155	1959 October–December, Visit by the Prime Minister, Mr Harold Macmillan, to Commonwealth countries in Africa.
CAB 21/3157,	1960 January, Visit by the Prime Minister, Mr Harold Macmillan to Commonwealth countries in Africa.
PREM11/3070	1959–60, Constitutional development in Africa: Federation of Rhodesia and Nyasaland, Part 1.
PREM 11/3075	1959–60, Constitutional development in Africa: Federation of Rhodesia and Nyasaland, Part 6.
PREM 11/3077	1959–60, Constitutional development in Africa: Federation of Rhodesia and Nyasaland, Part 8.
PREM 11/3085	1960, Correspondence from Lord Dalhousie, Governor-General, and Sir H. Gibbs on public opinion in Federation following visit by the Prime Minister.

Secondary sources

Books

Akyeampong, H. K., *Tributes to Dr J. B. Danquah* (Accra: State Publishing Corporation, 1967)

Altrincham, Lord, *Kenya's Opportunity* (London: Faber & Faber, 1955)

Anson, B. I., *The History of the Armytage or Armitage Family* (London: Hazell, Watson & Viney, n.d.)

Austin, D., *Politics in Ghana, 1946–1960* (London: Oxford University Press, 1970)

Baker, C., *Development Governor: A Biography of Sir Geoffrey Colby* (London: British Academic Press, 1994)

— *State of Emergency: Crisis in Central Africa, Nyasaland 1959–1960* (London: Tauris Academic Studies, I.B.Tauris, 1997)

Barker, D., *Grivas: Portrait of a Terrorist* (London: Harcourt Brace, 1960)

Brent, W. A., *Rhodesian Air Force: A Brief history, 1947–1980* (Kwambona, RSA: Freeworld Press, 1987)

Byford-Jones, W., *Grivas and the Story of Eoka* (London: Robert Hale, 1959)

Canry, C., *Encyclopaedia of Historic Places* (London: Mansell Publishing, 1984), vol. II

Chatham House Memorandum, *Cyprus, Background to Enosis* (London: Royal Institute of International Affairs, 1958)

Chiume, M. W. K., *Kwacha: An Autobiography* (Nairobi: East African Publishing House, 1975)

Churchill, R. S., *The Rise and Fall of Sir Anthony Eden* (London: MacGibbon & Kee, 1959)

Cohen, A., *British Policy in Changing Africa* (London: Routledge & Kegan Paul, 1959)

Crawshaw, N., *The Cyprus Revolt: An Account of the Struggle for Union with Greece* (London: George Allen and Unwin, 1978)

Durrell, L., *Bitter Lemons* (London: Faber & Faber, 1959)
Eden, A., *Full Circle: The Memoirs of the Rt Hon Sir Anthony Eden* (London: Cassell, 1960)
Firth, J. D'E., *Rendall of Winchester: The Life and Witness of a Teacher* (London: Oxford University Press, 1954)
Fisher, N., *Iain Macleod* (London: André Deutsch, 1973)
Foley, C., *Legacy of Strife. Cyprus from rebellion to civil war* (London: Penguin, 1964)
— *The Memoirs of General Grivas* (London: Longman, 1964)
Fry, G. K., *The Administrative Revolution in Whitehall* (London: Croom Helm, 1981)
Gray, D., *Spencer Perceval: The Evangelical Prime Minister* (Manchester: Manchester University Press, 1963)
Horne, A., *Harold Macmillan, Volume I, 1894–1956, Vol. I of the Official Biography* (London: Viking, 1989)
Horne, A., *Macmillan, 1957–1986, Vol. II of the Official Biography* (London: Macmillan, 1988)
Hunt, D., *On the Spot: An Ambassador Remembers* (London: Peter Davies, 1975)
Huxley, E., *Out in the Midday Sun* (London: Chatto & Windus, 1985)
Kelling, G. H., *Countdown to Rebellion. British Policy in Cyprus, 1939–1955* (London: Greenwood Press, 1990)
Kyle, K., *Cyprus* (Minority Rights Group, Report No. 30, 1984)
Kyriakides, S., *Cyprus: Constitutionalism and Crisis Government* (Philadelphia: University of Pittsburg Press, 1968)
Lapping, B., *End of Empire* (London: Paladin Grafton, 1989)
Macmillan, H., *Tides of Fortune* (London: Macmillan, 1969)
— *Pointing the Way* (London: Macmillan, 1972)
Maugham, R. C. F., *Africa As I Have Known It* (London: John Murray, 1929)
Mell, A., *Government House and the Old Residency, Zomba* (Zomba: The Government Printer, 1960)
Pike, J. G. and G. T. Rimmington, *Malawi: A Geographical Study* (London: Oxford University Press, 1965)
Rooney, D., *Sir Charles Arden-Clarke* (London: Rex Collings, 1982)
Ruvigny and Raineval, Marquis of, *The Plantagenet Roll of the Blood Royal* (London: Jack, 1905)
Sabben-Clare, J., *Winchester College, After 600 Years, 1382–1982* (Southampton: Paul Cave, 1981)
Sampson, A., *Macmillan: A Study in Ambiguity* (London: Allen Lane, The Penguin Press, 1967)
Shakespeare, W., *Othello*
Shepherd, R., *Iain Macleod* (London: Hutchinson, 1994)
Short, P., *Banda* (London and Boston: Routledge & Kegan Paul, 1974)
Stephens, R., *Cyprus, a Place of Arms* (London: Pall Mall, 1966)
Trench, C. C., *Men Who Ruled Kenya* (London: The Radcliffe Press, 1993)
Welensky, R., *Welensky's 4000 Days: The Life and Death of the Federation of Rhodesia and Nyasaland* (London: Collins, 1964)
Who Was Who, 1951–1960
Who's Who, 1995
Williams, T. D., *Malawi: The Politics of Despair* (London: Cornell University Press, 1978)
Wills, A. J., *The History of Central Africa* (London: Oxford University Press, 1964)

Wilson, D., *The Astors: The Life and Times of the Astor Dynasty, 1793–1992* (London, Weidenfeld & Nicolson, 1993)

Wood, J. R. T., *The Welensky Papers: A History of the Federation of Rhodesia and Nyasaland* (Durban: Graham Publishing, 1983). The very extensive collection of Welensky papers at Rhodes House, Oxford, had not been catalogued and made open to the public at the time the research for this book was undertaken. Reliance was, therefore, placed on Wood's book.

Journal articles

Arden-Clarke, C., 'Eight Years' Transition in Ghana', *African Affairs*, January 1958

Baker, C., 'Dr Banda's Arrest and Release from Detention, 1959–1960', *Society of Malawi Journal*, vol. 49, no. 3, 1996

Highfield School Magazine, The, Lent term 1917, vol. VI to Christmas term 1923, vol. XIV, *passim*

Saloway, R., 'The New Gold Coast', *International Affairs*, October 1955

Seaton, F., 'One Man's Emergency', *Outpost*, May 1959

Winchester College Calendar, August 1923

Wykehamist, The, vol. 589, 30 October 1920

Government publications

Colonial Office, September 1926, Pamphlet African No. 973, 15th edition, *Regulations for the Employment of Officers in the East African Dependencies*

Colonial Office List, 1955 (London: HMSO, 1955)

Dominions Office and Colonial Office List, 1929 (London: Waterlow & Sons, 1929)

Government of Kenya, *Life and Duties of an Administrative Officer in Kenya Colony* (Nairobi: Government Printer, 1929)

Hansard, Commons and Lords

Nyasaland: Despatch by the Governor Relating to the Report of the Nyasaland Commission of Inquiry, Cmnd. 815 (London: HMSO, 1959)

Nyasaland: Report for the Year 1956 (London: HMSO, 1957)

Nyasaland: Report for the Year 1957 (London: HMSO, 1958)

Nyasaland: Report for the Year 1960 (London: HMSO, 1961)

Nyasaland Government Gazette

Nyasaland State of Emergency, Cmnd. 707 (London: HMSO, 1959)

Proceedings of Legislative Council of Nyasaland

Report of the Nyasaland Commission of Inquiry, Cmnd. 814 (London: HMSO, 1959)

Report of the Nyasaland Constitutional Conference, Cmnd. 1132 (London: HMSO, 1960)

Southworth Commission Report, The (Zomba: The Government Printer, 1960)

Newspapers

Accra Evening News; *Cyprus Mail*; *Daily Express*; *Daily Mail*; *Daily Mirror*; *Daily Telegraph*; *Daily Times of Malawi*; *East Africa Standard*; *Ethnos*; *Evening Standard* (Salisbury); *Gold Coast Bulletin*; *Gold Coast Weekly Review*; *Kypriaki*; *Madras Mail*; *Manchester Guardian*; *Mombasa Times*; *News Chronicle*; *Nyasaland Times*; *Rhodesia Herald*; *Ross Gazette*; *Sunday Times*; *The Times*; *Times of Cyprus*

Index

Aberdare mountains, 18, 49
Aberdeen, 316
Abyssinia, 37, 39, 42–3, 338
Accra, 74–5, 79, 89, 96, 217, 271, 316, 331, 346
Accra Evening News, 78, 84
Acropolis, 103
Adams, W., 183
Aden, 30, 36, 223, 281, 312
Adu, Y., 330, 347
Africa, 281
African Progressive Association, 220
Afrikaans/Afrikaner, 178, 180
Aga Khan, 312
Aghios Georghios, 125, 127
Agros, 152
Algiers, 67
All-African People's Conference, 217
All Saints' Church, Ealing, 140
All Souls College, Oxford, 6, 16
Altrincham, Lord, 170, 344; *see also* Grigg, Henry Bidewell
Amery, Julian, 225, 319, 340
Amesbury Abbey, 337–8
Anderson, Colonel E. L. B., 21, 26
Antao, Dr, 277
apartheid, 173, 178–9, 186, 345–6, 348
Araouzo, I., 119, 138
Archer's Post, 37
Arden, Catherine, Baroness, 2
Arden-Clarke, Sir Charles Noble, 76–8, 80–1, 86–7, 96, 245–6, 270–1, 346, 355
Aristotelus, Kyriacos, 125
Armitage, Arthur (Robert's grandfather), 2
Armitage, Arthur (Robert's uncle), 41

Armitage, Frank (Robert's father), 1–2, 13, 41, 107, 159, 332, 340
Armitage, Harry (Robert's brother), 2, 9, 11–12
Armitage (née Meyler), Lyona (Robert's wife, Lady Armitage), 16–17, 22–4, 26–8, 33–6, 40–2, 46, 48–9, 53–4, 56–7, 60, 63, 66, 72, 78, 96, 166–7, 170, 177, 192–3, 194, 282, 303, 306, 311, 313–14, 317, 319, 322, 331–2
Armitage, Katherine (Robert's granddaughter), 313, 315
Armitage (née Byrde), Muriel (Robert's mother), 1–2
Armitage, Phoebe (Robert's daughter-in-law), 282, 313
Armitage, Richard Hugh Lyon (Robert's younger son), 41, 49, 281–2, 313
Armitage, Robert Jeremy (Robert's elder son), 33, 35–6, 49, 54, 56, 66, 163, 278, 282, 313–14, 332, 337–8, 353
Armitage (née Haworth), Susan, 281–2, 313
Armitage, Stephen (Robert's grandson), 313
Armitage Cup, 331
Asantahene, 88
Ashanti, 74, 78, 80, 88
Asian Convention, 219, 220
Astor, Lord and Lady, 9, 12, 15, 331, 340
Atatürk, 158
Athens, 101–3, 111, 117, 119, 121, 129, 145, 149, 152, 170; Athens radio, 131, 132, 134, 144, 151–2, 159–60, 165, 168

Aureol, MV, 97
Austin, Dennis, 79–80
Axminster, 314

Baker, Maxine, 333
Banda, Aleke, 299, 302, 304, 355
Banda, Dr Hastings Kamuzu, 216–23, 237–54, 263, 265–80, 282–7, 289–307, 309–10, 313, 318–19, 321–6, 328–30, 335–6, 340, 344–6, 350–3, 355
Banda, T. D. T, 204, 210, 309, 355
Barbados, 2
Barcelona, 312
Baringo, Lake, 49
Barotseland, 248
Barrow, Michael Palliser, 205–8, 222, 295–6, 356
Bates, A. F., 161
BBC, 314
Beira, 180, 281, 312, 328
Beit, Sir Alfred, 321–2, 331
Beit, Lady, 321
Beit Trust, 316, 318, 321, 324–7, 329–31
Bennett, Reginald, 247–8
Benson, Sir Arthur Edward Trevor, 189, 194, 222, 305, 344, 356
Berkeley, Humphry, 247
Birgi, Muharrem Nuri, 153, 155, 158, 356
Biscay, Bay of, 19, 33
Blackwood, Michael Hill, 184, 197–8, 205–6, 209–10, 213, 220–1, 244, 264–6, 272, 277, 279, 287–9, 292, 295, 304, 306, 353, 356
Blandford, 320
Blantyre, 180, 184, 194, 199, 201, 202, 205, 207, 227, 250, 253, 281–2, 293, 295, 297, 299, 304, 308–9, 326, 330
Bois de Boulogne, 10
Bombay, 2

Bombay Artillery, 2
Bonham, 10
Booker Brothers, 247
Boston, USA, 128
Boston Tea Party, 267
Boulogne, 33
Bournemouth, 33, 170, 319, 321
Bourton, 313
Bowker, Mr, 153
Boy Scouts, 41, 327
Bradford, 10
Branigan, Patrick Francis, 76, 78–9, 81, 87, 92, 110, 356
Bridport, 314
Bridstow, 2, 338
Brindisi, 282
British Council, 118, 328
British Honduras, 177
British Institute, 161, 163, 166
British Legion, 140
British South Africa Police (BSAP), 223
Brook, Sir Norman, 238, 255, 296
Brooke-Popham, Sir Henry Robert Moore, 46, 54, 356
Brumage, D. O., 29, 35–6
Bryanston School, 320, 329, 335
Bucquet, R., 196
Buganda, 261
Bulawayo, 320
Bunda Agricultural College, 326
Burden, Geoffrey, 213
Burns, Sir Alan, 74, 76, 177
Butler, Richard Austen (Rab), 318
Bvumbwe station, 308
Byrde, Muriel, *see* Armitage, Muriel
Byrde, Revd Frederic Louis, 2

Cacoyiannis, Sir Panayiotis, 138
Cairo, 14, 67
Calais, 170
Calcutta, 14
Caldicott, John Moore, 205, 207–8, 356

INDEX   403

Callaghan, (Leonard) James (Jim), 235
Cameronians, 75
Cameroon, 159
Campbell, Sir Jock, 247, 273
Canal Zone, 125, 150
Cape Town, 75, 177, 180, 345, 348
Cardiff, Maurice, 118, 130, 134, 137
Carlton Club, 103
Carrington, Peter (Alexander Rupert), 153
Castro, Fidel, 306
Cavendish-Bentinck, F. W., 66, 68–9, 71
Central African Federation, 171
Ceylon, 2, 88, 179
Chamberlain, (Arthur) Neville, 28
Chancellor College, 326
Charity, HMS, 127
Chauncey Maples, 323
Chelmsford, Frederick John Napier, 1st Viscount and 3rd Baron, 14
Cheltenham, 171, 313
Chequers, 9, 234, 298
Cherangani range, 18, 49
Cheshire, 171
Chijozi, D. W., 195, 204, 212–13
Chikumbula, Chief, 277
Chikwawa, 308
Chileka airport, 180, 233, 236–7, 251, 273, 275, 299, 311, 322
Chilwa, Lake, 193
China, Republic of, 326
Chinde, Chief, 276
Chinyama, J. R. N., 181, 204, 212–13, 276–7
Chipembere, H. B. M., 181, 194–5, 204, 210, 212–13, 216, 239, 250, 273, 284–6, 291–9, 301–2, 304–5, 322, 352, 356
Chiradzulu, 308
Chiromo, 180
Chirwa, O. E. C. (Orton), 299–301, 309, 357

Chirwa, W. M. (Manoah), 181, 185, 194–6, 204, 212, 220, 245, 357
Chisiza, D. K., 210, 216, 250, 273, 284, 286, 300, 304–5, 309, 357
Chisiza, Y. K., 273, 284, 286, 309, 322
Chitipa, 325; *see also* Fort Hill
Chiume, M. W. K., 194–5, 204, 210, 212–13, 216, 235, 250, 277, 284, 292–7, 299–300, 305, 322, 352, 357–8
Chokani, Willie, 316
Cholo, 308
Christian Democratic Party (CDP), 293, 309
Christianborg Castle, 74
Chudleigh, H. E, 160
Church House, 181
Church of England, 129
Church of Scotland church/Mission, 183, 230, 326
Churchill, Winston, 49, 116, 122, 340
City of Exeter, 180
City of York, 177
Clarence House, 338
Clark, William, 124–5, 134
Clemens, W. F. M., 104, 163, 166
Clerides, J., 147, 160–1, 167
Cliveden, 12
Cocoa Marketing Board, 86, 90
Codrington, Colonel William, 177
Cohen, Sir Andrew, 72, 75, 174, 358
Colby, Sir Geoffrey, 171, 173–7, 181–2, 184–5, 191, 205, 342, 347, 358
Colby, Lady, 171
Collins, F. G., 184
Colonial Development and Welfare Fund (CDWF), 64–5, 87, 89–90, 175
Colonial Office, 17, 23, 33, 59, 72, 74–5, 81–2, 88, 100, 103, 104, 110, 113–16, 118–19, 122–3, 126,

130–2, 134, 143–4, 147, 151, 154–5, 160, 171, 174, 177, 181, 189, 191, 206, 209, 213, 215–16, 219, 221–5, 227, 232–5, 242, 247, 252, 255–62, 266, 275, 280, 282–3, 290, 294, 296, 300, 305, 313, 318, 340, 343, 348, 350
Coloured Community Welfare Association, 220
Colvin, Revd Tom, 316
Comet, HMS, 125, 127
Committee for Education in the Forces, 321
Commons, House of, 2, 93, 101, 110, 112, 115, 145, 168–9, 224, 235, 238, 285, 354
Commonwealth, 61, 79, 179, 185, 189, 200, 236–8, 254, 261, 345
Commonwealth Relations Office, 348
Communist Party, 105, 129–30, 152
Congo, 275
Congress, *see* Congress Liberation Party (CLP); Malawi Congress Party (MCP); Nyasaland African Congress
Congress Liberation Party (CLP), 220, 284, 309
Connors, Peter, 333
Conservative Association, 318, 331
Conservative Party/government/ Conservatives, 110, 137, 144, 174, 234, 238, 246–7, 272, 301, 346, 351
Constitution Amendment Bill, 179
Convention People's Party (CPP), 77–80, 92, 94, 346
Coombes, H. P., 184, 212
Cormack, Mr, 44, 46
Coryndon, John, 28
Council for the Order of St John, 319
Country Gentleman's Association, 314
Coussey, Sir Henley, 76–8, 84

Craigmaddie, 11
Crawshaw, Nancy, 167
Creasey, Sir Gerald, 74–6, 358
Crete, 19, 117, 312
Crossman, Richard, 138
Crown Agents, 177
Crozier, Mr, 36
Cuba, 320
Cyprus, 97, 98–169, 170–1, 178–9, 188, 190–2, 194, 223, 255, 276, 286, 316, 319, 327, 331–5, 338–9, 341–5, 347–9, 353–4
Cyprus Airways, 103
Cyprus is Turkish Party, 151
Cyprus Mail, 108
Cyprus Turkish Association, 158

Dadnor, 2, 9, 11, 15, 171
Daily Mail, 161
Daily Mirror, 162, 268
Dalhousie, Lord Simon, 201, 235, 283, 312, 332, 340
Danquah, Dr J. B., 74–5, 78
Dar es Salaam, 241–2, 252, 255, 262, 269, 281, 312
Day, Francis, 1
Day, Miss, 4
Dayaram, P., 175
de Bromhead, P. J., 29
Dedza, 304, 326
Defence Act, 306
Derby, the, 33, 137
Dervis, Dr T., 106, 139
Devlin, Patrick Arthur, 228–34, 236–7, 239, 254, 261
Devlin Report, 231–2, 234–5, 254
Dickenson, Mr, 9
Dixon, A. C. W., 184, 197–8, 200, 205–6, 208–10, 213, 220–1, 245, 266, 272, 276, 279, 284, 287–9, 292, 295, 303–4, 353
Dodecanese, 154
Doig, Revd Andrew, 175, 188, 197
Dominion Party, 268

Dorchester, 282, 319
Dorset, 314–15, 319, 337
Dovas, General, 153
Drakos, Markos, 133, 140, 165
Durban, South Africa, 180
Durrell, Lawrence, 118–19, 124, 138–9, 141, 162–3, 358

East Africa, 18, 67, 171, 221, 227, 260
East Africa and Rhodesia, 196, 314
East Africa Standard, 33, 42, 47
East African Royal Commission, 259
East London, South Africa, 180
Eastern Highlands, Southern Rhodesia, 312
Eden, Sir Anthony, 54, 110–11, 114, 122, 132, 144–6, 154, 156, 159, 163–4, 168–9, 340, 344, 349, 358
Edinburgh, 316
Edusei, Krobo, 94
Egmont, John, Earl of, 2
Egypt, 2, 67, 98–9, 110, 151, 312, 349
Elder Dempster Line, 97
Elgeyo district, 48
Elgon, 22, 49
Elizabeth (Queen Mother), 201, 203–4, 280, 332, 338, 340
End of Empire series, 332, 334
English East India Company, 1
English Speaking Union, 321
enosis, 98–110, 112–16, 118, 121, 123, 125, 128–35, 137–9, 141–2, 144–5, 147, 150–1, 153–4, 156–7, 159, 167, 335, 343–5, 349
Eoka, 125–8, 135–6, 140–2, 146–7, 149–52, 155, 159–61, 165–6, 169, 351
Eritrea, 36, 42
Ethiopian empire, 42
ethnarchy, 105–6, 113–14, 130, 132, 134, 139, 155
Ethnarchy Council, 165, 168

Eton, 9, 36
Euro-African Association, 220

Fairclough, Anthony, 228–9
Falkland Islands, 71
Famagusta, 98, 133
Federal Party, 187, 198, 202; *see also* United Federal Party (UFP)
Finney, Philip, 217–18, 234, 293, 296, 298–9, 303, 358
Fisher (warden of New College), 16–17
Fisher, Lord Geoffrey, 317
Fletcher-Cooke, John, 122, 124, 130–1, 141, 160, 162–3, 165, 286, 358
Foot, Dingle, 250, 273
Foot, Sir Hugh, 319
Foot, John, 196, 198, 212
Footman, Charles W. F., 171, 182–3, 229, 235–6, 241, 254–65, 271, 281, 286, 358
Forbidden Cargo, 140
Foreign Office, 101, 114, 116, 119, 122, 132–3, 145, 153, 155, 163, 343, 348–9
Fort Hill, 305, 325; *see also* Chitipa
Fort Johnston, 308
Fort Manning, 304
Foster, Robin S., 258–62, 290, 306
Fox-Strangway, Vivian, 317
France, 10, 59
Freeman, Beryl, 191
Furneaux Pelham, 11

Gaitskell, Hugh, 93
Galla, 38
game policy committee, 56–7, 59
Gandhi, Mahatma, 102
Garba, 43
Gardiner, Gerald, 301
Garissa, 39
Garlake, General, 183
Gbedemah, K. A., 79, 81, 270

Genoa, 10, 33, 170
Germany, 57
Ghana, 73, 77, 214, 217, 248, 301, 330, 334, 355; *see also* Gold Coast
Gibbs, Sir Humphrey, 322
Gibraltar, 19, 75, 312
Gilgil, 56
Girl Guides, 327
Glasgow, 11, 316
Glenday, Vincent, 42, 44, 55, 359
Gold Coast, 72, 73–97, 104, 110, 148, 171, 177, 179, 189–90, 195, 270, 319, 321, 327, 331, 333–4, 338, 341–3, 345–8, 353–4; *see also under* Ghana
Golden Arrow, 170
Goldie, Archdeacon Donald N., 103, 338–9, 342, 349
Gorell Barnes, W. L., 181, 209, 218, 228, 231–2, 258, 345, 359
Government House, 24, 26–8, 55, 63, 96, 103, 108, 120–1, 140–1, 143, 147, 166, 171, 177, 181, 190–2, 195–6, 203, 215, 221, 229, 246, 250, 254, 270–4, 302, 307, 311, 316, 322–3, 328, 330, 332, 350–1
Granada television, 332, 334, 336
Grand National, 33, 54, 180, 309
Graylin, J. C., 208, 295
Greece, 99–109, 111, 114–15, 118, 121–3, 125–6, 128–32, 136–9, 144–7, 149, 154–9, 335, 344; Greek language, 3, 5, 9, 12–14, 99
Greece, King of, 121, 128
Green Howards, 167
Grenadier Guards, 192
Gridiron Club, 17
Griffiths, James, 173–4
Grigg, Edward William Macleay (Uncle Ned), 9–15, 18, 23, 24–8, 33, 36, 170, 359; *see also* Altrincham, Lord
Grigg, Henry Bidewell, 2

Grigg, John, 28, 177, 313, 353
Grigg, Lady, 26, 28, 33, 36
Grivas, General George, 101–2, 117–18, 121–2, 125–7, 133–5, 140–2, 144, 149, 152, 158, 165, 335
Grubb, Kenneth George, 128–30, 145, 359
Gunner's Hole, 10
Guy's Hospital estate, 2
Gwelo gaol, 239, 250, 272, 286, 290, 328, 355

Hale, W. H., 49, 54–5
Harar, 42
Harare, 328; *see also* Salisbury
Harding, Field Marshal Sir John, 150, 164, 166, 168–9, 171, 319, 349
Harding, Lady, 319
Harris, Mr, 40–1, 45
Harrison, Mr, 45
Haworth, Susan; *see under* Armitage, Susan
Haworth, Maurice and Mrs, 171
Hennings, Mr, 49
Highfield School, 2–5, 10, 15
Hitler, Adolf, 54
Hitler the Pawn, 49
HMS Pinafore, 237
Hobson, Basil, 182, 201
Hodgson, George, 201, 256, 258
Hola prison killings, 234
Home, Sir Alec Douglas-, 189, 201–2, 243, 251, 252, 255, 265, 266–9
Hone, Evelyn Dennison, 245, 252–3, 255, 259–60, 264, 282, 290, 359
Hopkinson, Henry, 110–12, 114, 132, 136, 149, 153–4, 159, 169, 174
Hoppers, 6–7, 11; *see also* Turner
Hoyle, Stephen and Mrs, 317

Huggins, Godfrey M., *see* Malvern, Lord
Hunt, Mr, 40–1
Hurst Park, 336
Hutton-Mills, Thomas, 331
Huxley, Elspeth, 37, 43
Hyde-Clarke, E. M., 52

Imperial Airways, 34
India, 1–2, 76–7, 88, 99, 305, 332, 340
Indian Association, 202
Indian Civil Service, 2
Indian Ocean, 67, 171
Indian Penal Code, 21
Ingham, John, 182–4, 195, 210, 258–62, 291–2, 294, 303, 307, 316, 322–3, 326
Institute of Commonwealth Studies, 336
Institute of International Affairs, 178, 316
Interracial Association, 202
Ionian Islands, 99
Ionnu, Alexi, 125
Iraq, 114
Isinger, 158
Isiolo, 36–7, 42–3, 45–8, 53, 69, 338, 340
Istanbul, 158
Italy, 54, 57, 59
Izzard, Ralph, 161

Jaffu, George, 324
Jairos Jere Association, 320
Jerusalem, 103
Jobidon, Bishop, 327
Joint East and Central Africa Board, 318, 331
Jones, Glyn S., 255, 260–5, 271, 279–82, 284–7, 290–2, 294, 298, 300, 305, 307, 310–11, 313, 319, 359
Juba River, 37

Jubaland, 38

Kabarnet, 52
Kadzamira, Cecilia, 309, 328
Kakamega, 19–20, 22, 27–9, 35–6, 69, 332
Kanaan, Soublis, 135, 147, 160
Kapsona, 54–5
Kariba, 312
Karonga, 293, 297, 299–300, 324–5, 352
Karpass peninsula, 98
Kasungu, 326; Kasungu nature park, 327; Kasungu plains, 172
Kasupe, 308
Katsonga, Chester, 293, 309
Kaunda, Kenneth (David), 282–3, 296, 325
Keightley, General, 141, 344
Kenya, 14, 17, 18–72, 74, 76, 82–3, 88–9, 159, 171, 182, 190, 225, 234, 242, 252, 258, 296–7, 313, 318–19, 332–4, 338, 340–1, 345, 353–4
Kenya, 312–13
Kenya, Mount, 18, 36, 49
Kenya Defence Force, 57, 61
Kenyatta, Jomo, 334
Kericho, 18, 29–31, 35–6, 311
Kettlewell, Mrs, 303, 316
Kettlewell, Richard Wildman, 182, 185, 210, 224, 292, 302–3, 316, 337, 351, 359
Khartoum, 14
Khlorakas, 102, 125
Kimble, Professor David, 327
Kimwengoi (witchdoctor), 52–3
King, R. M. M. (Donald), 201, 263, 292, 300, 303
King's African Rifles (KAR), 37, 41, 175, 181, 192, 199, 222–3, 244, 296, 307, 310
King's College (Taunton), 321
Kipsigis, 29–30, 32

INDEX

Kirk Range, 172, 326
Kisumu, 19, 33–6, 50
Koja, 41
Korea, 139
Korean war, 86
Kranidiotis, Nicos, 119, 145, 148, 154, 159
Kumbikano, Clement, 181, 194, 196, 204
Kütchük, Dr Fazil, 135, 151, 335
Kwenje, N. D., 195, 211–13, 284
Kykko, 102, 119–21
Kyrenia, 98, 165–6
Kyrenia, Bishop of, 106, 115, 160
Kyriacon, 150

Labour Party/government, 75, 111, 115, 136, 138, 173–5, 197, 232, 246, 346
Lag Bogal, 41
Lambert, Mr, 35
Lancaster House, 153, 276, 284, 286–7
Lapping, Brian, 332–4
Larnaca, 98, 133, 167, 170, 335
Lausanne, 99, 154
League of Malawi Youth (LMY), 292–3, 296–8, 300, 304–6, 351
Legum, Colin, 147
Lengwe, 323, 327–8
Lennox-Boyd, Alan, 113, 119–20, 122, 131–3, 138, 142–5, 147–50, 152–3, 155–6, 159–60, 163–5, 168–9, 171, 181, 187, 200–1, 204, 206–8, 210, 216–17, 221, 223–9, 232, 234–5, 237–8, 255, 259, 262, 340, 353–4, 359–60
Lewis, Desmond, 199
Libya, 114
Lilongwe, 201, 296, 304–5, 324–7
Limasol, 98, 114, 133, 165
Limbe, 180, 184, 206, 218, 237, 281, 308
Lingfield Park, 315

Liphook, 2
Little, L. A., 184
Livingstonia, 231, 247
Llandovery, 33
Llewellin, Lord, 180, 183, 201
Lloyd, Thomas Ingram Kynaston, 143, 171, 181, 360
Lloyd-George (of Dwyfor), David, 9, 11, 340
Lockhart, Mr, 44
Loizides, Savvas, 101
Loizides, Socrates, 101, 125–6, 136
London, 9–11, 14, 16–17, 33, 72, 74–5, 81, 90, 93, 103, 110, 112, 116–17, 122, 130, 132–4, 145–50, 152–4, 166, 169–70, 174, 177, 180, 192, 203–4, 219, 221, 226, 230, 233–4, 235, 237–8, 240, 247, 251–3, 264–6, 269, 273–5, 279, 282–3, 287, 291–9, 301, 307, 313–14, 319, 322, 331, 351–2
London conference (on Cyprus), 147–50, 152, 169
London conference (on Nyasaland), 174, 275, 296, 301, 351
London University, 321
Long, General Robert, 224
Longchamps, 10
Lourenço Marques, 180
Louw, E. H., 179
Low, M. W., 37
Lower River, 311
Luchenza, 284
Luo tribe, 20, 29–30, 35, 52
Lyceum Club, 10
Lypiatt, 170
Lyttelton, Oliver, 84, 110, 174–5, 340, 360

Maasai, 30
McGeagh, Mrs, 21
McGeagh, W. R., 20–2, 26
MacIntyre, Donald, 171
Mackintosh, Mr, 44

INDEX

Macleod, Iain, 238–50, 252–5, 261–83, 285, 290–301, 304, 306, 333, 340, 350–2, 354, 360
Macmillan, Harold, 134–5, 144–6, 152–8, 163, 168–9, 234–5, 237–8, 240, 243–4, 248–55, 265–70, 272, 275–6, 278, 283, 292, 296, 298, 301, 340, 345, 348–50, 360
Madras, 1–2, 4, 9, 13
Madras Mail, 1
Madura, 28, 33
Maitland, Patrick, 121
Makanjiri, Chief, 277
Makarios III, Archbishop, 101–2, 106–8, 113–25, 128–33, 135, 138–9, 144, 148–9, 152–4, 156–60, 165–6, 168–9, 179, 335, 340, 349, 360–1
Malawi, 321–30, 334–5; *see also* Nyasaland
Malawi, Lake, 172
Malawi, University of, 323
Malawi Congress Party (MCP), 276–7, 279, 289, 296, 299–300, 303–4, 306–7, 309–10, 321, 329, 347, 351, 353
Malawi News, 291, 300
Malaya, 164, 179, 189
Malda, 49
Malta, 76, 160
Malvern, Lord (Godfrey M. Huggins), 171, 183, 188–90, 194, 198–200, 251, 340, 349
Manchester Guardian, 220
Mandera district, 39–40
Manningham-Buller, Reginald Edward, 234–5, 361
Mantovani, 165
Marlborough College, 2, 10
Marnhull, 315–16, 318–20, 332
Marples, Ernest, 243
Marsabit, 44, 45
Marseilles, 19, 33, 36, 49, 312
Martin, Sir John, 148

Mashonaland, 223
Masula, Chief, 277
Matabeleland, 223
Matiana, 19
Matinga, Charles, 211, 213
Mau forest, 49
Mau hills, 18, 29
Mau Mau, 308
Maxwell-Lawford, Nicholas, 282
Mayfair Hotel, 322
Meru, 48
Mesaoria, 98
Messina, Straits of, 312
Metaxis Square, 161–3
Metkei, 51
Meyler, Lyona, 16; *see also* Armitage, Lyona
MI5, 126–7, 283
MI6, 127
Middle East, 61, 104, 110, 128, 143, 145–6, 151, 168, 348
Mills, Reverend W. D., 3–5, 10
Milward, V. G., 184, 196
Mitchell, Sir Philip, 67, 71
Mkumtumanji, G., 322
Mlanje, 308, 326; Mlanje mountains, 172, 193
Mlowe, 324
Moatise, 324
Mombasa, 18–19, 26, 28, 33, 36, 49, 67, 280–1, 312
Mombasa Times, 47
Monckton (of Brenchley), Walter Turner Monckton, 1st Viscount, 241, 245, 250–1, 253, 266–8, 278; Monckton Commission/Report, 241, 246, 252–4, 270–1, 282, 285, 349
Monson, Leslie, 258, 262
Moore, Sir Henry Monck-Mason, 59, 361
Morgan, James Conwy, 219, 232, 256–7, 361
Morgan, Revd, 46

Mountains of the Moon, Uganda, 24
Moyale, 37, 39, 41, 44
Mozambique, 180, 324, 326, 328–9
Mpiupiu mountain, 193
Mposa, Elerton, 175
Msonthi, John, 324
Mua mission, 323
Mullin, John, 224
Munir, M. N., 138, 161
Munro, Mr, 171
Murphy, Sir William, 201
Mussolini, Benito (Amilcare Andrea), 33
Muwamba, E. A., 175
Mzimba, 172
Mzuzu, 303, 325, 327

Nacala, 312, 324, 328
Nairobi, 14, 19, 27–9, 33, 36, 38, 48–9, 55–7, 59, 61, 69, 89, 96, 281, 312
Nakuru, 19
Nandi hills, 18
Nanyuki, 48
Naples, 170
National Farmers' Union, 209, 321
NATO, 114–15, 128, 145, 318, 320
Ncheu, 304
Ndirande, 293, 297
Ndirande Club, 201, 202
New College, Oxford, 9, 15–17, 331, 340
New York, 116
Ngoma, 41
Nicosia, 98, 103, 106, 127, 133, 140, 143, 149, 156, 161–2, 165, 335
Nigeria, 75, 179, 189, 191, 248, 290–1, 301, 331
Nile, River, 67
Nkata Bay, 172, 224, 293, 299–300, 323
Nkomo, Joshua, 296

Nkrumah, Kwame, 74–81, 84–8, 92, 95, 179, 195, 246, 270–1, 334, 339–40, 346, 361
Norman-Walker, Hugh, 261
Northern Frontier Districts, 23, 42
Northern Frontier Province, 36, 38, 47
Northern Rhodesia, 71, 173–5, 189, 197–8, 200, 205, 214, 222–3, 245, 248, 252, 255, 258–62, 266, 271, 275, 290, 304–5, 307, 346; *see also* Zambia
Northern Rhodesia Rifles (NRR), 223
Ntaja, Chief, 276
Nungumbankum, 1
Nutting, Anthony, 111, 132, 145
Nyambadwe House, 322
Nyanza province, 20, 40, 44
Nyasa, Lake, *see* Malawi, Lake
Nyasaland, 163–4, 167, 170–311, 313–14, 316–19, 321–2, 327, 329–33, 335–7, 339–51, 353–4
Nyasaland African Congress, 174, 181–5, 188, 195–6, 198–200, 204, 208–11, 213–14, 216–18, 220, 222–7, 230, 235–8, 250, 270, 284, 290–1, 293–301, 303–4, 306, 308, 322, 335, 349–50, 352
Nyasaland Association, 201, 220
Nyasaland Operations Committee, 224
Nyasaland Railways, 177, 291, 314
Nyasaland Times, 174, 282
Nyeri, 24, 28
Nyika Highlands, 172
Nyondu, Chief, 325

Observer, 124, 147, 183
Olympus, Mount, 98, 127
Operation Pursenet, 127
Orion, 67
Orthodox Church, 98–100, 120, 130, 158

INDEX

Ottoman Empire, 99
Outspan Hotel, 28
Oxford, 9, 13, 15–17, 34, 336–7, 340
Oxford and Cambridge Club, 9, 170
Oxford Development Research Project, 336

Pacific, 17
Paget, Archbishop, 183
Papadopoulos, Achilles, 138, 162
Papagos, A., 103, 111, 118, 121, 145, 152, 156
Papandreou, Georgios, 128
Paphos, 98, 125, 127
Paris, 10, 33, 170, 320
Paschalides, Paschales, 148
Pavlides, Paul George, 105, 138, 147, 160–1, 166
Peake, Sir Charles, 103, 111, 117, 119, 129, 145, 153, 170
Peake, Lady, 111
Perceval, Isabel Jane, 2
Perceval, Spencer, 2, 140
Percy, Norma, 333
Perham, Margery, 177, 196
Perth, Lord John David Drummond, 221–3, 227–8, 231–2, 238, 280, 294, 340, 351, 362
Phillips, Henry Ellis Isidore, 201, 260, 263–5, 290–2, 294, 303, 362
Phiri, Mattheus, 277, 284
Pinney, John, 281, 312
police mobile force (PMF), 222, 244, 296, 304
Pompeii, 170
Poole, 321
Poole Harbour, 282
Port Elizabeth, South Africa, 180
Port Herald, 292, 294, 300, 308, 352–3
Port Said, 19, 67, 282, 312
Poynton, Sir Hilton, 259–62, 290
Primrose, Sir John, 228, 231

Progressive Party, 211

Reading University, 16
Red Cross, 327
Red Sea, 19, 67
Reddaway, John, 151
Rendall, Montague John, 5, 6, 15
Renison, Sir Gilbert, 312
Rennie, Gilbert McCall, 171, 177, 362
Rhodes House Library, 337
Rhodes Trust, 14
Rhodesia, *see* Northern Rhodesia; Southern Rhodesia
Rhodesia African Rifles (RAR), 223, 244
Rhodesia and Nyasaland Club, 318–19
Rhodesia Club, 314
Rhodesian Herald, 183
Richards, C. A. L., 261
Richards, Norman, 191
Ricketts, General Abdi, 163
Rimmington, Gerald, 42–3
Roberts, Sir Bryan, 324
Roberts, Denys, 234, 362
Robertson, Sir James, 254
Robertson, Malcolm, 6–7, 15–16
Robins, George Herbert, 125–7, 134, 141–2, 150–3, 162–3, 165, 362
Robinson, Mr, 152
Robinson, Sir Albert, 313
Roman Catholic Church, 293, 323, 325
Romsey Abbey, 14
Ross, 2, 16
Rotary Club, 201, 206, 308, 321
Round Table, 321
Rowan, Major Russell, 192
Royal Air Force, 103
Royal Empire Society, 103, 170
Royal Engineers, 160
Royal Military Academy, 15

Royal Military College, 15
Royal Navy, 5
Royal Rhodesia Air Force (RRAF), 180, 183, 223, 272, 283, 311
Royal Rhodesia Regiment (RRR), 223, 227
Rumpi, 294–5, 297
Ruo River, 180
Ryall's Hotel, 250–1, 253

Sacranie, Sattar, 211, 307
St Andrew's School (Blantyre), 326, 330
Saint Germain, France, 10
St John's Ambulance, 195, 318–19, 327–8, 331
Saint Mary and Saint Melor church, 338
Salima, 324–5
Salisbury (Rhodesia), 181, 183, 205, 208, 213, 222, 248, 250–1, 268, 275, 283, 292, 295–6, 305, 311, 326; *see also* Harare
Salisbury (Wilts), 321, 338
Salonica, 158
Saloway, Reginald Harry, 76–9, 81, 87, 92, 362
San Thome, Mount, 1
Sandown races, 103
Sandringham, 243
Sandys, Duncan, 243
Sangala, J. F., 181, 204
Scotland, 11, 316
Scott, Reverend Michael, 177
Scott, Sir Robert, 76
Scottish Reformed Church, 247
Second World War, 54, 74, 100
Selbourne, Lord, 171
Seventh Day Adventists, 328
Seychelles, the, 159
Shifta, 39
Shire River/valley, 172, 180, 281, 324
Short, Philip, 276

Sierra Leone, 59
Simla, 14
Simmonds, Kenneth, 63, 182–3, 201, 281
Simon's Town, Cape Town, 177
Sinclair, George, 75–6
Siolo River, 47
Smith, Ian, 321
Smyrna, 158
Soche township, 184
Sofocleous, Neophytos, 166, 351
Somaliland (Italian), 39, 57
Somalis, 37–9, 41
Soskice, Frank, 301
Sotik, 30
South Africa, 2, 29, 34, 59, 153, 173, 176, 178–80, 184, 186, 223, 251, 268–9, 302, 306, 345–6, 348
South Staffordshire Regiment, 161
South Well, 315–16
Southampton, 2, 19
Southern Rhodesia, 57, 171, 174–6, 183, 188, 191, 194, 196, 198–200, 205, 213, 219, 221–3, 230, 237, 240, 245, 248, 251, 259, 263, 268–9, 283, 288–9, 290, 297, 312, 318, 320–2, 324–5, 333, 345–6; *see also* Zimbabwe
Spanopoulos, Dr George, 138
Spirindon, Archbishop, 102
Stallard, Peter, 290
State House, 323, 328, 330
Stephanopoulos, Stephanos, 121, 152–4, 157–9
Sterndale-Bennett, Sir John, 143
Storrs, Sir Ronald, 99
Stratos, George, 101
Strijdom, Johannes, 179
Stromboli, 170, 312
Sturminster Newton, 315, 321
Suez, 67, 110, 282; Suez Canal, 312
Sunbeaet, 55
Supply Board, 57–8, 66
Swahili, 21, 40

Sykes, J. W., 141
Syria, 98

Tambach, 48–50, 52–4, 69, 193, 332
Tana River, 38
Tanganyika, 30, 33, 261, 263–4, 312; *see also* Tanzania
Tanzam railway, 325
Tanzania, 329; *see also* Tanganyika
Tapsell, Peter, 246–7
Taunton, 314, 321
Tedzani Falls, 324
Teeling, William, 344
Tema harbour, 87
Thomas, A. R., 257
Thompson, C. B., 20–1, 26, 29
Thomson, J. K., 75
Thorne, Bishop Frank, 303, 317
Thorneycroft (of Dunston) (George Edward) Peter Thorneycroft, Baron, 267
Thrace, 154
Tilbury, 312–13
Times, The, 21, 103, 171, 192, 273
Todd, Sir (Reginald Stephen) Garfield, 183
Tomkinson, C., 29–30, 32
Tornaritis, Criton, 113, 124, 136, 141, 147, 160
Trades Union Congress, 77
Tredgold, Sir Robert, 183, 201
Troodos, 143–4
Troodos massif, 98, 121
Turkey, 98–9, 101, 107–9, 114, 118, 122–3, 132, 144–51, 154–60, 335, 344
Turkish Cypriots, 101, 108, 135–6, 141–2, 146–7, 167, 335
Turnbull, Richard G., 29–31, 35, 39, 45–8, 69–70, 312, 362
Turner, Mr, 6; *see also* Hoppers
Turner's House, 6

Uaso River, 38

Uganda, 24, 260–1
Umtali, 312
UN High Commission for Refugees, 341
United Federal Party (UFP), 207, 220, 277, 284, 300, 306, 309
United Gold Coast Convention (UGCC), 74–5, 78–9
United Kingdom (UK), 78, 99, 103, 111, 115, 123, 129, 211, 236, 242, 247, 249, 252, 265–7, 327
United Nations (UN), 102, 106–8, 112–19, 121–3, 128–31, 137, 139, 144–6, 149, 152, 156, 163, 165, 335; UNO, 103, 105, 117
United States (USA), 59, 96, 118, 128–9, 145, 273, 316, 322
University College (Accra), 79, 94, 96
University College (Salisbury), 183
Uploaders, 314
Usiene, 193
USSR, 106

Venice, 282
Victoria, Lake, 18–20, 29, 34
Victoria Falls, 173, 174, 248, 312
Victoria station, London, 33, 36, 170
Visanza, 304
Voice of the Fatherland, 151
Volta River, 87, 95

Wajir, 36–41, 43–5, 48, 53, 56, 69
Wales, Prince of, 12, 15, 340
Wall, Patrick, 318
Walpole, Sir Horatio, 2
Walters, John, 162
Watson, Aiken, 75–6, 282
Webster, J. L. H., 52
Welensky, Sir Roy, 176, 188–9, 196–7, 199–200, 206–8, 219, 222–3, 228, 230, 235, 243, 248–9, 251–4, 256, 261, 265–71, 273–5,

279, 283, 287–92, 295–300, 305–7, 311–12, 318, 340, 347, 362–3
Wellington, 10
West Africa, 73, 171, 261, 293, 305, 346–7, 352
Whitchurch, 33, 332
White, Mr, 45
White, Colonel 'Tiger', 162–3
White Highlands, 29
White's Club, 279
Whitehall, 104, 167
Whitehead, Sir Edgar, 222–3, 230, 251, 254, 265, 267–9, 283, 287, 289–91, 299, 312, 318, 340, 347, 363
Wild, J. V., 260
William-Powlett, Peveril Barton Reiby Wallop, 183, 363
Williams, Alwyn, 6, 15, 54
Williams, Sir Edgar, 228, 231, 387
Wilson (head gardener), 191–2
Wilson, H. W., 303
Wimbledon, 36
Wincanton races, 171
Winchester College, 5–16, 36, 66, 93, 340
Windsor, 177
Winster, Lord, 100–1
Winterton, Earl, 12
Wintringham, Mrs, 12

Wivelscombe, 170
Woods, Oliver, 103, 153, 177, 188, 192, 217, 273
Woodward, Dr, 16–17
World Bank, 325
World Council of Churches, 114, 128
Wright, Sir Andrew, 101–2, 127
Wylie, Mr, 45
Wyn-Harris, Sir Percy, 35–6, 70–1, 171, 228, 230–3, 363

Youens, Sir Peter, 208, 217, 271–2, 285, 290, 294, 296, 299, 302, 304–5, 307, 352, 363

Zambezi River, 281
Zambia, 322, 325–7, 329–30; *see also* Northern Rhodesia
Zanzibar, 255, 281, 312
Zimbabwe, 327, 329–30; *see also* Southern Rhodesia
Zomba, 171–2, 180–4, 190, 193–4, 199, 201, 226–7, 229, 237, 252, 265, 272, 281, 296–7, 302, 305, 308, 311, 313, 317, 323–6, 328, 337
Zomba Club, 201, 308
Zorlu, Fatim, 154–5, 158
Zurich, 262

1. ABOVE. Muriel and Frank Armitage with Robert, Madras, 1911.

2. BELOW. Sir Charles Arden-Clarke, Kwame Nkrumah and Robert Armitage, 1952.

3. ABOVE. Government House, Nicosia, Cyprus.

4. BELOW. Government House, Zomba, Nyasaland.

5. Lady Armitage, Cyprus, 1955.

6. Sir Robert Armitage, Nyasaland, 1957.

7. Sir Robert Armitage, Nyasaland, 1960.

8. Sir Robert Armitage, in retirement, 1984.

www.ingramcontent.com/pod-product-compliance
Lightning Source LLC
Chambersburg PA
CBHW070007010526
44117CB00011B/1449